Brussels Guide

Antwerp, Ghent & Bruges

Penguin Books

PENGUIN BOOKS

Published by the Penguin Group
Penguin Books Ltd, 27 Wrights Lane, London W8 5TZ, England
Penguin Books USA Inc, 375 Hudson Street, New York New York 10014, USA
Penguin Books Australia Ltd, Ringwood, Victoria, Australia
Penguin Books Canada Ltd, 10 Alcorn Avenue, Toronto, Ontario, Canada M4V 3B2
Penguin Books (NZ) Ltd, 182–190 Wairau Road, Auckland 10, New Zealand

Penguin Books Ltd, Registered Offices: Harmondsworth, Middlesex, England

First published 1996
Second edition 1998

Colour reprographics by Precise Litho, 34–35 Great Sutton Street, London EC1
Printed and bound by William Clowes Ltd, Beccles, Suffolk NR34 9QE

Edited and designed by
Time Out Magazine Limited
Universal House
251 Tottenham Court Road
London W1P 0AB
Tel + 44 (0)171 813 3000
Fax + 44 (0)171 813 6001
Email net@timeout.co.uk
http://www.timeout.co.uk

Editorial
Managing Editor Peter Fiennes
Editor Nicholas Royle
Deputy Editor Ian Cunningham
Researcher Eduardo Angelucci
Proofreader Tamsin Shelton
Indexer Julie Hurrell

Design
Art Director John Oakey
Art Editor Mandy Martin
Designers Benjamin De Lotz, Scott Moore
Scanner Operator Chris Quinn
Picture Editor Keri Miles
Picture Researcher Emma Tremlett

Advertising
Group Advertisement Director Lesley Gill
Sales Director/Sponsorship Mark Phillips
Advertisement Sales (Brussels) Addwittz

Administration
Publisher Tony Elliott
Managing Director Mike Hardwick
Financial Director Kevin Ellis
Marketing Director Gillian Auld
Production Manager Mark Lamond
Accountant Catherine Bowen

Features in this guide were written and researched by:

Introduction various. **History** Sarah Burnett. **Architecture** Bridget Hourican. **Surrealist Brussels** Eileen Cadman. **Brussels by Season** Joanne Fowler, Jodie K Hruby. **Sightseeing** Bridget Hourican (**Walk 1 The old centre, Walk 2 Palaces squares, gardens, Walk 3 Matonge to Merode** – Robin W Ratchford; **Famous Belgians no.1** – Nicholas Royle; **Famous Belgians no.2** – Tom Charity; **Famous Belgians no.3** – Linton Chiswick; **Famous Belgians no.4** – Ian Cunningham). **Museums** Sarah Burnett. **Art Galleries** Bridget Hourican. **Restaurants** Sarah Burnett. **Cafés & Bars** Sarah Burnett. **Shopping & Services** Lucy Leveugle. **Accommodation** Jodie K Hruby, Steven Tate. **Children** Bridget Hourican. **Clubs** Danny Roelens. **Film** Lucy Leveugle. **Gay & Lesbian** Danny Roelens. **Media** Thierry Denoël. **Music: Classical & Opera** Julius Stenzel. **Music: Rock, Folk & Jazz** Michael Leahy. **Sport & Fitness** Sarah Burnett. **Theatre & Dance** Bridget Hourican. **Trips Out of Town** Valerie De Rouaux (**Getting Started, Outside Antwerp, Outside Ghent, Outside Bruges, Wallonia** Steven Tate). **Directory** Ian Cunningham, Jane Evans, Joanne Fowler, Elisabeth Unna. **Further Reading** Sarah Burnett, Ian Cunningham, Peter Fiennes.

The Editor wishes to thank the following: Canon Richard Allington-Smith, Sarah Blee, Gail Bradley, Neil Carlson, Tom Charity, Linton Chiswick, Pippa Cragg, Ian Cunningham, Frédéric Dethoor, Bridget Hourican, Emily Hourican, Jodie K Hruby, Andrew Humphrey, David Jones, Michael Leahy, Alix Leveugle, Mike Meakin, Elisabeth Mertens, Eugene L Notkin, Peter B Overton, Nicola Pharoah, Perry Roberts, Danny Roelens, Julius Stenzel, Chris Tozer, Eva Vermandel, S Zammit.

Maps by Mapworld, 71 Blandy Road, Henley-on-Thames, Oxon RG9 1QB.

Photography by Sarah Blee except pages 7, 15, 16, 21 AKG; 9 Mary Evans Picture Library; 10, 12 ET Archive; 14, 82b MNAC; 22, 25, 27, 28 AHC - Arxiu Fotgrafic; 21 Galerie Christine et Isy Brachot; 31, 32 Arnhel de Serra; 35, 37 H Gruyaert/Magnum; 72 Marc Marnie; 74 Columbia-EMI-Warner Distributors; 192 Arwid Lagenpusch. Pictures on pages 80, 95, 99, 107, 163, 177, 194 supplied by featured establishments.

Contents

About the Guide

This is the second edition of the *Time Out Brussels Guide*, one in a series of 18 city guides. It paints a detailed picture of the *carrefour de l'Europe*, the crossroads of Europe. This edition has been completely updated and listings-checked and largely rewritten by a team of new writers and reliable Brussels-based experts. Some chapters have been rewritten from scratch, others have been revised and brought bang up to date.

ANTWERP, GHENT & BRUGES

More space is devoted to the **Trips Out of Town** section than in most other *Time Out City Guides* in order to reflect the importance of Antwerp, Ghent and Bruges as tourist destinations. The chapters relating to these three major centres are composed almost entirely of new material.

In certain chapters, such as **Music: Classical & Opera, Clubs** and **Gay & Lesbian**, listings for venues in Antwerp have been included alongside those for Brussels, because of the closeness of Antwerp to Brussels and because of the fact that the scene – if there *is* a scene, in *whatever* context – does not exist exclusively in Brussels. Listings for museums, restaurants, cafés, bars and hotels in Antwerp, Bruges and Ghent appear in **Trips Out of Town**.

PRESENT & CORRECT

All information was thoroughly checked and correct at press time, but please bear in mind that, even in the home of EU bureaucracy and red tape (or should that be *particularly* in the home of EU bureaucracy and red tape), listings details are liable to be complex and by no means set in stone. It is always wise to check details by phone first.

NAMES, ADDRESSES & LANGUAGES

Brussels is divided into *communes*, although these do not feature in the addresses in our listings. Postcodes are written in four figures: 1000 in the city centre, 1050 is Ixelles, and so on.

Although Brussels is officially bilingual, it is in fact about 80 per cent francophone and at the risk of upsetting Flemish speakers and Flemish nationalists, we have listed most names and addresses in French only. When something is located in a Flemish commune, we list it in Flemish. Given that it is impossible to please all of the people all of the time, we have taken a view on this infinitely complex problem and therefore can only apologise to anyone who feels we have got it wrong. Indeed, we may already – in the above few lines – have given offence to French-speakers by referring to the language spoken by the natives of Flanders as Flemish, when there is a strong argument for calling it Dutch, which it is, more or less, give or take a few differences in dialect. This is a thorny problem and different authorities we have consulted offer different advice. We make no political statement by doing things the way we have chosen to do them. Other than perhaps: Hey – can't we all just get on?

MAPS

While we have made every effort to provide a useful map of Brussels, some of the streets and galleries in the city centre are so small it simply has not been possible to include them all. Most chapters contain map references with listings. If there is no map reference where you might expect one, this is either because the street is not shown on the map (usually because it is too small) or because it is off the map entirely.

PRICES

The prices listed should be used as guidelines. Because of inflation and fluctuating exchange rates, prices in shops and restaurants are always subject to change. All are quoted in Belgian Francs (BF). If prices and services vary wildly from those quoted, you might ask if there's a good reason. If not, take your custom elsewhere and then, please, let us know. We endeavour to give the best advice, so we want to hear if you have been ripped off.

CREDIT CARDS

The following abbreviations have been used for credit cards: AmEx – American Express; DC – Diners Club; JCB – Japanese credit cards; MC – Mastercard; V – Visa.

RIGHT TO REPLY

The information we give is impartial. No organisation has been included in this guide because its owner or manager has advertised in our publications. We trust you'll enjoy the *Time Out Brussels Guide* and that it helps you make the most of your stay. But if you disagree with any of our assessments, let us know; your comments on places you have visited are always welcome. You'll find a reader's reply card at the back of this book.

> There is an online version of this guide, as well as weekly events listings for several international cities, at http://www.timeout.co.uk.

Introduction

What's the best way to find out what the best things are about living in Brussels – or Antwerp? Ask the people who live there.

BRUSSELS

Pinball at 2am in a blues café. Ordering a beer you've never heard of before and savouring the thrill. The smell of coffee beans roasting at Corica on rue Marché aux Herbes. Paving stones glistening under a steady drizzle. Rediscovering the Grand Place every time you visit it.

It's a truly cosmopolitan city. If you're Flemish and therefore have to speak French all the time it makes you feel as if you're on holiday every day. There are lots of relaxed restaurants and cafés. It's easy for people who travel a lot, with Eurostar and the airport. Some neighbourhoods feel like separate villages inside the city.

Moules-frites. Grand Place. Drinking until the early hours. Fresh bread. Taking a tram down avenue de Tervuren.

The beer. The modesty and lack of pretension. The conviviality. Belgians are very open to foreigners. There is a good awareness of culture and good integration of the past and present.

It's got the advantages of a capital without the inconveniences; it's less hectic than Paris or London. You can walk easily to places. Flats and houses are much less expensive. Many people, not only intellectuals, speak several languages. Foreigners can get along easily. Two hours on the train and you're in Paris or Amsterdam or Germany. The quality of food and restaurants. It's a much greener city than, say, Paris.

Resting your beer on a coffin lid in Le Cerceuil or playing chess between beers in Le Greenwich. The knowledge that as you walk through parts of the city, you see more or less the same skyline that Delvaux saw and reproduced in many of his paintings. The view down rue de la Régence towards the Palais de Justice. Getting a room at the Hôtel St Michel overlooking the Grand Place and not having to pay an arm and a leg for it. All that space devoted to Delvaux and Magritte in the Musée d'Art Moderne.

The Turkish and Moroccan shops with all their brightly coloured, crazily shaped produce; whole streets smelling of waffles and chocolate; the way these places open so early in the morning you can often catch them on your way home from a night out. It gets so hot and humid in the summer that the city centre parks are full of kids bathing in the fountains; and in winter the lakes freeze over and

you can skate almost all the way to Holland. The cinemas, too – although these are fading gradually, there are still some small, shabby, usually empty, cinemas which select their programme solely on the whim of the owner. The ordered society – the pace, the rhythm and predictability of life; the gentle formality between casual acquaintances which can go on for years despite almost daily contact; the Belgians' modesty about their country. Being able to step on a train, fall asleep and wake up almost anywhere in Europe.

ANTWERP

The lack of stress in day-to-day goings-on and being able to cycle to work. The scale of the town – it's small but has all the ingredients of a big city. The river setting. The attitude to the arts – there's something for everyone, it's there for the taking. Sitting on café terraces.

The European connections; good rail-links. It's a beautiful city with a medieval centre. It's a small enough town to be able to cycle everywhere and so maintain low stress levels. All the designers, architects and artists. The 4,000 bars and 2,000 restaurants. The cost of buying and renting is much cheaper than Brussels.

It's a day-and-night city, especially in the summertime when people come into town on Monday evenings just to hear the cathedral bells. It's got a lively music scene and is the perfect shopping city – all the top Belgian and international designers have shops here. Walking along the Scheldt on a sunny day. Heading out to Berchem (10 minutes on a tram from the city centre) to see some of the most beautiful art nouveau houses in the world.

£2.50 US$6

i-Deas,fashion,clubs,music,people

steady...

Subscribe now to i-D to receive 12 issues
full of the latest i-Deas, fashion, clubs, music and people.

In Context

Key Events

Early & medieval history

57-51 BC Julius Caesar fights Gallic Wars.
15 BC Establishment of the Roman province called Gallia Belgica.
5th century AD Collapse of Roman rule in northern Europe.
814 Death of Charlemagne.
843 Charlemagne's kingdom split between his three grandsons.
979 Official founding of Brussels (Bruocsella).
1041 Dukes of Brabant build palace at Coudenburg.
1302 Flemish army beats French armies in the Battle of Golden Spurs.
1337 Outbreak of Hundred Years War between England and France.
1338 Jacob van Artevelde leads pro-English revolution in Ghent.
1348-9 Black Death in Flanders.

Dukes of Burgundy

1369 Margaret of Male marries Philip the Bold, Duke of Burgundy.
1384 Philip and Margaret inherit Flanders, and it becomes part of Duchy of Burgundy.
1459 Philip the Good's court based in Brussels.
1467 Death of Philip the Good.
1477 Death of Charles the Bold.
1482 Mary of Burgundy dies and her husband Maximilian becomes regent.

The Spanish Netherlands

1500 The future Charles V born in Ghent.
1515 Charles declared of age by Netherlands Estates General.
1516 Charles inherits Spanish throne and becomes Charles I.
1519 Charles inherits the Hapsburg empire and becomes Emperor Charles V.
1555 Abdication of Charles V in the Netherlands in favour of his son Philip.
1565 Nobles in the Netherlands form the League of Nobles, opposing Spanish rule.
1566 Iconoclastic Riots in Antwerp and elsewhere.
1567 Appointment of Duke of Alva as governor.
1568 Execution of Count Egmont and Count Horne and outbreak of the Revolt of the Netherlands.
1576 Spanish Fury in Antwerp.
1579 Southern provinces form Union of Arras, in support of Philip II and Catholicism.
1581 Northern provinces form Union of Utrecht and declare they no longer recognise Philip or the Spanish.

Counter-Reformation

1598 Philip hands over the Netherlands to his son-in-law Archduke Albert.
1609-21 Twelve Year Truce between the Dutch and the Spanish Netherlands.
1621 The Netherlands revert to Spain after death of Albert.
1648 Spain recognises Dutch independence in the Treaty of Münster.
1695 The French bomb Brussels and destroy Grand Place.

The Austrian Netherlands

1701-13 War of the Spanish Succession. The Spanish Netherlands ruled by English and French.
1713 Spanish Netherlands pass to Austria in the Treaty of Utrecht.
1740-8 War of Austrian Succession. French troops occupy Austrian Netherlands 1744-8.
1780 Joseph II becomes Emperor of Austria.
1789-90 Brabançon Revolution against Joseph II.
1790 Austrian authority restored.
1792 France occupies Austrian Netherlands.
1795 Austrian Netherlands annexed into France and old provincial boundaries abolished.
1798 French introduce conscription and Belgian peasants riot.
1814 Napoleon exiled and Congress of Vienna starts to redraw European boundaries. Belgium and Netherlands merged into the United Kingdom of the Netherlands.

Unity & Revolution

1815 Napoleon defeated at Battle of Waterloo. William Prince of Orange declared King William I.
1830 Start of the Belgian Revolution.
1831 The Great Powers recognise Belgium as an independent state and Léopold of Saxe-Coburg-Gotha is invited to be king.
1839 The Dutch recognise independent Belgium.
1848 First Liberal government, after initial political domination by Catholics.
1885 Belgian Socialist Party founded.
1885 Berlin Declaration recognises Léopold II as head of state of the Congo.
1893 Introduction of universal male suffrage, with system of multiple votes.
1898 Flemish (Dutch) language given official equality with French.
1908 Léopold forced to hand Congo over to Belgium.

Belgium in the wars

1914 Germany invades Belgium.
1918 Belgium liberated by Allies.
1919 Universal male suffrage.
1930 University of Ghent becomes Flemish-speaking.
1940 Germany invades Belgium and Léopold III surrenders.
1944 Belgium liberated by Allies; sets up War Tribunals.

Post-war Belgium

1948 Benelux Customs Union comes into force.
1949 Women given the right to vote.
1950 Léopold III returns to Belgium but stands down because of national unease about his behaviour during the war.
1957 Brussels becomes the headquarters of the European Economic Community.
1962 Creation of the French-Flemish language frontier.
1967 Brussels becomes headquarters of NATO.
1970-94 Constitutional reforms change Belgium from a centralised state to a federal one.
1993 Death of Baudouin I and accession of Albert II.

History

France, Spain, Austria, Germany... Belgium has had so many owners over the centuries it's no wonder the country's divided.

Early & Medieval History

When Julius Caesar embarked on the Gallic Wars in 57 BC, most of the tribes in what is now Belgium were Celtic. The Romans called them the Belgae and Caesar complained that of all the peoples in Gaul, they were the toughest. He attributed this to the fact that they were the tribes furthest from the Mediterranean and had missed out on the civilising influence of visiting merchants. Nevertheless, they were not too tough to cook; the Flemish coast had become famous for its exported fish sauces.

Despite the toughness of the Belgae, Caesar's armies conquered the region. It became a Roman province called Gallia Belgica in 15 BC, and was later divided into administrative districts called civitates. The area was thinly populated and backward, and did not have as much economic importance for the Romans as other towns in Gaul. Even so, the districts paid taxes and provided troops to the Romans, who built a network of roads and army camps. Tournai (then Turnacum), in southwest Belgium, became an important quarrying town, as well as an early centre of Christianity. Salt was refined from sea water along the coast, and there was an ironworks near Ghent. Wool was also produced. No records relate to Brussels.

The Roman empire in the north began to founder in the third century, when Germanic tribes attacked the northern borders of Gallia Belgica. Excavations of Roman camps show that massive destruction took place in the third century. Severe flooding, a problem that recurred throughout the history of the Low Countries and often caused huge loss of life, also weakened the empire, and Roman Gaul collapsed in the fifth century.

The Germanic invasions of the third to fifth centuries were the first stage in the process that was to lead to the linguistic division of present-day Belgium. The northern areas slowly became German-speaking, while the southern part of the country continued to speak Latin-based languages. The division was by no means crystallised at this time, and it is premature to refer to a clear split before the tenth century, but the roots of the split do stretch back to here.

The Romans' successors were the Frankish kings, and Gallia Belgica formed the northern border of their authority. They in turn were succeeded by Charlemagne, who ruled from 768-814 and

Battle of the Golden Spurs

Throughout the thirteenth and fourteenth centuries, the townspeople of Flanders repeatedly rose against the counts of Flanders, who had to ask their French masters for armed assistance. The most famous battle of this time was the Battle of the Golden Spurs (Epérons d'Or in French, and Gulden Sporen in Flemish), or the Battle of Courtrai, which took place on 11 July 1302.

The people of Bruges rebelled over taxes, and they were soon joined by most of Flanders. The aristocratic French army fought a Flemish army of guild members, townsmen and peasants, who had no more than ten knights among them. The marshy battlefield was completely unsuitable for horses, and to the amazement of everyone involved, the French were roundly defeated.

It was the first time that an urban infantry had joined forces with the aristocratic cavalry, and it is seen as a milestone in Flemish resistance to the French. Consequently, the battle was hugely important in Flemish and Belgian consciousness. Almost immediately, it became the subject of mock epics, and it is also a popular theme for painters (in Brussels' Museum of Modern Art, there is a wonderful twentieth-century semi-abstract representation of the battle by Henri Michaux). More importantly, the date – 11 July – is still the day of the Flemish national holiday.

The name of the battle is a reference to the fact that the victorious Flemish took 500 pairs of golden spurs from the fleeing French knights.

Plagues, famines, floods

War was not the only problem to afflict Flanders in the Middle Ages. It also suffered a succession of natural disasters. There were two major famines in the twelfth century, when the counts of Flanders were feeding up to 100 paupers a day in Bruges alone. The major hazard of the fourteenth century was plague. About one third of Antwerp's population died in the outbreak of 1316 and a chronicler recorded that 'Dancing, games, song, all revels were done away with in those days'.

Three decades later, in 1348-9, the Black Death wiped out a quarter of the population of Flanders, although the area's dense population meant that the consequences were less severe than in England and France. In between plagues and famines, there were frequent and severe floods, causing many villages to be deserted.

built up a vast empire from Denmark to southern Italy, and from the Atlantic to the Danube.

When Charlemagne died in 814, his sons and grandsons went to war over their inheritance. Eventually in 843 his kingdom was split between his three grandsons following the Treaty of Verdun: Louis the German received East Francia, which roughly corresponds to Germany; Charles the Bald was given West Francia, which roughly equates to France plus Flanders; and Lothair received Middle Francia, or the Middle Kingdom. This was a thin strip comprising the land between the River Scheldt and Germany in the north, and stretching down to the Mediterranean. It would continue to be a source of contention between France and Germany in the twentieth century.

The grandsons of Charlemagne were not the only ones fighting over the region in the Dark Ages. Throughout the ninth and tenth centuries, the old Frankish kingdoms were subject to regular invasions by the Vikings, who took advantage of the power vacuum. There was a gradual disintegration of central power and a rise of feudal domains. Flanders became one of the most powerful of all, and although it was theoretically ruled by the kings of France, the Flemish counts were virtually autonomous. Other fiefdoms to emerge in the ninth, tenth and eleventh centuries were Liège, Hainaut, Namur, Luxembourg and Brabant.

Brussels was in Brabant. It is first mentioned in 695, when it was a stopping point on the trade route from Cologne to Bruges and Ghent. It was then known as Brocsella or Bruocsella, meaning 'village in the marshes'. However, the city was not officially founded until 979, when Charles of France built a fortress on the island of Saint Géry.

The history of the fiefdoms of northern Europe is a complex series of wars, shifting boundaries, trade disputes and intermarriages. Their contacts stretched beyond the borders of the domains themselves. One of the Flemish counts, Baldwin II, married the daughter of England's King Alfred the Great, while William the Conqueror married the daughter of another, Baldwin V. The Flemish were trading far beyond their own borders. Flanders was already exporting cloth to England in the tenth century and there is evidence of a slave trade between the two. By the twelfth century, Flemish cloth was being sold in France, Italy and England.

The economic health of Flanders depended not only on the state of its relations with England, but also on Anglo-French relations, with Flanders often suffering from English reprisals against the French. Despite the fact that the Flemish counts were vassals of the French kings, the Flemish were often hostile to the French and were dependent on English wool imports. In the thirteenth century Flemish towns resisted French influence, murdering French soldiers and Francophile noblemen until a French army was sent to quell resistance in 1302. Surprisingly, it was defeated (*see* **Battle of the Golden Spurs** *page 5*).

The balance of the English-French-Flanders triangle became even more fragile when the Hundred Years War between France and England broke out in 1337. At the time of the outbreak, a Flemish landowner called Jacob van Artevelde led a rebellion in Ghent against the pro-French counts of Flanders, who fled to France. Flanders had been officially neutral, but Van Artevelde actively allied it with the English until his murder in 1346.

Further problems arose in the thirteenth and fourteenth centuries because of unrest in Flanders, Brabant and Liège. Townspeople and merchants demanded new powers from their rulers, who often relied on French backing to quell disorder. Even so, the rulers were often forced to give in to their demands in order avoid full-scale rebellions. Guild power increased and the towns gained a share of the government. The new rights given to townspeople and the growth of trade caused cultural and economic disparities between the towns and the surrounding countryside. Ghent, Bruges, Ypres, Brussels, Louvain, Antwerp and Mechlin all became wealthier and more powerful, and in 1340

Ghent was the largest city in Europe after Paris. Regions such as Hainaut, Namur and Luxembourg in the south were mainly agricultural.

The growth of Brussels (still called Bruocsella) had started in the eleventh century, when it spread out from the marshy valley of the River Senne into the hills and plateaux around it. The forests surrounding the town provided materials for construction and fuel. They also provided hunting grounds for the Dukes of Brabant, who built a palace in 1041 on higher ground at Coudenburg. Wool was the most important trade from the thirteenth to fifteenth centuries, along with metalwork.

Dukes of Burgundy

A process of great cultural change began in the 1360s when Margaret of Male, daughter of the Count of Flanders, married Philip the Bold (Philippe le Hardi), Duke of Burgundy. When Margaret's father died in 1384, Flanders and, later, other provinces came together in a loose union under the authority of the Dukes of Burgundy.

The key figure in the rise of the Dukes of Burgundy was Philip the Good (Philippe le Bon), grandson of Margaret and Philip the Bold. Having inherited Flanders, Burgundy, Artois and other provinces, he then added Brabant, Holland, Hainaut, Namur and Luxembourg through a combination of politics, purchase and military action. The only part of the Netherlands that remained outside his realm was the prince-bishopric of Liège. Nevertheless, the Low Countries were by no means a country as such, merely a group of territories under the control of one family.

Although the Dukes of Burgundy ruled for less than a century, the cultural changes were huge. In addition to their ducal palace in Dijon, they had important residences in Lille (which housed the exchequer), Bruges and Brussels. The court moved between them, although from 1459 it was based mainly in Brussels. Keen to be viewed as the equals of the French court, the Dukes of Burgundy initiated their own court culture in the Netherlands, and were active patrons of the arts.

Parades, tournaments, jousting and pageants were a major part of city and court life under the Dukes, partly because they were a way of displaying their power and wealth. There also seems to have been a general taste for ostentatious fashion and bingeing. When Philip the Bold visited Bruges in April 1398, the festivities lasted a month, during which time the churches provided food for the poor every day.

The first university in the Low Countries was founded in Leuven (Louvain) in Brabant in 1425. Brussels Town Hall in Grand Place was started in 1402 and completed in 1455, and the awesome tower of Mechelen Cathedral was begun in 1452. The best-known evidence of the Dukes' patronage is the art of the fifteenth century. The painter Jan van Eyck (*pictured below*) was born in Brabant, and worked in Ghent and Bruges. Rogier van der Weyden was born in Tournai and worked in Brussels as the city's official painter. Hans Memling was born in Germany but settled in Bruges in 1465. Although the Dukes were the most prolific patrons, works were also commissioned by city governments, and by native and Italian merchants in Bruges.

Painters had to enrol in guilds in the city where they worked and were regarded as craftsmen. Many of them also painted banners for parades and festivals. In Bruges, sculptors belonged to the carpenters' guild. The merchant and artisan guilds had started as occupational organisations, set up to help people who were trading outside their home town. Later, guild statutes regulated hours and conditions of work, inspections, conditions of mastership and the length of apprenticeships (from two to eight years). Some also had courts that levied fines for breach of the statutes.

Most of the guilds were rigorous about restricting entry. The majority started excluding women in the fourteenth century, although some still allowed them to work as journeymen. In some guilds, entry was based on heredity, with fees often higher for 'external' candidates. The differences became exaggerated over time, so that in Bruges in 1441, the sons of master carpenters paid the equivalent of 5.2 days' work to join the guild, while applicants from outside Flanders paid the equivalent of 149 days' work. Not content with that, the guild raised it to 244 days in 1479.

The importance of the guilds in Belgium is most evident in Grand Place in Brussels. The scale of the guildhouses belonging to the haberdashers, boatmen, archers, tallow merchants and hosiery makers leaves little doubt about their wealth.

Although the textile industries were declining in the fourteenth and fifteenth centuries, mainly in the face of cheaper English competition, other industries were replacing them. Brussels was producing tapestries, Ghent had a growing leather industry, mainly producing gloves and purses, and the Flanders coastal towns were exporting pickled herring. Meanwhile, new agricultural techniques such as the single-handed plough were boosting production in the countryside. Yet floods and plagues continued to afflict the Low Countries throughout the century, and the average level of poverty in rural parishes was about 25 per cent.

There were repeated uprisings and rebellions in Ghent between 1400 and 1450, primarily because economic power had shifted from Flanders to Brabant. Not only were Brussels' industries more prosperous than Ghent's but Bruges' access to the sea had silted up and it had been superseded by Antwerp as a port and a centre of trade.

The Hapsburgs

The end of the rule of the Dukes of Burgundy began with the death of Philip the Good in 1467. He was succeeded by his son Charles the Rash (Charles le Téméraire) whose attempts at modernisation were unpopular, and there was no great grief when he was killed at the Battle of Nancy in 1477. He was succeeded by his daughter Mary whose death five years later left the Netherlands in disarray. Mary had married Maximilian von Hapsburg of Austria, the son of the German emperor, Frederick III. Their son Philip was only four when she died, so the Low Countries were ruled by Maximilian for the next ten years, making them part of the Hapsburg empire. Like his father-in-law Charles, Maximilian was unpopular in the Netherlands, and unrest in the provinces developed into civil wars in Holland and Utrecht, although he did eventually restore order.

Maximilian's son Philip married Juana (Joanna) the Mad, the daughter of King Ferdinand and Queen Isabella of Spain. Their son Charles was born in Ghent in 1500, and after an extraordinary series of premature deaths and childless marriages among the ruling families of Europe he had inherited most of Europe by the time he was 20. He became Lord of the Netherlands in 1506 (although his aunt Margaret of Austria was regent until 1515), and King of Spain in 1516, and he was made Emperor Charles V of Germany when his grandfather Maximilian died in 1519. In this way, a native of Ghent came to rule the Netherlands, Austria, the Tyrol, Spain, Mexico, Peru, the Caribbean, Sicily, Naples and the German Empire.

Charles spent much of his earlier reign in Brussels and spoke Flemish as his first language of choice. Though in later years he moved to

Ommegang

The Ommegang pageant in Brussels is held to commemorate the festivities that took place when Charles V visited Brussels, together with his son Philip (the future Philip II of Spain) and his sisters Eleanor of Austria and Mary of Hungary.

However, the first Ommegang procession took place in the mid-fourteenth century, long before the reign of Charles V. A statue of the Virgin was transported from Antwerp to the church of Notre Dame du Sablon in 1359, and representatives of the crossbowmen held an annual procession to celebrate the safe arrival of their patron. It was only when Charles V and his family watched the procession that it became a truly prestigious occasion.

The festival takes place on the first Thursday of July, and starts with a procession of historical figures from the court of Charles V, giants and guildsmen from the Sablon to Grand Place. Once it arrives at Grand Place, there is a horse parade and more pageantry, watched by the royal family, and it finishes up with a stilt-fighting tournament, a bizarre spectacle that is fairly common at Belgian festivals.

Spain, between 1506-55 he enlarged the territory of the Netherlands, adding Tournai, Friesland and Utrecht and severing the ties between the Count of Flanders and the French throne.

When Charles inherited the Low Countries, the province of Brabant had eclipsed Flanders. Brussels had a new town hall with a 300-foot (90m) steeple, and the Dukes of Brabant and other nobles had built palaces on the higher ground. The Netherlands were still booming culturally, and among his advisers during his late teens was the theologian and humanist Erasmus. Much of the court's leisure time was spent hunting wild boar and stags in the nearby Forêt de Soignes. The first regular international mail service was set up in Brussels in 1520 by Jean-Baptiste de Tour et Taxis.

Antwerp, also in Brabant, was even more prosperous than Brussels, because it was the crossroads of the trading routes between Spain, Portugal, Russia and the Baltic. Each day, as many as 5,000 merchants gathered in the exchange, while up to 500 ships came and went from the port. So euphoric was one Victorian historian about this golden age that he described the population of the Netherlands as 'three millions of people, the most industrious, the most prosperous, perhaps the most intelligent under the sun'.

*The **League of Nobles**, 1565, was opposed to Philip II's intolerance of Protestantism.*

But Charles's rule over the Netherlands and the other parts of his empire was far from trouble-free. Outside Brabant, provinces were drifting into poverty because of flooding, high taxes and racing inflation, and Charles had to crush a rebellion in Ghent in 1540. Far more serious was the fact that his reign saw the beginning of the Reformation, which had devastating consequences for the whole of Europe. Lutherans from Germany extended their influence westwards into the Netherlands, while Calvinism spread northwards from Geneva. The spread of Lutheranism and Calvinism would lead to a revolt against Charles's successor, and cause wars in France and England.

Although Charles was prepared to negotiate with Luther and his followers, he also dealt harshly with Protestants (or heretics as many preferred to label them). The first Lutheran martyrs were burnt in Brussels in 1523, and in 1550 Charles passed the Edict of Blood, which demanded the death penalty for all those convicted of heresy. Protestant propagandists claimed that 30,000 people died as a result of the Edict, although this is probably hugely inflated.

Charles abdicated in 1555, in a tearful ceremony at Brussels, and handed over the reins of the Netherlands to his son Philip. He had already abdicated in Austria in 1521 in favour of his brother Ferdinand, and three months after the Brussels ceremony, he abdicated in Spain, again in favour of his son, who became Philip II.

Like his father, Philip inherited a collection of provinces in the Low Countries, rather than a nation, and he was never crowned king. Instead, he was Duke of Brabant, Count of Flanders, Lord of Utrecht and Groningen, and so on. There was no common ancestry or language among the 17 provinces, and the French and Flemish language split was already evident. However, there was some administrative unity: provincial assemblies, the States, sent delegates to the central States General, and the rulers had personal representatives, *stadtholders*, in each state or group of states.

The problems afflicting the Netherlands during Philip's rule were similar to those suffered under Charles: heavy taxation and the spread of Protestantism. But whereas Charles had remained popular – partly because his roots and temperament belonged in the Netherlands – Philip was never liked. Spain was his birthplace and his home, and he had little affection for his subjects in the Low Countries. He was also more hardline in his defence of Catholicism than his father. In this he was aided by the Inquisition. Although the Spanish achieved the greatest infamy, their colleagues in northern Europe were hardly soft. A man in Bruges who trampled on a consecrated wafer had his hand and foot wrenched off by red hot irons and his tongue ripped out, before being slowly roasted over a fire.

DUTCH REVOLT

Philip's troubles in the Netherlands started fairly quickly. He appointed his half-sister Margaret of Parma as regent, but power was mainly in the hands of two pro-Spanish councillors, Cardinal

The Battle of La Hogue or Harfleur, 1692, between the French, English and Dutch.

Granvelle and Count Berlaymont. The former was hated in the Netherlands. Equally unpopular were Philip's attempts to reorganise the bishoprics, especially among the clerics and nobles who saw a threat to their power and wealth. Philip's most prominent opponents were Prince William of Orange, Count Egmont and Count Horne. Their demands for the removal of Granvelle were rejected by Philip.

In 1565 a group of nobles opposed to Philip formed the League of Nobles. Berlaymont referred to them disparagingly as *ces gueux* (those beggars) and *Vivent les Gueux* became their rallying cry. They objected to Philip's refusal to tolerate Protestantism, his attempt to centralise power, the heavy taxes imposed on the provinces, and the presence of Spanish troops in the Netherlands.

The spread of Protestantism was not confined to the League of Nobles. It burgeoned among the poor in the towns of Flanders, Brabant, Holland and Zeeland. In the 1560s, Calvinist 'field preachers' attracted huge crowds: about 14,000 people gathered outside the walls of Antwerp to listen to one preacher, while a preacher at Tournai had an audience of about 20,000. Part of their attraction to the poor was that the preachers railed against the wealth of the Catholic Church.

The preachers also criticised the imagery and art in the Catholic churches. In the Iconoclastic Riots of 1566, Calvinist mobs destroyed Catholic churches all over the Netherlands. In Antwerp, crowds attacked the cathedral with axes: they hacked up the Madonna, pulled down the statue of Christ at the altar, destroyed the chapels, drank the communion wine, burned manuscripts and rubbed the sacred oil on their shoes. They then did the same to 30 other churches in the city.

In 1567 Philip appointed a new governor in the Seventeen Provinces, and he arrived with an army of 10,000. The Duke of Alva was a ruthless army commander. He called the Netherlanders 'men of butter' and said he had come to tame them. One of his first acts was to set up the 'Council of Blood' (officially the Council of Troubles or Tumults). On 4 January 1568 alone, he had 84 people executed on the scaffold. In March of that year, there were 1,500 arrests, 800 of them in one day, and in June Count Egmont and Count Horne were beheaded in Grand Place in Brussels. Their deaths marked the start of a full-scale revolt in the Netherlands that would last for 80 years.

A major turning point was the Spanish Fury of 1576. A financial crisis in Spain meant that the troops had not been paid for three years,

Destruction of Grand Place

The low point of the seventeenth century for Brussels came towards the end of the War of the Grand Alliance (or League of Augsburg) in 1695. The French armies of Louis XIV had invaded the Spanish Netherlands but, having suffered a major defeat at the hands of the Dutch, were forced to pull back from the coast.

In order to divert the Alliance's resources, the French Duke of Villeroi bombarded Brussels for 36 hours, destroying 3,830 houses and 16 churches. His principal target was the Town Hall in Grand Place, which, surprisingly in view of its 300-foot (90m) steeple, the French somehow managed to miss. (They also missed the statue of the Mannekin Pis, which had been built in 1619, but given that the diminutive chap is barely two feet high, their having missed him is more understandable.)

Even so, the French guns damaged or destroyed most of the other buildings in Grand Place, including the Maison du Roi (which, in fact, had never been a royal residence) and several of the guildhouses. During 1696-7 there was extensive rebuilding and restoration work in the square, and some of the most famous buildings and façades date from then. What was a disaster at the time at least contributed to the elaborate style and unity of this famous square. There are several pictures of the bombardment and the devastation in the Musée Communal in Grand Place.

and Spanish soldiers in the Antwerp garrison went on the rampage, setting fire to almost a thousand buildings in the wealthiest quarter of Antwerp. Their behaviour strengthened the resolve of potential rebels.

But from 1578, when Philip sent Alexander Farnese (the future Duke of Parma) to govern in the Netherlands, the Spanish began to regain control over the southern Netherlands. Although Calvinism had first taken hold in the south, the southern provinces were now coming under the influence of the Counter-Reformation, and in 1579 the ten southern provinces formed the Union of Arras, accepting the authority of Philip, and Catholicism.

The north's response was the 1581 Union of Utrecht, which was essentially a declaration that the seven northern provinces no longer recognised Philip's authority. The boundaries were not yet fixed, however, and Parma reconquered Bruges, Ghent and, later, Antwerp. It is possible that he could have regained more territory in the north, but Philip II was preoccupied with the Spanish Armada and war against France, so Parma was forced to divert his troops to those campaigns. By the end of the century, the northern provinces had formed the Republic of the United Netherlands, also known as the United Provinces, while the southern provinces were known as the Spanish Netherlands.

Although the rebels were hostile to Philip and the Spanish and many of them were anti-Catholic, the general intention was not independence but merely to gain greater autonomy and religious freedom and to get Spanish troops out of the Low Countries. But the split became irreversible, particularly since continuing revolt was a unifying factor in the new republic in the north.

Counter-Reformation

In 1598 Philip handed over his remaining territories in the Netherlands as a 'fief of Spain' to Archduke Albert of Austria, husband of his daughter Isabella. The idea was that the removal of Spain might make reconciliation between north and south possible. However, when Albert died without an heir in 1621, the provinces reverted to Spanish rule, although Isabella remained governor until her death in 1633.

Isabella and Albert maintained an ostentatious court. Chief among its claims to glory was the court painter Pieter Paul Rubens, who lived in Antwerp. Among his contemporaries and students were Jacob Jordaens and Anthony van Dyke, who became court painter to Charles I of England.

Pieter Paul Rubens (1577-1640) studied in Italy, and worked in England (where he painted the ceiling of the Banqueting Hall in Whitehall), France and Spain as well as Antwerp. He was closely connected with the Catholic Counter-Reformation, and his work fused Italian and Flemish influences. There are plentiful examples of his work in Belgium: in the museums of Brussels, Antwerp and Mechelen, in Antwerp Cathedral and in his Antwerp home.

The political and military achievements of Isabella and Albert's rule were less notable. They negotiated a truce with the Dutch in 1609, but it lasted just 12 years, and the war then continued until 1648. During the last half-century of the war, the religious gap between the two sides widened, with the United Provinces becoming more firmly Calvinist and the Spanish Netherlands in the grip

of the Catholic Counter-Reformation, in particular the Jesuits. The Dutch developed a gruesome literature and art of martyrdom, portraying sufferings at the hands of the Spanish Inquisition. This, together with the reams of propaganda and treatises issuing from both sides, cemented the differences between north and south.

The war ended in 1648 with the Treaty of Münster in which Spain recognised the independence of the north's United Provinces. The borders agreed correspond to the present-day Belgian-Dutch border. One of the terms was that Antwerp's access to the sea be cut off by a Dutch blockade of the River Scheldt, rendering it redundant as a port. In the 1660s, Antwerp was allowed a sea outlet via a canal, but this was no substitute. The Scheldt would remain closed for nearly 150 years.

During the war, a flood of Calvinist and anti-Spanish merchants, workers and bankers had emigrated from the south to the north, taking with them their skills, contacts and wealth. The result was that the north (and Amsterdam in particular) flourished, becoming an affluent maritime and trading power. The south did not. Antwerp had been especially hard hit during the war by the Spanish Fury and the Dutch blockade. Its population fell from 100,000 in 1560 to 42,000 in 1589, and the post-war period brought little recovery.

Things were to become worse for the Spanish Netherlands in the second half of the seventeenth century. Louis XIV of France had ambitions to dominate Europe at the expense of the Dutch, the English and the Hapsburgs, and Spain's power had dwindled so far that it was no longer able to defend its territory. The late seventeenth century brought a succession of wars – the War of Devolution, the Dutch War, the War of the Grand Alliance (or League of Augsburg) – in all of which the Spanish Netherlands were either attacked or occupied.

Several of the ensuing peace treaties led to the territory of the Spanish Netherlands being whittled away. For example, France gained Artois and Ypres. Ironically, almost the only protection given to the southern Netherlands at this time came from the Dutch, who wanted a barrier between themselves and the French.

The semi-permanent state of war in the Spanish Netherlands caused serious economic decline in the late seventeenth and early eighteenth centuries. The only sector to prosper during those years was agriculture, and there was a shift of population from town to country. But the cities were not bereft of economic activity. Brussels, for example, was still producing a variety of luxury goods,

*Detail from 'La Chasse du Duc de Bourgogne' showing **Philip the Good**, Duke of Burgundy (1419-67).*

including lace, tapestries and porcelain, both for export and for the wealthy nobles and merchants still living in the Spanish Netherlands.

Austrian Netherlands

When Philip IV of Spain died in 1665, the Spanish throne passed to his sickly and feeble-minded four-year-old son Charles. Despite two marriages, Charles II remained childless and for most of the 1690s he seemed to be teetering on the verge of death. Eager to fill a vacuum, the French, English, Dutch and Austrians manœuvred over who would succeed him.

By the time Charles II died in 1700, there were two candidates: Archduke Charles of Austria and Philip of Anjou, grandson of Louis XIV of France. Charles favoured the Frenchman as his heir, partly, it is said, out of dislike for his own German wife, and in 1701 the French Duke of Anjou entered Madrid as King of Spain. Shortly afterwards, the French occupied Dutch-held 'barrier fortresses' in the Spanish Netherlands, and the English and the Dutch declared war on France.

The War of Spanish Succession lasted from 1701-13 and was fought in Germany, the Netherlands, Italy, Spain and their various colonies, as well as at sea. During the war, the Spanish Netherlands were governed by the French and the English. Peace was made at the 1713 Treaty of Utrecht and the 1714 Treaty of Rastatt. Philip of Anjou kept the Spanish throne, but the Austrians came away with the Spanish Netherlands, henceforth known as the Austrian Netherlands, and Spain's possessions in Italy. England gained Gibraltar, Minorca, Newfoundland and other land in America. The Dutch gained the right to keep a line of defensive forts in the Austrian Netherlands, with the cost borne by the Austrian emperors (and indirectly by the taxes of the inhabitants).

The main effect felt by the Austrian Netherlands during the first years of the eighteenth century was peace, for the country was no longer the prey of French armies. Only once during Austrian rule, which lasted until 1794, were the Netherlands invaded by the French. Otherwise, there was little change, for initially the Austrians allowed their new subjects a high degree of autonomy.

The single French invasion occurred in 1744. Emperor Charles VI of Austria wanted his daughter Maria Theresa to inherit his empire when he died, but the rest of Europe refused to accept this. France invaded and occupied the Austrian Netherlands until the Treaty of Aix-La-Chapelle (Aachen) restored Austrian rule in 1748 and gave the throne to Maria Theresa's husband, Francis I.

The real force, however, was Maria Theresa. Her rule, lasting until 1780, brought considerable economic renewal in the Austrian Netherlands. This was partly a result of peace, and partly of efforts by her governor, Charles of Lorraine, to build roads and waterways. There were also improvements in agricultural techniques, to the extent that the late eighteenth century was the only time in Belgium's history when it was self-sufficient in grain. A rural textile industry had grown up, with half the rural population of Flanders making their living spinning flax and weaving linen.

There were also new glass, coal and cotton industries which, unlike the trades that came before, did not revolve around the power of the guilds. Smaller industries such as paper mills, sugar refineries and silk factories grew up as well.

Cultural life also developed. Censorship was relaxed, French books circulated freely and bookshops were opened in the towns. There was a growing printing industry, too. However, the Austrian Netherlands were scarcely at the fore of the Enlightenment, and rural culture was still traditional, with companies travelling around the countryside performing medieval mystery plays.

Brussels also changed under the Austrians. In 1731 the Coudenburg Palace burnt down after a fire in the kitchens. Since this had been the residence of the Dukes of Burgundy and the scene of Charles V's abdication, the loss was emotive. In 1740 work began on a new palace, the Palais du Roi, which is now the town residence of the Belgian royal family. The neo-classical Place Royale and the Palais de la Nation, the seat of the Belgian parliament, were built in the 1770s and '80s.

Maria Theresa was succeeded by her son Joseph II in 1780. His rule was more zealous and more radical than his mother's. He immediately tried to modernise the country, closing monasteries and seminaries, taxing the Church and reforming the judicial system and the administration of the government. In 1781 he passed the Edict of Toleration, which recognised religious freedoms. He also tried, but failed, to unblock Antwerp's access to the sea.

Joseph was loathed by the conservative Belgians, who saw their traditional privileges and vested interests threatened. The result was the Brabançon Revolution of 1789-90, involving all the provinces except Luxembourg. The rebels, led by a Brussels lawyer, wrote a new constitution inspired by the US Articles of Confederation and formed the Confederation of the United Belgian States. But the revolution collapsed into chaos as a result of the widening split between conservative and progressive rebels. Around 100,000 peasants, led by priests, marched through Brussels to protest against the progressives, many of whom were forced to flee to France. Austrian authority was restored in 1791, and when Joseph II died, he was succeeded by the liberal Léopold II who had less enthusiasm for reform and was preoccupied with events in other parts of his tottering empire.

EUROPE'S REVOLUTIONARY WARS

In 1792 the French declared war on Austria and Prussia, occupying the Austrian Netherlands and Liège (until then an independent prince-bishopric). The French armies were initially greeted as liberators, but the welcome quickly faded, and when the French temporarily withdrew from Brussels after a defeat in 1793, the people of Brussels ransacked the houses of pro-French families. When France reoccupied the Austrian Netherlands in 1794, tens of thousands of Belgians emigrated.

The French exacted war levies and military requisitions and set up an *agence de commerce* to take anything from cattle to art back to France. Among their booty was Jan van Eyck's *Adoration of the Mystic Lamb*. Shortly afterwards, in 1795, the French absorbed the former Austrian Netherlands and set up a new administration. They abolished the old provinces and created nine new *départements*. Brussels became a departmental capital answering to Paris. Liège and the Netherlands were united for the first time, and the region was increasingly referred to by the French as Belgique.

The French passed laws suppressing feudalism and the guilds and from 1796 applied French law to Belgium. The Belgians accepted the occupation and annexation passively but unenthusiastically, and the French leaders complained of their apathy. Such protests as did occur were aroused by measures taken against the Catholic Church. In 1796 the French confiscated the property of the monasteries, making 10,000 people homeless. In 1797 they closed the Catholic University of Louvain (Leuven), and in 1798 some 600 priests were given the death sentence for refusing to swear loyalty to France (in the end most of them escaped death).

The main opposition to French rule came in 1798, after the French introduced conscription. There were riots in east and west Flanders and about 10,000 peasants formed an army in Brabant. The uprising was crushed brutally and bloodily, and hundreds were executed despite the fact that the peasants had been relatively restrained – they had burnt down pro-French houses and destroyed lists of taxpayers, but had not murdered anyone.

The last five years of the century saw industry in decline, the depopulation of towns, new taxes, economic hardship, and organised gangs of robbers roaming the highways. But from 1800, there was an economic resurgence. The French encouraged the growth of industries such as coal and cotton, which benefited from the new markets in

Musée Wellington – and Ferme du Caillou, where **Napoleon** *stayed – both contain plans relating to the Battle of Waterloo.*

Kings of Belgium

When the independent state of Belgium was created in 1831, the Belgians initially wanted Louis of Orléans, the second son of the French king, to be their monarch. However, the British prime minister, Lord Palmerston, resisted and said he was ready to go to war to prevent Louis from taking over. Louis's father forbade him to accept the throne.

The Belgians then opted for Léopold of Saxe-Coburg-Gotha who had already been asked by the Greeks to be their king in February 1830 and had turned them down. Léopold, as a Lutheran, conservative German, was not the most obvious choice for the Catholic Belgians, but he did repel Dutch attempts to reconquer Belgium; he also steadfastly observed the new constitution, and he encouraged Belgian politicians to work together.

Léopold was related to many of Europe's ruling families. His first wife, Charlotte, was heir presumptive to the English throne until her death in 1817; his second wife, Louise-Marie, was the daughter of Louis-Philippe of France. But his most famous relatives were his niece and nephew, Queen Victoria and her husband Albert, for whom he acted as matchmaker when they were both 17.

Léopold I was succeeded in 1865 by the ambitious Léopold II (*pictured above*). His ambitions for himself and his country were revealed in a letter he wrote to Prince Albert while he was still heir to the throne, saying that Belgium might be small, but that Rome, Carthage, Austria, Russia and Prussia had all started as small states and look what happened to them. He then began his search for territories for his empire, eventually settling on

the Congo, which was effectively his personal property from 1885-1908.

Léopold II initiated extensive building work in Brussels during his reign, including the monumental Palais de Justice, the Cinquantenaire Park and museums, and the African Museum in Tervuren.

When Léopold died in 1909, he was succeeded by his nephew Albert I. Known by the Belgians as le Roi Chevalier (the Soldier King), he fought with the Belgian army at Ypres after the Germans had invaded in 1914. He was killed rock climbing in the Ardennes in 1934.

Memories of his son Léopold III are less glorious. In 1940, he surrendered to the invading Germans after just 18 days, and although many Belgians supported this course of action, his behaviour was still contrasted with that of his predecessor. Léopold III was allowed to remain in his palace until 1944, when he was deported to Germany, and there was uneasiness in Belgium about his relationship with the Germans. After the war, Léopold moved to Switzerland and his brother Charles was made regent, until the government held a non-binding referendum in 1950 on whether the king should return to his country. Only 57 per cent voted in his favour. Léopold stepped aside in favour of his son Baudouin, who was crowned in 1951.

Baudouin was credited by many with preventing Belgium from splitting into two countries. Although he had a low profile outside Belgium, he was popular with his subjects, taking a deep interest in matters such as child welfare, homelessness and the lives of ordinary people. He died childless in 1993 and was succeeded by his younger brother, Albert.

France. Ghent became an industrial centre, and the number of people employed in the cotton industry there rose from 1,300 in 1806 to 12,000 in 1816. The new industries were capitalist, largely funded by entrepreneurial nobles and traders who had bought up former monastery lands cheaply.

One of the chief beneficiaries of the French occupation was Antwerp, which regained its access to the sea. Napoleon constructed a new harbour and port, which he described as 'a pistol aimed at the heart of England'. He also made his mark on Brussels, ordering the city's old walls to be demolished and replaced with open boulevards.

French rule of the Netherlands came to an end in 1814, when Napoleon was forced to abdicate as Emperor of France, following his defeat at the Battle of Leipzig. His opponents (Britain, Prussia, Russia, Austria) recaptured Brussels in February 1814 and appointed a council of conservatives to govern the city. The council was keen for Belgium to return to Austrian rule. In 1814 the Congress of Vienna began its work to break up and redistribute Napoleon's empire. However, in 1815, there was an interruption, when Napoleon made a final attempt at a comeback – his so-called Hundred Days. In early 1815 Napoleon left his exile on the Mediterranean island of Elba and landed near Cannes with a force of 800. By the time he reached Lyon these had grown to 7,000. Less than three weeks after landing, he triumphantly entered the capital with an army of thousands.

Condemning the landing, the Congress of Vienna said that Napoleon had made himself an enemy and disturber of the tranquillity of the world, and had rendered himself liable to public vengeance. Europe prepared for war, and the combined armies of the British, Spanish, Prussians, Austrians and Dutch numbered over one million men. Napoleon had gathered about 375,000.

The main Austrian armies massed along the Upper Rhine; the Spaniards were approaching the Pyrenees; the Prussians were in the Netherlands; and the Duke of Wellington, commander-in-chief of the British, Hanoverians and Belgians, established his headquarters at Brussels. Napoleon resolved to attack the Prussians and the British, convinced he had the secret backing of the Belgians and the Belgian army, and that they would swing round to his side if he won a single victory against Wellington or Blucher. The British and the Prussians were also apprehensive about the loyalty of the 17,000 Belgian and Dutch troops under Wellington's command.

The two sides met at Waterloo, about 12 miles (20km) south of Brussels. The battle lasted for ten hours and 50,000 soldiers were killed. Towards the evening the French broke ranks and fled, pursued by Prussian troops. Napoleon himself escaped by coach to Paris, where he eventually abdicated and surrendered to the British. He was banished to the island of St Helena, where he died in 1821. The Musée Wellington at Waterloo, and Ferme du Caillou, where Napoleon stayed, both contain maps and plans of how the battle was fought.

Unity & Revolt

In 1814-15 the Congress of Vienna redrew the map of Europe in the wake of Napoleon's military exploits. One of the dilemmas facing it was the future of the Netherlands. The north had been an independent state since 1648, but the former Spanish and Austrian Netherlands had no tradition of independence and Congress was reluctant to create one. Austria had no desire to recover these provinces, and there was no question of their going to France. So what was to become of them?

The Congress of Vienna opted to unite the Netherlands and the Austrian Netherlands and form the United Kingdom of the Netherlands, thereby creating a strong buffer between France and Prussia. It was a solution that few inhabitants had asked for, other than a few Belgian entrepreneurs who saw that union with the Dutch might compensate for the loss of markets in France.

The United Kingdom of the Netherlands was created as a constitutional monarchy ruled by William of Orange. He was installed as sovereign prince on 31 July 1814, and declared king in 1815. The new kingdom had 17 provinces and two capitals, the Hague and Brussels. William I was eager to promote prosperity and unity, and although he succeeded in the former, he failed in the latter.

The southerners found many reasons to resent the new state. The south of the kingdom was already industrialised and had become wealthy as a result. Although Brussels was joint capital, the new country was governed by a Dutch king, Dutch ministers and Dutch civil servants. Despite being more numerous and prosperous, the Belgians had little political power at the outset and gained little more over time: even 15 years later in 1830, only 18 out of the 119 generals and staff officers in the army were Belgian. Many Belgians took refuge in memories of the earlier grandeur of Antwerp and Brussels, regarding the Hague, Amsterdam and the Dutch as upstarts.

There was also fury at the government's attempts to introduce Dutch as the standard language. This resentment was not confined to French speakers: those who spoke Flemish dialects also protested against the use of Dutch. Belgium's Catholics were opposed to the new government because it had declared religious freedom and removed the Catholic bias in the education system.

Belgian liberals also opposed the new state, seeking freedom of the press and a less autocratic style of government. In 1828 Catholics and liberals formed an unlikely alliance, demanding that

When can you start talking about Belgium?

Belgium did not exist as an independent nation until 1830, but people had started using the name Belgium (la Belgique in French, and België in Flemish) at the end of the eighteenth century, to describe the area. Before that, it had gone under a variety of names depending on who happened to own it at the time.

While it was part of Spain in the sixteenth and seventeenth centuries, it was known as the Spanish Netherlands (les Pays-Bas espagnols, or de Spaanse Nederlanden). Later, it was to become known as the Austrian Netherlands

(les Pays-Bas autrichiens, or de Oostenrijkse Nederlandern). Just to confuse the issue, some historians also refer to the country during both those periods as the Southern Netherlands (les Pays-Bas méridionaux, or de zuidelijke Nederlanden).

The territory covered during those various incarnations roughly corresponds to that of modern Belgium, the chief exception being that the Principality of Liège remained an independent principality until the end of the eighteenth century.

---

the Belgians, not the Dutch, be the dominant force in the Netherlands. The government made concessions, repealing the language decrees in the south and guaranteeing freedom of education, but it would neither accept Belgian supremacy nor grant freedom of the press.

BELGIAN REVOLUTION

The winter of 1829-30 was severe, and farmers suffered accordingly. In addition, overproduction in the industries of the south had caused wage cuts, bankruptcies and unemployment. Workers in both sectors were mutinous, and there were regular protests and demonstrations in Brussels.

On 25 August 1830 (a month after the July 1830 revolution in France), an opera called *La Muette de Portici*, by Daniel Auber, was performed at the Théâtre de la Monnaie in Brussels. Its subject was the Naples rebellion of 1647 and the opera had been banned since being written in 1828. During an aria called 'L'Amour Sacré de la Patrie' ('Sacred Love of the Fatherland'), liberals and students inside the theatre started rioting, and then joined the workers who were protesting in the square outside. This marked the start of the Belgian Revolution.

The Dutch government negotiated with the leaders of the revolution and there seemed a possibility of administrative separation. But William I prevaricated and the impatient and disillusioned rebels decided to go for secession. William sent 10,000 troops into Brussels at the end of September, and while the numbers were insufficient to crush the revolution, they were enough to inflame the southern provinces into joining the uprising. Belgian soldiers deserted their regiments, and William's troops were driven out of Brussels.

A new government was rapidly assembled. On 4 October 1830, the rebels declared an independent state and provisional government; on 3 November they held elections for a National Congress. This met for the first time on 10 November and comprised 200 members, most of them intellectuals, lawyers and journalists. There were few men from industry or finance. On 22 November the new Congress decided on a constitution. Belgium was to be a parliamentary monarchy and unitary state of nine provinces, with freedom of religion, education, assembly, press and language, and a separate Church and State. On 3 March 1831, the Congress passed an electoral law defining the electorate, which consisted of about 46,000 men of the bourgeoisie. This meant that one out of every 95 inhabitants had the vote. At the time, this was a relatively high proportion – in France only one in 160 people could vote.

There was rapid recognition of the new nation in the rest of the world, and in January 1831 the Great Powers met in London to discuss the issue. Britain advocated the creation of a Belgian state, France and Germany agreed, and Belgium was duly recognised as an independent and neutral state. The choice of a new king was less harmonious, but eventually Léopold of Saxe-Coburg-Gotha was selected. He took an oath to the constitution on 21 July, now Belgium's National Day. Shortly afterwards, the Dutch invaded Belgium, and this helped prolong a sense of unity among the Catholics and liberals. The Dutch beat the Belgian rebels at Leuven and Hasselt but then retreated on hearing reports of an approaching French army of 50,000. The Dutch kept Maastricht and for a short time hung on to Antwerp as well, only surrendering it in December 1832. They did not recognise the new country until 1839.

Independent Belgium

It was inevitable that the coalition between liberals and Catholics in the new state of Belgium would be neither harmonious nor long-lived. The political history of Belgium in the nineteenth century consisted of a tug of war between the two sides, the main subjects of contention being the education system and the language split.

Belgium's history as a nation state began with the Catholics and the French speakers in the ascendant. The new constitution allowed people to use whichever language they preferred, but French was the language of the dominant class and was spoken in the courts, the education system (apart from some primary schools) and the administration. In the country as a whole, Flemish was more widely spoken, with 2.4 million Flemish speakers and 1.8 million French speakers. The majority of the population was governed in an alien language.

Intellectuals in Antwerp and Ghent soon began to resent the prevalence of French. In 1840 they organised a petition demanding the use of Flemish in the administration and law courts of Flemish-speaking provinces. However, this did not generate much popular support, for at this stage the Catholic-liberal split was a far more serious issue.

Initially, the Catholics were dominant at most levels. Membership of monasteries and convents more than doubled during the 1830s and '40s, and in 1834 a new Catholic university was founded at Mechelen, moving to Louvain (Leuven) in 1835. The Catholic Church also controlled much of secondary education. It was not until the 1840s that the Belgian liberals gained any impetus. In 1846 they held a congress in Brussels to clarify a political programme and to plan an election strategy. The sense of focus and organisation they gained from the congress gave them the upper hand over Catholics who did not organise themselves in the same way until the 1860s. Charles Rogier formed a liberal government in 1848, and the liberals governed, with a few gaps, until 1884.

Although Belgium lost the Dutch East Indies markets when it split from the Netherlands, there was industrial expansion in the 1830s, at a time when much of Europe had falling industrial prices. With its programme of railway construction, and large-scale investment in the coal, iron and banking industries, Belgium was the first country in continental Europe to undergo the Industrial Revolution. Nevertheless, there were still economic problems, such as a serious banking crisis in 1838. There was also crisis in the countryside. The rural linen and flax industries of Flanders were unable to compete with cheaper, more industrialised manufacturers in Britain. Matters weren't helped by a potato famine in Belgium in 1847. In that year 28 per cent of the population of East Flanders received poor relief.

As in the rest of Europe, a growing proletariat nurtured the rise of socialism. The Belgian Workers' Party was founded in 1885, and there were extensive strikes and protests by workers in 1886. Universal male suffrage was introduced in 1893, and in 1894 the socialists gained their first parliamentary seats. But the 1880s saw the Catholics regain power in Belgium, the bulk of their support in Flanders.

By the time the Catholics came to power in 1884, there had already been concessions to Flemish speakers, and the Catholics accelerated the process. In the 1870s and '80s there had been legislation introducing bilingualism in Flanders and strengthening the Dutch position in law and education, but the Flemish were still essentially governed and tried in French. But in 1898 Flemish was given official equality with French.

Despite constant dispute over particular issues, the Belgians did demonstrate a sense of unity in some areas of public life. Independence led to a building spree in Brussels. Among the earliest additions were the Galeries St Hubert in the 1840s. These were followed by a spate of official buildings and commemorative projects as Belgium celebrated its own existence, culminating in the construction of the Parc du Cinquantenaire for the fiftieth anniversary exhibition. The vast Palais de Justice was completed in 1883.

The main town-planning feat of the nineteenth century was covering over the River Senne. At first sight, Brussels appears to be an urban oddity in that it did not grow up around or near a river. In fact it did, but the Senne was slow flowing and narrow, and frequently caused flooding in low areas. It was also seen as a cause of disease and ill-health. So, in 1870, it was covered up, and thereafter Brussels shipping used the Canal de Willebroeck, which joins Brussels to the River Scheldt. A smaller river, the Maelbeek, was also covered over in Ixelles.

BELGIUM AS A COLONIAL POWER

The Belgian people expressed little appetite for imperialism or exploration in the nineteenth century, but Léopold II was eager to gain an empire. As Crown Prince, he had looked around for suitable territories, and considered British-run Borneo, the Philippines, South Africa and Mozambique. Finally, he decided to grab a piece of the 'magnificent African cake'. Much of central Africa was still unexplored and in 1876 Léopold set up the Association Internationale Africaine with the help of Henry Stanley (of 'Dr Livingstone, I presume?' fame). Although other European governments and the United States expressed qualms about Léopold's activities in Africa, he dismissed them sufficiently for the Berlin Declaration of 1885 to recognise the independent state of the Congo, with Léopold as head of state. He referred to himself as its proprietor. His new territory, over which he had absolute power, was 80 times the size of Belgium. From 1895, when he started exporting wild rubber, it generated massive revenue, much of which he passed back to Belgium in the form of public works such as the African Museum at Tervuren.

By the early twentieth century, Léopold's policy of extracting maximum profit from the Congo, regardless of ecological and human cost, was exposing Belgium to international criticism, particularly from Britain. In 1908 the Belgian government forced Léopold to hand it over to the nation, and it remained a Belgian colony until independence in 1960.

Belgium in the Wars

On its creation in 1830, Belgium declared itself perpetually neutral. But on 2 August 1914 Kaiser Wilhelm of Germany demanded that Belgium give German troops free passage on their way to invade France. Belgium had 12 hours to respond to the ultimatum, which it rejected. On 4 August German troops entered the country, and seven hours later Britain declared war on Germany. By midnight, five different empires were involved in war, and they all thought it would be over by Christmas.

Belgium suffered horribly in World War I. Snipers – known as *franc-tireurs* – shot at the Germans from ditches and outbuildings, and the Germans retaliated brutally. When snipers fired on Germans at the village of Hervé, they decided to set an example. Within a few days, only 19 of the 500 houses were still standing, the church was in ruins, and the shattered village was littered with corpses. Other massacres occurred elsewhere: the Germans shot 110 people at Andenne, 384 people at Tamines, and 612 people, including a three-week-old baby, at Dinant. Meanwhile, the German newspapers were full of stories about the torture and sadistic acts committed by the Belgian *franc-tireurs* against German troops.

Belgium fell and the government took refuge in Antwerp. The Germans entered Brussels on 20 August and held a military parade to celebrate. English nurse Edith Cavell, who had stayed on in the city and was later executed by the invaders, said that conversations with the Germans revealed they were surprised to find themselves there, having believed they were marching on Paris.

By the end of September, Antwerp was under siege and fell on 10 October, despite the arrival of British troops, including the poet Rupert Brooke, in a fleet of London buses. About 500,000 refugees left Antwerp, among them thousands of people who had fled there from elsewhere in Belgium.

Around 1.5 million had already left Belgium, although many later returned. The government went to Le Havre in France, while King Albert I took up position with the small Belgian army in the north-west of the country between Nieuwport and Ypres. There they fought in the deadly Ypres trenches alongside the French and British.

The four-year German occupation of Belgium had terrible consequences for the country. Its 44,000 war dead was hundreds of thousands less than Russia and France, but there was still great suffering. Around 700,000 Belgians were deported to Germany to work on farms and in factories, and the economy was devastated. Belgium had depended on other countries for its raw materials and its export markets, and it lost both. Much of its rail system was destroyed in an attempt to halt the German invasion, agricultural production fell, and there was widespread poverty and hunger.

The situation was prevented from becoming worse by the organisation of committees to provide food and relief. The National Assistance and Nutrition Committee (NHVC) was set up by the Belgians, while in the USA Herbert Hoover helped to set up the Commission for the Relief of Belgium.

Belgium was liberated in 1918, and until 1921 the main consideration of the post-war governments was how to rebuild the country. It is estimated that its losses represented about one-fifth of its national assets in 1914, and not all of them were recovered in war reparations.

The issues that had preoccupied the country before the war stagnated during and after it. The Flemish cause suffered a sizeable setback during the war: the Germans had been pro-Flemish, and a small group of Flemish politicians had been enthusiastic collaborators. In 1916, the Germans had given the Flemish lobby the prize they had been campaigning for since the turn of the century by declaring the University of Ghent Flemish-speaking. Not surprisingly, the university reverted to French when the Germans were defeated and did not become Flemish again until 1930.

Having recovered what they had lost during World War I, the Flemish made a series of language gains during the 1930s. In 1932 French and Flemish ceased to have equality in Flanders, where the official language became Flemish.

The period immediately after World War I had been marked by political unity, as Catholics, liberals and socialists worked together to rebuild the country. The unity quickly dissipated, however, particularly after the introduction of proportional representation. The first universal male suffrage elections without multiple votes for the bourgeoisie were held in 1919, and they resulted in a

King Albert I, *who reigned from 1909-34, didn't give in to the invading German armies without putting up a spirited fight.*

series of coalition governments. Between 1918-40, Belgium had 18 different administrations.

There was some economic recovery in the late 1920s, with Belgium's workers enjoying a standard of living much higher than before the war. But during the 1930s, Belgium slumped into depression, and its politics show much the same pattern as other European states. There was severe unemployment, social unrest and a move to the right. In the 1936 elections, Flemish nationalist and right-wing parties in Wallonia and Brussels made big gains, blaming the depression on the weak parliament, lack of strong leadership, and the unions.

After World War I, the Belgian government tempered its perpetual neutrality with an alliance with France. But towards the end of the 1930s, as Germany flexed its muscles, Belgium returned to its former position, reasserting its neutrality after Germany invaded Poland in 1939.

WORLD WAR II

Once again neutrality did Belgium little good, and on 10 May 1940 Hitler attacked. The Belgian response was different this time: whereas its stand in 1914 had led to international sympathy and admiration for the 'plucky' Belgians, this time there were raised eyebrows. Unlike his father Albert I, King Léopold III surrendered to the Germans after just 18 days. Much of the population supported Léopold's action, but the government itself did not. Believing that Belgium should commit itself to the Allies, it became a government-in-exile in Le Havre and then London.

Despite initially espousing a policy of normalisation in Belgium, the Germans became more authoritarian during the course of war. As the people became aware of this, there was greater resistance to the occupation. In the end, Belgium suffered many of the same problems as it had in WWI: deportations, forced labour, poverty and food shortages. Even so, there were both Walloons and Flemish who were deeply pro-German.

Belgium was liberated in September 1944 and one of the leaders' earliest tasks was to tackle the issue of collaboration. During 1944-9, the War Tribunals considered 405,000 cases, and reached 58,000 guilty verdicts, of which 33,000 were in Flanders. Most importantly the country had to deal with the behaviour of the King himself. The debate lasted five years, and eventually in 1950 the government held a non-binding referendum on whether Léopold should return. Only 57 per cent voted in his favour (72 per cent in Flanders and 42 per cent in Wallonia), and when he did come back there were serious disturbances. Léopold then stepped aside in favour of his son Baudouin who was crowned in 1951.

Even in the 1990s, the issue of collaboration is still sensitive. Up to 15,000 Belgians convicted of collaboration still receive reduced pension and property rights. In February 1996, a military court in Brussels reconsidered the case of Irma Laplasse, a Flemish farmer's wife who had betrayed resistance fighters to the Nazis in 1944. She was executed by firing squad in 1948. The court upheld her conviction, but ruled that the death sentence should have been commuted to life imprisonment. The judgment was met by protests from both sides. Concentration camp survivors and former members of the resistance and the Belgian secret army demonstrated outside the Palais de Justice in protest at any moves to rehabilitate collaborators. For their part, members of the nationalist Flemish Vlaams Blok party are campaigning for an amnesty for all those accused of collaborating, insisting that the War Tribunals were an attempt to victimise and repress the Flemish.

Post-war Belgium

World War II had made it clear that Belgium's traditional neutrality was pointless, and even before the war was over the government-in-exile set about rejecting the policy in favour of international alliances. It signed the Benelux Customs Union with Luxembourg and the Netherlands in 1944 (it came into force on 1 January 1948), abolishing all customs tariffs between the three countries and setting a common external tariff.

Belgium was also an enthusiastic participant in post-war international relations; partly it realised that as an export-driven economy it needed to belong to the growing international relations superstructure. Belgium was one of the first signatories of the UN Charter in June 1945, it participated in the Marshall Plan and it joined the Organisation for European Economic Co-operation in 1948. It joined the Council of Europe and the European Coal and Steel Community, and became the HQ of the European Economic Community (EEC) when it was set up in 1957. In 1960 Benelux countries abolished their internal borders. In 1967 Brussels became the headquarters of NATO.

The other important issue of the post-war years was the worsening of Flemish-Walloon conflict. As in 1918, the debate was initially dampened after the war by the awkward question of Flemish collaboration, but from 1960 onwards the split over language and community deepened. The language barrier between French-speaking Wallonia and Flemish-speaking Flanders was formally created in 1962 (Brussels is officially bilingual). In 1965 the political parties split into Flemish and Walloon wings. With the language question settled, the debate focused more on the constitution and the treatment of the Flemish and French communities.

The split between Flanders and Wallonia was exacerbated by economic developments. In the nineteenth and early twentieth centuries, Wallonia was the economic engine of Belgium because of its coal and steel. But these declined after WWI, and unemployment rose. Flanders, meanwhile, developed successful new industries, such as telecommunications, and complained that its wealth was being drained to prop up Wallonia. The Walloons in turn accused the government of economic favouritism towards the Flemish. In the 1971 elections, language-based parties such as Volksunie, Front des Francophones and Rassemblement Wallon achieved nearly a quarter of the vote.

Since 1970, the Belgian government has made a series of constitutional reforms, granting greater autonomy to the two communities and changing Belgium from a centralised to a federal state. There were prophesies of doom in 1993 when King Baudouin died, for he had been credited with holding the country together. So far, however, the country has not fallen apart and a new constitution was introduced in 1994. This created a new system of elected assemblies and governments representing the three regions of Flanders, Wallonia and Brussels, and the French, Flemish and German language communities. Belgian taxpayers complain bitterly about the cost of supporting these structures in addition to the national government, but at least the system has postponed any further split.

Brussels Today

If you had asked someone a couple of years ago to word-associate about Brussels, the answers would have been fairly bland. Tintin might have been mentioned, or beer, or perhaps something about mussels and chips. Ask the same question now and the response may involve phrases such as 'paedophile ring', 'corruption' or 'serial killer'.

After years of rarely earning a mention in the world's press, Belgium appeared to be the deviance capital of Europe for much of 1996-7. It started in August 1996 when the bodies of two missing girls were found in a dungeon in a house near Charleroi. The girls, 12 and 14, had been raped and tortured, and police arrested the owner of the house, convicted kidnapper and rapist Marc Dutroux.

Shortly afterwards, the bodies of four other missing girls, aged 8 to 19, were dug up. It quickly became clear that there had been massive police incompetence and/or corruption. Dutroux had been released early from prison against prosecutors' advice and his house had already been searched repeatedly by police who had failed to find the imprisoned girls, despite the fact that they had allegedly heard children crying. Furthermore, competing branches of the police had deliberately withheld information from each other. It was clear that the abductions were the work of an organised

ring, not of a lone pervert, and many people suspect that it had enjoyed high-level protection.

Belgium's response to the deaths of these girls and the circumstances leading to them was intense shock and outrage. Virtually every house and car in Belgium had black-bordered pictures of the girls in their windows; the funerals were broadcast on TV. Over 300,000 people took part in the 'White March' in Brussels to protest against corruption among Belgium's politicians, judiciary and police and the authorities' failure to prevent the tragedy.

But that was by no means all. In 1997, Brussels police found the body of a North African child, Loubna Benaissa, who had been missing since 1992. Her body was found less than a kilometre from her home, in a garage belonging to the father of a known paedophile. At the time of Loubna's disappearance, the police response had been dismissive – her family was told that the police could not use search dogs to look for her because the handlers were on holiday – and many Belgians attribute this to racism among the Ixelles police. Racism is also blamed for the fact that Loubna's face was absent from many of the posters of missing children displayed at the White March.

Later in the year, there were further unsettling discoveries. First, it seemed that a serial killer was at work in the Walloon town of Mons after human body parts were repeatedly found in carrier bags on the roadside (at the time of writing, nobody has been charged with the murders). And at the end of 1997, after the police had reopened their files on a number of unsolved disappearances, a quantity of human bones were found in the cellars of houses belonging to a Hungarian pastor, Andras Pandy, in the Molenbeek district of Brussels. He was charged with murdering six members of his family and at the time of writing is awaiting trial.

This sudden emergence of Belgium as a source of crime headlines has shaken existing preconceptions about the country, and forced many residents to reassess it. Is it still a complacent backwater somewhere between France and the Netherlands? Or a haven for the criminally insane?

If you ask a Belgian about the state of Belgium, the answer is likely to be gloomy. They will tell you about crime, corruption, high unemployment, and the terrible rise of either immigration or right-wing political parties such as the Vlams Blok. But if you ask many of the expats living in Belgium, they will tell you about the excellent health care, crèches and motorways, the numerous Michelin-starred restaurants, and the comfortable lifestyle of the Belgians. The only thing they will agree on is the cripplingly high taxes.

The answer, of course, lies somewhere between the two views. Life in Brussels has been good for many Belgians since 1945. Having suffered two German occupations this century, Brussels made a rapid recovery after World War

Belgian drivers

Belgians may grumble about rising crime in Brussels, but far more frightening to the average foreigner are the roads. The recklessness of Brussels drivers makes driving a fairly nerve-jangling experience at times, and it is rare to go a week without seeing some sort of accident. If you really want to get the adrenaline pumping in Brussels, a ride in a taxi should provide all the terror you want.

Brussels is enclosed by a huge network of excellent motorways (it is alleged that the lights of the Belgian motorway system are one of the few man-made structures that can be seen from space), which lead right into the centre of the city itself. Drivers arrive in central Brussels at high speed (except when the notorious 'Ring' is blocked by accidents), and are reluctant to slow down for anything. In particular, Belgium's *priorité à droite* law means that drivers do not have to give way when they approach a junction unless they slow down beforehand. Drivers therefore shoot straight out into the passing traffic at full speed, with the result that a significant number of Belgian cars have large dents in the right-hand passenger door or front wing.

Combine those factors with a tradition of low driving standards (there was no practical driving test until the 1970s) and a climate of regular rain, fog and snow, and it's not hard to imagine the results. Pile-ups on the motorway regularly involve dozens or even hundreds of cars.

II. The establishment of the EU and NATO headquarters in Belgium, and the service industries that grew up in their wake, helped create widespread affluence. Today, the city and suburbs are packed with excellent restaurants, designer shops are thriving, and the streets are jammed with BMWs and Saabs.

Brussels is the fulcrum of the EU and likes to think of itself as the capital of Europe. It is the home of the European Commission (basically the EU civil service) and the base for the Council of Ministers (made up of ministers from member states and the EU's main decision-making body). The EC is relatively small, with about 15,000 staff, but 100,000 non-Belgians work in jobs that have some direct or indirect connection to the EU. There are vast numbers of diplomats, lawyers, interpreters and journalists in Brussels; the city is also the international or European headquarters for many multinational companies and organisations.

So numerous are the associations and federations that there are even associations of associations: the Federation of International Associations and the Union of International Associations are both based in the city. These organisations support vast networks of catering companies (the cocktail party circuit is huge), cleaning companies, relocation experts, recruitment agencies and private schools, creating employment in Brussels and around.

However, the presence of the EU and its attendant professionals also creates problems, such as inflated house prices. Much of Brussels is completely unrepresentative of Belgium because the typical Belgian is unwilling or unable to pay rents or house prices designed for people on tax-free salaries and expense accounts. The fact that many Belgians feel financially excluded from Brussels leads some of them to regard it as a sort of overpriced Sodom and Gomorrah. 'You can't go out in Brussels after dark any more,' said one Belgian woman. 'It's not safe.' This might not be surprising from a speaker aged 75, but is strange from a 30-year-old. Stories abound of car-jackings, murder and drug-related crime, but to the former resident of London or Paris, the Belgian capital seems refreshingly safe and crime-free (apart from widespread car theft, which is not surprising in a city where there are so many expensive cars around). Reports of police incompetence and corruption tend to fuel the Belgians' pessimism about crime.

Another reason for pessimism is the economy. Belgium is suffering from rising unemployment and a huge national debt, and the government is struggling to tighten its belt. In order to combat the deficit, there are plans to cut back Belgium's generous social security and pensions system, creating a widespread sense of insecurity.

All this dismay and insecurity is very visible in Brussels. If you go near government or EU offices on a weekday, you have a fairly high chance of seeing a demonstration. Not all protests are specifically Belgian (French farmers occasionally flood the streets around the EC buildings with milk or block them with vegetables), but you are likely to see Belgian students, teachers, car and steel workers and pensioners demonstrating about redundancies, pension reductions or social security cuts. You may also come across the police and judiciary protesting about plans to reform them. When there is no demonstration, you can see the Brussels riot police sitting around with their riot shields and barbed wire blockades, reading the paper and eating crisps while they wait for another protest.

Elsewhere in Brussels, there are other signs of recession. The area around the Gare du Midi is depressed, if colourful, while the Marolles district in the centre of Brussels is poor and rundown, with high infant mortality rates and several hostels for the homeless. Rue Gray, virtually on the doorstep of the EC's Breydel building,

EU & NATO institutions

Most of the European Union institutions in Brussels are based around the Rond Point Schuman, near the Parc du Cinquantenaire. Until 1991, the European Commission was housed in the star-shaped Berlaymont building, but when it became clear that the asbestos in the 1960s building was a severe health threat, the staff were moved out. Some are now housed in the nearby Breydel building while others are scattered across different buildings in Brussels. The Berlaymont's glass front, which used to symbolise open government, is now tightly sheathed in plastic while the asbestos is stripped out. The fact that a building that used to act as pictorial shorthand for the EU is now deserted and dangerous is a convenient metaphor for Eurosceptics.

Journalists may use 'Brussels' as a synonym for the EU, but not all the European institutions are based here. Luxembourg houses the European Court of Justice, the Court of Auditors and the European Investment Bank, and it plays host to Council of Ministers meetings in April, June and October. The European Parliament is based in Strasbourg, in France, although most committees meet in Brussels. Many people have pointed out that these divisions lead to vast amounts of time and money being wasted on travel between Luxembourg, Strasbourg and Brussels, but not surprisingly France and Luxembourg are adamant that they will not cede their institutions to Belgium, or anywhere else.

In addition to housing the European institutions, Brussels is the headquarters of NATO and the secretariat of the European defence organisation, the Western European Union. These have a relatively low profile compared to the EU. Whereas the yellow stars and blue background of the EU are emblazoned all over the place in Brussels, you don't see people with car stickers or umbrellas bearing the NATO or WEU logos, nor do you see old-fashioned *quartiers* being destroyed to make way for yet more of their buildings. Nor indeed do you hear Brussels proclaiming itself the capital of the West's defences.

But then again, given that the former Belgian secretary-general of NATO, Willy Claes, had to resign because of a corruption scandal, NATO is probably not a subject many Belgians care to boast about.

---

is a shockingly neglected street of semi-derelict houses and high unemployment. The extreme right-wing parties have become increasingly popular in Belgium, although the problem of racism is far more serious in Antwerp than in Brussels. Even so, there have been racially motivated attacks in working class districts such as Schaerbeek and Molenbeek, and the police in these districts and Matonge are routinely accused of racism.

Another problem for Belgium is the unsettling question of its future. Following the constitutional reforms of 1980-94, Belgium is now a federalist monarchy with three regional governments: in Flanders, Wallonia and Brussels. Flanders is Flemish-speaking, Wallonia is Francophone, and the Brussels region is a bilingual (in practice mainly Francophone) enclave within the Flemish-speaking area. What should happen next is the subject of immense disagreement. On the one hand, there is a desire, particularly in Flanders, for further separation and an end to the federal state. The Flemish see Wallonia, with its dying coal and steel industries, as a burden on their healthier economy and they resent paying high taxes in order to pay for the social security benefits doled out to the Walloons. On the other hand, many Belgians regret the end of a unitary state, and the big show

of popular and patriotic mourning that followed the death of King Baudouin in 1993 was seen by many as a protest against the dismantling of the state of Belgium. Taxpayers also complain about the cost of supporting three regional governments in addition to the central government.

In daily life, the tensions are most evident in the language divide. In central Brussels, most people speak Flemish and French, but in the suburbs and elsewhere, the language issue can be more sensitive: people in Bruges and Ostend will often claim not to understand French and prefer to use English as their second language. In some of the more radical Flemish *communes* outside Brussels, there are reports that mail is torn up if the address contains French words such as 'rue' or 'Madame' instead of their Flemish equivalents.

Nevertheless, none of the above should lead anyone to think that Brussels is a collapsing city of the unemployed, the corrupt and the separatist. Whatever the Belgians say about their disabling taxes and their disintegrating state, they are adept at the business of living well and adapting to circumstance. Thus, the restaurants continue to flourish, the foie gras sellers prosper, and the Belgian bourgeoisie get on with business as usual. Look hard at the strikers and demonstrators and you will see that many of them are wearing fur.

Architecture

The Belgian capital's architecture has a glittering past – but an uncertain future.

Brussels' cocktail of styles has been shaken and stirred over the centuries by rousing Gothic, imperial pomp, industrial verve and EU modernity – with a dash of art nouveau lunacy thrown in for good measure. Brussels is finally waking up to its architectural heritage.

For a handsome city with at least two remarkable indigenous architectural styles – Flemish Renaissance and art nouveau – it held that heritage very cheap. The past 50 years have been a litany of demolition or neglect. Fanciful buildings that couldn't be turned into office blocks had no place in a city that aspired to be the capital of Europe. The lively Quartier Léopold was gutted and the Gotham City of the EU institutions put in its place. Victor Horta's masterpiece, the Maison du Peuple, was pulled down in 1964, despite international protests.

Other buildings were left to rot for years – the **Halles de Schaerbeek**, the **Magasins Old England**, the **Ixelles Radio Building**. In 1966, the first voices of protest were raised and the action group ARAU was formed. In recent years their concern has been shared by the entire population, and Brussels is suddenly in the business of cleaning up its image. The Fondation de l'Architecture in rue de l'Hermitage is to be enlarged; a good number of buildings – among them the **Palais des Beaux Arts** and the Halles de Schaerbeek – have been, or will be, renovated; and new buildings are now being designed with considerably more verve.

It's easy to make two immediate observations about architecture in Brussels. The first is that there is no such thing as homogeneity. That uniformity found in the terraces of other European cities does not exist here. On any one street the houses will be of various heights and widths and built with different stone; one will have a wrought-iron balcony, the next will not; one will have fanciful round windows, its neighbour will have discreet rectangular ones. This stylistic riot came about partly because Brussels was built more by private citizens, who had their own ideas about what they wanted, than by town councils or large building companies. Another important factor was the late nineteenth-century practice of having house-façade competitions, which meant architects were more concerned with showing off their flamboyant talents than developing conformity. This eclecticism has been compared to attending a concert in which the chords refuse to harmonise.

But it can also be regarded as invigorating: the eye does not grow tired at ceaseless repetition as it might elsewhere. The best way to take in this peculiarity of Brussels is simply to walk around the different *communes*, Ixelles, St Gilles and Uccle being particularly pleasant. Almost all the buildings date from the last 150 years, but within this limitation there are seemingly endless combinations. The other immediately striking point is the richness of the interiors. The blandest of façades will often turn out to contain the most sumptuous décor within. Mirrors, gilt edgings, trompe-l'œil, stained glass, ornamented ceilings... all are found in what appear to be the most ordinary-looking of homes. Keeping this lavishness and eccentricity inside is typically Bruxellois. It is the same spirit that leads to those clubs where you can dance till noon on Sunday while normal life goes on in the street above you.

To get the full feel of Brussels interiors you really have to know some inhabitants – preferably Belgians, since they have a habit of keeping beautiful things in the family and so are generally better able to adorn their houses than blow-in foreigners. Failing that, cafés and bars such as **La Chaloupe d'Or**, **A La Mort Subite**, **Le Falstaff** and **De Ultieme Hallucinatie** (*see chapter* **Cafés & Bars**) or public buildings such as the **Théâtre de la Monnaie** and **Centre Belge de la Bande Dessinée** give a good idea of the city's interiors through the ages.

Brussels, having been controlled at various times by the French, Spanish, Dutch and Austrians, reflects these different influences in its buildings. Most of the best examples of Dutch baroque and Renaissance architecture are to be found in other Belgian cities, but they survive in Brussels' churches and the **Grand Place**. Meanwhile French neo-classicism leaves its mark all around the **Royal Quarter**. From 1830, the two key styles in the city are Léopold II's imperial grandeur and the almost hallucinogenic swirlings of art nouveau at the end of the nineteenth century.

Luc Fayd'herbe's best work may lie outside the capital, but the honey-coloured **Eglise St Jean-Baptiste** *is a masterpiece.*

Gothic

Under the Burgundians of the fifteenth century, Brussels must have looked rousingly Gothic, but very few of the buildings remain. Churches are the main preserve of Gothic and baroque architecture in Brussels. Large-scale, arched, graceful and turreted, the two finest examples of Brabant Gothic architecture are the fifteenth-century **Notre Dame du Sablon** and **Cathédrale des Sts Michel et Gudule**. These impressive buildings, like St Peter's and St Guido's in Anderlecht and Bruegel's burial place (Notre Dame de la Chapelle), are faithful to the Brussels custom of superior interiors: all are beautifully proportioned inside, with tapestries, statues and breathtaking stained glass.

The **Hôtel de Ville** (Town Hall) is Brussels' sole secular example of this period, the only building in Grand Place to withstand the 1695 French bombardment. It stands among the later ornate buildings, its arches and its numerous sculptures clearly hailing from an earlier era. But, like the churches, it juxtaposes great size with surprising grace and sombre piety, though the latter impression could be due to the more recent addition of city grime. Cathédrale des Sts Michel et Gudule has now been cleaned, removing the association between Gothic and darkness, but the Hôtel de Ville retains its black exterior.

Flemish Renaissance

This is a loose term applied to the Italo-Flemish rococo baroque style of the seventeenth century (it's no wonder some shorthand label was thought to be needed), though the term Renaissance is misleading for such a late period. It's a style the Belgians are proud of because it's a home-grown one rather than one imported from their more powerful neighbours. Luc Fayd'herbe is the key name connected with this style in churches, though again his best work is to be found outside the capital. His Brussels masterpiece is undoubtedly the vigorous, honey-coloured Eglise St Jean-Baptiste, which, along with his other church, Notre Dame aux Riches Claires, has some of the features of a private house.

The gems in this style are the ornate and fanciful guildhouses of Grand Place, each with the distinctive markings of its guild. Remarkably, almost all of them were built in the four years following the 1695 bombardment and they are in impeccable condition. Remarkable, too, is the fact that the effect of all those decorative façades manages to be harmonious. Italo-Flemish baroque influenced the sculpture of this period, the chief example being **Manneken Pis**, who, it should be noted, has been as much admired for the grace of his design as vilified for its vulgarity.

Neo-classicism

The eighteenth century steadily gave way to a clean, creamy and symmetrical neo-classicism. This was at the prompting of the Austrians and French and coincided with the transformation of Brussels into a city for the aristocracy. The **Palais de Charles de Lorraine**, former residence of the governor of the Austrian Netherlands, is an early example of this style, though with its numerous statues, pillars and mouldings, it is more elaborate than those buildings that came at the end of the century. The great architect of these was Barnabé Guimard, who designed the **Palais de la Nation** (now the Belgian Parliament) and that carefully symmetrical group of stark white buildings around place Royale. Charles of Lorraine wanted to make Brussels look like Vienna, but it was overtaken first by Napoleon and then briefly by the Dutch before finally gaining independence. As a result, neo-classicism only left its chilly fingerprints on the Upper Town. Consequently, the old distinction between the Upper Town (French and aristocratic) and the Lower Town (Flemish and mercantile) is still immediately apparent.

Nineteenth century

The nineteenth century was a time of rapid and widespread construction, not least because of the huge population growth. The River Senne was efficiently buried and boulevards raised on its banks, leaving Brussels as one of the only European capitals to appear to be without a river. Until the explosion of art nouveau, it was a great century for reworking old styles. Everything can be described as 'neo': the prison of St Gilles imitates English Gothic; the town hall in Schaerbeek is neo-Renaissance. Private houses of the period are a cheerful mixture of styles, with Dutch, German and French influences visible everywhere.

The industrial age manifested itself in a profusion of iron- and glass-clad municipal buildings. Europe's first glass-covered shopping arcade, Jean-Pierre Cluysenaer's **Galeries St Hubert**, appeared in 1847; Charles Girault used iron and glass to give a feeling of space to his **Musées Royaux d'Art et d'Histoire** and the **Musée Royale de l'Armée et d'Histoire Militaire** in the Parc du Cinquantenaire; and Alphonse Balat was the most triumphant of all in his creation of the **Serres Royales** (Royal Hothouses) at Laeken.

Léopold II

If Brussels has some of the imperial feel of Paris and London, it is thanks to this man, who came to the throne in 1865. Treating the Congo as his personal playroom, he used the millions accrued there to endow Brussels with heroic dimensions.

Résidence Palace – *at 155 rue de la Loi.*

Everything monumental and imposing in the city can be credited to him. The enormous **Palais de Justice** is emblematic of his style: heavy and imperial. Léopold gave the city the great avenues de Tervuren and Louise, the **Arc de Triomphe** and the museums in the Parc du Cinquantenaire, and the **Museum voor Midden-Afrika** in the Parc de Tervuren. His style is little admired today: it smacks of imperial arrogance and one can't help thinking of the atrocities committed in the Congo during his reign. His style is held to be un-Belgian: many extol the virtues of the Flemish districts and condemn Léopold for giganticism in a city of miniatures. Certainly the style associated with him lacks Flemish wit and delicacy, but he opened up the city with a broad-minded coherence that this century's developers wholly lacked. Take, for example, the remarkable straight line (rue Royal Sainte Marie, rue Royale and rue de la Régence) which runs all the way from the railway station in Schaerbeek to the Palais de Justice. On the way it includes the great Schaerbeek Town Hall, the neo-Byzantine Eglise Sainte Marie, the lovely glass Jardins Botanique, the colonne du Congrés, the royal palace and place Royale. That's some chain of buildings. Take a taxi from one end to the other and spare some admiration for Léopold.

Art nouveau

At the end of the nineteenth century there was a sudden dam-burst of talent and Brussels for the first time was at the centre of a new architectural style. Brussels is full of handsome buildings, but most of them are on borrowed lines, using styles developed in other countries. Art nouveau originated in Britain in the 1880s, but it was Brussels that wholeheartedly seized upon it when architects such as Paul Hankar, Henri van de Velde, Paul Cauchie and, above all, Victor Horta made it their own. Art nouveau was inspired by the shapes of flowers and plants. It is about what Horta called 'maximum fluidity': the intertwining of all elements into a trembling whole. The effect is flowing and hallucinogenic. The hallmarks of art nouveau are sinuous lines, round windows, frescoes and sgraffiti (a mural design technique in which the top layer of glaze, plaster and other materials is cut to reveal parts of the material underneath).

The new style hit Brussels in 1893 with the house that Horta built for industrialist Emile Tassel at 6 rue Paul Emile Janson. This bears all the hallmarks of a Horta house. The bold exterior stands out from the propriety of its neighbours but doesn't go too far, maintaining a certain rectitude, while madness is given freer reign inside. In this way Horta was in the Belgian tradition and firmly avoided the showy flamboyance of Gaudí, his contemporary in Barcelona.

The best way to sample art nouveau in Brussels is to visit Horta's own house in rue Américaine (*see chapter* **Museums**). Or you could go on one of the ARAU trips, which get you inside some of the private art nouveau houses (*see chapter* **Sightseeing**: **Trips & tours**).

The large number of art nouveau houses in Brussels is due to a lucky confluence between talented architects and wealthy, enlightened patrons. Men such as Armand Solvay and Edmond van Eetvelde, industrialists and engineers who built the Congo Free State, commissioned these great houses with no regard for expense. They didn't need to: at the time, Brussels was richer than ever before or since. Art nouveau suited the individualistic temperament of wealthy Belgians. Their houses are all in isolated pockets, and there was no co-ordinated city planning. Ernest Blérot was alone in creating an entire art nouveau neighbourhood, building 25 houses around the Ixelles lakes.

The architects took the money and followed their visions, but many were committed socialists, and more interested in building for the people than for the elite. The Belgian Workers' Party gave its considered approval of the new style: such buildings were a concrete illustration of Marxist ideology. Art nouveau was therefore the preferred

Maison de St Cyr – built by a 22-year-old.

medium of free-thinkers and socialists, while Catholics condemned it as godless extravagance and turned to neo-Renaissance for their houses. Art nouveau was gradually brought to bear on municipal buildings, too. Louis Bertrand, mayor of Schaerbeek, then the fastest-growing *commune* in Brussels, decreed that all public buildings should be in the new style.

Paul Hankar designed numerous shopfronts, of which only the florist in rue Royale survives. The most famous and daring of the municipal designs was Horta's Maison du Peuple, a bold glass-covered building which was to house entertainment for the people. However, the people were not to be entertained for long. Having fallen into disuse, the Maison was pulled down in 1964. Alban Chaubon's theatres were similarly demolished, as were Hankar's shops and Blérot's own house.

Art nouveau was a short-lived phenomenon. Some of the most daring houses were built at the beginning of this century, such as Cauchie's sgraffiti-covered house in rue des Francs and the extraordinary **Maison de St Cyr** in square Ambiorix, built with quicksilver confidence by the 22-year-old Gustave Strauven. But by 1905, the style was fading fast. The rich began to move out to the countryside and the homes that were built for the mercantile classes had begun to betray the original spirit of art nouveau with their extravagant exteriors and bland interiors. Such ostentation was too much for Horta, who abandoned art nouveau for art deco, heralding the end of a great creative period. In just ten years art nouveau had entirely changed the face of the city.

Between the wars

Between 1918-39, Brussels seemed to be in the business of breaking records. All its municipal buildings had to be the first and best of their kind. The Palais des Beaux Arts was the first multipurpose entertainment centre in the world, uniting a concert hall, theatre, cinema, exhibition spaces, shops and cafés under one roof; the marvellous **Résidence Palace** was built as an apartment

block for the *haute bourgeoisie* and pre-dated New York's Rockefeller Center, which it closely resembles. It included within its 11 storeys a theatre, shops, Turkish baths, a dreamy green swimming pool and a roof garden. Presumably its inhabitants had no need to leave except to go to work. It is now hemmed in by EU buildings and has ceased to be a residential building. The Radio Building by the Ixelles lakes was built in 1938 and was then the most advanced communications building in the world.

By now the dominant style was art deco, its stern functionalism ideal for multipurpose buildings. Horta, having crossed styles with consummate ease, was continuing to make his presence felt: **Gare Centrale** and the Palais des Beaux Arts are both his. The latter has just been restored to its original appearance after years of suffering the indignity of scaffolding. Even so, one rather regrets that Horta gave up his dazzling art nouveau for these static, if admirably executed buildings.

Aside from record-breaking, the two main innovations between the wars were apartment blocks and *cité-jardins*. Blocks of rather stolid, geometrical buildings were designed to flank a small garden square and this became a feature of the city. The Tintin illustrations of the period reflect this development: well-brushed paving stones, straight buildings and a certain calm.

Post-war

Brussels' architectural fortunes since World War II are a sorry tale. Dual carriageways sliced through the *communes*. Useful though they no doubt were, they paid scant regard to the calm layout of the city. Having become the crossroads of Europe, Brussels was apparently determined to look like one. Post-war reconstruction continued piecemeal. Skyscrapers and the appalling **Tour du Midi** sprang up; the areas round Gare du Midi and Gard du Nord were demolished. Brussels was not short of good architects; it was just that they seemed to devote their talents to Antwerp and Ghent. Van Reeth's house in Antwerp and Van Impe's strange, curving, frankly sexual house in Ghent are more interesting than anything that was being built in the capital.

Today the picture is beginning to look hopeful again. True, the ludicrous *faux* baroque houses being built around Gare Centrale in supposed harmony with the older buildings are an example of the worst type of empty nostalgia. But the **Conrad Hotel** in avenue Louise has an opulent boldness, and the recently opened **European Parliament** has a gleaming, well-defined look and is a vast improvement on the 1970s-built Berlaymont. This century, much like the last one, is going out in a certain amount of style.

Surrealist Brussels

Some of the twentieth century's most astonishing visual art came out of the Belgian capital and its bourgeois suburbs.

The year 1998 was designated in Brussels as the year of René Magritte, with a major retrospective at the Musée d'Art Moderne (*see chapter* **Museums**). The show is the second of three important exhibitions mounted by the gallery. In 1997 a huge retrospective marked the centenary of Paul Delvaux, the other major Belgian surrealist painter fully the equal of Magritte. In 1999 the spotlight will fall on James Ensor, one of the oddest of Belgium's many expressionist painters, and a strong influence on Belgian surrealism.

To purists, a well-behaved, tasteful surrealist exhibition is perhaps a contradiction in terms. But surrealism is not Dada, and there's little likelihood of scandal. In fact, Belgium was little affected by the Dada movement. Dada was an act, born out of

René Magritte (1898-1967)

Cultural objects provide an infinite number of interpretations, and the surrealists would have been the last to claim definitive meanings for their work. Indeed, Magritte held that his own paintings had no meaning at all. One of the most challenging of his paintings is *Le Viol* or *The Rape* (1934; *see right*). The essential aspects of the female body – breasts and vulva – are transformed into a face, with the nipples for eyes and the vulva for the mouth. It appears at first an oppressive image, another instance of the masculine appropriation of the feminine body. (Men find it disturbing, too: at least one male member of the surrealist group could never avoid laughing uncomfortably when confronted with it.)

Although he never intended the work itself to be oppressive, Magritte has reproduced one of the oldest images in the world: an image of the feminine more profound than anything even Delvaux ever produced. There are few examples of the ancient image of Baubo available to us (there are fifth-century BC examples in Berlin's Museum für Völkerkunde), but once upon a time this image was one of the aspects of the Great Goddess, in the form of Baubo the Bellygoddess, who descended from the neolithic Belly-goddesses. Her eyes were nipples and she spoke through her vulva. She represented, among other things, active female obscenity. By displaying herself obscenely to the grieving goddess Demeter and telling her dirty jokes, she

gave Demeter new heart to continue the search for her lost daughter Persephone. In archaic ritual terms, the old was mocked to make way for the birth of the new – the essence of surrealism.

Paul Delvaux (1897-1994)

Though often described as a surrealist, Delvaux never considered himself part of the movement. There is a room dedicated to his work at the Musée d'Art Moderne (*see chapter* **Museums**). *Le Musée Spitzner* (1943; *see below*) contains many of the motifs that were to recur throughout Delvaux's career – the sleeping Venus, the skeleton, the moonlight, mountains, statues and classical architecture. The real Musée Spitzner was part of the Foire du Midi in Brussels and the fascinated Delvaux visited it several times. It included a lifelike, breathing wax model of a reclining Venus, and this image was transposed directly into his work from 1931 onwards. The men in suits on the right of the picture are portraits of Delvaux's friends and associates Paul-Gustave van Hecke, Gérard Bertouille, Emile Salkin, Olivier Picard and Yvan Denis.

the horrors of World War I, while surrealism is an idea, and so relatively safe. In the opinion of the critic Robert Hughes, 'Surrealism [is] a shining example of liberty on which, in principle, nobody acts.' However, surrealism did come out of Dada and rumour has it that, true to tradition, there may yet be a brouhaha brewing.

Like many revolutionaries, the Belgian surrealists often seemed to live out the petty-bourgeois existence they claimed to deplore. Magritte lived in a little suburban house in Jette and enjoyed a long and happy marriage to Georgette, his only muse. Delvaux, too, found his true love in Tam (having divorced his first wife, Suzanne Purnal), and then never looked elsewhere; he became a pillar of the Belgian art establishment. Magritte did not even have a studio, but painted in his sitting room. When his contemporaries commented on this, he replied that the paint was intended for the canvas, not the carpet. The Magrittes spurned bohemianism. Their house was impeccable and they kept a succession of Pomeranian dogs.

PARIS VS BRUSSELS

There were key differences between French and Belgian surrealism, resulting in a perpetually uneasy relationship between the two. The Paris group was strongly political and enjoyed close links with French left-wing parties, supporting calls for strikes and other political action. André Breton, the leader of the French surrealists, supported Trotsky when he was expelled from France. In contrast, the Brussels group was more interested in subverting the image rather than the political structure. Although briefly a member of the Communist Party, Magritte could not tolerate its doctrinaire attitudes to art and left quietly.

Breton was also fanatically anti-religion, despite the fact that his own pronouncements resembled papal decrees, and the Paris group tended to be as doctrinaire as any church. Relations between Breton and Magritte were always strained, particularly during Magritte's three-year stay in France in the late 1920s. René and Georgette attended meetings of Breton's group regularly, and Magritte, an agnostic, used to tease Breton mercilessly about his attitude to Roman Catholicism. One evening, Georgette came to the meeting wearing a small gold cross, a keepsake from her mother. Seeing it, Breton launched into one of his vitriolic denunciations. The Magrittes left, never to come back; shortly afterwards they returned to Brussels. Despite these differences, Breton came to Brussels in 1934 and gave an important talk entitled 'What is Surrealism?' at the Maison des Huit Heures in honour of a surrealist exhibition mounted by ELT Mesens.

Another difference between the French and Belgian movements was in their approach to artistic influences. The Paris group was particularly influenced by the art of Polynesia, whereas the Belgians (and Magritte in particular) did not take inspiration from 'exotic' cultures. Magritte's main influence was ordinary life (hence his conventional private life), and it was there that he sought the 'marvellous' that the surrealists so prized.

THE ODD COUPLE

Apart from their quiet, committed love lives, Magritte and Delvaux, almost exact contemporaries, had little in common. This isn't altogether surprising: Magritte's work has an intellectual quality that was foreign to Delvaux, the emotional and sensuous dreamer. Magritte had socialist beliefs, whereas Delvaux devoted himself to art. Magritte referred to him as 'Monsieur Delvache' and considered him a 'retina cretina' – a painter of pretty pictures. Yet he was impressed and disturbed by Delvaux's work and admitted he had been influenced by it.

The differences between the two were compounded by class. Delvaux came from a rich background (and so lowered his status by becoming

Delvaux's mural at **La Bourse** *Métro station.*

a painter), whereas Magritte's background was poor. Delvaux did not like Magritte, referring to the latter's 'disagreeable personality'. Some of their works have elements in common – the similarities between Delvaux's *The Window* (1936) and Magritte's *In Praise of Dialectic* (1937) are striking. Delvaux admired Jules Verne, whose characters from *A Journey to the Centre of the Earth* recur frequently in his paintings. Magritte enjoyed Poe. They even inhabited opposite areas of Brussels – Magritte in Jette to the north-west and Delvaux in Boisfort to the south-east.

CAFE SOCIETY

If you can tear yourself away from fine art, dawdle in some of the cafés and bars frequented or run by the surrealists themselves. One of the most popular of these spots is Le Greenwich (*see chapter* **Cafés & Bars**) in rue des Chartreux, where Magritte used to play chess. Forget the culture and enjoy the hushed, smoky, music-free atmosphere. Moon-shaped brass lights balloon out above the heads of its stolid patrons, who solemnly play chess on tables resembling sewing-machine stands. Marcel Duchamp came here as a professional chess player and member of the French national chess team and was annoyed at being defeated twice in a row by an 11-year-old boy named Bobby Fischer. Magritte must have found it a pleasant change after a hard day slaving over *Les Rencontres Naturelles* or the nth version of *The Empire of Lights*. The writer Louis Scutenaire tells how Magritte couldn't seem to keep away from the place, yet he found the habit of going there 'degrading' and announced he was never going to darken its doorway again. He was back the next day.

La Fleur en Papier Doré (*see chapter* **Cafés & Bars**) is a little surrealist museum-piece in rue des Alexiens, once run by Magritte's great friend Gerard van Brauene, the pixie of the Belgian surrealists. If you approach it after dark, bear in mind that the name is so faded as to be practically invisible. It's full of period charm, with an immense iron and brass stove, ephemera framed dustily on the walls and cobwebs dating from around 1950. The room upstairs is for exhibitions. It's so very period that the truth of the maxim scrawled on the wall, 'Nul n'est étranger comme moi-même', strikes home particularly forcefully: there's a slightly surreal feeling at being a tourist in such a place.

Le Cirio (*see chapter* **Cafés & Bars**) is a traditional café in rue de la Bourse that Magritte and the other surrealists used to frequent. It has a quiet, staid atmosphere, emphasised by the Regency stripe furnishings and art nouveau curls and mirrors. Other hangouts were Au Roi d'Espagne on Grand Place and the nearby Hulstkamp, which became La Taverne du Passage and is now very

expensive, and L'Imaige Nostre-Dame (*see chapter* **Cafés & Bars**) in rue du Marché aux Herbes.

TOURS

There are group and individual guided tours that take in the cemeteries in Ixelles and Schaerbeek where many of the surrealists are buried. Coach tours are also available. Contact the Tourist Information Office on 513 89 40 or 548 04 48. You need to book at least two weeks in advance. Events were scheduled throughout 1998 for many of the artists referred to in this chapter, both in Brussels and regionally. Contact Tourist Information for details.

Brussels sprouts

The Belgian surrealist movement did not begin and end with René Magritte and Paul Delvaux. Others, too, made their mark.

The influence of surrealism only showed in the work of **Rachel Baes** (1912-83) after 1945. She was friendly with Magritte, and ELT Mesens bought some of her paintings.

The poet **Paul Colinet** (1898-1957) met Magritte in 1930. Lecomte said of him that he was 'ill at ease in the presence of the too strictly rational'. He kept his own independence from the main group, his work having its roots deep within his childhood.

Camille Goemans (1900-60) was a writer and gallery owner of whom Magritte said: 'He set me the example of spiritual honesty.' He wrote a great deal but published very little. His role in the surrealist group was that of a questioner and a disseminator of ideas. He went to Paris and opened the Galerie Camille Goemans, which exhibited the works of artists such as Arp, Dali and Tanguy. After the gallery closed, Goemans left the surrealists in order to take up other interests.

Painter and collage-maker **Jane Graverol** (1905-84) was born in Ixelles of French parents. She studied at the Academy of Fine Arts in Brussels and met Magritte, Colinet, Goemans and Scutenaire in 1949. She founded the review *Temps mêlés* with André Blavier. In 1953 she published a small volume of writings by Magritte, Marien, Scutenaire, Lecomte, Colinet, Irene Hamoir and Van Brauene. She assisted Marien as editor of *Les Lèvres Nues*. Nougé, Marien and Lecomte were all enthusiastic about her painting, as was Breton, who took a particular interest in her work. She was strongly influenced by Magritte and, for a time, by Delvaux.

A poet and writer who had been influenced by Dadaism, **Marcel Lecomte** (1900-66) was one of Magritte's strongest supporters in his early years. He it was who showed Magritte a picture of De Chirico's *Song of Love* (1914), of which Magritte wrote: 'It was one of the most moving moments in my life; for the first time, my eyes saw thought.' He was a close friend of ELT Mesens. Along with Paul Nougé and Camille Goemans, he published a series of pamphlets called *Correspondence* that aimed to 'enlighten contemporary authors in regard to their own work'. He contributed to many reviews, including *Revue*

de l'Epoque, Disque Vert and *Adventure*. Jean Paulhan wrote that his work embodied 'a single primitive and mysterious state in which… idea and object were the same'.

A writer and maker of collages, **Marcel Marien** (1920-93) met Magritte in 1930 and collaborated with him on various works. He founded *Les Editions de l'Aiguille Aimantée* in 1941 and *Les Lèvres Nues* in 1954, which contained essays, articles and drawings by the surrealists. He and Magritte fell out in 1953 after Marien distributed a leaflet depicting Magritte's head on a banknote at the opening of the *Enchanted Realm* fresco in the casino at Knokke.

A French poet and writer – and biologist by profession – **Paul Nougé** (1895-1967) was active in the surrealist movement in Brussels. With a group of other surrealists, he founded the *Correspondence* group, which sometimes surpassed André Breton in its radical and subversive approach to literature. Nougé wrote a great deal about Magritte's paintings, including several prefaces to exhibitions. He was responsible for the title of Magritte's *The Empire of Lights*, and Magritte admired his work as much as he did that of Poe. However, they eventually fell out, and when asked in later years about Magritte, Nougé replied that he had nothing to say about him. Despite this, he wrote a deeply felt homage to his former mentor.

Louis Scutenaire (1905-88), the writer and poet, was born in Ollignies. He was introduced to Magritte and the other surrealists by Paul Nougé in Le Cirio in 1926. He lived in rue de la Luzerne and was known as 'Scute' to his friends. His book *Mes Inscriptions* (1945) was a collection of aphorisms, dialogues and odd facts, described by Waldberg as a book 'made from the stuff of wonder'. He wrote an essay on Magritte, who illustrated several of his poems. His insights into Magritte's work include the observations that 'he used his prison in order to escape' and 'he does not study objects, he utilises them'. Scutenaire collected a large number of Magritte's less publicly acceptable paintings.

In 1927, when composer and musicologist **André Souris** (1899-1970) was walking with a friend, they heard an organ-grinder churning out old romances. They bought the instrument, reversed the rolls of paper, and introduced these 'compositions' into a concert programme, causing quite a scandal. Souris also composed music to accompany a recording of Scutenaire's *Mes Inscriptions* in 1948.

Brussels
by Season

Brussels is a strange and wonderful city, all year round. Honestly.

It's easy to make the mistake of viewing Brussels as a haven for bureaucrats. Strip off its workaday suit, however, and you'll find that this is a city that likes to have fun. After all, Belgium has derived its character from its multifaceted neighbours and from its recent influx of international residents, and that is reflected in the culture of its capital city.

The joys of spring and the yearnings of summer bring out a multiplicity of events, ranging from the ultra-modern to the unashamedly provincial. The Tourist Information Board (513 89 40/fax 514 45 38) will provide you with all the information you need, including a useful annual brochure that can be posted or faxed to you free of charge. For activities beyond Brussels, the Belgian Tourist Information Office (504 03 90/fax 504 02 70) can offer specific tips to help you plan your trip.

Public holidays

	1998	1999
Easter Monday	13 Apr	5 Apr
Labour Day	1 May	1 May
Ascension Day	21 May	13 May
Whit Monday	9 June	24 May
National Day	21 July	21 July
Assumption Day	15 Aug	15 Aug
All Saints' Day	1 Nov	1 Nov
Armistice Day	11 Nov	11 Nov

Spring

Ars Musica
Date mid-Mar to early April. *Musiques Présentes, 25 Grand Place, 1000 (514 21 70/fax 512 66 49).*
For music-lovers of all cultures, this annual festival brings the finest modern musicians to Brussels. Many concerts are held in the Musée d'Art Ancien (*see chapter* **Museums**).

Serres Royales (Royal Hothouses)
61 avenue du Parc Royal (Domaine Royal), 1020 (513 89 40). Métro Heysel/tram 52, 92/bus 53. **Open** 9.30am-4pm Wed, Thur; 9-11pm Fri; 9.30am-4pm, 9-11pm, Sat, Sun. Note: only open two weeks around end April to early May, when the flowers are in bloom. Dates vary annually but are given out by the Tourist Office from Jan.
Admission free during day; 100BF at night.
For a few weeks Belgians get to peek into King Albert and Queen Paola's private world, when the royal hothouses are

opened to the public. The elegant complex known as 'the city of glass' was designed by nineteenth-century architect Alphonse Balat on a commission from Léopold II, who wanted it to be a showcase for the tropical plants he found in the Belgian Congo. The king later became so fond of the serene atmosphere within that he moved into one of the pavilions shortly before his death.

Scènes d'Ecran
Date 23-25 April. *Centre Culturel de la Communauté Française, 236 rue Royale, 1210 (218 37 32/fax 219 66 60).*
Second edition of this festival of films and videos about theatre, dance and opera. The intention is to bring the performance arts to a wider public, and the 1997 festival was a huge success. For the 1998 festival over 100 productions were submitted from all over Europe, with the selections made by a jury drawn from the great and the good.

Foire Internationale du Livre
Date late April to early May. **Admission** 200BF; 100BF students; 50BF groups. **Information** *72 rue A Campenhout, 1050 (646 38 90).* **Open** 9am-5pm Mon-Fri.
Although not on a par with Frankfurt's famed book fair, the Brussels five-day event does attract a significant crowd of readers. Some 80,000 visitors passed through in 1997. Don't expect to find many goodies in English as the fair focuses on European languages.

Festival van het Beeldverhal (Festival of the Comic Strip)
Date 8-10 May. *BD World, 3 rue des Mottes, 6230 Obaix (071 84 34 77/fax 071 84 34 77/festivalbd@ontonet.be).*
Fourth edition of this festival. In 1998 the theme was 'Animals in Comics', with over 50 authors in attendance.

Kunsten Festival des Arts
Date 9-31 May. *18 quai du Commerce, 1000 (219 07 07/fax 218 74 53).*
Now in its triumphant fourth year, the Kunsten Festival demonstrates all that Brussels has to offer by way of artistic expression. This ambitious exhibition is held at several venues in different parts of the city. Creation was the main theme for 1998. With contributions from the worlds of theatre and dance, the Festival has been compared to those of Edinburgh and Amsterdam.

Heilig-Bloedprocessie (Procession of the Holy Blood)
Date Ascension Day in May. Bruges. **Information** *Bruges Tourist Information Office, 11 Burg, 8000 Bruges (050 44 86 86/fax 050 44 86 00).*
Religion buffs will not want to miss the Procession of the Holy Blood, when the town of Bruges turns out to venerate a few drops of liquid thought to be blood from Christ's crucified body. Thousands of actors dressed in medieval garb parade through the streets, re-enacting how the vial arrived

in Bruges in the twelfth century. Floats, banners, musical instruments and choirs add to the atmosphere. Reserved grandstand tickets can be bought from the Tourist Office after 1 Feb. Bruges is an hour away from Brussels by train.

Concours Musical International Reine Elisabeth de Belgique (Queen Elisabeth International Music Competition)

Date May to mid-June. *Palais des Beaux Arts & Conservatoire Royal de Musique (see chapter* **Music***:* **Classical & Opera***).* **Tickets** 500-2,500BF.
Information *Palais des Beaux Arts, 23 rue Ravenstein, 1000 (507 82 00).* **Open** 9am-6pm Mon-Sat; *box office* 11am-6pm Mon-Sat.
Founded over 40 years ago by Belgium's former Queen Elisabeth, an avid violinist, this prestigious month-long competition is a must for classical music aficionados. Young musicians from around the world compete in the rotating categories of voice, violin and piano. Concerts are held at the Royal Music Conservatory and Palais des Beaux Arts, and for the most part tickets are available to the public. The 12 musicians who make it to the final have a chance to hobnob with King Albert and Queen Paola. Lesser mortals can catch a piece of the action on Belgian television.

Brussels 20km Run

Date last Sun in May. *Start & finish Esplanade du Cinquantenaire. Métro Merode or Schuman.* **Admission** 350BF participants; free spectators. **Information** *Syndicat d'Initiative – Bruxelles Promotion 1886, 17 rue de la Chapelle, 1000 (511 90 00/fax 511 37 15).* **Open** 9am-6pm Mon-Fri; 9am-4pm Sat.
Belgium's biggest track and field event attracts about 20,000 amateur and professional runners every year, the vast majority being Belgian. Competitors start at the Parc du Cinquantenaire and are led past many of Brussels' finer landmarks, including the Palais Royal, the Palais de Justice, avenue Louise and the Bois de la Cambre. If there's no rain, about 100,000 Bruxellois usually turn out to cheer on participants, especially those last panting stragglers. Winners receive a trophy, a medal and a certificate, but no cash.

Jazz Marathon

Date last weekend of May. *Venues throughout Brussels and nearby towns.* **Information** *Jazz Marathon, 34 rue Africaine, 1060 (concert details 534 22 00).* **Admission** three-day pass to all events 400BF in advance, 450BF on the day. Tickets also available at Fnac, TIB *(513 89 40/fax 514 45 38)* and participating venues.
In late May, music-lovers can enjoy non-stop jazz for three days straight. Little-known bands – mainly Belgian outfits – play at cafés and small clubs throughout Brussels and in nearby towns. To sample sounds at the 50 or so clubs in the city, buy a three-day pass. A special jazz bus will be on hand to shuttle you around at no extra cost. Marathon-goers also get the added bonus of reduced beer prices at participating venues. Several concerts held at Grand Place are free to the public and feature such luminaries as Maceo Parker (*see* chapter **Sightseeing** *page 72).*

Summer

Battle of Waterloo

Date mid-June. **Information** *Waterloo Tourist Information Centre, 149 chaussée de Bruxelles, 1410 (354 99 10/fax 354 22 23). Phone for directions.*
Open *1 Nov-31 Mar* 10.30am-5pm daily; *1 Apr-31 Oct* 9.30am-6.30pm daily.
War buffs will have to wait until the year 2000 to see the 1815 Battle of Waterloo re-enacted in this Brussels suburb. About 2,000 men get together every five years in June, don period uniforms, wield vintage guns and play war – with

some representing the troops of England's Duke of Wellington and Prussia's Marshall Blucher, while others act as French soldiers fighting under Napoleon's leadership.

Festival de la Musique

Date 20-21 June. *Conseil de la Musique, 236 rue Royale, 1210 (226 12 03).*
A massive annual party, with thousands of concerts and recitals – a journey through the world of music.

Couleur Café Festival

Date 26-28 June. *Halles de Schaerbeek, rue Royale Ste Marie, 1030 (227 59 60/fax 219 42 90).*
Three evenings of music and drama, with crazy rhythms, warm voices and exotic dances, interspersed with world music, acid-jazz and funk. Concerts are held on three podiums, with tents, bars, markets and food stalls nearby.

Ommegang

Date 30 June-2 July. *From place du Grand Sablon to Grand Place.* **Information** *TIB (513 89 40/fax 514 45 38).* **Admission** tickets for Grand Place performance 935-1,335BF.
The Ommegang, Flemish for 'Walkabout', is a medieval-style procession from place du Grand Sablon to Grand Place. The colourful parade originated in the fourteenth century as a religious event to celebrate the safe arrival of a statue of the Virgin Mary by boat from Antwerp. Over the years, the Ommegang became more secular and grew in stature when, in 1549, Charles V and his family watched the procession. Today's re-enactment ends in a dance (9pm-midnight) in an illuminated Grand Place. Tickets are expensive and are available from late May. Buy in advance as it always sells out. Those reluctant to fork out for the finale can watch from the streets along the way.

Brosella Jazz & Folk Festival

Date 2nd weekend in July. *Groen Theatre, Parc d'Osseghem, 1020 (269 69 56). Métro Heysel.* **Admission** free.
Organised by a group of unpaid music-lovers, the Brosella festival has been going strong for over 20 years, despite a shoestring budget. A sampling of jazz and folk from Belgian and international musicians is served up all weekend at the Parc d'Osseghem near the Atomium.

Festival d'Eté de Bruxelles

Date 30 June-19 Sept. *Selected venues.* **Admission** varies. **Information** *108 avenue de Tervuren, 1040 (735 06 13/fax 735 47 99).*
Lovers of Mozart, Schubert and Beethoven have a chance to listen to more than a dozen concerts over a three-month period. The performances are held at some of Brussels' finer halls and feature the Orchestre National de Belgique among others.

Foire du Midi (Brussels Annual Fair)

Date mid-July to mid-Aug. *Boulevard du Midi. Métro Gare du Midi.*
Every summer since 1885, Bruxellois have thronged to the annual fair near Gare du Midi. The family-oriented fair is one of the largest in Europe, spanning 2km with Ferris wheels, shooting galleries, dodgems, rollercoasters and fortune-tellers. Food stalls are on hand with traditional Belgian fare – from *moules-frites* to *boudin* (sausages) and *caricolles* (a poor man's escargot).

National Day

Date 21 July. *Parc de Bruxelles & other city parks.*
Belgium celebrates its independence and the accession of the first king of Belgium with festivities throughout the city. The biggest party takes place in the Parc de Bruxelles – across from the Palais Royal – with a military parade topped off by fireworks. On the outskirts, Bruparck runs family-oriented activities, with concerts geared to an easy-listening crowd.

Palais Royal Open Days
Date last week of July to 2nd weekend in Sept.
2 rue Ducale, 1000 (551 20 20/fax 512 56 85).
Métro Trône or Parc. **Open** 10am-4pm Tue-Sun.
Admission free.
Every year, just after Belgium's National Day, the King and Queen open up their home to the public. You won't catch a glimpse of the royal boudoir, though, or any of the rooms the couple actually inhabit – they're strictly off limits.

Meiboom (Raising of the Maypole)
Date 9 Aug. *From place du Grand Sablon to Grand Place.* **Admission** free. **Information** *TIB (513 89 40/fax 514 45 38).*
For a truly folksy experience of Belgian culture, stick around for the Raising of the Maypole, or *Meiboom*. This involves a festive procession of giant puppet-like and cartoon-style characters that winds through the streets from the Sablon to Grand Place. Legend has it that in 1213 a wedding party was celebrating outside the city when they were attacked by a gang from Leuven. The gang was chased out of town, and as a token of appreciation, the local duke allowed the victorious wedding party to plant a maypole on the eve of their patron saint's feast day.

Tapis des Fleurs (Floral Carpet)
Date mid-Aug. *Grand Place, 1000. Métro Bourse or Gare Centrale.* **Information** *TIB (513 89 40/ fax 514 45 38).*
Every other year (1998 and 2000) Brussels' main landmark, the Grand Place, is showcased even more than usual for three days when hundreds of thousands of cut begonias are carefully laid in a giant 1,860sq m floral carpet. The flowers of every hue imaginable are arranged to form significant symbols and pictures including a scene of Brussels' patron saint, St Michael, slaying a dragon.

Autumn

Journées du Patrimoine (Heritage Days)
Date 1st or 2nd weekend in Sept. **Admission** free. **Information** Brussels *Heritage Days Brussels, CCN, 80 rue de Progrès, 1030 (204 24 49/fax 204 15 22).* Flanders & Wallonia *Fondation Roi Baudouin, 21 rue Bréderode, 1000 (511 18 40/fax 512 00 35).*
Belgium, along with several other European countries, has a tradition of opening up several buildings – normally off-limits to the public – for one weekend of the year. Based around a different theme each year, these two days are meant to give ordinary citizens a rare glimpse into life on the farm, inside an abbey or even in a château. In Brussels, the event takes place during the second weekend in September. In the countryside it's a week earlier.

Les Nuits Botanique
Date 12-20 Sept. *Centre Culturel de la Communauté Français, 236 rue Royale, 1210 (226 12 17/fax 219 66 60).*
A festival of a wide range of music, enjoyed under the stars.

Rencontres d'Octobre
Date end Sept to mid-Oct. *Palais des Congrès, esplanade de l'Europe, 4020 Liège (04 343 42 47/ fax 04 344 49 66).*
A programme of dance, theatre and music striving to present works of originality from a variety of countries.

Audi Jazz Festival
Date mid-Oct to mid-Nov. *Venues throughout Belgium.* **Information** *Jazztronaut, 55 Boechtlaan, 1853 Grimbergen (534 22 00/fax 460 01 36).* **Open** 9am-7pm Mon-Fri.

This month-long musical jamboree offers a mixed bag of artists, both obscure and well-known. In its ten years of existence, the festival has featured the likes of Ray Charles and Herbie Hancock. Around 60 concerts are scattered throughout the country with the big names appearing at the Palais des Beaux Arts in Brussels.

Winter

Le Marché de Noël
Date three days in mid-Dec. *Grand Place, 1000.* **Information** *TIB (513 89 40/fax 514 45 38).* **Admission** free.
Brussels holds a European Christmas market every year in Grand Place, at which stalls representing various EU countries display their finest yuletide wares. If you're not in the mood for shopping, tuck into the multitude of ethnic food and booze. If you hate getting jostled in a crowd, avoid going in the middle of the day. Concerts featuring music from EU countries are held each night from 7.30-8pm.

Brussels Film Festival
Date mid- to late Jan. *Palais des Congrès de Bruxelles (513 41 30) & Actors Studio (218 10 55).* **Tickets** from 250BF; from 200BF students. **Information** *Brussels Film Festival, 50 chaussée de Louvain, 1210 (218 53 33/fax 218 18 60).* **Open** 9.30am-6pm Mon-Fri.
One of the lesser-known international movie fests, the Brussels Film Festival has gained more recognition in recent years by featuring first screenings and bringing in big-name stars. For example, in 1996 American actor-director Tim Robbins appeared as guest of honour. A competition for the best European feature film has also been initiated. Contact the organisers at the above address for a catalogue. For listings, check with TIB (513 89 40) or look in the *Bulletin*.

Binche Carnival
Date mid-Feb (including Shrove Tuesday). *Binche.* **Admission** free. **Information** *Belgian Tourist Office in Brussels (504 03 90/fax 504 02 70).*
Just over an hour's drive from Brussels, the town of Binche hosts Belgium's largest and wildest carnival. The highlight of the event takes place on Mardi Gras, or Shrove Tuesday, when the traditional *gilles* – dressed in clogs and embroidered costumes – don masks and dance in Grand Place carrying bundles of sticks to ward off evil spirits. They reappear later in the day, toting enormous head-dresses made from ostrich feathers, and toss oranges at the crowd as they pass through town – so look out.

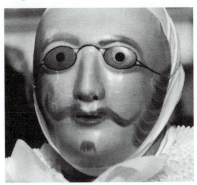

The **Binche Carnival** *is Belgium's biggest.*

MODERN PAINTERS

Major British and American writers contribute to the U.K.'s most controversial art magazine:

- JULIAN BARNES

- WILLIAM BOYD

- A.S.BYATT

- PATRICK HERON

- HILTON KRAMER

- JED PERL

- JOHN RICHARDSON

- PETER SCHJELDAHL

- RICHARD WOLLHEIM

Britain's best-selling quarterly journal to the fine arts.

Sightseeing

Sightseeing

Brussels' eventful history is reflected in the number and diversity of its buildings and monuments.

Something is moving in the centre of Brussels. You feel it immediately, that stir, that excited feeling that comes from people who know that they're Here Now. You feel it most at the heart of the old Lower Town, around Ste Cathérine, where clubs and bars are exploding into life.

But that is just the hip manifestation of a millennium fever that's gripping the city. The art scene, the contemporary ballet scene, the fashion scene – they're all on the up. Even the sleepy and cynical city authorities seem to have tapped into the energy. They're entering a feverish cycle of renovation – 1995-2000 will probably go on record for having the most renovations ever. Everything has been, is being, will be renovated: the Palais des Beaux Arts, the Halles de Schaerbeek, the Old England Department Store, even the long neglected and rundown place des Martyrs.

But let's not call this new. Let's just call it a dam-burst of pent-up energy – people who live in Brussels (as opposed to those who visit it) always loved it and always thought it kicked. They love it because you can go drinking anywhere you like till six in the morning, because you can dance from Saturday evening to Monday morning and never see the light of day, because you can watch a huge variety of films in six different languages, because you can eat better than anywhere else, because you get to live in beautiful apartments for much less than other major European capitals, because of the long, sticky summers, because of the international set that everyone complains about and secretly gets a kick out of.

So, if Brussels is hip, it's no news to the city's residents – they've just decided to share it with everyone else.

THE LAYOUT OF BRUSSELS

Brussels is neatly and logically set out, which means you can plan your sightseeing according to your interests. The city has an Upper and a Lower Town, which conjures up an image of important buildings and long avenues lording it over small, dark streets.

In fact, the two areas are within metres of each other. The Lower Town, the old Flemish quarter, contains the city's most famous sites, including its greatest landmark, **Grand Place**, and the **Manneken Pis**. It's also the ecclesiastical quarter, with around ten churches in chiming distance of each other; most of them are gems from the

Flemish Renaissance and baroque periods. If you're interested in royalty, go to the Upper Town, where you'll find the King's palace, royal squares and various palaces from the eighteenth-century neo-classical Austrian period.

The Upper and Lower town are the essential stopoff points for most visitors, but for the more adventurous there's plenty further afield. Almost all the 'attractions' are to be found in Laeken round the nine-balled **Atomium**: here are **Mini-Europe**, the **Planétarium**, the **Serres Royales**. It's an essential excursion if you're with children. The most modern buildings in the form of EU institutions are to be found round Rond-Point Robert Schuman, the great bureaucratic centre of Europe. St Gilles is where you go for art nouveau, this discreet *commune* having guarded its art nouveau heritage better than the others. And Tervuren is where you head for acres of green in the **Forêt de Soignes** and the **Parc de Tervuren**.

A huge amount of space – some 15 per cent – is given over to parks in Brussels itself. The built-up business and residential areas are scrupulously broken up by frequent patches of green, which probably help to account for the city's sedate, unfrenzied atmosphere. Around the city centre are congregated many small, carefully laid-out parks that provide settings for statues and national monuments. Many of these are now neglected and a little dispiriting, so you're often better off going just outside the centre to the larger, more attractive parks and woods. All parks tend to be quiet until the weekend. They are generally open from dawn to dusk, which means 6pm in winter and 8.30pm in summer.

Travel around as much as possible and discover that Brussels, like all great cities, has its secrets. Following one of our three suggested walks (*see pp 42, 52, 61*) would be one way to unearth a few of them.

The Lower Town

The Ilôt Sacré

The Lower Town begins magnificently with **Grand Place** (*see below*) and ends in tack at rue Neuve. Along the way it takes in some of the most interesting and least-known parts of inner-city Brussels. Just off Grand Place, to the east, is the Ilôt Sacré (Holy Isle), which was restored by the

Hidden churches

Scattered around the Grand Place are some of Brussels' oldest and most beautiful churches. The *commune* has been quite good about preserving them – the seventeenth-century Eglise de la Madeleine was transported stone by stone to another site when the construction of Gare Centrale on its former site threatened it with demolition. However, the churches' surroundings have been less well preserved: none of them has its own square and the area has been wholly given over to the demands of tourism and shopping, so walking amid the glitz, you are taken by surprise by these ancient buildings.

Eglise de la Madeleine
rue de la Madeleine, 1000 (511 28 45). Métro Gare Centrale. **Open** 7am-noon, 2-5pm, Mon-Fri; 7am-noon, 3-7pm, Sat; 7am-noon, 5-7pm, Sun. **Services** 7am, 7.30am, noon, 7pm, Mon-Fri; noon, 7pm, Sat; 7am, 9.30am, 10.30am, 7pm, Sun. **Map C3/C4**
A slightly bleak seventeenth-century church built in dark-brown brick. Transported to make room for Gare Centrale, it looks rather sad and isolated in its new upbeat surroundings. A chapel to St Rita was added in 1958.

Eglise Notre Dame de la Chapelle
place de la Chapelle, 1000 (512 07 37). Métro Gare Centrale. **Open** Oct-May 1-4pm daily; Jun-Sept 9am-4pm daily. **Services** 4pm Sat; 11.30am Sun. **Map B4**
A little way from the Grand Place, this is the burial place of Pieter Bruegel the Elder. Although there is no tomb, there is a memorial erected by his son Jan. This fine, large church stands at the beginning of rue Haute – where the painter was born – flanked on all sides by graceless, high-rise buildings. It boasts a wealth of styles: part of the chapel is twelfth-century; the transepts are seventeenth-century Romanesque; the nave is fifteenth-century Gothic. Most of the paintings date from the nineteenth-century, though there are some seventeenth-century de Clerks.

Eglise Notre Dame du Finistère
rue Neuve, 1000 (217 52 52). Métro De Brouckère. **Open** 8am-6pm Mon-Sat; 8am-noon Sun. **Services** 9.15am, 12.10pm, 5pm, Mon-Fri; 9.15am, Flemish 4.30pm, French 6pm, Sat; Flemish 9am, French 11am, Sun. **Map C2**
This eighteenth-century church (*pictured*) has found itself in the most incongruous setting of all: in the middle of the most famous and busiest of the downmarket high streets. Its very doors are splattered with graffiti. Within a metre of its porch, fluorescent sweets are sold and buskers strum their erratic tunes. Like the other churches, it has an air of long-suffering sanctity. The interior is ornate with a great carved pulpit and baroque paintings.

Eglise Notre Dame aux Riches Claires
21 rue des Riches Claires, 1000 (511 09 37/511 50 99). Métro Bourse. **Closed** for renovation except 9.30am-12.30pm Sun. **Services** French 11.15 am Sun; Spanish 10am Sun. **Map B3**
Tucked away down a small street, this is attached to buildings on every side. It is a charming, ruddy, asymmetrical building – also part of the Flemish Renaissance.

Unusually, it has a jutting gable, which is more common in a town house than a church, and is probably the work of Rubens' pupil, Luc Fayd'herbe.

Eglise St Nicolas
1 rue au Beurre, 1000 (513 80 22). Métro Bourse or De Brouckère. **Open** 7.45am-6.30pm daily. **Services** French 8am, 11.30am, 5pm, Sun; English 10am Sun; Flemish 6.30pm Sun. **Map C3**
The oldest church in Brussels is almost lost in the area's tourist and boutique glitz. Founded in the eleventh century, the oldest part of it dates from the twelfth; it managed to survive the 1695 bombardment, preserving a cannon ball in its wall. St Nicolas is – appropriately, in the light of the church's proximity to Grand Place – the patron saint of merchants. A calm model of medieval sanctity, its slightly curved shape follows the old line of the River Senne. The interior is invitingly dark and twisting with small, bluish stained-glass windows.

Notre Dame du Bon Secours
rue du Marché au Charbon, 1000 (514 31 13). Métro Bourse or De Brouckère. **Open** 9am-5pm daily. **Service** Flemish 11am Sun. **Map B3**
A strange little seventeenth-century baroque church behind boulevard Anspach, Notre Dame du Bon Secours is attached to a bar on one side. It was designed by Willem de Bruyn, who was also the architect of the Chaloupe d'Or and the Maison des Brasseurs on Grand Place. Like them it's a fine example of the Flemish Renaissance style. The interior contains a fourteenth-century wooden statue of Our Lady of Perpetual Succour.

Walk 1 The old centre

STARTING AT GRAND PLACE

Grand Place was laid out in the tenth century, on a drained swamp. Most buildings date from 1695-1700 when the original fifteenth-century guildhouses were rebuilt after Louis XIV's bombardment destroyed them. Work on the Town Hall began in 1402. Atop the spire is the archangel St Michael, patron saint of Brussels. In the mid-nineteenth century, the Grand Place was home to Marx, Engels and Victor Hugo.

Leave Grand Place by rue Charles Buls. For good luck, touch the reclining golden statue of Everard t'Serclaes on your left, a fourteenth-century hero who repeatedly defended the city from attack.

Proceed until rue du Lombard, then cross at the traffic lights and continue for 100m to the Manneken Pis (1619). He was given his first outfit in 1698 by the Elector Max Emmanuel of Bavaria. Today his 600-odd costumes are exhibited in the Musée de la Ville de Bruxelles (*see chapter* **Museums**) in Grand Place.

Retrace your steps back as far as the Amigo Hotel and turn right into rue des Brasseurs, leading to Marché aux Fromages, a lively street throughout the night. On your right is the narrowest house in Brussels. Now turn left along rue des Eperonniers and left again at le carrefour de l'Europe.

A few metres down the hill on the right are the three Galeries Royales St Hubert (1846), the first enclosed commercial arcade of its kind in Europe. In the Galerie de la Reine is the original nineteenth-century Neuhaus chocolate shop established by the inventor of the praline. Two doors along is the Delvaux leather goods shop (*see chapter* **Shopping & Services**).

At the end of the first gallery, turn left into rue des Bouchers, host to colourful restaurants and eye-catching displays of fresh fish or game (especially in the evenings). Turn first left into rue des Petits Bouchers. At the end, turn right into Marché aux Herbes and first left into rue au Beurre. At the end is the famous Dandoy shop (*see chapter* **Shopping & Services**), where speculoos biscuits are baked on the premises, and to your right stands the Stock Exchange or Bourse. Don't miss the thirteenth-century excavations as you pass by the right of the Bourse.

At place de la Bourse cross boulevard Anspach. In the distance to your right are the gleaming towers of Brussels' 'Little Manhattan'. Proceed along rue Auguste Orts, perpendicular to the Bourse. This part-rundown, part-renovated area is the centre of the city's avant garde, frequented by intellectuals, artists and students, and it has a distinct Flemish flavour.

At the junction with rue des Poissoniers, amble down rue Antoine Dansaert past shops selling the latest fashion designs from the 'Antwerp Four' before retracing your steps to rue des Poissoniers and then heading diagonally right to Pont di Carpe. Once a bridge spanning a branch of the now covered River Senne that encircled the Ile St Géry, this short street leads to place St Géry. Inside the renovated market hall (1881) are small, trendy shops. A few bars in the surrounding area open during the day, many more at night, attracting a lively, bohemian crowd.

Leave the square at the opposite end (rue de la Grande Ile) turning second left into rue des Riches Claires back to the big boulevard. Cross over and continue straight ahead along rue des Teinturiers until the traffic lights, passing an eclectic mixture of shops on your way. Head left and then first right past the police station until you reach the Town Hall at Grand Place.

---

commune in 1960. Now one of the liveliest areas, it's a medieval section of small streets almost entirely devoted to food. Fish restaurants display their wares tantalisingly on the street, with great ruddy lobsters and handfuls of shellfish reclining on mounds of ice.

Even the street names are appetising, with the likes of rue des Harengs and rue du Marché aux Herbes. Seeing these, it is easy to imagine the busy market trading of medieval times, and the agglomeration of restaurants is in keeping with tradition (Aux Armes de Bruxelles on rue des Bouchers is recommended – *see chapter* **Restaurants**). In the

lovely glass-covered Galeries St Hubert – Europe's oldest glass arcade – shops glitter with jewellery; the Arenberg Galeries cinema (*see chapter* **Film**) shows erudite films; and in the Taverne du Passage you can seat yourself at the long central table in the cream-coloured room for good honest Belgian food, and plenty of it.

The other side of the Grand Place is quieter, characterised by rather gloomy clothes shops and

The royal entrance to the **Palais des Beaux Arts** *on rue Ravenstein, which connects the Royal Quarter to the centre of Brussels.*

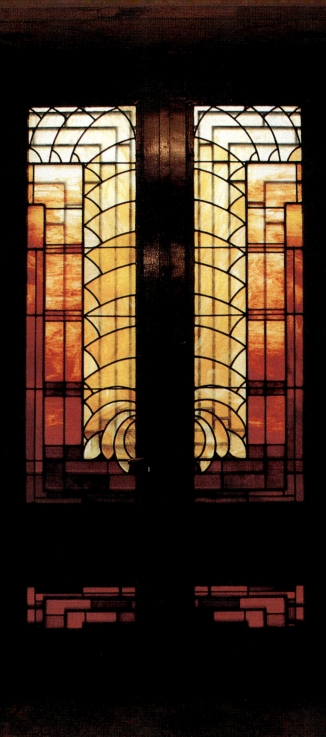

Smart bags
for
intelligent people

http//www.hedgren.be   Tel+32(0)3.226.26.06

HEDGREN
URBAN BAGS

Famous Belgians no.1

Possibly the most reluctant monarch ever to succeed to a throne, **Baudouin I** was crowned King of the Belgians in 1951 after the abdication of his father, Léopold III. A shy, lonely young man (b 1930) he faced huge problems both at home and abroad in the Congo. In May 1955 he toured the Congo for the first time and made a speech which received respectful comment around the world. He returned to the world stage in 1958 at the opening of the World Fair in Brussels, where he stated that 'technical know-how will not of itself create a civilised world. For technology to bring progress in its train it must be paralleled by corresponding changes in moral attitudes and by a firm will to work together in a common constructive effort.' Wise words, that are equally applicable 40 years later. Settling into his role, Baudouin came across as more relaxed and his popularity grew. He died childless in 1993 and was succeeded by his younger brother, Albert.

odd vendors of strange plastic figures. Only at the corner of rue de l'Etuve will you find a crowd, and quite a heaving crowd it tends to be: camera-clickers throng around the famous bronze boy statue, the **Manneken Pis** (*see below*).

The sights

Grand Place/Grote Markt

1000. Métro Bourse or Gare Centrale. **Map C3**
If Brussels is the crossroads of Europe and the Grand Place is the crossroads of Brussels, then presumably there is nowhere more central in Europe. But a crossroads does not sound like a place to linger and this is undoubtedly one of the most beautiful squares in the world. It is daily engulfed by swarms of tourists who, if they see nothing else in Brussels, will carry away the impression of baroque splendour, gilded façades (now stripped of grime) and firm cobbles. Almost totally destroyed by the French bombardment of 1695, Grand Place was triumphantly rebuilt by the guilds of Brussels in less than five years and emerged more distinctive than ever. It is the pivotal centre of the city: from here you could strike out on foot to almost all of the major sights. Grand Place undergoes seasonal transformations, with a great carpet of flowers in the summer and a Norwegian tree (a twin of the one in Trafalgar Square) together with a crib of live animals at Christmas, plus various pageants and parades throughout the year.

Guildhouses of Grand Place

Some of the buildings in Grand Place has been taken up for administrative purposes over the centuries, but the guildhouses remain the heart of it. Each guild left individual markings on its house and gave it a distinctive name, deriving from the façade. Looking at the array of ornate splendour, it is as well to reflect that its origins are neither royal nor aristocratic, but firmly and proudly mercantile. The grandly named 'Maison du Roi' (now the Musée de la Ville de Bruxelles) is known in Flemish as the Broodhuis, which is a more accurate title since it was owned by the bakers' guild and never by a king.
Nos.1-2 'Au Roi d'Espagne' – also the bakers' guild.
No.3 'La Brouette' (the wheelbarrow) – the grocers' guild.
No.4 'Le Sac' – the joiners' and coopers' guild.
No.5 'La Louve' (the she-wolf) – the archers' guild.
No.6 'Le Cornet' (the horn) – the bargees' guild.
No.7 'Le Renard' (the fox) – the haberdashers' guild.
No.9 'Le Cygne' (the swan) – the butchers' guild.
No.10 'L'Arbre d'Or' (the golden tree) – the brewers' guild.
No.24-25 'La Chaloupe d'Or' (the golden galleon) – the tailors' guild.
No.26 'Le Pigeon' – the artists' guild, where Victor Hugo stayed in 1852.

Hôtel de Ville

Grand Place, 1000 (tourist information 513 89 40). Métro Bourse or Gare Centrale. **Guided tours** 11.30am, 3.15pm, Tue; 3.15pm Wed; 12.15pm Sun. **Closed** *Sun Oct-Mar.* **Admission** 75BF. **No credit cards. Map C3**
The only building to survive the 1695 French bombardment, this magnificent Gothic structure, adorned with numerous sculptures, was begun in 1402, taken up again in 1444 and completed in four years. The architect, Jan van Ruysbroeck, then added the splendid 100m (328ft) tower, which upon its completion seemed to de-centre the rest of the building. Legend has it that the architect, in true Renaissance despair, climbed to the top of his masterpiece and threw himself off it. There are guided tours inside, which take in the elegant official rooms hung with famous tapestries and the gallery of the Spanish kings, with portraits executed after the monarchs were dead.

Detail of one of the **Guildhouses**.

Manneken Pis

corner of rue de l'Etuve and rue du Chêne, 1000. Métro Bourse or Gare Centrale. **Map B4**
Famous both as a national symbol and for the disappointment it causes visitors. 'But it's so small' is the inevitable cry. The tiny bronze statuette, perched on a stone façade and pissing cheerfully down, is certainly miniature, but if you go prepared for his diminutiveness, you might find him amusing. The idea is worth more than the execution. It says something for the irreverence of the Bruxellois that they chose this to embody their *esprit*. There are numerous legends (he was the son of a count, he extinguished a fire), but nothing much is known about his origins. The present statue was executed in the seventeenth century by Jerome Duquesnoy. It was stolen by the British in 1745, and again by the French in 1777; in 1817 it was taken and smashed by a French convict. The convict got hard labour for life and the little fellow was moulded together again. At the last count he had over 600 costumes (kept in the Musée de la Ville de Bruxelles in Grand Place), but don't expect him to stop there.

Ste Cathérine

The area from **La Bourse** down to Ste Cathérine is currently the coolest, sassiest part of the city. It still has a touch of sleaze – which is partly the reason why it's relatively tourist-free – and its shoddy bohemian feel is a refreshing discovery in Europe's bureaucratic capital. How long can this last? It's newfound popularity may well kill the place off in a few years' time, so catch it while you can. One of the best features of the area is its bars. Among the oldest and best is the Belgica on rue

Smart bags for intelligent people

HEDGREN
URBAN BAGS

http//www.hedgren.be   Tel+32(0)3.226.26.06

Théâtre de la Monnaie – *where the Belgian Revolution began in August 1830 – see p51.*

du Marché au Charbon (*see chapters* **Cafés & Bars** and **Gay & Lesbian**). It's small, packed, eccentric, Bruxellois and proud of it and serves its own lethal juniper-berry drink. Also nearby are (Au) Soleil, Pablo's and O'Reilly's (*see chapter* **Cafés & Bars**).

It's around place St Géry that the area is really taking off. Here you'll find Zebra (*see chapter* **Cafés & Bars**), with its stark, minimalist décor and young, hip, upmarket clientele; Coaster, which never gets going till two or three in the morning and is either packed with Brussels eccentrics or completely empty; Bison, for the grungy studenty types; and tiny **Java**, older then the rest, with its famous bottle-top-encrusted counter (*see chapter* **Cafés & Bars**).

Also here are two Brussels institutions, where the *vrais Belges* hang out, rather than the beautiful people. **Le Greenwich** (*see chapters* **Cafés & Bars** and **Surrealist Brussels**) on rue des Chartreux was much loved by René Magritte and remains gratifyingly surreal, with customers compulsively playing chess all day long. The Tuum is a gem of peculiarly Belgian seediness – it looks like a standard *taverne* with small tables and pinball, but stay a while and you'll see the living dead.

There are plenty of restaurants here, too. Check out Bonsoir Clara on rue Antoine Dansaert for nouvelle cuisine in intimidatingly slick surroundings; or Kasbah, next door, for delicious Moroccan food (*see chapter* **Restaurants**).

This area is also rapidly becoming the fashion centre of the city, though the bourgeois twin sets of avenue Louise are hardly competition. Studded discreetly along boulevard Antoine Dansaert are some of the most original designer shops in town. Check out the Stilj stores, one selling the latest designer clothes, the other specialising in underwear. Best of all are the shoe shops. (*See chapter* **Shopping & Services**.)

Ste Cathérine has some of Brussels' finest churches, and there is a gentle, dilapidated charm about its streets. Evocative names abound – such as place du Nouveau Marché aux Grains and quai au Bois à Brûler. The latter is a reminder that the River Senne once flowed right through this area before being buried in the nineteenth century (*see chapter* **History: Independent Belgium**).

One wonders at the lack of imagination of people who thought to deprive a city of its river. Only a trickle remains, at boulevard Barthelemy, though there's now a thriving art scene on what were once its banks (*see chapter* **Art Galleries**). Kanal 20, a building housing eight new galleries has recently opened (*see chapter* **Art Galleries: Kanal dreams**).

At place Ste Cathérine, the heart of the area, there is still a weekly fish market and the restaurants that line the rundown square specialise in seafood. **Eglise Ste Cathérine**, dominating the square, is a somewhat forbidding Joseph Poelaert creation, but the interior is surprisingly light and graceful. Around the corner is the splendid and very unusual **Eglise St Jean-Baptiste**, the greatest ecclesiastical example of Flemish baroque architecture in the city.

The sights

La Bourse
*Palais de la Bourse, 1000 (509 12 11). Métro
Bourse.* **Open** by prior arrangement for visits by
school parties, business people etc. **Admission** free.
Map B3
The Belgian Stock Exchange is set in a neo-classical building with a decorative frieze sculpted by Carrier-Belleuse and
statues by Rodin adorning the top. If you go inside, you discover that business is as methodical and unemotional here
as elsewhere in Brussels – it's a long way from Wall Street.
Perhaps when WH Auden was here the brokers were 'roar-
ing like beasts on the floor of the Bourse' but they're not,
unfortunately, any longer.

Eglise Ste Cathérine
*place Ste Cathérine, 1000 (513 34 81). Métro Ste
Cathérine.* **Open** 8.30am-5pm (summer until 6pm) Mon-
Sat; 9am-noon Sun. **Services** *chapel* 8am, *church* 10am,
Sun. **Map B2**
Looming over its own square, Eglise Ste Cathérine seems as
unkempt as its surroundings. It was designed in 1854 by
Poelaert, architect of the Palais de Justice. For-tunately, the
interior looks better: it's arched and graceful, with pretty
blue-and-yellow glass windows and a fifteenth-century
Black Madonna statue.

Eglise St Jean-Baptiste
*place du Béguinage, 1000 (217 87 42). Métro Ste
Cathérine.* **Open** 10am-5pm Tue; 9am-5pm Wed-Fri;
10am-5pm first, third and fifth Sat of the month; 9.30am-
noon Sun. **Services** *French* 5pm Sat; *Flemish* 10am Sun;
French 8pm Sun. **Map B2**
One of the best examples of Flemish baroque in Belgium,
this large church was designed by Luc Fayd'herbe, a pupil
of Rubens. It has a honey-coloured, vertical and symmetrical façade. Inside there is a beautiful pulpit and paintings by
the seventeenth-century Brussels painter Van Loon.

Marché St Géry
place St Géry, 1000. Métro Bourse. **Map B3**
Built by Dubois in 1881, the Marché St Géry used to be a
meat hall. The red-brick building is best seen from a distance
to appreciate its glass roof. Due to be knocked down in 1982,
it was saved by local protest and has been turned into a
shopping centre.

De Brouckère

Walking down boulevard Anspach, you lose
both the cool and the charm and reach the un-
abashedly Americanised area of De Brouckère,
where advertising billboards reign. This used to
be a more upmarket area and distinguished ves-
tiges remain. Café Métropole (*see chapter* **Cafés
& Bars**) is a magnificent turn-of-the-century bar
with *Casablanca*-style pianist. The opera house,
Théâtre de la Monnaie, is in place de la
Monnaie and appears to have given in to the surrounding tat, though this impression is dispelled
once you're inside.

The Théâtre de la Monnaie is horribly overshadowed by the awful Anspach Centre, which
dominates the skyline and dictates the business of
the area. The Centre is home to all manner of gar-
ish clothes shops, and the gaudy tone continues
along rue Neuve. Pedestrianised it may be, but it

is now infamous for its ugliness. Every conceiv-
able brand name (except the more upmarket ones)
is present and all the shops along its unrelenting
red expanse begin to feel the same.

Yet it was not always so. On the site of the concrete shopping complex, Inno, there was once 'A
sound of revelry by night/And Belgium's capital
had gathered then/Her beauty and her chivalry' for
the Duchess of Richmond's famous ball on the eve
of Waterloo. There Wellington danced gallantly
all night until 'Nearer, clearer, deadlier than
before!/Arm! Arm! It is – it is – the cannon's opening roar!' (Byron's *Childe Harold's Pilgrimage*,
Canto III, stanzas XXI and XXII.)

Rue Neuve ends, as it began, in a claustrophobic shopping centre, City 2. But there's an undeni-
able energy to the street. It is always packed, there
are numerous stands and buskers, and in summer
the hair-wrappers come out. It is a place to walk
through rather than linger in, as the crowds and
the glitz soon rankle. At night it empties somewhat, though Le Corbeau, off rue Neuve, is a lively
enough pub.

All around rue Neuve is seediness. Yet Brussels
often mixes sleaze with the sublime. The Flemish
theatre on rue de Laeken is a triumphant, flamboyant mock-baroque building surrounded by
sex shops and peepshows. Place des Martyrs,
with its monument dedicated to the 1830 revolutionaries who gave their lives for the *patrimoine*,
is bordered by fine neo-classical buildings.

Despite its grandeur and its patriotic associations, the square has for years been allowed to fall
into decay, to the total unconcern of the authorities. That's all changing and place des Martyrs is
one of the key places listed for renovation. The
monument's martyrdom is about to end.

The sights

Janneken Pis
*impasse de la Fidelité, 1000. Métro Bourse or De
Brouckère.*
Squatting, grinning and vulgar – if you didn't take to the
Manneken, don't distress yourself by going to see his female
counterpart. She was erected in 1985 in response to feminist
demands or in shameless exploitation of an existing famous
site – it's hard to know. Either way, she fails to inspire any
national pride, and the official tourist office-approved guide
doesn't even mention her.

Monument aux Martyrs de 1830
place des Martyrs, 1000. Métro De Brouckère. **Map C2**
Erected to commemorate the 445 rebels who died in the 1830
Revolution, this has an underground shrine containing the
names of the patriots. It ought to be a key national monument pertaining to the very foundation of the Belgian state.
In fact, the monument is unremarkable and has been terri-
bly neglected, as has the whole square. However, all this
is about to change as place des Martyrs looks forward to a
millennium facelift.

Théâtre de la Monnaie
*place de la Monnaie, 1000 (229 12 11). Métro De
Brouckère. (See chapter* **Theatre & Dance**.) **Map C3**

Walk 2 Palaces, squares, gardens

STARTING AT LE GRAND SABLON

This fine square (*see page 55*) is the centre of the arts and antiques trade in Brussels, with a market on weekend mornings and a great many antique/art shops in the adjoining streets (*see chapter* **Shopping & Services**). It is also host to numerous bars and cafés. Do go inside Notre Dame du Sablon to see the 11 stunning 14m-high stained-glass windows.

Leaving le Grand Sablon at the 'top', cross rue de la Régence. To your right stands the imposing Palais de Justice (1866-83; *see page 55*), one of the largest buildings of the nineteenth century.

Enter le Petit Sablon, the small park in front of you. Each of the 48 statuettes on the individually patterned pillars represents a guild. In the park is a statue of Counts Egmont and Horne, beheaded in 1568 for leading a Dutch uprising against the Spanish. Behind them on rue aux Laines, a street of majestic *maisons de maître*, stands the Palais d'Egmont (*see page 55*), now part of the Foreign Ministry.

Turn right along rue aux Laines and first left into rue du Grand Cerf. A few metres further to the left is the entrance to the Jardins d'Egmont, offering fine views of the inner courtyard of the palace. Return to rue du Grand Cerf, turn left and then right at the end of the street to place Louise.

Cross over left and follow the tramlines along avenue Louise. Named after one of the daughters of Léopold II, it was built as a tree-lined avenue from the city to the Bois de la Cambre (*see page 58*). Today some of the best Belgian shops, including Holemans, Bouvy, Olivier Strell and Scapa of Scotland (yes, it's Belgian), are here, as well as various chic cafés.

On the east side of the avenue, les Galeries Louise offer more shops and shelter from the not uncommon Brussels rain. Returning to place Louise, turn right towards the Hilton along avenue de la Toison d'Or or boulevard de Waterloo, depending which side of the road you are on. The most exclusive shops are on the left, while les Galeries de la Toison d'Or on the right also contain many notable stores, inlcuding Francis Ferent (*see chapter* **Shopping & Services**).

At the main junction, Porte de Namur (once a city gate), turn left and head down rue de Namur until you reach place Royale (1773-80). The statue in the middle is of Gottfried von Bouillon, leader of the First Crusade. To your left as you face the Palais de Justice is the splendid Cours de Comptes, opposite which is the Musée d'Art Ancien (*see chapter* **Museums**), housing works by Bruegel, Rubens and other Flemish masters. To the right is the Musée d'Art Moderne (*see*

The ornate interior of the opera house – built in 1819 to replace a fifteenth-century Brabant building – is splendid, though the exterior is undistinguished. Here it was, in August 1830, that the Belgian Revolution began. During a rousing performance of Auber's *La Muette de Portici*, the *Marseillaise*-style words of the duet 'Sacred Love of the Fatherland' so electrified the audience that they rushed head-long to the square outside where workers were protesting. It was a rare moment of class unity in Brussels and it secured independence in a remarkably quick time. By October the rebels were declaring an independent state; by 21 July 1831 (Belgium's National Day) the king of the new state was sworn in.

Théâtre de Toone

6 impasse Schuddeveld, petite rue des Bouchers, 1000 (511 71 37). Métro De Brouckère. **Open** noon-midnight Tue-Sat. **Box office** tickets available 8pm, just before performance. **Tickets** 400BF; 250BF under-12s, students (Tue-Thur only). **No credit cards. Map C3**
This puppet theatre is one of the best sights in Brussels and deservedly famous. The building is old and small and winding. Now in the hands of the seventh generation of the Toone family, there are performances about four times a week in Bruxellois, the regional dialect. There is also a charming café, a puppet museum – which includes the ancient collection of Marcel Wolfers – and a workshop where you can buy marionettes. Toone seems a name of Dickensian serendipity, when you recall that the cartoons in *Who Framed Roger Rabbit?* are referred to with wisecracking shorthand as Toons.

The Upper Town

Royal Quarter

The most elegant area of Brussels, the crowning glory of its eighteenth-century neo-classical period, is mercifully well preserved. It is the best approach to the centre of town: driving down the narrow, often traffic-choked rue de la Loi, you suddenly hit the Royal Quarter's great cobbled expanse and sweep magnificently around place Royale, then down the lovely curve of rue Ravenstein, into the heart of Brussels. This area was constructed in the eighteenth century, designed mostly by Guimard, to make Brussels a city suitable for royalty.

The **Parc de Bruxelles**, around which the palaces are spread, is the only disappointment in the area. It's a dingy and badly kept place. Numerous statues and the avenues in the shape of a compass are testimony to the fact that it was once well considered, although surely never beautiful. Thackeray wrote of it: 'Numbers of statues decorate the place, the very worst I ever saw. These cupids must have been erected in the

chapter **Museums**), home to paintings by more recent Belgian artists such as Paul Delvaux and Rané Magritte. Pass through the arch between the museums to the impressive courtyard of the former Austrian palace. Leaving by the bottom-right exit gives you a fine view over Mont des Arts to the old centre.

Turn back up the hill to place Royale, past the Old England Department Store (*see page 54*), to the excavations of the original fifteenth-century royal palace, burnt down in 1731. Around the

corner to the right, heading away from the Palais de Justice, is the Musée de la Dynastie (*see chapter* **Museums**) and the Palais Royal (1904; *see page 55*). Opposite the palace is Parc de Bruxelles, where brass bands sometimes play in summer; it leads to the Palais de la Nation, seat of the Senate and Chamber of Deputies.

Return to rue de la Régence. Continue towards the Palais de Justice, passing the Jardin des Sculptures on your right and the statue of Eros glistening aloft, until you reach the Sablon.

time of the Dutch dynasty, as I judge from the immense posterior developments.' The park saw great activity just before the Battle of Waterloo. Again according to Thackeray: 'The greatest folks in England walked in the Park – there was a per-petual military festival.' Fifteen years later, in the 1830 Belgian Revolution, its avenues ran with blood. There are neither festivals nor bloodshed now – the park is sleepy after being the scene of so much upheaval.

The square of palaces (in Brussels 'palace' can mean any important building) here comprises the Palais des Académies, the **Palais de la Nation** (the parliament) and the Horta-designed Palais des Beaux Arts, now returned to its former elegance. The entrance hall has been stripped of the scaf-folding to reveal art deco windows. Most impres-sive of all is the King's official residence, the **Palais du Roi**, where the guards stand impas-sively and the flag flies on the rare occasions when the monarch is home.

Directly behind the palace grounds is the nar-row rue Bréderode, where Joseph Conrad visited the Congo Trading Company in 1889, and which

still looks much as he described it in his most famous novel, *Heart of Darkness*.

West of the Palais du Roi lies **place Royale**, an even lovelier square because, instead of the dreary Parc de Bruxelles, there's Simonis's vigor-ous and triumphant figure of Godfrey of Bouillon, who led the first crusade. The square was sym-metrically designed by Guimard and its main building is Eglise St Jacques-sur-Coudenberg, which looks more like a Roman temple than a cradle of Christian piety.

The Royal Quarter is home to Brussels' great museums, palaces and libraries. The Musées des Beaux Arts housing both the old and modern art collections – the Musée d'Art Ancien and the Musée d'Art Moderne (*see chapter* **Museums**) – are the most impressive, with many Renaissance and seventeenth-century Flemish painters, and later Belgian surrealists.

On the Mont des Arts, created between 1956-8, are the modern Musée de la Dynastie (*see chapter* **Museums**) and the Palais du Congrès, as well as the Alfred I Library, which incorporates several manuscript museums. On rue Mont de la Cour is one of the great triumphs of art nouveau in the city: the **Old England Department Store**, long shuttered up but soon to be reopened as a museum of musical instruments. It is another surprisingly enlightened and exciting idea for the millennium.

Around the corner, off rue de la Régence, are the **Sablon** squares. These are unanimously celebrated and have a lovely easy grace, so the praise is well deserved. You can walk right around place du Petit Sablon's Paul Hankar-designed railings, with their figures of the proud Belgian guilds, or sit within them gazing at the elaborate fountain, dedicated to the martyrs Egmont and Horne. These two counts rebelled against the Spanish king, Philip II, in 1566, and were beheaded in 1568 in Grand Place by Philip's govenor, the ruthless Duke of Alva.

Behind the little square, Notre Dame du Sablon is one of the finest Gothic churches in the city. Place du Grand Sablon has an expensive antiques market on Saturdays and its shops overflow with ancient *objets*.

It also has interesting, if pricey, bars so it's one of Brussels' livelier areas at night. In **Chez Richard** (*see chapter* **Cafés & Bars**), one of the better Irish bars, Belgians are encouraged to dance on the tables till dawn. In **Le Pitt's Bar** (*see chapter* **Cafés & Bars**) the studiously hip knock back drinks along the counter.

Off the square, leading down towards Grand Place, is the cobbled, pedestrianised rue Rollebeek, which in the summer months becomes positively Mediterranean, its tables out on the street.

Rue de la Régence leads up to the largest site in the city, the monumental **Palais de Justice**. The biggest nineteenth-century building in Europe, it is Poelaert's masterpiece and was literally the death of him. Appropriately, it was built atop Galenburg Hill, where the medieval gallows used to stand. Its heaviness of style does not seem to be much admired, but by sheer dint of size it cannot fail to impress.

Beneath its enormous shadow is spread the **Marolles**, a poor area celebrated for its earthiness, lawlessness and Bruxellois patois. Seen from the Palais, the Marolles looks cowed – indeed many thousands of tiny homes were demolished to make way for the great building – but if you go into the Marolles, the Palais looks all washed up like a beached whale.

The sights

Cathédrale des Sts Michel et Gudule
place Ste Gudule, 1000 (217 83 45). Métro Gare Centrale or Parc. **Open** *April-Oct* 7am-7pm Mon-Fri; 7.30am-7pm Sat; 8am-7pm Sun. *Nov-Mar* 7am-6pm Mon-Fri; 7.30am-6pm Sat; 8am-6pm Sun. *Services* Flemish 4pm, French 5.30pm, Sat; 10am, 11.30am, 12.30pm Sun. **Admission** *crypt* 40BF; 30BF groups. **Map C3**

This magnificent cathedral, tactfully dedicated to the male and female patron saints of Brussels, would probably enjoy greater prominence were it not the victim of bad planning, which has left it hemmed in on three sides by ugly modern buildings. The scaffolding was recently removed from most of the exterior after countless years of work and it emerged gleaming from its chrysalis. It was completed by the end of the fifteenth century in the Brabant Gothic style, but was damaged by the French shelling of 1695. The interior is splendidly proportioned and stuffed with treasures, chiefly the wonderful pictorial stained-glass windows by Bernard van Orley, and the thirteenth-century choir. The altar is surprisingly cool and modern. The great Flemish painter Roger van der Weyden is buried nearby.

The Clock
Mont des Arts, 1000. Métro Gare Centrale. **Map C4**
A rather uninspiring title for this landmark, but there appears to be no proper name for this giant timepiece set into the wall at the lower end of Mont des Arts. It consists of 12 figures, each representing a historical personage. On the striking of the hour, the relevant figure emerges from his cubby hole and performs a mechanical action. If you're not there on the hour, it just looks like an ornate façade.

Eglise St Jacques-sur-Coudenberg
place Royale, 1000 (511 78 36/502 18 25). Métro Parc. **Open** 3-6pm Mon; 10am-6pm Tue-Sat; 9am-noon Sun. **Services** *French* 5.15pm Sun. **Map C4/D4**
The most important of the lovely neo-classical buildings in this exceptionally gracious square. The church was built in 1775 to resemble a Roman temple and has none of the Gothic piety exuded by most of the city's churches. The interior is just as imposing as the outside and one can easily imagine that it served perfectly as a Temple of Reason and then as a Temple of Law under the French Revolution, before being returned to Catholicism in 1802.

Hôtel Ravenstein
1 rue Ravenstein, 1000 (restaurant 512 77 68). Métro Gare Centrale. **Open** *restaurant* 11.45am-1.30pm, 6.45-8.30pm, Mon-Sat. **Credit** AmEx, DC, MC, V. **Map C4**
The last surviving building from the fifteenth-century Burgundy period, Hôtel Ravenstein is in what used to be the Jewish district, and is now occupied by science associations and a restaurant.

Old England Department Store
rue Villa Hermosa, 1000. Métro Gare Centrale or Parc.
With its curving black wrought ironwork framing large windows, this is one of the most distinctive and best known buildings in Brussels. Built by Paul Saintenoy in 1899, it has stood neglected for years, somehow escaping demolition, but someone was always going to do something for it. Now someone has: it is very shortly to open as the Musical Instruments Museum. The Instruments collection, comprising 600 works and one of the most important in the world, is currently housed in a building on place du Petit Sablon, where there is space for only one tenth of the collection. The Magasins Old England will provide four times more space, and the fanciful see-through metal lift may even start working again.

Palais de Charles de Lorraine
1 place du Musée, 1000 (519 53 71). Métro Gare Centrale or Parc. **Open** group visits, by prior arrangement only.
The Palais de Charles de Lorraine is a beautiful eighteenth-century palace whose interior has been remarkably well restored. The staircase is huge and has an imposing statue of Hercules. The state room has a star with 28 points on the floor, each one made of a different Belgian marble. Group visits may be made by prior arrangement.

Heritage Day

Brussels likes to stuff its treasures away like a sultan in charge of a harem. But for two days a year, the veil is cautiously lifted and the great public allowed in for a sniff. This takes place on the second weekend of September. It's incredibly popular, so you should not expect a private viewing. The full programme is available from May of every year (204 24 49). The 1998 theme is Les Lieux de Fêtes, which means places like old theatres and ballrooms will be decked out wistfully to relive for two days only their former gaiety.

Palais d'Egmont

off place du Petit Sablon, 1000 (515 16 11). Tram 20, 48/bus 34, 95. Not open to the public, except gardens. **Map C5**

Begun in the sixteenth century by the mother of the Count of Egmont, the Palais d'Egmont was enlarged in the eighteenth century and had to be rebuilt at the beginning of the twentieth century following a fire. It is now used for receptions by the Minister for Foreign Affairs. It was here that Britain, Ireland and Denmark signed the Treaty of Accession to the EEC in 1972. The rooms are magnificent, with rich tapestries and carpets, but unfortunately only the gardens are open to the public. These are lovely, if somewhat overshadowed by the Hilton Hotel, in a typical piece of bad town-planning. There are statues, including one of Peter Pan by Sir George Frampton, and a beautiful octagonal fifteenth-century well.

Palais de Justice

place Poelaert, 1000 (508 64 10/508 65 78). Métro Louise/tram 92, 93, 94. **Open** *Aug-Sept* 9.30am-noon, 1.30-3pm, Mon-Sat. **Admission** free. **Map B5/C5**

This mammoth building – bigger even than St Peter's in Rome – was purposefully situated on the Galenburg hill so that it could loom threateningly over the populace. One of Léopold II's key projects, it is frequently referred to by those who wish to denigrate his grandiose notions. It has a strong imperial air, deliberately modelled along the lines of the ancient Egyptian temples, and was so exhausting a project that the architect, Poelaert, collapsed and died in the middle of construction in 1879. The interior is equally imposing and equally good at overawing luckless criminals, with giant magisterial statues of Demosthenes and Cicero, and the echoing Salle des Pas Perdus (waiting room). You get a fine view of northern Brussels from the terrace at the front – try the telescopes.

Palais de la Nation

place de la Nation, 1008 (Parliament 519 81 36; Senate 515 82 11; visits 515 83 55). Senate entrance 7B rue de Louvain; Chamber entrance 11 rue de Louvain. Métro Arts-Loi. **Open** 10-11am, 2-3pm, Mon-Sat. **Admission** free. **Map D3**

To visit the seat of the Belgian Parliament you first have to ensure it is in session, and guided tours need to be arranged in writing at least two months in advance. The palace has a lovely eighteenth-century façade by Guimard, but the exchanges within make Britain's House of Commons sound like Plato's academy.

Palais Royal

place des Palais, 1000 (551 20 20). Métro Parc/tram 92, 94. **Open** *25 Jul-5 Sept* 10.30am-4.30pm Tue-Sun. **Admission** free. **Map D4**

The old seat of the dukes of Brabant, this was destroyed by fire in 1731 and rebuilt until it was given its final form in 1904 by Balat and Maquet at the request of the indefatigable Léopold II, who is largely responsible for the imperial feel of Brussels. Now it's the official residence rather than the home of the royal family. Only in late summer can you see inside the great state rooms and view the tapestries designed by Goya, but it's in a fine square with a broad sweep of cobbled road, overlooking Parc de Bruxelles and the Horta-designed Palais des Beaux Arts. Changing of the guard, which is not the great ceremonial occasion it is in London, occurs daily at about 2.30pm.

Parc de Bruxelles

entrances on rue de la Loi and place Royale, 1000. Métro Parc or Arts-Loi. **Map D3/D4**

This is an old park – designed in 1717 by Joachin Zimmer – and enjoys one of the best positions in town, in front of the Palais Royal, so it ought to be a small gem. Unfortunately, it's dirty and depressing, chiefly due to the ruthlessly trellised trees with branches tortured into geometric shapes. It's packed with bronze-green statues and none of these is remarkable. The park's most distinctive feature is its set of avenues, laid out in the masonic form of a compass. But that can be admired from a map and is little comfort when you find yourself trundling along the bleak, sandy paths.

Sablon

1000. Bus 20, 34. **Map C4**

Sablon – or Zavel in Flemish – is the elegant area comprising place du Grand Sablon, the church of Notre Dame du Sablon and place du Petit Sablon. Grand Sablon has flamboyant bars, numerous antique shops and a pricey flea market every Saturday. Notre Dame du Sablon is probably the loveliest Gothic church in Brussels. It was built in the fifteenth and sixteenth centuries; the interior, with its 11 14m-high exquisite stained-glass windows, is especially stunning (open 9am-5pm daily, entrance on rue de la Régence). Just across the road is Petit Sablon, a small park designed in 1890 by Henri Beyaert. Its railings were designed by the art nouveau architect Paul Hankar, and are divided by 48 columns, each with a statuette representing one of the ancient guilds of Brussels. Inside are statues of humanists and of the martyrs Egmont and Horne, who rebelled against Philip II in 1565 and so ended up on the scaffold in 1568.

The Marolles

This is a district of great poverty and fierce pride, such as you tend to find when an area has managed to retain its age-old local spirit against all the odds of urban expansion and standardisation. It stretches rather haphazardly from the Palais de Justice to Gare du Midi and avenue de Stalingrad. Two long streets run through it, the rue Haute and the rue Blaes. Off these are short, meandering streets with drying clothes and an air of rather seedy depression. Like other Brussels' streets their names proclaim their origins – rue des Orfèvres (Goldsmiths' Street), rue des Tonneliers (Barrelmakers' Street), rue des Ramoneurs (Chimney Sweeps' Street).

The Marolles is not what it used to be. In the seventeenth and eighteenth centuries, it was a thriving area, populated by artisans. Earlier, Pieter

Bruegel, who was born around 1525 and lived at 132 rue Haute, must have drawn inspiration for his great peasant feasts and skating crowds from the energy around him.

But ever since the Senne was buried in 1870 the district has been in steady decline. Since the Middle Ages it has been a refuge for the persecuted – a leprosy centre was founded here in the twelfth century and today it is a haven for illegal immigrants. Apparently, it is now acquiring a chic charm rather like New York's East Village – one of the forbidden places that yuppies want to get into – so there is an uneasy mixture of pine shops and fashionable boutiques rubbing shoulders with out-and-out poverty.

Its future poses a real dilemma, as the 'genuine' inhabitants – that ever-decreasing number of locals who still speak the dialect, or indeed those illegal immigrants who are part of Marolles tradition – are in no position to save the crumbling buildings or revive the once-thriving trade. There are numerous concerned action groups, but their well-meaning presence could in itself be perceived as a portent of doom.

The Marolles is threatened on one side by property and development sharks, and on the other by chichi shops, spuriously proclaiming their local flavour. In the meantime, the corner bars still serve their chips and beer while the early hours are peopled by the nightshifters and those who are still up for it after a night at the **Fuse** (*see chapter* **Clubs**), the most famous techno club in Brussels. Techno should never be too easily accessible. Clubbers feel better for having to make a trek.

The place du Jeu de Balle is the district's spiritual centre, and the easiest way to soak up the atmosphere is to head for the flea market held there early in the morning. An exciting confusion of people and wares, it's highly recommended for genuine bargains.

The sights

Maison de Bruegel

132 rue Haute, 1000 (no phone). Bus 20, 48. **Open** *May-Oct* groups by prior arrangement only (with written request). **Map B5/C4**
This sixteenth-century house has now been restored as authentically as possible. It does not, however, contain any precious prints or old letters, so it is better as an illustration of what the painter's living quarters would have been like than as a museum.

Ixelles & Avenue Louise

Ixelles, stretching from the uptown glamour of Porte de Namur to the student bars around the university, has pockets of energy and a rambling charm. It also has some of Brussels' best examples of art nouveau houses, particularly on the borders with St Gilles. Avenue Louise, which provides a straight boundary to Ixelles, hardly belongs to its

twisting streets and, in fact, is technically in the *commune* of Brussels.

In 1864 land was sliced from Ixelles and St Gilles so that a suitably magnificent avenue could tie the centre of town to the pleasant grounds of the Bois de la Cambre. Yes, it's Léopold II again. You soon get to know his imperial feel and this avenue, named after his eldest daughter, begins beside his Palais de Justice (not on the Marolles side, of course), the great building sheltering the bourgeoisie from the irreverence of the poor.

Gucci, Versace and Chanel have boutiques on avenue Louise, clashing somewhat with Häagen-Dazs, Hamburger Quick and various other fast-food joints. But the start of avenue Louise is quite pretty. From place Louise you can see the dome of the Palais de Justice, then as you go down the avenue there are small pedestrianised streets sloping off to the right, where cafés put their tables out on the street and give the area a relaxed, Mediterranean feel.

However, as soon as you hit place Stéphanie, you are into avenue Louise proper and you understand why it generally fails to arouse enthusiasm (apart from that of well-heeled sex-shoppers who target a small and rather expensive red-light area around, and just behind, this part of avenue Louise). It seems to be an exercise in how to make pedestrians feel small: the avenue is very long and wide (six lanes of traffic), the buildings very tall (the shortest about ten storeys), the shops out of any decent price range. The only people about are young executives in a hurry and squat, middle-aged wives of the rich, every one of them with dyed blonde hair, two inches of make-up and floor-length mink.

The avenue has been parcelled up between travel agencies, large companies, hotels, haute couturiers and interior decorators. It's the interior decorators who have the edge – you can get to see some extremely beautiful furniture. The clothes shops offer little temptation; there's something unremittingly bourgeois about them – all soft suits and low-heeled shoes.

Of the hotels, only the Conrad, resembling an inspired New York apartment block, is interesting. The avenue has few bars or restaurants, so there's not a great deal to detain you except for the Horta-designed Hôtel Solvay at no.224. Peer through the glass in the front door to get a glimpse of the delights within.

If you persist to the very end (and trams 93 and 94, which run the length of the avenue, will whisk you quickly past the most soulless parts), the Bois de la Cambre is a treat. A large and charming park of beautiful trees, it is especially pleasant around the lake and is bordered by the magnificent, embassy-lined avenue Franklin Roosevelt.

Chaussée d'Ixelles is separated from avenue Louise by the lavishly named Galeries de la Toison d'Or (Golden Fleece Galleries), which have a good mixture of shopping opportunities: some of the Louise-style designer shops, but also some of Ixelles's more downmarket brand names such as Ici Paris. No.15 does good, though expensive, club clothes. Here, too, is the UGC Acropole (*see chapter* **Film**), pioneer of Sunday-morning cinema, where you can enjoy coffee and croissants with your film.

Lively Porte de Namur, at which the chaussée begins, is where Africans arriving from the Congo were housed, and the tradition has continued. Here and especially further on, around chaussée de Wavre, is the African area known as **Matonge**.

The sights

Abbaye de la Cambre

avenue Emile Duray, 1050 (648 11 21). Tram 23, 90, 94. **Open** 9am-noon, 3-6pm, Mon-Fri; 3-6pm Sat; 8am-12.30pm, 3-6pm, Sun; 9am-noon Catholic feast days.
Founded in the twelfth century by a noblewoman called Gisèle for the Cîteaux Order, the abbey was badly damaged during the Wars of Religion and was rebuilt in the sixteenth and eighteenth centuries. There is also a fourteenth-century church attached to the abbey. The buildings are set in elegant French gardens and now house the National Geographical Institution and an art exhibition centre.

Bois de la Cambre

main entrance on avenue Louise, 1050. Tram 93, 94.
This used to be part of the old Forêt de Soignes and was the favoured strolling spot of the well-to-do. Set at the southern end of avenue Louise, it retains some of that atmosphere with its restaurants, tearooms and boating on the lake. The peripheries tend to be used as through roads, so you have to penetrate quite far in for tranquillity. It's a good size at 124 hectares (50 acres), and has plenty of handsome old trees – the beeches are especially beautiful. The avant-garde Théâtre de Poche is situated just inside its borders.

Matonge

This area is just a stone's throw from avenue Louise, but could hardly be more different; it's further proof of Brussels' constantly changing cityscape. The population here is predominantly Zairean (most are students), but you also have Indians and North Africans. The shops – mostly selling food, clothes and cosmetics – are wholly exotic. Great bunches of tiny bananas spill on to the street, alongside mangoes and guavas. Hanging in windows and clothing passers-by are richly patterned dresses and traditional Zairean menswear. Scattered about are hairdressing salons advertising dreadlocks and displaying additional tresses. In the galerie d'Ixelles is **Musicanova** (*see chapter* **Shopping & Services**), a record shop that has its own label and helps to promote new African artists.

Matonge really comes to life at night. On wintry days the area's distinctive colours can seem sad under grey skies, but at night the bars fill up with regulars from all over, and clubs such as Mambo go on all night. The area has its problems, too: rents

are very high, so many students have to move to cheaper Schaerbeek; work permits are difficult to come by, and the Belgian police are notoriously unsympathetic to those without proper papers.

Chaussée d'Ixelles itself really has little to commend it other than its pleasantly undulating shape, representative of the rest of Ixelles, which weaves and ducks, disappears up hills and round corners. The chaussée has all the ubiquitous middle- and low-range names, the likes of C&A and Nopri. It is narrow and uneven, but the streets running off it are more charming.

On rue St Boniface is a spacious and lively café, **L'Ultime Atome** (*see chapter* **Cafés & Bars**). Round the corner from this is the blackened, sinister, turreted Eglise St Boniface, which has the peculiarity of being attached to the houses on either side of it. Halfway down chaussée d'Ixelles is place Fernand Cocq, an uneven square that seems to have appeared without design. However, the Maison Communale, set in a garden at the end of the square, is a large, pleasant building, which formerly belonged to the violinist Bériot and his Spanish wife, the famous singer La Malibran – they bought the house as an inspired monument to their newly-wed love.

By night the square is home to some interesting bars, including cybercafé L'Amour Fou (*see chapter* **Cafés & Bars**) and, on rue des Tulipes, jazz bar Sounds (*see chapter* **Music: Rock, Folk & Jazz**). As the chaussée goes on, it becomes drearier and the shops fizzle out. Near the end, up the steep rue Van Volsem, is Ixelles's art gallery, the **Musée Communal d'Ixelles** (*see chapter* **Museums**), which boasts Belgian impressionists, Toulouse-Lautrec posters and frequently remarkable exhibitions. The chaussée ends at the Ixelles ponds, which are pretty in spring and summer when there are ducks and fishermen. At the edge of the lake is a large, rather ugly mustard-coloured building in the shape of a *paquebot* or package boat. You can't miss it. You wouldn't know it from the outside but this building is on the New-York-based World Monuments Fund's '100 most endangered sites for 1998-9' list. What brought it to the vigilant attention of the Fund is its interior. Constructed in 1938 by Joseph Diongre, it was then the largest, most advanced communications building in the world. Its vast Studio Four is still reckoned to be one of the best anywhere. It has 19 studios, so well insulated that recording goes on absolutely undisturbed. It's long-since fallen into disuse and is in a lamentable state, so it needs as much of the world's concern as it can get. Take a long look at it (you won't get inside): this is currently the most important building in the city.

*The baroque splendour of Brussels' **Grand Place** – see page 47 – undoubtedly one of the most beautiful squares in the world.*

Further down and to the east of chaussée d'Ixelles is the bilingual university (*see chapter* **Directory: Students**), the French side being the ULB and the Flemish the VUB. They are both enclosed by boulevard de Triomphe within a pleasant campus. This is a very lively area, though it can be quiet at weekends when the students retreat home.

Along chaussée de Boondael, by place de la Petite Suisse, there are some good, reasonably priced Vietnamese restaurants, and **L'Atelier**, a bar serving about 300 types of beer, is around the corner (*see chapter* **Cafés & Bars**). The area opposite the Ixelles cemetery is a hub of activity, with small bars and bistros such as Le Campus (*see chapter* **Directory: Students**), which serve good, cheap Belgian food late into the night.

St Gilles

Parts of St Gilles merit its inclusion on any list of Brussels' most beautiful spaces. It's a small *commune*, running from Porte de Hal, touching avenue Louise, continuing down to Uccle and across to Gare du Midi, and its less alluring side is often forgotten. Not surprisingly, the avenue Louise-Uccle end is very beautiful and the Gare du Midi side is rundown.

It is an area of uneven squares and gentle angles; the short, wide streets lead to small squares or charming crossroads. It is as if the *commune* were designed around the principle of 'pause and contemplate'. Everything is brought to a considered conclusion, whether it is the Barrière de St Gilles at the centre, where the main avenues converge and slope off down exciting-looking hills, or a smaller square such as parvis de la Trinité, where elegant houses face the lovely church, which looks as if it might belong in Latin America. Nothing has been allowed to spring up haphazardly. If you avoid the main thoroughfares (chaussées de Waterloo and de Charleroi), you can remain among quiet, composed streets where almost every corner has a bar and the small shops are discreetly interesting and expensive.

St Gilles is largely residential, and the main reason why people visit is its unequalled number of art nouveau houses (*see chapter* **Architecture**). It has always been a rich *commune* and all the houses are elegant, but at the turn of the century a few wealthy men commissioned fabulous art nouveau residences that have mercifully escaped destruction. Most of these are to be found in the area between rue Defacqz and the prison.

Victor Horta's house, the only one fully open to the public and known as **Musée Horta**, is at the centre of it all in rue Américaine. With their swirling, daring lines and elaborate friezes, the houses appear flamboyant and *insouciant* beside their more stalwart neighbours.

The art nouveau houses often come in pairs and, oddly, one is invariably more brilliant and lavish than the other. Perhaps the architects worked on the principle of foils or, more probably, one industrialist could afford to pay more than the other. In rue Defacqz, at nos.48 and 50, are the Hankar-designed Hôtels Ciambarlani and Janssens. No.48 has a marvellous frieze and a beautiful row of dormer windows; no.50 has only an interesting arrangement of brick to proclaim its architect.

The same is true of nos.83 (by Roosenboom) and 85 rue Faider (by Van Waesberghe). The first is a marvellously bold design with a curving trapeze balcony; the second only has a few twirls to its railings. All of the houses are now protected and most are used as embassies or for functions, but a few are rented to the public. It seems that you can live in them, so long as you don't change them; 92 rue Africaine, designed by B de Lestré in 1905, is residential and, with its great round windows, grilled railings in the shape of compasses and view on to the delightful Eglise de la Trinité, it has to be one of the best addresses in Brussels.

There are more such houses further down towards the prison. The prison itself seems to have been carefully integrated to avoid disturbing the harmony around it. The walls are fairly low and the complex is divided into two, intersected by the pleasant rue de la Jonction so that you don't get a huge walled mass. Softening a prison is a strange exercise, but it is perhaps better to face up to its existence in this elegant *commune* than to stick it in the darkest corner where the bourgeoisie could ignore it.

At the beginning of rue de la Jonction is the only art nouveau house other than Horta's that you can get into on a daily basis: the Hôtel Hannon, built by Brunfaut in 1902 and now called Contretype (*see chapter* **Art Galleries**), is now open as a photography gallery. The great breadth of the interior hints at what we are missing in the other houses.

Around the corner from the Hôtel Hannon is the charming square Larousse. Here, for those sick of the lavishness of art nouveau, are houses by Dewin (nos.12, 20 and 22). These are simpler, paler, flatter and more calming to look at.

Straight up from the prison towards the Barrière, occupying a commanding position, is St Gilles's **Hôtel de Ville**, an impressive nineteenth-century building in the French Renaissance style. This is a good, though little visited, museum, open weekdays until 4pm. Designed by Albert Dumont, in 1900-4, its most arresting features are its frescoes, on the ceiling above the main staircase and in the Marriage Room.

To the west of the prison are the Parc de Forest and **Parc Duden**. The second of these is the more attractive and was once famously elegant, but both are now rather ramshackle. You are now in the *commune* of Forest or Vorst and you can feel the

Walk 3 Matonge to Mérode

STARTING AT PORTE DE NAMUR

Porte de Namur was once a city gate, and the inner ring road follows the line of the now demolished medieval walls. Head along the bustling chausée d'Ixelles. Turn first left into chausée de Wavre to find colourful African shops, including les galeries d'Ixelles, selling everything from vivid fabrics to tropical vegetables. Matonge is the centre of the city's Congolese community but also attracts many other West Africans.

Turn first right along rue Francart. At no.9 is Yamato (*see chapter* **Restaurants**), a Japanese noodle bar. Literature café Comptoir Florian at 17 place St Boniface serves speciality teas and coffees. Across the square is L'Ultime Atome (*see chapter* **Cafés & Bars**), a lively bar.

At L'Eglise St Boniface turn left into rue de la Paix. The pedestrianised rue Longue Vie to your left contains African restaurants whose tables spill out on to the pavement on summer evenings. At the traffic lights turn right to rejoin the chausée de Wavre, one of the city's better shopping streets. At no.174, Bière Artisanale (*see chapter* **Shopping & Services**) sells more than 400 varieties of Belgian and other beer.

Go straight ahead at the next lights and continue down the hill. To your left towers the gleaming new European Parliament building. Turn up rue Wiertz, named after the nineteenth-century painter, go first right into rue Vautier and Parc Léopold. Originally laid out in the 1950s as a zoo, at the beginning of this century the park became a centre for science. Today the Institut Royal des Sciences Naturelles de Belgique (*see chapter* **Museums**) and the Musée Wiertz are here. Head downhill through this oasis of green and leave at the bottom right-hand corner with the carp pond to your left.

Cross over. A few metres to your right is place Jourdan with many interesting bars and cafés, a market at weekends and a frites stand reputed to be the best in town.

Leaving place Jourdan by the northern corner, walk up rue Friossart. Beyond the traffic lights at rue Belliard, to your left stands the monolithic European Council building.

Opposite, at Rond Point Robert Schuman (named after one of the European Union's founding fathers) is the star-shaped Berlaymont. Built on the site of a convent, the former European Commission headquarters is now under renovation and sheathed by a Christo-style white shroud. The European Quarter is eerily deserted at weekends, but bustling with Eurocrats, civil servants, lobbyists and journalists during the week.

East of Rond Point Robert Schuman is the imposing Arc de Triomphe (*see page 68*), commissioned by Léopold II and built in 1905, and the refreshing greenery of Parc du Cinquantenaire (*see page 68*). Laid out to commemorate Belgium's fiftieth anniversary in 1880, this large park is home to the Musée Royal d'Art et d'Histoire, the Musée Royal de l'Armée et d'Histoire Militaire and Autoworld (*see chapter* **Museums**) and more.

Walk through the park and beneath the Arc de Triomphe to the tree-lined avenue de Tervuren, also set out at the behest of Léopold II. At the main junction, rue des Tongres rising to the left contains some interesting shops and cafés. A little further from the main junction, in rue Abbé Cuypers on the right of avenue de Tervuren, is perhaps the finest row of *maisons de maîtres* in Brussels. To return to the city centre, catch the métro from Mérode (direction Heysel or Bizet).

difference. The houses are less graceful and the shops cheaper. There is a good local atmosphere, but as an outsider you are likely to feel something of an intruder, which is also true of the parks.

Back in St Gilles, towards Gare du Midi, you are also away from the wealthy district, in a part of the *commune* that tourists don't visit. Here the shops cease to display delicate ornamental goods and become more humdrum, and the restaurants – mostly Spanish, Greek, Portuguese and North African – are cheaper.

Off the depressing place Bethlehem, on rue Vanderschrick, are more art nouveau houses, but these, too, have given in to their surroundings:

they are not as well tended as their counterparts on the other side. The last of them has been turned into a charming café, the Porteuse d'Eau (*see chapter* **Cafés & Bars**). At Porte de Hal, you are back into open territory. There is a tower here, like something out of a Grimm fairytale, which houses the folklore museum.

The sights

Hôtel Hannon
1 avenue de la Jonction, 1060 (538 42 20). (See chapter **Art Galleries**.)
Now the Espace Photographique Contretype, this house is all staircase and light, lofty salons. The immense fresco

decorating the staircase (by PA Baudouin) immediately arrests your eyes and steals all the glamour from the discreetly beautiful photos. Stripped of its original furniture, the house has the echoing impersonality of a grand showpiece studio, built as a backdrop to beautiful exhibitions for beautiful people. Jules Brunfaut built it in 1902 for the industrialist Edouard Hannon, who was also a keen amateur photographer. His photos are here, alongside other classically lovely works. No gritty urban realism here.

Musée Horta

25 rue Américaine, 1060. (See chapter **Museums**.)
Built between 1898 and 1901, this was the architect's home and atelier, and was grudgingly preserved by a state that knocked down most of his masterpieces. The authorities must be congratulating themselves now, for this is one of the most visited museums in the city and one of the most rewarding. The exterior is plain enough, and nothing compared with the Hankar-designed house round the corner in rue Defacqz. This external reticence is fairly typical of an architect who was Belgian enough to want to keep his delights hidden away indoors. The interior is astonishingly light, flowing, graceful and harmonious. It's clearly a place to live in; there's no attempt to dazzle, startle or disturb as there is in art nouveau elsewhere. You're not struck in crazed amazement; you just want to lean back, let the light pour over you, shut out the voice of the guide, and float.

Parc Duden

entrances on square Lainé and chaussée de Bruxelles, 1190. Bus 48, 54.
An elegant city space, though it has become somewhat ramshackle. It used to be part of the Forêt de Soignes, and was where Emperor Charles V went hunting. It has tall trees and is set on a slope from which you get a good city view. A bit out of the way, the park is imbued with the atmosphere of the *quartier*, which can either be a good or a bad thing.

Parc de Wolvendael

entrances on avenue Wolvendael and rue Rouge, 1180. Tram 92/bus 41.
A small, beautiful park in the elegant *commune* of Uccle, it was owned by successive members of royalty through the centuries. There is a restaurant in an enchanting seventeenth-century Louis XV-style pavilion. *Mini-golf.*

Porte de Hal

boulevard du Midi, 1000 (534 15 18). Métro Porte de Hal. **Open** 10am-5pm Tue-Sun. **Admission** 150BF; 100BF groups; 70BF children; free disabled. **No credit cards. Map B6**
This fourteenth-century tower, embellished in the nineteenth century, has something of a fairy-tale appearance. It has been a prison, a toll house, a grain store, a repository for archives and is now the museum of folklore. It houses a rather hazy collection of popular images and documentation of the area's history.

Anderlecht

Above St Gilles and over to the south-west of the city, Anderlecht is a poor *commune* but an unusual one in having almost no immigrant population. It is a large district, with small, haphazardly arranged houses – there are no high-rises. It does not look appealing, yet it is frequently invaded by

The origins of the **Guildhouses** *in Grand Place are neither aristocratic nor royal, but firmly and proudly mercantile – see p47.*

visitors drawn by a happy juxtaposition of highbrow and lowbrow culture. The name 'Anderlecht' is roughly translated as 'love of Erasmus' and the house where the great humanist lived in 1521 is situated here. But this district is also home to the best football team in the country, RSC Anderlecht.

Most of the interesting bits are around Métro St Guidon. On emerging from the station, the first thing you see, standing gracefully aloof from the standard-issue shopping arcade, is the beautiful **Collégiale des Sts Pierre et Guidon**. The architecture is late fifteenth-century Gothic, and inside is a long altar illuminated by light filtering through the stained glass above.

Behind it is the seventeenth-century *béguinage*, now a museum. (*Béguinages* were lay sisterhoods whose members lived in religious communities but were not bound by nuns' vows. Often widows or spinsters, they did charity work and existed in large numbers in Belgium and the Netherlands. There are still some *béguinages* in Flanders.) The atmosphere of quiet sanctity is also present in the **Maison d'Erasmus** around the corner, a small, well-preserved, red-brick seat of learning set in a shady garden. Up from the church is a charming lane, rue Porselein, that has cottage-style houses, climbing plants and Jacques Prévert poems written on the wall beside Miró drawings. It ends at a good local bar, the high-windowed Le Porcelain.

Five minutes' walk from the church, in the pleasant and hilly Parc Astrid, announced by its proud purple-and-white flag, is the Anderlecht stadium (*see chapter* **Sport & Fitness**). The stands are regularly packed with enthusiastic supporters singing strange versions of English football songs. The stadium used to have what was known as the 'O-Side', a standing-room-only area frequented exclusively by the heavies, but it's now fully seated and quieter.

Moving towards the town side of Anderlecht and the seedy Gare du Midi area, you come across other pockets of interest. There is a sliver of canal on which you can take occasional boat excursions – they should be called 'urban excursions' to forewarn anyone expecting long grass and dragonflies. On quai de Mariemont you can find food and entertainment at the Fool Moon Café (*see chapter* **Music: Rock, Folk & Jazz**), which has an upbeat line-up of music and theatre. Below this are spread the industrial-looking nineteenth-century abattoirs and markets designed by Tirou.

Finally, Anderlecht boasts some key museums. On rue Gheude is the great **Musée Bruxellois de la Gueuze** (*see chapter* **Museums**), last brewer of the naturally fermented beer and more than just a stop on the culture trail. On rue Van Lint you'll find the small and incomplete Musée de la Résistance, which tells some of the important and hidden tales of Belgium's World War II experience.

The sights

Collégiale des Sts Pierre et Guidon

place de la Vaillance, 1070 (521 84 15). Métro St Guidon. **Open** 9am-noon, 2.30-6pm, Mon-Fri. **Closed** holidays and Sun during services.

A fine example of the Brabant Gothic style, it was built between the fourteenth and sixteenth centuries but has a crypt dating from the eleventh, which is one of the oldest in Belgium. However, the spire is a youthful nineteenth-century addition. Inside the crypt is a Celtic stone called the tombstone of St Guidon. There are other ancient tombs in the church, as well as medieval wall paintings. To the left of the church, in rue de Chapelain, is the thirteenth-century Béguinage of Anderlecht, whose surviving seventeenth-century buildings have been turned into a museum.

Maison d'Erasmus

31 rue de Chapitre, 1070 (521 13 83). Métro St Guidon/tram 56/bus 49. **Open** 10am-noon, 2-5pm, Mon, Wed, Thur, Sat, Sun. **Admission** 20BF. **No credit cards**.

The great humanist only spent five months here in 1521, but there is an impressive collection of documents, including first editions of *In Praise of Folly* and *Adages*, and letters from Charles V and Francis I. The house itself, with its Renaissance furnishings, is well worth seeing. There are portraits of Erasmus by Dürer and Holbein, and a medal by Cellini.

Monument aux Martyrs Juifs

rue Emile Carpentier, 1070. Bus 47, 103.

On the walls of this moving monument are imprinted the names of 23,838 men, women and children who were taken from Malines between August 1942 and July 1944 and sent to Nazi concentration camps. Not one of them survived.

Schaerbeek & St Josse

Schaerbeek has some of Brussels' most interesting sights, but not a lot of people know that. It's just not on the tourist trail and it doesn't have a Métro, which means knowledge of difficult things like trams is involved.

It's a visibly poor *commune* – bad street lighting, erratic refuse collection and no glamorous shops – so maybe the authorities are not too eager for you to see it, but don't let that put you off. Jump on the 93 or 94 tram and make for the Centre Communal. Stick around there – it's a huge *commune* but you don't have to see all of it.

Schaerbeek runs from the Gare du Nord up to Laeken and across to avenue de Woluwe St Lambert. It has three stations: Gare du Nord, Schaerbeek and Josaphat. Schaerbeek's image ranges from the seediness of its downtown area to the sedateness of its houses near the EU area. It is a commune that grew with the new Belgian state: at independence in 1830 there were 1,600 people living here; by 1900 there were 65,000.

Schaerbeek's population is now for the most part North African and Turkish. The women tend to sport the full yashmak, while the men are more Europeanised. On the streets you will hear strange combinations of Moroccan/Flemish and Turkish/ Flemish being spoken (Schaerbeek is a Flemish district).

The heart of Schaerbeek – the area around its Hôtel Communal (town hall) – is most impressive. It is all built on a rather grandiose scale, with long avenues sweeping down to monumental buildings and churches overlooking the city.

The Hôtel Communal is a mighty work, inaugurated in 1887 by Léopold II, who is sure to have approved of its massive dimensions. Badly damaged by fire at the beginning of the century and twice occupied by the Germans, the Flemish Renaissance-style building is constructed from red brick, with numerous towers and windows. Inside, it maintains a stately air, hiding dull bureaucracy behind heavy doors.

Place Colignon was constructed around the Hôtel and a contest was held in 1896 for the design of the house façades lining the square. These complement the town hall well with their substantial proportions and numerous turrets and gables. Many have flagpoles and just the right degree of solemnity to carry them off.

Just around the corner from the Hôtel Communal is Eglise St Servais, a large and beautiful, though decaying, church that holds services in Spanish and Italian and has a commanding view over avenue Louis Bertrand. Facing the Hôtel, across lengthy rue Royale Ste Marie, is the neo-Byzantine Eglise Ste Marie. This mosque-like building is curvaceous and arched, with an octagonal dome, and set up high so that it looks over Schaerbeek and down rue Royale.

On one side of rue Royale, nearest the Hôtel Communal, are the **Halles de Schaerbeek**. A rare example of nineteenth-century industrial architecture, the Halles are also a rare example of a Brussels renovation success story. Or let's not say rare. Let's say it's a sterling example for the future, as the city has thrown itself so enthusiastically into renovation, and there's hope for any number of buildings that five years ago were on death row. Millions were spent on converting this former meat and vegetable market into a fully functioning theatre and concert hall.

Further down rue Royale is one of the loveliest of Brussels' myriad cafés, the art nouveau De Ultieme Hallucinatie (*see chapter* **Cafés & Bars**). The exterior is peeling badly and a glum notice warns you not to leave anything in your car, but inside, the floating lines are indeed hallucinatory. It has a long and fierce Flemish tradition, so don't ever call it by its French name.

Further towards town is the Gare du Nord, which used to have great pull when it was the red-light district. Girls sat in the windows of dark houses; small bars had jukeboxes and more girls. It was unequivocally sleazy, but had a certain

The Clock at Mont des Arts – see page 54. *Be there on the hour to see the relevant figure emerge from his cubby hole.*

*The **EU area** has its admirers, but a great many more detractors. See page 67.*

downbeat energy. A few years ago, that all ended. Everything was closed down and many of the buildings were razed to the ground to make way for high-rise office blocks.

Now a few sad peepshows with bleak neon lights nestle in the ruins around the station, and tacky little sex shops are tucked into odd corners. However, it has retained its seedy connotations. You are unlikely to see any women around, for the good reason that hopeful men still hang about. Don't these guys realise the glory days are over? Soon, no doubt, you will alight from the train at Gare du Nord and see nothing but respectably ugly and cheap examples of late twentieth-century office architecture.

The rest of Schaerbeek is residential and offers little of particular interest to the visitor, though it's a good place for markets. Lying not far from the town hall is **Parc Josaphat**, a reasonably pretty space with ponds, an animal reserve and various sporting facilities.

St Josse is a tiny *commune* into which Schaerbeek seems to melt. This is true of certain Brussels *communes*. Only a small neat sign tells you that you have officially crossed into another area. St Josse is now almost completely North African and Turkish, though as the cheapest area near the European Commission and Parliament, it has its share of shrewd EU officials. Its trademark seems to be fruit shops. These are everywhere, especially along rue Verbist, where the shopfronts are decked out with identical lavish displays of seasonal fruit and vegetables.

St Josse is bounded by chaussée de Louvain, a long, narrow, ugly and energetic road whose shops are shabby but do seem to throw up great bargains from time to time. The clothes store DOD has expanded to at least five branches here. It deals in factory-reject designer clothes but is erratic, sometimes offering great Italian designers, at other times pushing lines of boring Bally shoes. The charming baroque Eglise St Josse stands on this chaussée, looking bewildered by the bustle and rubble around it. Inside is a beautiful altar with a round ornate roof.

At place Madou, St Josse borders on the city centre. A few minutes' walk along from here is the **Colonne du Congrès**, with the eternal flame burning at its foot. If you head up boulevard Bischoffsheim, you reach the wonderful-looking **Botanique**, an inspired mixture of neo-classicism, glass and iron. Formerly the city's greenhouse, it is now a cultural centre – with a cinema, theatre and exhibition halls – that maintains a hothouse atmosphere. (*See chapter* **Music: Rock, Folk & Jazz**.)

The sights

Botanique

236 rue Royale, 1210. (226 12 11). Métro Botanique. **Open** 9am-6pm daily. **Map D4/E1**
This long and beautiful neo-classical building was built in 1826 as a botanical garden. Now the cultural heart of the French community, it's also a centre for theatre, films (especially cartoons) and exhibitions. It also retains a hothouse atmosphere and has some impressively fleshy plants.

Colonne du Congrès
place du Congrès, 1000. Métro Madou. **Map D2/D3**
Another Poelaert piece. This one was built in 1850 to commemorate the National Congress of 1831 that proclaimed the Belgian constitution. A statue of Léopold I tops the column, which has that heaviness associated with so much of Poelaert's work. At the foot burns the eternal flame, a homage to the Unknown Soldier of the two World Wars.

Halles de Schaerbeek
22 rue Royale Ste Marie, 1030. Tram 90, 92, 93, 94.
(*See chapter* **Music: Rock, Folk & Jazz**.) **Map E1**
A rare example of Brussels' nineteenth-century industrial architecture, the Halles (there is a Grand and a Petit Halle) have just opened triumphantly after many years of renovation and are now being used as a concert hall and a theatre. They were built in 1865, burned down in 1898 and then reconstructed according to the original design. Like the Galeries St Hubert near the Grand Place, the Halles are all glass and iron, with light pouring in through the huge sheets of glass in the façade. They must have been some place to shop for carrots in; they're now some place to hear concerts in, too.

Parc Josaphat
entrances on avenue des Azalées and avenue Louis Bertrand, 1030. Tram 23. **Map G1**
The main park in the huge *commune* of Schaerbeek has lots of bonuses, such as a small animal reserve (with deers, goats and lambs), sporting facilities, a sculpture museum and free concerts on Sundays in July and August.
Archery. Café. Mini-golf.

EU area – Schuman & environs

This is Gotham City, Belgian-style. Walk through the **Parc du Cinquantenaire** towards the Rond-Point Schuman, take a left to rue Froissart and look down. You're on a height here and the EU's institutions are spread out before you. To the right is the distinctive 1970s starfish-shaped Berlaymont, the Commission headquarters. Vacated these past five years because of obscene amounts of asbestos, it's still ghostly white and plastic-covered like Berlin's Reichstag. Straight in front of you is the 1995 Council of Ministers' Justus Lipsius building, sprawling across a huge area in peach granite.

Away to the left, just visible through the trees of the **Parc Léopold**, is the very recent (officially opened in February 1998) European Parliament, shining blue-green in the distance like the Emerald City. Check out the odd, covered, geometric bridge on rue Belliard by which EU officials walk from one building to another. Look for the large, elegant, honey-coloured shape of the **Résidence Palace**, Brussels' finest art deco building and a remnant of another age, mercifully preserved amid all this modern bureaucracy. Take in the panoramic view and don't necessarily go down and walk among the buildings – it's pretty encroaching at street level. But make your way to the open-air platform of Schuman railway station for another fine view – the incongruous juxtaposition of the Berlaymont, the Parliament, the Résidence Palace and the railway lines. The area is crying out for a great chase movie to be shot here.

The EU area has its admirers, but it has a great many more detractors. People will refer nostalgically to pre-EU days when it was the lively quartier Léopold, with plentiful local bars and beautiful houses. There are those who are still enraged at the way this area was picked off to make way for Europe. Perhaps it's a casualty of progress, but it's certainly Europe now, not a Brussels *commune*. The thing to be grateful for is that the 1970s are over and the '90s have some architectural style, so those heavy grey office blocks that line the streets may one day be replaced by more daring buildings with glass curves, like the undulating Parliament.

Three long, narrow roads cut through the area: rue de la Loi, rue Joseph II and rue Belliard. Walking along these three traffic-heavy thoroughfares is no pleasure, so it is good that there are three Métro stops on rue de la Loi. The area has a quiet sense of mighty work going on behind concrete blocks and expansive panes of glass. Only at lunchtime and between 6pm and 8pm could it be described as bustling. (At weekends it becomes a ghost town, the only people on view being a few security guards.) At night there is some activity in a few places: the Irish bars Kitty O'Shea's, the James Joyce and the Wild Geese (*see chapter* **Cafés & Bars**). Full of the international set and a few Belgians looking for *craic*, these are the Greek Chorus to the EU institutions. If you want a job in Brussels, go hang out in one of them.

As soon as you move away from these three main streets, you are almost immediately back in the familiar cobbled enclaves of central Brussels. On one side, at the end of rue Archimède, are the twin squares of Ambiorix and Marie-Louise, both of them small and graceful, if unfortunately victim to the national mania for trellised trees. These are squares of beautiful, listed houses. Don't miss 11 place Ambiorix, although a reminder is probably unnecessary. Long and thin, with its spidery balconies and bronzed, rounded façade, it stands out like a fairy-tale home of a captive princess.

Just behind the square is the sloping rue des Confédérés. Here, in a red-brick house at no.83, WH Auden spent five months in the late 1930s 'bathing and café-crawling'. His poems, 'Musée des Beaux Arts' and 'Brussels in Winter', contain some of his impressions of the city.

On the other side of rue de la Loi, dominated by the Parliament, is place de Luxembourg, a square of great charm where the numerous bars have Stella and Jupiler signs rather than Guinness and Murphy's. Quartier Léopold railway station is here, small and dirty with open-air platforms, evoking the atmosphere of a black-and-white film, while clinging to it still is the age-old, oily, excited smell of departure and arrival.

Behind the Parliament on the other side lies **Parc Léopold**, a somewhat bedraggled bit of green with a bleak lake and basketball court. This

Famous Belgians no.2

Belgium's biggest movie star – affectionately known as 'the muscles from Brussels' – **Jean-Claude Van Damme** was born Jean-Claude Van Varenberg, 18 October 1960. His father was an accountant, and his mother ran a florist's shop. A skinny child, he took up karate at nine years old, and fell in love with the sport. He also studied ballet for a number of years, to professional standard. Before he was 20, he was the European Professional Karate Association's middleweight champion, as well as the owner of his own, very lucrative, gymnasium, the 'California Gym'.

'Belgium is a beautiful but sad country,' he said. 'It is always raining and grey.' After a small role in a French film, *Rue Barbar*, he sold up and lit out for Hollywood, where he struggled in a variety of odd jobs – pool cleaner, carpet layer, limo driver – and changed his name ('It's better in America, Van Damme: Hot Damme, Damme Good…'). Eventually, he landed a role in the martial arts quickie *No Retreat, No Surrender* (1985), and was subsequently cast in the title role for Arnold Schwarzenegger's *Predator* – from which he was fired after he complained about his costume. Inevitably, it was Menahem Golan, the colourful Cannon studio boss, who made Van Damme a star. Awed by a demonstration of the splits – a staple of every subsequent Van Damme flick – Golan gave him the lead in *Bloodsport* and made a killing, especially in the Asian market, but also in France, and on video in the US and the rest of the world.

With his grace and good looks, Van Damme might have been a good bet to take over from Schwarzenegger in the mainstream action man stakes, but his severely limited acting range, coupled with a thick Continental accent he can't seem to shake, has hampered his career. Perhaps all he needed was a larger-than-life role like *The Terminator* – or a director like James Cameron – to compensate, but that's never materialised and Van Damme's fan base remains strictly hardcore action fans (supplemented by the gay audience). Something of a movie buff himself, Van Damme has imported three highly regarded Hong Kong film-makers to direct him (John Woo, Ringo Lam and Tsui Hark) but the results have been disappointing. He also directed himself in *The Quest*.

and the monumental Parc du Cinquantenaire at the end of rue de la Loi are proof that although Brussels might recklessly destroy houses to make way for Europe, it has no intention of losing its parks. At the end of Parc Léopold is the Institut Royal des Sciences Naturelles, through the gates of which you can see the huge canvases in the **Musée Wiertz**, twisted into what Thomas Hardy would call their 'staring and ghastly attitudes'.

Amid all the European extravagance, the best place to eat is still firmly Belgian: **La Bonne Humeur** (*see chapter* **Restaurants**) does the best *moules-frites* in town. Despite its fame, it has resisted the urge to expand, so you still eat at long tables in a small room and booking is a necessity.

The sights

Arc de Triomphe

Parc du Cinquantenaire, 1000. Métro Mérode.
Obviously inspired by the great monument of the same name in Paris, this imposing structure was built by Girault in 1905. It is located in the city's most famous park, the Parc du Cinquantenaire, and stands like a gateway from the peripheries into the centre. Avenue de Tervuren rushes from the suburbs to meet it and the long, narrow, gloomy rue de la Loi takes over to bring you in a straight line to the centre of town. Most of the European Union buildings are to be found grouped at the town end of the park on Rond-Point Robert Schuman.

Maison de Cauchie

5 rue des Francs, 1040 (673 15 06). Métro Merode.
Open 11am-6pm, first weekend of the month and by appointment for groups (minimum 20 people).
Admission 150BF. **No credit cards. Map H5**
On a quiet, unremarkable street leading onto the Parc du Cinquantenaire, this is immediately arresting and worth going to look at even if you're not in Brussels the first weekend of the month. It was the home of the painter Cauchie, built in 1905 in the twilight of the Brussels art nouveau period. It's not, in fact, typically Belgian – but it's the only real example of sgraffiti in the city, and, like the Palais Stocklet, was much influenced by the Viennese Sezession movement.

Parc du Cinquantenaire

main entrances on avenue de Tervuren and rue de la Loi, 1000. Métro Merode or Schuman. **Map G4**
The largest, most impressive and most famous of the city parks was commissioned by Léopold II, who had 300 labourers working day and night to finish it in time for Belgium's fiftieth anniversary in 1880. It has all the trappings of an imperial park. The Arc de Triomphe is flanked on either side by the Royal Museums of Art, History and Military History as well as Autoworld (*see chapter* **Museums**). There are sculptures, a fairy-tale tower and, most interesting of all, Horta's Pavilion, which houses Lambeaux's *Haut-Relief des Passions Humaines*. This is kept locked out of respect for the nearby mosque, but a tantalising peephole will allow you a

Built in 1826 as a botanical garden, the **Botanique** *– see page 66 – is now the cultural heart of the French community.*

glimpse of a thigh or a breast on a carved fresco. Beside the pavilion is a monument to the Belgian soldiers who 'freed' the Congo: it shows black people in attitudes of ecstatic gratitude to the soldiers and is being allowed quietly to decay. Aside from these sights, the park itself is pleasant to walk in, if rather unkempt, with long avenues and a cobbled centre. Typically, there's now a tunnel running through it, which makes the whole park feel somehow impermanent. The park has a bad reputation for muggings around dusk, so take care. *Café (in museum). Running track. Sandpit. Tennis.*

Parc Léopold
entrance on chaussée de Wavre, 1040. Métro Schuman.
Map F5
On the side of a steep hill, the Parc Léopold has more character and less grandeur than its near neighbour the Parc du Cinquantenaire. It also conatins a small lake and a museum of natural history (*see chapter* **Museums**).

Résidence Palace
155 rue de la Loi, 1040 (231 03 05). Métro Schuman.
Map F4
This is the most stunning art deco building in a city where art nouveau reigns and many art deco examples are – like the Palais des Beaux Arts and Gare Centrale – heavy and unimaginative. The 11-storey Résidence Palace was built in the 1920s as a deluxe apartment block and has a theatre, a roof garden and an incomparable indoor swimming pool. It's not exactly open to the public and there are no guided tours, but if there happens to be a spectacle showing, you pays your money and you're in, though you won't get to see all of it.

Outside the centre
Laeken

There is far too much in Laeken not to include it, but it always seems like an unreal city hovering outside Brussels. Its giant amusement park, brimming with treasures that are constantly updated and expanded, efficiently streamlines the populace's leisure time. But it's like a bland spaceman's idea of what humans require for time out. Not our idea. One resents the efficiency of the Kinepolis's endless screens and faultless Dolby stereo that so quickly sucked audiences from the city auditoria that tiny cinemas such as the Marivaux had to close. It's hard to rejoice in that latest obsession with miniatures, **Mini-Europe**, which is a very poor cousin to the Manneken Pis and marionettes.

There are far too many attractions to list them all here. The Atomium is worth a drive up from the city centre, especially if you go very early in the morning. The exposition park beside the trade mart is something to wonder at – a reminder that Brussels is the fourth largest conference city in the world. The King lives up in Laeken, but in a palace you don't get to see. So, too, do other wealthy Belgians, in streets that fan out behind the park.

You can now take the Métro right to the centre of this leisure realm. The station is called Heysel, also the former name of the nearby stadium that was the scene of terrible tragedy in 1985 – still the most shocking football hooliganism ever witnessed – and is a sober reminder of real life in the midst of Laeken's careful construction of fun.

The sights
Atomium
boulevard du Centenaire, 1020 (477 09 04/477 09 77). Métro Heysel/tram 81. **Open** *Sept-Mar* 10am-6pm daily; *Apr-Aug* 9am-8pm daily. **Admission** 200BF; 160BF groups (minimum 20); 140BF children. **Credit** AmEx, MC, V.
Probably the second most famous monument in Brussels, the Atomium is the city's equivalent of the Eiffel Tower, but it has aged less well and was never as impressive anyway. It's a 102m (335ft) representation of the nine atoms of a molecule, done in steel and aluminium. It was designed by André Waterkeyn for the 1958 World Fair and has a dated feel. You can go inside and view the Biogénium exhibition about human life, which is not that remarkable. The best thing about the visit is travelling to the spheres by long escalators, and the view of the city from the top, which is one of those indisputably modern phenomena like New York from the Empire State Building and Paris from the Eiffel Tower.

Eglise Notre Dame de Laeken
parvis Notre Dame, 1020 (479 96 61). Tram 81/bus 53. **Open** guided visits 2-6pm Sun. **Services** 5pm first Fri of month; 5pm Sat; 9.15am, 10.15am, 11.30am, Sun.
This is the burial place of Belgium's kings and queens and opening times are firmly restricted to days of national significance. But the huge, neo-Gothic exterior, designed by Poelaert in 1851, is well worth a look. In the cemetery behind are tombs of important Belgians – including Poelaert himself – and a cast of Rodin's sculpture *The Thinker*. There are also a couple of incongruities: a mosque and an Egyptian temple. If you do get in, make sure to look out for the wonderful thirteenth-century Madonna on the altar.

Mini-Europe
Bruparck, boulevard du Centenaire, 1020 (478 05 50). Métro Heysel/tram 18, 19, 81, 91. **Open** *1 Apr-30 June* 9.30am-6pm daily; *1-19 July* 9.30am-8pm daily; *20 Jul-19 Aug* 9.30am-midnight daily; *20-31 Aug* 9.30am-8pm daily; *1 Sep-6 Jan* 10am-6pm daily. **Closed** 6 Jan-31 Mar. **Admission** 395BF; 355BF groups (minimum 20); 295BF children. **Credit** V.
Lying at the foot of the Atomium is the kitsch manifestation of Brussels' Europhilia. The whole of Europe is laid out here over 2.5 hectares (6 acres). The models are exact copies, on a scale of 1:25, of the major European monuments, including the Acropolis, the Brandenburg Gate and Big Ben. Similarly shrunk cars, buses and trains speed along the roads and under the tunnels. At the last count there were about 300 monuments, but the number has to keep growing to keep up with the ever-expanding EU.

Palais du Centenaire
Parc des Expositions, place de Belgique, 1020 (477 02 11). Métro Heysel.
Eleven *palais* were built here, the first in 1935 to commemorate a century of Belgian independence. They allow Brussels to offer a unique European venue for trade fairs. They cover 120,000sq m and have parking space for 15,000 cars. The largest of them, the Grand Palais built by Van Neck, is a triangular composition with ever-decreasing pavilions flanking the imposing, four-columned centre building.

Parc de Laeken
entrance on boulevard de Smet de Naeyer, 1020. Métro Heysel.
A visit here is inevitable whatever your interests, and there is enough here to keep you amused all day. In the adjacent

The neo-classical glass-and-iron **Botanique** *– see page 66 – contains a cinema, theatre and exhibition halls.*

Famous Belgians no.3

'Long, long ago, before the invention of the saxophone' was how F Scott Fitzgerald looked back from twentieth-century America's first flush of jazz age youth culture to a duller, less fabulous time. The saxophone was patented in 1845, but that doesn't matter. It found its voice, its musical home, in America in the late 1920s, and is as modern an acoustic instrument as you'll find.

It wasn't invented in America, however; it was invented in Brussels, by **Antoine Joseph Sax** (commonly known as Adolphe Sax). The new instrument blended the bell of a trumpet or trombone with the reed and mouthpiece of a clarinet, to create something that merged the power and edge of the brass family with the rich, mellow sound of the woodwinds. Sax also invented the sax-horn, the saxtromba and the

sax-tuba; but none of these quite caught on. The saxophone developed in a number of sizes, from the tiny, screechy sopranino to the rough, boomy bass saxophone, and interested a few composers, but not enough to develop a serious repertoire. After Sax's death in 1894, it fell into the hands of vaudevillians, who used it to play a kind of showy ragtime hybrid.

The jazz musicians rescued it. In a gutsy music where improvisation reigns, the opportunity to play an instrument so close to the human voice was an attractive prospect, and the lush texture that a few alto and tenor saxophones could give to a jazz orchestra soon meant that clarinettists were expected to double on the newer horns. Coleman Hawkins, Johnny Hodges and Sidney Bechet gave the instrument its own voice, and when an alto saxophonist called Charlie Parker set the modern jazz revolution in motion, he did it on an alto sax.

Today it is also popular in soul and funk (*see left* ex-James Brown alto star, Maceo Parker), the axe of choice for generations of jazz innovators and an instrument with a uniquely romantic image.

Bruparck is the Atomium, Mini-Europe, Kinepolis and water slide complex Océade (*see chapter* **Children**). If none of these twentieth-century amusements suits your mood, stroll along the attractive footpaths, keeping a lookout for glimpses of the Château Royal.

Pavillon Chinois

44 avenue Jules van Praet-Iaan, 1020 (268 16 08). Tram 23, 52, 92. **Open** 10am-4.40pm Tue-Sun. **Admission** 80BF (120BF tour of Pavillon Chinois and Tour Japonaise). **No credit cards**.

Inspired by the 1900 Paris Exhibition, Léopold II had this delicate house built from plans by the French architect Marcel. The ornamented façade was made in Shanghai. It stands incongrously but classically between solid Belgian trees. Fortunately, it has the Japanese Tower across the road to keep it company. Inside there is a fine porcelain collection.

Planétarium National

10 avenue de Bouchot, 1020. Métro Heysel/tram 18, 19, 81. **Open** 9am-4pm Mon-Fri. **Shows** 1.30pm Tue; 9.45am, 3.30pm, Wed; 11am Thur; 9.45am, 2.30pm, Fri; 3.45pm first and third Sun. **Admission** 120BF; 80BF groups. **No credit cards**.

Like so many other attractions, this is right beside the Atomium. Besides the telescope trained on the sky, there is a huge cupola – 24m (79ft) in diameter – on which is projected the movements of the planets and stars.

Serres Royales (Royal Hothouses)

61 avenue du Parc Royal (Domaine Royal), 1020 (tourist info 513 89 40). Métro Heysel/tram 52, 92/bus 53. **Open** *end of April/beginning of May when flowers are in bloom* 9.30am-4pm Wed, Thur; 9-11pm Fri; 9.30am-4pm, 9-11pm, Sat, Sun. **Dates** vary annually but are given out by the tourist office from Jan. **Admission** free during day; 100BF at night. **No credit cards**.

Magnificent sequence of 11 linked greenhouses built on the orders of Léopold II by Balat and the young Horta. Sometimes called 'the City of Glass', they rise up from the royal grounds like the Emerald City in *The Wizard of Oz*. The largest is 60m (197ft) long and 30m (98ft) high. Exotic plants bloom within, but like so much else in Brussels, their opening days are strictly limited. However, the exterior can be viewed from Parc de Laeken – for the best aspect, turn left at the main exit on avenue du Parc Royal and look down on them from the left-hand pavement.

Tour Japonaise

44 avenue Jules van Praet-Iaan, 1020 (268 16 08). Tram 23, 52, 92. **Open** 10am-4.40pm Tue-Sun. **Admission** 80BF (120BF tour of Pavillon Chinois and Tour Japonaise). **No credit cards**.

Across the road from the Chinese Pavilion, this fanciful red tower also rises up from between sturdy trees and it, too, was designed by Marcel. But the details were executed in Yokohama this time. Closed for 50 years, it is now run by the Musées Royaux d'Art et d'Histoire and exhibits Japanese art.

From Montgomery to Tervuren

There are several compelling reasons to visit Tervuren. The first is that you get to take the 44 tram from Montgomery all the way down the avenue de Tervuren, through the **Forêt de Soignes** to the final destination. It's a great ride. Montgomery is one of the busiest traffic junctions in Brussels, with three lanes of traffic whizzing recklessly round the grass roundabout. A jaunty statue of Monty stands just above the tunnel facing the Cinquantenaire, reminding motorists that

the British field marshal marched along here from France, rolling up the German right flank.

The tram emerges from underground and trundles down the wide and beautifully tree-lined avenue de Tervuren. It's best to sit on the right-hand side of the tram since then you get a good view of the brilliantly geometric **Palais Stocklet**. You also see the lovely hills and lakes of Parc de Woluwe and, further on, catch glimpses of the embassy houses through the trees.

During the summer months the splendid Musée de Transport Urbain Bruxellois (*see chapter* **Museums**) sends its old trams trundling through the forest. In autumn, the chestnut trees along the avenue rain down conkers on the tram roof. Once in the Forêt de Soignes, you are sheltered by tall, spindly trees and cross through Quatre Bras, where the elegant Hussar regiment met Napoleon's troops in 1815 and fled precipitately back to town.

On reaching the final stop of Tervuren, you see Léopold II's Museum voor Midden-Afrika (*see chapter* **Museums**) immediately before you, announced by a large stone statue of an elephant atop a roundabout. Everyone condemns the way in which this museum came about, while simultaneously praising its treasures and booty. Proudly displayed are the art, minerals and wildlife of the Congo. The park around the museum has formal gardens and, further down, a sequence of canals. Below the park is an arboretum with old trees and delicate-looking Japanese plants.

Past the boathouse, where you can hire paddling boats, is the small village of Tervuren. The cobbled main square has been recently renovated and traffic has been restricted in order to encourage people to linger. The square's focus is provided by the eighteenth-century church of St Jan, and you can pause for excellent ice-creams in the glacerie Mont Blanc. All around the village are fine big houses, which help make this the home of many British and Irish Eurocrats.

Tervuren is quiet and charming, and a good way to escape the city for a healthy dose of greenery. When you've had your fill, take the 44 tram back to the metropolis, heading for the magnificent Arc de Triomphe lighting up the sky.

The sights

Forêt de Soignes

Boitsfort, 1170. Tram 44.

This huge beech woodland stretched over 12,000 hectares (4,800 acres) in 1822. Now it's been reduced to 4,000 (1,600 acres), which is still impressive for such a built-up capital. In summer, old trams from the Musée de Transport Urbain Bruxellois (*see chapter* **Museums**) make their way through the trees. The forest includes the Tervuren Arboretum (769 20 81), which is full of old and new forest flora; the Groenendaal Arboretum (657 03 86), which has about 500 exotic species, as well as a forest museum and a high-class restaurant in what used to be an abbey; and the Jean Massart Experimental Garden (673 84 06), a research centre holding approximately 5,600 species.

Famous Belgians no.4

A bit of a cheat, really, as he never actually existed, but like most great fictional detectives, **Hercule Poirot** has a knack for seeming more real than his creator. Indeed, had Agatha Christie thought to provide her famous sleuth with a permanent address, there can be little doubt that he would even now be receiving mail from would-be clients, just as letters continue to arrive for Sherlock Holmes at 221B Baker Street.

On the face of it, Poirot, with his egg-shaped head, painstakingly waxed moustache and habit of flicking microscopic specks of dust from his clothing, is an absurd creation – the more so when one realises that his very name constitutes one of the feeblest jokes in English literature (in the early novels we are told that Poirot has come to England to spend his retirement growing leeks, or *les poirots*). Yet his character and background were constructed shrewdly. A more 'obvious' Poirot would have been a Frenchman, but Christie calculated, correctly, that her readers would warm to him more readily if he were Belgian. For this was in 1915, when Belgium had existed as a state for only 76 years – far too shallow a national soil for British prejudice to take root. Besides, it was the height of World War I, when 'gallant little Belgium' was taking her stand against the Kaiser.

Poirot made his début in *The Mysterious Affair at Styles*. There he uses the detective skills he had acquired on the Brussels police force to solve one of the those quintessentially English murders which, far from threatening the immutability of provincial life, actually accentuates it. This is a world in which vicars are still pillars of the community, where housemaids speak in a kind of sub-cockney argot which existed only in the imaginations of middle-class novelists, and in which, the killer unmasked, everyone repairs to the drawing room for a nice cup of tea. It's a world into which Poirot fits

perfectly. For, as Colin Watson points out in his history of British detective fiction, *Snobbery with Violence*, Poirot 'was an altogether English creation – as English as a Moorish cinema foyer or hotel curry or comic yodellers'. That comically literal diction, with its liberal sprinkling of schoolboy French *Eh bien*s and *Voyons*, wasn't fooling anybody. Yet it had a purpose: to make Poirot sufficiently ridiculous for his innate intelligence – his much-vaunted 'little grey cells' – to be acceptable to a readership who, as Watson noted, 'is inclined to be in awe of knowledge but to distrust intelligence'. On the page, Poirot's eccentricities are both useful to the author and, in the main, entertaining to the reader. On screen they tend to be merely irritating: Albert Finney's hammed-up Poirot in *Murder on the Orient Express* wouldn't have survived the journey from Victoria Station to Carshalton Beeches without being ejected by his fellow passengers. Peter Ustinov (*see left*), who took over in the role, had the good sense to sketch in the accent and the innate fastidiousness as lightly as he could without merely playing himself.

Tour Japonaise – *see p73 – built by the French architect Marcel, like the Pavillon Chinois.*

Moulin de Lindekamaele

*6 avenue JF Debecker, 1200 (770 90 57). Métro
Roodebeek.* **Open** *visits* 9am-noon, 3-6.30pm, Tue-Fri;
restaurant noon-3pm, 6.30-9.30pm, Mon-Fri.
This fifteenth-century mill was originally owned by the
Hannecart family and was first a paper then a flour mill.
Bought by the *commune* in 1932, it is now a restaurant and
conference centre.

Palais Stocklet

281 avenue de Tervuren, 1150. Tram 39, 44. Not open
to the public.
Brussels' most interesting palace has now unfortunately
closed to the public after it was discovered that visitors had
been making off with the treasures. It's a marvellous geometric building designed by the Austrian Josef Hoffmann,
and is in deliberate opposition to the lavishness of art nouveau. It is, in its sparseness and purity, entirely modern. Only
old black-and-white photos, with the Klimts in the dining
room, give a clue to the interior. It's still worth taking the 44
or 39 tram from Montgomery for a look at that exterior.

Parc de Tervuren

entrance on chaussée de Louvain, 1380. Tram 44.
Notable mainly for the African Museum, which was built by
Girault to house Léopold II's Congo booty. Even if you don't
venture in, the building itself and the huge statue of the elephant give you a lift. The museum is surrounded by formal
gardens, but the park around these is large and attractive,
with a series of canals and woods. The grounds originally
belonged to a palace and there are still remains of eighteenth-
century stables and the Renaissance Chapelle St Hubert.

Parc de Woluwe

entrance on avenue de Tervuren, 1160. Tram 39, 44.
This is one of the most attractive parks close to the city. Like
so many others, it was commissioned by Léopold II, but was
renovated after 1945. It has an easy grace, is well tended and
clean, and has none of the stuffy flower beds and tortured
arrangements of the formal parks. It's large, with woods,
lakes and slopes, and if it snows, you can skate and sledge.
Boats. Café. Fishing. Mini-golf.

Additional sights

Basilique Nationale du Sacré Cœur

*1 parvis de la Basilique, 1083 (425 88 22). Métro
Simonis then bus 87.* **Open** *Apr-Sept* 6am-6pm Mon-Sat;
Oct-Mar 8am-5pm Mon-Sat. **Guided tours** by
appointment. **Services** *French* 9am Mon-Fri; *Flemish*
5.30pm Sat; *French* 6.30pm Sat; *Flemish* 9am, with
Gregorian choir 10am, Sun.
This twentieth-century basilica (not actually completed until
around 1970) is impressive for its commanding position and
its size – 167m (548ft) x 89m (292ft). It's a national monument dedicated to the memory of patriots, but the dull red-
brick style is heavy and it fails to move the beholder. The
interior is rather better, though, with its chapels, large choir
and statue of Our Lady by Goosens.

Butte du Lion (Lion Hill)

*252-254 route du Lion, 1420 Braine-l'Alleud (tourist
information 354 99 10).* **Open** *1 Apr-14 Oct* 9.30am-
6.30pm daily; *15 Oct-31 Mar* 10.30am-4.30pm daily.
Admission 40BF; 20BF children. **No credit cards**.
Just outside Brussels, the site of Waterloo is an essential pilgrimage for British visitors. It's one of the most impressive
battle commemorations around. The Lion is set on an 45m
(147ft)-long slope and weighs 28 tonnes. It was built by Van
Geel ten years after the battle and stands on the spot where
the Prince of Orange fell. It's a good climb to the top – 230
steps – but when you do go for it, you get a fine view of the
surrounding fields, which have fortunately been left much

as they were, so you can mentally reconstruct the battle. If
you have problems doing that, there are audio-visuals in the
museum at the foot of the hill to do it for you.

Château Malou

*45 chaussée de Stockel, 1200 (761 27 66/gallery 762
21 05). Bus 28.* **Open** when gallery has exhibition;
phone to check.
Now an art gallery and cultural centre, this is a fine eighteenth-century castle set by a lake in the elegant Parc Malou.
It was built in 1776 by Baron Lambert, but then passed to
the Malou family, who lived in it until 1951. The stables have
been turned into an art exhibition centre.

Walibi

Wavre, 1300 (010 42 15 00). **Getting there** *by train*
Ottignies-Louvain-la-Neuve line from Schuman to Gare
de Bierges (the station is 300m from Walibi); *by car* take
the E411 Bxl-Namur motorway to exit 6. **Open** *4 Apr-30
Jun* 10am-6pm daily; *1 July-18 Oct* 10am-7pm daily.
Admission 760BF; 680BF children up to 1m 30cm tall;
free children under 1m tall. **Credit** MC, V.
Before Disneyland Paris brought America right into the
heart of a reluctant France, this was the biggest theme park
in mainland Europe. It has the usual assortment of stomach-
churning rollercoasters, gentle carousels and elaborate river
rides. It also boasts an enormous slide and splash complex,
Aqualibi, which is open all year round and costs 480BF when
Walibi is closed (*see chapter* **Children**).
Disabled: toilets.

Trips & tours

ARAU (L'Atelier de Recherche
et d'Action Urbaine)

*55 boulevard Adolphe Max, 1000 (219 33 45/fax 219 86
75). Métro De Brouckère or Rogier.* **Duration** 3 hrs.
Departures *Mar-Nov* (in English) 9.45am first, second,
fifth Sat of month. **Pick-up** Hôtel Métropole, place de
Brouckère. **Tickets** 600BF (booking advised). **No credit
cards. Map C2**
ARAU is a committee of Brussels' citizens, created in 1969
to safeguard the city's heritage. An adjunct of its activities
is the bus and tram tour of the city. This is highly recommended, as ARAU has the whole thing sewn up and is the
only way into some of the loveliest of the private houses.
Also on offer on the third Saturday of the month is a tour of
art deco buildings.

Arcadia

17 rue Wafelaerts, 1060 (534 38 19/fax 534 60 73).
Duration 3 hrs. **Departures** 9.45am Sun. **Pick-up**
depends on tour.
Arcadia organises nine different tours, including art nouveau, baroque and classic, and nineteenth-century Brussels.

De Boeck's Sightseeing Tours

*8 rue de la Colline, 1000 (513 77 44/fax 502 58 69).
Métro Gare Centrale.* **Duration** 3 hrs. **Departures** *Apr-
Oct* 10am, 11am, 2pm, 3pm, daily; *Nov-Mar* 10am, 2pm,
daily. **Pick-up** Grand Place. **Tickets** 780BF; 630BF
students; 380BF children.
Take your pick of daily tours, in most European languages
and Japanese, which go to all the major sights. De Boeck's
also does trips to Waterloo, Bruges and Antwerp.

Guides TIB-GBB

*Hôtel de Ville, Grand Place, 1000 (513 89 40/fax 514 45
38). Métro Gare Centrale.* **Pick-up** depends on tour.
Map C3
Tours include a comic book trail, a tour of Jewish Brussels
and an underground tour of the archaeological sites. Reserve
in groups by fax or writing two weeks in advance.

Museums

What Brussels' museums lack in quantity they make up for in diversity and charm.

The chances are that you were not drawn to Brussels for its museums – there is no Louvre, no Hermitage, no MOMA here. Scoff if you will, but take note: beautiful plants have been known to sprout when towering trees don't steal all the light. There is no shortage of smaller-scale museums with well-presented permanent displays, excellent temporary exhibitions and uncrowded spaces. Unlike other capital cities, there is no museum-mob scene here and it is always possible to see permanent and temporary collections without endless queuing and bruised ribs. And even if you tire of the museums in the Belgian capital, it is within day-trip distance of the museums of London, Paris, Amsterdam and Cologne.

The largest museums in Brussels are the two **Musées des Beaux Arts** (the **Musée d'Art Ancien** and the **Musée d'Art Moderne**) and the **Musée Royal d'Art et d'Histoire**. But some of the city's smaller museums – such as the **Musée Horta** and the **Centre Belge de la Bande Dessinée** – have more character and are more uniquely Bruxellois. As well as art nouveau and the comic strip, other aspects of Belgium that are well represented in Brussels museums are art deco, surrealism, and the works of Rubens, the Brueghel family and Ensor.

In addition to the permanent collections in Brussels, you will also find good temporary exhibitions. The **Palais des Beaux Arts** (*see chapters* **Art Galleries** and **Music: Classical & Opera**) in rue Ravenstein holds regular art exhibitions, while the **Musée Communal d'Ixelles** organises strong and often controversial shows.

For a full list of the city's museums, as well as details of temporary exhibitions, contact the Tourist Information Office at 61 rue Marché aux Herbes (504 02 70).

Musée d'Art Moderne – *see page 79.*

Art & architecture

Centre Belge de la Bande Dessinée

20 rue des Sables, 1000 (219 19 80). Métro Botanique, De Brouckère or Rogier/tram 55, 58, 81, 90/bus 38, 61, 71. **Open** 10am-6pm Tue-Sun. **Admission** 180BF; 120BF groups (of 15 or more); 60BF under-12s. **No credit cards. Map D3**

This excellent museum combines two of the Belgian capital's most appealing traditions: art nouveau and the comic strip. An unholy union, some might say – would Horta and Hergé approve? – but most people agree that this museum is pure joy. The building, a *grand magasin* from the early 1900s, was designed by Victor Horta, but in typical Brussels fashion was virtually in ruins by the early 1980s. Unlike much of the Belgian heritage, it was saved from the wrecking ball and restored, and now serves as a shrine to the ninth art (the seventh and eighth being cinema and television). Although *la bande dessinée* did not originate in Belgium, Belgian artists have been at the forefront of the comic strip ever since Hergé brought Tintin into the world in 1929. Spirou, Lucky Luke, Gaston Lagaffe and the Smurfs were all born of Belgian ink. The museum recreates the worlds of these and other cartoon heroes through photos, original documents and 3D props in an engaging display called the Museum of the Imaginary. In another display, visitors follow the progress of the comic strip from initial conception to finished product, and there are original drawings by Belgian and other artists including Hergé, HG Wells and Jules Verne. It also has regular exhibitions of other comic strip artists. Those who come here for the Horta and not the *bande* might want to save themselves the entrance fee and restrict themselves to the small display on Horta and the wonderful entrance hall, rather than venturing further inside. *Bookshop. Restaurant.*

Weapons and
Armour Hall

Aviation
Department

Royal Military History and Army Museum Brussels

**Jubelpark 3
B-1000 Brussels**

Guided tours
in French, Dutch,
English or German

32-2/732 34 49
32-2/732 35 86

Beautiful view on
Brussels from
the Arcade

Historical Hall
Belgium 1831-1914

Fondation pour l'Architecture
*55 rue de l'Ermitage, 1050 (649 02 59). Tram 81, 82,
93, 94/bus 54, 38, 60, 71.* **Open** 12.30-7pm Tue-Fri;
11am-7pm Sat, Sun. **Admission** 200BF; 150BF students,
over-60s. **No credit cards**.
A converted pumping house between avenue Louise and
chaussée d'Ixelles that has good exhibitions of Brussels' dis-
appearing recent architectural heritage. Displays are varied
and well put together, with models, photos, videos and
furniture, and the interpretation of architecture is not too
restrictive: recently there was an excellent exhibition about
the great liners of the 1930s. Look out for posters around
Brussels showing current exhibitions.
Bookshop.

Musée d'Art Ancien
*3 rue de la Régence, 1000 (508 32 11). Métro Gare
Centrale or Parc/tram 92, 93, 94/bus 20, 34, 38, 60,
71, 95, 96.* **Open** 10am-noon, 1-5pm, Tue-Sun.
Admission free. **Map C4/C5**
An extensive collection of works dating from the fifteenth
century and continuing up to the nineteenth century.
Highlights include an important collection of Pieter Bruegel
paintings, including *Landscape with the Fall of Icarus* and
Winter Landscape with Skaters and a Bird Trap, as well as
a fine collection of paintings and sketches by Rubens. Other
notable works include a medieval copy of *St Anthony's
Temptation* by Hieronymus Bosch, paintings by Lucas
Cranach the Elder, Memling and Jordaens, and Jacques-Louis
David's depiction of Marat's death, plus several of Ensor's
macabre masks and skulls. Since the museum is very large
and also contains some mediocre works – for example, some
appallingly mawkish nineteenth-century depictions of dogs
and children – it is best not to try to see all of it in one go
(and since it's free, you can make several trips). One good
strategy is to follow the museum's Blue (fifteenth-sixteenth
centuries), Brown (seventeenth-eighteenth centuries) and
Yellow (nineteenth century) routes, which steer visitors past
some of the highlights. The museum is connected to the
Musée d'Art Moderne by an underground passage.
Shop.

Musée d'Art Moderne
*3 rue de la Régence, 1000 (508 32 11). Métro Gare
Centrale or Parc/tram 92, 93, 94/bus 20, 34, 38, 60, 71,
95, 96.* **Open** 10am-1pm, 2-5pm, Tue-Sun. **Admission**
free. **Map C4/C5**
The museum is dominated by Belgian artists, of whom the
most prominent are the Surrealists Magritte and Delvaux.
Other Belgian artists are also well represented, including Pol
Bury and his moving sculptures, and the fauvists Léon
Spilliaert and Rik Wouters. There are also a few works by
non-Belgian artists, including Raoul Dufy, the video artist
Nam Jun Paik, Francis Bacon, Marc Chagall, Georges Braque
and Picasso, but be warned that some of these are by no
means their best works. The museum is well laid out in a
spacious, subterranean design that spirals down eight floors.
The signposting can occasionally be confusing, but crowds
are rare and the atmosphere is restful and quiet (apart from
some of the clankings made by the kinetic sculptures near
the entrance). The museum entrance is closed at weekends,
so use the Musée d'Art Ancien entrance on rue de la Régence
and follow the signs through the underground tunnel to the
twentieth-century collection.
Shop.

Musée Charlier
*16 avenue des Arts, 1210 (218 53 82). Métro Arts-Loi
or Madou/bus 29, 63, 65, 66.* **Open** 9am-6pm Mon-Fri.
Admission 100BF. **No credit cards. Map D4/E3**
Guillaume Charlier was an active figure in the artistic world
of Brussels in the late 1900s. Trained at the Beaux Arts
in Brussels, he was taken under the wing of Henri van
Cutsem, a collector and patron of the arts. Charlier actually

moved into Van Cutsem's house, the site of this museum,
where he organised concerts and salon discussions for the
city's intellectual and artistic circles. The *fin-de-siècle* house
is crammed with beautiful tapestries, furniture, silverware,
and works by Ensor, Meunier and Charlier himself. Concerts
are still held in the concert hall: contact the museum for a
full programme.

Musée Communal d'Ixelles
*71 rue van Volsem, 1050 (511 90 84). Bus 38, 54, 60,
71.* **Open** 1-6.30pm Mon-Fri. **Admission** 200-250BF. **No
credit cards**.
This excellent little museum is housed in a former abattoir
just off the chaussée d'Ixelles. Founded in 1892, it is well-
known in Brussels for its exhibitions of mainly modern art,
but it also has a good permanent collection, including works
by Belgian artists Magritte, Delvaux, Spilliaert, de Smet
and Van Rysselberghe, and original posters by Toulouse-
Lautrec. It also has Picasso's *Guitar and Fruit Bowl*, which
was stolen a few years ago but later recovered. A new wing,
opened in 1994, blends perfectly with the older part, creating a well-lit and interesting space for the paintings. Slightly
off the usual tourist track, the museum is rarely crowded.
Bookshop.

Musée Constantin Meunier
*59 rue de l'Abbaye, 1050 (648 44 49). Tram 93,
94/bus 38, 60.* **Open** 10am-noon, 1-5pm, Tue-Sun.
Admission free.
The former house and studio of Constantin Meunier (1831-
1905) contains more than 170 sculptures and 120 paintings,
the best known of which are the bronze figures of industrial workers. Meunier began his artistic career painting
religious scenes, but changed tack in his fifties, turning
to sculpture and social realism. His later works feature
farmers, miners and industrial workers labouring heroic-
ally in fairly grim surroundings. Although much of his
work appears rather worthy and monumental, his figures
do convey a sense of dignity and suffering, and in small
doses it can be quite moving. Don't come here looking for
anything frivolous, cheering or fashionable, but do drop in
if you're passing.

Musée David et Alice van Buuren
*41 avenue Leo Errera, 1180 (343 48 51). Tram 23,
90/bus 60.* **Open** 2-5.30pm Mon; 1-5.30pm Sun; *garden*
2-6pm daily (group visits for 12-30 people any day by
appointment only). **Admission** 300BF; 200BF students.
Credit V.
As you walk along the sedate, suburban Uccle streets leading to the Van Buuren Museum, it is difficult to believe that
you are approaching one of the most remarkable houses in
Brussels. The house was built in 1928 for David van Buuren,
a wealthy Dutch banker who became enamoured of the art
deco style, and it has been run as a museum since 1973. It
contains a remarkable collection of paintings, including one
of several versions of Bruegel's *Landscape with the Fall of
Icarus*, and works by Ensor, Van Gogh and Braque, as well
as paintings by Gustave van de Woestyne, a close friend of
the Van Buurens. The art deco piano and carpets on the
ground floor are wonderful, as is the dining room. Unlike
many museums of this type, the house is one that you would
actually like to live in. Brussels weather permitting, the garden is also worth a tour, particularly the maze designed by
Belgian landscape architect Réné Péchère.
Bookshop.

Musée Horta
*25 rue Américaine, 1060 (537 16 92). Tram 81, 82, 91,
92/bus 37, 38, 54, 60.* **Open** 2-5.30 pm Tue-Sun.
Admission 200BF. **No credit cards**.
Victor Horta was one of the founders of art nouveau, a new
architectural language that combined glass, iron, wood and
organic shapes to create airy, fluid and rhythmic spaces. He

After a humbling visit to the **Musée de la Dynastie** *– see page 82 – a subject takes time out.*

was responsible for some of the finest art nouveau architecture in Brussels, although some of his most famous buildings were demolished – his Maison du Peuple, for example, was torn down in 1965 during Brussels' wrecking ball period. Horta built this house in rue Américaine in 1899-1901 as his home and studio. The attention to detail is astonishing and every functional element, down to the last door handle, is designed in the fluid, sensuous art nouveau style. The staircase and stairwell are particularly breathtaking – an extravaganza of wrought iron, mirrors and floral designs, topped by a stained-glass canopy. The only problem about the museum is that it gets very crowded, and even the wonderful staircase loses its appeal when you have to queue for ten minutes to climb it. Try to visit on a weekday.

Musée Royal d'Art et d'Histoire

10 parc du Cinquantenaire, 1000 (741 72 11). Métro Merode or Schuman/tram 81, 82/bus 20, 28, 36, 67, 80. **Open** 9.30am-5pm Tue-Fri; 10am-5pm Sat, Sun. **Admission** 150BF; 100BF students and groups; 50BF children; free Wed. **No credit cards**. **Map G4**
This vast museum has one of the world's largest antiquity departments, with a huge collection of artefacts from the ancient worlds of Egypt, Greece, the Near and Far East, and pre-Columbian America. Items of interest include the Roman Apamea mosaic, discovered in Syria in the 1930s by a team of Belgian archaeologists, and the amazing feather cloak (and other feather art) made by Amazon Indians in the early seventeenth century. Other collections include European art from the Middle Ages, art deco, glass and metalwork, lace, and eighteenth-century carriages. Visiting a collection this enormous and ancient can be hard on the feet, and you'll see a fair number of bored and bad-tempered families traipsing around collection after collection. It's best to identify a few areas of interest, and stick to them.
Bookshop.

Institut Royal des Sciences Naturelles de Belgique *in rue Vautier – where dinosaurs and children gather in large numbers.*

Musée Wiertz

62 rue Vautier, 1050 (648 17 18). Métro Trône or Maelbeek/bus 20, 34, 38, 60, 80, 95, 96. **Open** *Apr-Oct* 10am-noon, 1-5pm, Tue-Sun; *Nov-Mar* 10am-noon, 1-4pm, Tue-Sun. **Admission** free.
The paintings of Antoine Wiertz (1806-65) are chiefly known nowadays for their size and often gruesome themes. Some of the canvases in this museum (the painter's home and studio) are over 11 metres high, and subjects include *Thoughts and Visions of a Decapitated Head*, *The Suicide* and *The Burned Child*, as well as a portrait of Quasimodo. The paintings, of which this museum has about 160, have mostly religious or philosophical themes, and the style is dynamic and tortured, with deep colours and plenty of Herculean musculature. Some of the larger paintings appear laughable to the modern visitor, but the smaller studies and sketches are more appealing. It's certainly not the pick of Brussels' museums, but it's an interesting (and amusing) enough experience for a rainy afternoon.

Science

Institut Royal des Sciences Naturelles de Belgique

29 rue Vautier, 1000 (627 42 38). Métro Trône or Maelbeek/bus 20, 34, 38, 60, 80, 95, 96. **Open** 9.30am-4.45pm Tue-Sat; 9.30am-6pm Sun. **Admission** 150BF; 100BF students, groups, over-60s; 50BF disabled; free under-5s. **No credit cards**.
The recommended first stop for anyone with children is the dinosaur department, which has the skeletons of 29 iguanadons discovered in a Belgian coal mine at the end of the nineteenth century. Thanks to the robotic wonders of 'dinamation', you can also watch full- and half-scale dinosaurs blink, wriggle and snarl. Look out, too, for the whale room (with 18 whale skeletons), and the insect department, which is informative and well-mounted and has 5,000 butterflies and beetles. Other parts of the museum await renovation.
Bookshop.

*Transports of delight await motor fans at **Autoworld** – possibly the world's finest car park.*

Koninklijk Museum voor Midden-Afrika/Musée Royal de l'Afrique Centrale

13 chaussée de Louvain, Tervuren 3080 (769 52 11). Tram 44. **Open** 10am-5pm Tue-Fri; 10am-6pm, Sat, Sun. **Admission** 200BF; 80BF students. **No credit cards**. **Map E3/H2**

At its inception in 1897, the Museum voor Midden-Afrika was devoted to glorifying the Belgian presence in Africa. In fact, that presence was less than glorious – to the extent that the world did not need the benefit of late twentieth-century hindsight to be shocked at how Belgium's Léopold II (1865-1909) treated the Belgian Congo. International outrage at the atrocities – murders, mutilations, the destruction of entire clans – committed against the Africans forced the monarch to hand over the reins to the Belgian state in 1908. It is estimated that between 1896-1906 Leopold earned his country $15 million from the Congo, at the expense of at least three million lives. As for the museum, its permanent display is a mixture of dusty cases of somewhat motheaten stuffed animals, jars of giant earthworms and other creepy-crawlies, and collections of African masks, utensils, art and ceremonial clothes and items. The presentation of the latter collections is dull – a shame, since much of it could be fascinating and impressive if it was displayed and labelled better. If ever this museum is given a makeover, it will be excellent. In the meantime, children enjoy the animal and insect sections, and the temporary exhibitions, which usually focus on one African country, are livelier than the permanent displays. The beautiful grounds are another redeeming feature and make an excellent place for a walk or picnic.

History

Musée de la Dynastie

7 place des Palais, 1000 (511 55 78). Métro Gare Centrale or Parc/tram 92, 93, 94/bus 20, 34, 71, 95, 96. **Open** 10am-4pm Tue-Thur, Sat, Sun. **Admission** free. **Map D4**

Dynasty refers to the beloved Belgian royal family, and memorabilia, photographs and documents chronicle the history of the Belgian monarchy since 1831. Unlikely to be your first stopping place in Brussels, but OK if you have an interest in this sort of thing.

Musée Royal de l'Armée et d'Histoire Militaire

3 parc du Cinquantenaire, 1000 (733 44 93). Métro Merode or Schuman/tram 81, 82/bus 20, 28, 36, 67, 80. **Open** *museum & library* 9am-noon, 1-5pm, Mon-Fri; 10am-5pm Sat, Sun. **Admission** free. **Map G4**

Guns, swords, cannons, grenades, uniforms and artillery are arranged in somewhat haphazard displays with special emphasis on the Belgian army. There's an interesting section on the 1830 Belgian Revolution, with weapons, posters and paintings. Of more universal appeal is the aviation section's enormous hangar. This houses 130 aircraft from World War I to the present, with a special focus on World War II planes used by the Allies and the Luftwaffe. Also included are MIG fighter jets, Douglas Dakotas and Sikorsky helicopters. *Bookshop.*

Musée de la Ville de Bruxelles

Maison du Roi, Grand Place, 1000 (511 27 42). Métro Bourse or Gare Centrale. **Open** *May-Sept* 10am-12.30pm, 1.30-5pm, Mon-Thur; 10am-1pm Sat, Sun. *Oct-Apr* 10am-12.30pm, 1.30-4.30pm, Mon-Thur; 10am-1pm Sat, Sun. **Admission** 80BF. **No credit cards**. **Map C3**

One of the most interesting aspects of this slightly dowdy museum is the building itself. Situated opposite the Town Hall on Grand Place, the Maison du Roi (King's House) occupies the site of the thirteenth-century Bread Hall. The building was rebuilt in the sixteenth, eighteenth and nineteenth centuries. The museum contains a mixture of paintings, photographs, documents, tapestries and models chronicling the history of Brussels. Much of it is interesting if you make the effort to read the explanatory texts and study the displays, but it does require some diligence. There are interesting sections on the destruction of Grand Place in 1695, and King Léopold's ambitious nineteenth-century building programme, and the displays give a good idea of just how many invasions Brussels has suffered in its history. The museum also contains the vast wardrobe of the Manneken Pis, and, less tackily, examples of the art (including Pieter Bruegel's *Marriage Procession*) and stonework produced over the centuries by Brussels' artists and craftsmen.

Transport

Autoworld

11 parc du Cinquantenaire, 1000 (736 41 65). Métro Mérode or Schuman/tram 81, 82/bus 20, 28, 38, 67, 80. **Open** *Apr-Oct* 10am-6pm Tue-Sun; *Nov-Mar* 10am-5pm Tue-Sun. **Admission** 200BF; 150BF students, groups, over-60s. **No credit cards. Map G4**

Cars, cars and more cars in what some claim is the world's most prestigious collection. Starting from 1886, the exhibition traces the development of the automobile through hundreds of incarnations, including the glamorous 1928 Bentley and the 1930 Bugatti. There is a sad display of pre-World War II cars produced by Belgium's now-defunct car industry, and there are cars driven by various members of the Belgian royal family. It's possible to hire cars from the collection – not to drive, unfortunately, but to display at receptions or other events.

Musée du Transport Urbain Bruxellois

364 avenue de Tervuren, 1150 (515 31 08). Tram 39, 44. **Open** *Apr-Aug* 1.30-7pm Sat, Sun, public holidays; *July, Aug* 2-6pm Wed-Fri; 1.30-7pm Sat, Sun, public holidays. **Closed** *Sept-Mar.* **Admission** 150BF (includes tram ride to Tervuren or Cinquantenaire); 75BF 6-11s; free under-6s. **No credit cards.**

More commonly known as the Tram Museum, this is not as dull as it sounds because the museum depot is linked to the Brussels tram network. Visitors can travel to Tervuren or the Parc du Cinquantenaire and back in an antique tram, and the journey through the forest to Tervuren is particularly fine. There are also static exhibits. Some of the trams can be hired for private parties; Belgians, for reasons best known to themselves, often use them as a backdrop for wedding photographs.

Children

Musée des Enfants

15 rue du Bourgmestre, 1050 (640 01 07). Tram 23, 90, 93, 94/bus 71. **Open** by arrangement only; phone 9.30am-noon Mon-Fri. **Admission** 200BF. **No credit cards.**

You'll want to be a child again when you accompany one through this wonderful and intelligent museum. The guiding principle here is that doing is everything and that only by actively participating in exhibits will children discover themselves and the world around them. Children who are accustomed to being admonished in other museums for touching anything or making a noise will find this museum a joy. There are cooking, painting, modelling and puppet workshops, and the displays and activities are completely rearranged every three years so that children don't tire of the place. The next reorganisation was scheduled for 1998, so the museum will be shut until mid-October 1998, when a new exhibition, Imagine, will open. The displays are in French or Flemish, so bring a friend to translate if you don't speak either of these languages.

Beer

Musée Bruxellois de la Gueuze

56 rue Gheude, 1070 (520 28 91). Métro Gare du Midi or Clemenceau/tram 18, 52, 55, 56, 81, 82/bus 20, 47. **Open** *June-Sept* 8.30am-5pm Mon-Fri; 10am-1pm Sat. *Oct-May* 8.30am-4.30pm Mon-Fri; 10am-5pm Sat. **Admission** 100BF. **No credit cards.**

In the 1930s there were at least 50 independent lambic breweries in Brussels. Today, the Cantillon Brewery, which dates back to 1900, is the only one that remains, and it is now a museum as well as a working brewery. Hidden away in a rather dreary part of Anderlecht, the brewery produces a range of traditional lambics and gueuzes (*see chapter* **Cafés & Bars**). Visitors to the museum get a tour around the brewery, followed by a sampling of the product.

Musée Bruxellois de la Gueuze – *visit the museum, tour the brewery, sample the beer.*

Art Galleries

Though overshadowed by Antwerp, Brussels galleries are starting to assert themselves.

After a long hibernation, Brussels' art scene is finally beginning to stir. It still has a hesitant, provincial feel, but it's starting to acquire a sassy self-confidence. Gallery owners have at last seen the point of combining forces, and as a result that ephemeral, unconnected feeling that used to hang over the art scene, in which good art was produced in isolated pockets, has largely passed. The most significant event of the past few years has been the opening of eight separate galleries under one roof, in a house on the canal called Kanal 20 (*see below* **Kanal dreams**). This could represent the beginnings of an art quarter, something Brussels has never really had before.

Belgium is a country with a long and proud art tradition, as witness its consecutive celebrations in 1997 and 1998 of the centenaries of the great surrealist painters Paul Delvaux and René Magritte. The country continues to produce fine artists such as Panamarenko and Didier Vermeiren, but most of these prefer to work in the more traditional art cities in Flanders – especially Antwerp, which is the undoubted leader for fashion and art. But with this new encouragement, some may be tempted into the capital.

The international political status of Brussels makes it a magnet for big names, and there are generally interesting exhibitions on show. The weekly *Bulletin* (*see chapter* **Media**) gives information about all current exhibitions, while *Art Brussels*, which can be picked up in most galleries, gives a seasonal list of what's on.

Horta's swansong – **Palais des Beaux Arts**.

Public galleries & spaces

Atelier 340

340 drève de Rivieren, 1090 (424 24 12). Métro Beekkant/tram 84. **Open** 2-7pm Tue-Sun (when exhibiting). **Admission** 150-200BF. **Credit** V.
Non-profit-making, artist-run and assembled in a block of condemned houses, Atelier 340 celebrated its fifteenth anniversary in 1995 and currently looks more secure than at any time in its fraught history. In 1980 Wodek Majewski, a Polish sculptor in search of a space, set up in a house here and has been developing it ever since, emerging triumphant from his run-ins with the demolition squads. Atelier 340 has now been accepted as an established space and plans are ongoing for further development. It has become a great forum for sculpture and shows the best new Belgian works, which are then circulated among galleries abroad. Majewski has also acquired a permanent collection through buying directly from his artists.

L'Autre Musée

place des Martyrs, 41 rue St Michel, 1000 (640 84 37). Métro De Brouckère. **Open** 2-6.30pm Tue-Sat (when exhibiting). **Admission** free. **Map C2**
An enthusiastic showplace for contemporary work, L'Autre Musée has two spaces. The one in place des Martyrs is for large sculptures, while the rue du Viaduc site is for paintings and engravings. Both show mainly Belgian and northern European artists, and are a much-needed forum for young unknowns.
Branch: 22 rue du Viaduc, 1050.

Centre d'Art Contemporain

63 avenue des Nerviens, 1040 (735 05 31). Métro Merode or Schuman. **Open** 9am-1pm, 2-5pm, Mon-Fri; 1-6pm Sat (when exhibiting). **Admission** free. **Map G5/H5**
An information centre for modern Walloon art, with a small exhibition space. The Centre d'Art Contemporain organises themed shows of Belgian and European artists and remains one of the few places in the country where young artists can get a start. Seeing the delicacy and originality of the works here is a timely reminder of the strength of Belgian talent, perhaps somewhat unfocused at the moment but still following in a great tradition.

Palais des Beaux Arts

23 rue Ravenstein, 1000 (507 84 86). Métro Gare Centrale. **Open** 10am-6pm Tue-Sun. **Admission** 250BF; 200BF over-60s; 150BF students. **No credit cards.** **Map C4**

Built in 1928, the Beaux Arts was the great architectural feat of its time, being the first building in the world to put concert halls, exhibition spaces, theatres, cinemas, shops and restaurants under one roof. Stripped of his fanciful art nouveau whirlings and reduced to clean art deco lines, the great architect Victor Horta made his swansong a spacious, functional municipal building that gracefully combined its separate elements. The Beaux Arts was luckier than some art deco masterpieces – it was too useful a space to be demolished – but in the 1960s the lovely roof windows that gave the entrance hall its lofty elegance were covered with scaffolding. In 1996 the entire hall was finally renovated and can now be seen in its original state. Eleven interlinked hexagonal and circular rooms ensure that there is space for even the largest sculptures – you can get lost wandering round a show. So far there has been a well-thought-out and impressive programme of events, ranging from Man Ray's photographs to Christo's conceptual sculptures. Until July 1998, the Austrian visionaries – Klimt, Egon Schiele and Kokoschka – will be on display. The Palais also hosts the regular Europalia festival, which focuses on a different theme each year, and serves as an information point about other exhibitions in the city.

Contretype – Hôtel Hannon *for photography.*

Photography

Contretype – Hôtel Hannon

1 avenue de la Jonction, 1060 (538 42 20). Tram 90, 92. **Open** 1-6pm Tue-Sun. **Admission** 50BF; 30BF groups. **No credit cards.**

This is one of the few art nouveau houses – other than the Musée Horta (*see chapter* **Museums**) – that is open to the public. Light and spacious with its alcoves and marble, it was the home of Edouard Hannon, an amateur photographer, and has been a photography gallery since 1989. The choice tends towards artistic, beautiful photographs rather than gritty realism.

Commercial galleries

Abel Joseph Gallery

89 avenue Maréchal Foch, 1030 (245 67 73). Tram 23. **Open** 11am-7pm Tue-Sat. **No credit cards.**

Opened in October 1996, this is one of the exciting new galleries that is helping to give energy to the Brussels scene. It's a small, friendly space on the ground floor of a fine townhouse. Renovations are still going on, but the plan is to invite different artists to live in upstairs rooms for about three months and contribute by their work and presence to the artistic life of the community.

Christine et Isy Brachot

8 rue Villa Hermosa, 1000 (511 05 25). Métro Gare Centrale. **Open** 2-6pm Tue-Sat. **No credit cards.**

It's a New York-style set-up: you have to ring the bell and announce your intentions – browsers are not encouraged. Artists who haven't been vetted are not encouraged either, but if you want to buy a Magritte or a Delvaux, there is probably nowhere better to present yourself. The Brachots' other great artist is Panamarenko, whose weird and delicate flight-obsessed sculptures are worth braving that bell for. In 1998, the centenary of Magritte's birth, they are hosting a retrospective of his works.

Kanal dreams

Could **Kanal 20** possibly be the first site in a new art quarter for Brussels? Will the success of this recently opened space encourage others to set up galleries along the banks of the Canal de Charleroi? In spring 1996, one long, narrow *maison de maître* became home to eight galleries: Albert Baronien, Argos, Artiscope, Crown Gallery, Encore… Bruxelles, Guy Ledune, La Lettre Volée and Windows. The division of space is unequal – some have light pouring in through great windows, others are way up in the attic – but the use of space is always creative, and after more than two years the collective enthusiasm is undimmed.

The response to this co-operative has been overwhelming, with cars lining the canal on opening nights. The galleries co-ordinate all their shows so that there are five openings a year, and those coming to look in one gallery will almost invariably check out another.

The galleries function as separate commercial enterprises, so the range is diverse; but all are modern and contemporary and have a messianic need to bring artists to public attention. So far the public seems more than happy to pay attention, and the rumour is that two galleries from Paris are about to open in adjacent houses. Meanwhile, the excellent Meert Rihoux gallery has been operating successfully for a number of years in the nearby rue du Canal, so perhaps Brussels already has its art quarter…

Kanal 20, 20 boulevard Barthelemy, 1000 (735 5212). Métro Comte de Flandre. **Open** 1-7pm Wed-Sat. **No credit cards.**

Sabine Wachters Fine Arts – *the verve.*

Damasquine
62 rue de l'Aurore, 1000 (646 31 53). Tram 93, 94. **Open** 1-7pm Thur-Sat; 11.30am-2pm Sun. **No credit cards.**
This small gallery has been showing mostly new Belgian work since 1981. It has six exhibitions a year and the range is wide, including video and lasers. It is cautiously willing to take on young artists.

Fred Lanzenburg
9 avenue des Klauwaerts, 1050 (647 30 15). Tram 23, 90/bus 71. **Open** 10am-12.30pm, 2-7pm, Tue-Sat. **No credit cards.**
For 30 years, Lanzenburg has been making careful and erudite choices, presenting artists of international standing in a discreet gallery overlooking the Ixelles lakes. Recent selections include the Japanese Takayoshi Sakabe and the Pole Malgorzata Paszko.

Meert Rihoux
13 rue du Canal, 1000 (219 14 22). Métro Ste Cathérine or Yser. **Open** 2.30-6pm Tue-Sat. **No credit cards.** **Map B2**
In this spacious third-floor gallery, the speciality is conceptual work, especially German and American artists from the 1970s. Meert Rihoux handles about 16 artists and is good at taking on young Belgians who have already cut their teeth elsewhere.

Rodolphe Janssen
35 rue de Livourne, 1050 (538 08 18). Tram 93, 94. **Open** 2-7pm Tue-Sat. **No credit cards.**
One of the galleries at the forefront of strong, original contemporary art, it does about six shows a year, covering everything from photography to sculpture. A simple, whitewashed space with an outstanding collection of art books.

Sabine Wachters Fine Arts
26 avenue de Stalingrad, 1000 (502 39 93). Métro Lemonnier. **Open** 11am-7pm Tue-Sat. **No credit cards.** **Map A4/B4**
One of the few commercial galleries that will show young unknowns, Sabine Wachters has two large, airy galleries with mostly themed exhibitions. The work here is experimental and erratic, but it has a verve and energy that make it compelling and unexpected. The ambience has something of an end-of-year art school show.

Salon d'Art et de Coiffure
81 rue de l'Hôtel des Monnaies (537 65 40). **Open** 9.30am-noon, 2-6.30pm, Tue-Sat. **No credit cards.** **Map B6**
A surreal image greets you as you enter the Salon d'Art ed de Coiffure: snippets of hair piling up on the floor in front of elegant prints and unbound limited editions of avant-garde writers. The man behind it, Jean Marchetti, started off as a hairdresser and continues as one, but somewhere

along the way he discovered art and in 1976 transformed his salon into a smart, whitewashed gallery. After all, he had what gallery-owners long for: a captive audience. Marchetti's choice of artists and writers is daring. He brings out limited editions under three publishing imprints: La Pierre d'Alun, La Petite Pierre and La Haute Pierre. In these he pairs writers with artists to produce books that are as much works of art as pieces of text. A place of rare, dedicated enthusiasm, and the haircuts are pretty good, too.

Xavier Hufkens
8 rue St Georges, 1050 (646 63 30). Tram 23, 90, 93, 94. **Open** noon-6pm Tue-Sat. **No credit cards.**
Here you'll find an interesting choice of Belgian and international artists in painting, sculpture and photography. The gallery attracts big names, such as Robert Mapplethorpe, as well as those of national repute such as Didier Vermeiren and Geert Verheuren.

Antwerp

Brussels may be on the up, but Antwerp is still where it's at. Artists, fashion designers and film-makers mushroom in Antwerp as effortlessly as bureaucrats do in Brussels. If you're interested in modern art, a visit to Antwerp is a must. This is where most Belgian artists choose to live or work, and the city has a brash, optimistic attitude towards encouraging new talent.

Middelheim Open-air Sculpture Museum
61 Middelheimlaan, 2020 Antwerp (03 828 13 50). **Open** *1 Oct-31 Mar* 10am-5pm Tue-Sun; *Apr, Sept* 10am-7pm Tue-Sun; *May, Aug* 10am-8pm Tue-Sun; *June, July* 10am-9pm Tue-Sun. **Admission** free.
There are works here by major sculptors from Rodin to the present day, including the Belgians, Panamarenko and Vermeiren. This open-air venue is also well worth visiting for its biennial summer exhibition of international sculpture.

Provincaal Museum voor Fotografie
47 Waalse Kaai, 2000 Antwerp (03 216 22 11). **Open** 10am-5pm Tue-Sun. **Admission** free.
Opened quite recently in a warehouse, the gallery has a permanent collection of historic photographs, including views of old Antwerp. There are some generally excellent temporary exhibitions of European photographers. Also on show are antique cameras and a turn-of-the-century photographer's studio.

Ronny van de Velde
3 Lizerenpoortkai, Antwerp (03 216 30 47). **Open** 10-6pm Tue-Sun. **Admission** varies. **Credit** V.
Antwerp's leading gallery, Ronny van de Velde has held major retrospectives of Marcel Duchamp and Francis Picabia, among others. In an immaculate old house on four levels, it specialises in classic modern art.

Zwarte Panther
70-74 Hoogstraat, Antwerp (03 233 13 45). **Open** 2-6pm Thur-Sun. **No credit cards.**
In the centre of town, this is a small, discreet gallery with one of the best reputations in the country. It specialises in figurative rather than realistic art and is the best place in Belgium for Art Brut.

*There's not mush room for anything else when **Alison Gill** exhibits her sculpture at Sabine Wachters Fine Arts.*

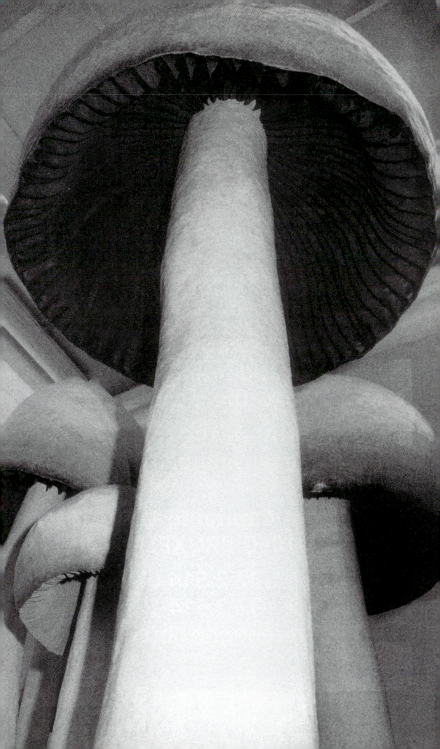

Consumer

Restaurants

Venture beyond the narrow streets around Grand Place and you'll encounter a wider choice of quality restaurants than can be found in many other European capitals.

Most people who visit Brussels expect to subsist on mussels, chips and chocolates. This they can do very happily, but the city has far more to offer. There are countless restaurants in Brussels serving modern French/European food, with not a mussel or a *frite* in sight. Equally, for those who do want traditional food, there are large numbers of bistros and brasseries serving steaks, mussels and Flemish stews and casseroles.

Not surprisingly, beer plays an important part in traditional Belgian cuisine. *Carbonnade flamande* is beef braised with beer, onions, carrots and thyme, while *lapin à la gueuze* is a casserole of rabbit, beer, onion and sometimes prunes. You'll also find *lapin à la kriek*, where cherry beer is used instead of gueuze.

If you go to Belgium during the autumn or winter, most restaurants will have game on the menu. Pheasant, venison and wild boar are all standard items during the hunting season, and rabbit and hare appear all year round. The standard of game in many Belgian restaurants is outstanding and really worth a try. Another seasonal favourite is wild mushrooms, which grow plentifully in the forests around Brussels and in the Ardennes.

A much more basic speciality is stoemp, which is mashed potato mixed with different vegetables and occasionally meat. You can get carrot stoemp, cabbage stoemp, and others. It is usually served with sausages. You can often buy stoemp and sausages in bars and cafés, along with *tête pressée* (brawn), *kipkap* (jellied bits of meat), *croque monsieur* (cheese and ham on toast) and toast *cannibale* (raw minced beef on toast). On the subject of meat, don't expect to get a hamburger if you ask for *steak à l'américaine*. Instead you'll be given a large plate of raw minced steak, perhaps with some raw onion, capers, black pepper and Tabasco to help it down.

The large numbers of expats living in Belgium have helped make it an excellent place for international cuisine. The EU district in Etterbeek, which is centred around the Rond Point Schuman, is one of the best places for Italian, Spanish and Greek restaurants. At lunchtime, they are crowded with journalists, lawyers, lobbyists and diplomats, but they are usually quieter in the evening. If you want cheaper Mediterranean food, the streets around the Gare du Midi and place Flagey

have plenty of Portuguese and North African cafés and bars, although the atmosphere in many of them is not immediately welcoming.

Brussels also has growing numbers of Asian restaurants, and these will be useful if your money is running low, or if you are looking for vegetarian food. They are not concentrated in any particular area, although Ixelles has a fair number near the university. The commonest type of Asian food is from francophone countries such as Vietnam, though many British visitors complain about the lack of Indian restaurants. (There is a handful of curry houses, described later in this chapter.)

Brussels is very strong on fish and seafood. Specialist fish restaurants are mainly to be found in the north of the city around the fish market at Ste Cathérine. Most offer good-value set menus, and if you want to eat lobster or turbot the set menu will usually be hundreds or thousands of francs cheaper than ordering à la carte. The square at Ste Cathérine is rather touristy, but is far less so than most of the fish restaurants around Grand Place. The restaurants lining streets such as rue des Bouchers have tanks of lobsters and amazing displays of fish and seafood outside, but as a general rule these restaurants are mediocre and stories of food poisoning are common. Therefore, having gawped at the specimens of foul catfish and other marine monsters, it might pay to eat elsewhere. Note, however, that there are honourable exceptions to this rule, such as the famous Aux Armes de Bruxelles (*see below*).

Eating in Brussels is by no means cheap, and visitors from the UK will find the restaurants generally more expensive than those at home (although the strong pound does help on this score). Nevertheless, most Brussels restaurants offer excellent value, whatever the prices. The ingredients are usually high quality, portions are generous (more so than in France) and design and ambience can be impressive.

The average prices given for each restaurant are based on one person eating three courses – starter, main course and dessert – and do not include drink or coffee. But much of the time, you'll find that you do not want a dessert, since the first two courses will be ample. Very expensive means an average of 2,000BF or more; expensive means 1,500BF and upwards; moderate

*You will need to book weeks ahead to get into **Comme Chez Soi** – but it is worth it.*

means 1,000BF and over; inexpensive means less than 1,000BF. Many restaurants, particularly those in residential areas such as Ixelles, offer cheap set lunches, with two or three courses for under 500BF. These are definitely worthwhile if you want to experience Brussels gastronomy on a tight budget.

French & Belgian

Very expensive

Comme Chez Soi

23 place Rouppe, 1000 (512 29 21). Métro Anneessens. **Open** noon-2pm, 7-10pm, Tue-Sat. **Menu** 2,150-5,000BF (minimum four people). **Credit** AmEx, DC, MC, V. **Map B4**
It is universally agreed that this is the best restaurant in Brussels. Chef Pierre Wynants may not have his own BBC show yet, but he's a star of European cooking all the same. The place is often booked up weeks ahead, so advance planning is required if you want to go there and eat food such as fillets of sole with a mousseline of Riesling and prawns.

La Maison du Cygne

9 Grand Place, 1000 (511 82 44). Entrance 2 rue Charles Buls. Métro Gare Centrale. **Open** noon-2.30pm, 7-10.30pm, Mon-Fri; 7-10.30pm Sat. **Average** 3,500BF. **Menu** 1,400 (lunch only)-2,600BF. **Credit** Amex, DC, MC, V. **Map C3**
It's not just the wonderful location in Grand Place that makes this a place for a special treat. The food is also luxurious, with a menu dotted with ingredients such as foie gras and truffles. The cooking is excellent and rich, but the portions are not enormous, making the menu less daunting than it sounds. Its popularity with expense-account diners gives it a somewhat corporate atmosphere at lunchtime.

Expensive *aux armes de Bruxelle*

Le Fils de Jules

35 rue du Page, 1050 (534 00 57). Tram 81, 82/bus 54. **Open** noon-2.30pm, 7-11pm, Mon-Fri; noon-2.30pm, 7pm-midnight Sat. **Average** 1,500BF. **Menu** 395BF (lunch only). **Credit** AmEx, DC, MC, V.
An Ixelles brasserie with cooking based on the Basque country and south-west France, combining classics such as cassoulet and confit de canard with more imaginative dishes. There's a good regional wine list. The decoration is fairly standard for this part of Brussels, with art deco touches and plenty of space.

L'Idiot du Village

19 rue Notre Seigneur, 1000 (502 55 82). Bus 20, 48. **Open** noon-2pm, 7.30-11pm, Mon-Fri. **Average** 2000BF. **Credit** AmEx, DC, MC, V.
L'Idiot du Village is a small and very popular bistro hidden away in a side street off rue Blaes. The chairs and tables are the type of furniture you hope to find in the nearby Jeu du Balle flea market (but never do), the walls are midnight blue, there are dried herbs and roses around the place, and the chandelier looks like a leftover from Christmas. It sounds faintly clichéd, but works perfectly, as does the food. Booking is essential.

Inada

73 rue de la Source, 1060 (538 01 13). Métro Louise. **Open** noon-2.30pm, 7-10.30pm, Tue-Fri; Sat 7-10.30pm. **Average** 2,500BF. **Menu** 820 (lunch only)-1,580BF. **Credit** AmEx, DC, MC, V. **Map B6**
This small French restaurant is run by a Japanese chef, and the combination – light French cooking with Japanese flavours – is superb. The game, if you visit during the season, is particularly good. The restaurant is spacious and low-key with tiny Zen pebble gardens on each table. When you want a break from the increasingly prevalent Brussels restaurant style of gilded mirrors, iron chandeliers and baroque paintwork, this is a perfect antidote.

Au Chat Perché

A friendly, cosy,
candlelit restaurant.
Fine French cuisine
and world wines.

"SABLON"

Rue de la Samaritaine, 20
1000 Brussels
Tel & fax: 02/ 513 52 13

Closed on Saturday and Sunday midday
Monday all day

La Manufacture

12 rue Notre-Dame du Sommeil, 1000 (502 25 25).
Métro Bourse. **Open** noon-2pm, 7-11pm, Mon-Fri; 7-11pm Sat. **Average** 1,600BF. **Menu** 1500BF. **Credit** AmEx, DC, MC, V. **Map A3**
Well-known restaurant housed in an old leather factory (hence the name). The food at La Manufacture is modern European with Japanese influences, and it's all wonderful. The factory conversion was tastefully done, using restrained wood, leather and metalwork. The lighting and dark blue and orange colour scheme are flattering, and the customers are sleek and middle class. Unusually for Brussels, there's a good selection of New World wines, and there are tables in the courtyard in summer.

L'Ogenblik

1 galerie des Princes, 1000 (511 61 51).
Métro Gare Centrale. **Open** noon-2.30pm, 7pm-midnight, Mon-Sat. **Average** 2,100BF.
Credit AmEx, DC, MC, V.
L'Ogenblik is a grown-up but informal bistro in the Arenberg Galeries in central Brussels. The atmosphere suggests it's the sort of place you might go on the spur of the moment, when the fridge is empty, but you will almost certainly have to empty your wallet when you get there: the food is sophisticated and involves ingredients such as lobster, turbot and wild mushrooms. Excellent if you want a gastronomic treat without having to be too starched and formal about the whole thing.

La Quincaillerie

45 rue du Page, 1050 (538 25 53). Tram 81, 82/bus 54.
Open noon-2.30pm, 7pm-midnight, daily. **Average** 2000BF. **Credit** AmEx, DC, MC, V.
Of the numerous restaurants around the place du Châtelain in Ixelles, La Quincaillerie is the best known and perhaps the most stylish. Housed in a former hardware shop, it attracts quite a variety of affluent customers from all over Brussels and beyond. However, it now tends to rest on its reputation somewhat, at least in terms of service. The food is mainly traditional and modern French, and the fish and seafood are especially good.

La Table de l'Abbaye

62 rue de Bellevue, 1000 (646 33 95). Tram 93, 94.
Open noon-2.30pm, 7-11pm, Mon-Fri; 7-11pm Sat.
Average 2,000BF. **Credit** AmEx, DC, MC, V.
Upmarket restaurant in an old townhouse just off avenue Louise. Although the decoration is slightly precious and lacy and the well-heeled clientele is by no means young, the atmosphere is pleasant. The menu is imaginative, with especially good fish, and the wine list is excellent. On summer evenings, try to eat in the garden at the back.

Moderate

Amadeus

13 rue Veydt, 1050 (538 34 27). Tram 91, 92. **Open** noon-3.30pm, 6.30pm-1am, Tue-Sun. **Average** 1,200BF. **Credit** AmEx, DC, MC, V. **Map C6**
A popular restaurant, with separate wine bar, Amadeus is housed in Rodin's studio. The high-ceilinged rooms are painted in dark colours and lit with candles, and it's good for romantic dinners as well as a standard night out with friends. The menu is divided into two sections: petite faim and grande faim, and includes a mixture of traditional food such as waterzooi and steak tartare, more modern alternatives including scampi and white truffle casserole, and a couple of vegetarian options. There's also a good Sunday brunch (10am-2pm), where you can eat as much as you want. The choice includes cold meats, smoked fish, croissants, pain au chocolat, cheese and tartes. The food is generally good but staff can be slapdash.

Mussels & chips

Mussels are cooked in a variety of ways in Brussels. A main course usually comprises about a kilo of mussels, plus some chips. The most common versions are: provençale (cooked with tomato, garlic and herbs); marinières (with shallot, carrot, parsley and celery); with white wine; with white wine and cream; and gratinée (with cheese on top). You can also have them in breadcrumbs or batter.

The chips that will accompany your mussels in Belgium are the best in Europe. The secret of Belgian chips is that they are cut fairly thin (but not too thin), and they are fried twice. This may not be good for the health or the diet, but it makes the chips much crisper than you'll find in other countries.

The other secret is the choice of potato, and Belgians are very particular about this, using varieties such as bintje, which are floury and slightly sweet.

Another essential aspect of eating chips in Belgium is the mayonnaise that goes with them. Most people quickly retract any scepticism about the combination once they have tried it. But mayonnaise is not the only sauce you will be offered with your moules-frites. Most chip shops offer a bewildering choice of sauces: américaine, andalouse, banzai, cocktail, curry, hawaii, hili-pili, mustard and tartare, to name a few. Most of them taste like mayonnaise with a few E numbers added. Américaine and andalouse both have tomatoes, herbs and spices (in theory), with américaine having more of a barbecue flavour than andalouse. Cocktail has a touch of whisky flavouring, a combination that does take a bit of getting used to.

Other seafood is also popular in Belgium, in particular the crevette. These pink or grey shrimps (crevettes roses or crevettes grises) appear all over the place: in salads, in croquettes, in stuffed tomatoes, in sauces and so on. Ostend is well known for oysters (huîtres), and in most restaurants on the coast you will also find solettes (young sole about 12 centimetres long). Eels in green sauce (anguilles au vert) are another favourite dish.

Bonsoir Clara

22-26 rue Antoine Dansaert, 1000 (502 09 90). Métro Bourse. **Open** noon-2.30pm, 7-11pm, Mon-Fri; 7pm-midnight Sat, Sun. **Average** 1,200BF. **Menu** 450BF (lunch Mon-Fri only). **Credit** AmEx, MC, V. **Map A2/B2**
Large and airy restaurant in the fashionable rue Antoine Dansaert. With bare brick and high ceilings, the basic design is similar to others in this neighbourhood, but the velvet patchwork drapes and the modern stained glass make it stand out from the crowd. The food is modern European – carpaccio, salmon tartare, calves' liver and so on – and it is better for vegetarians than many Brussels restaurants. Service is slow, so it's wise to order your next bottle of wine before your previous one is exhausted. It's usually wise to book in advance.

Café Camille

559 chaussée de Waterloo, 1060 (345 96 43). Bus 37, 38, 60. **Open** noon-2.30pm, 7pm-midnight, Mon-Fri; 7pm-midnight, Sat. **Average** 1,200BF. **Credit** AmEx, MC, V. **Map B6**
Café Camille has never grabbed any headlines, but it produces classic French cooking with a twist and is well away from the tourist circuit. At lunchtime, you'll find the chattering classes and their expense accounts; in the evening it has a more local feel. Starters include seafood brioche, and goat's cheese in pine nuts; main courses include *magret de canard* with mango, and sole with saffron. There's a small gravel garden at the back.

Le Canterbury

2 avenue de l'Hippodrome, 1050 (646 83 93). Bus 71. **Open** noon-midnight Mon-Sat. **Average** 1,500BF. **Credit** AmEx, DC, MC, V.
Comfortable and modern brasserie with a shaded terrace overlooking the Ixelles lakes. A favourite with urbane and affluent middle-aged Belgians, so there are numerous fur coats, Hermès ties and well-fed poodles. It specialises in chicken, and although the food is not particularly adventurous, it is based on excellent ingredients and perfectly prepared. The chips are superb, and the bacon club sandwich is a wonderful Saturday lunchtime revitaliser if you overdid it the night before.

Le Grain de Sel

9 chaussée de Vleurgat, 1050 (648 18 58). Tram 81, 82/bus 38, 60, 71. **Open** noon-2pm, 7.30-10pm, Tue-Sat. **Average** 1,100 BF. **Menu** 850BF. **Credit** MC, V.
The unprepossessing exterior does the Grain de Sel a disservice, for this small Ixelles restaurant is engaging, unpretentious and offers excellent value. The three-course menu, at 850BF, gives a choice of six or seven starters and main courses, such as tuna carpaccio, tiân of courgettes and pigeon with lentils. If you go in the summer, try to get a table in the small rose garden at the back: it makes you feel you're miles away from the busy traffic of nearby avenue Louise and place Flagey.

La Grande Ecluse

77 boulevard Poincaré, 1070 (522 30 25). Métro Comte de Flandre/bus 63. **Open** noon-2pm, 7-11pm, Mon-Fri; 7pm-midnight Sat, Sun. **Average** 1,500BF. **Menu** 890-1,300BF. **Credit** AmEx, DC, MC, V. **Map A4**
The latest in a line of Brussels restaurants to use the city's derelict industrial heritage, the fashionable Grande Ecluse is built on a converted lock in out-of-the-way Anderlecht. The interior is based on the original and the effect is spectacular. Although the food (standard Belgian and French) is pleasant enough and ingredients are fresh, this is more a place to go for the setting than for the food itself.

Translating the menu

Virtually all menus in Brussels are in French, though some restaurants in the centre also have versions in Flemish and English.

Meat

Viande meat; **Agneau** lamb; **Biche** venison (doe); **Bœuf** beef; **Boudin noir/boudin blanc** black or white pudding; **Biche** venison (doe); **Caille** quail; **Canard** duck; **Magret de canard** duck breast; **Caneton** duckling; **Cerf** venison (stag); **Cervelle** brain; **Cheval** horse; **Chevreuil** venison; **Dinde** turkey; **Faisan** pheasant; **Foie** liver; **Gibier** game; **Jambon** ham; **Jambonneau** ham on the bone; **Lapin** rabbit; **Lièvre** hare; **Marcassin** boar; **Perdreau** partridge; **Pintade** guinea fowl; **Porc** pork; **Poulet** chicken; **Ris** sweetbreads; **Rognon** kidneys; **Sanglier** boar; **Veau** veal; **Volaille** chicken; **Suprême de volaille** chicken breast. **Saignant** rare (ie steak), **à point** medium rare, **bien cuit** well done.

Fish & seafood

Poisson fish; **Anguille** eel; **Brochet** pike; **Cabillaud** cod; **Coquille Saint Jacques** scallop; **Crevette** shrimp; **Dorade** sea bream; **Ecrevisse** crayfish (freshwater); **Espadon** swordfish; **Homard** lobster; **Huître** oyster; **Lotte** monkfish; **Loup de mer** sea bass; **Moule** mussel; **Palourde** clam; **Plie** plaice; **Raie** skate; **Rouget** red mullet; **Saumon** salmon; **Scampi** prawn; **Thon** tuna; **Truite** trout;

Waterzooi creamy rich fish stew (can be prepared with chicken instead of fish).

Vegetables

Légume vegetable; **Herbes** herbs; **Ail** garlic; **Artichaut** artichoke; **Asperge** asparagus; **Champignon** mushroom; **Chicon** chicory/Belgian endive; **Chou** cabbage; **Echalote** shallot; **Epinard** spinach; **Fève** broad bean; **Haricot** bean; **Haricot vert** French bean; **Oignon** onion; **Poireau** leek; **Poivron vert/rouge** green/red pepper; **Pomme de terre** potato; **Truffe** truffle.

Herbs

Aneth dill; **Basilic** basil; **Cerfeuil** chervil; **Ciboulette** chive; **Estragon** tarragon; **Fenouil** fennel; **Persil** parsley; **Romarin** rosemary; **Sauge** sage; **Thym** thyme.

Fruit

Fruit fruit; **Ananas** pineapple; **Banane** banana; **Cassis** blackcurrant; **Cerise** cherry; **Citron** lemon; **Citron vert** lime; **Fraise** strawberry; **Framboise** raspberry; **Groseille** redcurrant; **Marron** chestnut; **Pamplemousse** grapefruit; **Pêche** peach; **Poire** pear; **Pomme** apple; **Prune** plum; **Raisin** grape.

General

Beurre butter; **Escargot** snail; **Fromage** cheese; **Gaufre** waffle; **Œuf** egg; **Pâtes** pasta; **Poivre** pepper; **Sel** salt; **Sucre** sugar.

*Swan around at **Maison du Cygne** – see p91.*

Lola

33 place du Grand Sablon, 1000 (514 24 60). Tram 92, 93, 94/bus 34, 95, 96. **Open** noon-3pm, 6.30-11.30pm, daily. **Average** 1,500BF. **Credit** AmEx, DC, MC, V.
A long, narrow restaurant in the Sablon, with modern design, and classic French cooking with a twist. Main courses include duck with mango and rabbit with almonds and orange blossom, and there are a couple of vegetarian starters and main courses. Customers are mainly in their thirties and are of the chattering and designing variety. Prices are somewhat inflated by its location in the Sablon.

Majestic

33 rue du Magistrat, 1050 (639 13 30) Tram 93, 94. **Open** noon-midnight daily (sandwich menu 2.30-7pm). **Average** 1,500BF. **Credit** AmEx, DC, MC, V.
Newish restaurant and bar in a converted townhouse just off avenue Louise. The menu is French/Belgian, with a few ostentatious touches such as *foie d'oie* pizza. But the most notable aspect of the Majestic is not the food, but the styling: long cocktail bar, red velvet walls, vast mirrors, and waitresses who wear chainmail vests over black tops. The gallery upstairs is an excellent place to observe the flash clientele, who spend a lot of time inspecting other people's clothes. Whether you think they are tacky or stylish depends on how attractive you find chunky gold jewellery and perma-tans.

Mieux Vaut Boire Ici Qu'en Face

40 rue Alphonse de Witte, 1050 (644 30 31). Tram 81, 82/bus 71. **Open** noon-2pm, 7-10.30pm, Mon-Sat. **Average** 1,500 BF. **Credit** AmEx, MC, V.
Good-value Ixelles restaurant, with the same owners as Bonsoir Clara (*see above*) and Kasbah (*see below*) and with an equally stylish design, but smaller and more intimate than the others. The name ('Better to drink here than opposite') refers to the church across the road, and certainly there is a greater choice of wine, including an excellent selection of dessert wine. Food is modern European; service is friendly.

La Meilleure Jeunesse

58 rue de l'Aurore, 1050 (640 23 94). Tram 93, 94. **Open** noon-2.30pm, 7pm-1am, Mon-Sat. **Average** 1,100BF. **Credit** AmEx, DC, MC, V.
Fashionable restaurant and bar on the corner just off avenue Louise. The furniture is bric-a-brac with comfortable sofas at the entrance and art on the walls. The food is French bistro cooking with a few exotic touches, and is mostly good. The service is slow, possibly because the waitresses are more concerned with their modelling or acting careers. There's a pleasant terrrace at the back with a wonderful view of the Abbaye de la Cambre.

Les Salons de l'Ataläide

89 chaussée de Charleroi, 1060 (537 21 54). Tram 91, 92. **Open** noon-3pm, 7pm-midnight, daily. **Average** 1,500BF. **Menu** 400BF (lunch only). **Credit** AmEx, DC, MC, V. **Map C6**
A former auction house converted into a vast and spectacular baroque restaurant with drapes, shell-encrusted mirrors, candles and huge paintings. One of the most popular restaurants in Brussels, so it's usually necessary to book beforehand. A good place for a first date because you can always talk about the decoration if you run out of conversation, but not a place for a secret liaison because you'll probably bump into someone you know. Bistro cooking, with navarin of lamb, seafood salad and other staples.

Inexpensive

Bazaar

63 rue des Capucins, 1000 (511 26 00). Métro Porte de Hal. **Open** 2pm-1am Tue-Sun. **Average** 800BF. **No credit cards. Map B5**
On the site of an old monastery in the Marolles district, Bazaar has very Brussels styling: brick walls, large mirrors, exotic bric-a-brac, old sofas and carpets. The food is equally eclectic, with a menu that features dishes from all over the world. On Friday and Saturday evenings, there's also a popular bar and club.

Aux Bons Enfants

49 place du Grand Sablon, 1000 (512 40 95). Tram 92, 93, 94. **Open** noon-2.30pm, 6-10.30pm, Mon, Tue, Thur-Sun. **Average** 800BF. **No credit cards. Map C4**
Basic restaurant that is unusually good value for this part of Brussels. The style is heritage and rustic, with heavy wood tables and a beamed roof, and it's warm and comforting on a cold or rainy evening. Particularly useful on Sunday evenings, when many Brussels restaurants are closed. The menu is mainly steak, pizza and pasta.

Le Campus

437 avenue de la Couronne, 1050 (648 53 80). Bus 95, 96. **Open** noon-3am Mon-Fri; noon-5am Sat, Sun. **Average** 900BF. **Credit** AmEx, DC, MC, V. **Map F6**
As the name suggests, Le Campus is close to the university in Ixelles, and it's a perennial favourite with students. The food is standard – spaghetti, steak and the like – but it's excellent value and open at most hours of the day and night. A useful filling station.

Au Charlot

1 rue Froissart, 1040 (230 33 28). Métro Schuman. **Open** 11am-11pm Mon-Fri. **Average** 800BF. **Credit** AmEx, DC, MC, V. **Map F4/F5**
This brasserie on the corner of place Jourdan has a Charlie Chaplin motif, but fortunately the theme is not too obtrusive. It's good for lunch and, despite the area, the customers are not exclusively people who work in the European institutions. The menu has few surprises, with substantial salads, steaks and omelettes. In the unlikely event that you are still hungry afterwards, visit the excellent chip stall in place Jourdan.

Ixelles brasserie **Le Fils de Jules** *– see p91.*

in the wrong direction. In fact, the atmosphere is minimalist and modern with bright lighting and an orange, light blue and white colour scheme, and functional Ikea cutlery. The menu is small but imaginative, with six or seven main courses and starters, and the cooking is mostly French with eastern influences. The service is pleasant, the wine list eclectic.

Marilou

104 avenue Adolphe Buyl, 1050 (647 80 99). Tram 93, 94/bus 71. **Open** noon-2.30pm, 7pm-midnight, Mon-Thur; noon-2.30pm, 7pm-1am, Fri, Sat. **Average** 900BF. **Credit** AmEx, DC, MC, V.
Small bistro near the university, popular with students and lecturers. The menu is simple bistro-style – carpaccio, tomatoes stuffed with prawns, salads and steak. All very charming and French with small tables, candles and tins of salt.

Raconte-Moi des Salades

19 place du Châtelain, 1050 (534 27 27). Tram 81, 82/bus 54. **Open** noon-3pm, 7pm-1am, Mon-Sat. **Average** 600BF. **No credit cards.**
As the name suggests, it specialises in salads, but it has plenty to offer both the vegetarian and the carnivore. As well as an imaginative list of substantial salads, there are omelettes, pasta, sandwiches, several types of carpaccio, and a few meat and fish dishes. There are tables outside on the square, and a very pleasant garden at the back.

Touch and Go

12 rue St Boniface, 1050. Métro Porte de Namur/bus 54, 71, 34, 80. **Open** noon-2.30pm, 6.30-midnight, daily. **Average** 600BF. **No credit cards.** **Map D5**
This expanding chain of restaurants focuses on stuffed pitta bread, and there's a huge choice of salads and fillings. Customers vary according to the branch and the time of day, with lots of office workers in the daytime and younger customers in the evening. The most interesting branch is the new one in rue St Boniface, with dark blue and pink walls, lights made out of industrial pipes, and large abstract paintings and collages. Best for summer days and evenings is the one in rue de Livourne, which has a large garden at the back. **Branches:** 12 rue St Boniface, 1050; 131 rue de Livorne, 1050 (640 55 89); 113 rue Edith Cavell, 1180 (347 54 94).

En Face de Parachute

578 chaussée de Waterloo, 1050 (346 47 41). Bus 37, 60. **Open** noon-2pm, 7.30-11pm, Tue-Sat. **Average** 1,000BF. **No credit cards**. **Map B6**
Small bistro in a former chemist's, with the original wooden shelves. The seats are old tram seats; it's all very pleasant, cosy and intimate. The food is good but fairly standard for Brussels: goat's cheese, bruschetta, stoemp, spinach ravioli, scampi à la Provençale, with one or two vegetarian choices.

Le Jardin de Nicolas

137 avenue de Tervuren, 1150 (732 24 49). Métro Montgomery. **Open** 10am-1am daily. **Average** 800BF. **No credit cards**.
A popular restaurant for lunch or a snack in the evening. The salads are good, the pasta respectable and there are good-value plats du jour. There are tables in the front garden in summer, but the situation on one of the busiest roads out of Brussels means that a certain amount of carbon monoxide is inhaled. Popular with ladies who lunch, but also with office workers and journalists.

L112

112 avenue Lesbroussart, 1050 (640 83 43). Tram 81, 82, 93, 94. **Open** noon-3pm, 7pm-midnight, Mon-Sat. **Average** 1,000 BF. **Credit** MC, V.
Just off avenue Louise, L112 describes itself as a 'restaurant atmosphérique'. If this conjures up images of some olde worlde cellar with beams and serving staff dressed up as monks or peasant girls, your train of thought is taking you

Traditional

Expensive

La Belle Maraîchère

11 place Ste Catherine, 1000 (512 97 59). Métro Ste Catherine. **Open** noon-2.30pm, 6-10pm, Mon, Tue, Fri-Sun. **Average** 2,000BF. **Menu** 950-1,700BF. **Credit** AmEx, DC, MC, V. **Map B2**
Small and famous fish restaurant by the fish market in place Ste Cathérine. The cooking is traditional French, as is the ambience, and there are few surprises. It sounds dull, but it isn't. The fish is excellent, the set menus are good value, and if the customers aren't particularly young or chic, who cares?

Les Brasseries Georges

259 avenue Winston Churchill, 1180 (347 21 00). Tram 23, 90. **Open** 11.30am-midnight daily. **Average** 1,300BF. **Credit** AmEx, DC, MC, V.
A traditional Parisian-style brasserie on the borders of Ixelles and Uccle, with gleaming brass, stained glass and towering flower arrangements. The menu comprises classics such as steak, seafood, game, oysters and cassoulet, and although none of it is cheap, it is all good value, as is the house wine. An excellent place to observe the Belgian bourgeoisie: fur-coated widows with small dogs, affluent families with well-scrubbed children, and lawyers taking their parents out to lunch. Very much a Brussels institution and an excellent treat for Sunday lunch.

La Marie-Joseph

47-49 quai au Bois à Bruler, 1000 (218 05 96). Métro Ste Cathérine. **Open** noon-3pm, 6.30-11pm, Tue-Sat. **Average** 1,600BF. **Credit** AmEx, DC, MC, V. **Map B2**
Fish restaurant near the Ste Cathérine fish market, with the same owners as Le Canterbury. It's bright, modern and comfortable with leather chairs and everything you'd expect from a Brussels fish restaurant: oysters, lobster, sole, turbot, mussels, *crevettes* and so on. Nothing earth-shattering, but the ingredients are high quality and the cooking reliable.

La Sirène d'Or

1A place Ste Cathérine, 1000 (513 51 98). Métro Ste Cathérine. **Open** noon-2.30pm, 6.30-10pm, Tue-Sat. **Average** 1,700BF. **Menu** 1,300BF. **Credit** AmEx, DC, MC, V. **Map B2**
Famous and plush fish restaurant, decorated with ships' prows and busts of mermaids. Specialises in bouillabaisse. None of it is particularly original, but if you want perfectly cooked fish and seafood, with rich, classic French sauces, and you have plenty of money to spend, then this is certainly a good place to come. The 1,700BF menu includes an apéritif and wine.

De Ultieme Hallucinatie

316 rue Royale, 1210 (217 06 14). Métro Botanique. **Open** noon-2.30pm, 7-10.30pm, Mon-Fri; 7-10.30pm Sat. **Average** 2,500BF. **Menu** 1,450-2,750BF. **Credit** AmEx, DC, MC, V. **Map D4/E1**
Smart restaurant in an amazingly well-preserved art nouveau house, though in a dingy and somewhat threatening area of northern Brussels. All the original details are there: curving wood and iron, mirrors and stained glass. The cooking is sophisticated and French; it's also expensive, and most people confine themelves to the cheaper and more relaxed café section.

Moderate

Aux Armes de Bruxelles

13 rue des Bouchers, 1000 (511 21 18). Métro Bourse. **Open** noon-11.15pm Tue-Sun. **Average** 1,500BF. **Menu** 495 (lunch)-1,695BF. **Credit** AmEx, DC, MC, V. **Map C3**
Many of the fish restaurants in the streets around Grand Place are lacklustre and overpriced, but Aux Armes de Bruxelles is a notable exception. It's a stickler for tradition, with starched white tablecloths, good service and a menu of Belgian classics such as *waterzooi*, steak and, best of all, vast buckets of mussels, complete with chips and mayonnaise.

La Roue d'Or

26 rue des Chapeliers, 1000 (514 25 54). Métro Bourse. **Open** noon-12.30am daily. **Average** 1,500BF. **Credit** AmEx, DC, MC, V.
A small brasserie in the centre of town that has survived mass tourism. It's in one of the streets leading off Grand Place and has the usual ingredients: brass fittings, a long polished wooden bar and tables, and traditional Brussels food, although the Surrealist murals are a break with tradition. The menu includes *waterzooi*, stewed eels, rabbit, steak and good mussels and chips.

In 't Spinnekopke

1 place du Jardin aux Fleurs, 1000 (511 86 95). Métro Bourse. **Open** noon-3pm, 6-11pm, Mon-Fri; 6-11pm Sat. **Average** 1,200 BF. **Credit** AmEx, DC, MC, V. **Map B3**
It looks small, but with its numerous rooms the capacity is surprisingly big. The building has been here since 1762, and

L'Idiot du Village – *tucked away down a side street, but so good and so popular that you always need to book – see p91.*

it's warm and comfortable with log fires, red flagstones, low ceilings and check tablecloths. The food is very Belgian: *waterzooi, lapin à la kriek* and steaks. Not surprisingly, it's quite touristy.

La Taverne du Passage

30 galerie de la Reine, 1000 (512 37 32). Métro Gare Centrale. **Open** noon-midnight daily. **Average** 1,500BF. **Menu** 395-400 BF (lunch only). **Credit** AmEx, DC, MC, V.
A somewhat dowdy Brussels institution that looks as if nothing has changed since the 1920s. Like the original mirrors and lights, the menu has conceded little to the passage of time, with traditional Belgian food such as *waterzooi*, steak and *crevettes*.

Le Volle Gas

21 place Fernand Cocq, 1050 (502 89 17). Bus 54, 71. **Open** 11am-1am daily. **Average** 1,000BF. **Credit** AmEx, DC, MC, V. **Map D6**
Traditional Belgian food in what was formerly a jazz bar called the Bierodrome. The menu is fairly short but dependable, with half a dozen or so classic Belgian starters such as *salade aux lardons* and *salade au roquefort*, and about ten classic main courses, including stoemp, cassoulet, *lapin à la kriek* and steak. There's a terrace in front in spring and summer. It's recently acquired new management, so watch out for changes.

Cheap

L'Achepot

1 place Ste Cathérine, 1000 (511 62 21). Métro Ste Cathérine. **Open** 11am-midnight Mon-Sat; *food served* noon-3pm, 6.30-10.30pm. **Average** 800BF. **No credit cards. Map B2**
Small and basic family-run *estaminet* or tavern that looks as if it hasn't changed for several generations. The food is traditional Belgian and French, with dishes such as stoemp and goat's cheese salad, and plenty of offal, including kidneys, brain, tripe and liver.

La Bonne Humeur

244 chaussée de Louvain, 1030 (230 71 69). Bus 29. **Open** noon-2pm, 6.30-9.30pm, Mon, Thur-Sun. **Average** 900BF. **Credit** MC, V. **Map E3/H2**
A traditional family-run restaurant in St Josse that produces wonderful mussels and chips, as well as a few other Belgian classics such as shrimp croquettes. If you want *moules-frites* and are fed up with the hordes of tourists around Grand Place and the centre, this is the place to come. It's also cheaper than the more central restaurants.

Chez Léon

18 rue des Bouchers, 1000 (511 14 15). Métro Bourse. **Open** noon-11pm daily. **Average** 850BF. **Menu** 595-970BF. **Credit** AmEx, DC, MC, V. **Map C3**
One of Belgium's most successful culinary exports, Chez Léon works to a simple formula: big portions of mussels and chips, paper tablecloths, brisk (sometimes impatient) service and a quick turnover. Locals sneer at it, and it's certainly not the place for a romantic tryst, but it's good value and popular with every nationality but the Belgians. There are other branches in the Bruparck in Heysel, and at Waterloo.

Au Stekerlaplatte

4 rue des Prêtres, 1000 (512 86 81). Métro Hotel des Monnaies. **Open** 7pm-1am Tue-Sun. **Average** 1,500BF. **Credit** V.
The street outside is rundown, and the façade is unassuming to say the least, but this traditional bistro is always full. Inside it's dark and labyrinthine, and the atmosphere is convivial. There's a long menu, most of it traditional Belgian food and all of it good value.

Aux Armes de Bruxelles – *see page 99* – *a high-quality fish restaurant near Grand Place.*

Caribbean

Canne à Sucre
12 rue des Pigeons, 1000 (513 03 72). Tram 92, 93, 94/bus 34, 95, 96. **Open** *7.30-1.30am Tue-Sat.*
Average 1,500BF. **Credit** AmEx, MC, V.
Caribbean restaurant near the Sablon, with Antilles and Creole cooking and hundreds of rum-based cocktails. Most of the main courses involve fish, seafood or chicken, and much of it involves spices or coconut. On Thursday, Friday and Saturday, there is live music.

Greek

L'Atlantide
73 rue Franklin, 1040 (736 20 02). Métro Schuman.
Open noon-2.30pm, 6-11pm, Mon-Fri; 6-11pm Sat.
Average 800BF. **Credit** MC, V. **Map G4**
A straightforward and very well-known Greek restaurant, popular with the Greeks who work in the European district. There's no plate-smashing or Greek dancing, just plain white and blue walls, and excellent meze and more substantial food, plus retsina and Greek desserts.

L'Ouzerie
235 chaussée d'Ixelles, 1050 (646 44 49). Bus 71.
Open 7pm-midnight Mon-Thur; 7pm-1am Fri, Sat.
Average 900BF. **Credit** AmEx, DC, V. **Map D5/E6**
On the chaussée d'Ixelles, L'Ouzerie is a lively and modern Greek restaurant that attracts quite a mixture of ages and nationalities and serves delicious versions of all the staple dishes: houmous, saganaki, squid, octopus, and so on. It's not the place to go for if you want plate-smashing, moussaka, and waiters in Greek national costume. The menu is good value and you'll need to book.

Indian

Mumtaz
64 chaussée de Wavre, 1050 (512 54 27). Métro Porte de Namur/bus 54, 71. **Open** noon-3pm, 6pm-midnight, daily. **Average** 700BF. **Menu** 350 (lunch only)-1,000BF.
Credit AmEx, DC, MC, V. **Map D5/H6**
British-style curry house in the Matonge, with tacky lamps and décor, and all the old favourites such as madras, vindaloo, korma and so on. Traditional curry houses are thin on the ground in Brussels and this is a useful and cheap address for expats who want to be reminded of their student days and the concept of curries after closing time.

Au Palais des Indes
263 avenue Louise, 1050 (646 09 41). Tram 93, 94.
Open noon-2.30pm, 6-11.30pm, Mon-Sat; 6-11pm Sun.
Average 1,400BF. **Menu** 695BF (lunch only).
Credit AmEx, DC, MC, V. **Map C5/D6**
Upmarket Indian that is definitely not the place to go after 12 pints of lager or lambic. It produces classy versions of all the old favourites, and specialises in tandoori. All dishes can be made in varying degrees of hotness; the set menu comes in vegetarian and meat versions. Service is very pleasant.

La Porte des Indes
455 avenue Louise, 1050 (647 86 51). Tram 93, 94. **Open** noon-2.30pm, 7-10.30pm, daily.
Average 1,800BF. **Menu** 650 (lunch only)-1,850BF.
Credit AmEx, DC, MC, V. **Map C5/D6**
Even further upmarket Indian, which is part of the same international chain as London's Blue Elephant Thai restaurant. The food involves dishes such as prawns with saffron, rather than vindaloos and onion bhajis, and like the nearby Au Palais des Indes (*see above*), this is not somewhere to eat when you're tired and emotional; rather, it's a luxurious place where you might be given lemon sorbet between courses.

La Porte des Indes – see p101 – upmarket.

La Fin de Siècle
*3 avenue de l'Armée, 1040 (732 74 34). Métro
Montgomery.* **Open** noon-2.30pm, 7-11pm, Mon-Fri; 7-
11pm Sat. **Average** 900BF. **Credit** MC, V.
Not to be confused with the bar of the same name near the
Bourse. The food at La Fin de Siècle is Italian and not exclusively traditional, with pastas such as tagliatelle with white
truffle oil. The decoration is kitsch, with *trompe l'oeil* paintings, chandeliers and dark walls, and classical music is
played. The avenue Louise branch is particularly busy, so
you'll need to book.
Branch: 423 avenue Louise, 1050 (648 80 41).

Gioconda-Store
*76 rue de l'Aqueduc, 1050 (539 32 99). Tram 81,
82/bus 54.* **Open** noon-3pm, 6.30-10.30pm, Tue-Sat;
6.30-10.30pm Sun. **Average** 900BF. **Credit** AmEx, DC,
MC, V.
A modern and convivial Italian restaurant and deli, just off
place Châtelain. The atmosphere is friendly, and the customers fairly young and well heeled, but it's not pompous or
self-satisfied. The best thing on the menu is the excellent
antipasti: for 340BF you help yourself from a large table of
delicious and tasty salads and vegetables. Main courses are
less remarkable but the choice of pasta is perfectly adequate
and helpings are generous. Desserts are also good.

Rosticceria Fiorentina
45 rue Archimède, 1040 (734 92 36). Métro Schuman.
Open noon-2.30pm, 6.30-10.30pm, Mon-Fri, Sun.
Average 1,000BF. **Credit** AmEx, MC, V. **Map G3/G4**
A good-value, family-run restaurant that has been in the
European district far longer than most of the Europeans
who work there. The food is simple and tasty: home-made
pasta, risotto, and daily specials such as saltimbocca and
osso bucco. At lunchtimes, it tends to be full of Italians,
right from the loftiest EU bureaucrat down to his lowliest
photocopier operator.

Le Shimla
67 place Jourdan, 1040 (230 71 58). Métro Schuman.
Open 11.30am-3pm, 6.30pm-midnight, Mon-Sat.
Average 800BF. **Credit** AmEx, DC, MC, V. **Map F5**
Reasonably priced curry house with a touch of flock wall-
paper that's much more down-to-earth than, say, La Porte
des Indes (*see above*). All the usual curries are available –
vindaloos, biryanis, kormas – and there are plenty of vegetarian dishes. The service is very friendly and pleasant.
Another good place for homesick Brits pining for curry.

Rugantino
*184-186 boulevard Anspach, 1000 (511 21 95). Métro
De Brouckère.* **Open** noon-3pm, 6.30pm-midnight, Mon-
Fri; 6.30pm-midnight Sat. **Average** 900F. **Credit** AmEx,
DC, MC, V. **Map B3**
Traditional Italian restaurant near the Bourse, with bustling
waiters, art deco interior, and young customers. The food is
basic pasta, pizza and meat, but it's good value and good
quality, and the pizzas are cooked in a wood-burning oven.
In this busy road where food options mainly comprise
branches of McDonald's, Pizza Hut and the like, this is very
much a haven.

Italian

Cosi
95 rue Américaine, 1050 (534 85 86). Tram 81, 82. **Open**
noon-2.30pm, 7-11pm, Mon-Fri; 7-11pm Sat. **Average**
1,000BF. **Menu** 395BF (lunch only). **Credit** MC, V.
Another modern Italian restaurant in Ixelles, with fresh
pasta and starters including bruschetta, involtini, or parma
ham with pears. The lighting is low, with an assortment of
classy bric-a-brac and old radios and clocks around the walls,
and staff are engaging and friendly. Good for vegetarians.

Fellini
*32 place du Châtelain, 1050 (534 47 49). Tram 81,
82/bus 54.* **Open** noon-2.30pm, 7-11pm, Mon-Fri; 7-11pm
Sat, Sun. **Average** 1,250BF. **Credit** AmEx, DC, MC, V.
The streets round place du Châtelain are packed with restaurants, and this modern Italian is always crowded with the
Ixelles bourgeoisie. It can be frenetic at times, and both staff
and customers are highly satisfied with themselves, but the
food is good, particularly the pasta with smoked salmon and
vodka. Pastas are available as starters or main courses.

North African & Middle Eastern

Al Barmaki
*67 rue des Eperonniers, 1000 (513 08 34). Métro Gare
Centrale.* **Open** 7pm-midnight Mon-Sat. **Average**
900BF. **Credit** AmEx, DC, MC, V. **Map C3**
Lebanese restaurant near Grand Place in an enticing street
full of tattoo parlours and Goth jewellery shops. Al Barmaki
offers the usual Middle Eastern staples – felafel, houmous,
aubergine salad, tabbouleh, chickpeas and so on – but the
quality of the food is well above average and helpings are
generous. A very useful place for vegetarians.

Kasbah
*20 rue Antoine Dansaert, 1000 (520 40 26). Métro
Bourse.* **Open** noon-2.30pm, 7-11pm, Mon-Fri; 7-11pm Sat.
Average 1,000BF. **Credit** AmEx, MC, V. **Map A2/B2**
Far removed from your average backstreet couscous house,
Kasbah is stylish and fashionable, and lit by dozens of
Moroccan lanterns. The menu includes tagines, couscous and
green Moroccan tea. Booking is essential.

North American

Pablo's
51 rue de Namur 1000 (502 41 35). Métro Porte de Namur. **Open** noon-2am Mon-Sat; *food served* noon-3pm, 6pm-midnight. **Average** 100BF.
Credit AmEx, DC, MC, V. **Map D4**
Very popular restaurant and bar serving standard Tex-Mex food such as burritos, chilli con carne and burgers, which you can wash down with Margaritas and other cocktails. The ambience is more suited to groups than couples, and it's popular with office outings and hen nights, so there's invariably a posse of would-be gigolos hanging out at the bar.

Rick's
344 avenue Louise, 1050 (647 75 30). Métro Louise/tram 93, 94. **Open** 11am-midnight daily. **Average** 1,300BF.
Credit AmEx, DC, MC, V. **Map C5/D6**
A well-known avenue Louise bar and restaurant that is populated by US businessmen and frat boys, and goes rather heavy on the *Casablanca*/classic movies theme. The menu of burgers, chilli and steaks is predictable but it's very good quality, as is the excellent weekend brunch. Although the whole package is somewhat clichéd, Rick's is curiously comforting and appealing. The large walled garden at the back is idyllic on summer lunchtimes and evenings.

Russian & Eastern European

Les Ateliers de la Grande Ile
33 rue de la Grande Ile, 1000 (512 81 90). Métro Bourse.
Open 8pm-1.30am Tue-Sat. **Average** 1,200BF. **Credit** AmEx, DC, V. **Map B3**
Noisy Russian and Slav restaurant in an old foundry, with small ramshackle rooms leading off each other, candles and gypsy violinists. The food is hearty – blinis, roast meat and lashings of vodka – and not for someone who wants to pick at a Caesar salad.

South-east Asian

Apocalypse
20 avenue Adolphe Buyl, 1050 (647 07 18). Tram 93, 94. **Open** noon-midnight daily. **Average** 650BF. **Credit** AmEx, DC, V.
Cheap Vietnamese restaurant near the university, which is popular with students. The turnover is rapid and the food is straightforward and very good value. Don't go if you want a long romantic dinner, and don't be put off by the name.

Da Kao
38 rue Antoine Dansaert, 1000 (512 67 16). Métro Bourse. **Open** 11am-3pm, 7pm-1am, daily. **Average** 600BF. **No credit cards. Map A2/B2**
No-frills Vietnamese restaurant in the centre of Brussels. The turnover is fast, the service brusque and lighting harsh, but the food is excellent value by Brussels standards, and it is justifiably popular. It's also a refreshing contrast to its more fashionable and self-conscious neighbours, such as Bonsoir Clara and Kasbah. There's Tsingtao beer, and as well as Vietnamese dishes, you can get tempura and dim sum.

Indochine
58 rue Lesbroussart, 1050 (649 96 15). Tram 81, 82. **Open** noon-2.30pm, 7-11.30pm, Mon-Sat. **Average** 600BF. **Menu** 280 (lunch only)-695BF. **Credit** MC, V.
Small and friendly restaurant near Flagey, with old tram seats and a 'journal mural' stuck to the window and walls, consisting of texts and drawings intended to stimulate thought or discussion. Recent examples include a thesis by the Unabomber. There's a good choice of meat, seafood and vegetarian dishes, and the owners are smiling and friendly.

La Quincaillerie – *see p93* – *good seafood.*

My-Tai
110 chaussée de Malines, 1970 (731 27 26). Bus 30, 39. **Open** noon-2.30pm, 7-10.30pm, Tue-Sat; 7-11pm Sun. **Average** 900BF. **Credit** AmEx, DC, MC, V. **Map C3**
A Thai restaurant out of the way in suburban Wezembeek-Oppem, but well worth a visit , particularly if you have children. A downstairs playroom means you can park your offspring downstairs and eat good Thai classics, such as red chicken curry, in peace. The staff are pleasant and helpful and the chef can make dishes less or more hot if asked.

Samourai
28 rue du Fossé aux Loups, 1000 (217 56 39). Métro De Brouckère. **Open** noon-2pm, 7-10.30pm, Mon-Sat; 7-10.30pm Sun. **Average** 1,800BF. **Menu** 1,400-2,300BF. **Credit** AmEx, DC, MC, V. **Map C3**
Upmarket and labyrinthine Japanese restaurant hidden away in an unenticing shopping arcade. It's certainly not cheap, but the food is really excellent, and for a special occasion it's a worthwhile alternative to the better-known European restaurants in Brussels. There's a range of set sukiyaki, teriyaki and other menus, which offer the best value.

Takesushi
21 boulevard de Charlemagne, 1040 (230 56 27). Métro Schuman. **Open** noon-2.30pm, 7-10.30pm, Mon-Fri; 7-11pm Sat, Sun. **Average** 900BF. **Menu** 450BF (lunch only). **Credit** AmEx, DC, MC, V. **Map F4**
The outside looks inauspicious, with fading photographs of Japanese food, but this is deceptive since it is highly popular. You'll find Japanese people plus a good smattering of Eurocrats, and you can choose between sashimi, teriyaki, sukiyaki, sushi and tempura. The sushi lunch menu is a particular bargain. There's a fairly large garden at the back.

Yamato
11 rue Francart, 1050 (502 28 93). Bus 54, 71.
Open noon-2pm, 7-10pm, Tue-Fri. **Average** 600BF. **No credit cards. Map D5**
A simple Japanese noodle bar just off the chaussée d'Ixelles. The noodles are served at a plain wooden counter and the turnover is rapid. Not somewhere to linger, but it's good value and very popular with Japanese living in Brussels.

Yamayu Santatsu
141 chaussée d'Ixelles, 1050 (513 53 12). Bus 54, 71.
Open noon-2pm, 7-10pm, Tue-Sat. **Average** 1,000 BF.
Credit AmEx, DC, MC, V. **Map D5/E6**
Very popular Japanese restaurant, usually full of a mixture of students and Japanese people of all ages. The atmosphere is bright, noisy and convivial. The sushi and sashimi are excellent and very fresh, and there are multi-course takesushi and sukiyaki menus.

Spanish

Las Castanuelas
132 rue Stévin, 1040 (280 00 81). Métro Schuman.
Open noon-2.30pm, 7-10.30pm, Mon-Fri. **Average** 800BF. **No credit cards. Map F4**
A tapas restaurant in the European district that is always crowded at lunchtime, but less so in the evening. The tortilla is wonderful, and all the usual tapas are on the menu: calamares, octopus, meatballs, chorizo, prawns with garlic and so on, plus some more substantial Spanish cooking. The house Rioja is good value.

La Grillange
7 avenue Eudore Pirmez, 1040 (649 26 85). Tram 81, 82. **Open** noon-3pm, 7-11pm, Tue-Sat. **Average** 1,300BF.
Menu 1,200BF. **Credit** AmEx, DC, MC, V. **Map G6**
A good Spanish restaurant in a nondescript part of Etterbeek. Popular with well-heeled Spaniards, the food is traditional, and the four-course set menu is based on the food of a different region each month. If you don't opt for the set meal, it's often a good idea to ignore the menu and let the owner tell you what's good that day.

Turkish

L'Ottomanie
97 rue des Alexiens, 1000 (512 08 90). Bus 34, 48, 95, 96. **Open** 11am-midnight Tue-Sun. **Average** 1,000BF.
Credit AmEx, DC, MC, V. **Map B4**
A modern Turkish restaurant, with good-value meze and surprisingly drinkable Turkish and Middle Eastern wine. It caters for young Europeans rather than Turks, and the decoration is odd in places: stencil-painted walls, and lights that resemble the teats of milking machines. Odd touches such as having the menu in the form of a play script lay it open to charges of pretentiousness, but it remains popular and relaxed.

Vegetarian

Dolma
329 chaussée d'Ixelles, 1050 (649 89 91). Tram 81, 82/bus 71. **Open** noon-2pm, 7-10pm, Mon-Sat. **Average** 800BF. **Credit** AmEx, DC, MC, V. **Map D5/E6**
Owned by the same people as Tsampa (*see below*), Dolma (formerly called Le Paradoxe) also has an adjoining health-food shop. The food is vegetarian, with an emphasis on tofu, seitan and quorn (it tastes better than it sounds) as well as more straightforward quiches and *tartes*. Best value is the eat-as-much-as-you-want buffet, which costs 440BF at lunchtime and 490BF in the evening.

*Check out the pasta at **Fellini** – see p102.*

Shanti
68 avenue Adolphe Buyl, 1050 (649 40 96). Tram 93, 94/bus 71. **Open** noon-2pm, 6.30-10pm, Tue-Sat.
Average 1,000BF. **Menu** 400BF (lunch only). **Credit** AmEx, DC, MC, V.
Mainly vegetarian restaurant above a health-food shop. It's near the university, so it's popular with affluent students, but the customers also include a good smattering of Ixelles and Uccle thirtysomethings. The food is a relief for vegetarians weary of having to eat omelette after omelette in Brussels' more traditional restaurants: grilled tofu with pleurottes (wild mushrooms) and fruit and mustard sauce, plus staples such as vegetarian curry. You usually need to book.

Totem Natural Kitchen
6 rue des Grands Carmes, 1000 (513 11 52). Métro Bourse or Gare Centrale. **Open** 7-11pm Wed-Sun.
Average 900BF. **No credit cards.**
It is rare to find a vegetarian restaurant in central Brussels, and even rarer to find one that has no hint of ethnicity in its styling. Totem serves organic food such as ragout of seven vegetables with polenta, vegetable sushi, a gratin of the day, and dishes based on tempeh and seitan. The restaurant is tiny, and the interior very calm and plain.

Tsampa
109 rue de Livourne, 1050 (647 03 67). Tram 93, 94.
Open noon-2pm, 7-10pm, Mon-Fri; 7-10pm Sat.
Average 800BF. **Menu** 350 (lunch only)-430BF. **Credit** AmEx, DC, MC, V. **Map C6**
Walk through the health-food shop in front to reach this imaginative vegetarian restaurant. The menu has eastern influences; there is plenty of seitan and quorn, and the wines are organic. There's a garden at the back.

Cafés & Bars

If Belgium produces 400 different beers and the average bar or café serves around 20, it may take you a while to taste them all.

The bars and cafés of Brussels are by far the liveliest part of the city. Anyone who has spent a day wandering around almost-deserted streets, bemused by the relative lack of sightseeing opportunities, might wonder why they have come to Brussels. But as soon as they start visiting the bars, they understand the attraction.

Quite simply, Brussels is a superb place to drink. There are hundreds of bars and cafés, catering for every taste. You can sit in art nouveau splendour and drink coffee or champagne in the company of the Brussels bourgeoisie and their poodles. You can hang out in comfortable old bars with wooden booths and surly old men and drink dozens of different beers in bizarrely shaped glasses. You can drink Guinness in Irish pubs, bottles of Budweiser in all-American bars, or cups of hot chocolate in chess bars. You can pose with a *citron pressé* and a novel at one of the Parisian-style pavement tables in the Sablon. You can salsa in Latin American bars, bop to Euro-pop, and be chic against a backdrop of velvet drapes and candles. And you can do any of these things from breakfast until dawn.

Most visitors' first destinations are the touristy bars and cafés on all sides of the Grand Place. These offer an excellent view of the square, and their interiors give a clue to the wealth and power of the medieval guild houses, but you may find high prices and a distinct lack of Belgians, so it's worth looking further afield. For example, a few paces to the north, the streets around the Bourse are good for turn-of-the-century cafés **Le Cirio** and **Le Falstaff**, as well as the more fashionable **Pp Café** (*see below*). Be warned that if you visit the toilet in any of the larger bars around here, you will find an ancient woman demanding 10BF or 20BF for the privilege.

Just beyond Grand Place are important drinking streets such as the meandering rue Marché au Charbon, which are virtually deserted during the day but come alive late in the evening. At weekends, streets such as rue Marché au Charbon, rue Antoine Dansaert and place St Géry are packed until well after 3am, with many bars not filling up until past midnight.

Another fruitful area is further to the south, in Ixelles, which stretches out on either side of avenue Louise. The places around the university are studenty, while closer to the centre you will find chic cafés and bars for twenty- and thirtysomethings.

Food on offer includes French staples such as *croque monsieur*, and you will also find open sandwiches, delicious pâtisserie and occasionally more substantial salads and steaks.

Sadly, in whatever area you drink, you will also notice the 'Irish' pubs – Brussels, like most other European cities, has seen an explosion of them in the last few years. It's not that there's anything wrong with them, but to talk to some British expats, you would think they were the only type of bar available. It's a shame to let their growing presence obscure the fact that Brussels does have much more interesting alternatives.

The average Belgian bar or café sells around 20 types of beer, but a few of the traditional ones sell 100 or more, and this, of course, is the reason why many people visit Brussels in the first place. Between 400 and 600 beers are brewed in Belgium, and although not all of them are available in the capital, you will probably find more than you are physically able to drink. Although Belgian beer is now widely exported, and brands such as Chimay and Hoegaarden are easily available in the UK, you will doubtless make new discoveries. You can also sit and wonder at the almost lyrical names, such as Verboden Frucht (Forbidden Fruit), Delirium Tremens, Guillotine, Mariage Parfait and Mort Subite (Sudden Death). Others, however, may present more of a challenge: Bokrijks Kruikenbier, Huyghe and Breda's Begijntje can be difficult to pronounce, even on the first glass.

You can also wonder at, and occasionally struggle with, the beer glasses. Many Belgian beers have their own glasses, and it is anathema to most barmen to serve a beer in the wrong kind of glass. Some of these glasses, such as the kwak glass with its bulbous bottom and wooden stand, are marketing devices, but there is a rationale for having different shaped glasses, just as there is for wine. According to beer-lovers, aromatic beers require a wide-rimmed glass, thick glasses keep light beers cool, broad-rimmed glasses help keep the sediment of heavy beers in the glass, and so on. If you are a stickler for such rules, most specialist beer shops in Belgium stock the glasses as well as the beers themselves.

Although over 75 per cent of the beer sold in Belgium is lager, such as Stella and Jupiler, it is becoming better known for its Trappist and abbey ales. The Trappist ales are made by monks, and 'lay brothers' working with them, at just five breweries: Chimay, Orval, Rochefort, Westmalle and Westvleteren. The abbey (*abbaye* in French and *abdij* in Flemish) ales are modelled on the Trappist ales, but are produced by brewers rather than monks (although the quaint pictures of monasteries and monks on the labels suggest otherwise). The quality of abbey ales varies: some are excellent, while others are simply cashing in on the fame of the Trappist breweries.

Monastic beers fall into two main types: *doubel* (double), which are dark and sweet with six or seven per cent alcohol, and *tripel* (triple), which are eight or nine per cent proof. Other types are stronger still, such as the black and heavy Rochefort 100, and Westvleteren 120, which tastes similar to barley wine. Chimay ale comes in three different strengths: Chimay red (seven per cent alcohol), Chimay white (eight per cent) and Chimay blue (nine per cent).

Belgium is also famous for its lambic beers, which are 'spontaneously' fermented and have no yeast added. Instead, the yeast comes from microbes and micro-organisms in the air as the wheat, barley and hops are left to cool. To facilitate this process, breweries such as Cantillon have hundreds of vents in the roof. Next time you find yourself standing chill and damp at a Brussels tram stop, try to console yourself with the fact that the air around you is contributing to a unique type of beer.

A mixture of old and young lambic is used to make gueuze, which is the best or worst of Belgian beers, according to taste. The blend of old and new beer is put in champagne bottles and re-fermented, and the resulting concoction is fizzy and dry with a sourish taste. There is some sediment at the bottom of the bottle, so it must be poured carefully, but you can also buy a partially filtered version, which is sweeter.

Both lambic and gueuze are used to make Belgium's fruit beers. The most traditional fruit beers are cherry (*kriek*) and raspberry (*framboise*), but in recent years breweries have experimented with other fruits. Damson and peach are fairly successful, and it is also possible to buy less palatable alternatives such as banana and mint flavours.

A more easily acquired taste is *witbier* or *blanche*. This wheat beer is delicious and refreshing on a hot summer afternoon or evening and is often served with a slice of lemon, but beware – it can cause lethal hangovers.

If you are visiting Brussels in winter, some of the seasonal and Christmas ales may be more appropriate. These are often spiced with coriander, ginger or cinnamon, and there are also honeyed versions.

If beer is not to your taste, Belgian bars and cafés always have a good choice of wine by the bottle or glass. Most wine on offer is French, and Brussels is very good for white and red Burgundy, but New World and Mediterranean wine is scarce and over-priced. Cocktails are widely available, and flavoured vodkas are popular, particularly in the younger bars.

Opening times for many Brussels bars and cafés are purely theoretical, and in practice they may indeed close much earlier or later, depending on the state of their relations with the police and the *commune* authorities and on how many customers are in that night.

Bars

L'Acrobate
14 rue Borgval, 1000 (513 73 08). Métro Bourse.
Open 9pm-dawn Fri, Sat.
The style of this bar is Central American kitsch, with primary colours, fairy lights, shrines, lanterns and plastic flowers, although it's often too crowded and dark to see much of this. It's usually empty until well past midnight, and then rapidly becomes packed out. There's a small dance-floor at the back, with music ranging from Latin American to hip- hop and 1970s disco.

L'Amadeus
13 rue Veydt, 1050 (538 34 27). Métro Louise/tram 91, 92. **Open** *wine bar* 6.30pm-2am Tue-Sat. **Map C6**
A wine bar and restaurant (*see chapter* **Restaurants**) housed in the former studio of the sculptor Auguste Rodin. Built around a courtyard, with dark colours, exposed brick and tall candles, it's popular with all ages. There's a good wine list (many wines available by the glass) and there are oysters in season.

L'Amour Fou
185 chaussée d'Ixelles (at place Fernand Cocq), 1050 (514 27 09). Métro Porte de Namur/bus 54, 71. **Open** 9am-3am daily. **Map D6**
Long, narrow, modern bar in Ixelles with art on the walls and two pinball machines at the entrance. Fairly crowded in the evenings, but more relaxed during the daytime, and there are various French and Flemish newspapers on wooden sticks on the tables. Customers are young and casual.

L'Archiduc
6 rue Antoine Dansaert, 1000 (512 06 52). Métro Bourse. **Open** 4pm-dawn daily. **Map A2/B2**
Elegant and chic bar, decorated in 1930s liner style. Mellow without being sedate, it occasionally has a piano player or live jazz. Close to the centre, it's a good place to start or, even better, finish the evening.

L'Archipel
163 chaussée de Charleroi, 1060 (538 91 91). Tram 92. **Open** 7.30pm-2am Tue-Sat. **Map C6**
Bookshop in St Gilles that turns into a bar and restaurant in the evening. Since the food (quiches, pasta etc) can be variable, the bar is the more attractive option. L'Archipel specialises in genièvres: deceptively refreshing fruit gins in dozens of flavours. The alcohol level and hangover potential mean it's usually best to fight the temptation to taste half a dozen different flavours.

L'Atelier
77 rue Elise, 1050 (649 19 53). Tram 93, 94/bus 71. **Open** 6pm-3am daily.
Don't even think of going to L'Atelier if you want peace or sophistication: it's right next to the university in Ixelles and is invariably crammed with beery students, playing pinball and talking about life, alcohol and everything. There's also occasional live music. Since there are over 200 beers available at reasonable prices, the place also attracts plenty of beer tourists.

Belgica

32 rue du Marché au Charbon, 1000 (no phone). Métro Bourse. **Open** 10am-3am Thur-Sun. **Map B3**
The Belgian flag is outside and there's a bust of King Léopold inside, but this is no traditional bar for patriotic old Belgians. It's predominantly gay (*see chapter* **Gay & Lesbian**) but if you go late at weekends, it's by no means wholly so. The music is loud, it's bustling and crowded, and it's popular as a pre-club bar.

Beursschouwburg

22 rue Auguste Orts, 1000 (513 82 90). Métro Bourse. **Open** 7pm-3am Thur-Sat.
Huge, cavernous, post-industrial bar next to a theatre and ballroom. Slightly arty and predominantly Flemish, it's usually empty until about 11, and then becomes packed. Music is mostly acid jazz and funk, with occasional live bands.

Le Bois Sans Soif

60 avenue Adolphe Buyl, 1050 (649 44 73). Tram 23, 90, 93, 94/bus 71. **Open** noon-4am Mon-Fri; 4pm-4am Sat, Sun.
Pleasant bar near the university in Ixelles where you can play games including Scrabble, Pictionary and Rummikub. The interior has distressed, tangerine paintwork, and beech tables and counter, a style that seems popular in this part of Brussels. There's a garden at the back.

Le Cerceuil

10-12 rue des Harengs, 1000 (512 30 77). Métro Bourse or Gare Centrale. **Open** 11am-2am daily.
Just off Grand Place, Le Cerceuil (which means coffin in French) looks like an undertaker's from the outside and has coffins for tables, ultra-violet lighting to bring out customers' pallor, and a mixture of Gregorian chant and funeral marches. Customers are mainly tourists, students, Goths and horror fans.

Le Châtelain

17 place Châtelain, 1050 (538 67 94) Tram 81, 82, 93, 94. **Open** 10.30am-1am Tue-Sat; 5pm-1am Sun.
Unpretentious neighbourhood bar, just off avenue Louise, of a type that is rare in this district of Brussels. There are old theatre posters and photos of Hollywood stars on the walls, but generally there is little sign of conscious design. Customers are a mixture of Belgians and expatriates, youngish and middle-aged. It also serves food, such as omelettes, *croques* and steaks.

Chez Richard

2 rue des Minimes, 1000 (no phone). Tram 92, 93, 94/bus 34, 95, 96. **Open** 7am-late daily. **Map B5/C4**
Bar/café near the Sablon whose character changes as the day progresses. You'll find lawyers and businessmen at weekday lunchtimes, and visitors to the Sablon antique shops and stalls at weekends. In the evening, the average age drops by several decades, and people happily drink and dance to Euro-pop.

Le Corbeau

18-20 rue St Michel, 1000 (219 52 46). Métro De Brouckère or Rogier. **Open** 10am-12.30am Mon-Fri; 10am-2am Sat. **Map C2**
This bar's main claim to fame is its glasses. The 'chevalier' is a glass of beer about half a metre high, so a certain dexterity is required if you want to avoid a faceful. The music gets louder and the customers rowdier as the evening wears on, and if you've always wanted to stand on a table and sing pop songs with young Belgians on a Saturday night, the opportunity may well present itself here.

L'Entrée des Artistes

42 place du Grand Sablon, 1000 (502 31 61). Tram 92, 93, 94/bus 34, 95, 96. **Open** 8am-2am daily. **Map C4**

Another of those bars that line the Sablon where you can while away some pleasant hours at the counter or at one of the tables outside. It's convenient for posing with a book or people-watching, particularly during the Sablon antiques market at the weekend, and a good place to start with a coffee and then move on to something stronger as lunchtime approaches. Prices are reasonable considering the location, and the only downside are the mobile phones trilling all around you.

Fin de Siècle

9 rue des Chartreux, 1000 (no phone). Métro Bourse. **Open** 4.30pm-1am daily. **Map B3**
A long old bar in the centre of town that has been given a makeover of distressed paint and plasterwork, lanterns on the tables, and art (for sale) on the walls. The music is classical, and there's a small stage at the back where there are occasional flamenco shows among other entertainments. Crowded at weekends, it is quiet and civilised during the week.

Le Greenwich

7 rue des Chartreux, 1000 (511 41 67). Métro Bourse. **Open** 11am-2am daily. **Map B3**
Big, bright, old-fashioned bar in the centre of town, with marble tables and wooden panelling. What distinguishes it from other bars of this type is the lack of talking and the intense games of chess played at the tables by old and young. The silence makes it a good bar in which to sit and read.

Le Garde-Manger

151 rue Washington, 1050 (346 68 29). Bus 37, 60. **Open** noon-3pm, 4pm-1am, Mon-Fri; 4pm-1am Sat, Sun.
In a small square by the pretty parc Tenbosch, Le Garde-Manger has gilded mirrors, candelabras, velvet and attractive burgundy walls. Service can be offhand and many of the

*Authentic art deco – **L'Espérance** – see p111.*

customers are of the convertible-driving, mobile-carrying variety, but it's a pleasant enough place, particularly in the summer if you can get one of the coveted tables on the small terrace at the front. It also does a small selection of imaginative salads, pasta and other food.

Goupil Le Fol

22 rue de la Violette, 1000 (511 13 96). Métro Bourse.
Open 8pm-dawn daily. **Map C3**
Eccentric bar near the Mannekin Pis that looks like a junk shop from the outside. It looks like one inside, too: every surface, including the ceiling, is covered in old books, pictures and LPs. As well as standard Belgian beers, there are fruit wines and gins, which can lead to severe hangovers.

H2O

27 rue du Marché au Charbon, 1000 (512 38 42). Métro Bourse. **Open** 7pm-2am daily. **Map B3**
Fairly sophisticated bar in an excellent street for drinking. With candles, drapes, and ambient or classical music, it is quieter and older than many of its neighbours, and is the scene of many a thirtysomething seduction. There is a also a small food menu.

Le Java

14 rue St Géry, 1000 (512 37 16). Métro Bourse.
Open 8pm-3am Mon-Sat. **Map B3**
Small wedge-shaped bar, with red marbled walls, huge windows and an almost Gaudi-esque bar-top encrusted with old bottle-tops. Noisy, crowded, interesting, and right in the middle of an area that is excellent for bars.

Kafka

6 rue de la Vierge Noire, 1000 (513 54 89). Métro De Brouckère or Bourse. **Open** noon-3am Mon-Fri; 5pm-3am Sat, Sun. **Map B2/B3**
Smoky old bar with brown walls and a bare tiled floor, selling 18 types of vodka and a fairly long list of Belgian beers. Customers are mainly Flemish, with a strong contingent of barflies and eccentrics. Scruffy and relaxed, it can be a good antidote to the more style-conscious bars around the Bourse.

La Kartchma

17 place du Grand Sablon, 1000 (512 49 64). Tram 92, 93, 94/bus 34, 95, 96. **Open** 10am-4am daily. **Map C4**
Some people think this is the most pleasant of the bars and cafés with tables outside that line one side of the Sablon, although in summer it is hard to distinguish which tables belong to which. A good place to sit in your shades on summer lunchtimes or evenings and watch the Sablon types and their Porsches.

Le Maldorore

91 rue Américaine, 1050 (539 22 26). Tram 91, 92, 93, 94. **Open** 8pm-late daily.
This calls itself a 'night bar', and the hours it keeps have led to occasional run-ins with the Ixelles authorities and the police. The music is loud, and it's popular as a place to drink pre- or mid-clubs. It's not the sort of place where you make an evening of it.

Orange-Bleu

29 rue Antoine Dansaert, 1000 (no phone). Métro Bourse. **Open** 4pm-3am daily. **Map A2/B2**
Cocktail bar and café near the Bourse that has latched on to the Brussels style of velvet drapes, classical statues, rich-coloured paint effects and antique furniture. It's pleasant enough, though somewhat self-conscious, and it has a good cocktail list. Although drink prices are relatively high, measures are large.

Le Pantin

355 chaussée d'Ixelles, 1050 (640 80 91). Bus 71. **Open** 11am-2am Mon-Sat; 5pm-2am Sun. **Map D5/E6**

Slightly scruffy bar right at the bottom of the chaussée d'Ixelles near the ponds, where students hang out and old and young Belgians play chess. If you're going on a Saturday morning, combine it with a visit to the food market at place Eugene Flagey.

Le Pitt's Bar

53 rue des Minimes, 1000 (514 41 74). Tram 92, 93, 94/bus 34, 95, 96. **Open** 8pm-2am Tue-Sun. **Map B5**
A small bar near the Sablon with trompe l'oeil décor and a varying character. At weekends, DJs play loud garage music and the male customers pose as if waiting to be spotted by a model agent. On weekdays it's altogether quieter, with a log fire.

Poechenelle Kelder

5 rue du Chêne, 1000 (511 92 62). Métro Bourse. **Open** 10am-midnight Mon-Thur; 10am-2am Fri-Sun. **Map B4**
The name means 'puppet cellar' and the theme is Brussels in general and puppets in particular. Since it is situated right opposite the Manneken Pis, this is perhaps not surprising. There are puppets all over the place, together with postcards and other *objets* relating to Brussels folklore, and the snacks include specialities such as *tête pressée* (a type of brawn).

(Au) Soleil

86 rue Marché au Charbon, 1000 (513 34 30). Métro Bourse. **Open** 10am-2am daily. **Map B3**
A former men's clothing shop with the original signs outside and old wooden fittings inside, although some of the fading ads on the walls are actually recent additions. It's crowded in the evenings, with a fair number of stubbly artist types and an excellent atmosphere. A good choice of beer, some food, and tables outside in summer.

Sounds

28 rue de la Tulipe, 1050 (512 92 50). Métro Porte de Namur/bus 54, 71. **Open** 11.30am-4am Mon-Sat. **Map D5/D6**
Comfortable bar just behind place Fernand Cocq, with live jazz four or five nights a week. There's a small supplement on drinks during the jazz, but otherwise it's free. It also has occasional tango sessions.

Le Sud

43 rue de l'Ecuyer, 1000 (513 37 65). Métro Gare Centrale. **Open** 10pm-2am Tue-Fri; 10pm-6am Sat, Sun. **Map C3**
The combination of popularity and bureaucracy has somewhat tarnished the appeal and originality of Sud, but it remains an excellent bar/club all the same. Opened a few years ago in an abandoned building, it used to have the feel of a large squat, and although the candles remain, it now has luxuries such as fire exits. The small club section in the cellar plays a wide variety of eccentric and more mainstream dance music.

Tierra del Fuego

14 rue Berckmans, 1060 (537 42 72). Métro Louise. **Open** noon-2am daily. **Map B6/C6**
Bar and café on the ground floor of a Latin American cultural centre just off avenue Louise. The décor is baroque and exotic, with drapes, candles, glittery embroidered chairs, and murals. You can drink caipirinhas (Brazilian cocktails served with lime, sugar syrup and vodka, with plenty of ice) or generous glasses of Dominican, Haitian and Cuban rum, buy coffee from Costa Rica, Mexico, Jamaica, Honduras, Haiti and Brazil, and smoke cigars, or you can stick to more standard beers and spirits.

Ceci n'est pas un bar. **La Fleur en Papier Doré** *– see page 111 – was a haunt of Magritte and other Belgian surrealists.*

*Hommage au Sentim
l'inconstance origin
Sais-tu, Lorenzo, ce que v
as-tu jamais étudi
philosophie des
Larmes ?*

Zebra Bar

33 place St Géry, 1000 (511 09 01). Métro Bourse.
Open 11.45am-2.45am daily. **Map B3**
Fashionable bar (and café), run by the owners of Pp Café (*see below*), Bonsoir Clara and Kasbah (*see chapter* **Restaurants**), with a big, posy terrace, a long list of beers and cocktails, and food. The mood changes depending on the time: peaceful and relaxed in the daytime, noisy and bustling in the evening. Whatever the mood, it's definitely worth a visit.

Traditional bars

L'Albertine

53 rue de la Madeleine, 1000 (513 56 71). Métro Gare Centrale. **Open** *Apr-Sept* 7am-7.30pm daily. *Oct-Mar* 7am-7.30pm Mon-Fri. **Map C3/C4**
An unspectacular but pleasant bar near Mont des Arts. It's warm, comfortable and central, and doesn't have the touristy or desolate air that some Brussels bars take on during the daytime. The beer is good and there's a decent wine list; it also does some snacks and spaghetti throughout the day.

A La Bécasse

11 rue de Tabora, 1000 (511 00 06). Métro Bourse or De Brouckère. **Open** 10am-1am Mon-Thur; 10am-2am Fri, Sat; 11am-midnight Sun. **Map B3**
An ancient and popular drinking hall hidden away in an alley in the centre of Brussels. Customers squeeze together on long narrow tables, and aproned waiters serve lambic and gueuze beer in pottery jugs.

La Chaloupe D'Or

24 Grand Place, 1000 (511 41 61). Métro Bourse or Gare Centrale. **Open** 10am-1am daily. **Map C3**
One of the most famous Grand Place bars/restaurants in the guildhouse of the tailors. It's opposite the Town Hall, and there's a fine view of this and other buildings from the upper rooms. One of the best of the Grand Place bars.

Le Cirio

18 rue de la Bourse, 1000 (512 13 95). Métro Bourse. **Open** 10am-1am daily. **Map B3**
Large, dark, turn-of-the-century café near the Bourse that attracts a good cross-section of Brussels life: tourists, Eurocrats, and old women with poodles. There's a big choice of beers, and it's well known as a place to drink *half-en-half*, a mixture of champagne and white wine.

L'Espérance

1-3 rue du Finistère, 1000 (217 32 47). Métro De Brouckère or Rogier. **Open** 11am-1am Mon-Fri.
Authentic art deco bar to the north of the centre, with wood panelling, some chrome fittings and a comfortable atmosphere. After a dodgy start in the 1930s – there were bedrooms upstairs for the bargirls and their customers – it is now highly respectable, and it's a fine place to sit and sip a glass of *half-en-half*.

La Fleur en Papier Doré

53 rue des Alexiens, 1000 (511 16 59). Bus 34, 48, 95, 96. **Open** 10.30am-1am Mon-Thur, Sun; 11.30am-3am Fri, Sat. **Map B4**
Dark old bar in a seventeenth-century building. It was the local of Magritte and the Belgian surrealists and Dadaists in the 1920s, and the walls are covered with pictures, clippings, writings and graffiti by them. Customers are a mixture of gnarled old men, putative intellectuals and tourists.

*Not usually a place to sit and reflect in peace and quiet, **Rick's Bar** – see p113 – does good Sunday brunch and cocktails.*

À L'Imaige Nostre-Dame

8 rue Marché aux Herbes, 1000 (219 42 49). Métro Bourse/bus 25, 60, 65, 66, 71. **Open** 11.30am-1am Mon-Sat; 4pm-1am Sun. **Map C3**
An old inn owned by the same people as A La Bécasse (*see above*), and similar in style. It, too, is hidden down an alleyway and has a heritage feel, with old wooden tables, stained glass and leather benches. The beers are good, and there is some traditional food. Good for cold days or gloomy Sunday evenings.

La Lunette

3 place de la Monnaie, 1000 (218 03 78). Métro De Brouckère. **Open** 8am-1am Mon-Thur; 8am-2am Fri, Sat; 10am-1am Sun. **Map C3**
The Belgian revolution of 1830 started in this square, when opera-goers were inflamed with patriotic fervour. This traditional bar (and café) with mirrors and wooden panels is a pleasant place to sit and read your history books or watch the world go by. Watch out, however, if you order a 'lunette' of beer – it's a litre glass.

Moeder Lambic

68 rue de Savoie, 1060 (539 14 19). Métro Horta. **Open** 4pm-4am daily.
Moeder Lambic, which means Mother Lambic, is beer heaven. It claims to offer over a thousand types, although not all may be in stock at once. Given the size of the beer menu, the actual bar is surprisingly small (perhaps the storerooms are very large), but it's pleasant enough, particularly at quieter times. The neighbourhood is not especially picturesque, but if you're only here for the beer, that doesn't present a problem.

A La Mort Subite

7 rue des Montagnes aux Herbes Potagères, 1000 (512 86 64/513 13 18). Métro Gare Centrale or De Brouckère. **Open** 10.30am-1am Mon-Fri; 11am-1am Sat; 12.30pm-1am Sun. **Map C3**
Famous and traditional Brussels bar with surly waiters, noisy customers, mirrors and smoke-yellowed walls. Passive smoking hell (or heaven, depending how you look at it). The beer list is somewhat short for a traditional Belgian bar, but most of the classic ones are there, including La Mort Subite.

La Rose Blanche

11 Grand Place, 1000 (513 64 79). Métro Bourse or Gare Centrale. **Open** 10am-1am daily; *food served* 11.30am-11pm daily. **Map C3**
La Rose Blanche is another famous Grand Place bar and restaurant with a terrace in front. There's a long list of beers, which might prove tempting if you've just worked up a thirst in the beer museum next door, and there is also traditional Belgian food.

Le Roy d'Espagne

1 Grand Place, 1000 (513 08 07). Métro Bourse or Gare Centrale. **Open** 10am-1am daily. **Map C3**
Famous Grand Place bar that is housed in one of the grandest guildhouses (the bakers'). Waiters wear traditional aprons, pigs' bladders hang from the ceiling, and it's firmly on the tourist trail. But it's still worth a look, and there's an excellent view of Grand Place from the upper rooms. *See also chapter* **Surrealist Brussels**.

Le Stoemelings

7 place de Londres, 1050 (512 43 74). Métro Trône. **Open** 11am-2am Mon-Fri; 5pm-2am Sat, Sun. **Map E5**
Le Stoemelings is a cosy traditional bar, whose position on the borders of Ixelles and the European district makes for a varied atmosphere. There are some lawyers and lobbyists in the daytime, but a more local feel in the evening. In addition to some unusual beers, there are small snacks such as *croque monsieur*.

La Librairie des Etangs – *see page 114* – *has a small tearoom at the back of the shop.*

La Térrasse

*11 avenue de Tervuren, 1040 (733 22 96). Métro
Mérode.* **Open** 10am-11pm daily.

Old-fashioned and comfortable bar/café with leather ban-
quettes and wooden panelling. There's a large, vine-covered
terrace in front, although its location on a busy junction
means it can be noisy. It sells dozens of Belgian beers, and
specialises in savoury *tartes*, among them tuna, salmon,
chicken, leek, artichoke and roquefort (200-250BF).

Toone

*21 Petite rue des Bouchers, 1000 (513 54 86). Métro
Bourse.* **Open** noon-midnight daily; *théâtre* 8.30pm
Tue-Sat. **Map C3**

The bar of the Toone theatre, where puppets perform plays
in the Brussels dialect. The road, which is just off the Grand
Place, is packed with (mostly mediocre) fish restaurants, so
you have to keep your eyes open if you want to find it.
Puppets hang from the ceiling, and it's warm and cosy, but
not a bar to visit if you want to avoid tourists.

Anglophone bars & pubs

The Bank

79 rue du Bailli, 1050 (no phone). Tram 81, 82, 93, 94.
Open noon-1am daily.

Newish Irish pub, off avenue Louise, in a converted bank
that still has safe deposit boxes lining the walls. Unlike
many Irish pubs in Brussels, it's not dominated by people
watching sport, so the atmosphere is less macho. Saturday
nights are crowded, with live Irish music or predictable
record selections like U2.

Conway's

*10 avenue de la Toison d'Or, 1050 (511 26 68/502 29
10). Métro Louise or Porte de Namur.* **Open** noon-2am
Mon-Sat; 11am-5am Sun. **Map C6/D5**

Noisy New York-style Irish bar with Kilkenny and Guinness
on tap and a big selection of whiskey and bourbon. The
upstairs sports bar is a very popular place for watching
rugby internationals, Superbowl and so on. Happy Hour is
from 6-9pm daily, and women get half-price cocktails and
spirits at the bar on Thursdays. Also serves burgers and
Cajun food.

James Joyce

34 rue Archimède, 1040 (230 98 94). Métro Schuman.
Open 11am-5am daily. **Map G3/G4**

Irish pub in the European quarter that is usually quieter
(some say more miserable) than the other Irish pubs, but is
possibly the most authentic. There is Irish folk music on
Tuesday evenings. The food is not much to write home
about, except for the Sunday brunch.

Kitty O'Shea's

*42 boulevard Charlemagne, 1040 (230 78 75). Métro
Schuman.* **Open** noon-3am daily. **Map F4**

One of the first Irish pubs to open in the EU district,
Kitty's is very popular with Eurocrats, lawyers and journalists, and quieter than some of its newer counterparts in
the city centre. It has a snug at the back, a separate restaurant section serving Irish stew and the like, and it also does
an acceptable Sunday brunch fry-up.

MacSweeney's

24 rue Jean Stas, 1060 (534 47 41). Métro Louise. **Open**
noon-1am daily. **Map C6**

MacSweeney's is yet another Irish pub in central Brussels.
Its location in a popular shopping area means it's usually
frequented by men watching English Premiership football
on Sky Television while their wives/girlfriends shop. The
atmosphere is friendly, particularly on weekend afternoons
when it's not too crowded, and the bar staff are pleasant,
although they do tend to get a little overstretched at times.
The Guinness is good and relatively cheap – by Brussels
standards anyway.

O'Neill's
11 avenue de la Toison d'Or, 1050 (511 26 68/502 29 10). Métro Louise or Porte de Namur. **Open** 6pm-2am Mon, Tue, Sun; 6pm-3am Wed; 6pm-4am Thur; 6pm-5am Fri, Sat. **Map C6/D5**
Popular ersatz Irish pub. There's the usual Kilkenny's, Guinness and so on, and it's a popular place for watching English football, rugby and other sport. The location near the Porte de Namur and the Brussels Hilton means there's usually a smattering of Scandinavian businessmen at the bar trying to chat people up. Bar staff are pleasant.

O'Reilly's
1 place de la Bourse, 1000 (552 04 80). Métro Bourse. **Open** 11am-2am Mon, Tue, Thur, Sun; 11am-5am Fri, Sat. **Map B3**
Large 'Irish' pub opposite the Bourse that's always packed and noisy, and a sea of green whenever the Irish football team are in town. Certainly not a place for a quiet (or cheap) pint of Guinness.

Pablo's
51 rue de Namur, 1000 (502 41 35). Métro Porte de Namur. **Open** noon-2am Mon-Sat; *food served* noon-3pm, 6pm-midnight, Mon-Sat. **Map D4**
Cocktail bar serving good Tex-Mex food. Several types of tequila are available, and there are pitchers of Margaritas (800BF for a small one, 1,700BF for a large one). The ambience is more suitable for groups than for an intimate evening. There are cheaper cocktails at the bar for women on Saturdays from 6-11pm.

Rick's Bar
*344 avenue Louise, 1050 (647 75 30). Métro Louise/tram 93, 94. * **Open** 11am-midnight daily; *food served* 11am-11pm daily. **Map C5/D6**
American bar that seems to exert a magnetic force on every US businessman and frat boy in Brussels. Not the place to go if you want somewhere quiet or Continental, but it does a good Sunday brunch, the garden is pleasant in summer, and the cocktails are good.

Wild Geese
2-4 avenue Livingstone, 1040 (230 19 90). Métro Maelbeek. **Open** 11am-1am daily. **Map F3**

An Irish pub in the European district that opened on St Patrick's Day 1995. Packed most evenings with Eurocrats, secretaries, lawyers and students, with a bit of a meat-rack air, especially Friday evenings. Tables outside in summer.

Cafés & tearooms

L'Atelier de la Truffe Noire
300 avenue Louise, 1050 (640 54 55). Tram 93, 94/bus 38, 60. **Open** 8.30am-7pm Mon-Sat. **Map C5/D6**
L'Atelier de la Truffe Noire (it's owned by the grand restaurant, La Truffe Noire, next door) opened at the beginning of 1998, and was immediately highly popular. The menu features sandwiches and pâtisserie, as well as delicacies such as carpaccio, foie gras, and dishes involving truffles (you can also have truffles added to sandwiches for an extra 100BF). There's also a breakfast menu from 8.30-11am. The décor is minimalist – almost Japanese – with leather chairs and simple blinds, but the mix of rich autumnal colours gives it warmth. It all sounds rather precious, but the atmosphere is relatively relaxed, and it's definitely a welcome addition to avenue Louise.

Café Metropole
31 place de Brouckère, 1000 (219 23 84). Métro De Brouckère/bus 29, 60, 65, 66, 71. **Open** 9am-1am daily. **Map C2**
The café of the five-star Hôtel Metropole is sophisticated and elegant, with *fin-de-siècle* high ceilings, stucco, tinted mirrors and plush upholstery. Not somewhere to go and drink pint after pint of traditional Belgian beer; more a place to sip champagne, eat pâtisserie and watch the traffic go by.

Cybertheatre
4-5 avenue de la Toison d'Or, 1050 (500 78 11). Métro Porte de Namur. **Open** 10am-1am Mon-Thur, Sun; 10am-2am Fri, Sat; *food served* noon-2pm, 7-10.30pm, daily. **Map C6/D5**
Huge cybercafé and bar in a converted theatre at Porte de Namur. It's divided into different sections, with one zone for a restaurant, another for free Internet surfing, one for training and homepage building, and one for games. It also stages events such as graphic art exhibitions, video evenings and concerts of ethnic music.

Genever juniper

Discussions of Belgium's alcoholic specialities usually begin and end with the beer, but it's also worth exploring other sections of the drinks menu. The other native alcoholic product of Belgium (and the Netherlands) is genièvre or genever. This, of course, is the origin of gin.

Genièvre is made from pure fermented grain, and ranges from 30 to 50 per cent in strength. It is drunk neat and cold, and you are most likely to come across it in a variety of fruit flavours. Red fruit flavours, such as redcurrant, raspberry, plum and blackcurrant, are particularly refreshing, to the extent that it's tempting to gulp it down like fruit juice. Big mistake…

One drink that appears on virtually every drinks menu in Belgium is *half-en-half*. The exact ingredients of this vary according to the price and the bar, but it's essentially a mixture of white wine and sparkling wine or champagne. It tends to be popular with the old women who frequent places such as Le Falstaff and Le Cirio (*see above*), and certainly worth trying: not only is it cheaper than champagne, but many prefer the taste.

A final word of warning about the Belgian drinks menu: Gordon's and Scotch are not at all what they seem. Both are rich, dark ales, made in Scotland and exported to Belgium (it seems that they are too strong to be sold successfully in the UK). If you want gin and tonic, order *un gin-tonic*; if you want Scotch, order *un whisky* or *un whisky pur malte*.

Le Falstaff

19-25 rue Henri Maus, 1000 (511 87 89/511 98 77).
Métro Bourse. **Open** 10.30am-3am Mon-Fri; 10.30am-
5am Sat, Sun. **Map B3**
Vast and famous art nouveau and art deco café spread across
several rooms, with a covered terrace in front. The customers
are a mixture of young and old, tourists, fur-coated Brussels
bourgeoisie, businessmen and expats. There is a dazzling
choice of Belgian beers and a lengthy menu, if unexciting
food; the long opening hours make it worth bearing in mind.

Le Gallery

7 rue du Grand Cerf, 1000 (511 80 35). Métro Louise.
Open noon-3pm, 6pm-1am, Mon-Sat; 6pm-1am Sun. **Map
C5**
Large, halogen-lit cocktail bar and Vietnamese restaurant
with a sophisticated, slightly 1980s design. It serves good
dim sum and Vietnamese food costing around 350BF per
portion. The art and photography on the walls are for sale.

Hallowe'en

*10 rue des Grands Carmes, 1000 (514 12 56). Métro
Bourse/bus 34, 48, 95.* **Open** 4pm-midnight Mon; noon-
2am Tue-Sat.
A central café based on a horror theme, featuring a monster
sculpture as you go in, candles in skulls and events such as
horror-film screenings and magic shows. Fortunately, the
menu no longer sticks to the theme, and dishes with names
involving young virgins and black widows are no more. The
food itself is innocuous: smoked salmon, endive salad etc.

Indigo

160 rue Blaes, 1000 (511 38 97). Bus 20, 48. **Open**
10am-3pm Tue-Fri; 9.30am-4pm Sat, Sun. **Map B4/B5**
Quirky tearoom very close to the Jeu du Balle flea market
and furnished with junk: rickety tables and fold-up chairs
that the flea market itself might have rejected as too precarious. It serves home-made cakes, breakfast, brunch, salads
and quiches, and is useful for vegetarians.

La Librairie des Etangs

*319 chaussée d'Ixelles, 1050 (646 97 86). Tram 81/bus
71.* **Open** 10am-7pm Mon-Sat; 10am-2pm Sun. **Map
D5/E6**
Small tearoom at the back of an 'international' bookshop near
the Ixelles ponds. There are regular exhibitions of art, which
is for sale, as well as occasional events such as poetry readings in French or English. The shop sells books in English,
French, German, Dutch and Spanish.

Loplop Café Expression

*29 rue de l'Ecuyer, 1000 (512 18 89). Métro Gare
Centrale.* **Open** 9am-4am daily. **Map C3**
Opinions about this 'international pub' vary – some people
rave about the cosmopolitan, multilingual atmosphere, the
organised and impromptu music sessions and the happen-
ings; others think it is best left to foreign students and back-
packers. Either way, there are dozens of beers on offer,
including Guinness and Kilkenny, as well as Scrumpy Jack
and Snakebite. Named after the artist Ferdinand Lop.

The Lunch Company

*18 rue de Namur, 1000 (502 09 76). Métro Porte de
Namur/tram 92, 93, 94/bus 71.* **Open** 10.30am-6pm
Mon-Fri; 11am-7pm Sat.
A 'tearoom' that serves breakfast and excellent and imaginative salads and quiches, as well as sandwiches, cakes and
flavoured teas. The atmosphere is slightly effete and possibly someone's idea of English style, with the menu featuring Whittard's tea, English muffins, and cheese and pickle
toasted sandwiches. Actually, the food and atmosphere far
outstrip any tearoom you are likely to find in England. There
are comfortable wicker chairs, slightly precarious tables and
a little garden at the back.

A Malte

30 rue Berckmans, 1060 (537 09 91). Métro Louise.
Open 10am-2am daily; *food served* 7am-midnight Mon-
Sat, noon-3pm Sun. **Map C6**
Stylish, whimsically decorated café selling delicious sandwiches and tarts, plus some more substantial brasserie food.
Good for whiling away rainy afternoons (of which there are
plenty in Brussels), particularly if you can get the table in
the harem-like gallery at the back. There are tables in the
back garden in the summer. Service can be slow.

Le Pain Quotidien

*16 rue Antoine Dansaert, 1000 (no phone). Métro
Bourse.* **Open** 7am-7pm daily. **Map A2/B2**
A growing chain of bakeries/cafés, Le Pain Quotidien has
spawned several imitators. All branches share a common
design: simple rooms with large wooden tables, and wood-
en dressers containing jams, chocolates and coffee to buy.
Food to eat in includes delicious bread and jam, croissants,
tartines with carpaccio or cheese, *tartes aux pommes* or
aux poires, ice-cream, and stunning chocolate cake and
chocolate brownies.
Branches: 515 chaussée de Waterloo, 1060; 11 rue de
Sablon, 1000; 125 avenue Louise, 1050.

Le Perroquet

*31 rue Watteau, 1000 (511 57 90). Tram 92, 93,
94/bus 34, 95, 96.* **Open** 10.30-1am daily; *food served*
noon-1am daily. **Map C4**
Authentic art nouveau bar just off the Sablon, with mirrors,
stained glass, a black and white tiled floor, and tables outside in summer. Describes itself as a 'resto-bar', and serves
dozens of different stuffed pitta breads (200BF) and various
salads (250-350BF). Popular with young British and Irish
expats.

La Porteuse d'Eau

*48A avenue Jean Volders, 1060 (538 83 54). Métro
Porte de Hal.* **Open** 10am-1am daily. **Map B6**
Renovated art nouveau café in a grimy, unassuming street
in St Gilles. It's light and airy with stained glass, wooden
floor, spiral staircase and a slightly shiny feel. Customers are
a mixture of ages, and smarter than at most bars in the neighbourhood. It's a pleasant enough place to have a drink or
some pâtisserie if you happen to be in the area.

Pp Café

28 rue Van Praet, 1000 (514 25 62). Métro Bourse.
Open noon-3am daily; *food served* noon-2.30pm, 6.30pm-
1am daily.
A relatively new, and highly popular, extension of the empire
of Fred Nicolay, the Terence Conran of Brussels who started Bonsoir Clara, Kasbah (*see chapter* **Restaurants**) and
Zebra (*see above*). Pp Café is housed in the former Pathé
Palace Cinema and has a mixture of original and replica art
nouveau fixtures like gilded lights and William Morris-style
borders on the walls. Customers are young and old, fashionable and not-so-fashionable. The drinks menu caters for
everyone, with a good choice of beer, wine, flavoured vodka,
tequilas, cocktails and fruit juices. The food involves standard Brussels fare like goat's cheese salad, *boudin blanc* and
noir, and steak, as well as more unusual dishes like carrot
cake with saffron and basil. There's a large covered terrace
in the front.

Le Schievelavabo

20 rue Egide Van Ophem, 1180 (332 20 91).
Tram 55. **Open** noon-2pm, 7pm-1am, Mon-Fri;
7pm-1am Sat, Sun.

An oasis in an otherwise unpromising
*corner of St Gilles, **La Porteuse d'Eau***
benefits from the fluid lines of art nouveau.

*The vegetarian options at **L'Ultime Atome** are more extensive than at many Brussels cafés.*

In an ancient building in the southern suburb of Uccle, this is not somewhere you'll stumble on in your peregrinations around the Grand Place, but is a good place to know about if you're staying in this area. Youngish customers sit on old wooden settles and choose from a sizeable list of beers, and the atmosphere is convivial.

SiSiSi

174 chaussée de Charleroi, 1060 (534 12 72). Tram 81, 91, 92. **Open** *10am-2am daily; food served noon-3pm, 6pm-12.30am, daily.* **Map C6**

Once very fashionable, this bar and café has now acquired more of a neighbourhood feel, although the nature of the neighbourhood means that customers are still young, chic and reasonably affluent. Large windows and a site on a road junction make it a good spot to watch the world passing by, and it's popular at lunchtime.

De Skieven Architek

50 place du Jeu de Balle, 1000 (514 43 69). Bus 20, 48. **Open** *9am-1am daily.* **Map B5**

Café overlooking the Jeu de Balle flea market that does breakfast, croissants, sandwiches, ice-cream and oysters. It also sells magazines and newspapers at the front door. There's a garden at the back, and it's less rough-and-ready than the other bars around the square, but service can be non-existent.

De Ultieme Hallucinatie

316 rue Royale, 1210 (217 06 14). Métro Botanique. **Open** *11am-2am daily; food served 11am-2.30pm, 6pm-midnight, daily.* **Map D4/E1**

Famous café (and separate restaurant), with a dingy, inconspicuous exterior and an ornate art nouveau interior of rich wood and pale green ironwork. There is a lengthy beer list and the café menu comprises delicious Belgian staples such as prawn croquettes. A slight drawback is the area, which is well known for thefts, particularly car break-ins.

L'Ultime Atome

14 rue St Boniface, 1050 (511 13 67). Métro Porte de Namur/bus 34, 54, 71, 80. **Open** *9am-12.30am Mon-Fri; 10am-12.30am Sat, Sun; food served noon-12.30am daily.* **Map D5**

Airy and popular L-shaped café with wooden tables and very yellow walls. The relaxed atmosphere makes it a good place to have a drink/wait for someone on your own, but it is equally appropriate for groups, both during the day and in the evening. The food – salads and a few more substantial meals – is good and the vegetarian options more extensive than many places in Brussels. Customers are mostly in their twenties and thirties, but the atmosphere is sufficiently relaxed and cosmopolitan for most ages to feel at home here.

La Vâche Qui Aime Regarder Les Trains

6 rue Jean Stas, 1060 (no phone). Métro Louise. **Map C6**

A tearoom and café just off avenue Louise that sells quiche, salads, tarts, cakes and milkshakes throughout the day. Its setting and the quality of the food make it popular with ladies who shop, and on Saturdays it's always heaving with middle-class women and their daughters. At other times, it is somewhat more relaxed, and it's a useful place for Sundays when much of this area can seem a bit desolate. The place is best known for its ice-cream, which is sold in Le Pain Quotidien (*see above*), and comes in exotic flavours such as vanilla with honey and lavender.

Vert de Gris

63 rue des Alexiens, 1000 (514 21 68). Bus 34, 48, 95, 96. **Open** *noon-2.30pm, 7pm-midnight, Mon-Fri; 7pm-midnight Sat, Sun.* **Map B4**

Bar, restaurant and deli that has no sign outside but is conspicuous enough. The light and airy front room has a modern iron chandelier and large wooden tables. The style changes at the back, with a working humidor, stuffed animals, ancient and modern sofas and palm trees. The food – mainly pasta – is OK but not exceptional.

Shopping
& Services

Shop till you drop, in the consumer society that is Brussels.

Each of the *communes* has retained its local shopping area, with food shops, craft shops, boutiques, and chains such as Di (a kind of second-class Boots without the pharmaceuticals). In St Josse the chaussée de Louvain has a strong ethnic element, reflected in the food stores and clothing outlets. Woluwe and Westland Shopping Centres are two malls housing all the mainstream stores and are frequented by Belgian and expat middle to high income suburban families. Unless you are one of the above, these places should be strictly avoided.

The main shopping districts are concentrated in two areas: uptown and the centre. For the latter, leave the Métro at Gare Centrale or De Brouckère. Although shop-types are concentrated in particular quarters (all the photo shops are on rue du Midi, all the fish shops on the *quais* at Ste Cathérine), each quarter is only a few streets away from another. Uptown is more spread out.

Overall, Brussels has everything you would find in most other major cities, but you should certainly not overlook Antwerp or Ghent (*see chapter* **Trips Out of Town**). Antwerp is trendier and livelier, just a short trip away from Gare Centrale, and many big names have chosen to open there rather than in Brussels.

Sales run only in January and July. Shopkeepers are told exactly on which days to start and which to end, although you will often find unadvertised sales starting a few days before and lasting till a few days after the official dates. 'Promotions' – specific discounts – are allowed and tend to coincide with seasonal events, such as special offers on perfume and chocolates around Valentine's Day.

Shopping districts

Uptown

Boulevard de Waterloo and avenue Louise are the city's answer to Knightsbridge or Fifth Avenue. Foreign business money and vulgar Belgian inheritances are spent in the boutiques of Armani, Chanel, Gucci, Yves Saint Laurent, Cartier, Cacharel and Hermès, which are just some of the names that dot the two avenues. Avenue de la Toison d'Or, with its galleries, is more mid-range, and if none of the shops can be enthused about for originality, neither can they be slated. Bouvy, at no.52, is one of the designer label shops selling the likes of Ralph Lauren and Calvin Klein.

Parallel with avenue Louise is the chaussée d'Ixelles, which branches off to the left towards the Galeries d'Ixelles and the chaussée de Wavre. Chaussée d'Ixelles has most of the main high-street shops, though its more interesting gift shops are found as you approach place Fernand Cocq.

The antiques trail

This leads you from behind boulevard de Waterloo, down through the Petit Sablon, to the Grand Sablon, then along rue des Minimes and rue des Petites Minimes, and on to rue Blaes via rue Haute. At 63 rue Blaes you will find a good source of upmarket bric-a-brac, as well as period furniture (shops also do restorations). Rue Blaes and the place du Jeu de Balle, the centre of the Marolles, has an eclectic mix of shops, combining trendy clothing stores with local bakeries and grocers.

Centre

Rue Neuve is an embarrassment for residents and confounds tourists, being desperately in need of a facelift. Fortunately, this now appears to be on the cards. However, all the international high-street stores such as Morgan, Benetton and Esprit have branches here. The horror culminates in the City 2 mall, with much the same sort of consumer traps, though to its credit you will also find the large record and bookstore **Fnac**. Rue des Fripiers, on the other side of place de la Monnaie, has a more bearable selection of the generic stores.

Behind the Bourse, St Géry, an old market hall, was at one point a huge streetwear shopping centre, but lack of custom forced it to close its doors. The neighbourhood is an interesting mix: a shift down and to the right leads you into the two streets that make up Chinatown. A turn to the left takes you to a few trendy streetwear and record stores. Rue Antoine Dansaert functions as a consortium of young designers and label stores, catering for the trendy yuppie with a large disposable income.

Bright young things

Take a trip down rue Antoine Dansaert, and look at the young designers based there. Most of them are of appeal to twenty- or thirtysomethings; prices tend to be reasonable but not for those on a budget.

Nathalie Vincent at no.84 (502 75 64) has been designing for nearly ten years now, with her distinctive red and black sheer-dominated women's clothes (she also sells jewellery and other accessories).

Nathalie R at no.71 (511 20 06) remains a bastion of women's shoes with square and round toes, only slightly giving in to the fashion for pointed toes. She has recently started designing men's shoes, too.

Nicolas Woit at no.80 (503 48 32) uses new and old silky materials, which he cuts up and patches together to make lovely, soft-lined, slinky clothing.

Patrick Pitschon at no.82 (512 11 76) has a bit of an attitude – and it certainly shows in his clothes.

Bernard Gavilan pour L'Homme Chrétien

1 rue du Marché au Charbon, 1000 (502 01 28). Métro Bourse/tram 23, 52, 55, 56, 81/bus 34, 48, 95, 96. **Open** 11am-7pm Mon-Sat. **Credit** MC, V. **Map B3**
Bernard is a 'transformer' rather than a creator (but not the small silver robot kind, although he is very dinky!). He sells a mixture of customised vintage clothes, mixed with 'new old', a result of strategic raids on warehouses. A lot of the clothes are his own designs: a combination of the latest high-street trends and quirky innovations. He crosses 1970s boogie flared fashion with a marked oriental influence, and he's pushing for an '80s glam revival with lots of stiletto boots. His packed little shop, just off Grand Place, is a shrine to kitsch, and has the most stylish window displays in town. He does a couple of extravagant fashion shows a year.

Johanne Risse

35 place du Nouveau Marché aux Grains, 1000 (513 09 00). Métro Bourse/bus 47, 63. **Open** 10am-6.30pm Mon-Sat. **Credit** AmEx, MC, V. **Map B2**
The minimalist Japanese look of everything in this store is misleading. In fact, it contains everything necessary for a trousseau, including fully fledged wedding dresses, though they have very pure lines. Prices are high.

Jonathan Bernard

53 rue du Midi, 1000 (512 46 20). Métro Anneessens. **Open** 11am-6pm Wed-Thur; 11am-7pm Fri, Sat. **Credit** MC, V. **Map B4**
Loved by hipsters, the ground floor of this boutique holds mainly black, sober but revealing clubwear, along with accessories such as handbags. The first-floor studio does makeovers, costume rentals and design.

Kaat Tilley

4 galerie du Roi, 1000 (514 07 63). Métro Gare Centrale/bus 29, 60, 63, 65, 66, 71. **Open** 10am-6.30pm Mon-Sat. **Credit** AmEx, DC, MC, V.
Her store (*pictured*) is as faerie-like and whimsical as some of the designs, with twinkling lights and hanging branches. Kaat's womenswear is ingeniously constructed with lots of different materials; she also sells very beautiful antique-looking wedding dresses of her own design. This is her flagship boutique, although she sells in France, the Netherlands, the USA and Japan. She tends to send her male customers to another young designer, who specialises in suits, particularly for weddings. These have understated lines and appeal to a thirtysomething crowd. He is: Michel de Mulder, 11-13 rue Léon Lepage, 1000 (512 55 33).

Qu'art by Rita H Valcke

100A rue Africaine, 1060 (537 91 98). Tram 81, 82/bus 54. **Open** 11am-6pm Mon-Tue, Thur-Sat. **Credit** AmEx, DC, MC, V.
This Flemish designer uses fluffy wools in winter and sheers in summer. Her women's clothing is unextravagant, but usually very colourful, and of appeal to all ages.

Ste Cathérine is an up-and-coming area, frequented by art students, but the food shops, such as the Maison du Caviar on quai des Usines, are filled with upmarket fish and luxury goodies. A short walk up is boulevard d'Ypres, with lots of North African foods and cooking essentials.

Rue du Midi offers a good detour, with stamp, coin and art shops. Boulevard Lemonnier, which runs parallel, has old-fashioned wig and fur shops, grocers, and second-hand book and record stores. Perpendicular to rue du Midi, around rue Marché au Charbon and rue Plattesteen, are a host of vintage clothes stores, trendy delis, and boutiques owned by hatter extraordinaire **Elvis Pompilio**.

Up towards Grand Place, around the Manneken Pis, are the tourist-dependent chocolate and lace shops. Rue des Eperonniers has a mixture of bad rock shops and quirky old-fashioned gift stores (La Courte Echelle at no.12 sells dolls' houses and other miniatures). To find the Galeries Agora, a hell-hole of tacky stores selling hippy-dippy grunge, trashy boots and cheap piercing and jewellery, follow the smell of incense.

The beautiful glass-roofed architecture of the Galeries St Hubert arcade dates back to 1846. It now houses upmarket, old-fashioned boutiques (notably the lace store at nos.6-8) and modernist design stores (Ligne at no.12).

The large chocolate store Neuhaus at no.25, Häagen-Dazs at the entrance of the Galeries on the Grand Place side, and a few Parisian-style cafés provide limited sustenance for the tuckered-out retail therapist.

Department stores

Inno
111 rue Neuve, 1000 (211 21 11). Métro Rogier/tram 23, 52, 56, 81, 90/bus 58. **Open** 9.30am-7pm Mon-Thur, Sat; 9.30am-8pm Fri. **Credit** AmEx, DC, MC, V. **Map C2**
Inno now holds the monopoly as the only large Belgian-owned department store. Walking in on the ground floor, you are hit by scents from the omnipresent maze of big-name perfume counters and the rest of the cosmetics department. The five floors feature miscellaneous merchandise from cheap to chic, but the staff clearly want minimal contact with customers. Men's, women's and children's apparel and underwear, bedlinen, bath towels, luggage, toys, crystal, silver, home furnishings and a hairdresser are all nevertheless represented within.
Café. Money-changing service.
Branches: 12 avenue Louise, 1060 (513 84 94); 699 chaussée Waterloo, 1180 (345 38 90); Woluwe Shopping Centre, 1200 (771 20 50).

Marks & Spencer
17-21 rue Neuve, 1000 (218 50 55). Métro De Brouckère/tram 23, 52, 55, 56, 81/bus 29, 60, 63, 65, 66, 71. **Open** 9.30am-6pm Mon-Thur; 9.30am-8pm Fri; 9.30am-6.30pm Sat. **Credit** V. **Map C2**
Things have come to a sad state of affairs when Marks & Spencer does good business out of selling Belgian chocolates in Brussels, but expats will be expats, and some food habits die hard. Having said this, the men's, women's and children's clothing, which make up most of the store, remain

inexpensive and of good quality, with certain items even passing as fashionable these days.
Export tax scheme. Money-changing service.
Branches: 89-95 Meir, 2000 Antwerp (03 203 45 90); 15 place St Lambert, 4000 Liège (04 221 19 90).

Tati
39 rue Neuve, 1000 (223 76 70). Métro De Brouckère/tram 23, 52, 55, 56, 81/bus 29, 60, 63, 65, 66, 71. **Open** 9.30am-6.30pm Mon-Thur, Sat; 9.30am-7pm Fri. **Credit** AmEx, DC, MC, V. **Map C2**
Aptly named, French-owned cheap but not very cheerful department store. Push your way through the crowds to buy clothing, crockery, toys, linen and other household goods, displayed on two floors, mostly in large bins.

Fashion

Designer

Adolfo Dominguez
118 avenue Louise, 1050 (503 18 15). Tram 93, 94. **Open** 10am-6.30pm Mon-Sat. **Credit** AmEx, DC, MC, V. **Map C5/D6**
Elusive Spanish designer sets up shop in Brussels. Long elegant lines for women make for somewhat sober attire but the men's Mao, single-breasted and box suits are trendy.

Balthazar
22 rue du Marché aux Fromages, 1000 (514 23 96). Métro Gare Centrale/bus 34, 48, 95, 96. **Open** 11am-6.30pm Mon-Sat. **Credit** AmEx, DC, MC, V. **Map C3**
Menswear boutique offers ready-to-wear Paul Smith, John Smedley and Comme des Garçons, plus accessories for the image-conscious dandy, at prices you would expect.

Emporio Armani
37 place du Grand Sablon, 1000 (551 04 04). Tram 92, 93, 94/bus 20, 34, 48, 95, 96. **Open** 10.30am-7pm Mon, Wed-Sat; 11am-6pm Sun. **Credit** AmEx, MC, V. **Map C4**
This huge new shop is decked out in traditional Armani minimalist colours. The ground floor is men's clothing and accessories; the first floor has women's clothes, underwear and jeans. Staff are helpful and the clothes stylishly cut.

Francis Ferent
443-445 galeries de la Toison d'Or, 1050 (513 12 49). Métro Louise or Porte de Namur. **Open** 10am-6.30pm Mon-Sat. **Credit** AmEx, DC, MC, V. **Map C5/D6**
A good source for women's labels such as Joseph, DKNY or D&G, but all are still overpriced. The sales assistants are Harvey Nicks assistants *manquées* and they don't pull it off.

Gerald Watelet
268 avenue Louise, 1050 (647 35 50). Tram 93, 94/bus 38, 60. **Open** 10am-6pm Mon-Sat (and by appointment). **Credit** AmEx, DC, MC, V. **Map C5/D6**
Belgian designer Watelet has recently had a return to fortune after being forced to sell, and then buy back, his label. He still works in a studio above his showroom, receiving important (ie loaded) customers only upon appointment for haute couture. Prices are stratospheric, starting at 200,000BF for suits. Items from his classic prêt à porter collections (entitled 'Almost Couture') are available in the downstairs shop.

Gianni Versace
64 boulevard de Waterloo, 1000 (511 85 59). Métro Louise/tram 91, 92, 93, 94/bus 34. **Open** 1-6.30pm Mon; 10am-12.30pm, 1.15-6.30pm, Tue-Sat. **Credit** AmEx, DC, MC, V. **Map B6/D5**
You either love or hate the Eurotrash Versace look, but since his death his collections have had an even higher profile. This opulent boutique is surprisingly airy, with women's

clothes and leather goods on the ground floor, while the sweeping white staircase leads to the men's department. **Branch:** 3 De Keyserlei, 2018 Antwerp (03 232 03 03).

Massimo Dutti
22 avenue de la Toison d'Or, 1050 (289 10 50). Métro Porte de Namur/bus 34, 54, 71, 80. **Open** 9.30am-6.30pm Mon-Fri; 10am-6.30pm Sat. **Credit** AmEx, DC, MC, V. **Map** C6/D5
Upmarket clothing by the same Spanish company that owns Zara (*see below*). Smart, conservative clothes for working men, with some women's clothing and accessories, are of good quality and are well presented in this chrome and silver shop. Prices average around 10,000-15,000BF for a suit; shirts and blouses start under 2,000BF.

Natan
158 avenue Louise, 1050 (647 10 01). Tram 93, 94. **Open** 10am-6pm Mon-Sat. **Credit** AmEx, DC, MC, V. **Map** C5/D6
A cross-pollination of Armani's minimalist refinement and Saint Laurent's glamour best describes the creations of Edouard Vermeulen, the designing force here. Top-of-the-market, ready-to-wear clothes for women with cash to spare.

Nicole Kadine
28 rue Antoine Dansaert, 1000 (503 48 26). Métro Bourse/tram 23, 52, 55, 56, 81/bus 47, 63. **Open** 10am-6.30pm Mon-Sat. **Credit** AmEx, MC, V. **Map** A2/B2
Medieval-look velvets and layers, combined with more oriental hues, make up the long, loose-fitting womenswear at this French-born, Antwerp-based designer store.

Olivier Strelli
72 avenue Louise, 1050 (512 56 07). Tram 93, 94. **Open** 10am-6.30pm Mon-Sat. **Credit** AmEx, DC, MC, V. **Map** C5/D6
A more brightly coloured Calvin Kleinish look is the best way to describe the classic suits from this well-established Belgian designer (even Mick Jagger wears Strelli). A look at the uniforms that he designed for the Sabena air hostesses might give you an idea of his style. The two floors in this shop cover all his men's and women's creations, as well as the lower-cost and more casual line 22 Octobre.
Branches: 14 galerie Louise, 1050 (511 43 83); 62 Frankrijklei, 2000 Antwerp (03 233 51 36); 24 Huidevetterstraat, 2000 Antwerp (03 231 81 41).

Stijl Men/Women
74 rue Antoine Dansaert, 1000 (512 03 13). Métro Bourse/tram 23, 52, 55, 56, 81. **Open** 10.30am-6.30pm Mon-Sat. **Credit** AmEx, MC, V. **Map** A2/B2
Helmut Lang, Raf Simons, Alexander McQueen, Martin Margiela, Ann Demeulemeester, Dries Van Noten and Dirk Bikkembergs all have a patch in this downtown mecca for the trendy professional. A one-stop shop for young professionals in the know.

Thierry Mugler
80 avenue Louise, 1050 (502 64 22). Tram 93, 94. **Open** 10am-6.30pm Mon-Sat. **Credit** AmEx, DC, MC, V. **Map** C5/D6
Walking in, you catch a whiff of Mugler's perfume Angel and realise that this is possibly why the staff's noses are so stuck up. Produce the platinum card and they'll become ever so obsequious. Still, Mugler's clothes are as perfect as the perfectly formed bodies they are made for.

Via della Spiga
42 avenue Antoine Dansaert, 1000 (502 20 97). Métro Bourse/tram 23, 52, 55, 56, 81. **Open** 10.30am-6.30pm Mon-Sat. **Credit** AmEx, DC, MC, V. **Map** A2/B2
Another shop for young champagne trendies with Vivienne Westwood, Jean Colonna, Romeo Gigli and D&G. It is the

only shop in Belgium to sell the exclusive clothes made by Stephen Sprouse, who inspired Warhol and has sole rights of reproduction of the artist's work on clothes.

Mid-range

La Fée Clochette
24 rue du Midi, 1000 (514 18 85). Métro Bourse/tram 23, 52, 55, 56, 81/bus 34, 48, 95, 96. **Open** 11am-6.30pm Mon-Sat. **Credit** AmEx, V. **Map** B4
Solely responsible for the unfortunate but highly successful introduction of Buffalo platform trainers to Brussels youth, which was immediately copied and picked up on by the high-street stores and shows no sign of leaving the capital. Top-priced club gear, costume jewellery and glittery make-up is sold in this haven of kitsch, much loved by drag queens and fashion victims. From 1-6pm Wed-Sat, there is a sale section on the first floor with bewitching prices.

Ming Tsy
124 rue Blaes, 1000 (424 29 68/427 90 29). Métro Porte de Hal or Louise/bus 20, 48. **Open** 10am-6pm Wed-Sat; 10am-4pm Sun. **No credit cards. Map** B4/B5
Taiwanese clothes designer and artist Ming Tsy opened this beautiful shop in April 1997. She uses oriental fabrics to create Audrey Ang-like clothes, scarves and bags, and will make to measure providing you allow her to come up with the design. She also sews together cotton-based paper to make exquisite stationery sets, books, photo albums and paper gift bags. The paper is also sold by the metre.

Privé Joke
8-10 rue des Riches Claires, 1000 (502 73 68). Métro Bourse or Anneessens/bus 34, 47, 48, 95, 96. **Open** 10.30am-7pm Mon-Sat. **Credit** DC, MC, V. **Map** B3
Overpriced but priceless streetwear shop rules the teenage roost in Brussels. It sells Carhartt, E-pure, Greda and Lady Soul, as well as D&C and New Balance shoes, and whatever the latest trendy street label is. The staff are friendly, there's a DJ booth and the place is a good source for flyers.

Zara
8-10 avenue Louise, 1050 (511 37 60). Métro Louise/tram 91, 92, 93, 94. **Open** 9.30am-7pm Mon-Thur; 9.30am-7.30pm Fri-Sat. **Credit** V. **Map** C5/D6
This Spanish high-street chain went down a storm when it first opened and is continuing to create turbulence. One of the attractions of this shop is that there is constant upheaval of stock, and you never seem to see the same item two weeks running, although there is nothing exactly wild about any of the clothes. The whole family can come here to be kitted out, but the women's section is the most successful.
Branches: 48-50 rue Neuve, 1000 (219 87 47); 58 Meir, 2000 Antwerp (03 226 44 25).

Budget

Hennes & Mauritz
123 rue Neuve (City 2), 1000 (0800 999 93/223 23 31). Métro Rogier/tram 23, 52, 55, 56, 81, 90/bus 58. **Open** 9.30am-6.30pm Mon-Thur; 9.30am-7pm Fri, Sat. **Credit** AmEx, DC, MC, V. **Map** C2
The staff and the clothes in this hugely successful Swedish store look like MTV castoffs, which is not to disparage them. There is something for everyone here, whatever your particular fashion statement. Ahead of every high-street trend, H&M does a quality, budget version. The underwear is also excellent for the price, as are the many accessories. Of the four branches in Brussels, the huge garage-like store in City 2 is the trendiest. The 36 rue Neuve branch specialises in 'Big is Beautiful'; no.80 has a maternity section, as well as the basics. All items can be exchanged in any of the H&Ms in

The cutting edge of blade purveying, **Au Grand Rasoir – Maison Jamart**. *See page 125.*

Europe, regardless of which branch they are bought in. Refunds, however, operate within Belgium only, within 14 days of purchase. Stores accept all major European currencies (but not foreign cheques).

Branches: 36 rue Neuve, 1000 (219 48 14); 80 rue Neuve, 1000 (219 03 40); 41-43 chaussée d'Ixelles, 1050 (514 46 66).

Liquidoma

38 rue des Bogards, 1000 (511 52 69). Métro Anneessens/tram 23, 52, 55, 56, 81. **Open** 9.30am-6.30pm Mon-Sat. **Credit** AmEx, DC, MC, V. **Map B4**
The nearest Brussels gets to an army surplus store sells all the army-cum-amateur junglist essentials. Happy campers can also find hiking gear and survival rudiments. Other assorted items include Eastpack rucksacks, jeans, a good selection of combat boots and Airwalks, as well as cowboy chic, with boots, fringed jackets and silver belt-buckles.

Second-hand

Coco

45 rue St Jean, 1000 (512 53 77). Métro Gare Centrale/bus 35, 48, 95, 96. **Open** varies. **No credit cards. Map C4**
A hidden treasure trove, nestling behind a façade of ivy, awaits the retro bargain hunter. But Coco herself is no wallflower and will offer to alter clothes or embark on a lengthy quest for a coveted item in her attic. Upstairs has topsy-turvy 100BF bargain bins containing a mixture of accoutrements. Dusty bronze candlesticks, dark rooms and a fairy-tale atmosphere make it look like a Sleeping Beauty palace, as if everything had been left as it was for 50 years. There is an excellent men's jacket section, a fine selection of hats, and lots of old dresses. Downstairs has shoes, tops, bags and a little showcase crammed full of trinkets and bric-a-brac. Ring to be let in if the front door isn't open.

Les Enfants d'Edouard

175-177 avenue Louise, 1050 (640 42 45). Tram 81, 82, 93, 94/bus 54. **Open** 9.30am-6pm Mon-Sat. **Credit** AmEx, MC, V. **Map C5/D6**
In a swanky (ie tacky) location, this is a large store specialising in designer second-hand items and end of line stock, all in excellent condition, but not at excellent prices.

Idiz Bogam

162 rue Blaes, 1000 (502 83 37). Métro Porte de Hal/bus 20, 48. **Open** 10am-6.30pm daily. **Credit** AmEx, DC, MC, V. **Map B4/B5**
This cubby hole of a store, hiding in the trendy and characterful Marolles, has been around since 1990. It sells 'fripes de luxe': second-hand and vintage clothing at a price, originating from London, New York and Paris. The vast new showroom-sized branch in the centre has even more preserved or updated stock (lots of sequins), including furniture for sale and wedding dresses.
Branch: 76 rue Antoine Dansaert, 1000 (512 10 32).

Look 50

10 rue de la Paix, 1050 (512 24 18). Métro Porte de Namur/bus 54, 71. **Open** 10am-6.30pm Mon-Sat. **No credit cards. Map D5**
Although there is some second-hand mod-style clothing here, the best items are in the window display. Most people come here for the selection of vintage Levis.

Peau d'Ane

37 rue des Eperonniers, 1000 (513 84 37). Métro Gare Centrale/bus 35, 48, 95, 96. **Open** 11am-7pm Mon-Sat. **Credit** MC, V. **Map C3**
Sells a mixture of men's and women's vintage clothes and the shop's own designs. The beauty of this place is that staff will alter the clothes for a perfect fit for just a little extra.

R&V

19 rue des Teinturiers, 1000 (511 05 10). Métro Bourse/tram 23, 52, 55, 56, 81/bus 34, 48, 95, 96. **Open** 11am-7pm Mon-Sat. **Credit** MC, V.
Ramón's mission is to make fashion junkies happy, with a good selection of mainly vintage girls' clothing and lots of shoes. Despite nice clothes, the stock never seems to change.

Shoes & hats

Elvis Pompilio

60 rue du Midi, 1000 (511 11 88). Métro Bourse/tram 23, 52, 55, 56, 81. **Open** 10.30am-6.30pm Mon-Sat. **Credit** AmEx, DC, MC, V. **Map B4**
The interior of this hat shop is Aladdin-meets-Alice in Wonderland. The Mad Hatter is Elvis (the name is real) who hails from Liège, and is never without his trademark cowboy hat. His creations, however, are of all shapes, forms and colours, and not for the shrinking violet. The men's collection next door, with permutations of classic styles such as caps and woolly hats, are similarly extravagant, although all are street-smart wearable. Feathers, net, fake flowers, velvet, felt… are all garnishings on these lavish items, which sell for around 5,000BF. Accessories such as candy-coloured frilly parasols and umbrellas cost around 3,000BF.

Hatshoe

89 rue Antoine Dansaert, 1000 (513 80 90). Métro Bourse/tram 23, 52, 55, 56, 81/bus 63. **Open** 10.30am-6.30pm Mon-Sat. **Credit** DC, MC, V. **Map A2/B2**
Hats and shoes, as the name indicates. The footwear walks a fine line between trendy and traditional (Patrick Cox addicts take note). Hats are by designer Cécile Bertrand.

Preiser

78 chaussée de Wavre, 1050 (511 27 19). Métro Porte de Namur/bus 34, 80. **Open** 9am-6.30pm Mon-Sat. **Credit** AmEx, DC, MC, V. **Map D5/H6**
This store specialises in out-of-the-ordinary sizes. These range from European men's 35 to 52 and from women's 31 to 46. The conservative brands go from the affordable to the downright expensive, with Bally, Clarks and Church alongside the ubiquitous Timberland.
Branch: 59 rue du Midi, 1000 (511 26 02).

Sacha

27-31 rue des Fripiers, 1000 (218 79 65). Métro De Brouckère/tram 23, 52, 55, 56, 81/bus 29, 60, 63, 65, 66, 71. **Open** 10am-6pm Mon-Thur; 10am-7pm Fri-Sat. **Credit** AmEx, DC, MC, V. **Map C3**
Sacha serves up trash for cash but the designs are nevertheless innovative and add spice to Belgian shoelife. Platforms, boots, trainers and docs are all found here.

La Silla

52 rue Antoine Dansaert, 1000 (513 80 90). Métro Bourse/tram 23, 52, 55, 56, 81/bus 47, 63. **Open** 11am-6.30pm Mon-Sat. **Credit** AmEx, DC, MC, V. **Map A2/B2**
Chic, trendy shoes are well displayed in little portholes in the pastel-toned walls of this shop. Italian shoes (mainly for women) start at 5,000BF up to boots at 11,000BF.

Virgin

13 rue des Eperonniers, 1000 (513 14 56). Métro Gare Centrale/bus 35, 48, 95, 96. **Open** 11am-12.30pm, 1.30-6.30pm, Mon-Sat. **Credit** AmEx, DC, MC, V. **Map C3**
Small boutique that does a good and original line in shoes but especially in boots of all sorts, from silver Gary Glitter extravaganzas to the plain black ankle-boot. Some clubby clothes are also sold. Staff are relaxed and friendly.
Branch: 10 rue Antoine Dansaert, 1000 (511 46 03).

Tailors

Maison de Gand
415 avenue Louise, 1050 (649 00 73). Tram 93, 94.
Open 10am-7pm Mon-Sat. **Credit** AmEx, DC, JCB, MC,
V. **Map C5/D6**
Housed in an early twentieth-century private house with
most of its original interior preserved, Maison de Gand has
been creating luxury apparel for men and women since 1981.
Snobbery is required merely to enter this establishment, but
if you have the cash and attitude to spare, you could very
well feel at home. Cufflinks in semi-precious and precious
stones, cravats and other accessories are also on offer.

Underwear

Boutique Minuit
*60 galerie du Centre, 1000 (223 09 14). Métro De
Brouckère/tram 23, 52, 55, 56, 81/bus 29, 60, 63, 65,
66, 71.* **Open** 10.30am-6.30pm Mon-Sat. **Credit** AmEx,
DC, MC, V.
This shop allows you to indulge in your wildest fantasies.
Downstairs has trashy lacy underwear, fluorescent jock-
straps and wild patterns. Upstairs has more hardcore fetish
gear, French maid outfits and rubber. Piercing jewellery is
also sold, along with accessories. Staff are mainly amiable
middle-aged women, so no fear of embarrassment.

Patricia Shop
*158 rue Blaes, 1000 (513 36 48). Métro Porte de Hal/bus
20, 48.* **Open** 9.30am-5.30pm Tue-Sat. **No credit cards.**
Map B4/B5
Most lingerie in Belgium is overpriced, but bargain-hunting
women should not despair. Patricia Shop has bins outside
that have very cheap (we're talking 99-199BF) attractive
bras. End-of-line deals can be caught inside on quality bras
and other underwear, some tacky, some tasteful in design.

Stijl Underwear
*47 rue Antoine Dansaert, 1000 (514 27 31). Métro
Bourse/tram 23, 52, 55, 56, 81.* **Open** 10.30am-6.30pm
Mon-Sat. **Credit** AmEx, DC, MC, V. **Map A2/B2**
Stylish undergarments for guys and gals and beachwear by
the likes of John Smedley, André Sarda, Helmut Lang and
Crummay. It's on the pricey side, but if you like to be avant-
garde in your inner layers, too, then Stijl is where it's at.

Undressed
*58 rue de l'Aqueduc, 1050 (544 08 44). Tram 81,
82/bus 54.* **Open** 1-6.30pm Mon; 10am-6.30pm Tue-Sat.
Credit AmEx, DC, MC, V.
Dutch designer Marlies Dekkers is making her name with a
very idiosyncratic range of women's underwear. Be prepared
to bare all, as her product reveals more than it hides, with a
mainly black, bondage-inspired design, while retaining a
sober, minimalist quality. Prices are reasonable, the beautifully presented shop is well worth the detour, and owner
Nathalie Burhenne and her assistants aren't overbearing.

Entertainment

John Kennis
*12 avenue Marnix, 1000 (512 23 03). Métro Porte de
Namur.* **Open** 9.30am-1pm, 2.5pm, Mon-Fri; 9.30am-1pm,
2-5pm, Sat. **Credit** AmEx, DC, MC, V. **Map D5**
Men's formal attire for hire, with all the trimmings. Black tie
costs 2,400BF (3,000BF with accessories). White tie penguin-
suits are 2,700/3,700BF. Service is efficient and amiable.

Picard
*71-75 rue du Lombard, 1000 (513 07 90)). Métro Gare
Centrale/bus 34, 48, 95, 96.* **Open** 9am-6pm Mon-Sat.
Credit AmEx, DC, MC, V. **Map B3**

For carnival all year round, try this large jam-packed store,
whose colourful window display is hard to miss. The stock
spills over like Mardi Gras, with boas, masks, costumes and
wigs. There is an excellent stage make-up selection and a
practical joke and magic tricks counter.

Fashion accessories

Christa Reniers
*28 rue du Vieux Marché aux Grains, 1000 (514 17
73). Métro Bourse/tram 23, 52, 55, 56, 81/bus 63.*
Open noon-7pm Thur-Sat. **Credit** AmEx, DC, MC, V.
Map B3
Selling in Paris and New York, Belgian jeweller Reniers uses
each new collection as an extension of the old: models are
never deleted, which gives a sense of continuity to the cufflinks, rings, bracelets and keyrings. These are often in silver, but with hints of other metals. The rounded popcorn
shapes mix austerity with extravagance.

Delvaux
*27 boulevard de Waterloo, 1000 (513 05 02). Métro
Louise/tram 91, 92, 93, 94/bus 34.* **Open** 10am-6.30pm
Mon-Sat. **Credit** AmEx, DC, MC, V. **Map B6/D5**
It seems that one of these Belgian-made expensive quality
leather bags with the telltale 'D' is owned by every middle-
class, middle-aged woman in Brussels, but the new collections are an attempt to modernise. Will they stand up to the
competition from the huge Louis Vuitton store opening down
the road in 1998?
Branches: 22 boulevard Adolphe Max, 1000 (217 42 34);
31 galerie de la Reine, 1000 (512 71 98).

Lorenzo Lebon
200 chaussée d'Ixelles, 1050 (646 35 01). Bus 54, 71.
Open 11am-7pm Thur-Sat (and by appointment). **Credit**
AmEx, V. **Map D5/E6**
Ostend-born Lorenzo Lebon creates backpacks and handbags with quirky details (the latest collection has velcro
attachments for mobile-phone leather cases) and whimsical
shapes (an accordion or violin case for instance).

Patrick Anciaux
*7-9 galerie de la Reine, 1000 (511 52 15). Métro Gare
Centrale/bus 29, 60, 63, 65, 66, 71.* **Open** 2-6pm Mon;
11am-6pm Tue-Sat. **Credit** AmEx, DC, MC, V.
Antique jewellery that is glamorously decadent, if a little
pricey. Turn-of-the-century and 1930s costume jewellery are
best represented, and Patrick Anciaux also shows contemporary designers, selling their work in the shop.

Swatch Store
*42 rue du Marché aux Herbes, 1000 (512 98 16). Métro
Gare Centrale or De Brouckère.* **Open** 10am-6.30pm Mon-
Sat. **Credit** AmEx, DC, MC, V. **Map C3**
In the heart of the tourist trail, in an eighteenth-century house
near Grand Place, this cyberspace flagship shop sends off
the right signals. Admire the designs and check the time.

Children

Fashion

Kid Cool
*30 avenue Louise, 1050 (513 39 45). Métro Louise/tram
91, 92, 93, 94/bus 34.* **Open** 10am-6.30pm Mon-Sat.
Credit AmEx, DC, MC, V. **Map C5/D6**
Gap-style comfortable and colourful clothes made for cool
kids from three months to 12 years. A Belgian home-grown
make, the prices are mid-range to expensive, but the clothes
are a nice alternative to the classic Dujardin, which is for the
Belgian young conservative child.

Peau d'Zèbre

*40 rue du Midi, 1000 (513 05 28). Métro Bourse/
tram 23, 52, 55, 56, 81/bus 34, 48, 95, 96.* **Open**
11am-1pm, 2-6pm, Mon-Sat. **Credit** AmEx, DC, MC, V.
Map B4
For trendy tots, miniature versions of high-street fashion and
clubwear are available at moderate prices. The staff were a
little unfriendly on our last visit, but the clothes are definitely
worth a peek.

Toys

In den Olifant

*47 rue des Fripiers, 1000 (219 72 07). Métro De
Brouckère/tram 23, 52, 55, 56, 81/bus 29, 60, 63, 65,
66, 71.* **Open** 10am-6.30pm Mon-Sat. **Credit** AmEx, DC,
MC, V. **Map C3**
This small store sells more wooden, crafted toys than the big
chains, and at reasonable prices. Each level is for a different
age group (the older kids have to climb more stairs) and there
are also magic tricks, poster paints and crayons.

Serneels

*69 avenue Louise, 1050 (538 30 66). Tram 91, 92, 93,
94.* **Ope** 9.30am-6.30pm Mon-Sat. **Credit** AmEx, DC,
MC, V. **Map C5/D6**
Its 300sq m are filled with life-size stuffed (baby) giraffes and
the rest of the jungle. Dolls, electronic gear and all the necessary contents of the BCBG (Bon Chic Bon Genre – Belgium's equivalent of Sloanes) child's playroom are sold at
BCBG prices. A large gambling-game section is attractive to
all age groups. Operates a *carte de fidelité* system with reductions for loyal customers.

Gifts

Au Grand Rasoir – Maison Jamart

*7 rue de l'Hôpital, 1000 (512 49 62). Métro Gare
Centrale/bus 35, 48, 95, 96.* **Open** 9.30am-6.30pm Mon-
Sat. **Credit** AmEx, V. **Map C4**
Supplier to the Royal Court of Belgium, Au Grand Rasoir has
a real old world feel (it's existed since 1821), with excellent
service and a window display filled with quality razors of
every variety. There are mother-of-pearl and bone-crafted
handles on many of the blades, which lie next to Swiss
Army knives of all types. Will carry out repairs, sharpening,
silver-plating.

Bali-Africa

*154-156 rue Blaes, 1000 (514 47 92). Métro Porte de
Hal/bus 20, 48.* **Open** 9am-6pm Mon-Sat; 9am-3pm Sun.
Credit AmEx, DC, MC, V. **Map B4/B5**
Two stores merged into one to create 1,000sq m of display
space, with items crammed on to various levels. Stocking
mainly African art, jewellery and kalimbas (buffalo-skin
drums) but with some Latin American input, too, the owner
claims that all proceeds go to help the developing countries
from which the merchandise originates.

Candar

*164 rue Blaes, 1000 (514 58 77). Métro Porte de Hal/bus
20, 48.* **Open** 10am-6pm Tue-Sat; 10am-4pm Sun.
Credit AmEx, DC, MC, V. **Map B4/B5**
Scented candles and intricate candleholders mix with gleaming, metallic kitchen design items and glow-in-the-dark toys.
The staff are friendly, and the Marolles area is one of the
most interesting in Brussels.

Wittamer – *for all your pastry and
chocolate needs, head to place du
Grand Sablon – see page 128.*

Courrier Sud

*34 rue du Marché au Charbon, 1000 (514 57 09).
Métro Bourse/tram 23, 52, 55, 56, 81/bus 34, 95,
96.* **Open** 11am-6.30pm Mon-Sat. **No credit cards**.
Map B3
Beautiful, well-priced jewellery with ethnic and novelty
items, made mostly from silver with semi-precious stones.
Coloured lanterns and bottles, wallets, bags, picture frames
and other knick-knacks from different parts of the world are
carefully strewn around the shop. The painted parrots on the
shopfront bear no relation to the quality of goods inside.

Dans la Presse ce Jour-là

*23 rue du Lombard, 1000 (511 43 89). Métro Bourse/
tram 23, 52, 55, 56, 81.* **Open** 11.30am-6.30pm Mon-Fri;
11.30am-5pm Sat. **Credit** MC, V. **Map C5/D6**
Novelty birthday gift shop offers a copy of a French, Belgian,
Swiss or British newspaper printed on a specific birthdate.
The shop also does gift packages that include wine, port or
Armagnac from the relevant year.

Histoire d'Eau

646 chaussée de Waterloo, 1050 (343 63 27). Bus 38.
Open 11am-7pm Mon-Sat. **Credit** MC, V. **Map B6**
Luxury toiletries on sale here include almond shaving soap,
shampoos in little bottles, and lots of other potions to lather
yourself in. Bathroom essentials and accessories make for
an upmarket Body Shop – less PC, but more refined.

Maison d'Art G Arekens

*15 rue du Midi, 1000 (511 48 08). Métro Bourse/tram
23, 52, 55, 56, 81/bus 34, 48, 95, 96.* **Open** 10am-1pm,
2-6pm, Mon-Sat. **No credit cards**. **Map B4**
A haven for kitsch collectors with a variety of religious icons
on offer such as crucifixes or triptychs, with a few Buddhas
to make up the balance. There are lots of small plaster-cast
reproductions of non-religious statues, but the shop's real
strength is its 55,000 postcards and reproduction etchings.

La Maison du Bridge

64 rue du Bailli, 1050 (537 43 85). Tram 81, 82, 93, 94.
Open 10am-1pm, 1.30-6.30pm, Tue-Sat. **No credit
cards**.
The name is a bit misleading because every board game
imaginable is sold here, along with larger table games.
Paraphernalia such as card mats and gambling chips are
also sold, plus deluxe chess and backgammon sets.

Ma Maison du Papier

*6 galerie de la rue de Ruysbroek, 1000 (512 22 49). Bus
34, 48, 95, 96.* **Open** 1-7pm Wed-Fri; 3-7pm Sat; and by
appointment. **Credit** MC, V. **Map C4**
This feels like a store of treasures waiting to be unearthed,
with its drawers of prints, plaques and posters of art exhibits
and adverts from the late 1800s to the present.

Nature Gallery

*3 rue de la Reinette, 1000 (502 67 66). Métro Porte de
Namur.* **Open** 10am-6.30pm Mon-Sat. **Credit** MC, V.
This eco-friendly shop sells trinkets with a nature theme
such as botanical prints, aboriginal art and birdsong whis-
tles. Films are projected in the shop and there is an in-store
information desk that can offer advice (but not bookings) on
out-of-bounds nature-themed travel to untouched climes.

Rêves d'Art et de l'Orient

*146 rue Blaes, 1000 (514 31 40). Métro Porte de Hal/bus
20, 48.* **Open** 9am-6pm Tue-Sat; 9am-2pm Sun. **Credit**
AmEx, DC, MC, V. **Map B4/B5**
An outpost of Far and Middle Eastern decorative objects,
from Persian carpets to Indian carvings. Enriched with
Buddha figures, modern and antique, as well as different collectibles such as netsukes (Japanese kimono toggles), the display makes for varied perusal, and purchase at a price.

Rosalie Pompon

65 rue Lebeau, 1000 (512 35 93). Bus 34, 48, 95, 96.
Open 10.30am-6pm Tue-Sat; 10.30am-6.30pm Sun.
Credit DC, MC, V.
Papier mâché Niki de St Phalle statue replicas balance dangerously on the shelves, and you have to avoid the perilous mobiles and hanging bells in this shop cluttered with novelty gift and design items (heart-shaped hand-warmer keyrings, feather-filled transparent inflatable cushions).

Yannart-Remacle

11 rue du Marché au Charbon, 1000 (512 12 26).
Métro Bourse/tram 23, 52, 55, 56, 81/bus 34, 95, 96.
Open 9am-noon, 2-5pm, Mon-Fri. **No credit cards.**
Map B3
All sorts of supplies for jewellers. Best of all, though, are the walls of drawers selling crystals and semi-precious stones. Staff will also do engravings on the stones, and settings.

Flowers

Fleurop-Interflora

(0800 99 669). **Open** 24 hours daily. **Credit** AmEx, DC, MC, V.
The head office of this international florist has a 24-hour hotline for those who feel the need to say it with flowers.

Het Witte Gras

7 rue Plétinckx, 1000 (502 05 29). Métro Bourse
or Anneessens/tram 23, 52, 55, 56, 81/bus 34, 47,
48, 95, 96. **Open** 9am-6pm Mon-Sat. **Credit** AmEx, DC, V.
Fresh flowers spill out of terracotta pots and vases that are also for sale. Competitive prices.

Hobbies, arts & crafts

L'Estampe

71 rue Blaes, 1000 (512 87 27). Métro Porte de Hal/bus 20, 48. **Open** 10am-12.15pm, 2-5pm, Tue, Thur-Sat; 10am-2pm Sun. **No credit cards. Map B4/B5**
Fashion sketches, hunting and historical scenes, and nature prints of animals, insects and fruit are arranged in a carefully calculated clutter to give the shopper the impression of sifting through rubble.

La Fiancée du Pirate

118 rue Blaes, 1000 (502 11 93). Métro Porte de Hal/bus 20, 48. **Open** 10am-2pm Tue, Thur, Sat, Sun. **Credit** MC, V. **Map B4/B5**
The smell of the sea hits you as you enter. Chests, lanterns, aged maps and portholes from old wrecks are just some of the nautical items on display.

Fig's

5 rue des Grandes Carmes, 1000 (512 02 80).
Métro Anneessens/tram 23, 52, 55, 56, 81/bus 34,
48, 95, 96. **Open** 11am-6.30pm Mon-Sat. **Credit** AmEx, DC, MC, V.
At first sight, this looks like a small hardware store, but on closer inspection you realise that each packet contains not nails but dozens of tiny silver figurines. It also sells games, helmets and swords for role-playing aficionados.

Fourmi

211 rue Vandekindere, 1180 (345 84 65). Tram 23, 90.
Open 10am-6pm Mon-Sat. **Credit** V.
Nothing in this shop is ready-made. Beads of all varieties, silk-paints, plaster, boxes, cane, threads, paper, silk sold by the metre, felts and other materials, as well as books to read up on all sorts of hobbies and crafts, are available for the craft-oriented.

Markets

Each of the 19 *communes* in Brussels has a local market. They are usually one of two types: brocante (rommelmarkten in Flemish), which sell bric-a-brac; or markets that sell food, plants and other items, sometimes with brocante. The following are the most popular in the city. Credit cards are not accepted.

Sablon

The area around the Grand Sablon (*tram 92, 93, 94/bus 20, 48*) is where old money (or discreet new money) shops for antiques, art and home furnishings. A small market featuring mostly collectibles (coins, china, stamps and so on) is held at weekends (9am-6pm Sat; 9am-2pm Sun).

Grand Place

Grand Place (*Métro Gare Centrale/bus 34, 48, 95, 96*) is the site of a medium-sized daily flower market (8am-6pm) and a bird market on Sundays (9am-1pm).

Gare du Midi

The Marché du Midi (*Métro Gare du Midi/tram 23, 52, 55, 56, 81, 82, 90/bus 20, 49, 50, 78*) is one of the largest markets in Europe, attracting throngs of residents and out-of-towners every Sunday morning, although the building work on the Eurostar terminal impedes it somewhat. From 6 or 7am, stalls selling fresh and dried fruit, veg, fish and meat set up on disused train tracks, under flyovers, and in parking lots adjacent to the station. There's a heavy Mediterranean and North African flavour, with a maze of stands selling a wide variety of produce: olives, cheeses, fresh herbs and spices. Cheap clothing, cassettes of rai music, plants and flowers are also sold, the latter going for a song as the market draws to a close, usually around 1pm. If you are a woman it is best not to (a) wear a short skirt or (b) go alone.

Marolles

The flea market in the cobblestoned place du Jeu de Balle (*Métro Porte de Hal/bus 20, 48*) is held every day (7am-2pm depending on the weather) and features a lot of junk that is worth sifting through. Records, costume jewellery, army coats, assorted furniture and home accessories make up the bulk of the goods on offer. Tuesday and Thursday are the best days, while on Friday and Saturday prices seem to increase.

Historic Marine

39A rue du Lombard, 1000 (513 81 55). Métro Bourse/ tram 23, 52, 55, 56, 81/bus 34, 95, 96. **Open** 10.30am-7.30pm Mon-Sat. **Credit** AmEx, DC, MC, V. **Map B3**
Selected nautical paraphernalia, with models from the Maritime Museum in Paris; can't really be described as the bargain hunter's dream but will appeal to marine fans. Down the road is the aviation equivalent, with the same owners, and there will be a surprise themed shop opening late 1998.

Kasoeri

31 rue de la Paix, 1050 (514 22 51). Métro Porte de Namur/bus 71. **Open** 10.30am-6.30pm Mon-Sat. **Credit** AmEx, DC, MC, V. **Map D5**
The spools of Indian cottons, wools, silks and linen range from subdued materials to richly hued patterns, many of them hand-woven. Also sells buttons of bamboo, coral, coconut and shell, and hand-painted comforters and scarves.

La Maison du Timbre – Belgasafe

24 rue du Midi, 1000 (512 63 49). Métro Bourse/tram 23, 52, 55, 56, 81/bus 34, 48, 95, 96. **Open** 9.30-11.30am, 1-5.30pm, Mon-Fri; 9.30am-noon Sat. **No credit cards. Map B4**
One of the many specialised stamp stores along rue du Midi, selling necessary aids such as cutters and display books.

Sougné

33 rue Antoine Dansaert, 1000 (511 03 07). Métro Bourse/tram 23, 52, 55, 56, 81/bus 63. **Open** 8.30am-6.30pm Mon-Sat. **No credit cards. Map A2/B2**
Since 1929 Sougné has been selling a fine selection of fishing gear and outerwear for angling enthusiasts. The art deco interior has a timeless charm and the service, although sometimes glacially slow, is more personal than larger stores.

Tissus du Chien Vert

2 rue du Chien Vert, 1080 (411 54 39). Tram 18. **Open** 10am-6pm Mon-Sat. **No credit cards. Map A1**
Two windowed floors for fake-fur enthusiasts and lovers of material comforts. A pool table on which to cut fabric, a boat to store it in, a lifesize plane, and a punch-bag for customers' amusement make up the quirky decor.
Branch: 50 quai du Charbonnage (opening June 1998).

Art supplies & stationery

Ali Photo Video

150 rue du Midi, 1000 (511 71 65). Métro Anneessens/tram 23, 52, 55, 56, 81/bus 34, 48, 95, 96. **Open** 9am-6pm Mon-Sat. **Credit** AmEx, MC, V. **Map B4**
Just one of the many photo-video shops along this road, selling mainly new cameras of all makes. If any of the others don't have what you are looking for, you are sure to be sent here. It also buys, sells and exchanges second-hand cameras – look out for offers posted on the board – as well as developing photos (slides are a speciality).

Ordning & Reda

44 rue des Fripiers, 1000 (223 49 90). Métro De Brouckère/tram 23, 52, 55, 56, 81/bus 29, 60, 63, 65, 66, 71. **Open** 10.30am-7pm Mon-Sat. **Credit** V. **Map C3**
Swedish stationery shop with primary-coloured paper, notebooks, sketchbooks and photograph albums, all with pure, minimalist design. Everything is excellent quality and environment-friendly. Staff are helpful, which makes the prices you pay for the sake of style a little easier to swallow.

Schleiper

151 chaussée de Charleroi, 1060 (538 60 50). Tram 91, 92. **Open** *supplies* 8.30am-6.15pm Mon-Fri, 9.30am-6.15pm Sat; *framing* 9.30am-12.15pm, 1.30-6.15pm, Mon-Sat. **Credit** AmEx, DC, MC, V. **Map C6**

This mammoth art shop has all types of art supplies organised on several floors, and an efficient framing department. Prices are not low, but goods are cheaper than in most art shops and the shop operates a loyalty card system.
Branch: 135A rue du Midi, 1000.

Auctions

Galerie Moderne

3 rue du Parnasse, 1050 (511 54 15). Métro Trône/bus 38, 54, 60, 95, 96. **Sales** twice monthly. **Viewing** preceding Fri-Sun. **Map E5**
One of the largest auction venues in Brussels, its first sale of the month features top-of-the-market arts and antiques. The second sells bric-a-brac and household odds and ends, often obtained through the owners' having gone bankrupt or owing back taxes.

Galerie Vanderkindere

685 chaussée d'Alsemberg, 1180 (344 54 46). Tram 23, 55, 90/bus 48. **Open** 9am-noon, 2-5pm, Mon-Fri. **Sales** phone for dates of the monthly auctions and catalogue.
If seventeenth- and eighteenth-century art and *objets* are your cup of tea, this auction house is a must. Items coming under the hammer include museum-quality collectibles.

Palais des Beaux Arts

10 rue Royale, 1000 (513 60 80). Métro Parc or Gare Centrale/tram 92, 93, 94/bus 29, 38, 60, 63, 65, 66, 71. **Open** 10-11.30am, 2-6pm, Tue-Fri. **Sales** monthly, plus specials (phone for schedule). **Map D4/E1**
The sales held here have the largest collection of fine art and antiques, elegantly displayed in huge exhibition rooms. The auctions are also among the most expensive.

Food

Maison du Miel

121 rue du Midi, 1000 (512 32 50). Métro Anneessens/tram 23, 52, 55, 56, 81/bus 34, 48, 95, 96. **Open** 9am-6pm Mon-Sat. **No credit cards. Map B4**
The shop, open since 1887, is about the size of a beehive, buzzing with every type of honey imaginable.

La Truffe Noire

300 avenue Louise, 1050 (640 54 55). Tram 81, 82, 93, 94. **Open** 10am-7pm Mon-Sat. **Credit** MC, V. **Map C5**
This upmarket *traiteur* service linked to the restaurant really thinks a little too much of itself. However, the food is worth the expense, and is exquisitely refined.

Bakeries

Dandoy

31 rue au Beurre, 1000 (511 03 26). Métro Bourse/tram 23, 52, 56, 81/bus 34, 96. **Open** 8.30am-6.30pm Mon-Sat; 10.30am-6.30pm Sun. **Credit** DC, MC, V. **Map C3**
The best melt-in-your-mouth speculoos (traditional Belgian biscuits baked in wooden moulds), *frangipanes* (almond-flavour cakes) and *pains à la grecque* in town.

Le Pain Quotidien

16 rue Antoine Dansaert, 1000 (502 23 61). Métro Bourse/tram 23, 52, 55, 56, 81/bus 47, 63. **Open** 7.30am-7.30pm daily. **No credit cards. Map A2/B2**
Tearoom-bakery chain with pseudo-rustic décor and large common dining table. Croissants, brownies, tartes au citron and many other delicacies. *See also chapter* **Cafés & Bars**.
Branches too numerous to list.

La Wetterenoise
*12 rue de Tabora, 1000 (512 15 19). Métro De
Brouckère/tram 23, 52, 55, 56, 81/bus 29, 63, 66, 71.*
Open 7am-7pm Mon-Sat. **No credit cards. Map B3**
Cutest shop in the chain. It's a tiny place containing rustic-
looking stone-baked breads and scrummy baguettes.
Branches too numerous to list.

Chocolate

Léonidas
*46 boulevard d'Anspach, 1000 (218 03 63). Métro De
Brouckère/tram 23, 52, 55, 56, 81/bus 29, 60, 63, 65,
66, 71.* **Open** 9am-6.30pm Mon-Sat; 10am-6pm Sun. **No
credit cards. Map B3**
Sweet and sickly pralines at a good quality-to-price ratio (relatively cheap). Although a tad too creamy for connoisseurs,
they are perfectly palatable. Service is assembly-line style
and main foreign currencies are accepted.
Branches too numerous to list.

Mary's
*73 rue Royale, 1000 (217 45 00). Tram 92, 93, 94/bus
29, 63, 65, 66.* **Open** 9am-6pm Tue-Fri; 9am-noon, 2-
5pm, Sat. **Credit** MC, V. **Map D4/E1**
For *la crème de la crème*, Mary's is altogether a classier alternative to the mid-range Corné, Neuhaus or Godiva, which
have branches all over town. The beautiful décor is matched
by the care taken in the box presentation.

Pierre Marcolini
*39 place du Grand Sablon, 1000 (538 42 24). Tram 92,
93, 94/bus 20, 34, 48, 95, 96.* **Open** 10am-6.30pm daily.
Credit AmEx, DC, MC, V. **Map C4**
Young prize-winning chocolate-maker fast making a name
for himself with his many chocolate and sugar sculptures.
Branch: 137 avenue Reine Astrid, 1950 (721 24 71).

Planète Chocolat
*57 rue du Midi, 1000 (511 07 55). Métro Bourse/tram
23, 52, 55, 56, 81/bus 34, 48, 96.* **Open** 10am-6.30pm
Tue-Sat; 1-6.30pm Sun. **Credit** MC, V. **Map B4**
A mini-Willy Wonka factory where you can see the chocolate pouring out of taps into huge barrels, ready to be made
into reasonably priced, sculpted chocolates. Confectioner
Frank Duval gives group tours explaining the history of
chocolate-making and culminating in a sampling, all for
220BF a head. Relax with fellow chocoholics in the tearoom.

Wittamer
*6 & 12 place du Grand Sablon, 1000 (512 37 42). Tram
92, 93, 94/bus 20, 34, 48, 95, 96.* **Open** 7am-7pm daily.
Credit AmEx, DC, MC, V. **Map C4**
The pastry cook and chocolate-maker *ne plus ultra* is in a
snooty central location. The delicious light pastries and pralines are a treat for the eyes. No.6 is the chocolate shop and
no.12 the bakery.

Delicatessens

L'Atelier Gourmand
470 rue Vandekindere, 1180 (344 51 90). Tram 23, 90.
Open 8.30am-7pm Mon-Sat. **No credit cards.**
A little out of the way, but worth the effort. Chef Richard
Kopp prepares almost everything himself, from the breads
used for the sandwiches to the gleaming platters of French,
Greek and other European specialities. All quite expensive.

Au Suisse
*73-75 boulevard Anspach, 1000 (512 95 89). Métro
Bourse/tram 23, 52, 55, 56, 81/bus 34, 48, 95, 96.*
Open 10am-8pm Mon-Fri; 10am-9pm Sat, Sun and public
holidays. **No credit cards. Map B3**

A Brussels institution since 1876, this is the place to nip into
for real Belgian fare, either to take out or to eat in. There's
nothing Swiss about this place, despite the name and the
flags. The staff resemble Mesdames Pipis (loo attendants)
but get in their good books and you might be able to skip
the very long queue at lunchtime. Customers are an eclectic
mix of authentic gruff Belgians and young trendies. The deli
has two long counters serving a large selection of salads,
cheeses, cold meats, traditional Belgian maatjes (herrings),
tête pressée (brawn), filet américain (a raw minced beef concoction) and other sandwich fillings. The other counter
serves hot and cold drinks, including home-made milkshakes
and freshly pressed juices, and a small selection of pastries.

Health food

Den Teepot
*66 rue des Chartreux, 1000 (511 94 02). Métro Bourse/
tram 23, 56, 81.* **Open** 8.30am-7pm Mon-Sat; *restaurant*
noon-2pm Mon-Sat. **No credit cards. Map B3**
A good selection of healthy snacks and more substantial
food, frozen and fresh produce, as well as natural eastern
health and beauty products. Organises vegetarian cooking
lessons, and is considering giving them in English, too.

Shanti
*68 avenue Adolphe Buyl, 1050 (647 88 60). Tram 93,
94/bus 71.* **Open** 9am-7pm Mon-Fri; 10am-6.30pm Sat.
No credit cards.
Vegetarian shop attached to a restaurant of the same name
(*see chapter* **Restaurants**).

International cuisine

African Asian Foods
*25 chaussée de Wavre, 1000 (514 03 86). Métro Porte de
Namur/bus 34, 80.* **Open** 9am-8pm Mon-Sat. **No credit
cards. Map D5/H6**
In the heart of Matonge, AAF is one of many grocers selling
African produce including salted fish, oils, fruits and veg.

La Ferme Landaise
*41-43 place Ste Catherine, 1000 (512 95 39). Métro De
Brouckère or Ste Cathérine.* **Open** 8.30am-6pm Mon-Sat.
Credit AmEx, DC, MC, V. **Map B2**
Duck liver pâté, Sauternes and rich prepared specialities of
the south of France. Special orders are also made up as gifts.

Tagawa Superstore
*119 chaussée de Vleurgat, 1050 (648 59 11). Tram 81,
82, 93, 94/bus 38, 60.* **Open** 9.30am-7pm Mon-Sat. **No
credit cards.**
Japanese expats and japanophiles congregate in this upmarket supermarket with two floors of food, including fresh and
frozen fish, Japanese cookies and salted biscuits.

MTM
*25-27 boulevard d'Ypres, 1000 (217 71 49). Métro Yser/
tram 18.* **Open** 8am-5pm Mon-Thur, Sat. **No credit
cards. Map B1**
The warehouse for the former 'morning market' of the neighbourhood, MTM sells a variety of strong-smelling North
African fresh herbs, spices and other ingredients, ranging
from coriander (its is exceptional) to couscous grains.

Sun Wa Chinese Supermarket
*2-4 rue de la Vierge Noire, 1000 (512 58 33). Métro
Bourse/tram 23, 52, 55, 56, 81/bus 47.* **Open** 9am-7pm
Mon-Sat. **No credit cards. Map B2/B3**
This large supermarket is the place to shop for your oriental essentials. And that doesn't mean the selection of Chinese
porn that sits by the cash desk, but the choice of Chinese fruit
teas, tinned and dried fuits, spices, noodles, rice etc.

Delve for bargains at **Pêle-Mêle** *– see p133.*

Drink

Ak'wa
16 place St Géry, 1000 (513 15 70). Métro Bourse/ tram 23, 52, 55, 56, 81/bus 34, 48, 95, 96. **Open** 4-8pm Thur; 11am-6.30pm Fri, Sun. **No credit cards**. **Map B3**
Opened in April 1997, this shop is taking off slowly. Only bottles of water and non-alcoholic and sugar-free drinks are sold. The limited stock may be reflected in the idiosyncratic opening times. Home delivery service is available.

Alexopoulos Frères
17 boulevard d'Ypres, 1000 (218 74 85). Métro Ste Cathérine/tram 18. **Open** 8.30am-6pm Mon-Sat. **No credit cards**. **Map B1**
If you're a big retsina or ouzo fan, this store is worth a visit. Other Greek wines and spirits are also sold, but there is a slight catch: most are sold in quantities of minimum 6 or 12 bottles. Get stocked up.

Bière Artisanale
174 chaussée de Wavre, 1050 (512 17 88). Métro Porte de Namur/bus 34, 80. **Open** 11am-7pm Mon-Sat. **Credit** MC, V. **Map D5/H6**
Welcome to beer heaven, which is getting bigger and better all the time. There are over 400 different types of beer available, along with the essential matching glasses, and gift packages. Owner Nasser Eftekhari also runs beer-tasting sessions and classes, in several languages including English. The Internet site is worth checking out for more information on the store and to place an order for home delivery (you can also telephone): http://users.skynet.be/beermania/. The shop even delivers internationally (600BF per 30kg is added to the basic price for postage to the UK); the beer's so good it's easily worth the extra expense.

De Boe
36 rue de Flandre, 1000 (512 32 26). Métro Ste Cathérine. **Open** 9am-1pm, 2-6pm, Tue-Fri; 7am-6pm Sat. **Credit** AmEx, DC, MC, V. **Map A2/B2**
For over 100 years, De Boe has been selling coffee (both new mixes and traditional flavours such as arabica) and teas from all around the world. Fine wines and chocolate are also sold.

La Maison du Thé
11 rue Plattesteen, 1000 (512 32 26). Métro Bourse/ tram 23, 52, 55, 56, 81/bus 34, 48, 95, 96. **Open** 9am-6pm Tue-Sat. **Credit** MC, V.
For a special cuppa choose from one of the 50 teas on offer in this old-fashioned shop. Also sells teapots, coffeepots etc.

Le Comptoir des Eaux
129 rue Franz Merjay, 1050 (346 43 90). Tram 91, 92/bus 54. **Open** 10.30am-7pm Tue-Sat. **No credit cards.**
Over 100 different types of water, still or fizzy, flavoured with therapeutic Chinese herbs and other extras.

Home furnishings
Design
100% Design
30 boulevard Anspach, 1000 (219 61 98). Métro De Brouckère/tram 23, 52, 55, 56, 81/bus 29, 60, 63, 65, 66, 71. **Open** noon-6.30pm Mon; 10am-6.30pm Tue-Sat. **Credit** AmEx, DC, MC, V. **Map B3**
Inflatable chairs and cushions in acidic greens and pinks.

Coutellerie du Roi
27 passage du Nord, 1000 (217 54 94). Métro De Brouckère/tram 23, 52, 55, 56, 81/bus 29, 60, 63, 65, 66, 71. **Open** 9.30am-6.30pm Mon-Sat. **Credit** AmEx, DC, MC, V.
This shop has been at the cutting-edge since 1750 and even has cigar and sugar-cube cutters, as well as more traditional knives and scissors. It also does repairs.

Cristallerie Anspach
123 boulevard Anspach, 1000 (512 76 96). Métro Anneessens or Bourse/tram 23, 52, 55, 56, 81/bus 34, 48, 95, 96. **Open** 9am-6.30pm Mon-Sat. **Credit** AmEx, DC, MC, V. **Map B3**
If you're a fan of crystal statuettes, a trip to this shop where Baccarat, Waterford, Lalique and Val Saint Lambert (the token Belgian effort) are all represented is worth it.

Max
90-101 rue Antoine Dansaert, 1000 (514 23 27). Métro Bourse/tram 23, 52, 55, 56, 81/bus 47, 63. **Open** 10.30am-6.30pm Tue-Fri; 11am-6pm Sat. **Credit** AmEx, DC, MC, V. **Map A2/B2**
Kidney-shaped coffee tables and colourful high-backed Jetsons-style chairs. Smaller home furnishings such as lamps and vases are more affordable.

L'Objet du Désir
14 rue de Tabora, 1000 (512 61 47). Métro De Brouckère or Bourse/tram 23, 52, 55, 56, 81/bus 29, 60, 63, 65, 66, 71. **Open** 10.30am-6.30pm Mon-Sat. **Credit** AmEx, DC, MC, V. **Map B3**
Gadget and novelty appliance design shop, with ideal items for the yuppie wedding lists it also organises.
Branch: 21 place du Sablon, 1000 (512 42 43).

Au Tapis Magique
7-8 place du Jeu de Balle, 1000 (511 01 63). Métro Porte de Hal/bus 20, 48. **Open** 9.30am-6pm Tue-Sat; 9.30am-3pm Sun. **Credit** AmEx, DC, MC, V. **Map B5**

Hole-in-the-wall shop on the edge of the market place with a good selection of carpets. Haggling should be attempted.

La Vaisselle au Kilo
8A rue Bodenbroek, 1000 (513 49 84). Tram 92, 93, 94/bus 20, 34, 48, 95, 96. **Open** 10am-6pm Mon-Thur, Sat; 10am-6.30pm Fri; 10am-5.30pm Sun. **Credit** JCB, MC, V. **Map C4**
A bull in this china shop would have to be careful, as it's chock-full. Cheap crockery and glassware are mostly priced by the kilo, but items in some ranges can be bought singly.

Music & video

BCM
6 Plattesteen, 1000 (502 09 72). Métro Bourse/tram 23, 52, 55, 56, 81/bus 34, 48, 95, 96. **Open** 11am-6.30pm Mon-Sat. **No credit cards.**
An excellent selection, which specialises in techno (with the industrial Belgian edge), house and drum 'n' bass on vinyl. It's possible to come across some real finds here. There's also a more limited CD section. Staff are very helpful and relaxed.

Caroline Music
20 passage St Honoré, 1000 (217 07 31). Métro De Brouckère/tram 23, 52, 55, 56, 81/bus 29, 60, 63, 65, 66, 71. **Open** 10am-6pm Mon; 9.30am-6.30pm Tue-Sat. **Credit** MC, V.
This varied and extensive range of CDs continues to resist the invasion of the megastores. Huge sections are devoted to indie rock and French music. A good source for gig tickets.

Doctor Vinyl
1 place St Géry, 1000 (512 73 44). Métro Bourse/tram 23, 52, 55, 56, 81/bus 34, 48, 95, 96. **Open** 10.30am-6.30pm Mon-Sat. **Credit** DC, MC, V. **Map B3**
New vinyl, techno, house and drum 'n' bass.

Fnac
City 2, rue Neuve, 1000 (209 22 11). Métro Rogier or De Brouckère/tram 23, 52, 55, 56, 81. **Open** 10am-7pm Mon-Thur, Sat; 10am-8pm Sat. **Credit** MC, V. **Map C2**
Branch of the French chain, carrying CDs and cassettes (*see also below* **Newsagents & bookshops**).

Free Record Shop
18 rue Fossé aux Loups, 1000 (217 88 99). Métro De Brouckère/tram 23, 52, 55, 56, 81/bus 29, 60, 63, 65, 66, 71. **Open** 10am-7pm Mon-Sat; noon-6pm Sun. **Credit** AmEx, DC, MC, V. **Map C2**
Huge selection and the helpful assistants will order anything you want. There are 15 listening booths, and a huge collection of videos for sale, many in English. **Branches:** 147 rue Wayez, 1070 (523 49 18); 42 chaussée d'Ixelles, 1050 (512 13 54).

Médiathèque
Passage 44, 44 boulevard du Jardin Botanique, 1000 (218 26 35). Métro Rogier/tram 23, 52, 55, 56, 81, 90/bus 58. **Open** 10am-6pm Mon-Thur, Sat; 10am-9pm Fri. **No credit cards. Map C2/D2**
This large, dark institution rents out all media, with an extensive and eclectic selection of CDs and videos. The non-subtitled 'version originale' section is quite small but more arthouse than the average local video shop.

Mélopée
12 rue Plattesteen, 1000 (502 33 83). Métro Bourse/tram 23, 52, 55, 56, 81/bus 34, 48, 95, 96. **Open** 10.30am-7pm Mon-Sat. **Credit** DC, MC, V.
A gold mine for film soundtrack buffs. The selection runs from classics to kitsch, with the latest blockbuster themes, too. Mainly stocks CDs, with some vinyl and laserdisc films.

Musicanova
24 galerie d'Ixelles, 1050 (511 66 94). Métro Porte de Namur/bus 34, 71, 80. **Open** 10am-7pm Mon-Sat. **Credit** MC, V.
Located in Matonge, the lively African quarter, this small shop boasts a fine selection of African, Caribbean and Latin American music and a lively rumbustious atmosphere.

Music Mania
4 rue de la Fourche, 1000 (217 53 69). Métro De Brouckère/tram 23, 52, 55, 56, 81/bus 29, 60, 63, 65, 66, 71. **Open** noon-6.30pm Mon-Fri; 11am-6pm Sat. **Credit** MC, V. **Map B3**
The best independent music shop in town mainly sells vinyl, and is much loved by DJs. Staff are way too cool with their vast knowledge, but this is part of the attraction of a shop where you can spend hours sorting through records and listening to them on the decks at the counter.

Orbit
99-103 rue du Marché au Charbon, 1000 (503 41 20). Métro Anneessens/tram 23, 52, 55, 56, 81/bus 34, 48, 96. **Open** 10am-6pm Tue-Sat. **Credit** MC, V. **Map B3**
Mainly sells microphones, decks, samplers, mixing tables and some other professional studio equipment.

Virgin Megastore
Anspach Shopping Centre, 1000 (219 90 04). Métro De Brouckère/tram 23, 52, 55, 56, 81/bus 29, 60, 63, 65, 66, 71. **Open** 10am-7pm Mon-Thur, Sat; 10am-8pm Fri; noon-7pm Sun and public holidays. **Credit** AmEx, MC, V. **Map C3**
Only one floor, albeit vast, with 50 listening stands. However, it does stock vinyl.

Newsagents & bookshops

Adagio
7-9 rue des Eperonniers, 1000 (511 12 46). Métro Gare Centrale/bus 35, 48, 95, 96. **Open** 9am-6pm Mon-Fri; 9.30am-6pm Sat. **Credit** MC, V. **Map C3**
Scores of scores, books about instruments and music theory.

Darakan
9 rue du Midi, 1000 (512 20 76). Métro Bourse/tram 23, 52, 55, 56, 81/bus 34, 48, 95, 96. **Open** 11am-6.30pm Mon-Sat. **Credit** MC, V. **Map B4**
Books on film and photography. It's a good place to track down detective novels and obscure comics.

Fnac
City 2, rue Neuve, 1000 (209 22 11). Métro Rogier or De Brouckère/tram 23, 52, 55, 56, 81. **Open** 10am-7pm Mon-Thur, Sat; 10am-8pm Sat. **Credit** MC, V. **Map C2**
The book stock is excellent in all languages. The French and English sections are strong, and the prices aren't too bad. Smaller publishing houses are represented in all languages, which is rare for such a generic store.

Grande Muraille
5 galerie de la rue de Ruysbroek, 1000 (512 14 56). Tram 92, 93, 94/bus 20, 48, 95, 96. **Open** 2-6pm Mon; 10am-6pm Tue-Sat. **Credit** AmEx, V. **Map C4**
For its wealth of choice, this is the best store in Brussels for books, video cassettes and brochures on traditional Chinese medicine, philosophy and cooking.

Stijl Underwear *is where it's at for stylish smalls for guys and gals – check out rue Antoine Dansaert. See page 123.*

Your permanent domicile is outside the European Union. (E.U.)

You spend more than BEF 5001,- VAT included in one shop.

You export the goods outside the E.U. within three months after the month of purchase.

Your Global Refund Cheque/Tax-free Shopping Cheque needs a Customs stamp when you exit the E.U.

YOU ARE EXITING THE EUROPEAN UNION

• From Brussels National Airport

⇨ The goods are in your luggage

1. First of all go to the Customs (to the right of Passport Control) and show your goods before checking in.
2. Leave your Global Refund Cheque/Tax-free Shopping Cheque with the Customs and check in your luggage.
3. Pass through passport control and take back your Cheque stamped by Customs.
4. Go to INTERCHANGE counter and cash your Cheque.*

⇨ The goods are in your and hand luggage

Get your Custom stamp in the latest location when exiting the E.U.

• From another airport or border crossing

Where you are exiting the E.U. ask Customs to stamp your Cheque and look for the Global Refund Office and cash your cheque.

You can also mail your Cheque to Global Refund Belgium and mention your complete home address and/or credit card number of Belgian bank account number.

*Rate of VAT 21% = 17,35% of selling price. In some cases the rate is 6%. Global Refund service = VAT amount less an administration charge. No refunds available on purchases of tobacco.

 GLOBAL REFUND™

House of Paperbacks

813 chaussée de Waterloo, 1180 (343 11 22). Tram 23, 90/bus R, W. **Open** 10am-6pm Tue-Sat. **Credit** AmEx, DC, MC, V. **Map B6**
Situated on the first floor of a townhouse, this English-language bookstore has a homey feel. The shelves are well stocked and the staff extremely helpful.

Librairie de Rome

50B avenue Louise, 1050 (511 79 37). Métro Louise/ tram 91, 92, 93, 94. **Open** 7.30am-9pm Mon-Fri; 8.30am-9.30pm Sat; 8.30am-8.30pm Sun. **Credit** AmEx, DC, MC, V. **Map C5/D6**
The best place to get international fashion and special interest mags and newspapers.

Sterling Books

38 rue du Fossé aux Loups, 1000 (223 62 23). Métro De Brouckère/tram 23, 52, 55, 56, 81/bus 29, 60, 63, 65, 66, 71. **Open** 10am-7pm Mon-Sat; noon-6.30pm Sun. **Credit** MC, V. **Map C2**
This latest addition to the English-language literary scene operates an interesting system whereby the books are sold at the sterling cover price at that day's exchange rate, plus 6% VAT. Alternatively, staff accept payment in sterling. Two airy floors cater for eclectic reading habits. The ground-floor fiction selection offers a few trashy bestsellers and an excellent selection of contemporary fiction, including fringe publishers. The first floor has well-stocked computer, travel and dictionary sections. The manager, who used to work in an Islington bookshop, hopes to hold poetry readings and similar events to attract a more artsy crowd. A good selection of English-language magazines and newspapers is on sale, as are children's books. Staff will order books.

Tropismes

galerie des Princes, 1000 (512 88 52). Métro Gare Centrale/bus 29, 60, 63, 65, 66, 71. **Open** 1.30-6.30pm Mon-Sun; 10am-6.30pm Tue-Thur; 10am-8pm Fri; 10.30am-6.30pm Sat. **Credit** AmEx, DC, MC, V.
A convincing take on an airy Parisian Left Bank bookshop, with philosophy, fine art, architecture and like topics making up the bulk of the material.

L'Univers Particulier

194 chaussée de Charleroi, 1060 (538 17 77). Tram 81, 82, 91, 92. **Open** 10am-7pm Mon-Sat. **Credit** AmEx, DC, MC, V. **Map C6**
The place for occult and New Age books in French, as well as tarot cards and other spiritual/psychic paraphernalia.

WH Smith

71-75 boulevard Adolphe Max, 1000 (219 27 08). Métro Rogier/tram 23, 52, 55, 56, 81, 90/bus 58. **Open** 9.30am-6.30pm Mon; 9am-6.30pm Tue-Thur, Sat; 9am-7pm Fri. **Credit** AmEx, MC, V. **Map C2**
A good selection of English reading materials does not really justify the exorbitant prices charged here. Nevertheless, a steady stream of folk make their way to the shop to flick through the wide choice of magazines and newspapers, which staff do allow you to skim (and sometimes even read). The book sections stretch over two floors. Books can be ordered, but expect a fortnight's wait.

Comics

La Boutique Tintin

13 rue de la Colline, 1000 (514 45 50). Métro Gare Centrale or De Brouckère. **Open** 11am-6pm Mon; 10am-6pm Tue-Sat. **Credit** AmEx, DC, MC, V.
This flagship store sells Tintin strips and memorabilia such as clothes, statuettes, mugs and stationery, as well as albums of Hergé's other cartoon creations.

Bière Artisanale – *beer heaven – see p129.*

Brüsel

100 boulevard Anspach, 1000 (502 35 52). Métro Bourse/tram 23, 52, 55, 56, 81/bus 34, 48, 95, 96. **Open** 10.30am-6.30pm Mon-Sat. **Credit** AmEx, DC, MC, V. **Map B3**
One of the best out of the multitude of comic shops in the area, selling perennial Belgian favourites such as *Tintin, Lucky Luke, Quick* and *Flupke* or *Le Chat*, as well as *The Far Side* or *Calvin & Hobbes*, in most major European languages. Brüsel also sells tea-sets, figurines, posters and other collector's items.

Le Dépôt

108 rue du Midi, 1000 (513 04 84). Métro Anneessens/ tram 23, 52, 55, 81/bus 34, 48, 95, 96. **Open** 10am-6.30pm Mon-Sat. **Credit** V. **Map B4**
Large store selling and dealing in new and second-hand comic strips, plus vinyl and CDs.
Branches: 120-122 chaussée d'Ixelles, 1050 (511 75 04); 142 chaussée d'Ixelles, 1050 (513 46 22).

De Schaar

24 place Fontainas, 1000 (512 47 82). Métro Anneessens/tram 23, 52, 55, 56, 81. **Open** 11am-7pm Mon-Fri; 11am-6pm Sat. **No credit cards. Map B3**
Strips, comics, manga, vinyl, CDs, posters, books and videos (120BF/2 days rental of cult classics from directors such as David Lynch or Visconti) to tickle the fancy of cult fans of all types.

Schlirf

752 chaussée de Waterloo, 1180 (648 04 40). Bus 38. **Open** 10.30am-7.30pm Mon-Sat; 10.30am-6.30pm Sun. **No credit cards. Map D5/H6**
Specialising in American comics, as well as a wide choice of Belgian comic strips, this bookshop also sells art books.

Second-hand bookshops

De Slegte
*17 rue des Grandes Carmes, 1000 (511 61 40). Métro
Bourse/tram 23, 52, 55, 56, 81/bus 34, 48, 95, 96.*
Open 9.30am-6pm Mon-Sat. **Credit** AmEx, DC, MC, V.
Claims to have the largest selection of second-hand books in
Belgium. The five floors cover mainly Flemish, but also
French, English and German books.

Pêle-Mêle
*55 boulevard Maurice Lemonnier, 1000 (548 78 00).
Métro Anneseens/tram 23, 52, 55, 56, 81.* **Open** 10am-
6.30pm Mon-Sat. **No credit cards. Map A4/B4**
Pêle-Mêle buys and sells. The French section is huge and
chaotic, and paperbacks are very cheap at 15-55BF, while
Flemish, as usual, gets short shrift. The large English section comprises a high proportion of romance, sf and crime
fiction, but delving and browsing reveals bargain classics
and surprise treasures.

P Genicot
*6 galerie Bortier, 1000 (514 10 17). Métro Gare
Centrale/bus 35, 48, 95, 96.* **Open** noon-7pm Mon-Sat.
Credit AmEx, DC, MC, V.
This gruff literary connoisseur has a selection of antique and
second-hand books arranged alphabetically in this gallery
behind Grand Place. About 90% of the stock is in French,
although there is a small English-language crime section.

Postcards

Plaizier
*50 rue des Eperonniers (513 47 30). Métro Gare
Centrale/bus 35, 48, 95, 96.* **Open** 11am-1pm, 2-6pm,
Tue-Sat. **Credit** AmEx, MC, V. **Map C3**
A bit different from your average card shop, with an artsy
Flemish twist. Good selection of beautiful novelty postcards
by photographers, arranged alphabetically.

Health & beauty

Hairdressers

Burlesque
*64 rue du Midi, 1000 (513 01 22). Métro Bourse/tram
23, 52, 55, 56, 81/bus 34, 48, 95, 96.* **Open** 10am-6pm
Tue-Sat. **No credit cards. Map B4**
Hairdresser Lorenz dexterously wields a pair of scissors and
a bottle of hair dye to produce good cuts and flamboyant
colouring, and he will create extravagant coiffures for the
adventurous. With his international multilingual touch he
has built up a faithful if gullible clientele: prices seem to vary
depending on his appreciation of you.

Nicole & Jocelyn
*37 chaussée de Wavre & 18-19 galerie d'Ixelles, 1050
(511 28 74). Métro Porte de Namur/bus 34, 71, 80.*
Open 9.30am-7pm Mon-Fri; 8.30am-7pm Sat. **Credit**
AmEx, DC, MC, V. **Map D5/H6**
Specialises in Afro hair, including dreads and extensions.

Saunas

Bio Etna Centre
*31 place de Brouckère, 1000 (219 24 68). Métro De
Brouckère/tram 23, 52, 55, 56, 81/bus 29, 60, 63, 65,
66, 71.* **Open** 10am-10pm daily. **Credit** V. **Map C2**
Billed as a relaxation centre where visitors can avail themselves of a sauna, Turkish steam bath and other facilities.
Massage, shiatsu, reflexology, facials and peelings are some
of the other comforts with which you can pamper yourself.

Cosmetics

Ici Paris XL
*63 rue Neuve (219 22 07). Métro De Brouckère/tram 23,
52, 55, 56, 81/bus 29, 60, 63, 65, 66, 71.* **Open** 9.30am-
6.30pm Mon-Sat. **Credit** AmEx, DC, MC, V. **Map C2**
One of the largest stores in the chain, carrying a wide selection of men's and women's fragrances. A lot of the toiletries
are cheaper than at other stores around town.
Gift-wrapping. Tax-free for exports worth over 7,000BF.
Branches *too numerous to list; phone 511 33 06.*

Make-Up Forever
*62 rue du Midi, 1000 (512 10 80). Métro Bourse/tram
23, 52, 55, 56, 81/bus 34, 48, 95, 96.* **Open** 9.30am-
7pm Mon-Sat. **Credit** AmEx, DC, MC, V. **Map B4**
All the colours of the rainbow in little pots. Ostensibly for
professional make-up artists and hairdressers, this shop is
also frequented by those who like quality cosmetics. It is a
beauty salon as well, offering all the essentials such as man-
icures, waxing, facials and make-up sessions. If you go ten
times you get the eleventh session for free – worth taking
advantage of, as the prices are also colourful.

Opticians

Optic No 1
*25 avenue de la Toison d'Or, 1050 (514 53 34). Métro
Louise/tram 91, 92, 93, 94.* **Open** 10am-6.30pm Mon-
Sat. **Credit** AmEx, DC, MC, V. **Map C6/D5**
Just one of the many spectacles supermarkets in town, this
one claims to be the cheapest. See what you think; compare
the prices for names such as Versace, Armani and Trisadi.

Tattooists & piercers

European Tattoo Academy
*23 boulevard Maurice Lemonnier, 1000 (502 43 52).
Métro Anneessens/tram 23, 52, 55, 56, 81.* **Open** 2-
10pm Mon-Sat. **No credit cards. Map A4**
The environment in this tattoo surgery is sterile and reas-
suringly antiseptic. Ring to enter and browse through the
catalogues or bring your own design and the two tattooists
will do it justice. Some piercing also done, but limited to ears,
eyebrows, noses and navels. Prices are extortionate.

Piercing Arkel
*1 avenue Brigade Piron, 1080 (410 87 99). Bus 63, 82,
85.* **Open** by appointment only. **No credit cards.**
This piercer's reputation has spread by word of mouth. She
runs a private piercing parlour, charging reasonable rates:
usually 1,000BF + jewellery (which starts at 200BF, and
which she orders from the renowned Wildcat in Brighton).
She will do all piercings, in a very sterile environment (don't
be intimidated when she leads you down to the cellar).

Sporting goods

Heaven
58 rue des Minimes, 1000 (502 45 60). Bus 20, 34, 48.
Open noon-5pm Mon; 10am-6.30pm Tue-Sat. **Credit**
MC, V. **Map B5**
Multicoloured kites, frisbees, boomerangs and other flying
objects are sold for beginners and seasoned fanatics. The
designs range from the decorative (butterflies) to the stylised
aerodynamic (Cayman sport kites) to the plain silly (cows).

Inline
*12 rue des Riches Claires, 1000 (502 73 68). Métro
Bourse/tram 23, 52, 55, 56, 81/bus 34, 48, 95, 96.*
Open 10.30am-7pm Mon-Sat. **Credit** MC, V. **Map B3**
Sells inline skates (from about 5,000BF), which haven't quite

*Fancy a cuppa? Over 50 different teas are on offer at **La Maison du Thé** – see page 129.*

taken off in Brussels as yet (too many cobbles). Apart from blading accessories, they also stock Casio G-shock watches.

Olympus Sports
54A rue Neuve, 1000 (227 51 02). Métro De Brouckère/tram 23, 52, 55, 56, 81/bus 29, 60, 63, 66, 71. **Open** 10am-6.15pm Mon-Sat. **Credit** AmEx, MC, V. **Map C2**
Trainers, clothing, children's sizes and equipment. Rivals the more established Footlocker, with friendlier staff and prices.

Ride all Day
39 rue St Jean, 1000 (512 89 22). Métro Gare Centrale/bus 35, 48, 95, 96. **Open** noon-6.30pm Mon-Sat. **No credit cards. Map C4**
One of the original and best skateboarders in town, Yves Tchao has it really sussed. His excellent skatestore caters for the hardcore of faithful groupies who use it as a hangout just a short cruise away from the skate hotspot that is neighbouring Mont des Arts. He has monopolised the market by cashing in on the Japanese and Scandinavian skaters. RAD focuses on selling the boards themselves but also has clothes and shoes. Staff (all diehard skaters) offer tips and advice.

Pets

Tom & Co
200 avenue Georges Henri, 1200 (779 28 90). Métro Gribaumont/bus 20, 28, 80. **Open** 9am-6.30pm Mon-Sat. **No credit cards.**
Pet supermarket for those who like to pamper.
Branches *too numerous to list; phone 481 25 27.*

Dry-cleaning

De Geest
41 rue de l'Hôpital, 1000 (512 59 78). Métro Gare Centrale/bus 35, 48, 95, 96. **Open** 8am-7pm Mon-Fri; 8am-6.30pm Sat. **No credit cards. Map C4**

Fur, suede, leather, carpets, curtains and upholstery. There's a pick-up and delivery service.

Mister Minit
City 2, rue Neuve, 1000 (223 34 70). Métro Rogier/tram 23, 52, 55, 56, 81, 90/bus 58. **Open** 10am-7pm Mon-Sat. **No credit cards. Map C2**
Fast shoe-repairs, key-cutting and rubber stamps. Most areas have a local *cordonnier*, but this is a good alternative.
Branches *too numerous to list.*

Travel agents

Connections
19 rue du Midi, 1000 (550 01 00). Métro Bourse/tram 23, 52, 55, 56, 81/bus 34, 48, 95, 96. **Open** 9am-7pm Mon-Fri; 10am-4pm Sat. **Credit** MC, V. **Map B4**
Excellent, friendly, trilingual service, offering cheap deals for students as well as for the over-26s. Staff have information and can make reservations on buses, planes, trains, boats and accommodation, and they sell ISIC cards.
Branch: 78 avenue Adolphe Buyl, 1050 (647 06 05).

Pharmacies

Look for the green crosses for your nearest chemist, who has a monopoly on pharmaceuticals – even aspirin can't be bought anywhere else. Phone 0900 105 00 for the nearest chemist on night duty and open at weekends.

Internet access

Best bets for hooking up are:
Belgacom's Skynet *(0800 933 20).*
Ping *(070 23 37 72).*

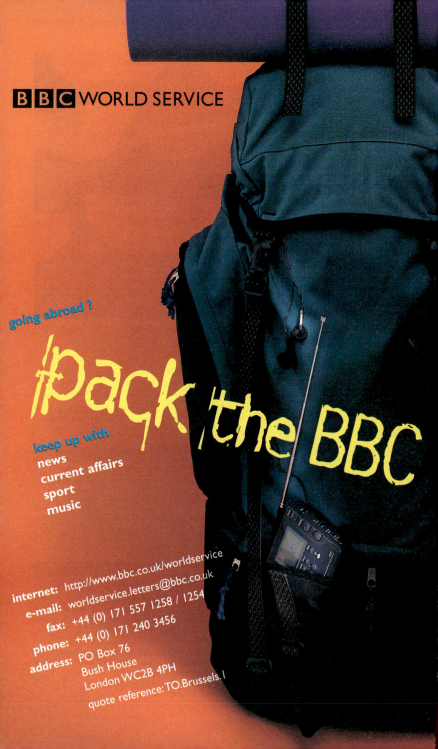

Accommodation

**From the spectacular to the sterile to the downright dodgy...
Brussels has rooms for just about everyone.**

One of the advantages of living in a city that's been taken over by Eurocrats is the plethora of hotels. – far more of them than you would normally find in a city of this size. Many hotels specialise in clients who come for less than a week and are content with cleanliness, efficiency and lack of character. If you value individuality over uniformity, it pays to choose your hotel carefully.

The Belgian Tourist Reservation Office (513 74 84/fax 513 92 77) is a free service, using a comprehensive list of hotels and quoting relevant discounts, which can be up to 50 per cent or more. For those on a more modest budget, there are bargains to be had: many hotels offer cheap deals at weekends and over the summer. If you prefer to book accommodation yourself, you can get the Tourist Reservation Office hotel list from the Tourist Information Office (504 03 90/fax 504 02 70).

STAR RATINGS

Star ratings are given to hotels by the government. Stars are a guide to the number of services the hotel offers, rather than the innate quality of the establishment. A good hotel offering many services will have more stars than an excellent one that offers fewer services. All prices quoted here are standard charges for rooms with a WC and a shower or bath. Cheaper hotels frequently offer the option of communal facilities, which can be a boon if you're on a tight budget. Equally, if you are going the bargain route, make sure that you specify if you want en suite facilities when reserving.

Most of the hotels listed here will have no difficulty in dealing with your enquiries in English.

Hotels

Very expensive

Conrad Brussels

71 avenue Louise, 1050 (542 42 42/fax 542 43 00). Tram 93, 94. **Rates** *single* 13,000-17,500BF; *double* 14,000-18,500BF; *suite* 30,000-75,000BF; *breakfast* 350-900BF. **Credit** AmEx, DC, JCB, MC, TC, V. **Map C5/D6**
The Conrad has the distinction of being one of the largest hotels in Brussels that aspires to luxury and elegance as much as efficiency. From the vast, chandliered ground-floor lounge furnished with tapestried wing-back chairs, chintz sofas, polished maple tables and marble floors, to the well-appointed rooms that live up to the lobby's promise, the Conrad's old-style restrained opulence almost makes you forget it has only been open since 1993. If it has one fault, it is

that the ultra-professional approach can leave you a bit cold; cosy it ain't. Otherwise, it is one of Brussels' finest.
Hotel services *Air-conditioning. Babysitting. Bar. Car park. Conference facilities. Currency exchange. Disabled: rooms. Fax. Gift shop. Laundry. Lifts. Multilingual staff. Non-smoking floors/rooms. Sauna. Shoe shine. Sport/fitness facilities. Restaurants.* **Room services** *Bath robes. Data communication facilities. Electrical transformer & adapters. Fax. Hairdryer. Toiletries kit. Telephone (3 extensions, voicemail). TV.*

Hilton Brussels

38 boulevard de Waterloo, 1000 (504 11 11/fax 504 21 11). Métro Louise or Porte de Namur/bus 34. **Rates** *single* 9,500-12,900BF; *double* 9,500-12,900BF; *suite* 23,000-46,000BF; *breakfast* 690-890BF. **Credit** AmEx, DC, JCB, MC, TC, V. **Map B6/D5**
To slag off a Hilton for its lack of individual character is to miss the point: this is the hotel for the frequent traveller who wants the feeling of instant familiarity, whether in Abu Dhabi or Albuquerque. And let's face it: it does excel at providing comfort. The Sunday brunch has become a Brussels institution with the city's expat community.
Hotel services *Air-conditioning. Babysitting. Business*

Conrad Brussels – *one of the city's finest.*

HOTEL ★★
"Accueil Stéphanie"

→ Town Center: Royal Palace Area

→ Bed & Breakfast

→ Single: 1.400 BF - Double: 2.000 BF - Triple: 2.200 BF
Group (+ 10 persons): 900 BF/person in double room

→ 10% reduction for your inquiry + reservation by fax

11, Rue de la Grosse Tour

1000 Brussels Ⓜ Louise

Tel.: 32-2-511 82 26

Fax: 32-2-513 82 16

Mobilphone: 32-75 94 30 60

On avenue Louise, the four-star, Norwegian-owned **Hôtel Bristol Stéphanie** – see p140.

centre. Car park. Conference facilities. Currency exchange. Disabled: room. Fax. Garage. Gift shop. Gym. Laundry. Lifts. Multilingual staff. Non-smoking floors. Piano bar. Sauna. **Room services** Hairdryer. Minibar. Radio. Refrigerator. Room service. Safe. Telephone. TV.

Le Meridien
3 carrefour de l'Europe, 1000 (548 42 11/fax 548 40 80/info@meridien.be). Métro Gare Centrale. **Rates** *single* 10,000BF; *double* 12,000BF; *suite* 17,500-32,000BF; *breakfast* 850-950BF. **Credit** AmEx, DC, JCB, MC, TC, V. **Map C3**
Another hotel that's cashed in on the business boom, and on the jaded traveller's yearning for familiarity. The cavernous colonial-style lobby features a giant brass chandelier suspended from the ceiling, while a pianist tinkles nightly for guests. The rooms are spacious and warmly decorated in English Victorian repro style. Ultra-convenient and efficient. **Hotel services** Air-conditioning. Babysitting. Bars (2). Business centre. Conference facilities. Currency exchange. Disabled: rooms (2). Fax. Fitness machines. Gift shop. Ice-machines on each floor. Laundry. Lifts. Multilingual staff. Non-smoking floors (2). Restaurants (2). **Room services** Bath robes. Fax. Hairdryer. Minibar. Modem. Radio. Room service. Safe. Telephone. TV (pay & cable). Toiletries kit.

Radisson SAS Hotel
47 rue Fossé aux Loups, 1000 (219 28 28/fax 219 62 62). Bus 29, 63, 65, 66, 71. **Rates** *single* 11,000-13,000BF; *double* 12,000-14,000BF; *suite* 18,000-40,000BF; *breakfast* 590BF. **Credit** AmEx, DC, JCB, MC, TC, V. **Map C2**
Finished in 1991, the Radisson SAS is a joint venture of the American and Scandinavian companies that form its name – and it exemplifies the ultra-professional (if a tad too programmed) approach that you'd expect from these two companies. Crisp, clean, efficient: it's the perfect hotel to stay in if you're in town on business. With glass lifts travelling up the atrium and a seven-floor-high skylight with a lounge and goldfish pond below, the Rad SAS feels like the swankiest mall you've ever been in. Each room is decorated in one of

four styles – Italian, Scandinavian, Oriental or Royal Club – which is apparent mostly in the carpeting, curtain or bedspread selection (if you're expecting a futon or tatami mat in the oriental room you're out of luck: the only Asian touches are the gingko leaf patterned rug and vaguely Japanese-styled lamps and cupboards). The Scandinavian room does feature teak floors, which combat allergies because, unlike carpeting, they don't hold dust. The Royal Club rooms are finer versions of the single and double rooms, with art deco-esque furniture and a more intimate atmosphere. The Radisson has rooms that are among the most spacious in Brussels, and it's just a five-minute walk to Gare Centrale. **Hotel services** Air-conditioning. Babysitting. Business centre. Bars (2). Car park. Conference facilities. Currency exchange. Disabled: rooms. Fax. Gym. Hairdryer. Ice-machine on each floor. Jacuzzi. Laundry. Lifts. Massage. Multilingual staff. Non-smoking rooms. Sauna. Shoe shine. Restaurants (2). **Room services** Fax. Hairdryer. Minibar. Modem. Trouser press. Radio. Refrigerator. Room service (24 hours). Safe. Telephone with voicemail. TV (pay & cable).

Expensive

Amigo
1-3 rue de l'Amigo, 1000 (547 47 47/fax 513 52 77). Tram 23, 52, 55, 56, 81/bus 34, 48, 95. **Rates** *single* 6,700-7,300BF; *double* 7,750-9,000BF; *executive* 12,450BF; *suite* 16,500-28,600BF; *extra bed* 1,200BF. **Credit** AmEx, DC, JCB, MC, TC, V.
If your first impression upon walking into the Amigo is that it has been around for ages, you're half right: the hotel was built for Brussels' 1958 World's Fair, but much of the materials and furnishings used were taken from buildings as old as sixteenth century – flagstones and tiling from medieval abbeys, Aubusson tapestries, Empire and colonial-styled armoires and chairs, and Flemish paintings. For many the Amigo is the most Belgian of the city's larger hotels (only the Métropole comes close in catching the city's character). Built on the site of an old jail (another jail still sits across the

Le Dixseptième – *23 rooms – see p145.*

way), the Spanish Renaissance-style 'mansion' hotel is a favourite of opera singers, French stars and starlets, and ministers. A two-minute walk from Grand Place.
Hotel services *Air-conditioning. Babysitting. Bar. Car park. Conference facilities. Currency exchange. Disabled: rooms. Laundry. Multilingual staff. Non-smoking rooms. Restaurant.* **Room services** *Hairdryer. Minibar. Radio. Room service. Safe. Telephone. TV/VCR.*

Carrefour de l'Europe
110 rue du Marché aux Herbes, 1000 (504 94 00/504 95 00/hotelcde@hotelcde.com). Métro Gare Centrale. **Rates** *single* 8,100-11,100BF; *double* 9,100-12,100BF; *suite* 18,100BF. **Credit** AmEx, DC, JCB, MC, TC, V. **Map B3**
One of four hotels that sprawl inter-connected across from the Gare Centrale like a theme park. Borderline swanky.
Hotel services *Air-conditioning. Babysitting. Bar. Beauty salon. Conference facilities. Currency exchange. Laundry. Lifts. Multilingual staff. Non-smoking floor/rooms. Restaurant.* **Room services** *Fax/computer plug-in. Hairdryer. Minibar. Radio. Refrigerator. Room service. Safe. Telephone. Trouser press. TV/VCR. Website: http://www.hotelcde.com*

Château du Lac
87 Château du Lac, 87 avenue du Lac, 1332 Genval (655 71 11/fax 655 74 44). Train to Genval. **Rates** *single* 5,825-9,825BF; *double* 7,050-11,050BF; *suite* 22,000-25,550BF. **Credit** AmEx, DC, JCB, MC, TC, V.
South of Brussels in the upscale community of Genval, this hotel is worth noting as a place to get away from it all. On a small lake, this four-star deluxe pile has all the regal charm you would expect from its name, but its 98 spacious rooms have all modern creature comforts. The fitness centre housed in the building's newer addition is a separate entity from the hotel, but is used by many guests.

Hotel services *Aerobics. Air-conditioning. Babysitting. Bar. Body styling. Conference facilities. Currency exchange. Disabled: rooms. Gym. Jacuzzi. Laundry. Lifts. Massage. Multilingual staff. Non-smoking floor/rooms. Relaxation pool. Sauna. Sporting facilities. Restaurants. Sunbed. Yoga.* **Room services** *Fax/computer plug-in. Hairdryer. Minibar. Radio. Refrigerator. Room service. Safe. Telephone. Trouser press. TV/VCR.*

Crown Plaza
3 rue Gineste, 1210 (203 51 51/203 44 44). Métro Rogier/tram 23, 52, 55, 56, 81, 90. **Rates** *single* 6,800-9,900BF; *double* 7,800-10,900BF; *suite* 12,000-19,000BF; *extra bed* 1,000BF; children under 12 free with parents. **Credit** AmEx, DC, JCB, MC, TC, V. **Map D1/D2**
Formerly the Palace Hôtel, this 1910 art deco building has recently been renovated to combine its glorious architectural heritage with all the modern comforts. Rita Hayworth, Orson Welles, Brigitte Bardot and Grace Kelly are among its former guests.
Hotel services *Bar. Conference facilities. Laundry. Lifts. Multilingual staff. Restaurant.* **Room services** *Hairdryer. Radio. Telephone. TV.*

Hôtel Bristol Stéphanie
91-93 avenue Louise, 1050 (543 33 11/fax 538 03 07). Tram 93, 94. **Rates** *single* 8,200-9,200BF; *double* 9,200-10,200BF; *suite* 15,000-35,800BF; *extra bed* 1,000BF; *breakfast* 600BF. **Credit** AmEx, DC, JCB, MC, TC, V. **Map C5/D6**
Though this four-star hotel was bought four years ago by a Norwegian group, it has retained an English name evoking its original owners. The anglo-inspiration remains in its decor, in the airy but intimate lobby of tapestry-upholstered armchairs and blue-and-gold curtains. The rooms have an efficient but spartanly elegant feel, while the suites on the tenth floor are more personable: each is individually decorated in the style of a Scandinavian chalet, with features such as a seashell-shaped bath and a sauna. Cute. Right on avenue Louise, which is the closest thing Brussels gets to New York's Fifth Avenue.
Hotel services *Air-conditioning. Babysitting. Bar. Car park. Conference facilities. Currency exchange. Disabled: rooms. Garage. Laundry. Lifts. Multilingual staff. Non-smoking floor/rooms. Swimming pool. Restaurants (2).* **Room services** *Free tea & coffee. Hairdryer. Kitchenette (in 17 rooms). Radio. Refrigerator. Room service. Safe. Telephone. Trouser press. TV (satellite & cable).*

Métropole
31 place de Brouckère, 1000 (217 23 00/fax 218 02 20). Métro De Brouckere/tram 23, 52, 55, 56, 81. **Rates** *single* 9,500-12,500BF; *double* 11,000-14,000BF; *suite* 15,000-35,000BF; *extra bed* 1,000BF; *pet in room* 500BF. **Credit** AmEx, DC, JCB, MC, TC, V. **Map C2**
Opened in 1895, the Métropole Hôtel was actually an afterthought when it was built: it's still owned by the brewery family that originally added it on to the café it had opened to promote its range of beers. Today, it stands as one of the grandest hotel interiors in Brussels. The main entrance is all French Renaissance flourish, leading to an Empire-style reception hall replete with gold stained-glass windows characteristic of the city's art nouveau heritage. The rooms mix art deco, art nouveau and modern style with a subtle flourish – some bathrooms still have the original tiling from the turn of the century, preserved to perfection. The restaurant downstairs offers opulence and value-for-money meals, and the piano bar-lounge even attracts locals, which is a ringing endorsement for any hotel bar.

Hôtel Sema – *see page 147 – so cosy and so well soundproofed, it's easy to forget you're so close to the centre of the city.*

Hotel services *Air-conditioning. Babysitting. Lifts. Conference facilities. Currency exchange. Disabled: rooms. Laundry. Lifts. Multilingual staff. Fitness facilities. Laundry. Massage. Non-smoking rooms. Piano bar. Restaurant. Sauna. Shoe shine.* Room services *Hairdryer. Minibar. Radio. Room service. Safe. Telephone with voicemail. TV/VCR.*

Palace Hôtel

See above Crown Plaza.

President World Trade Centre

180 boulevard Emile Jacqmain, 1000 (203 20 20/fax 203 24 40). Métro Rogier/tram 23, 52, 55, 56, 81, 90. Rates *single 7,500BF; double 8,000BF; suite 13,000BF.* Credit AmEx, DC, JCB, MC, TC, V. Map C1/C2

This hotel stands as a testament to the property speculation from the late 1960s to the '80s that led to the destruction of many of the city's most beautiful buildings to make way for the business boom that is only now beginning to happen. Taking its name from Brussels' version of New York's twin towers (the Belgian WTC made it to 27 storeys before running out of money), the President World Trade Centre stands amid glass-and-steel office buildings – just about the worst place you could imagine building a hotel. Which makes the fact that it is actually quite a good hotel all the more strange. Like a second-string Hilton, the WTC has a mildly Las Vegas gleam in its spacious lobby and rooms. WTC's one standout is its garden, possibly the largest in Brussels.

Hotel services *Babysitting. Conference facilities. Currency exchange. Fax. Garden. Gym. Laundry. Lifts. Multilingual staff. Non-smoking rooms. Piano bar. Safe. Sauna. Sunbed. Restaurant.* Room services *Hairdryer. Minibar. Radio. Room service. Trouser press. TV (cable)/VCR.*

Royal Crown Hôtel Mercure

250 rue Royale, 1210 (220 66 11). Métro Botanique/tram 92, 93, 94. Rates *single 9,650BF; double 10,300BF; suite 12,500-32,000BF; extra bed 1,000BF; breakfast 650BF.* Credit AmEx, DC, JCB, MC, TC, V. Map D4/E1

What used to be the Scandic Crown Hotel has merged with the Hôtel Mercure to create one of the most predictable good hotels in Brussels. Not the top of the heap, but the service and accommodation are professional enough.

Hotel services *Air-conditioning. Babysitting. Beauty salon. Car park. Conference facilities. Currency exchange. Disabled: rooms. Fax. Laundry. Lifts. Multilingual staff. Non-smoking floor/rooms. Piano bar. Sauna. Sport/fitness facilities. Restaurants.* Room services *Hairdryer. Minibar. Radio. Refrigerator. Room service. Safe. Telephone. TV.*

Sheraton Brussels Airport

Brussels National Airport, 1930 Zaventem (725 10 00). Train from Gare Centrale to Zaventem. Rates *single 10,400-11,400BF; double 11,400-12,400BF; suite 19,000BF-29,000; extra bed 900BF; breakfast 575BF.* Credit AmEx, DC, JCB, MC, TC, V.

The sister hotel of the larger city centre location.

Hotel services *Air-conditioning. Babysitting. Business centre. Bars (2). Car park. Conference facilities. Currency exchange. Disabled: rooms. Garage. Laundry. Lifts. Multilingual staff. Non-smoking rooms. Restaurant. Sport/fitness facilities.* Room services *Bath robe & slippers. Hairdryer. Minibar. Radio. Refrigerator. Room service. Safe. Telephone. TV/VCR.*

Sheraton Brussels Hotel & Towers

3 place Rogier, 1210 (224 31 11/fax 224 34 56). Métro Rogier/tram 23, 52, 55, 56, 81, 90. Rates *9,500-10,500BF; suite 15,500-20,500BF; extra bed free; breakfast 570BF.* Credit AmEx, DC, JCB, MC, TC, V. Map C1

The biggest hotel in Brussels and, as with the Hilton, if you've seen one Sheraton, you have seen them all. But that's the hotel's strength: you know exactly what you're getting yourself into when you book at one. Thirty floors of standardised comfort, with what are among the largest rooms in Brussels. A great view of the city from most floors. Close but not too close to the city's red light district, for those so inclined.

Hotel services *Air-conditioning. Business centre. Babysitting. Car park. Conference facilities. Currency exchange. Disabled: room. Fax. Fitness facilities. Laundry. Lifts. Multilingual staff. Non-smoking floors (5). Piano bar. Restaurants (2). Sauna. Swimming pool.* Room services *Bath robe & slippers. Hairdryer. Radio. Minibar. Room service. Safe. Trouser press. TV (pay & cable). Telephone with voicemail.*

Stanhope Hôtel

9 rue du Commerce, 1000 (506 91 11/fax 512 17 08). Métro Trône. Rates *single 9,900BF; double 12,900-14,900BF; suite 17,500-35,000BF; extra bed 1,000BF.* Credit AmEx, DC, JCB, MC, TC, V. Map E4

Three turn-of-the-century townhouses were converted into this intimate hotel seven years ago, retaining much of its original architectural splendour while providing modern comfort. No two rooms are exactly the same, but the decor is mostly late nineteenth-century English – all the rage in Brussels hotels these days. The lobby evokes the country home salon that most of us wish we had, while the basement bar is pure gentlemen's club. If you're willing to spend, check into a junior suite: the layout is duplex, with a small sitting room with TV on the first level and bedroom on the second. Off the beaten path, but still very accessible to the centre.

Hotel services *Air-conditioning. Babysitting. Bar. Car park. Conference facilities. Currency exchange. Disabled: rooms. Fitness. Garage. Garden. Laundry. Lifts. Multilingual staff. Restaurant. Sauna. Sports facilities. Tearoom.* Room services *Fax. Hairdryer. Minibar. Radio. Room service. Safe. Telephone. Trouser press. TV (satellite & cable)/VCR.*

Medium range

Alfa Sablon

2-8 rue de la Paille, 1000 (513 60 40/fax 511 81 41). Tram 91, 92, 93, 94. Rates *single 5,300BF; double 6,800BF; suite 12,000BF.* Credit AmEx, DC, JCB, MC, TC, V. Map C4

Efficient if unexceptional hotel whose principal attraction is probably its proximity to the Sablon, where Brussels' old and new money change hands over antiques, art and over-priced espressos.

Hotel services *Air-conditioning. Babysitting. Bar. Currency exchange. Disabled: rooms. Laundry. Lifts. Multilingual staff. Non-smoking rooms.* Room services *Hairdryer. Radio. Refrigerator. Room service. Safe. Telephone. TV.*

Arenberg

15 rue d'Assaut, 1000 (501 16 16/fax 501 18 18). Bus 29, 60, 63, 65, 66, 71. Rates *single 4,200BF; double 5,000BF; suite 6,500BF.* Credit AmEx, DC, JCB, MC, TC, V.

Renovated in 1997, but at this price, you could do with better service. Stay here only if everything else is booked.

Hotel services *Bar. Car park. Conference facilities. Lifts. Parking. Restaurant.* Room services *Minibar. TV (cable).*

Aris

78-80 rue du Marché aux Herbes, 1000 (514 43 00/ fax 514 01 19). Tram 23, 52, 55, 56, 81. Rates *single 3,500-5,000BF; double 4,000-6,000BF.* Credit AmEx, DC, JCB, TC, V. Map B3

http://www.timeout.co.uk

Les Bluets – see p148 – personal touch.

The bleached-out salmon-coloured lobby welcomes you to the mass-produced, sterile charm of this decent hotel. Here again is a hotel whose location is its basic attraction: the rooms are spotless and the furniture new (the hotel opened in June 1995), but there is an overall lack of character. The beds are smallish, if firm.
Hotel services *Air-conditioning. Breakfast room. Currency exchange. Lifts.* **Room services** *Hairdryer. Telephone. TV (cable).*

Diplomat

32 rue Jean Stas, 1060 (537 42 50). Métro Louise/tram 91, 92, 93, 94. **Rates** *single 4,200BF; double 4,900BF.* **Credit** AmEx, DC, JCB, MC, TC, V. **Map C6**
Uninspiring but practical hotel for visitors doing business in the area. Clean, comfortable – but nondescript.
Hotel services *Lifts.* **Room services** *Hairdryer. Minibar. Radio. Telephone. TV (cable).*

Le Dixseptième

25 rue de la Madeleine, 1000 (502 57 44/fax 502 64 24). Métro Gare Centrale. **Rates** *single 5,600-7,200BF; double 6,400-7,800BF.* **Credit** AmEx, DC, JCB, MC, TC, V. **Map C3/C4**
In a word: gorgeous. This 23-room hotel is housed in a seventeenth-century building that once served as the residence of the Spanish ambassador to Belgium, and the current proprietor has taken care to retain the building's former grandeur while providing comfortable accommodation. When the building was bought in the late 1980s by a Swedish consortium, the plan was to turn the building into apartments – which is the reason why the majority of the rooms feature fully fitted kitchens. Now owned by a Belgian family, the conveniently located hotel (a scenic five-minute walk from Gare Centrale) features a burnished, listed staircase leading up to the individually decorated rooms, which

are mostly decorated in Louis XVI or French Renaissance style. Alabaster-white walls create an airiness, while antique furnishings (a four-poster bed in one room, an ornate oak dining table in another) create an instant feeling of home. Very comfortable. Highly recommended.
Hotel services *Bar. Conference facilities. Garden. Lift. Kitchenette.* **Room services** *Minibar. TV (cable).*

Le Dôme

12-13 boulevard du Jardin Botanique (218 06 80/218 41 12). Métro Rogier/tram 23, 52, 55, 56, 81, 90. **Rates** *single 4,000BF; double 4,500BF.* **Credit** AmEx, DC, JCB, MC, TC, V. **Map C2/D2**
There are actually two parts to this hotel: the original Dôme, on the corner of the major thoroughfare boulevard Adolphe Max and boulevard du Jardin Botanique, dates back to 1902, with the original façade of the ten-floor building maintained, while Le Dôme II, added on 20 years ago, is a few doors down. The rooms are basically identical, functional and with small flourishes (framed Gustav Klimt posters, faux art deco furnishings) to diminish the overall sterile atmosphere. The newer Dôme II attracts a mostly American, business clientele, who appreciate its air-conditioning.
Hotel services *Babysitting. Bar. Lifts. Conference facilities. Currency exchange. Disabled: rooms. Laundry. Trouser press. Multilingual staff. Non-smoking rooms. Restaurant.* **Room services** *Free tea & coffee. Hairdryer. Minibar. Radio. Room service. Safe. Telephone. TV (cable).*

Hotel Ibis

100 rue du Marché aux Herbes, 1000 (514 40 40/fax 514 50 67). Métro Gare Centrale. **Rates** *single 4,350BF; double 4,650BF; triple 5,350BF.* **Credit** AmEx, DC, JCB, MC, TC. **Map B3**
Efficiency overrules aesthetics at the Ibis. From the spacious salmon and mint-green lobby with plastic plants and brass accents to the efficient if a tad institutional rooms, the Ibis is an experience in familiarity to anyone who has stayed in an Ibis anywhere in the world. One of the most appealing features about the hotel is its 15-minute contracts, whereby if there is a problem with your room and it has not been seen to in 15 minutes, your stay is free.
Hotel services *Currency exchange. Lifts. Meeting room. Restaurant. Parking.* **Room services** *Minibar. Telephone. TV (cable).*

New Hotel Siru

1 place Rogier, 1000 (203 35 80/fax 203 33 03). Métro Rogier/tram 23, 52, 55, 56, 81, 90. **Rates** *single 3,700-5,900BF; double 4,400-5,900BF.* **Credit** AmEx, DC, JCB, MC, TC, V. **Map C1**
Although it's been around since 1935, the Siru got a new lease of life in the 1980s when it decided to model itself on New York's famed Chelsea Hotel and feature works by local artists in every room. The rooms themselves are compact but well laid-out – think neat student room at the beginning of the school term, and you've got the picture. An excellent view of Brussels is available from the higher floors. The hotel is located a few metres away from Gare du Nord and the red light district – but the area is safe.
Hotel services *Bar. Car park. Conference facilities. Currency exchange. Laundry. Lifts. Multilingual staff. Non-smoking rooms. Restaurant.* **Room services** *Hairdryer. Radio. Telephone. TV (cable).*

Inexpensive

L'Agenda

6-8 rue de Florence, 1000 (539 00 31/fax 539 00 63). Métro Louise/tram 91, 92. **Rates** *single 3,300BF; double 3,600BF; suite 4,100BF; extra bed 500BF.* **Credit** AmEx, DC, JCB, MC, TC, V.

This 15-year-old hotel was renovated in June 1995, giving the set of apartment-like rooms a fresh feel. Clean and comfortable with personable desk staff, this is a great place for a couple planning to stay a few days. Near avenue Louise.
Hotel services *Babysitting. Currency exchange. Fax. Multilingual staff. Non-smoking rooms.* **Room services** *Free tea & coffee. Hairdryer. Kitchenette. Minibar. Trouser press. Telephone. TV (cable).*

Argus

6 rue Capitaine Crespel, 1050 (514 07 70/fax 514 12 22). Métro Porte de Namur or Louise. **Rates** *single* 3,200BF; *double* 3,500BF. **Credit** AmEx, DC, JCB, MC, V. **Map C5**
The practically but not lavishly sized rooms resemble motel rather than hotel accommodation, with inoffensive modern furniture and a cosy feel. A few steps away from the Toison d'Or, a popular promenade of mid-range clothing stores, and the more upmarket boulevard de Waterloo.
Hotel services *Babysitting. Bar. Fax/Internet access. Laundry. Lift. Parking (limited).* **Room services** *Hairdryer. Minibar. Telephone. TV (cable).*

Arlequin

17-19 rue de la Fourche, 1000 (514 16 15/fax 514 22 02/arlequin@skynet.be). Métro De Brouckère/tram 23, 52, 55, 56, 81. **Rates** *single* 2,750BF; *double* 3,600-3,900BF; *triple* 4,750BF; *suite* 4,000-5,700BF. **Credit** AmEx, DC, MC, V. **Map B3**
Don't let the graffiti-covered corridor leading to the hotel entrance scare you off – this is a fine place to stay if your needs are modest. The student-sized rooms have just enough space to pack and unpack, with the decor being nondescript enough not to annoy.
Hotel services *Lift. Meeting room.* **Room services** *TV (cable).*

Armorial

101 boulevard Brand Whitlock, 1200 (734 56 36/fax 734 50 05). Tram 23, 90. **Rates** *single* 2,800BF; *double* 3,100BF. **Credit** AmEx, DC, MC, V.
Another hotel whose principal attraction is its location. This one is on a tree-lined boulevard leading to square Montgomery, which has an Arc de Triomphe arch and one of the most dangerous intersections in the city – much like Paris's place de la Concorde.
Room services *TV (cable).*

Ascot

1 place Loix, 1050 (tel/fax 538 88 35). Tram 91, 92. **Rates** *single* 2,300-2,700BF; *double* 3,000BF. **Credit** AmEx, DC, MC, V. **Map C6**
Charmless service unfortunately diminishes an otherwise charming hotel's appeal. Unless you are a masochist on holiday, you could do better.
Hotel services *Airport shuttle. Bar. Lift. Meeting room. Parking.* **Room services** *Minibar. TV (cable).*

Balladins

600 avenue Houba de Strooper, 1020 (476 15 14/fax 476 13 96). Tram 18. **Rates** *single or double* 3,200BF; *extra bed* 700BF. **Credit** AmEx, DC, MC, V.
If you want to see one of the most attractive residential districts in Brussels with tree-lined avenues and friendly shops then the Balladins is a good choice. It's near the Atomium and Mini-Europe, popular tourist attractions.
Hotel services *Bar. Lift. Meeting room. Parking. Wheelchair: access.* **Room services** *Minibar. Telephone. TV (cable).*

Rembrandt *– reasonably priced pension-type accommodation near avenue Louise with blond wood and frills. See page 150.*

De Boeck's

40 rue Veydt, 1050 (537 40 33/fax 534 40 37). Tram 91, 92, 93, 94. **Rates** *single* 2,500-2,800BF; *double* 2,300-3,200BF. **Credit** AmEx, DC, MC, V. **Map C6**
We had a complaint about this renovated townhouse from a reader of the first edition of this guide, although the desk clerk was singled out for praise. The jury is still out.
Hotel services *Airport shuttle. Garden. Meeting room. Lift. Parking.* **Room services** *Telephone. TV (cable).*

Du Congrès

40-42 rue du Congrès, 1000 (217 18 90/fax 217 18 97). Métro Madou. **Rates** *single* 2,750BF; *double* 3,150BF; *triple* 3,550BF. **Credit** AmEx, DC, MC, V. **Map D3**
Tastefully renovated mansion near place Madou, with fine ceilings, wood panelling and 52 rooms.
Hotel services *Parking.* **Room services** *TV (cable).*

Galia

16 place du Jeu de Balle, 1000 (502 76 19/fax 502 76 19/hotel.galia@skynet.be). Bus 20, 48. **Rates** *single* 1,600-2,500BF; *double* 1,800-2,500BF; *suite* 4,000BF; *breakfast* included.* **Credit** AmEx, JCB, MC, TC, V. **Map B5**
Standard hotel with spartan amenities for the person who needs a clean, safe room as a base while in Brussels. The restaurant downstairs is filled in the mornings not only with backpacking travellers but also with local bargain hunters and merchants from the daily flea market, just a few steps outside the front door. Recently enlarged to 25 rooms.
Hotel services *Bar. Lifts. Restaurant. Currency exchange.* **Room services** *TV.*

La Grande Cloche

10-12 place Rouppe, 1000 (512 61 40/fax 512 65 91). Tram 23, 52, 55, 56, 81. **Rates** *single or double* 2,850BF. **Credit** MC, V. **Map B4**
La Grande Cloche is situated on the charming place Rouppe, which gives on to the wide avenue Stalingrad leading to Gare du Midi, where you can take advantage of the city's best-known flea market every morning. It's only a two-minute walk away from your hotel room.
Hotel services *Bar. Lift. Parking.* **Room services** *TV.*

Hôtel St Michel

15 Grand Place, 1000 (511 09 56/fax 511 46 00). Métro Gare Centrale/tram 23, 52, 55, 56, 81. **Rates** *single* 2,400-4,250BF; *double* 3,850-5,100BF; *suite* 4,550BF; *extra bed* 900BF. **Credit** AmEx, MC, V. **Map C3**
When visiting the city, you can't get a much better location in Brussels for sightseeing than this… and the price is dead cheap for the neighbourhood. The catch? Windows are not double-glazed, which means that light sleepers might have problems with traffic and rowdy carryings-on outside, but to be able to open floor-to-ceiling double windows on to the Grand Place at these prices is quite something. The hotel itself? A mixed bag: booking here is a lottery, with attractive low-rent versions of Louis XV furniture in some rooms containing the bare necessities, and other rooms resembling something from a halfway house – garage-sale sofas, saggy mattresses and threadbare carpets. Housed in the sixteenth-century home of the Duke of Brabant, which makes it sound a lot grander than it is today: the façade is massive and impressive, with inlaid gold and all that, but the hotel only takes up a minuscule portion of the building. Near everything you want to see in Brussels.
Hotel services *Lift.* **Room services** *Minibar. TV.*

Hôtel Sema

6/8 rue des Harengs, 1000 (548 90 30/fax 548 90 39). Tram 23, 52, 55, 56, 81. **Rates** *single* 3,000BF; *double* 3,500BF. **Credit** MC, TC, V.
Intimacy is the operative word for this converted private home opened in April 1995 and boasting 11 cosy, wood-beamed-ceiling rooms so quiet it's easy to forget that you're

in the centre. You have to pass two doors to enter each room: an outer, more soundproofed one followed by an ornate, older version. At press time, the chalet-styled breakfast room was in the midst of becoming a crêpe restaurant.
Hotel services *Currency exchange.* **Room services** *Hairdryer. Radio. TV (cable).*

Lambeau
150 avenue Lambeau, 1200 (732 51 70/fax 732 54 90). Métro Georges Henri. **Rates** *single* 2,600-2,900BF; *double* 3,100-3,600BF; *suite* 3,600BF. **Credit** AmEx, MC, V.
This is as suburban as you can get without a picket fence. Quiet and with rooms a little on the smallish side – but with more facilities than most establishments in this price range.
Hotel services *Airport shuttle. Bar. Lift. Parking.* **Room services** *Fax. Hairdryer. Minibar. Safe. Telephone. Trouser press. TV (satellite)/VCR.*

La Légende
35 rue du Lombard, 1000 (512 82 90/fax 512 34 93). Tram 23, 52, 55, 56, 81. **Rates** *single* 2,300-2,700BF; *double* 2,500-2,950BF; *triple* 3,700BF. **Credit** AmEx, DC, MC, V. **Map B3**
If you want to be in the centre of Brussels nightlife, this is ideal: salsa clubs, most of the city's gay bars, and bistros for thirtysomethings are all within spitting distance. There are 45 rooms, only half of which have bath or shower and WC.
Hotel services *Lift.*

Lloyd George
12 avenue Lloyd George, 1050 (648 30 72/fax 646 53 61). Tram 23, 90, 93, 94. **Rates** *single* 1,850BF; *double* 2,200BF; *suite* 2,800-3,600BF. **Credit** AmEx, DC, MC, V.
Away from the hubbub of the city centre, this small hotel is good value for money. Near the lush Bois de la Cambre.
Hotel services *Bar. Garden. Lift. Restaurant.* **Room services** *TV (cable).*

La Madeleine
22-24 rue de la Montagne, 1000 (513 29 73/fax 502 13 50). Métro Gare Centrale. **Rates** *single* 2,695BF; *double* 2,995BF. **Credit** AmEx, DC, MC, V. **Map C3**
Don't expect much, that way you won't be disappointed: all the basic necessities in a no-frills hotel that's less attractive for what it is than for where it is. Five minutes on foot from Gare Centrale, with the architecturally impressive Galeries Royales St Hubert and the bustling restaurant street rue des Bouchers even closer. Clean enough.
Hotel services *Breakfast room. Lift.* **Room services** *Telephone. TV (cable).*

Maison du Dragon
158-160 boulevard Adolphe Max, 1000 (218 82 15/fax 218 18 25). Métro Rogier/tram 23, 52, 55, 56, 81, 90. **Rates** *single* 3,500BF; *double* 4,200BF; *breakfast* 180BF. **Credit** DC, MC, V. **Map C2**
So-so smallish hotel on one of the city's main strips, which can be noisy at night. Near WH Smith so at least you can pick up something to read for nights without sleep.
Hotel services *Bar. Lift. Restaurant.* **Room services** *TV (cable).*

Mozart
15A rue du Marché aux Fromages, 1000 (502 66 61/fax 502 77 58). Bus 34, 48. **Rates** *single* 2,500BF; *double* 4,200BF. **Credit** AmEx, DC, MC, TC, V. **Map C3**
Not as scary as the name would lead you to believe – in fact, quite nice. A speckled grey marble staircase leads you up to the first-floor reception of this tiny hotel squeezed in between two of the many pitta shops on this street. The rooms are mostly duplexes, with a small sitting room and bathroom on a different level than the bedroom. As you would expect, classical music emanates throughout the lobby and hallways, but the room furnishings are mostly Ikea – good Ikea, but

Ikea nonetheless. The street outside is a bustling area of activity at night, so it might be wise to get a room at the back.
Hotel services *Lift. Currency exchange. Multilingual staff.* **Room services** *Radio. Hairdryer. Minibar. Telephone. TV.*

Opéra
53 rue Grétry, 1000 (219 43 43/fax 219 17 20). Métro De Brouckère/tram 23, 52, 55, 56, 81/bus 29, 63, 65, 66, 71. **Rates** *single* 2,300BF; *double* 2,700-2,800BF; *suite* 3,450-3,950BF. **Credit** AmEx, JCB, MC, TC, V. **Map B3**
Opéra follows the rule of thumb that the posher the name, the more modest the accommodation is likely to be. Thinking of how much money you're saving by staying here makes your visit more bearable.
Hotel services *Lift.* **Room services** *Telephone. TV.*

Les Tourelles
135 avenue Winston Churchill, 1180 (344 02 84). Tram 23, 90/bus 38. **Rates** *single* 2,900BF; *double* 3,500BF; *suite* 3,900-4,600BF. **Credit** AmEx, MC, TC, V.
Super comfortable inn where the feel is more that of a country home than a hotel. In the elegant Uccle quarter of town on a tree-lined street where many in the city aspire to reside. Child-friendly.
Hotel services *Babysitting. Bar. Meeting room. Restaurant.* **Room services** *Hairdryer. Radio. Telephone. TV.*

Van Belle
39 chaussée de Mons, 1070 (521 35 16/fax 527 00 02). Bus 47. **Rates** *single* 2,215BF; *double* 2,460BF. **Credit** AmEx, DC, MC, V. **Map A4**
Near Brussels' garment district, this is another hotel built in anticipation of Brussels' business boom: 126 rooms in an area of town you'd only want to stay in if you had business there.
Hotel services *Bar. Car park. Lift. Meeting room. Restaurant.* **Room services** *TV (cable).*

Windsor
13 place Rouppe, 1000 (511 20 14/fax 514 09 42). Tram 23, 52, 55, 56, 81. **Rates** *single* 1,800BF; *double* 2,500BF. **Credit** AmEx, DC, MC, V. **Map B4**
Another hotel on the lovely place Rouppe with 24 rooms but only ten have bath and toilets, so specify when reserving.
Hotel services *Bar. Parking. Lift.* **Room services** *TV.*

Cheap

Les Bluets
124 rue Berckmans, 1060 (tel/fax 534 39 83). Métro Hôtel des Monnaies. **Rates** *single* 1,650BF; *double* 2,250BF. **Credit** AmEx, MC, V. **Map B6/C6**
The geraniums spilling out of flower boxes outside this converted townhouse give you an idea of the personal touch given here. Run by a lovely couple, the atmosphere is more that of a country house than a hotel. Popular with Belgians.
Hotel services *Garden.*

De France
21 boulevard Jamar, 1060 (522 79 35/fax 522 11 11). Métro Gare du Midi/tram 23, 52, 55, 56, 81, 90. **Rates** *single* 1,600BF; *double* 1,900BF. **Credit** AmEx, DC, MC, V. **Map A5**
The kind of hotel that you'd expect to rent by the hour, if you know what we mean. But it's cheap and close to the Gare du Midi, so handy for the Eurostar.
Hotel services *Bar. Lift.*

La Tasse d'Argent – 17 rooms, popular at weekends and Duvel is served at the bar. Your cup runneth over. See page 150.

Duke of Windsor

4 rue Capouillet, 1060 (539 18 19). Tram 91, 92.
Rates *single* 1,500BF; *double* 2,250BF. **Credit** AmEx,
DC, MC, V.
A minimum two-night stay is required to lodge at this private home converted to a five-room inn. Reserve well in advance by phone and confirm by letter. Speaking French helps. Non-smokers only.

George V

23 rue 't Kint, 1000 (513 44 93/fax 513 44 93). Tram
18. **Rates** *single* 1,980BF; *double* 2,200-2,400BF; *triple*
2,000BF; *quad* 3,200BF. **Credit** MC, V. **Map A3**
Modest hotel that is in one of the few areas of the centre that actually has the feeling of a neighbourhood: a mix of long-time city residents, immigrant families and artists. A good selection of bars and cafés within walking distance.
Hotel services *Bar. Lift. Parking.* **Room services** *Tea & coffee facilities. Telephone. TV (in double rooms).*

Hôtel des Eperonniers

1 rue des Eperonniers, 1000 (513 53 66/511 32 30).
Métro De Brouckère/tram 23, 52, 55, 56, 81. **Rates** *single*
1,895BF; *double* 2,195BF. **Credit** AmEx, MC, V. **Map C3**
The kind of hotel that fugitives from justice would stay in. Most of the furnishings look as if they came from someone's attic, the building itself, situated conveniently near Gare Centrale and the Galeries Royales St Hubert, is squeezed in between other buildings that make it easy to miss. If you do stay here, specify that you would like a room with a bath and a toilet – those lodging in rooms without facilities can take advantage of the communal showers and WCs, which can be an interesting way to get to know people.
Hotel services *Lift.*

Madou

45 rue du Congrès, 1000 (218 83 75/fax 217 32 74).
Bus 63. **Rates** *single* 1,600BF; *double* 2,050BF. **Credit**
MC, V. **Map D3**
This old townhouse has been converted into nine rooms that offer a homely atmosphere. Often booked out, which is the best indication of a hotel's popularity.

New Galaxy

7A rue du Progrès, 1210 (203 47 76/fax 203 45 54).
Tram 23, 52, 55, 56, 81, 90. **Rates** *single* 1950BF;
double 2,700BF. **Credit** DC, MC, V. **Map C1/D1**
The name alone should give you pause, but if you really want to be a stone's throw from Gare du Nord, then pitch your tent here. Only two-thirds of the hotel's rooms have bath or shower and WC, so specify when booking. A reader of our first edition found it adequate and good value.
Hotel services *Lift. Parking.* **Room services** *TV.*

Rembrandt

42 rue de la Concorde, 1050 (512 71 39/fax 511 71 36).
Tram 93, 94. **Rates** *single* 1,800-1,950BF; *double* 2,500-
2,700BF; *suite* 2,300-3,100BF. **No credit cards**. **Map D6**
Pension-type accommodation near avenue Louise, which means that there is a chichi factor at work. Decor borders on cutesy-quaint and kitschy twee: lots of blond wood and frills. Check out the lobby of antique bric-a-brac, lace doilies and antique lamps.
Hotel services *Lift.*

Royotel Brussels

312 rue Royale, 1210 (218 30 34/fax 219 93 79). Tram
91, 92, 93, 94. **Rates** *single* 2,100BF; *double* 2,500BF.
Credit AmEx, DC, MC, V. **Map D4/E1**
Chain hotel with very reasonable prices and good enough service. Out-of-the-way location in an area that has not yet been fully gentrified.
Hotel services *Bar. Lift. Meeting room.* **Room services** *TV (cable).*

La Tasse d'Argent

48 rue du Congrès, 1000 (217 83 75/fax 217 32 74).
Métro Madou. **Rates** *single* 1,500BF; *double* 1,750-
1,900BF. **Credit** MC, V. **Map D3**
Seventeen rooms in a slightly tacky style reminiscent of the 1950s, which only adds to its charm. Popular at weekends.
Hotel services *Bar.*

Youth hostels

Auberge de Jeunesse Bruegel

2 rue de St Esprit, 1000 (511 04 36/fax 512 07 11).
Métro Gare Centrale. **Open** 7.30am-1am daily. **Rates**
double 650BF per person; *quad* 550BF per person; *12 beds*
495BF per person.
More central than others, which makes it more suitable for those who like to enjoy a little nightlife before turning in.
Hostel services *Currency exchange.*

Auberge de Jeunesse Jacques Brel

30 rue de la Sablonnière, 1000 (218 01 87/fax 217 20
05). Métro Botanique/tram 91, 92, 93, 94. **Open** 8am-
1am daily. **Rates** *single* 660BF; *double* 550BF per person;
triple or quad 450BF per person; *6-14 beds* 395BF per
person. **Map D2**
Near the Botanique but accessible by foot from the centre, this hostel has 140 beds and ranks as one of the cleanest.
Hostel services *Currency exchange. Laundry.*

CHAB – Hôtel des Jeunes

Centre Vincent van Gogh, 8 rue Traversière, 1210 (217
01 58/fax 219 79 95) Métro Botanique/tram 91, 92, 93,
94. **Open** 7.30am-2am daily. **Rates** 300-550BF. **Credit**
MC, V. **Map E2**
Trendy hostel with 220 beds in quirky spaces such as a former concert hall, where there are beds on the stage. Rooms for two to four people with dormitories taking from six up to 16; bigger savings to be had the more you share.
Hostel services *Bedlinen rental. Left luggage. Phone booth. Private garden access. TV. Washing machine. Website http://www.ping.be/chab*

La Fonderie – Auberge de Jeunesse Jean-Nihon

4 rue de l'Eléphant, 1080 (410 38 58/fax 410 39 05).
Métro Comte de Flandre. **Open** *reception* 7am-noon,
2pm-1am, daily. **Rates** *double* 550BF per person; *quad*
450BF per person; *8 beds* 395BF.
The name translates as foundry – former incarnation of this hostel. What it lacks in character it makes up for in comfort.
Hostel services *Bedlinen rental. Dining room. Garden. Laundry room. Parking.*

Sleep Well Youth Hostel

23 rue du Daimier, 1000 (218 50 50/fax 218 13 13).
Métro Botanique/tram 91, 92, 93, 94. **Open** 10am-1pm
(later entry 50BF) daily. **Rates** *single* 690BF; *double*
560BF per person; *triple or quad* 450BF per person; *6-8*
beds 395BF per person.
If you want hotel-style accommodation but still to pay hostel rates, then this former YMCA is the place for you.
Hostel services *Bar. Bedlinen rental. Currency exchange. Guided tours. TV (cable, in lobby).*

Bed & breakfast

Bed & Brussels

2 rue Gustave Biot, 1050 (646 07 37/fax 644 01 14).
Tram 93, 94. **Reservations** 9am-6pm Mon-Fri. **Rates**
single 850-1,650BF; *double* 1,470-2,730BF.
Book B&Bs throughout Belgium with this agency.

Arts & Entertainment

Children

Brussels offers enough amusement to keep even the most demanding young visitors occupied for a month of Sundays.

Children's activities in Brussels are a rather bewildering mixture of the quaint and the cutting edge. On one hand there are the puppet shows in the park, the toy museums, the carnival parades, the crib with live animals… nothing to tell you you're not in the Victorian era. Then there are the Brussels children themselves, with their wonderfully controlled manners, their habit of addressing you formally and the endearing and unself-conscious way they kiss you on meeting.

On the other hand, however, there are stomach-churning rides at Aqualibi and Océade, and there's skateboarding up the stairs and ramps of Mont des Arts. Brussels is rather proud of its quaint side, but unless your offspring have been brought up on wooden toys and the Ovalteenies, you're likely to find yourself seeking out the hard, commercial edge of child entertainment.

Museums

Brussels has exceptionally good museums for children, some of which are listed below. For adult museums with a high degree of interest for children, such as the Museum voor Midden-Afrika, Institut Royal des Sciences Naturelles de Belgique (Natural History Museum), Centre Belge de la Bande Dessinée, Musée des Enfants, Autoworld and the Musée Royal de l'Armée et d'Histoire Militaire, *see chapter* **Museums**.

Lilliput Belgium Centre de la Miniature
59 rue Colonel van Gele, 1040 (732 24 71). Tram 81, 82. **Open** 10am-5pm Tue-Fri; 2.30-5pm Sat. **Admission** 100BF. **No credit cards.**
In their enthusiasm for all things small, perhaps the Belgians don't realise that Swift was being satirical about the Lilliputians. This is just another miniature place in the city of miniatures. There are tiny toys and dolls' houses, complete with mini-dolls and furniture. Most usefully, it runs all-day workshops through July and August where children can make their own figures and furniture, and learn the art of things small and delicate.

Musée de Cire (Wax Museum)
1st floor, Anspach Centre, place de la Monnaie, 1000 (217 60 23). Métro De Brouckère. **Open** 10am-6pm daily. **Admission** 190BF; 150BF groups, children, students. **No credit cards.**
If your child has seen Madame Tussaud's, this probably won't impress them. Otherwise, the fascination of lifelike models should work its magic, even if the museum does take itself a little too seriously – what children want to see is Michael Jackson or a chamber of other horrors. Instead, it goes for the historical trip: 20 scenes are laid out from

Roman times to the early twentieth century, or Julius Caesar to Hergé. Still, the models are good and the attention to detail is impressive.

Musée du Jouet (Toy Museum)
24 rue de l'Association, 1000 (219 61 68). Métro Botanique or Madou. **Open** 10am-6pm daily. **Admission** 100BF; 60BF groups, 5-12s; free under-5s. **No credit cards.**
Belgium, like the Netherlands, has a worldwide reputation for toy-making, and the examples on display here range from delicate 1850s dolls in glass cases to present-day streamlined and glossy machines. There's a shop selling rather superior toys and the museum will put on birthday parties for 295BF per child.

Scientastic Museum
Level 1, Métro Bourse, 1000 (715 91 30). Métro Bourse. **Open** 2-5.30pm Sat, Sun. **Admission** 150BF; 130BF students; 90BF groups; free under-4s. **No credit cards.**
Located in the Bourse Métro station, this is an interactive museum, all about having a tactile experience of science. There are 36 hands-on exhibits involving optical illusions, making your friend's face disappear and being suspended in mid-air.

Films & TV

Brussels has a good number of cinemas and most films are shown in their original language, so there are generally a few children's films in English to choose from. Films for over-16s are indicated as CNA or ENA, which means children not admitted. At UGC De Brouckère on Saturdays at 9.30am parents can leave their children to watch a suitable film under supervision. However, it's likely to be in French.

With 30 or so channels, finding English television in Brussels is not a problem. The BBC and the numerous Dutch channels are your best bet if you don't have satellite. *See chapter* **Media**.

Puppets

Théâtre Royal le Peruchet, Musée International des Marionettes
50 avenue de la Forêt, 1050 (673 87 30). Petite Gare du Boondael/tram 94. **Open** Sept-Jun Wed, Sat, Sun. **Admission** *museum* 30BF; *show & museum* 175BF. **No credit cards.**
This theatre-cum-museum has a good collection of puppets and lively interactive performances, but opening times are erratic so you need to phone beforehand to check.

Théâtre de Toone
6 impasse Schuddeveld, petite rue des Bouchers, 1000 (513 54 86). Métro De Brouckère. **Open** noon-midnight

Tue-Sat. **Box office** tickets available 8pm, just before performance. **Tickets** 400BF; 250BF under-12s, students (Tue-Thur only). **No credit cards.**
Despite most of the shows being held in Bruxellois, the regional dialect, this is a gem of a puppet theatre to which all children respond, even if they don't understand a word. There are occasional performances in English; check the listings magazine *Bulletin* or phone for details. There is also a puppet museum, which you can enter free during the interval, and a workshop where you can buy marionettes.

Miscellaneous fun

Brussels Formula One
62 rue de Lusambo, 1190 (332 37 37). Tram 18, 52. **Open** 3-11pm Mon, Tue; noon-11pm Wed-Sun. **Admission** 500BF. **Credit** MC, V.
For those who want to whizz round in go-karts, and indulge in Formula One dreams.

Ecole du Cirque de Bruxelles
104 chaussée de Boondael, 1050 (640 15 71). Tram 23, 90/bus 71. **Open** 9am-5pm Mon-Fri. **Admission** 6,000BF for one year. **No credit cards.**
This is one summer class children can easily be persuaded to attend. Children are taught acrobatics, trapeze artistry, acting and how to act the clown. Day courses during school holidays.

Labyrinthes de Q-Zar
36 boulevard de l'Empereur, 1000 (512 08 74). Métro Gare Centrale. **Open** 3pm-midnight daily. **Admission** 150BF. **Credit** MC. **Map C4**
For the modern child, who may just be having it up to here with all these cute miniatures. Activities include state-of-the-art war games. A good place for birthday parties.
Branch: 43 quai au Foin, 1000 (217 28 01).

Mont des Arts
Close to place Royale. Métro Gare Centrale. **Map D4**
For the skateboarding enthusiasts and indulgent parents, this artificial slope was built to provide access to Brussels' museums and exhibition centres, but the steps and marble surface turned out to be ideal skateboarding terrain.

Seasonal activities

Binche Carnival
mid-Feb, including Shrove Tuesday.
This is the biggest of the carnivals held in towns around Brussels. Almost every town has its carnival, where costumes are taken out of the museum and a quantity of oranges is brought to be thrown at the crowd. It's an essential Belgian experience but don't expect children to be riveted for too long.

Drive-in Movies
parc du Cinquantenaire (346 59 49). **Open** *July, Aug* 8pm; *film* 10.30pm. **Admission** 500BF per car.
An all-American experience, but can your family stand being holed up in a car together for two hours?

Foire du Midi
boulevard du Midi, mid-July-mid-Aug. **Map A4/A6**
Ferris wheels, dodgems, rollercoasters, hot dogs till late into the night.

Georges Henri Fair
avenue Georges Henri.
Modest, relaxed, enjoyable fair down the long length of Georges Henri, held for three days in the second week of September. It's about food and fairground rides.

Grand Place
At Christmas there's a crib with live animals and, for the past two years, an ice rink. This was hugely popular and looks like being a fixture.

Parks & playgrounds

No area in Brussels is without its regimented patch of green, but many are too small, too flat or too formal to interest any self-respecting child. The following selection does have some tot appeal, with plentiful games and ice-cream on tap.

Bois de la Cambre
main entrance on avenue Louise, 1050. Tram 23, 90, 93, 94.
This is one of the best inner-city parks for children. It's expansive, with beautiful lakes and woods, there's a skating area and in the centre is the Halle du Bois, a large and tempting games centre complete with bouncy castle. The Halle is open at weekends and on holidays from 2-6pm for children aged 3-12 years.

Parc du Cinquantenaire
main entrances on avenue de Tervuren and rue de la Loi, 1000. Métro Merode or Schuman/tram 20, 80. **Map G4**
The layout is a little formal, but it has lawns for football, paths for inline skating and a sandpit. Autoworld and the Musée Royal de l'Armée et d'Histoire Militaire (*see chapter* **Museums**) are guaranteed to impress youngsters for a while, and the small, mock-medieval tower is amusing, though you can no longer climb it. An ice-cream van can usually be found tinkling in the centre.

Parc de Tervuren
entrance in chaussée de Louvain, 1380. Tram 39, 44.
The Museum voor Midden-Afrika (*see chapter* **Museums**) is one draw, and those stuffed animals always excite attention, though today's children may find them wholly unethical. The park is large and airy and you can hire boats from the boathouse.

Parc de Woluwe
entrance in avenue de Tervuren, 1160. Tram 36, 39, 42, 44.
This is one of the best parks to take children to, simply because it's so attractive. Set on slopes, it engenders an immediate feeling of freedom. It's ideal in winter for skating or tobogganing, and good for kite-flying on a windy day. There are walks and woods, lawns for games, crazy golf and a lake with rowing boats.

Square Ambiorix
entrance in square Ambiorix, 1000. Métro Schuman/tram 23, 50. **Map G3**
This small, attractive playground, just beside the EU area, has climbing frames and slides.

Animals & amusement parks

Belgium has a huge number of amusement parks and attractions, most of them outside Brussels. A full list can be obtained from the Belgian Tourist Office at 63 rue du Marché aux Herbes (*see chapter* **Directory**).

Antwerp Zoo
26 Koningen Astridplein, 2018 Antwerp (03 202 45 40/fax 03 231 00 18). **Open** *Dec, Jan* 9am-4pm daily; *Feb, Oct, Nov* 9am-4.30pm daily; *Mar-June, Sept* 9am-6.30pm

daily; *July, Aug* 9am-6.30pm daily. **Admission** 450BF;
290BF 3-11s, over-60s, disabled; free under 3s (no pets
allowed). **No credit cards.**
Belgium's main zoo is in Antwerp. It's one of Europe's oldest, set right in the city beside the old railway station. The
number of animals is impressive, the conditions less so,
though they are steadily improving. It has that dated and
rather depressing feel of city zoos, where there just isn't the
space needed by the animals, and the big cats pace dement-
edly behind bars. The choice of captive creatures ranges
from amphibians to monkeys, and you can catch a show of
dolphins leaping through hoops.

Aqualibi
Wavre, 1300 (010 42 16 00). **Open** *Apr-Sept* 10am-6pm
Wed, Thur, Sun; 10am-11pm Fri, Sat (reserved for Walibi
visitors during the day). *Oct-Mar* 2-10pm Wed-Fri; 2am-
11pm Sat, Sun. **Admission** 495BF. **Credit** MC, V.
Attached to Walibi (*see below*), this extravagant water attraction offers a wildly wet experience with its array of chutes,
huge waves, pools and Jacuzzis, plus an adventure trail
called Rapido.

Plankendael Animal Park
582 Leuvensesteenweg, Mechelen 2812 (015 414 921).
Open *summer* 9am-6.15pm Mon-Sat, 9am-7pm Sun;
winter 9am-5pm daily. **Admission** 420BF; 270BF 3-11s,
over-60s, disabled (no pets allowed). **Credit** MC, V.
This large, attractive farm with over a thousand animals in
40 hectares has a great deal more space and freedom than a
zoo. It's children-oriented, with cuddly animals in the 'pet-
ting farm', a superior playground and an adventure trail.
There's also a 'creeps and other horrors' corner, which dwells
on the scarily fascinating world of spiders, rats and insects
and demonstrates an astute awareness of what children
want. The farm also caters for birthday parties.

Walibi
Wavre, 1300 (010 42 15 00). **Getting there** *by train*
Ottignies-Louvain-la-Neuve line from Schuman to Gare
de Bierges (the station is 300m from Walibi); *by car* take
the E411 Bxl-Namur motorway to exit 6. **Open** *4 Apr-30
Jun* 10am-6pm daily; *1 July-18 Oct* 10am-7pm daily.
Admission 760BF; 680BF children up to 1m 30cm tall;
free children under 1m tall. **Credit** MC, V.
The nearest theme park to Brussels, and the best. Walibi is
constantly expanding, adding more stomach-churning rides
and opportunities to get soaked. It also has roundabouts and
slow trains for smaller children. Be warned: it is usually
uncomfortably crowded, and during school holidays you can
queue up to an hour for the most popular rides.

Bruparck & Laeken

The whole Atomium area seems to have been created for the round-the-clock amusement of your
children. They can go up the nine-balled wonder
itself for a great view. They can see a film in
the Kinepolis (*see chapter* **Film**), which, with 30
screens and mostly American films, is usually
showing something suitable. Then there are cafés
in the Village, the lilliputian Mini-Europe, which
has trams that run and boats that sail, and there's
Océade for slide-and-splash fun.

Atomium
*boulevard du Centenaire, 1020 (474 89 77). Métro
Heysel/tram 81, 19, 81, 91.* **Open** *Apr-Aug* 9am-8pm
daily; *Sept-Mar* 10am-6pm daily; **Admission** 200BF;
150BF groups (minimum 20); 160BF children. **Credit**
AmEx, MC, V.
See also chapter **Sightseeing**.

Mini-Europe
*Bruparck, 20 boulevard du Centenaire, 1020 (478 05
50). Métro Heysel/tram 18, 19, 81, 91.* **Open** *1 Apr-30
June* 9.30am-6pm daily; *20 July-19 Aug* 9.30am-midnight
daily; *1 Sept-6 Jan* 10am-6pm daily. **Closed** 6 Jan-31
Mar. **Admission** 395BF; 340BF groups (minimum 20);
295BF children. **Credit** V.

Océade
*Bruparck, 20 boulevard du Centenaire, 1020 (478 43 20).
Métro Heysel/tram 18, 19, 81, 91.* **Open** *Apr-Jun* 10am-
10pm Fri-Sun; 10am-6pm Tue-Thur. *July, Aug* 10am-10pm
daily. *Sept-Mar* 10am-6pm Tue-Fri; 10am-10pm Sat, Sun.
Admission 460BF; 360BF children 1.25m-1.5m tall; free
children under 1.25m tall. **Credit** MC, V.

You have to be a member to use many of Brussels'
sports centres. Not these.

Centre de Danse Choreart
985 chaussée d'Alsemberg, 1180 (332 13 59). Tram 55.
This is the city's biggest dance school, with classes in
modern and classical ballet, jazz and tap-dancing. It runs
classes for children from three-and-a-half upwards.

Centre Sportif de Woluwe St Pierre
2 avenue Salomé, 1150 (762 12 75). Tram 39. **Open**
8am-7pm Mon-Thur, Sat, Sun; 8am-8pm Fri. **Admission**
pool 100BF; 90BF under-14s. **No credit cards.**
The Olympic-size pool has lanes and diving boards. The
shallow children's pool has a water chute and inflatable
rings. There's also tennis, squash, mini-football and basketball. All can be arranged by the hour except tennis, for which
you have to be a member.

Pompom Ponies
1,512 chaussée de Waterloo, 1180 (374 84 49). Bus 38.
Rates 450BF per hour.
Attractive setting for pony classes for children. They can
attend all-day sessions for a week, at the rather hefty price
of 7,500BF.

Poseidon
*2 avenue des Vaillants, 1200 (762 16 33). Métro
Tomberg.* **Open** 8am-7pm Mon-Fri; 8am-7.30pm Sat, Sun.
Admission *pool* 75BF; 60BF under-14s; *ice rink* 250BF;
210BF under-13s. **No credit cards.**
Poseidon's 25m pool and small children's pool can become
seriously overcrowded, as can the ice rink, which should be
avoided at peak times (weekends and Wednesday afternoons). The good news is that the ice is well maintained and
there are children's skates available for hire.

Christiansen
*City 2, rue de la Blanchisserie, 1000 (218 09 28).
Métro Rogier.* **Open** 10am-6.30pm Mon-Sat. **Credit**
AmEx, DC, V.
Belgium's largest toy-shop chain has large and all-encom-
passing stores that run the gamut from Barbie dolls to
Nintendo games, but it's all a little mass-produced.

In den Olifant
159 rue de Linthout, 1200 (736 70 68). Métro Merode.
Open 10am-6.30pm Mon-Sat. **Credit** AmEx, DC, MC, V.
Map H3
The beautiful wooden toys and Victorian-looking games pur-
veyed at In den Olifant are possibly more parent- than child-
friendly.

*It's raining cats and dogs at **Maison Picard**.*

Chi-Chi's
541 Brüsselse Steenweg, 3090 Overijse (657 57 00).
Open 11.30am-10pm Mon-Thur, Sun; 11.30am-11pm Fri,
Sat. **Average** 600BF. **Menu** 250BF (lunch), 695BF,
795BF. **Credit** AmEx, DC, MC, V.
A little outside the centre of town but hugely popular.
Children's menus are 140BF and include chicken, burgers or
stew. On Sundays this is reduced to 99BF with a free drink.

La Maison d'Attila
*36-42 avenue Prince du Ligne Nile, 1080 (375 05 70/375
38 05). Bus 60.* **Open** noon-midnight daily. **Average**
885BF. **Credit** AmEx, DC, MC, V.
This has a buffet with a wide range of pasta, salads, grills
and fondues. An inspired system of payment operates whereby up to the age of 14 you multiply the child's age by 59BF,
so for a one-year-old you pay 59BF and for a ten-year-old
590BF. At 15, the adult charge of 850BF kicks in.

L'Orchidée Bleue
*99 boulevard Brand Whitlock, 1200 (734 59 12). Métro
Georges Henri/tram 23, 90.* **Open** noon-2.30pm, 6-11pm,
daily. **Average** 650BF. **Menu** 395BF, 495BF, 695BF.
Credit AmEx, DC, MC, V.
Good Chinese food at reasonable prices. Its best option is the
Sunday brunch (noon-2pm), which offers an enormous choice
of dishes at 295BF for under-12s and 495BF for adults.

Childminding

The Ligue des Familles, 127 rue du Trône, 1050
(507 72 11), organises daytime childminding services for children aged up to six. It may also provide night-time sitters, or you can phone the local
commune for a full list of childcarers.

It can be hard to find an English babysitter at
short notice. Your best bet is to call Kids 'n' Carers
(653 39 24), where staff will do their best to send a
suitable, qualified person. For longer-term visitors,
there are a number of English-language crèches.
The City International School, 101-103 boulevard
Louis Schmidt, 1040 (734 88 16), runs a full-time
weekday crèche.

Maison Picard
*71-75 rue du Lombard, 1000 (513 07 90). Métro Gare
Centrale.* **Open** 9am-6.30pm Mon-Sat. **Credit** AmEx,
DC, MC, V. **Map B3**
Maison Picard and Le Palais des Cotillons (*see below*) are
two great magic and theatrical shops that face each other
across rue du Lombard. This one specialises in serious
make-up and masks.

Le Palais des Cotillons
*66 rue du Lombard, 1000 (512 23 20). Métro Gare
Centrale.* **Open** 9.30am-6pm Mon-Sat. **Credit** AmEx, DC,
MC, V. **Map B3**
Full of lurid tricks such as fake flies and whoopee cushions,
as well as the best fireworks around and a very extensive
dressing-up section.

Prémaman
*Woluwe Shopping Centre, rue St Lambert, 1020 (770 58
97). Métro Roodebeek.* **Open** 9.30am-7.15pm Mon-Sat.
Credit AmEx, DC, MC, V.
Brussels' answer to Mothercare has all the usual maternity
and baby clothes, plus simple educational toys.

Child-friendly restaurants

Because Belgian children are generally so well
behaved, there is seldom any difficulty about
bringing children into restaurants. However,
Brussels seems to be too gastronomically proud to
cater much for children and special menus are
not generally offered. Listed below are some exceptions, but don't expect your children to sample
great Belgian cooking.

Health

For emergencies, dial 100 and speak slowly in
English. There are two paediatric emergency numbers – 535 43 60 and 648 40 14. There is a 24-hour
English-speaking helpline for all problems of any
nature on 648 40 14.

International schools

British School of Brussels
19 Leuwensesteenweg, 3080 Tervuren (767 47 00). Tram 44.
Mostly British, but 60 nationalities are represented. Exams
offered include GCSE and A levels.

International School of Brussels
19 Kattenburg, 1170 (672 27 88). Bus 95.
Fifty-five nationalities, from nursery age upwards.

St John's International School
146 drève Richelle, 1410 Waterloo (354 11 38).
St John's ecumenical school has a special department for
children with learning difficulties.

Clubs

Only the most desperate turn up before midnight.

Being at the centre of Europe makes Brussels a good city for clubbing. The multitude of nationalities living here means that most musical tastes are catered for.

Bruxellois are less attitudinal than New Yorkers, Londoners or Parisians; rather, they are influenced and impressed by them, and unless you're a soccer hooligan, being a foreigner is likely to get you more easily into a private club. Exceptions to this rule persist, especially for North Africans (xenophobia shows its face more boldly at night), but this, too, is improving in Brussels. Antwerp, however, remains more intractable: the ultra-right racist party, the Vlaams Blok, is strong there.

Although most clubs open at around 11pm, only the most desperate arrive before midnight. Before then, clubbers congregate at cafés and bars to decide which spots to hit. If you are out with Belgians, remember that buying rounds is the custom, with everyone taking their turn. The larger the group, the more drinks bought… and the more likely everyone is to end up thoroughly gone before the night's end.

Speaking of getting pissed, about the only time being anglophone (particularly British or Australian) works against you is when it comes to drinking. Because of limited licensing hours back home, some visitors, used to cramming in the pints before 11pm, get rat-arsed long before everybody else. Belgians get just as drunk but take their time over it, allowing ample opportunity to witness other people's excesses. Pace yourself.

Dress codes are laid-back: in a city where jeans and a blazer can pass muster for formal, the trend is to be stylish but comfortable. Remember, though, that certain looks which might afford instant entrée into certain soirées (nose-ring or chartreuse mohican, say) will get you turned away from others. If a Brussels doorman doesn't want to let you in, you won't get in, and any attempt at persuasion is a waste of breath. Doormen also expect a tip. Don't give less than 50BF and, in a lot of clubs, don't expect any gratitude either. They'll show their appreciation by recognising you next time and letting you in immediately. But if you're thinking of trying to blag your way in for free, forget it.

'Club privée', or private club, is the excuse most doormen give when denying entry. Although many clubs do have a membership scheme, most people in any given club are not part of it – 'members only' filters out the undesirables. If you look like everybody else, getting in shouldn't be a problem.

Bear in mind that most public transport stops around midnight and doesn't resume till about 5.30am. Taxis can be hired, but there's a 95BF supplement for all fares beginning between 10pm and 6am.

Antwerp clubs

Café d'Anvers
15 Verversrui, 2000 Antwerp (03 226 38 70).
Open 11pm-6am Fri, Sun; 11pm-7.30am Sat.
Admission 250BF; free on regular nights before midnight and an hour before closing.
Used to be Antwerp's hottest spot, but lost most of its trendy clientele when the management changed. Those who still come bought the wrong guidebook.

Café Local
25 Waalsekaai, 2000 Antwerp (no phone). **Open** 11pm-6am Thur-Sun. **Admission** from 200BF.
Gorgeous venue… shame about the punters. If Café Local took as much care over its door policy as it has with decor, the club would be perfect. Modelled on a Cuban market square, the bar area is impressive: the stands of fresh fruit and vegetables, shelves of coffee beans, toys and tins of produce and the *cantina*-like central bar all look pretty authentic to anyone who's never been to Havana. The dance area resembles an old-style tango hall, with bead-curtained entrances and softly lit tables around the edge. Music ranges from salsa to world to pop, which reflects the crowd: a little too much of everything to create any real atmosphere.

Red & Blue
13 Lange Schipperskapellestraat, 2000 Antwerp (03 231 47 13). **Open** 10pm-5am Sat.
The newest club in Antwerp. Every Saturday it holds one of the biggest gay events in Belgium, which has Dutch punters flocking across the border. *See chapter* **Gay & Lesbian**.

Clubs

L'Acrobat
14-16 rue Borgval, 1000 (513 73 08). Métro Bourse/ tram 23, 52, 55, 56, 81. **Open** 9pm-4am Fri, Sat. **Admission** free.

La Démence – the biggest gay rave in Brussels – blows the **Fuse** *on the third Sunday of the month. See page 158.*

House music and an easygoing door policy attract a trendy crowd to **Mirano Continental**.

A late-twenties and thirtysomething crowd flock to this unpretentious disco bar that falls neatly between alternative and mainstream – perfect for 1980s trendies who have grown up in the last few years. The interior is eclectic kitsch: an Indian-inspired gold-leaf painting here, a Fabergé-egg design there. The DJ spins rap, rock, world music, disco and soul in a thoroughly engaging mix.

Le Bal
47 boulevard du Triomphe, 1050 (649 35 00). **Open** 10pm-4am Thur-Sat. **Admission** 100BF.
Very popular disco with commercial music and mainstream clientele. Flemish people call this a disco for 'Johnny and Marina', which is the same as saying it's a bit tacky. Fine if you like this sort of thing.

Cercle 52
52 rue des Chartreux, 1000 (514 30 78). Métro Bourse/tram 23, 52, 55, 56, 81. **Open** 10pm-6am Thur-Sun. **Admission** 150BF. **Map B3**
The dark room is the main attraction at Cercle 52. *See also chapter* **Gay & Lesbian**.

La Démence
208 rue Blaes, 1000 (511 97 89). Bus 20, 48. **Open** from 11pm third Sun of month. **Admission** varies (check flyers in the bars). **Map B4/B5**
The biggest gay rave in Brussels attracts disco queens from all over Belgium. Muscle boys, clones and fashion victims mix on two floors, with house dominating the ground floor, and garage upstairs. *See also chapter* **Gay & Lesbian**.

D-Light
208 rue Blaes, 1000 (511 97 89). Métro Porte de Halle/bus 20, 48. **Open** 11pm-6am last Fri of month. **Admission** 300BF. **Map B4/B5**
D-Light is the femme alternative to La Démence (*see above*). *See also chapter* **Gay & Lesbian**.

La Doudingue
5 clos Lamartine, 1420 Braine-l'Alleud (384 02 81). **Open** 10pm-6am daily. **Map C3**
Very good music, in a pleasant venue south of Brussels. The clientele is young and fashionable. Worth a visit if you don't mind driving (it's 30-45 minutes from the centre of town) or paying over the odds for a cab.

Espace de Nuit
10 rue Marché aux Fromages, 1000 (502 76 89). **Open** 10pm-6am daily. **Map C3**
Small disco on several floors in a historic house behind the Grand Place, catering mostly for tourists. The music is generally good, though.

The Fuse
208 rue Blaes, 1000 (511 97 89). Métro Porte de Hal/bus 20, 48. **Open** 11pm-7.30am Sat. **Admission** 300BF. **Map B4/B5**
This self-proclaimed 'first techno club in Brussels' has been around since 1993, and keeps getting better. DJs from Detroit, New York, London and Amsterdam spin regularly for the technoheads who turn out a thousand strong every Saturday. The Fuse wins few points on decor, though: the former

Spanish disco relies on the music and the crowd to attract punters in. A smaller dancefloor on the second level takes care of crowd overflow, and 'Cosmos', the chill-out room hidden away on the first floor, plays deep garage and ambient music while video monitors show Japanese animation. Attracts mainly a very young crowd (16+). Check flyers in bars for special events.

Jeux d'Hiver

Bois de la Cambre, 1 Chemin Croquet, 1000 (649 08 64). **Open** varies. **Admission** varies.

A Brussels institution established by three graduates from Solvay, one of the most famous business schools in the world, and still going strong after more than a decade. The place where parents like their daughters to go, as the rich and famous meet here. With its terrace and children's playground, the restaurant is popular during the day, especially in summer.

Mirano Continental

38 chaussée de Louvain, 1030 (218 57 72). Métro Madou/bus 29, 63. **Open** 11pm-late Sat. **Admission** 300-500BF midnight-4am depending on event; free on non-special nights before midnight and after 4am. **Map E3/H2**

For years the only disco in town, this former cinema has undergone a rebirth as other clubs have sprung up. With a reduced attitude quotient, the Mirano crowd runs from yuppie to trendy, while the music is mainly house. Door policy is easygoing, though it helps if you don't look like a dealer or a druggy. Advance screenings of films are also shown here once a month.

Pitt's Bar

53 rue des Minimes, 1000 (514 41 74). Bus 34. **Open** 8pm-3am Wed, Thur; 8pm-5am Fri, Sat. **Admission** free. **Map B5/C4**

Aimed at house, techno and garage lovers, Pitt's Bar (pronounced 'Pete's bar' by locals) is frequented by a mostly sedentary crowd of students and early-twentysomethings.

Scandal Bar

7 rue Borgval, 1000 (no phone). Tram 23, 52, 55, 56, 81/bus 34, 48. **Open** from 11pm daily. **Admission** varies.

Tacky but fun. *See also chapter* **Gay & Lesbian**.

Strong

17 rue Poinçon, 1000 (75 46 22 60). Tram 23, 52, 55, 56, 81/bus 34, 48. **Open** varies. **Admission** varies (see flyers in bars). **Map B4**

The hottest club in town, preferred by many to the Amsterdam club circuit. Sunday night is gay night.

Tour-Taxi

5 rue Picard, 1000 (420 55 05). Métro Ribaucourt. **Open** 5am-5am first Fri of month. **Admission** 200BF; free before midnight.

Huge spectacular space with 40-foot ceilings, aimed at the over-25s. On the first Friday of the month, Tour-Taxi presents 'Manhattan': the best of soul, funk and latino house from the 1970s to the '90s. MCM (the French version of MTV) has its parties here. A restaurant is due to open soon.

TAO After Club

18 place Simonis, 1081 (no phone). **Open** varies. **Admission** varies.

The 5am opening time makes this the place for those who don't want to go home after clubbing on a Saturday night. There's a different event every Sunday. Leave your mobile phone at home.

Who's Who's Land

17 rue Poinçon, 1000 (511 93 88). Tram 23, 52, 55, 56, 81/bus 34, 48. **Open** 9pm-3am, Fri, Sat. **Admission** 300BF. **Map B4**

The place to be, described by its fans as the best and most beautiful club in Europe, with its much-photographed interior. An absolute must. Mixed on Friday and Saturday, exclusively gay on Sundays (when it's called Strong). Check flyers for special events and speak English to the doormen.

Club venues open around 11pm when most clubbers are still gathering in bars and cafés.

Film

From **Man Bites Dog** *to free choc ices, Belgian cinema is a toothsome prospect.*

The first public screening of a film in Belgium took place on 1 March 1896 in the King's Gallery in Brussels. A century on, Belgian cinema's most famous export, like it or not, is the Muscles from Brussels, Jean-Claude van Damme. Meanwhile, Belgian film itself is quietly attaining cult status. The industry's problem is the linguistic divide, which has effectively created two, mutually exclusive national cinemas. Jan Bucquoy's 1995 hit *La Vie Sexuelle des Belges*, which sent up provincial Belgian attitudes, received money from its backers only on condition that it was made in French.

Flemish cinema, too, has done well in the international market, with films such as Stijn Coninx's epic *Daens* (nominated as Best Foreign Film at the 1992 Oscars) about a priest in 1893 Belgium fighting for the rights of the working classes. Robbe de Hert's *Blueberry Hill* and *Brylcreem Boulevard* and Frank van Passel's quirky *Manneken Pis* are all coming-of-age love stories.

Jaco van Dormael became Belgium's best-known director after *Toto le Héros* successfully combined biting childhood reminiscence with Hollywood pathos. Van Dormael's more recent offering, *Le Huitième Jour*, saw French star Daniel Auteuil and talented Down's syndrome actor Pascal Duquenne jointly awarded the Palme d'Or at Cannes. Other 1990s hits include Rémy Belvaux's 1992 *Man Bites Dog* (*C'est arrivé près de chez vous*), an excellent mock-doc-cum-film-noir about a serial killer, which shows the black Belgian sense of humour to a tee. In *Crazy Love*, Dominique Deruddere merged three Charles Bukowski stories into one film. His latest work, *Suite 16*, is a voyeuristic pseudo-existential drama featuring Pete Postlethwaite and lots of sex and death (persisent themes in Belgian cinema).

Moviegoing in Brussels

Good news for purists is that if foreign films are dubbed, they are often shown in the original version (with subtitles) as well. Cinema quality is generally high, seats comfortable, legroom extensive and prices reasonable. In addition to the cinemas listed below, there are occasional events and festivals at local cultural centres and *communes* (try St Gilles on 538 90 20). German films are shown regularly at the Goethe Institut (230 39 70). To receive a newsletter listing Hispanic cultural events contact the Maison de l'Amérique Latine (538 19 12).

Cinemas

Films change on Wednesdays in Brussels. For details, check listings published in *Le Soir*'s Wednesday cultural supplement *MAD*, or the *Bulletin* (*see chapter* **Media**), or the Belgian cinema Internet site at http://www.cinebel.com/ which gives comprehensive listings for the whole country. Abbreviations to look out for are:

EA under-16s admitted
CNA or ENA under-16s not admitted
St subtitles
V angl English version
V fr French version
VO original version, ie not dubbed.

You will find officious ushers and usherettes guarding the doors at most cinemas. It's customary to tip them 20-30BF, and failure to do so may result in a torrent of quite incomprehensible abuse until you pay up. Tickets usually cost 200-280BF, often with concessions for students, OAPs and the unwaged. Some cinemas also offer reductions to everyone on Mondays. Unless otherwise stated, none of the cinemas listed below accepts credit cards.

Actors' Studio

16 petite rue des Bouchers, 1000 (0900 29 969/512 16 96). Métro De Brouckère/tram 23, 52, 55, 56, 81/bus 29, 60, 63, 65, 66, 71. **Tickets** 180-220BF; *season 720BF four films for one person, 1,080BF six films for two people.* **Map C3**
Located in a passageway just off the tourist trail near the Grand Place, the two screens at the Actors' Studio each show four or five films a day, usually an interesting combination of prizewinning arthouse movies, such as Atom Egoyan's *The Sweet Hereafter*, and a few mainstream Hollywood and foreign films.

Arenberg Galeries

26 galerie de la Reine, 1000 (0900 29 550/512 80 63). Métro Gare Centrale/bus 65, 66, 71, 29, 60, 63. **Tickets** 190-240BF; *season 2,000BF ten films.*
This converted art deco theatre in the Galeries St Hubert is elegant and comfortable, with good air-conditioning. Its two auditoria show three or four films at a time, usually high-quality arty foreign films. It sells film posters, a few arthouse videos and Häagen-Dazs ice-cream, as well as other frozen treats and a free monthly programme with reviews. Its annual festival, Ecran Total (1 July-15 Sept), offers a daunting choice of independent films.

A converted art deco theatre in the Galeries St Hubert, **Arenberg Galeries** *offers you comfort, quality movies and Häagen-Dazs.*

Aventure

57 galerie du Centre (entrances in rue des Fripiers & rue de la Fourche), 1000 (219 17 48). Métro De Brouckère/ tram 23, 52, 55, 56, 81/bus 29, 60, 63, 65, 66, 71. **Tickets** 150-200BF. **Map B3/C3**

The three screens lack quality projection and digital sound and the air-conditioning/heating tends towards the extreme but the deluxe seating offers some compensation. Aventure shows an eclectic mixture of mainstream Hollywood and foreign product and is also a good place to catch rare independent features and sneak previews. The ushers and usherettes are particularly vitriolic if crossed.

Kinepolis

Bruparck, 1 avenue du Centenaire, 1020 (bookings 474 26 00; information French 0900 35 241, Flemish 0900 35 240). Métro Heysel/bus 84, 89. **Tickets** 200-250BF.

A 28-screen multiplex, part of a themed complex, Bruparck, which is invariably filled with 13-year-olds on group outings. Since Kinepolis opened, Brussels cinemas have been forced to raise their standards to match its excellent levels of comfort (double armrests on all seats) and sound and picture quality. It also boasts the largest Imax screen in Europe, with full sensurround effects. Films tend to be mainstream Hollywood fare and all the big hits.

Wheelchair access.

Movy Club

21 rue des Moines, 1060 (537 69 54). Tram 52/bus 49, 50. **Tickets** 130-200BF; *membership card* 10BF (and normal prices for films), 12th film free.

A favourite with students, playing a mixture of classics (Bergman) and quirky mainstream favourites (Mike Leigh). The location means that you should plan your journey carefully, though the unique 1934 interior is worth the trip.

Wheelchair access.

Musée du Cinéma

Palais des Beaux Arts, 9 rue Baron Horta, 1000 (507 83 70). Métro Parc or Gare Centrale/tram 92, 93, 94/bus 38, 60, 71, 95, 96. **Open** 5.30-10.30pm daily. No under-16s. **Tickets** 50-80BF by phone 24 hours in advance; 60-90BF on the day. **Map D4**

The permanent exhibition traces the development of cinema, up to its actual invention, including interactive eighteenth- and nineteenth-century zoetropes. The cinema has two screens, both undubbed; the second shows two silent movies a day, with piano accompaniment. There are several themes each month; a typical week's programme might include Chaplin, Hitchcock, Cronenberg, Resnais, Antonioni and Fassbinder. Weekly classes in film analysis are taught in French and Flemish, and the cinema organises the Ciné-découvertes festival every 1-15 July, screening films that haven't found Belgian distributors.

Nova

3 rue d'Arenberg, 1000 (511 27 74). Métro Gare Centrale/bus 29, 60, 63, 65, 66, 71. **Tickets** 150-200BF; *season* 900BF six films. **Map C3**

This trendy one-screen cinema boasting 200 seats, a stage, balcony and post-atomic décor is housed in the old Théatre des Capucines. The programme concentrates on the more challenging end of recentish international releases. Every Friday at midnight, Nova hosts 'Nocturne': variously, film noir, sf or *The Rocky Horror Picture Show*. Look out, too, for the free monthly 'Open Screen' where anyone can bring their amateur efforts in Super 8, 15mm, 35 mm or video; 15 minutes maximum) to be shown to all and sundry on the big screen. 'Live Soundtracks', where DJs and/or musicians create a soundtrack to a film of their choice, is held regularly and costs 250BF. During the summer months, Nova also organises street projections on to old buildings. If you're not in the mood for a film, try out the lively bar, which features DJs every Thursday.

Styx

72 rue de l'Arbre Bénit, 1050 (0900 29 969). Métro Porte de Namur/bus 54, 71. **Tickets** 170-200BF.

The two tiny screens in Ixelles show arthouse staples such as *A Clockwork Orange*, *Brazil* and *Wings of Desire*. There are not many staff: occasionally you'll find the same person selling tickets, providing refreshments and manning the projector, so be patient if the door is still locked ten minutes before the film's due to start.

UGC Acropole

Entrances at 17 Galerie de la Toison d'Or & 8 avenue de la Toison d'Or, 1050 (French 0900 104 40; Flemish 0900 104 50). Métro Porte de Namur/tram 34, 80. **Tickets** 180-240BF; *season* 730BF four films for one person, 1,080BF six films for two people. **Map C6/D5**

This 11-screen cinema is not quite as glitzy or as stylishly designed as UGC De Brouckère. Queuing is confusing as there are two queues to the two entrances, both often very long. Mainstream Hollywood fodder and a lot of French blockbusters await you within, and the air-conditioned auditoria are comfortable.

UGC De Brouckère

38 place de Brouckère, 1000 (French 0900 10 440; Flemish 0900 104 50). Métro De Brouckère/tram 23, 52, 55, 56, 81/bus 29, 60, 63, 65, 66, 71. **Tickets** 180-240BF; *season* 730BF four films for one person, 1,080BF six films for two people. **Credit** AmEx. **Map C2**

Bang in the city centre, this building somehow fits 12 screens into a stripped-brick and exposed-metal interior. It's all very cyberspace as you zoom up the escalators, past the bars, to your film. The flagship screen is the lavish 70mm Gran Eldorado. The queues tend to be on the long side, and the ushers seem to double up as bouncers on Friday and Saturday nights. It shows big Hollywood mainstream films, plus a few arty European offerings such as the movies of Pedro Almodóvar.

Vendôme

18 chaussée de Wavre, 1050 (0900 29 909/502 37 00). Métro Porte de Namur/bus 34, 54, 71, 80. **Tickets** 190-240BF; *season* 1,020BF six films for one or two people. **Map D5/H6**

Mid-size cinema with five screens, all featuring digital sound and comfortable seating and showing a mixture of mainstream and a few big arthouse films.

Cinema specials

Special screenings – especially late at night or early in the morning – are a Brussels speciality. See above for venue details unless listed.

Ciné-Apéro

Espace Delvaux, place Keym (entrance at 3 rue Gratès), 1170 (672 13 01). Bus 41, 95, 96. **Times** 6pm, 8.30pm, Wed. **Tickets** 160BF; 120BF concessions.

A film (one of the big hits from the previous year), served with a free apéritif (from 7.30-8.30pm) in a venue more often used as a theatre.

Ciné-Famille

Espace Delvaux (see above). **Times** 3pm every other Sun. **Tickets** 160BF; 120BF concessions.

Children's classics and animation fairy-tales from the likes of Walt Disney, dubbed into French.

Ciné-Loisirs

Botanique, 236 rue Royale, 1000 (226 12 09/226 12 10). Métro Botanique/tram 92, 93, 94/bus 58. **Tickets** 60-140BF. **Times** 3pm Wed. **Map D4/E1**

A recent French-language film (admittedly of somewhat variable quality) is shown weekly at this very conveniently located francophone cultural centre.

Dive In

Cybertheatre, 4-5 avenue de la Toison d'Or, 1050 (500 78 11). Métro Porte de Namur/bus 34, 80. **Tickets** free. **Times** 9.30pm Mon. **Map C6/D5**

Classic cinema (Godard, Spike Lee, David Lynch) shown with remixed soundtracks by live DJs in this cavernous cybercafé. Recent attractions have included British director Anthony Minghella interviewed by video-conference about Shakespeare's *The Tempest*. The Cybertheatre is also involved with the Brussels Film Festival, and is a good information point on film in general. Its Internet homepage is at http://www.nirvanet.com/

Drive-in Movies

Esplanade du Cinquantenaire, 1040 (346 59 49). Métro Merode/tram 81, 82/bus 20, 61, 80. **Times** *July-Aug* 8pm for screening at 10.30pm Fri-Sat.

A summer favourite that brings out every pink Cadillac in town. Pedestrians are not left out: headphones and deck-chairs are provided. Films are mainstream hits.

Le Documentaire

Espace Delvaux (see above). **Times** *Sept-June* 8.30pm Tue once a month. **Tickets** 160BF; 130BF concessions.

Belgian and foreign documentaries, shorts and features, on a wide variety of topics, sometimes followed by a debate.

Matinées Classiques pour Jeunes

Musée du Cinéma (see above). **Times** 3pm every other Sun. **Tickets** 50BF. **Map D4**

An introduction to classic all-time favourites such as *West Side Story*, Buster Keaton's *Sherlock Junior* and films by Chaplin and Tati. Worth knowing about, as under-16s are not admitted to the Museum's other screenings.

Midnight Screenings

UGC De Brouckère (see above). **Times** midnight Sat. **Tickets** 180-240BF. **Map C2**

You get to see a preview of a big film about a fortnight before the official release date. Usually very popular: it's best to queue for tickets earlier in the evening.

Les Petits Déjeuners du Cinéma

UGC Acropole (see above). **Times** 10am Sat. **Tickets** 240BF. **Map C6/D5**

The ticket price covers coffee, croissant and the film, which is usually a big hit from the previous year.

Proximus Sneak Preview

Kinepolis (see above). **Times** 8pm Tue. **Tickets** 200BF.

Kinepolis's version of Sneak Preview (*see below*), with a greater emphasis on standard Hollywood fare that's already been shown in the US.

Samedis du Cinéma

UGC De Brouckère (see above). **Times** 9.30am Sat. **Tickets** 60BF (free choc ice). **Map C2**

Two films, one a mainstream family movie, the other a more eccentric offering.

Sérénades en Chambre Noire

Espace Senghor, 366 chaussée de Wavre, 1040 (230 31 40). Métro Schuman. **Times** *Oct-Mar* 4.30pm Sun. **Tickets** 170BF; 140BF concessions; *season* 1,000BF eight screenings. **Map D5/H6**

Relaxed winter Sunday event showing mainly European films (the audience has a say in voting for films they want to see in the forthcoming season), with some token Hollywood blockbusters, usually last season's hits. You get a free drink at the end.

Sex and death Belgian style in **Suite 16**.

Sneak Preview

Cinédit, 26 Arenberg Galeries, 1000 (512 80 63). Métro Gare Centrale/bus 65, 66, 71, 29, 60, 63. **Times** *Sept-June* 9.30pm Thur. **Tickets** 240BF; 190BF Mon.

A surprise film shown pre-release, the main purpose being to gauge the audience's reaction. Results of the poll are posted on a chart outside.The guinea pigs watch mostly arthouse or mainstream fare from the UK, USA or France, with the odd obscure international production thrown in, too. It soon fills up, so arrive early and enjoy the charged atmosphere.

Festivals

Belgium has a busy calendar of film festivals dotted around the country. The main event is the **Brussels Film Festival** in January (227 39 80). Dennis Hopper, Neil Jordan and Bertrand Tavernier were guests at the 25th Festival in 1998.

February is a always a busy time. The **Festival du Dessin Animé et du Film d'Animation** is held in the last two weeks of February at Passage 44 (218 27 35/534 41 25), and the **Romantic Film Festival** in Mons starts around St Valentine's Day (065 36 37 99).

March brings the **Social Film Festival** to Charleroi (071 47 34 53) while the **African Film Festival** is at Brussels' Palais des Beaux Arts (507 82 00) in June. The **Flanders Film Festival** (09 221 89 46) arrives annually in October, and come December, there's a **Short Films Festival** in Louvain (016 35 67 77).

Gay & Lesbian

Its profile may have remained lower than in other countries for somewhat longer, but the gay scene in Belgium has been catching up apace.

Belgium's first national lesbian and gay pride event was only held in 1996, more than a quarter of a century after Stonewall in New York, the uprising that led to gay pride events around the world. However, gays and lesbians enjoy more rights here than in countries such as the US and Britain, simply because they've been largely ignored by the legal system. Furthermore, the government, and most other political parties, are in favour of legalising gay marriages.

Broad-mindedness in government has not, however, always been reflected at grass-roots level. Bitter disagreements between gay organisations recently degenerated into farce, when a government-backed commission that would have represented the various groups had to be abandoned because of the refusal of rival gay (though not lesbian) organisations to work together.

An unofficial apartheid exists between male and female gays. Male bars are sniffy about admitting women; female bars – notably L'Archange (*see below*) – will cheerfully admit gay men. The men have the best of the deal, with a reasonable choice of bars and clubs; the lesbian scene is more or less confined to a couple of bars near the Bourse.

Bars

L'Archange
9 rue Borgval, 1000 (no phone). Tram 23, 52, 55, 56, 81/bus 34, 48. **Open** from 10pm Tue, Thur-Sat.
One of only two lesbian bars in Brussels, the other being Sapho (*see below*). It's a dark, cosy, nondescript bar, frequented by every lesbian in the city who goes out. Men allowed.

Le Belgica
32 rue du Marché au Charbon, 1000 (no phone). Tram 23, 52, 55, 56, 81/bus 34, 48. **Open** 10pm-3am Thur-Sat. **Map B3**
The most fashionable gay bar in Brussels and the place to find out where the best parties are. Neither as prissy nor as raunchy as most of the competition, Le Belgica still sports the designer dilapidation that has characterised it since the 1980s: yellow, peeling walls, functional wood chairs, and tables that look as if they've been salvaged from a garage sale. The house drink, a genever cocktail served in shot glasses, is more potent than it looks.

Chez Flo
25 rue au Beurre, 1000 (513 31 52). Tram 23, 52, 55, 56, 81/bus 34, 48, 95, 96. **Open** 8pm-midnight Wed-Sun. **Show** 9.30pm. **Map C3**
A drag show with dinner thrown in, it's one of the most touristy gay places in Brussels, but none the worse for that.

Chez Maman
7 rue des Grandes Carmes, 1000 (no phone). Métro Bourse. **Open** 7pm-2am Wed,Thur; 10pm-late Fri, Sat. **Map B3**
Tiny bar, famous for its drag shows on Fridays and Saturdays and attracting a predominantly but not wholly gay crowd. 'Maman' and her entourage perform a limited range of numbers, such as 'Que Sera, Sera' and 'Nine to Five' on the bar-top, which is no more than eight feet long. What's impressive is not so much the acts themselves, but the fact that the stiletto-wearing performers avoid breaking ankles.

Le Comptoir
24-25 place de la Vieille Halle-aux-Blés, 1000 (514 05 00). Métro Gare Centrale/bus 34, 48. **Open** 7pm-midnight Mon-Thur; 7pm-1am Fri-Sun daily.
A landmark building housing a precious crowd: cravats, kept boys and their keepers, and yuppies in dry-cleaned jeans. Upstairs, the restaurant serves nouvelle cuisine and stylish updates on more traditional European fare in an environment best described as *haut paysan*.

*A mixed crowd is over the moon at **La Luna**.*

Totem – cosy and friendly – see page 166.

Le Duquesnoy
*12 rue Duquesnoy, 1000 (502 38 83). Métro Gare
Centrale.* **Open** 8pm-4am Mon-Sat; 6pm-4am Sun.
Map C4
Very 1980s and very raunchy, with a TV playing borderline
S&M porno and leather-clad barmen. A back staircase leads
up to two floors of dark rooms. The music ranges from gener-
ic divas belting out disco versions of familiar tunes to the
Pet Shop Boys. Every gay man in Brussels denies going here,
but the customers must come from somewhere.

H₂0
*27 rue du Marché au Charbon, 1000 (512 38 43). Tram
23, 52, 55, 56, 81/bus 34, 48.* **Open** 7pm-2am daily.
Map B3
Whether the decor is a failed attempt at Gothic or baroque
is hard to say. Still, this cosy dark bar serving a light menu
of salads and snacks, as well as a more rounded drinks menu,
does have considerable charm, with plenty of intimate corners for têtes-à-têtes. It welcomes women as well as men,
which is saying a lot for any gay establishment in Brussels.

Het Hessenhuis
53 Falconrui, 2000 Antwerp (03 231 13 56). **Open** May-
Feb 5pm-late Tue-Sun.
Part of a museum, 'Het Hessenhuis', this serves by day as a
tearoom for elderly straights. After the museum closes, it
becomes a busy meeting place for gays on their way to a
party or club. Recommended.

Het Rijk der Zinnen
*14 rue des Pierres, 1000 (511 26 59). Tram 23, 52, 55,
56, 81/bus 34, 48.* **Open** 11am-7am Mon-Fri; 3pm-7am
Sat, Sun. **Map B3**
The English translation, the Empire of the Senses, is rather
grand for this bar: however appropriate it once was, Het Rijk
der Zinnen now has a sort of down-at-heel charm. Definitely

not a fashion bar, it's where you end up when everywhere
else is closed and you're still trying to get laid. Pasta and
other light dishes served.

Incognito
*36 rue des Pierres, 1000 (513 37 88). Tram 23, 52, 55,
56, 81/bus 34, 48.* **Open** 11am-4am daily. **Map B3**
Smoked-glass windows allow for one-way people-watching:
patrons can see out, but passers-by can't see in. Clientele is
mainstream, the music mostly French pop and disco (Celine
Dion is a patron saint), heavy aftershave is *de rigueur*.
Incognito is one of the only bars in Brussels to have been
firebombed, but it remains highly popular.

Sapho
*1 rue St Géry (512 45 52). Tram 23, 52, 55, 56, 81/bus
34, 48.* **Open** 10pm-6am Fri, Sat.
There's a constant boomeranging between L'Archange (*see
above*) and here. Men are quite welcome if accompanied by
a convincing-looking lesbian.

Shakespeare
*24 Oude Koornmarkt, 2000 Antwerp (03 231 50 58).
Tram 23, 52, 55, 56, 81/bus 34, 48.* **Open** from 10pm
Fri, Sat.
Catering to a largely butch crowd, this small, dark pub is the
oldest survivor in the Antwerp lesbian landscape. Music is
a mixture of rock, soul, house and disco; men are welcome if
accompanied by a woman.

The Slave
*7 Plattesteen, 1000 (513 14 14). Tram 23, 52, 55, 56,
81/bus 34, 48.* **Open** from 9pm daily.
Sleaze-wise, the only bar that gives Le Duquesnoy (*see above*)
a run for its money. Breaking the very 1980s gloom are
monitors playing porn and music videos (the ubiquitous
Madonna, Barbra and Liza) competing with the thumping
house tapes. Down below, dark rooms are provided for those
who want to get a little more personal.

Eating & drinking

Lola
*33 place du Grand Sablon, 1000 (514 24 60). Tram 92,
93, 94/bus 34, 95, 96.* **Open** noon-3pm, 6.30-11pm, daily.
Map C4
Highly popular international brasserie that has become a
meeting place for the gay arty jet set (interior designers, art
dealers, dilettanti). The only straight restaurant in Brussels
where you'll see the entire staff cheerfully singing 'Happy
Birthday' for an all-male table.

La Luna
177 Italiëlei, 2018 Antwerp (03 232 23 44). **Open** noon-
2.30pm, 6-11pm, Mon-Fri; 6-11pm Sat.
Fabulous interior and fabulous food. Never intended as a gay
venue, but since it's the newest and trendiest place in Antwerp,
all fashion-conscious gay men and women want to be there.

L'Orange-Bleu
*29 rue Antoine Dansaert, 1000 (513 98 29). Tram 23, 52,
55, 56, 81/bus 63.* **Open** 7pm-3am Tue-Sat. **Map A2/B2**
Greek and Roman statues, art deco prints and burnished oak
and redwood turn-of-the-century furnishings make L'O-B so
aesthetically entrancing that you probably won't notice that
you're paying an arm and a leg for the experience.

Le Petit Boxeur
*3 rue Borgval, 1000 (511 40 00). Tram 23, 52, 55, 56,
81/bus 34, 48.* **Open** 8pm-11pm Tue-Sat.
Tiny but exquisite restaurant next to L'Archange (*see above*),
with trendy gay/straight clientele. The owner (dentist by day)
provides a warm welcome; food is delicious but not cheap.

La Démence – *the biggest gay rave in town attracts punters from all over the country.*

Tels Quels

81 rue du Marché au Charbon, 1000 (512 32 34). Tram 23, 52, 55, 56, 81/bus 34, 48. **Open** 5pm-2am Mon-Thur, Sun; 5pm-4am Fri, Sat. **Map B3**

A Brussels institution: the only place in town that caters equally to lesbians and gay men (though some nights cater exclusively to one or the other). Tels Quels has a strong political slant: it includes an archive of gay rights and history (open evenings Mon, Tue) and hosts group discussions.

Totem

42 rue de la Grande Ile, 1000 (514 46 10). Tram 23, 52, 55, 56, 81/bus 34, 48. **Open** 7pm-midnight Wed-Sun. **Map B4**

A restaurant-cum-art gallery, close to most of the gay and lesbian bars, in one of the small streets around the Bourse. It isn't exclusively gay, but none of the straight customers will stare if you feel like holding hands. Perhaps not the best food in town, but very cosy and friendly.

Le Troisième Acte

28 rue des Pierres, 1000 (502 56 49). Tram 23, 52, 55, 56, 81/bus 34, 96. **Map B3**

The secret of Le Troisième Acte is its unvarnished charm: gingham tablecloths, sepia-toned walls and no-nonsense furnishings provide a refreshing change from overdone gay restaurants. The clientele is mostly downtown and trendy, with some uptown yuppies making a sojourn every now and then for the simple Belgian and French cuisine.

Clubs

Cercle 52

52 rue des Chartreux, 1000 (514 30 78). Tram 23, 52, 55, 56, 81. **Open** 10pm-6am Thur-Sun. **Admission** 150BF. **Map B3**

It used to be a disco, but Cercle 52 has now become a club quite similar to the Slave (*see above*) and Le Duquesnoy (*see above*).The dark room is the main attraction.

La Démence

208 rue Blaes, 1000 (511 97 89). Bus 20, 48. **Open** from 11pm third Sun of month. **Admission** varies (check flyers in the bars). **Map B4/B5**

The biggest gay rave in Brussels, attracting disco queens from all over Belgium. Muscle boys, clones, hairdressers and fashion victims mix on the two floors, with mainstream house dominating the ground floor, and more solid garage keeping bodies moving on the upper level. A dark room and chill-out room are also available.

D-Light

208 rue Blaes, 1000 (511 97 89). Métro Porte de Halle/bus 20, 48. **Open** 11pm-6am last Fri of month. **Admission** 300BF. **Map B4/B5**

D-Light is the femme alternative to La Démence (*see above*), but with a more exclusive following. The music, however, is a more accessible brand of house than you will find at most venues.

Red & Blue

13 Lange Schipperskapellestraat, 2000 Antwerp (03 231 47 13). **Open** 10pm-5am Sat.

The newest club in Antwerp. Every Saturday it holds one of the biggest gay events in Belgium, which has Dutch punters flocking across the border.

Scandal Bar

7 rue Borgval, 1000 (no phone). Tram 23, 52, 55, 56, 81/bus 34, 48. **Open** from 11pm daily. **Admission** varies.

Not an official lesbian or gay disco, but sufficiently easy-going to make you feel comfortable. The music is largely rai (North African pop). Tacky but fun.

Strong

17 rue Poinçon, 1000 (no phone). Tram 23, 52, 55, 56, 81/bus 34, 48. **Open** varies (see flyers in bars). **Map B4**

The hottest club in town, preferred by many punters to the Amsterdam club circuit. Enough said?

Private clubs

Atthis
7 Volkstraat, 2000 Antwerp (03 216 37 37).
Open 8.30pm-2am Fri, Sat.
A women-only private club that's a little more refined than the majority of lesbian clubs in Belgium. There's a video library and a lesbian centre that's run under the same name.

Boots
22 Van Aerdstraat, 2060 Antwerp (03 233 21 36).
Open 10.30pm-5am Fri, Sat. **Admission** free.
Without a doubt the raunchiest, sleaziest bar in Belgium: tell someone that you're a regular here, and you immediately have a reputation to live up to. Rooms are designated for any sexual activity you could imagine (well, almost: no llamas yet) and the crowds are completely oblivious to anything but their own pleasure.

Saunas

Macho 2
106-108 rue du Marché au Charbon, 1000 (513 56 67).
Tram 23, 52, 55, 56, 81. **Open** noon-2am Mon-Thur; noon-4am Fri, Sat; 2pm-2am Sun. **Admission** 450BF; 300BF under-25s. **Map B3**
Macho 2 offers hygienic facilities for those who might be in the market for a legitimate sauna. You'll find a large steam room, workout space, a small movie theatre and plenty of cabins to rest in. Clientele covers all ages but is typically slightly younger than Oasis (*see below*).

Oasis
10 rue Van Orley, 1000 (218 08 00). Métro Botanique/ tram 91, 92, 93, 94. **Open** noon-1am daily. **Admission** 450BF Mon, Wed-Sun; 250BF Tue.
Pretty boys and sugar daddies flock to this sauna to work up a sweat. The space is one of the most appealing in Brussels – an old converted townhouse that has retained some of its original splendour. Buffet on Saturdays, and special days for the less sylph-like patrons.

Hairdressers

Man to Man
9 rue des Riches Claires, 1000 (514 18 23). Tram 23, 52, 55, 56, 81. **Open** 10am-6.30pm Tue-Sat.
Map B3
The window features an ever-changing display of nipple clamps, handcuffs and other S&M hardware, which gives Man to Man a more menacing impression than it really merits. Basic haircutting and styling are on offer, and there are fetish items on sale.

Sex shops

Le Classix
13 rue des Riches Claires, 1000 (514 55 62). Tram 23, 52, 55, 56, 81. **Open** 5-11pm Mon-Sat. **Map B3**
A sex supermarket of videos, magazines and other paraphernalia. In a more discreet street than Erot'X (*see below*), which makes entering and leaving a less public affair.

Erot'X Stars
40 boulevard Maurice Lemonnier, 1000 (513 93 44).
Tram 23, 52, 55, 56, 81. **Open** 11am-9pm daily. **Map A4/B4**
Erot'X Stars offers two floors of male videos to buy or rent, with private cabins for in-store viewing, plus a limited range of poppers, latex and other accessories.

Associations

Education about and action against AIDS are the *raison d'être* of the organisations **Aide Infor Sida** (514 29 65/hotline 511 45 29), **Act Together** (511 33 33/512 05 05) and **Act Up** (512 02 02). Aide Infor Sida concentrates on combating ignorance surrounding the disease, while Act Together is more a support system for sufferers, their families and friends. Act Up campaigns for more funding and research and better treatment for the ill.

For those embarking on a long-term stay in Brussels, there's the **English-Speaking Gay Group** for lesbians and gay men, which publishes a newsletter, *The Group*, listing its activities. Write to EGG, BP 198, 1060 Bruxelles 6.

Egalité
200 rue de la Loi, 1049 (295 98 97). **Lines open** 10am-5pm daily. **Map D3/G4**
This coalition of gays and lesbians working at EU institutions aims to fight discrimination in their workplace rather than in society as a whole.

International Gay & Lesbian Association
81 rue du Marché au Charbon, 1000 (502 24 71). Tram 23, 52, 55, 56, 81. **Open** by appointment. **Map B3**
Housed in the same building as Tels Quels (*see above*), the IGLA has been working for equal rights for lesbians and gay men since 1978.

Tel'Egal
Postbox 1969, 1000 (502 79 38). **Lines open** 8pm-midnight Mon-Fri.
This hotline serves the gay and lesbian community, dispensing legal and social advice.

Clean facilities for legit sauna at **Macho 2**.

Media

Being at the centre of Europe gives Brussels a wealth of choice when it comes to reading, listening or viewing.

As an international city, Brussels rightly enjoys international media. Even the humblest news-stands sell periodicals in English and German, as well as French and Flemish, with the larger ones selling Spanish, Italian, Greek, Portuguese and Arabic publications, too. The numerous terrestrial, satellite and cable television stations that can be received in Brussels are similarly polyglot.

Quantity is not, of course, an indicator of quality. Newspapers range from the lurid to the soporific, but the paedophile scandal (*see chapter* **History: Brussels Today**) that has rocked the nation for the past two years has encouraged the national media to take themselves more seriously, and journalistic standards have noticeably risen as a result.

Newspapers

La Dernière Heure

This popular right-wing daily is the closest thing Brussels has to a tabloid in French. Sports coverage is its chief strength, which even its detractors concede is excellent.

L'Echo

Crammed with balance sheets, economic predictions and Stock Exchange movements. An acquired taste.

European Voice

Published by the usually acerbic *Economist*, this upstart weekly provides an insider's view of EU policies and politics, while eschewing overly critical comment. Style-wise, *European Voice* looks like a student newspaper, but if you know how to read between the lines, you might learn something of interest.

Het Laaste Nieuws

Once renowned as *the* traditionally liberal Flemish daily, with both bourgeois and populist leanings, *Het Laaste Nieuws* has lately entered the tabloid fray, going in for sensationalist coverage of crime stories and star interviews. Though nowhere near as extreme as, say, the *News of the World*, it's nothing like the paper it used to be.

La Libre Belgique

Very Catholic French daily. *La Libre Belgique* has the distinction of being the only francophone paper to have maintained its editorial independence during World War II. If you don't mind wading through moralising editorials and articles about the papacy, it's a better read than anything else you'll find in French.

Le Matin

This French newcomer resulted from the merging of two left-wing papers, *La Wallonie* and *Le Peuple*. Close to the Socialist Party, *Le Matin* considers itself as a progressive publication and is working hard to become Belgium's answer to France's *Libération*.

De Morgen

Once the staple of socialist workers, *De Morgen* has evolved into a more general Flemish left-wing daily, covering the arts, fashion and human interest, as well as national and international news. Reputation for investigative journalism.

Le Soir

The most widely read francophone daily, known for its quality and its independent views. Good on Wednesdays for the cultural supplement *MAD* and on Fridays for its accessible economic section *Eco Soir*.

De Standaard

The quality Flemish daily is very Catholic and conservative in its approach to reporting, which means that while its accuracy is usually unimpeachable, it can also be very boring.

Magazines

Bulletin

The only English-language weekly in Brussels, this is the magazine to read if you don't understand French or Flemish but still want to know what's going on in the country. It contains *What's On*, a supplement of comprehensive cinema, concert and television listings.

Dag Allemaal

If you've wondered how *Hello!* magazine would read in Dutch, *Dag Allemaal* is the answer. Its frothy interviews, entertaining articles and glossy photo spreads (bought in from other publications) make it the biggest-selling magazine in Belgium.

Humo

Originally a Flemish mag with television listings, *Humo* has become an irreverent, ironic, intellectual and anarchistic publication, rather like a lefty student who never grew up. Music, film, politics and the arts all get a weekly going-over.

Kiosk

If you read French, this paperback-sized monthly is a must for finding out what's going on. Cafés, bars, art shows, clubs, films, exhibitions and other events are all covered.

Télémoustique

Previously a TV/leisure weekly, *Télémoustique* came of age when it reported on the paedophile scandal that broke in the summer of 1996. Since then it has continued to demonstrate a flair for scoops and investigative reports.

Le Vif-Express/Knack

These sister publications – the former in French, the latter in Flemish – are the only news magazines in Belgium. Both publish glossy weekend supplements covering fashion, travel and lifestyle.

Brussels news-stands bulge with papers and periodicals in French, Flemish, English, German, Italian and many other languages.

BRUSSEL-HALLE

Vlan

Emploi - Immo - Auto - Loisi

Hebd

J'ANNONCE

J'AN
le journal des

Deuxième année • Paraît chaque semaine le vendre

AUTO/MOTO/
RUBRIQUE 3

1 EMPLOI

2 IMMO

3 AUTO-VELO-MOTO

4 LA MAISON

5 LOISIRS-HOBBY

6

Radio

To keep the 'cultural imperialism' of American and British music at bay, radio stations receiving subsidies must make at least 60 per cent of their music broadcasts in the language of the region from which the station is funded. For the outsider, it's a good way to pick up some linguistic tips. Bear in mind that frequencies for the same station differ in other parts of the country.

Bel RTL
104 mhz
News, music and games are the mainstay of this French-speaking station, which began as a spin-off from the TV channel RTL-TVi (*see below*). Some star presenters continue to appear on both.

BFM
107.6 mhz
A new talk-only station in French, with news bulletins every 50 minutes and programmes on a variety of issues, including politics, the economy, culture and the environment.

Bruxelles-Capitale
99.3 mhz
News station, available only in Brussels, which makes the most of the intimacy of its listener-base.

Musique 3
91.2 mhz
French-owned classical music station.

La Première
92.5 mhz
The French state-owned station now has a distinctly old-fashioned air but continues to schedule news programmes, political debates, game shows, sporting events and serials.

Radio 21
93.2 mhz
Francophone pop-rock station that tends to play music that's neither new enough to be current nor old enough to be nostalgia. However, it's also the place to catch up on music that you're unlikely to hear anywhere else.

Radio Contact
102.2 mhz
The most visible radio station in Brussels. Its blue dolphin logo is on the back of every Renault Clio, its (never *quite* up-to-the-minute) pop output on the PA of every boutique.

Studio Brussel
100.6 mhz
Popular Flemish station aimed at those with eclectic and international musical tastes. Slots are dedicated to genres ranging from rock 'n' roll to reggae and rai (North African pop). Jazz (acid, freestyle and old school), hip-hop, alternative rock and other sounds are all tossed into the mix. This is as hip as Brussels gets.

VRT1
91.7 mhz
The most serious of the three Flemish state-owned radio stations, VRT1 features political discussions as well as classical music.

VRT2
93.7 mhz
The popular station in the Flemish state-owned VRT (formerly BRTN) triumvirate, generally concentrating on oldies and some Top 40 hits.

VRT3
89.5 mhz
High culture is this Flemish station's forte: profiles of composers, choral, chamber and classical concerts, and opera.

Television

Belgium is the most cabled-up country in the world, giving viewers access not only to national and local stations, but also to French, German, Dutch, British, Italian, Spanish, Portuguese and Arabic TV. Among the most popular stations are France's TF1, France 2 and France 3 stations, the pay-film channel Canal Plus, the cultural channel Arte, and MCM, the Gallic version of MTV. Holland 1, 2 and 3 provide a wide variety of chat shows, educational programmes and entertainment. Because of their general fluency in English, Flemish-speaking viewers tune in regularly to BBC1 and BBC2, NBC Superchannel and CNN.

Eurosport 21
Sport-only, state-run, francophone station, on from 8am till midnight.

Kanaal 2
Sister station to VTM, showing mainly anglophone series and made-for-TV films. Broadcasts from 5pm to midnight.

RTBF
The state-run francophone station has retained respectability due to the lack of competition. It plays on two complementary channels. La Une has a varied programme, including news, popular films and game shows; La Deux offers more cultural programming, with documentaries, cookery shows and undubbed films. Broadcasts from 6am to midnight.

RTL-TVi
The commercial French station is beginning to give state-owned TV a run for its money with its current-affairs coverage. Otherwise, it's undemanding: soaps, sitcoms and talk shows. Its sister station, Club-RTL, shows cartoons and old movies. Both stations broadcast from noon till midnight.

Télé-Bruxelles/TV Brussel
Twin public-access French and Flemish stations covering local news with more streetwise flair than the state-owned and commercial stations. Done on a shoestring budget, which makes it more compelling. Broadcasts from 6pm to 2am.

VRT
The Flemish version of RTBF, this state-owned station (formerly BRTN) is fighting a prolonged ratings war with the commercial channels – hence the number of soaps, serials and game shows. Even in its news coverage, VRT has lost its old dominance. Broadcasts from 6am to midnight.

VT4
This independently owned station started out in the early 1990s as a cultural alternative to the populist VTM and stodgy VRT. Unfortunately, its experiments with off-the-wall chat shows and would-be innovative series failed to attract sufficient ratings to justify costs, and it's since resorted to cheaper, largely American programming, with a plethora of soaps. Broadcasts from 7am to midnight.

VTM
This popular, privately owned station offers the best Flemish news coverage, as well as its own talk shows, soap operas and game shows. Broadcasts from 7am to midnight.

Music: Classical & Opera

Despite soaring prices, audiences are still flocking to excellent venues in Brussels and Antwerp.

Less than ten years ago, Brussels was home to La Monnaie (the opera orchestra), several chamber groups and three full-sized symphony orchestras: the National Orchestra and two radio orchestras, one Flemish, one French. The National Orchestra struggles on; the French orchestra folded in 1991; and the Flemish one has been moved somewhat ignominiously to Leuven, a medium-sized town about 35km (20 miles) east of the capital. The splendid broadcast hall on place Flagey, which both radio orchestras had shared since the 1930s, is still boarded up and abandoned. Although it has been placed on a list of the world's 100 most endangered monuments, its fate remains uncertain.

Yet the picture is not niformly bleak. The once-threatened National Orchestra (Orchestre National de Belgique) is still thriving under Yuri Simonov (formerly of the Bolshoi Opera). Under the baton of rising star Antonio Pappano, the radically reformed La Monnaie plays symphonic concerts as well. The Ensemble Orchestral de Bruxelles, formed three years ago by Jacques Vanherenthals, is a promising attempt to give the capital city a symphony of its own again.

Most importantly, audiences continue to flock to concerts both big and small. Because of the budget cuts of the last few years, ticket prices have soared for prestige events at major venues. Nevertheless the choice is still vast, thanks to the continuing popularity of early music and original-instrument ensembles, an area in which Belgium has traditionally excelled. La Petite Bande, one of the first authentic baroque ensembles in the world, is still flourishing after more than 30 years. Philippe Herreweghe and his Chapelle Royale are also regular performers, as are Anima Eterna, Il Fondamento and many other fine groups. Such concerts often take place in the many smaller venues found throughout Brussels and outlying areas.

Belgian concert-goers are likely to be amateur musicians themselves. Besides its six conservatories, the country has an extensive network of preparatory academies where anyone can learn an instrument for a modest fee. Graduates unable to find professional work often end up in one of the many amateur orchestras and choirs.

This may explain the excitement generated every May by the world-class Concours Musical International Reine Elisabeth de Belgique (Queen Elizabeth International Music Competition), which changes focus each year between violin, piano and voice. Founded by the great Belgian violinist Eugène Ysaÿe in collaboration with the then Queen Elisabeth (herself a keen amateur violinist), the contest's first winner was David Oistrakh in 1937. The level of virtuosity has remained high. The final-round gala concerts – always sold out – are broadcast live on both French- and Flemish-speaking television.

Contemporary music fans should check out the yearly Ars Musica festival, which stages events throughout Brussels, featuring Belgian and international performers. Recent years have seen the flourishing of several fine local groups specialising in new music, including Ictus Ensemble, Oxalys and Musique Nouvelle.

Details of all concerts can be found in *What's On*, a supplement to the *Bulletin* (*see chapter* **Media**).

Tickets

Ticket prices vary from one event to another, even for the same venue. Philharmonic Society prices range from about 350-2,500BF, with gala concerts such as the Queen Elisabeth finals costing up to double the normal price. At Théâtre de la Monnaie (*see below*) expect to pay at least 400BF and up to 2,000BF for orchestra seats. Prices at other venues range from 150-1,500BF, but there are no strict guidelines. Listed below are the two main ticket agencies.

Tourist Information Brussels (TIB)

Hôtel de Ville, Grand Place, 1000 (513 83 20/fax 514 45 38); see chapter **Directory** *for opening times. Métro Bourse or Gare Centrale.* **Credit** DC. **Map C3**
The Brussels tourist information office can furnish all necessary information, including addresses and telephone numbers, for most events in the city. Reservations should be made at the Grand Place office. Many (but not all) tickets can be purchased directly from TIB.

Fnac

City 2, rue Neuve, 1000 (reservations 209 22 39). Métro Rogier/tram 23, 52, 55, 56, 81 90. **Open** 10am-7pm Mon-Thur, Sat; 10am-8pm Fri. **Credit** MC, V. **Map C2**
Like TIB, Fnac can sell tickets to selected events in Brussels, Antwerp and even France.

Major venues

Palais des Beaux Arts

23 rue Ravenstein, 1000 (box office 507 82 00/24-hour information French & Flemish 507 84 44). Métro Parc. **Box office** 11am-6pm Mon-Sat. **Tickets** 350-2,500BF; 25% reduction students, elderly, unemployed with ID; 245BF under-12s, disabled. **Credit** MC, V. **Map C4**
Home of the National Orchestra, the Palais is also the seat of the Philharmonic Society, which organises and co-ordinates the bulk of big-name concerts throughout Brussels. The society puts out a glossy brochure of its events, which include many foreign orchestras, soloists and chamber groups. Acoustics in both the splendid Salle Henri LeBoeuf and the smaller, 400-seat chamber-music hall are excellent. The entire complex, Brussels' most prestigious venue, is a fine example of art nouveau design. The finals of the Concours Musical International Reine Elisabeth de Belgique are held here.

Conservatoire Royal de Musique

30 rue de la Régence, 1000 (box office 507 82 00/24-hour information French & Flemish 507 84 44). Métro Gare Centrale. **Tickets** one hour before performance or ten days in advance from Palais des Beaux Arts (*see above*). **No credit cards. Map C4/C5**
Smaller than the Palais des Beaux Arts and slightly shabby, but also with great acoustics, the Conservatoire Royal de Musique's hall was partially designed by the French organ-builder Cavaillé-Coll. The stage is too narrow for symphonic orchestras but perfect for chamber formations and voice recitals. It is here that the preliminary rounds of the Queen Elisabeth competition are held – the most interesting part, according to contest connoisseurs.

DeSingel

25 Desguinlei, Antwerp 2015 (03 248 38 00). Gare Berchem. **Box office** 10am-7pm Mon-Fri; 4-7pm Sat. **Tickets** 400-1,200BF. **Credit** MC, V.
DeSingel is Antwerp's modern equivalent to the Palais des Beaux Arts. The huge Blue Hall can accommodate major philharmonic orchestras. The Red Hall is ideal for smaller groups. Acoustics are excellent.

Churches

Cathédrale des Sts Michel et Gudule

place St Gudule, 1000 (217 83 45/343 70 40). Métro Gare Centrale or Parc. **Open** Apr-Oct 7am-7pm Mon-Fri; 7.30am-7pm Sat; 8am-7pm Sun. Nov-Mar 7am-6pm Mon-Fri; 7.30am-6pm Sat; 8am-6pm Sun. **Admission** crypt 40BF; 30BF groups. **No credit cards. Map C3**
Brussels' largest church – too large, in fact, to be acoustically ideal for music much more complicated than Gregorian chant. Nevertheless it's the venue for quite a few major events. The interior is just as grandiose as the exterior, and audiences of a thousand or so help absorb some of the ten-second echo. Sunday noon masses feature special concerts during much of the year.

*Book early for concerts at the **Chapelle Royale**, among Brussels' best venues in terms of acoustics and architecture.*

Chapelle Royale

Eglise Protestante, 5 Coudenberg, 1000 (673 05 81). Métro Gare Centrale. **Open** varies. **Tickets** varies. **No credit cards.**
The favourite hall of many musicians, and a jewel both acoustically and architecturally. It's too small for anything larger than a baroque chamber orchestra, but ideal for authentic instruments. As maximum audience size is about 150, early booking is advised. It's also Brussels' best-heated church in winter.

L'Eglise des St Jean et St Etienne aux Minimes

62 rue des Minimes, 1000 (511 93 84). Bus 48. **Open** varies. **Admission** varies. **No credit cards. Map B5**
This high-baroque church, near the Sablon and Marolles quarter, has medium-quality acoustics but hosts a huge number of concerts. The Philharmonic Society produces most of its early-music recitals here. During most of the summer, the Midi-Minimes concerts attract a mixed crowd of tourists and locals on their lunch hours. One Sunday morning a month during the rest of the year, a mixed amateur and professional ensemble called La Chapelle des Minimes does fine performances of Bach cantatas. The admission fee is voluntary, and you get erudite programme notes translated into four languages. It's always advisable to arrive a half-hour before the 10.30am starting time for these often standing-room-only events. A much-needed new heating system was recently installed.

Occasional venues

Some interesting places, such as museums, *châteaux* and large townhouses, hold concerts sporadically. Catch a summer opera production at Château de La Hulpe (south of Brussels), for example, and try to recognise the setting of the film *The Music Teacher*. Also, many of Brussels' outlying *communes* have their own cultural centres, whose halls may be used for concerts (*see chapter* **Theatre & Dance**).

L'Atelier

51 rue du Commerce, 1040 (511 20 65). Métro Trône. **Open** concerts 8.30pm. **Tickets** 250BF. **No credit cards. Map E4**
Definitely the funkiest recital hall in Brussels. The former workshop of a music-loving painter and his wife, L'Atelier is filled with canvases, old posters and sundry memorabilia. Despite the somewhat down-at-heel aspect, the place has hosted many great musicians, often before they made names for themselves. A venerable coal stove standing in the middle of the room keeps audiences toasty even in the dead of winter.

Hôtel Astoria

103 rue Royale, 1000 (513 09 65/217 62 90). Métro Parc. **Open** concerts 11am Sun. **Admission** 250BF. **No credit cards. Map D4/E1**
Magnificent turn-of-the-century elegance in a working hotel that hosts Sunday brunch concerts. A small, opulent hall ideal for chamber music – suitable ambience guaranteed.

Hôtel de Ville – Salle Gothique

Grand Place, 1000 (tourist information 279 43 11). Métro Bourse or Gare Centrale. **Open** varies. **Tickets** usually free. **No credit cards. Map C3**
Although concerts here are rare, it's worth looking out for a performance, if only to savour the interior of the Grand Place's most grandiose building. The Gothic Hall can accommodate a chamber orchestra and the acoustics are fine, although the ornate décor is almost a distraction.

*The look of the **Lunatheater** may be modern, but the music also goes back to Renaissance.*

Lunatheater

20 place Sainctelette, 1000 (201 59 59). Métro Yser.
Box office 9am-6pm Mon-Fri. **Tickets** 480BF; 300BF
students. **Credit** MC, V. **Map B1**
A medium-sized hall with a wide range of programmes, from
Renaissance to modern.

Maison du Spectacle de la Bellone

*46 rue de Flandre, 1000 (513 33 33). Métro Ste
Catherine.* **Open** *exhibition & library* 10am-6pm Tue-Sat.
Admission free. **Map A2/B2**
Located in a rear courtyard behind an unprepossessing street
entrance, the stunningly ornate baroque façade is as splendid as those of the Grand Place. Menaced with destruction
15 years ago, La Bellone was saved by the efforts of the late
painter and scene-designer Serge Creuz. The courtyard was
recently glassed over, enabling the façade to be used as a
spectacular backdrop for concerts.

Musée Charlier

*16 avenue des Arts, 1210 (220 28 19). Métro Arts-Loi or
Madou/bus 29, 63, 65, 66.* **Open** *museum* 1.30-5pm Mon,
Wed, Thur; 12.30-5pm Tue; 1.30-4.30pm Fri. **Concerts**
12.30pm, Sun. **Admission** *museum* 100BF; *daytime
concerts* 150BF; 120BF under-26s; *evening concerts* 300-
500BF. **No credit cards. Map D4/E3**
The modest recital hall is part of an ancient stately home
now surrounded by faceless office buildings. Sunday concerts usually begin at 12.30pm. It's too small for anything
larger than a chamber-music format.

Musée d'Art Ancien

*Auditorium, 3 rue de la Régence, 1000 (508 32 11/512
82 47). Métro Gare Centrale or Parc/tram 92, 93, 94/bus
38, 60.* **Open** 10am-noon, 1-5pm, Tue-Sun. **Admission**
free Tue, Thur-Sun; 100BF 12.30-1.30pm Wed. **Credit**
AmEx, DC, MC, V (minimum purchase 500BF). **Map
C4/C5**
This museum features regular lunchtime concerts on weekdays, which can make a nice break during a tour of the
exhibits. The museum guides have been encouraging musical events with themes, such as baroque concerts played on
original instruments in the Rubens paintings hall.

Opera

Théâtre de la Monnaie

*place de la Monnaie, 4 rue Léopold, 1000 (229 12
11). Métro De Brouckère.* **Box office** 11am-5.30pm
Tue-Sat. **Tickets** 300-3,000BF. **Credit** AmEx, DC,
MC, V. **Map C3**
The national opera house is the jewel in the Brussels cultural
crown and soaks up the lion's share of arts subsidies. Its
lavish interior reveals its glorious past; a recent and costly
renovation shows confidence in the future. Former director
Gerald Mortier, principal architect of its current success,
has since moved to Salzburg, but his influence is still felt.
Mortier steered the repertoire towards more contemporary
works and innovative productions of the classics. He also
tried to hire fine singers not yet famous enough for their
prices to be out of reach. Current director Bernard Foccroulle,
himself a musician, has had notable success with baroque
works played by period-instrument ensembles. Perhaps
most importantly, he hired Antonio Pappano, a conductor
appreciated by audiences, critics and performers themselves.
Results are consistently first-class, which means it's almost
impossible to obtain tickets for many productions. Last-
minute possibilities exist, but there are always more people
than seats.

Vlaamse Opera

8 Van Ertbornstraat, Antwerp 2080 (03 233 66 85).
Box office 11am-5.45pm Tue-Sat. **Tickets** 250-
2,500BF. **No credit cards.**
The Flemish Opera has also recently undergone a radical
overhaul, especially the orchestra, which is now excellent.
Productions are divided between the newly revamped opera
house in Ghent (3 Schouwburgstraat; 09 225 24 25) and the
old but acoustically splendid Antwerp Hall. The latter is a
mere 35-minute train ride from central Brussels. From the
station in Antwerp, five minutes' walk down the café-lined
DeKeyserlei brings you there. As with the Brussels opera,
the emphasis is on quality rather than big names and productions are usually thoroughly rehearsed. The management
encourages orchestra players to participate in weekday
lunchtime chamber concerts in the foyer.

Music: Rock, Folk & Jazz

Brussels may never quite make it to be the music capital of Europe – but don't tell it that.

In rock as in so many other areas, Brussels is spoilt by its location. Lying strategically between Amsterdam, Paris and Cologne means that the city is included in most north European tours.

Forest National is the venue of choice for most large gigs short of mega-events of the Rolling Stones/Michael Jackson variety, which are held out of town. For those without a car, this can be a drag, although late-night trains are often laid on. Medium-sized gigs are held in the **AB**, **Botanique** or **Cirque Royale**.

Deep down, however, Brussels is not the best city for rock. The clubs are surprisingly small, often running on a shoestring in hastily renovated buildings. A remarkable exception is the AB (Ancienne Belgique). Having undergone major renovation in 1996, it now boasts a main hall for 2,000 and a smaller club that is used to showcase an endless procession of bands from out of town (usually Flanders).

Of the other clubs, **Magasin 4**, **Le Sud** and **Thunderbird Café** are worth checking out. Bands to look out for include Jaune Toujours, Betty Goes Green, Marka and the triumphant return of Front 242. Gig information can be found in the free monthlies *Ticket* and *MoFo*, available from venues and record shops.

Rock venues

AB – Ancienne Belgique
114 boulevard Anspach, 1000 (201 58 58/201 59 59). Métro Bourse/tram 52, 55, 81/bus 48, 95, 96. **Admission** varies. **No credit cards. Map B3**
The busiest venue in town, AB – Ancienne Belgique puts on shows every week. The smaller gigs in the first-floor club include Wednesday midday showcases, which are incredible value at 100BF (includes a sandwich). The same people also run the **Boterhammen in het Park** summer festival. Their café is located around the corner on the corner of rue des Pierres and Steenstraat.

Beursschouwburg
22 Auguste Ortsstraat, 1000 (513 82 90). Métro Bourse/bus 34, 47, 48, 63, 95, 96. **Admission** varies. **No credit cards.**
The tiny 'theatre of the stock exchange' is a pretty leftover from the nineteenth century, now run with considerable flair

as a venue for the performing arts. Avant-garde theatre used to predominate, but the organisers have decided to run the place as an experiment in juxtaposition. Fervently devoted to inner-city life, they also programme rap, North African music and jazz. If that sounds too formidable for a Saturday night, try the café on the ground floor, which is the venue for frequently silly parties (including Tupperware). Worth looking out for is the annual Spoken Tongues festival, featuring rock's literate fraternity (we're talking Richard Hell, Gavin Friday and others) in surprising readings.

Botanique
236 rue Royale, 1210 (226 66 60). Métro Botanique/tram 92, 93, 94/bus 38, 61. **Admission** 500BF approx. **No credit cards. Map D4/E1**
The former botanical gardens of Brussels are the French-speaking community's cultural centre. The Orangerie hosts an increasing number of rock and world music events, as well as a good selection of quality French acts and local hopefuls such as the wry Marka. Don't miss the highly rated Nuits Botanique festival, held in September. Note: as the sign on the door is at pains to point out: 'Tourists, there are no botanical gardens here'.

Cirque Royal
81 rue de l'Enseignement, 1000 (218 20 15). Métro Madou/bus 29, 63, 65, 66. **Admission** varies. **No credit cards. Map D3**
The former indoor circus is a great seated venue, as the circular structure allows audience and performer to come close together. This is one of the few venues that still has usherettes (who expect a tip) and a bell to announce the beginning of the show. Notable also for the excellent Bier Circus bar next door.

Esseghem Blues
329 rue Léopold Ier, 1090 (427 80 39). Métro Bockstael/tram 18/bus 49. **Open** varies. **Admission** varies. **No credit cards.**
This club has been a haven for international blues artists for years – but don't expect to meet Eric Clapton at the bar. The organisers (and audience) prefer the rootsier performers. Note: the entrance is on rue d'Esseghem.

Flanagan's
59 rue de l'Ecuyer (no phone). Métro Monnaie/bus 29, 63, 65. **Open** 10pm Tue-Sat; 7pm Sun. **Admission** varies (200-300BF). **No credit cards. Map C3**
This venue has moved from its previous quarters to an improbably genteel neo-classical building whose main function is as a drum shop. The concert hall on the ground floor has regular gigs at 10pm. The Long Island Bar upstairs has pool tables and is popular with skateboarders. Flanagan's has perhaps yet to find its niche, but at least it is within easy walking distance of a number of other music venues. So should things get dull…

Fool Moon
26 quai du Mariemont, 1080 (410 10 03). Métro Gare de l'Ouest/tram 18/bus 63. **Open** varies (10pm on gig nights). **Admission** 300-500BF. **No credit cards.**
A warehouse that has been successfully transformed into a music venue, with a preference for dance-based acts. Expect soul, acid-jazz or dub to be high on the agenda. The Fool Moon is off the beaten track by a long mile. Spare some cash for a taxi home if you hang around after the show.

Forest National
36 avenue du Globe, 1190 (347 03 55). Forest-Est rail/tram 18/bus 54. **Open** varies. **Admission** varies. **No credit cards.**
The city's major venue overhauled its acoustics and layout to handle 11,000 spectators. Parking, however, remains a major problem. Local police are unsympathetic towards badly parked cars. Get there early or take public transport.

Halles de Schaerbeek
rue Royale Ste Marie, 1030 (227 59 60). Tram 92, 93, 94/bus 58. **Open** varies. **Admission** varies. **No credit cards. Map E1**
A splendid nineteenth-century vegetable market that narrowly escaped demolition and was a major music venue for many years despite a leaking roof and sleepless neighbours. This is where the summer **Couleur Café** festival was spectacularly unveiled. The renovated water- and almost soundproofed roof has given the hall a new lease of life. Given its cavernous size, the sound is not too bad. The managers run it as a multi-discipline arts centre. One of the opening acts last year was Björk, complete with string quintet. Smaller gigs sometimes take place in the cellars.

KK (Kultuurkaffee)
VUB Campus, Triomflaan (629 23 26). Tram 23, 90/bus 34. **Open** weekday lunchtimes, evenings 7.30pm (gigs 9pm). **Closed** summer holidays. **Admission** free.
A student club at the Flemish university with free weekly gigs, usually from left-field indie bands such as local heroes PPz30. Exhibitions and art movies are shown upstairs. The KK gets zero points for ventilation (bring your own oxygen mask), but ten for the choice of bands.

Magasin 4
4 rue du Magasin, 1000 (223 34 74). Métro Yser/tram 18/bus M, F, G. **Open** varies; 9pm approx on gig nights. **Admission** 200-400BF. **No credit cards.**
A small club on two levels with a good selection of alternative rock bands. These are the acts that will break over the next few months and will probably move up to the VK or AB (*see above*) on their next visit. Photo exhibitions are also organised, as well as the occasional free concert.

Le Sud
43 rue de l'Ecuyer, 1000 (no phone). Métro Monnaie/bus 29, 63, 65. **Open** 10pm-3am Thur, Fri; 10pm-6am Sat. **Admission** 200BF. **No credit cards. Map C3**
This labyrinthine club started life as a secret venue built in the alleyways between a number of semi-abandoned buildings. The Balkan decor is worth a look. Choice of bands is just as eclectic and usually good. Clo-Clo, the cellar club named after Claude François, revels in the tackier moments of the 1970s. Best enjoyed after a few drinks. Don't forget to tip the doorman on the way out.

Thunderbird Café
48 quai du Commerce, 1000 (219 39 80). Métro Yser/tram 18. **Open** 10pm-2am Fri, Sat. **Admission** free. **No credit cards. Map B1**
'There are lots of great things about Brussels. Tex-Mex food is not one of them.' So said Texan rock historian Ed Ward before the Thunderbird opened, but don't take this as gospel. In addition to the commendable grub, the venue also boasts

gigs roughly twice a week. The owners have tapped into the Texan music scene, regularly featuring some of rock and country's most colourful performers. Recommended locals include Roland, the Electric Kings and the Seatsniffers.

VK
rue de l'Eglise, 1080 (414 29 07). Métro Comte de Flandre/bus 89. **Open** varies. **Admission** 600BF approx. **No credit cards.**
A mecca for the international indie scene. VK is tucked away in a back street of Molenbeek. It makes up for this by coming up with the hottest bands and one of the better selections of beer at the bar. A shuttle bus is sometimes organised from the centre of town – call for details.

Folk venues

Brussels enjoys a healthy world music scene. The award-winning a cappella outfit Zap Mama grew out of an African vocal workshop in Brussels, and the influx of English-speaking residents has swelled the ranks of the local amateur (largely Irish) groups. Concerts, however, are still advertised very much by word of mouth. Must-see world acts include Barly Baruti's Trio; folkies include Orion and Fluxus. More successful world music artists regularly appear at venues such as the AB (*see above*), Auditorium 44 (*see below*) and Salle de la Madeleine (*see below*).

Auditorium 44
Passage 44, boulevard du Jardin Botanique, 1000 (201 06 03). Métro Botanique/tram 93, 94/bus 38, 61. **Open** varies. **Admission** varies. **No credit cards. Map C2/D2**
The Auditorium was part of a 1960s utopia: an office block with a shopping gallery, cinema and theatre in the basement. The cinema folded many years ago, but the smallish theatre remains, most notably as the venue for the highly recommended annual cartoon and science fiction festivals. More recently, it has become a home of sorts for a number of mid-sized folk events that cater for various communities in Brussels. Notable shows have included Finland's Varttina and Ireland's Dervish.

Can Can
95 rue de Jérusalem, 1030 (215 91 30). Bus 59. **Open** 7pm Wed-Sat; 5.30pm Sun. **Admission** free. **No credit cards.**
In parallel to the rise of karaoke, the old café-concert is making a minor comeback. Originally intended as a place where anyone could step up and regale punters with their amateur or semi-pro talents (usually in French), it has now become one of the few outlets for less commercial acts.

James Joyce
34 rue Archimède, 1000 (230 98 94). Métro Schuman/bus 20, 28, 36, 67. **Open** 5pm-midnight daily **Admission** free. **Map G3/G4**
An Irish pub in the European quarter with live folk music every second Thursday from 9pm. Bring your fiddle, and a notebook to catch all the details of upcoming gigs elsewhere around town. Other cafés with Irish music include Kitty O'Shea, the Wild Geese (*see chapter* **Cafés & Bars**) and La Pinte d'Argent (*see below*).

La Movida
3 rue St Géry, 1000 (502 02 84). Métro Bourse/bus 47, 48, 95, 96. **Open** 8pm-2am Tue-Sun **Admission** free. **No credit cards.**
Tapas bar that was once popular for its flamenco music (and

Local hopeful Marka is well worth catching on his next visit to **Botanique** *– see page 175.*

occasional dancing). Guitarist Nono Garcia was a regular before returning to Spain. Movida has since declined somewhat in popularity and cut back on the live music.

Paradoxe
329 chaussée d'Ixelles, 1050 (649 89 81). Tram 81/bus 71. **Open** noon-2pm, 7-10pm, Mon-Sat. **Admission** free. **Credit** DC, MC. **Map D5/E6**
One of the city's first vegetarian restaurants, and a place to catch highbrow world, jazz and folk acts.

Salle de la Madeleine
rue Duquesnoy, 1000 (no phone). Métro Gare Centrale/bus 34, 48, 95, 96. **Open** varies. **Admission** varies. **No credit cards. Map C4**
A venue that has never really taken off, despite its handy central location. In between the book fairs, there are occasional concerts by African artists – notably a seemingly endless procession of bands from the Zaiko Langa Langa family.

White Horse Inn
9 place du Luxembourg, 1050 (230 33 26). Bus 95, 96. **Open** varies **Admission** free. **No credit cards. Map E4/E5**
Every first Friday of the month, this nondescript fake Brit pub brings a bit of life to a rather pretty square that is otherwise dead at night. The best of Belgium's amateur and semipro folk players meet to swap a few tunes and talk shop. The quality is very high, which only confirms the fact that the Commission is actually full of hidden talents. The sessions are managed by fiddle-player Oliver Gray, of the group Crossroads. Ring ahead if you actually want to play.

Jazz venues

As early as 1896, touring American minstrel shows were playing ragtime music in Belgium. Local pioneers such as Geo Deltal and Louis Frémaux (big hit: 'Bruxelles Cake Walk') and the American Arthur Briggs played across Europe and helped train the first bona fide Belgian jazzmen. The peak of the swing and big bands coincided with the outbreak of WWII and gave local musicians an open market. Ever since, Belgium has been a good source of musicians (in the 1960s Bobby Jaspar and Jacques Pelzer played with most of the American greats), without ever coming up with a recognisable style. The ageing bop generation is still standing: the New Look Trio handle two gigs a day despite being over 60, while Toots Thielemans is enjoying one of the busiest retirements ever seen. Pianists Charles Loos and Nathalie Loriers and avant-garde outfit Aka Moon guarantee good listening for years to come.

Airport Sheraton Hotel
Brussels National Airport (725 10 00). **Open** noon to 3pm Sun. **Admission** free. **Credit** AmEx, V.
The idea of listening to jazz in a soundproofed atrium as planes take off over your head may or may not appeal, but it's certainly a different way of spending a Sunday afternoon. The quality of food and music make it increasingly popular. Brunch, at 1,250BF, is reasonable given airport prices.

L'Archiduc
6 rue Antoine Dansaert, 1000 (512 06 52). Métro Bourse/bus 47, 63. **Open** 2pm-midnight Mon-Sat; 5pm-midnight Sun. **Admission** varies for concerts, otherwise free. **Credit** AmEx, MC, V. **Map A2/D2**
Built in the 1930, this superb little bar was for a long time a secret after-hours club for jazz fans. Nat 'King' Cole and troops of others dropped by for an après-gig drink. The new owner has restored the place to its former glory and now hosts the occasional concert by people such as Mal Waldron. Jumping genres, Tori Amos and Norwegian wunderkind Espen Lind also played here. Ring the doorbell to enter.

Marcus Mingus Jazz Spot

10 impasse de la Fidélité, 1000 (502 02 97). Métro Monnaie/bus 29, 63, 65. **Open** 9pm Tue-Sun. **Admission** varies. **No credit cards**. **Map C3**
The jury is still out on this one, as it only recently opened. To find it, walk up the touristy rue des Bouchers and turn left down a tiny lane following the sign for the appalling Janneken Pis statue (*see chapter* **Sightseeing**). The small two-room club is trying to generate some action with a combination of Latin and modern jazz and a handful of genre-bending local bands.

New York Café Jazz Club

place Stéphanie, 1050 (534 85 09). Métro Louise/tram 91, 92, 93, 94. **Open** 10pm Thur-Sat. **Admission** free. **No credit cards**. **Map C6**
The New York Café is a swish, brasserie-type restaurant. The club behind it is a comfortable venue for catching local acts. Pass the time by spotting celebrities.

Phil's Jazz Kitchen Café

189 rue Haute, 1000 (513 95 88). Bus 20, 48. **Open** noon-2pm, 6-11pm Tue-Sun. **Admission** free. **No credit cards**. **Map B5/C4**
Smallish, modern venue that gets crowded with a young international crowd on weekend nights. Food is available at lunchtime and from 6.30pm onwards. Phil's is also handy on Sunday mornings: it's not far from the flea market and serves Sunday brunch accompanied by live ambient music (recently all didgeridoo and electric guitar). There's an interesting selection of paintings on the walls.

La Pinte d'Argent

place des Bienfaiteurs, 1030 (241 03 14). Tram 90/bus 54, 65. **Open** 8pm-midnight daily. **Admission** free. **No credit cards**.
Since opening only three years ago, this place has been transformed from a grotty neighbourhood café to one of the friendliest gigs in town. Don't let the American and British flags put you off: this is as Belgian as they come, and the mix of ages, nationalities, music and drinks is heady. Each drink only costs 80BF, whether it's a whisky, a coffee or one of the many special beers (La Chouffe on tap is recommended). The bad news is that you have to buy five vouchers worth 400BF. Most of the jazz happens during the week, with musicians dropping by and tuning in to the night's theme, which might be a homage to Django Reinhardt or Ella Fitzgerald. At weekends, the musical net is cast wider. If you're only interested in the jazz, ring in advance to find out what's on.

Sounds

28 rue de la Tulipe, 1050 (218 40 86). Bus 54, 71. **Open** 6-11pm daily. **Admission** usually free. **No credit cards**. **Map D5/D6**
The bar at the front resembles a fairground attraction. At the back, a small stage features a healthy selection of local and touring jazz musicians, usually playing modern styles. There is a good selection of beers and a better-than-average choice of snacks and light meals (the owners are Italian).

Au Travers

11 rue Traversière, 1210 (218 40 86). Métro Botanique/tram 92, 93, 94/bus 38, 61. **Open** 8pm-midnight Mon-Sat. **Admission** 300BF. **Map E2**
The Travers has been on the brink of going bust for as long as anyone can remember. Its reputation is built on music that makes no concessions to commercial considerations. The Monday night jam sessions are an institution. The Travers is small, untidy and fiercely proud of its role in jazz.

Putting on rock and pop gigs every week, **AB – Ancienne Belgique** *is the busiest venue in Brussels. See page 175.*

Festivals

For a country that is known for its rain, Belgium has an outstanding number of festivals every year, many of them open-air. Brussels hosts comparatively few of them, but then the idea is presumably to get away from cities rather than bring people to them. Having said that, there is still plenty of music around if you care to check the local press.

Brosella is a jazz and folk festival held every July in a pretty park almost in the shadow of the Atomium (*see chapter* **Sightseeing**). As the fest is a freebie, don't expect to find big names, but the organisers are very particular about the quality of the acts. Very relaxed atmosphere.

Jazz Marathon is the new name for an old idea: setting up some 400 musicians in cafés, clubs and restaurants around town and then organising a network of old-time buses to ship the audience from one venue to another. It usually happens around May.

World music has always been strong in Belgium, and **Couleur Café** is the best way to catch it. Over a weekend in July, a whole village springs up in the decaying splendour of the former customs depot Tour et Taxis. The organisers are always anxious to create bridges between styles and age, finding the missing link between Burundi Black and Zap Mama.

Viva Brazil welcomes the greatest stars of Brazil for a week in June, making it one of the very few of its kind in Europe.

Klinkende Munt – also free – features rock and avant-garde fare in front of Théâtre de la Monnaie (*see chapter* **Theatre & Dance**) each July.

Boterhammen in het Park (literally, sandwiches in the park) is a lunchtime festival of Flemish-language music held in the park opposite the Royal Palace in July.

Out of town

Regular rock shows are held at the following.

Antwerp

Koningin Elisabethzaal *Koningin Astridplein (03 233 84 44).* **Box office** noon-6pm Mon-Sat.

Bruges

Cactus Cultuur Café *121 Langestraat (050 33 20 14).*

Charleroi

Backstage *rue du Grand Central (071 30 91 80).*

Dour

Rockamadour *10 rue du Marché (065 65 91 32).*

Ghent

Vooruit *23 Sint-Pietersnieuwstraat (09 225 56 43).*
Flanders Expo *1 Maaltekouter (09 240 92 11).*

Werchter

The site of an annual festival, held over the first weekend in July (info & tickets 09 243 77 77). Also major open-air gigs.

Sport & Fitness

From chess to cricket, it's all here.

The presence of so many foreign nationals in Brussels means there are opportunities to play games and sports that you might not necessarily expect to be on offer in Belgium (cricket, for example). Organised sport is especially popular here, while cycling seems to have become part of the Belgian psyche – at weekends you will have your work cut out just trying to dodge the whizzing hordes of lycra-clad middle-aged pedallers around town. If mountain biking is more your thing, however, many of Brussels' parks and forests (*see also* chapter **Sightseeing**) are ideal for cyclists, as well as walkers and riders.

Brussels has comparatively little to offer on the spectating side, because it actually has few world-beating teams in any sport. In sporting terms, the Belgian capital is still synonymous with the 1985 Heysel Stadium disaster. During the European Cup Final between Liverpool and Juventus, fighting between supporters caused a wall to collapse, killing 39 fans. Hopefully, the European Championships due to be held in 2000 (*see below* **Football**) will create happier memories of the place.

Armchair spectators are well served here: most Brussels homes receive BBC1, as well as major French, Dutch, Italian and Spanish stations (*see* chapter **Media**). Cricket fans can also pick up commentaries on BBC Radio 4, and a number of Irish pubs (*see chapter* **Cafés & Bars**) in Brussels have Sky Television.

For up-to-the-minute details of major sporting events in and around Brussels, contact the Tourist Information Office at 61 rue Marché aux Herbes (504 02 70).

Spectator sports

Athletics

The Ivo van Damme Memorial athletics meeting is held each August in Brussels and attracts some of the world's most famous athletes. The event is named after the winner of the 800m silver medal at the 1976 Montreal Olympics, who died in a car crash soon after the competition.

The annual Brussels 20km Run, which attracts more than 20,000 runners, is held on the last weekend of May and passes through the centre of Brussels and the nearby Bois de la Cambre. Information on dates is available from the Tourist Information Office.

Cycling

In recent years, the Tour de France has occasionally made a detour through Belgium, with Brussels being one of the stopoff points. The Grand Prix Eddy Merckx, named after Belgium's most famous cyclist, is a speed race held annually in Brussels, usually in May or June.

Football

Belgium and the Netherlands are co-hosting the 2000 European Championships. Supporters visiting the tournament should be warned that, following the Heysel Stadium tragedy, the police are – fairly or unfairly – liable to pay particular attention to British and Irish fans. And, if the handling of ticket sales for the Ireland-Belgium World Cup qualifier is anything to go by, ticketing arrangements for Euro 2000 will be anything but efficient.

Although the Belgian national team eventually qualified for the World Cup, the domestic league is far from thriving. Several members of the national team play abroad, especially in the Netherlands, and Belgian teams fared disastrously in Europe in the 1997/98 season, failing to get beyond the preliminary rounds in any of the tournaments. The atmosphere at Belgian league games also leaves something to be desired: even the most popular club, RSC Anderlecht, has attendances of fewer than 10,000, while another first division Brussels team, the fabulously titled Racing White Daring Molenbeek, draws average gates of under a thousand and languished at the bottom of the first division for much of the 1997/98 season. Another Brussels team, Union St Gilleois, has long seen better days, and is struggling in the third division. Of the major teams outside Brussels, Club Brugge and Standard Liège are only about an hour away from Brussels by train.

RSC Anderlecht

Van den Stock Stadium, 2 avenue Théo Verbeeck, 1070 (522 15 39). Métro St Guidon. **Tickets** 500-1,000BF; *season tickets* 6,500-11,000BF.

Horse racing

Horse racing has only quite recently become a popular Belgian pastime, and many events involve chariot-style racing rather than mounted jockeys. There is also a major international show jumping event at Heysel each November. For dates of

Brussels International Show Jumping, contact the Tourist Information Office, or look out for posters. For details of racing events in the vicinity of Brussels, contact the following courses:

Hippodrome de Boitsfort *51 chaussée de la Hulpe, 1180 (660 28 39).*

Hippodrome de Groenendael *4 St Jansbergen, 1560 Hoeilaart (657 44 84).*

Renbaan de Sterrebeek *43 du Roy de Blicquylaan, 1933 Sterrebeek (767 54 75).*

Rugby

There are Flemish and French rugby leagues, both run by the Belgian Rugby Federation, and teams are spread all over Belgium. Annual cup finals are held at King Baudouin (formerly Heysel) Stadium.

Fédération Belge de Rugby *239 avenue Rogier, 1030 (216 40 24).*

Tennis

The European Community Championships are held in Belgium every February. The event is by no means a Grand Slam, so don't expect all the stars to be there, but there's usually a smattering of the world's top ten players, particularly the European contingent. In 1997 Tim Henman reached the final. The event is held at the Sportspaleis in Antwerp, about 40 minutes by train or car from Brussels.

Activities

Since the turnover of expatriates in Brussels is high, contact details for British and American sporting clubs tend to change from year to year. The best way to find out about teams and events in Brussels is to keep an eye on the *Bulletin* and similar publications. Clubs such as the British and Commonwealth Women's Club (772 53 13) and the American Women's Club (358 47 53) are also a good source of information about expatriate sports activities – for both sexes. Other good sources are the specialist sports press in Belgium, and there's also a growing number of websites with information about cycling and walking in Belgium.

Badminton

Brussels British Badminton Club holds matches in Brussels (Woluwe St Lambert) and at nearby Waterloo. There are also badminton courts at some of Brussels' gyms, such as the Ixelles branch of **Winners** (*see below* **Health & fitness**).

Basketball

Basketball is popular in Belgium, and the annual NBA European street basketball tour usually comes to the city in August. Events include three-on-three tournaments and interactive activities such as ball skills sessions. Also very popular in

Belgium is korfball, the mixed-sex cross between basketball and netball. The korf, or net, is 3.3m (11ft) high, which eliminates height advantage and makes it popular with both sexes.

Olympic Anderlecht Korfball *73 rue des Fruits, 1070 (523 92 39).* One of the most active korfball clubs in Brussels, this has teams for a range of age groups and abilities.

Bowling

For the more indolent, bowling offers the chance to drink and relax while you compete.

Crosly Super Bowling *36 boulevard de l'Empereur, 1000 (512 08 74).*

Bowlmaster *45 rue van Zande, 1080 (465 05 10).*

Chess

For people who like to play in relaxed surroundings, **Le Greenwich** and **Le Pantin** are the best-known chess cafés in Brussels (*see chapter* **Cafés & Bars**). There are also more formal clubs for the budding grand master, including:

Cercle Royal des Echecs de Bruxelles *rue Roger Vanderweyden, 1000 (514 29 47).*

Climbing

Clearly, Brussels doesn't have any natural climbing spots, but there are climbing walls for people who want to practise or learn from scratch. Those in search of the real thing should head south to the Ardennes and the rocks near Namur.

Escalade New Rock *136 chaussée de Watermael, 1160 (675 17 60).* An indoor climbing centre with an 18m climbing wall and around 800sq m of climbing space. It runs beginners' courses and organises climbing courses in Belgium and abroad.

Roc' House *277 chaussée de Boondael, 1050 (648 86 77).* 420sq m of climbing space, with a 16m wall.

Winners (*see below* **Health & fitness**) also has a 13m climbing wall.

Cricket

Cricket has a long history in Brussels: as long ago as 1815, British regiments had a few overs at the Bois de la Cambre on the eve of the Battle of Waterloo. These days the expatriate cricket clubs play host to visiting sides from the UK, enabling you to hear the familiar sound of leather against willow on soft summer days (a sound you had perhaps hoped to escape). For details of teams and nets, check in the *Bulletin*.

Royal Brussels Cricket Club *Ground 51, Centre-Ohain, 117 vieux chemin de Wavre, 1328 Ohain-Lasne (764 75 24).*

Curling

If you were inspired by the hype about the UK's near-success in the curling at the 1998 Winter Olympics and fancy trying your hand at 'chess on ice', contact:

Curling Club de Bruxelles *125 avenue des Chênes, 1180 (374 51 12).*

Cycling

Bikes can be hired fairly cheaply from most railway stations and returned to any station – ask at stations for details of the Train-Plus-Vélo scheme. Cycling in town is not particularly recommended, because of the cobbled and potholed roads as well as the habits of some drivers (when cycling on any road, watch out for the *prioritité à droite* rule). Fortunately, there are plenty of cycle tracks, and Bois de la Cambre and the Forêt de Soignes offer excellent cycle rides.

Fédération Belge du Cyclotourisme *34 avenue du Limbourg, 1070 (521 86 40)*. Organises more than 600 cycles a year all over Belgium.

Vélos Pipette *47 rue de l'Hospice Communal, 1170 (672 16 98)*. For bike hire.

Football

Playing football in Brussels, from park games to amateur leagues, is easy. The two British expatriate clubs – British United Football Club (732 77 77) and Royal Brussels British Football Club – are usually looking for new players. Look in the *Bulletin* for contact details of these and other clubs.

Golf

With more than 60 courses in Belgium, a clubhouse is never far away. There are five or six courses in Brussels itself and plenty in nearby towns such as Waterloo. Expect the usual contingent of international businessmen. For details of golf courses in Belgium, contact the Fédération Royale Belge de Golf (*see below*). For more frivolous entertainment, there are mini-golf courses in Parc Josaphat, Parc de Woluwe and Parc de Wolvendael.

Fédération Royale Belge de Golf *110 chaussée de la Hulpe, 1000 (672 23 89)*.

Health & fitness

If you want to work out while you're in Brussels, there are plenty of gyms to choose from. Most offer a range of aerobics, step and fitness classes, plus a good selection of fitness equipment. Some offer extras such as sunbeds, martial arts classes, or squash and badminton courts. The most popular include:

American Gym *144 boulevard Général Jacques, 1050 (640 59 92)*.

Golden Club *33 place du Châtelain, 1050 (538 19 06)*.

John Harris Fitness *47 rue du Fossé aux Loups, 1000 (219 82 54)*.

Winners *13 rue Bonneel, 1210 (280 02 70); 12 rue Général Thys, 1050 (644 55 44)*.

Ice skating

Grand Place sometimes has a small, temporary ice rink in December. While it is obviously not the place for Olympic speed-skating, it is quite probably the most picturesque ice rink in the whole of Europe. Otherwise, there are public ice rinks at the following:

Patinoire de Forest *36 avenue du Globe, 1190 (345 16 11)*.

Poseidon *2 avenue des Vaillants, 1200 (762 16 33)*.

Martial arts

A variety of courses is on offer. The **Golden Club** (*see above* **Health & fitness**) is well known for its martial arts classes and the fact that Jean-Claude van Damme used to train there before he hit the big time. The **American Gym** (*see above* **Health & fitness**) also has a range of martial arts classes, including boxing.

Centre de la Culture Japonaise *44 rue des Augustines, 1090 (426 50 00)*. English-speaking classes in judo, karate and the like.

Ligue Royale Belge de Lutte *6 place de Dinant, 1000 (512 24 27)*. Not lute-playing but Graeco-Roman wrestling for those who prefer western traditions of violence to oriental ones.

Rambling

The Forêt de Soignes and the smaller Bois de la Cambre offer excellent rambling opportunities and are quickly reached by bus or tram from the centre of Brussels. The forests and paths are well maintained, and separate paths for riders, cyclists and walkers mean you don't get mown down by horses and mountain bikes when you're out for a leisurely stroll. Both forests are easily reached by bus and tram. Trams 93 and 94 and buses R, W and 365A (from Bascule) stop at several places along the edge of the Bois de la Cambre. Tram 44 is useful for getting into the Forêt de Soignes.

Rollerblading

Cobbled streets and dug-up pavements don't offer the perfect environment, but there are one or two purpose-built locations. There is also a public outdoor rollerskating rink in the Bois de la Cambre.

Roller Park *300 quai de Beistbroeck, 1070 (522 59 19)*. Offers rollerblading and skateboarding, and stays open until 10pm on weekdays, midnight on Fridays and Saturdays. On Sunday, it closes at 7pm.

Rugby

Brussels British Rugby Club (759 23 78) plays against Belgian and other, expatriate teams. Players tend to come from Ireland, South Africa and Australasia, as well as the UK, so there is a good mix.

Running

The annual 20km run in May is popular with keen runners of all levels, and the route is very pleasant, through the Bois de la Cambre and up avenue Louise. There are also shorter events: the Nike 10km Vincent Rousseau Run and the Nike 5km Run (for women). In between times, most runners

*Brussels' **skateboarders** make tracks for Mont des Arts or place Stéphanie or Roller Park.*

pound the picturesque paths in the Bois de la Cambre, the Parc de Woluwe, and the grounds of the Koninklijk Museum voor Midden-Afrika (*see chapter* **Museums**).

Skateboarding

The Mont des Arts, near place Royale in central Brussels, is the main spot, and its marble surface and stairs of different heights will test most skateboarders. Place Stéphanie on avenue Louise is smaller and easier but still attracts crowds, especially on Sunday afternoons. **Roller Park** (*see above* **Rollerblading**) in Anderlecht also caters for skateboarders in the evenings.

Squash

A number of gyms and tennis clubs have squash courts. They include:
Castle Club *16 avenue de la Bécasse, 1970 (731 68 20).* Although it's a bit out of the way in Wezembeek-Oppem and you'll need a car to get there, this club is a favourite among English-speaking squash players.
Centre Sportif de Woluwe St Pierre *2 avenue Salomé, 1150 (762 12 75).*
Liberty's Squash Club *1068 chaussée de Wavre, 1160 (734 64 93).*
Winners *(see above* **Health & fitness***).*
Wimbledon Tennis & Squash *220 chaussée de Waterloo, 1640 Rhode St Genèse (358 35 23).* Midway between Brussels and Waterloo, this club is easy to reach by car or bus.

Swimming

The number of pools in and around Brussels makes swimming one of the most accessible sports there is. Swimming caps are compulsory at most pools (you can hire them), and most of them insist that men wear trunks rather than shorts.
Océade Bruparck *20 boulevard du Centenaire, 1020 (478 43 20).* This impressive sports complex at Heysel offers everything to keep youngsters happy, including a wave machine and water slides. *See also chapter* **Children**.
Poseidon *2 avenue des Vaillants, 1200 (771 66 55).* Poseidon has a separate children's pool (as well as an ice rink), but it gets very crowded, particularly at weekends.
Centre Sportif de Woluwe St Pierre *2 avenue Salomé, 1150 (762 12 75).* This massive complex offers an Olympic-sized pool and water slide. It also has squash, volleyball, a solarium and steam baths.

Tennis

There are plenty of tennis courts around Brussels, but most belong to private clubs. A few, however, still rent out courts by the hour, including:
Tennis Couverts Montjoie *91 rue Edith Cavell, 1180 (345 22 68).*
Tennis Panorama *95 Hengstenberg, 3090 Overijse (687 55 33).*
Of the many tennis clubs in Brussels, the following are popular with expatriates:
Brussels Lawn Tennis Club *890 chaussée de Waterloo (374 92 59).*
Castle Club *(see above* **Squash***).*
Wimbledon Tennis & Squash *(see above* **Squash***).*

Theatre & Dance

The Brussels boards are trod by singularly talented feet.

Belgium has a great tradition of both theatre and dance, but dance – unhampered by language and more likely to draw in the international crowds – is currently taking centre stage.

Modern ballet is especially strong in Brussels. For years it was the stronghold of Maurice Béjart, one of the fathers of contemporary dance. When he left, New York's equally adventurous Mark Morris took his place as choreographer in residence in the **Théâtre de la Monnaie**. That's some legacy and Belgium now feels it has a reputation for dance radicalism to protect. The range and quality of choreography is extraordinary. As well as established names such as Anne Teresa de Keersmaeker and Wim Vandekeybus are Michèle Anne de Mey, Mairo Paccagnella, José Besprosvany, who danced with Béjart, and Abdelaziz Sarrokh, who performs with young street dancers.

Belgian theatre is an inspired mixture of French realism and German grotesquerie. In the famous **Théâtre de Toone**, puppets perform bizarre antics, gabbling in Bruxellois dialect, while at the **Théâtre National** perfect productions of Racine are classically staged. Here the Belgian genius for painting and interior design comes out in the stage sets, which are either incredibly surreal – including gargoyles and fairgrounds – or conventionally but stunningly beautiful. They justify a visit even if you don't understand the language.

Despite all the long-running problems of poor arts funding and a tradition of exporting its talent, Belgian theatre has remained buoyant through its 150 years, though apart from the brief flowering of Maurice Maeterlinck at the end of the nineteenth century, there have been few national playwrights. Theatres survived on French plays until after World War II, when they turned to translating American and British works, sustaining themselves through the 1970s on Alan Ayckbourn, Tom Stoppard and Harold Pinter. Continental playwrights have only recently returned to favour. The recent trend is for co-productions, notably with nearby Strasbourg, and this has helped to maintain quality. Most of Brussels' 30 theatres perform in French, though the much smaller Flemish scene is reputed to be more creative.

The curtain rises all over Brussels at 8.30pm. There is no central booking office, so tickets have to be booked from individual venues. Box offices are generally open all day, Tuesday to Saturday. Tickets are generally not expensive and there are always good discounts for students, groups and the over-60s.

For up-to-date information about both theatre and dance, consult the *Bulletin* (*see chapter* **Media**).

Theatre

Main venues

Koninklijke Vlaamse Schouwburg

146 rue de Laeken, 1000 (219 49 44). **Box office** noon-7pm Mon-Fri; 3-7pm Sat. **Tickets** 900BF; 700BF under-26s; 450BF standby. **Credit** MC, V. **Map B2/C2**

The national theatre for the Flemish community is housed in far more flamboyant style than its French counterpart, though it's surrounded by seedy peepshows. The vigorous mock-baroque building, designed by Baes in 1887, has an outstanding programme of Dutch-language plays. It's also the choice for many touring English companies.

Rideau de Bruxelles

Palais des Beaux Arts, 23 rue Ravenstein, 1000 (box office 507 82 00). Métro Parc. **Box office** 11am-6pm Mon-Sat. **Tickets** 300-700BF; 300BF students, disabled. **No credit cards. Map C4**

One of the Palais des Beaux Arts' multiple entertainment outlets, this theatre has a safe, established, Belgian feel. Set up in 1953 to promote Belgian talent, it shows a lot of work by new young writers, and is a good venue for touring Belgian companies. The staple diet is Mamet, Stoppard and Hare; generally good, solid fare. It also stages plays in sign language, using deaf actors.

Théâtre 140

140 avenue Eugène Plasky, 1030 (733 97 08). Tram 23, 90/bus 29, 63. **Box office** noon-6pm Mon-Sat. **Tickets** 520-800BF. **No credit cards. Map H3**

The brainchild of Jo Deckmine, one of the great radicals of the Belgian arts who's been causing havoc in the Brussels theatrical world since the 1970s. Théâtre 140's seats are scuffed and the carpet is studded with cigarette butts, but its subscribers are devoted and the entertainment is world

The exquisite **Chapelle des Brigittines** *in Les Marolles – a centre for co-productions and Belgian dance companies – see page 187.*

class. Used for theatre, music and dance, it doesn't have a repertory company, but effortlessly attracts the best touring groups. The theme is contemporary art, and within that you get just about everything, from Pink Floyd to New York Living Theatre.

Théâtre National
Centre Rogier, place Rogier, 1210 (203 53 03).
Métro Rogier. **Box office** 11am-6pm Tue-Sat.
Tickets 325-750BF; 325BF students. **Credit** AmEx, DC, MC, V (credit card bookings by telephone after 7pm only). **Map C1**
The 'National' Theatre, which only serves the French community, is very much into co-productions. It recently enticed the French director Jean-Marie Villégier from Strasbourg, which means that the current standard of productions is exceptional. It is also a host venue for major touring companies such as Britain's RSC.

Théâtre Royal du Parc
3 rue de la Loi, 1000 (512 23 39). Métro Arts-Loi or Parc. **Box office** 11am-6pm daily. **Tickets** 180-850BF; 330BF students under 26. **No credit cards**.
Map D3/G4
One of the most beautiful theatres in western Europe, the Théâtre Royal puts on fine classical productions, but its best feature is the performance of hopelessly dated 1930s comedies or *boulevards* that are not seen anywhere else. No attempt is made to update them. It's gruesome, riveting and unique.

Théâtre de Poche
chemin de Gymnase, Bois de la Cambre, 1000 (649 17 27). Tram 23, 90. **Box office** 10am-5.30pm Mon-Sat.
Tickets 350-550BF. **No credit cards**.
An avant-garde and erudite menu of central European playwrights and others – including the likes of Bukowski. The theatre often works with English directors and writers, such as John Godber. It hosts the annual Premières Rencontres festival in September, which shows end-of-year work by Belgian and international drama schools.

Théâtre de Toone
6 impasse Schuddeveld, petite rue des Bouchers, 1000 (511 71 37). Métro De Brouckère. **Open** noon-midnight Tue-Sat. **Box office** tickets available 8pm, just before performance. **Tickets** 400BF; 250BF under-12s, students (Tue-Thur only). **No credit cards**.
Located in the centre of town, this charming theatre, which has been in the Toone family for seven generations, is world famous and a must for any visitor. Marionette productions of works such as *Cyrano de Bergerac* and *Hamlet* are performed in Bruxellois, a regional mixture of French and Flemish. Its equally charming café is open all day. (*See also* chapters **Children** *and* **Sightseeing**.)
Café.

Théâtre de Vaudeville
15 galerie de la Reine, 1000 (514 16 00). Métro Gare Centrale. **Box office** 1-6pm daily. **Tickets** 400-500BF.
No credit cards.
Those of us who used to dance all night in this beautiful theatre during its brief years as one of Brussels' hottest clubs rather begrudged its return to its original use. Still, the result has been triumphant – it was chosen by Deborah Warner and Fiona Shaw for the première of *The Wasteland*. No doubt its founders would be relieved.

Outside Brussels

DeSingel
25 Desguinlei, Antwerp 2015 (03 248 38 00). **Box office** 10am-7pm Mon-Fri; 4-7pm Sat. **Tickets** 400-900BF. **Credit** MC, V.

This is an international centre for dance and theatre in a huge concrete setting with a consistently intelligent programme of events. Four international companies are chosen every season, with the emphasis very much on innovation and originality.

Théâtre Jean Vilar
rue du Sablon, Centre Urbain, Louvain-la-Neuve, 1348 (010 450 400). **Box office** 11am-6pm Mon-Sat.
Tickets up to 900BF; 300BF students. **Credit** AmEx, DC, MC, V.
In the heart of the university town, Jean Vilar has the verve you would expect from playing to student audiences. It puts on a wide variety of plays, both contemporary and classical. Past productions include a play by and with Benoit Poelvoorde of *Man Bites Dog* fame (*see chapter* **Film**).

Café-Theatre

For more intimate, relaxed theatre over a drink, check out the venues below. Most of them work with young Belgian companies, but they also take in lesser-known touring groups. Box office opening times vary.
Théâtre 'Le Café' *158 rue de la Victoire, 1060 (538 75 24). Métro Porte de Hal.*
Café-Théâtre du Botanique *236 rue Royale, 1210 (226 12 11). Métro Parc.*
Comiqu'Art *1 rue de la Victoire, 1060 (537 69 37). Métro Porte de Hal.*
La Fleur en Papier Doré *53 rue des Alexiens, 1000 (511 16 59). Bus 20, 48.*
Le Fool Moon Théâtre *26 quai de Mariemont, 1080 (410 10 03). Bus 63.*

English-language groups

Brussels has some extremely dedicated amateur theatrical groups, and in a city where they are often the only chance to see English-language theatre, performances are packed out. They have become a must for the claustrophobic expat community. The oldest of these, the English Comedy Club, has a very respectable tradition, having been founded in 1909; others, such as the English Shakespearean Society, the Irish Theatre Group and the American Theatre Group, were started about 20 years ago and have flourished ever since. Productions are generally safe renditions of established plays. The quality is erratic, but there's often a surprising amount of talent in evidence.

Most societies don't have a fixed venue, but listings of plays and dates of society meetings can be found in the *Bulletin*. If you have thespian proclivities and are planning to stay in Brussels for a while, it's worth phoning to see if you can get involved.

Dance

Brussels not only has some of the most exciting new dance companies in Europe, it also has some of the best festivals and a number of beautiful venues in which to stage them, be it the classical **Théâtre de la Monnaie**, the exquisite **Chapelle des Brigittines**, or the newly renovated **Cirque Royale**. The only problem is that these are modest in size, so you have to book for the most exciting shows. For those who haven't got the message yet, here it is again – go and see a dance performance in Brussels. If you're not into contemporary ballet, you admittedly have fewer options.

The only classical ballet company in Belgium is based in Antwerp, the excellent Royal Ballet of Flanders; and South American, Asian and folk dance can be hard to come by.

Main venues

Atelier Ste Anne
75-77 rue des Tanneurs, 1000 (548 02 60). Bus 20, 48.
Box office 2-6pm Mon-Sat. **Tickets** 280-480BF. **No credit cards. Map A5/B5**
This centre for music, theatre and dance opened in 1973 as a base for young choreographers and directors. The choreographer in residence at the moment is the Béjart-trained José Besprosvany, who uses legends from his native Mexico in his innovative dances.

Chapelle des Brigittines
rue des Visitandines, 1000 (511 99 66). Bus 20, 48. **Box office** 8.30am-5.30pm Mon-Fri. **Tickets** 400BF; 250BF students. **No credit cards. Map B4**
An exquisite chapel set incongruously in the rundown Marolles area, the Chapelle des Brigittines is a centre for co-productions and Belgian companies. It co-produces the annual Festival Bellone-Brigittines (Aug-Sept) of dance, theatre and music, in which the programme revolves around one particular theme each year.

Cirque Royal
81 rue de l'Enseignement, 1000 (218 20 15). Métro Madou. **Box office** 11am-6pm Tue-Sat. **Tickets** price varies. **No credit cards. Map D3**
This is the only good large dance venue in Brussels, with a capacity of about 1,700. It's a renovated circus with a pleasing round shape. The exciting programme is a mix of classical and contemporary dance, and the venue is the most common host for touring companies.

Lunatheater
20 place Sainctelette, 1000 (201 59 59). Métro Yser. **Box office** 9am-6pm Mon-Fri. **Tickets** 480BF; 300BF students. **Credit** MC, V. **Map B1**
The Lunatheater used to be a cinema, but now boasts an upbeat dance programme and is the preferred venue for Wim Vandekeybus and his ferociously energetic company. His *Live Project 1996* had musicians and dancers performing against a backdrop of moving film images and featured blind dancer Saïd Gharbi.

La Movida
3 rue St Géry, 1000 (649 59 14). Métro Bourse or Ste Catherine/bus 47, 48, 95, 96. **Open** *flamenco* 10pm approx. **Admission** free. **Credit** DC, MC, V. **Map B3**
Authentic rather than touristic, this vibrant bar hosts weekly flamenco shows *(see chapter* **Music: Rock, Folk & Jazz: Folk venues**).

Palais des Beaux Arts
23 rue Ravenstein, 1000 (507 82 00). Métro Parc. **Box office** 11am-6pm Mon-Sat. **Tickets** 500BF approx but price varies. **Credit** MC, V. **Map C4**

Palais des Beaux Arts *– theatre and dance.*

Together with the Paleis (the Flemish arm of the Beaux Arts), this co-ordinates music, theatre and dance events and is an umbrella for numerous organisations. It runs a strong modern and classical dance programme, called La Série, in September.

Théâtre de la Balsamine
1 avenue Felix Marchal, 1030 (735 64 68). Bus 29, 54. **Box office** 10am-6pm Mon-Fri. **Tickets** 450BF; 250BF students. **No credit cards.**
A very avant-garde venue covering both theatre and dance, Théâtre de la Balsamine was erected on the site of a ruined barracks, and for the first few productions actors systematically destroyed different parts of the barracks. Enter stage left and a wall would fall in. At dance performances the spectators are invited to choose one of the dance solos and confront the dancer. The theatre also hosts the experimental Danse à la Balsa festival in February. This is a festival better reserved for diehards: these dancers are more interested in confronting you than entertaining you. Too much thought, not enough fun.

Théâtre de la Monnaie
place de la Monnaie, 4 rue Léopold, 1000 (229 12 11). Métro De Brouckère. **Box office** 11am-5.30pm Tue-Sat. **Tickets** 300-3,000BF. **Credit** AmEx, DC, MC, V. **Map C3**
The beautiful centre of opera and ballet where Maurice Béjart held sway for 30 years. Anna Teresa de Keersmaeker and her company, Rosas, are now in residence with their contemporary ballet. (*See also chapters* **Sightseeing** and **Music: Classical & Opera**.)

Centre for music, theatre and dance opened in 1973, **Atelier Ste Anne** – see page 187.

Smaller venues

The cultural centres of the different Brussels *communes* have small dance, theatre and film programmes. The most active are the Centre Culturel de Woluwe St Pierre (773 05 88), the Centre Culturel d'Anderlecht (522 74 07) and the Halles de Schaerbeek (218 00 31).

Outside Brussels

Vlaamse Opera
3 Frankrejklei, Antwerp 2000/postal address 8 Van Ertbornstraat, Antwerp 2080 (03 233 66 85). **Box office** 11am-5.45pm Tue-Sat. **Tickets** 250-2500BF. **No credit cards**.
This and the Stadsschouwberg (070 233 244), also in Antwerp, are where to see the Royal Ballet of Flanders and other touring classical ballet companies. The Vlaamse Opera also plays host to Israeli and Brazilian dance companies.

Festivals

Kunstenfestivaldesarts
Information 219 07 07. **Date** every other May; next festival 2000.
A key international festival of tremendous vitality, and virtually unique in including both French and Flemish works. It's held in theatres all round Brussels and is concerned with all the performing arts. It's also exceptionally well endowed and sponsors special co-productions.

Rencontres D'Octobre
Information 511 04 60. **Date** Sept-Oct.

Held in Liège and Brussels, this fest is an annual chance for Belgian artists to interact with outside companies. The theme is modernity.

Classes & information

Centre de Danse Choreart
985 chaussée d'Alsemberg, 1180 (332 13 59). Tram 55.
The city's biggest dance school has its own professional dance company. Classes in classical ballet, jazz and tap.

Ecole de Danse Universelle
277 chaussée de Boondael, 1050 (649 77 40). Tram 90.
Ballroom, rock 'n' roll, tango, samba and other dances can be learnt here for 3,500BF per batch of 15 lessons. There are reductions for students and partners.

Maison du Spectacle – La Bellone
46 rue de Flandre, 1000 (513 33 33). Métro Ste Cathérine. **Map A2/B2**
The Maison is a centre for dance and theatre, and has a library with all current periodicals. It also brings out a seasonal magazine, *Nouvelles de Danse*, which is sold in major bookshops.

Rhapsodie
28 rue Defacqz, 1050 (539 12 04). Métro Louise/tram 93.
The place for belly-dancing, African and Latin American dance, plus yoga and meditation.

Yantra Académie
16B rue de la Cuve, 1050 (646 25 64). Tram 91, 92/bus 38, 59, 60, 71.
With the exception of classical ballet, all classes at the Yantra Académie are for adults only. Jazz (six ability levels), contemporary dance and a form of African dance are all offered.

Trips Out of Town

Getting Started

Belgium may be a small country but its riches are many and varied.

The linguistic confusion in Brussels becomes even more pronounced when you travel outside the city. With French, Dutch and German the three national languages (the last is only spoken by fewer than 100,000 of the country's 10 million citizens), even the natives get a little tongue-tied, so don't kick yourself for at times being at a loss for words. This much is clear: when in Wallonia, speak French or, failing that, English. Generations of Walloons never took the time to learn Dutch as it wasn't necessary: for ages French was the country's dominant language. But the current concentration of economic power in Flanders has meant that the younger generations are beginning to learn Flemish. And any Walloon who speaks good Dutch is bound to speak better English, generally learned from films, TV and pop songs.

What to speak becomes more complicated for the foreigner in Flanders. Depending on the region, speaking French can be considered a political statement, as many Flemings still have bitter memories of the suppression of their language and culture. In other regions, such as Ghent, Knokke-le-Zoute and Antwerp (but only among the upper class in the latter), it is a mark of class. Although most Flemings speak good to excellent English (again, courtesy of American and British pop culture as much as schooling), it is still a good idea to begin each new encounter with 'Do you speak English' ('Spreekt u engels?' in Dutch) before launching into a monologue.

Rail travel
Belgian railways

Brussels is one of the few cities with three major train stations: the newly renovated Gare du Midi, where the TGV and Eurostar depart and arrive, Gare Centrale and Gare du Nord. Express routes exist between most major cities, with local routes stopping in spots easy to miss on a map. Due to the country's small size (two hours is the longest ride between two connecting stations), the trains are utilitarian in comfort.

Because rail travel is still a major means of transport in Belgium, train tickets are inexpensive. From Monday morning to Friday late afternoon, return tickets cost the same as two one-way tickets and are valid for the day of purchase only. From early Friday evening to Sunday evening, a 40 per cent discount is offered on return tickets;

you have to depart the day you bought the ticket, and the return is valid until Monday evening. Tickets can be purchased at the station.

Train information

Belgium has long had a reputation for Eastern bloc efficiency and bonhomie when it comes to service, but the SNCB is actually showing signs of improving customer service. When you telephone them for schedule and fare information, they actually pick up, though still after a good wait. For information on services in and out of Brussels, phone 203 28 80 or 203 36 40.

Coach travel

The importance of train travel means that the bus is the last resort of transportation for the tourist: the schedules seem to be written in hieroglyphics that only the most seasoned commuter can get his head around. And even then, buses are used more for connections to villages and suburbs outside cities than for travel between major points. For further information on buses, TEC (410 21 00) is the bus line for Wallonia, while De Lijn (526 28 28/526 28 11) handles Flanders. For trips outside Belgium, most people choose Eurolines (218 29 93).

Day trips
Taxistop

28 rue Fosse-aux-Loups, 1000 (223 22 31/fax 223 22 32). **Open** 10.30am-6pm Mon-Fri.
This agency offers a variety of services that save travellers money. The central service is their car service, which goes to destinations throughout Belgium and Europe for a fee of 1.3BF/km, plus 200BF for administration costs. The only catch is that there must be a car already sheduled to depart for your destination when you call to reserve in advance… and there has to be space. Other services include Airstop and Eurostop, through which airlines and coach companies respectively offer cut-rate tickets on trips as a means to fill otherwise empty seats.

Bed & breakfast
Bed & Brussels

58 rue Victor Greyson, 1050 (646 07 37/fax 644 01 14). Tram 93, 94. **Reservations** 9am-6pm Mon-Fri.
B&Bs throughout Belgium can be booked through this agency. If you phone and get their answering service, leave a message and they'll get back to you. They publish a guide of bed & breakfasts, suitably entitled *Bed & Breakfast. See also chapter* **Accommodation**.

Antwerp

Belgium's second city is its unofficial capital of culture.

For many years Europe's diamond capital and second largest port, Antwerp has recently begun to assert itself in other ways. Its young fashion designers have hit the catwalks of France and Italy. Its museums and art galleries are a point of reference in Belgium. Its clubs and bars are now rivalling those of Brussels.

A few years ago Antwerp was one of the best-kept secrets in northern Europe. The turning point came as recently as 1993, when the city was named Europe's Culture Capital. So far, it hasn't lost any of its charm; instead, it has been getting fresher and acquiring more of a buzz than at any other time in its history.

Antwerp's long-neglected southern side is also beginning to come to life. The area around the **Koninklijk Museum voor Schone Kunsten** (Royal Museum of Fine Arts) and the **Museum van Hedendaagse Kunst Antwerpen** or **MUHKA** (Museum of Contemporary Art) is scattered with new nightclubs, restaurants, bars (*see below* **Eating & drinking**). As for the art world, the trend is for local artists to eschew the commercial gallery scene and open their own homes to the public. Unfortunately for visitors, these openings tend to be advertised by word of mouth, so you either need to know Antwerp very well or have good connections in the art world.

Other aspects of Antwerp life remain timeless. A Sunday walk by the River Scheldt or in one of the parks. A visit to Antwerp Zoo, the biggest in Belgium. The weekend markets and cafés around the Grote Markt. The diamond industry, based around the area of Pelikaanstraat, is vital to the Belgian economy and represents seven per cent of the gross national product. The city's prosperity, however, has always depended on the port.

LINGUA BELGICA

Throughout its history, Antwerp has been a place of exchange, and as a consequence language has never been a problem here. Everyone seems to be fluent in Flemish, English, French and German. Yet despite this, Antwerp can seem provincial and reserved. Walking around the city you may notice abrupt changes between one street and another. From the clean and intact historical centre you can easily step into what remains of the red light district. It's as if these different worlds are juxtaposed but never actually meet, or at the very least tolerate but completely ignore each other.

History

According to legend, a giant used to cut off the hand of any sailor who could not pay the toll to sail on the Scheldt. The giant carried on chopping off hands and terrifying sailors until he was defeated by a Roman, Silvius Brabo. It was after accomplishing this feat that the brave Roman became the Duke of Brabant. Although the legend curiously fits the name of the city (with slight alteration the Flemish name means 'hand throwing'), and the statue of this heroic citizen stands in the middle of the Grote Markt, the truth is somewhat more prosaic. Antwerp was founded by Christian missionaries in the seventh century. Its Golden Age did not begin until the fifteenth century, when its port began to flourish. This was due to two factors. One was that the city profited from Charles V's policies of expansion. The second was that, having silted up, the rival port of Bruges had become completely inactive. Antwerp became a major trading centre for spices, wool, salt and precious stones.

Furthermore, having discovered the route to the East, Portuguese merchants began to use Antwerp as a point of exchange, and Jews who had been fleeing Portugal moved to Antwerp and founded the city's diamond industry. Banks were established in the city and in 1460 the first stock exchange was built. Commerce was thriving and it was a period of expansion for the arts.

This era of prosperity came to an end around the sixteenth century, and a period of savage religious conflict and repression followed. The city was divided by religious quarrels and in 1566 the Calvinist Iconoclasts destroyed numerous churches in the city. Philip II, not known for his religious tolerance, sent the faithful and feared Duke of Alva to sort out the situation. Thus began the period of 'Spanish Fury'. In 1577 Calvinists took control of the city and banned the public practice of the Catholic faith until 1585 when the Spanish regained power over the city.

As with the rest of Belgium the period of rule of Albert and Isabella was more sedate, but with the Treaty of Munster and the closing of the Scheldt, the city's downfall was guaranteed. For the next hundred years Antwerp no longer had access to the sea. With its wealth entirely founded on trade and exchange this meant the city was economically devastated, much to the delight of Amsterdam. Not only did the Dutch capital gain from the

St Anna Strand *on the left bank of the Scheldt, thought to be safer for a stroll than a swim.*

closure of the port, but many Protestant merchants left Antwerp for Amsterdam.

In the nineteenth century, having come to realise the important position of Antwerp, Napoleon constructed docks and used the city as a strategic point in his war against Britain. After the downfall of Napoleon and the Treaty of Vienna (1815), Antwerp, like the whole of Belgium, came under the rule of William of Orange and enjoyed a new period of prosperity.

With the coming of independence in 1830, however, Antwerp suffered further hard times, as the Dutch imposed a heavy tax as a condition of independence. In the following century, Antwerp suffered greatly during both World Wars.

Sightseeing

Bonaparte Docks & St Anna

It's possible to visit Antwerp's historical centre or walk around the shopping streets on a Saturday afternoon and not notice that the city even possesses a port. Yet the River Scheldt is a mere three-minute stroll away from the Grote Markt, and some of the nineteenth-century docks are also within walking distance.

It may be a good idea to begin a tour of Antwerp by taking a quick look around this area. You are not going to encounter huge cranes, monstrous industrial activity or the seedier side of the port, but at least you will get a general impression of the city's activity.

Strolling along the Scheldt, you'll come to the **Steen** (National Maritime Museum). On one side of the Steen you can walk under the hangars and around the Bonaparte Docks. These docks, built by Napoleon, are the closest to the city centre and are now practically at a standstill. Few ships remain and those that do are used for tours or leisure. Despite this, you will still be able to get a fair picture of what this part of the port must have been like in the nineteenth century.

St Paulus' Church & Butchers' Hall

Not far away, near Vervesrui, is the red light district, or what remains of it. Perhaps because it is so close to the historical centre, many of the prostitutes are being persuaded to move elsewhere. This seems a little harsh, especially since many women working in the red light district helped rescue works by Rubens, Jordaens and Van Dyck when fire broke out in St Paulus' Church in 1968.

St Paulus' has since been restored. It is in Gothic style but with a baroque bell tower. The interior has beautiful paintings by Flemish masters and wonderfully carved wood panelling. There are major works by Rubens, Jordaens, Van Dyck and other Flemish masters.

St Paulus' is on a lively square. It may not be as neat as other squares in the centre but it seems to

Built in iron and glass just over a century ago by De la Censerie, Antwerp's **Centraal Station** *is itself one of the city's sights.*

Made in Belgium

Belgium is most emphatically on the fashion map, not only because of the long-established Olivier Strelli or Gerald Watelet, who have dressed Queen Paola and show in Paris, but also for a whole new generation of exciting young designers. Look out for fashion schools La Cambre, St Lukaas and, of course, the Antwerp Academy.

The players

The Antwerp Six

Here's the legend: six graduates of the classes of 1980 and 1981 at the Antwerpse Kunstaka-demie hired a truck in 1987 and went to London Fashion Week to present their clothes. First they took London by storm, then Paris, and now they are all famous and living happily ever after.

Ann Demeulemeester

Along with Martin Margiela and Dries van Noten, Ann Demeulemeester was credited in the 1980s with the not very Derridean 'fashion deconstruction', in which seams and linings were deliberately left on the outside. She now creates clothes that flow while remaining close to the body, using ribbons and lots of asymmetry to create movement. Her simple designs, usually in monochrome shades, redefine the boundaries of femininity (one of her shows involved male and female models identically dressed as Patti Smith clones) and have been extended to a menswear range.

Shops *Coccodrillo, 9A/B Schuttershofstraat, 2000 Antwerp (shoes); Louis, 2 Lombardenstraat, 2000 Antwerp (clothes);* **Stijl** (*see chapter* **Shopping & Services: Fashion***).*

Dirk Bikkembergs

Black leather, studs, slit clothes and military-style cuts, for men and women.

Sold at *Stijl; Verso for men, 39 Huidevetterstraat, 2000 Antwerp (03 226 92 92); women's at SN3, 49 Frankrijklei, 2000 Antwerp (03 231 08 20).*

Dirk van Saene

The media seem to forget Dirk van Saene but he makes women's clothes with a trendy, utilitarian, wearable feel. Greys, blues and reds all cohabit peacefully, but he doesn't like to mix them too much.

Dries van Noten

A few years back Dries van Noten was into deconstruction with a vengeance, but he has since moved on. Known for layering, he makes a habit of putting coats over chiffon dresses, the chiffon print dresses over trousers and so on. Patterned, dark, rich colours (aubergines,

---

be more integrated into city life. Not far away, on Vleeshouersstraat, is the Butchers' Hall, built by the Butchers' Guild at the beginning of the sixteenth century. It was the only place in the city where meat could be sold. It is a puzzling construction, in late Gothic style, with little turrets and walls that alternate red brick and white stone. Today the hall is used as a museum for archaeological finds and objects pertaining to local history.

Much of the area in the immediate vicinity of the Butchers' Hall has been renovated, but the style of the new houses is insipid. The intention must have been to build in a style that would not be at odds with the medieval and Renaissance architecture nearby. The policy is understandable but the end result makes you wish the city fathers had had the stomach for something a little more more daring.

Along the river

On the other side of the Steen, walking towards the city centre, there are large terraces on the riverfront. Here you can stroll by the river and enjoy a cup of coffee either on the terrace or in any of the nearby cafés.

A little further on, in St Jansvliet, is the entrance to the St Anna pedestrian tunnel, which takes you to the left bank. Wooden escalators take you underground, then it's a ten-minute walk to the other side of the river. As you emerge, you will notice a traditional café that is unremarkable other than for its mussels, at which it excels.

Antwerp was built mainly on the right bank of the Scheldt and the left bank is consequently not particularly lively. The twentieth-century architect Le Corbusier had an ambitious plan to move all the administration buildings to the left bank, thinking that this was the only way in which it might have a chance to develop. The project was turned down and the left bank never did pick up.

Nevertheless, the left bank can claim the only beach in Antwerp, the St Anna Strand. Years ago, people used the strand as the local beach. It was popular and busy during the summer until it was considered unsafe because of high levels of pollution. The beach was destroyed.

Recently Antwerp has rediscovered the strand and decided to restore it to its original use. Once again, the beach can get rather crowded when the

midnight blues, chocolate browns, smoky greys) mix with camels and muted shades. It's just as well he's into coats: he's been known to sit his fashion-show audience outside in a snow storm. His smart but simple menswear is favoured by the (well-off) new lad and has a strong northern European feel.
Sold at *Stijl; Het Modepaleis, 16 Nationalestraat, 2000 Antwerp (03 233 94 37).*

Martin Margiela

The most reclusive of the crew, refusing to be photographed or to give face-to-face interviews. He surprised the fashion world by being appointed design director of the women's ready-to-wear collection at Hermès, the first collection being shown in 1998. His CV reads like a script: he worked as a fashion assistant to Gaultier from 1984-7, has been showing in Paris since 1989 (his shows are always in out-of-the-way locations) and he recently helped design the costumes for Peter Greenaway's *The Pillow Book*. They called him a deconstructionist, which he isn't really: he just likes recycled, lived-in clothes, using mixed-media techniques (he screen-prints photos of clothes on to materials and makes them into clothing) and leaving unfinished seams hanging. His designs (including allusions to bacteria, and a blouse made of shards of pottery) have been consecrated in museums in Rotterdam and Venice. His trademark white square identifies his simply-cut layered clothes.
Sold at *Coccodrillo (shoes only), Louis (clothes only) and Stijl (clothes and shoes).*

Walter van Beirendonck

Van Beirendonck's label says it all: Wild & Lethal Trash (W&LT) is a collection of futuristic, brightly coloured synthetics shaped into strong lines. Punk-trash and superhero influences and fairy- and children's tale references are inherent in his iconography (so much so that he has started creating children's collections, too). His feel for redefining popular culture led him to design the costumes for U2's Pop Mart tour. Directly inspired by the violent trash cartoon culture, Van Beirendonck has created a website with his cyber-icon Puk Puk, an alien from the Planet Dork. You can even design the face of the future and your own T-shirts; log on to http://www.walt.de/ Basically upmarket clubwear, W&LT took off in 1994 when he secured the financial backing of German company Mustang. Walter's graduation collection was insect-based, and although he's now very urbanistic, he's not forgetting his roots – he's been teaching in the fashion department at the Antwerp Academy since 1985.
Sold at *Closing Date, 15 Korte Gasthuisstraat, 2000 Antwerp (03 232 87 22).*

Raf Simons

Raf Simons' school uniform-inspired designs are a mishmash of punk and sober cotton shirts. He uses lots of machine-knit wools, which he hand-assembles into sweaters. Up-and-coming Antwerp designer who's the hot tip to take over at Versace.
Sold at *Stijl.*

---

weather permits but, although some fish have now returned to the river, it is still considered unsafe to swim in it.

No one would deny that the most fascinating parts of Antwerp are on the opposite bank. Nonetheless, from the left bank you can enjoy excellent views of the historic part of the city, particularly in the evening.

Our Lady's Cathedral

Antwerp's historical centre stretches all around the Grote Markt. In the centre of the market square is the statue of Brabo, legendary symbol of the city. The houses around the square mostly date from the Renaissance, including the Stadhuis (Town Hall).

The majestic Onze Lieve Vrouwkathedraal (Our Lady's Cathedral) is just off the square. Although a chapel was built here in the thirteenth century, work on the cathedral itself began in the fourteenth century, before Antwerp's Golden Age. With trade and wealth steadily increasing in the following centuries, ambitions for the cathedral grew and plans were drawn up to make it one of the most

gigantic in Europe. Construction was interrupted several times by fires and the city's changing fortunes; these same fires, iconoclastic fury and destruction carried out at the time of the French Revolution also caused the destruction of many of the cathedral's original features. Renovation, however, is now complete and the building can be viewed in its full glory.

The most famous works in the cathedral are those by Pieter Paul Rubens. It's hard to avoid the baroque master in Antwerp. Some of his most stunning works are kept in his house and in the Koninklijk Museum voor Schone Kunsten (Royal Museum of Fine Arts). Many of the works that are displayed in the city are inspired by religion rather than by Greek mythology, so those who are not great fans of the ample sensuous ladies for which he is renowned may find themselves drawn to his work in Antwerp.

There are four paintings by Rubens in the cathedral: *The Raising of the Cross*, *The Descent from the Cross*, *The Resurrection* and *The Assumption*. The last of these is located directly over the altar and can only be seen from a distance. Its

dynamism and dazzling colours can be appreciated but it is difficult to get a good idea of the detail. The other paintings are more dramatic. *The Raising of the Cross*, one of the first works painted by Rubens after his return from Italy, is a rich and emotional work. The real masterpiece, though, is *The Descent from the Cross*.

St Carolus' & St Jacob's

The narrow, tortuous streets behind the cathedral will take you to St Carolus' Church. On one side of this square stands the baroque church, and opposite is the city library. Built by the Jesuits, St Conscienceplein is one of the prettiest squares in Antwerp; it is admittedly far less imposing than the Grote Markt, but is peaceful and intimate. Everything here seems quiet: little evidence can be heard of the activity of the city, even though you're at its very centre.

St Carolus' dates from the seventeenth century. The façade is elaborate and ornate, with columns and statues. Rubens worked on this church, which was the only existing baroque construction – his contemporaries were still working in Gothic mode. Rubens also painted the ceilings of the church, but these, tragically, were destroyed by fire.

Another church that is nearby and well worth visiting is St Jacob's in Lange Nieuwstraat. As you walk towards it from a distance the church looks big and impressive, but the closer you get the more it seems to disappear. The church is not on a square and rises up from the nearby streets. What is even more peculiar is that little houses completely surround it, barely making space for the main and side entrances.

St Jacob's attracts many visitors because it is Rubens' burial place. The painting over his tomb, *Our Lady Surrounded by Saints*, was painted by the artist for this very purpose. The painting of St George is believed to be a self-portrait, while the Virgin is a portrait of Isabelle Brant, Rubens' first wife. Mary Magdalene is a portrait of Hélène Fourment, his second wife.

The church is heavily decorated in baroque style. It was built in a wealthy part of Antwerp and the parishioners made sure the church reflected their status.

Antwerpen Centraal, diamond district & the Meir

Built in iron and glass, with an impressive dome, Antwerp's central railway station is a surprising construction. With its majestic stairs and gold decorations, it is splendidly ostentatious. Created

*One of the largest zoos in Europe and housing over 4,000 animals, **Antwerp Zoo** can take a whole day to visit. See p198.*

by the architect De la Censerie, it was built just over a century ago.

The diamond district, which begins on Pelikaanstraat, borders the station. This predominantly Jewish area has the highest concentration of jewellers in the country. The Bourse aux Diamants in Pelikaanstraat is heavily guarded, access is limited and there is strict control of identity cards. Nearby lies the much more accessible **Diamond Museum**. The area itself glitters rather less than the stones it sells; in fact its appearance has been completely rundown. There is also a highly visible police presence in these streets.

The Meir, Antwerp's main shopping street, takes you from the station to the historical centre. As with most major shopping streets, the shop window displays are such that they tend to draw the attention away from some remarkable nineteenth-century façades just overhead. Don't miss, for example, the art deco Boerentoren, one of Europe's first skyscrapers.

The Handelsbeurs (Stock Exchange) in Hofstraat is the site of one of the oldest stock exchanges in Europe. The original building was replaced in the sixteenth century. In 1858 a fire destroyed the replacement building as well and the present one was put up in 1872.

Green Antwerp

Antwerp Zoo is next to the station on the opposite side of the Meir. It forms a vast green area right in the middle of the city. Antwerp has a profusion of parks. The Botanical Gardens in Leopoldstraat are perhaps the most charming and also the most neglected by visitors. The herb garden in particular is not to be missed.

Further away from the centre, in the Middelheim, there is a huge park as well as an open-air sculpture museum. It mounts temporary exhibitions, but is most notable for its permanent collection, which includes works by Rodin, Minne, Moore and Zadkine.

The Nachtegalenpark, in the same area, is an excellent park for children, very busy during weekends and at any time the weather happens to be fine. If you are interested in architecture, don't miss Cogels Osylei. Wide and lined with trees, this wonderful street, in the Berchem area, has art nouveau and turn-of-the-century houses built by Victor Horta's pupil, Jos Bascourt.

Getting there

By train from Gare du Nord, Gare Centrale or Gare du Midi; *by car* A1 or A12.

Tourist information

15 Grote Markt (03 232 01 03/fax 03 231 79 37). **Open** 9am-6pm Mon-Sat; 9am-5pm Sun.
One of the best tourist offices in Belgium, with information about where to eat, sleep and amuse yourself. If you're seeking information about the Antwerp province in general, try the tourist office at 11 Karel Oomstraat (03 216 28 10).

Museums & places of interest

Antwerp Zoo

26 Koningen Astridplein, 2018 Antwerp (03 202 45 40/ fax 03 231 00 18). **Open** *Dec, Jan* 9am-4pm daily; *Feb, Oct, Nov* 9am-4.30pm daily; *Mar-June, Sept* 9am-6.30pm daily; *July, Aug* 9am-6.30pm daily. **Admission** 450BF; 290BF 3-11s, over-60s, disabled; free under 3s (no pets allowed). **No credit cards.**

Founded at the end of the nineteenth century, Antwerp Zoo is one of the oldest and largest in Europe. Some of its most inspired buildings date from its earliest days, such as the giraffes' Egyptian temple and the immense aviaries for birds of prey. As the zoo houses over 4,000 animals, it can take a full day to visit. Some of its more popular attractions are the nocturama where night birds are kept in semi-darkness, the reptilarium, the aquarium and dolphinarium. Make sure you get there a little ahead of feeding time because seals and dolphins tend to attract large crowds and adults sometimes only grudgingly make room for children. Some of the animals kept here belong to species that are almost extinct (for instance some of the gorillas), but the zoo does take part in international breeding programmes to help guarantee the survival of threatened species.

Diamond Museum

31-33 Lange Herentalsestraat, 2000 Antwerp (03 202 48 90). **Open** 10am-4.45pm Tue-Sun. **Closed** public holidays. **Admission** *15 May-31 Aug* 100BF; *1 Sept-14 May* free. **No credit cards.**

Although the Diamond Museum offers a comprehensive history of the diamond industry and trade, most visitors come here to see the end product. Dazzling jewellery is on show, and it's even possible to see the diamonds being cut on Saturday afternoons.

Ethnografisch Museum

19 Suikerrui, 2000 Antwerp (03 232 08 82). **Open** 10am-4.45pm Tue-Sun. **Closed** public holidays. **Admission** 75BF; 30BF concessions. **No credit cards.**

Antwerp's Ethnographic Museum has an excellent reputation. It is arranged on several floors, each representing a certain part of the world. The top floor is generally reserved for temporary exhibitions. Each floor has its own reading section, with relevant books and comfortable seats where you can read up on the artefacts displayed. The atmosphere is cosy, if a little too dark, and visitors range from elderly ladies to intense students. The one problem with this museum is that the information is exclusively in Flemish.

Koninklijk Museum voor Schone Kunsten (Royal Museum of Fine Arts)

Leopold de Waelplaats, 2000 Antwerp (03 238 78 09). **Open** 10am-4.45pm Tue-Sun. **Admission** 150BF; 120BF concessions; Fri free. **Closed** public holidays. **No credit cards.**
See p203 **Arty facts.**

Museum voor Fotografie

47 Waalse Kaai, 2000 Antwerp (03 216 22 11). **Open** 10am-4.45pm Tue-Sun. **Closed** public holidays. **Admission** free. **No credit cards.**

The Museum of Photography is on the same square as the Museum van Hedendaagse Kunst Antwerpen (MUHKA). There are temporary exhibitions and a permanent section that has photograhs by Man Ray, Cartier-Bresson and Wiliam Klein. There are also excellent portraits, including one of Picasso. Much of the museum is devoted to the history and evolution of the art of photography. There are gigantic cameras and old snapshots of Belgium in general and Antwerp in particular.

Museum van Hedendaagse Kunst Antwerpen (MUHKA)

16-30 Leuvenstraat, 2000 Antwerp (03 238 59 60). **Open** 10am-4.45pm Tue-Sun. **Closed** public holidays. **Admission** 150BF; 100BF concessions. **No credit cards.**

The MUHKA (Museum of Contemporary Art) is unlikely to convert non-fans of modern art, but for aficionados and the open-minded it is definitely worth visiting. The museum focuses on works from the 1970s onwards and organises temporary exhibitions that run, on average, for two months. The museum has its own collection but this is only occasionally displayed. The first floor is given over to temporary exhibitions, and on the top floor a space is reserved for young contemporary artists. The strength of this museum lies in the way in which space is used. Rooms are flooded with natural light and are mostly painted white. The result is a relaxed and soothing atmosphere, ideal for contemplating works that are not always effortlessly accessible. Like most museums in Antwerp, the MUHKA organises activities for children; these change with every new exhibition.

Plantin-Moretus Huis

22 Vrijdagmarkt, 2000 Antwerp (03 233 02 94). **Open** 10am-4.45pm Tue-Sun. **Closed** public holidays. **Admission** 75BF; 30BF concessions. **No credit cards.**

It was in this immense sixteenth-century house that Christophe Plantin established his printing workshop. Here you can discover all the intricacies and difficulties of printing. There are huge presses, a beautiful proofreading room and a foundry. The house was also a centre for intellectuals. Proofreaders were all university-educated and fluent in several languages. Books were printed in Latin, Flemish, French, Hebrew, German and Spanish. Justus Lipsus, a contemporary of Erasmus, spent time here. If the technical aspects of printing do not fascinate you, the house itself probably will. There are some fine paintings, Mercator maps, Plantin's *Regia Bibla*, one of the rare Gutenberg Bibles, and other invaluable manuscripts.

Rubenshuis

9 Wapper, 2000 Antwerp (03 232 47 47). **Open** 10am-4.45pm Tue-Sun. **Closed** public holidays. **Admission** 75BF; 30BF concessions. **No credit cards.**

With works displayed in the Koninklijk Museum voor Schone Kunsten (Royal Museum of Fine Arts; *see p203* **Arty facts**), as well as in several churches of the city, and with a whole souvenir industry dedicated to him, Rubens is completely unavoidable in Antwerp. Several of his works are displayed in Rubenshuis (Rubens' house). Born in 1577, Rubens began his career in Antwerp, where he became an apprentice to several outstanding artists. In 1600 he went to Italy, where he studied the Italian masters. He bought this house in 1611, shortly after his return from Italy, and soon after being appointed city painter by Archdukes Albert and Isabella. Numerous souvenirs from his time in Italy decorate the house.

A visit begins with a look at the Master's studio, which is overlooked by a mezzanine where his work could be admired by potential buyers. Rubens was an exceptionally prolific painter – chiefly because he didn't do all the painting himself. Works were mass-produced by staff in his workshop; Rubens would direct proceedings and add the necessary brushstrokes. With pupils such as Jordaens and Van Dyck, he could afford to limit the extent of his contribution to attentive supervision.

The baroque façade of the workshop can be seen from the inner courtyard. It's one of the few baroque buildings in

Koninklijk Museum voor Schone Kunsten *(Royal Museum of Fine Arts) has a fine collection of fifteenth-century Flemish art.*

Antwerp, which, in Rubens' time and much to his regret, was predominantly Gothic. The house passed through the hands of several owners before the city of Antwerp eventually managed to buy it. It has been extensively renovated and the garden entirely reconstructed. Much of the furniture dates from the seventeenth century but was not originally in the house.

Steen (National Maritime Museum)

1 Steenplein, 2000 Antwerp (03 232 08 50). **Open** 10am-4.45pm Tue-Sun. **Closed** public holidays. **Admission** 75BF; 30BF concessions. **No credit cards.**
The Steen is almost as old as Antwerp itself and has become a symbol of the city. Built in 1200, it was originally part of the fortifications. Later it served as a prison, where inmates had to pay the guards for their stay. This meant that the wealthier prisoners lived in better conditions than poorer ones, regardless of the seriousness of the offences. For a while it served as a sawmill before being turned into a maritime museum. Today you'll find maps, maritime *objets* and countless models of ships. Real ships can be found in the outdoor section of the museum.

Shopping

Antwerp's new-found role in the world of fashion has made it the most exciting shopping city in Belgium. Clothes by young stylists can be found in all the smarter boutiques. Dries van Noten's Het Mode Paleis has become an Antwerp attraction in its own right, although many come just to admire the sumptuous nineteenth-century buildings.

Although Antwerp's main shopping street is the Meir, there are other areas that are just as inviting and conducive to spending money – for example, the smarter Huidevetterstraat, Schutterhofstraat and Leopoldstraat. Eiermarkt has some beautiful shops, as does Korte Gasthuisstraat. Antwerp has a well-deserved reputation for its fine antique shops, most of which can be found around Lombardvest and Steenhouwersvest.

Fashion

For world-class Antwerp-based designers *see page 194* **Made in Belgium.**

A Boon

4 Lombardvest, 2000 Antwerp (no phone). **Open** varies. **No credit cards.**
Delightfully old-fashioned glove shop, with hundreds of different gloves for men and women, displayed on dark wooden shelves. Staff still soften the leather gloves by putting them on wooden hand models before you try them on.

Anvers Shop

53 Leopoldstraat, 2000 Antwerp (03 213 28 08). **Open** 10.30am-6.30pm Mon-Sat. **Credit** AmEx, V.
Impeccable clothes set against a minimalist décor. Anvers sells elegant women's casual wear, ranging from classic cuts to more inventive looks. Prices are relatively accessible.

Closing Date

15 Korte Gasthuisstraat, 2000 Antwerp (03 232 87 22). **Open** 11am-6.30pm Mon-Sat. **Credit** AmEx, DC, MC, V.

Museum van Hedendaagse Kunst Antwerpen (MUHKA) – *see page 198 for the city's museum of contemporary art.*

Bright lights, flashes of colour, steel racks and vast, factory-like rooms. Closing Date sells clothes for men and women, and attracts thirtysomething customers. Prices are upper mid-range.

Coccodrillo

9A/B Schuttershofstraat, 2000 Antwerp (03 233 20 93). **Open** 10am-6pm Mon-Sat. **Credit** AmEx, DC, MC, V.
The collections of Prada, Dirk Bikkembergs, Patrick Cox and Joan & David are well represented at this mecca of fashion footwear.

Corakemperman

9 Schrijnwerkerstraat, 2000 Antwerp (03 231 27 22). **Open** 10am-6pm Mon-Thur; 10am-7pm Fri, Sat. **Credit** MC, V.
The grey slate look of the interior contrasts with the colourful clothes hanging on the racks. The clothes are influenced by African and Asian styles, both in colour and choice of materials. Though some of the items may look difficult to wear, the choice is huge and varied, and endless combinations are possible.

Dany-May

36 Frankrijklei, 2000 Antwerp (03 233 97 35). **Open** 10am-6.30pm Mon-Sat. **Credit** AmEx, DC, MC, TC, V.
Showcasing the younger, trendier (but still traditionally chic) lines of Calvin Klein, Byblos and Iceberg, as well as other designers.

De Puzzel

43 Kammenstraat, 2000 Antwerp (03 233 90 69). **Open** noon-6.30pm Mon; 10am-6pm Tue-Sat. **Credit** AmEx, DC, MC, V.
Postcards and women's shoes are sold in De Puzzel, which takes advantage of its colonial décor by providing a café and lounge area for weary shoppers. Thigh-high leather and utilitarian work boots, platform trainers and sensible brogues are stocked. The postcard styles include art deco and Roy Lichtenstein.

Dierckx

108 Frankrijklei, 2000 Antwerp (03 233 23 93). **Open** 9.30am-6.30pm Mon-Fri; 9.30am-6pm Sat. **Credit** AmEx, DC, MC, TC, V.
For over a century, Dierckx has been the pre-eminent name in Belgian bespoke tailoring. Men's and women's suits are sold in this finely appointed shop.

Dries van Noten

16 Nationalestraat, 2000 Antwerp (03 233 94 37). **Open** 10am-6.30pm Mon-Sat. **Credit** AmEx, DC, JCB, MC, V.
One of the designers who helped launch world interest in Flemish fashion, Van Noten sells his own collections and selected items from Paul Smith in this landmark building dating from 1886. The men's and the women's floors are decorated with late nineteenth-century furniture, complemented by contemporary lighting and furnishings. Jewellery by Belgian duo Wouters & Hendrickx is also on sale.

Esprit

52 Meir, 2000 Antwerp (03 233 60 20). **Open** 10am-6pm Mon-Fri; 10am-6.30pm Sat. **Credit** AmEx, DC, MC, V.
A bargain-priced store that has spent on its interior: three floors of steel tubing and grating give the Antwerp branch an industrial feel. The Brussels stores are blander, with blond wood that lets the clothes grab your attention.

SN3

48 Frankrijklei, 2000 Antwerp (03 231 08 20). **Open** 10am-6.30pm Mon-Sat. **Credit** AmEx, DC, MC, V.

Called 'Snoopy 3' with something less than affection by some locals, this designer boutique carries the principal collections by the likes of Chanel, Prada, Lacroix and Claude Montana. Despite a tradition of being snobbish and a touch sterile (two floors of streamlined plate glass and flattering soft lighting), SN3 is still worth a visit.

XSO

13-17 Eiermarkt, 2000 Antwerp (03 231 87 49). **Open** 10am-6pm Mon-Fri; 10am-6.30pm Sat. **Credit** AmEx, DC, MC, V.

The décor is a mix of Japanese purity (white walls, slate floors) and Italian flourishes (lanterns), which is appropriate with two sections, one dedicated to Issey Miyake and the other to Romeo Gigli. The lower-priced G Gigli collection is housed in a boutique within XSO.

Jewellery & watches

Ginotti

3 Appelmansstraat, 2018 Antwerp (03 231 56 92). **Open** 2-6pm Mon; 10am-12.30pm, 2-6.30pm, Tue-Sat. **Credit** AmEx, DC, MC, TC, V.

These days it's hard to impress anyone with a Rolex, Cartier or Breitling – with so many good counterfeits around, it's difficult to tell who's wearing the genuine article. That's why Ginotti sells the really exclusive names in watches – Blancpain, Audemars Piguet and relative newcomers Daniel Roth and Franck Muller – that start at about £3,000 a pop.

Nadine Wijnants

26 Kloosterstraat, 2000 Antwerp (03 226 45 69). **Open** 11am-6pm Tue-Sat. **Credit** MC, V.

One of the top young jewellery designers in Belgium, Wijnants creates charming trinkets with semi-precious stones and oxidised or sterling silver, bronze and gold plate. Incorporating influences that run from India to street style, Wijnants always aims to make her collections affordable. She does customised jewellery, too.

Health & beauty

Il Trucco

1 Vlasmarkt, 2000 Antwerp (03 232 08 22). **Open** 1-6pm Wed-Sat. **No credit cards**.

Il Trucco sells make-up for everyday wear. Its products, Visiora (Christian Dior's professional line), Screenface and Paris-Berlin, are top of the range. They are high in pigments, which means smaller quantities can be used and the make-up never looks as if it has been pasted on. Prices are very reasonable.

Optometrix

43 De Nieuwe Gaanderihji, 2000 Antwerp (03 231 93 21). **Open** 10am-6pm Mon-Sat. **Credit** AmEx, DC, V.

High-fashion spectacle frames such as Calvin Klein, Matsuda, Alain Mikli and Beausoleil are sold at this Antwerp branch of a Belgian chain.

Sirenzo

61 Leopoldstraat, 2000 Antwerp (03 231 29 68). **Open** noon-6pm Mon; 11am-6pm Tue-Sat. **Credit** MC.

A recent addition to the New Age scene, Sirenzo sells crystals and tarot cards in addition to herbs and vitamins. Books are also sold, but almost exclusively in Dutch.

Soap

13 Plantinkaai, 2000 Antwerp (03 232 73 72). **Open** 9am-8pm Tue-Fri; 9am-5pm Sat (booking advisable). **No credit cards**.

The salon in Belgium where the ultra-stylish get their hair dyed, fried or laid to the side. The interior features large paintings of Japanese superhero art and milky fluorescent

colours, and it has been the backdrop for more than a few fashion shoots. Unlike Brussels salons, everyone speaks fluent English – a must if you're trying to get your hairdresser to understand what look you're striving for.

Flowers

Plantaanrdige Verbeelding

12 Schuttershofstraat, 2000 Antwerp (03 226 10 42). **Open** 11am-7pm Mon; 9am-7pm Tue-Fri; 9am-6pm Sat. **Credit** MC, V.

The shop is as beautiful as the flowers it sells. Built in grey stone, the rooms are big and spacious and are filled with bucketfuls of flowers, marvellous plants and arrangements. A designer's answer to boring bouquets.

Interiors

HaZorFim

20 Schupstraat, 2018 Antwerp (03 227 16 66). **Open** 10am-6pm Mon-Fri; 10.30am-2pm Sat. **Credit** AmEx, DC, MC, V.

This is a factory outlet of the 43-year-old Israeli manufacturer, which explains the reasonable prices for high-quality silver pieces. Platters, gondola-shaped bowls, picture frames, champagne buckets and jewellery boxes are just some of the merchandise on offer.

Jos Hofmans

42 & 53 Kloosterstraat, 2000 Antwerp (03 233 89 29). **Open** 11am-6pm daily. **No credit cards**.

The chances of getting a bargain here are increased by the fact that there is so much junk on offer: you have to dig deep through these two depots of bric-a-brac to reach something of value, but it's also worth a stop just to have a peek in.

Nine D

9B Schuttershofstraat, 2000 Antwerp (03 232 42 99). **Open** noon-6.30pm Mon; 10.30am-6.30pm Tue-Sat. **Credit** MC, V.

Natural fabrics, comfortable wooden furniture and wholesome food in a soft-hued setting as cosy as your own living room. Most of the furniture is designed by proprietor Nathalie van Reeth, but French tableware is also on offer.

N Vrouyr

6-8 Komedieplaats, 2000 Antwerp (03 232 36 87). **Open** 2-6pm Mon; 9.30am-12.30pm, 2-6pm, Tue-Fri; 10am-12.30pm, 2-6pm, Sat. **Credit** AmEx, MC, V.

Since 1920, this spacious Antwerp store has been selling luxury carpets from the Near, Middle and Far East. N Vrouyr is a member of the prestigious Belgian Chambre des Antiquaires.

Oude Bureaus, Oude Spiegels

68 & 79 Kloosterstraat, 2000 Antwerp (03 238 73 62). **Open** noon-6pm Mon-Sat; 2-6pm Sun. **No credit cards**.

The name translates as 'Old desks, old mirrors', which pretty much sums up the late nineteenth- and early twentieth-century English and German office furniture and French ornate mirrors on sale.

Scapa of Scotland

16 Huidevetterstraat, 2000 Antwerp (03 227 38 54). **Open** 10am-6.30pm Mon-Sat. **Credit** AmEx, DC, MC, V.

Ralph Lauren is the name that actually springs immediately to mind upon entering this two-floor store: Turkish, Irish and Austrian are a few of the many cultures influencing the clothes and home furnishings on display. The ground floor is mostly British-inspired apparel, while upstairs you find patchwork cushion and duvet covers, Indian brass statuettes and teak and walnut cupboards arranged in the perfect home setting.

Arty facts

The **Koninklijk Museum voor Schone Kunsten** (Royal Museum of Fine Arts) is the focal point of southern Antwerp. Fifteenth-century Flemish painting is well represented, with works by Van Eyck, Van der Weyden and Hans Memling.

Van Eyck improved significantly on old oil painting techniques, moving away from the limitations of tempera – hence the glowing colours of his paintings. There are works from the same period by Simone Martini, Antonello da Messina and France's Jean Fouquet. The sixteenth century is often considered a period of transition, probably because a number of different styles were developing at the same time. There are instances of mannerism in the work of Van Orley, while Quinten Metsys is clearly influenced by the Italian Renaissance. Note the use of colours and light, and the minute attention to detail. The influence of Michelangelo can be clearly seen in the work of Frans Floris, especially in his portrayal of the human body.

The museum contains no original works by Peter Bruegel the Elder. There are several paintings by his school and these works, like those of Bruegel himself, are fascinating for their details of contemporary working-class life. Many of the works here are landscapes, some of them Belgian. If the countryside they depict doesn't look remotely Belgian, the reasons are twofold: urbanisation, and the fact that the landscapes were largely imagined and idealised.

The most stunning section of the museum is that devoted to the seventeenth century. There are marvellous paintings by Rubens, Jordaens and Van Dyck. The Rubens paintings are mostly religious works, though *Venus Frigida* is a notable exception. The idea that hunger and cold cool the fire of love is clearly reflected in the attitude of the goddess. *Adoration of the Magi* is another impressive work. Highly theatrical, mobile and expressive, it is a beautiful representation of baroque art. Lovers of historical detail should take note of *The Disbelief of Saint Thomas*. The painting was ordered by Rockox, mayor of Antwerp in Rubens' time, and the portraits on the side panels of the triptych are those of himself and his wife.

Jordaens' compositions are less dramatic. The colours are darker, the movement less dynamic, but his subjects convey a great generosity and sensuality. The range of his subjects is also more varied. His themes are often joyous, even uproarious, apparently like the artist himself.

Van Dyck's work is less vigorous and flamboyant than that of either Jordaens or Rubens. The emotion is more subdued and contained, but also more intimate. This can best be seen in works such as *Portrait of the Painter Marten Pepyn*. Van Dyck spent a lot of time in England, where he was court painter to Charles I.

The eighteenth-century section seems a little drab in comparison to the seventeenth century. Many artists were happy to follow in Rubens' footsteps, and there was little innovation, apart from the growing importance of historical and flower painting. In the nineteenth century, Belgian artists found fresh subject matter in their country's newly acquired independence, and several works in the museum depict significant historical events. Meanwhile, artists such as Joseph Stevens and Constant Meunier were depicting scenes of daily life. Antwerp-born Henri de Braekeleer is an important figure of the nineteenth century, and the city is one of his recurrent themes. His realism is delicate and moving.

The museum's extensive collection of paintings by James Ensor gives an overview of the artist's development. His first works, such as *Le Salon Bourgeois* and *La Mangeuse d'Huître*, are influenced by the French impressionists and by Turner. His more disturbing and impressive works came later on, when his world becomes filled with skeletons, masks and puppets. These paintings are haunting, vivid and occasionally grotesque.

The works of Rik Wouters, exhibited in the same room, are less haunting. Filled with sunlight, his colours are more those of fauvism than of impressionism. He is influenced by Cézanne, but his use of rich reds and blues puts one in mind of Matisse. Wouters was painting during World War I, when he saw active service and lost his sight. Strangely, his suffering rarely surfaces in his paintings and sculptures. Even *Rik au Bandeau Noir*, though clearly sadder than the festive *La Repasseuse*, has a definite optimistic quality.

The modern section of the museum includes works by internationally renowned artists such as Modigliani and Chagall, and paintings by the Belgian surrealists René Magritte and Paul Delvaux (*see chapter* **Surrealist Brussels**). There are sculptures by Ossip Zadkine, and elegant works by George Minne. A section is devoted to Flemish expressionism, the Cobra movement and the *groupe zero*.

't Koetshuis (Chelsea)

62 Kloosterstraat, 2000 Antwerp (03 231 36 43).
Open noon-6pm Tue-Fri; 1-6pm Sat, Sun. **No credit cards**.

This store's official name is Chelsea, but 't Koetshuis (literally 'the carriage') is what you'll find written in large letters over the front door. The art deco and art nouveau furnishings – large and small – are chosen and displayed with care, which means the proprietor clearly knows the value of the pieces, therefore bargain hunters beware. On the first floor there is a cosy, rustic café-bar that serves soup and drinks.

Leisure

Ganesh & Co

19 St Katelijnevest, 2000 Antwerp (03 226 95 59).
Open 10am-6pm Tue-Sat. **No credit cards**.

Started by Johan Declerck and Peter Auwrex as a green alternative to city travel, Ganesh & Co provides Indian bicycles for rent and for sale. Indian jewellery and trinkets are also on sale here, with proceeds going to a variety of relief projects in India.

USA Import

75 St Jacobsmarkt, 2000 Antwerp (03 232 04 29). **Open** 10am-6.30pm Mon-Sat. **No credit cards**.

A favourite of DJs, USA Import sells mostly vinyl dance music, including house, techno, garage, jungle and ambient. For the most part, prices are surprisingly competitive with those in New York and London, the cities from which most of USA Import's stock originates.

Toys

De Stal

5 Gorendaalstraat, 2000 Antwerp (03 233 40 93). **Open** 10am-6pm Tue-Sat. **No credit cards**.

A piglet greets you at the door and invites you in to the wood-and-straw emporium. Half of De Stal is dedicated to pigs, the other half to cows, some more original than others. Amusing for kids and of interest to collectors, and it has some good decorative ideas.

Sjokkel

4 Wijngaardstraat, 2000 Antwerp (03 234 28 27).
Open 11am-6.30pm Mon-Sat. **No credit cards**.

Set on two floors, this charming toyshop has a magical quality. As in every child's dream attic, there are toys everywhere: wooden toys, beautiful Victorian dolls, mechanical contraptions. Children and adults alike will want to spend hours rummaging through everything. Very much the antithesis of, say, Segaworld.

Food

Confiserie Burie

41 Korte Gasthuisstraat, 2000 Antwerp (03 233 13 08). **Open** 10am-6pm Mon-Sat. **No credit cards**.

Colourful sweets, huge lollipops, but mostly row after row of chocolates and pralines in this small confiserie. You can choose a selection yourself but if this proves to be a task beyond your capabilities the shopkeeper is very willing to help out.

Goosens

31 Korte Gasthuisstraat, 2000 Antwerp (no phone).
Open varies. **No credit cards**.

This small and popular traditional bakery offers a good choice of pastries and cakes, all displayed on metal racks, and served by two efficient elderly ladies.

Restaurants

Cantina Macondo

6 Grote Goddaard, 2000 Antwerp (03 232 42 89). **Open** 7-11pm Tue-Sat. **No credit cards**.

Chilean-owned restaurant serving a variety of South American dishes. Specialities include *pollo molle poblano* and enchiladas. The music and warm rustic style complete the authentic Latin American feel.

Kei Kei Oriental Canteen

34-36 Mindebroedersui, 2000 Antwerp (03 213 22 26).
Open noon-2pm, 6.30-11pm, daily. **Credit** MC, V.

Kei Kei offers a selection of noodle soups and fried or steamed rice dishes in a clean, minimalist environment, and includes cuisine from a number of Far Eastern countries. Clients are young, trendy and health-conscious. Set menus start at around 500BF.

Lenny's

47 Wolstraat, 2000 Antwerp (03 233 90 57).
Open 11.30am-2.30pm, 6pm-10pm, Tue-Sat. **No credit cards**.

Lenny's serves huge sandwiches in brown bread or baguettes, great salads and a variety of hot dishes. Friendly and relaxed, it has newspapers and magazines to read and a steady flow of customers, especially at lunchtime.

Pottenbrug

32 Mindebroedersui, 2000 Antwerp (03 231 51 47).
Open noon-2pm Mon, Fri; noon-2pm, 6.30pm-10pm, Tue-Thur; noon-2pm, 6.30pm-11pm, Sat; 6.30-10pm Sun.
Credit AmEx, MC, V.

A beautiful restaurant with an old-time Parisian bistro atmosphere, Pottenburg has served its simple and sophisticated cuisine for over 20 years. Popular with artists and local workers, its *cuisine gourmande* is always fresh and tasty. Excellent lunch menus.

Santatsu Yamayu

19 Ossenmarkt, 2000 Antwerp (03 234 09 49). **Open** noon-2pm, 6.30-10.30pm Tue-Sat; 6.30-10.30pm Sun.
Credit AmEx, DC, MC, V.

Small but very good Japanese restaurant in the Ossenmarkt, specialising in sushi and sashimi but also serving soba and udon noodles. The style is modern Japanese, with a bar and counter in the middle of the room. The excellent lunch menu offers a good choice of dishes. Reservations are advisable in the evening.

Sir Anthony van Dyck

16 Oude Koornmarkt, 2000 Antwerp (03 231 61 70).
Open sittings at 7pm, 10pm. **No credit cards**.

A wonderful, exclusive restaurant, owned by an antiquarian and displaying impeccable taste. There are two sittings in the evening, at 7pm and 10pm, but you can linger in the bar. Booking essential.

Spaghettiworld

66 Oude Koornmarkt, 2000 Antwerp (03 234 38 01).
Open 4pm-midnight daily. **No credit cards**.

Artsy coffee-house/restaurant/meeting place for Antwerp's bright young things. Acid house, trip hop and soul are just some of the sounds bubbling from the PA as diners tuck into their pasta.

Ulcke van Zurich

50 Oude Beurs, 2000 Antwerp (03 234 04 94). **Open** 6-11pm daily. **No credit cards**.

The happening restaurant for club kids, DJs and fashion victims. The menu is rib-sticking meat and fish, to provide sustenance for the night ahead.

Het Swing Café – *great not only for people-watching, but also for jazz, blues and soul.*

Zuidterras

37 Ernest van Dijckkai, 2000 Antwerp (03 234 12 75).
Open 9am-midnight daily. **Credit** AmEx, DC, MC, V.
Designed by architect Bob van Reeth, Zuidterras is right on the River Scheldt. Décor is a combination of metal fittings and black and white tiles, but with huge, heated windows all around it is the river that really dominates the place. Salads and seafood, and mussels in season, are its strong points. Also a good place for afternoon coffee.

Cafés & bars

Bourla

7 Komedieplein, 2000 Antwerp (03 231 07 50). **Open** early-late daily. **No credit cards.**
Always open, always full of people passing through, Bourla is the ideal place for meetings and coffee.

Café Au Lait

8 Oude Beurs, 2000 Antwerp (03 225 19 81). **Open** 3pm-4am Mon-Fri; 8pm-4am Sat, Sun. **No credit cards.**
Soi-disant Afro-Belgian bar, with African-style paintings on the wall and a billiard table. Plays funk, R&B, soul and salsa. There's no dancefloor but that's no deterrent to the young, lively crowd. There are DJs on most week nights.

Café Hopper

2 Leopold de Waelstraat, 2000 Antwerp (03 248 49 33). **Open** 11.30am-2am daily. **No credit cards.**
This bright, street-corner jazz café on the southern side of the city has good concerts on week nights and Sunday afternoons. Music ranges from post-bebop to modern contemporary jazz. Highly popular, particularly with artists.

Den Engel

3 Grote Markt, 2000 Antwerp (03 233 12 22). **Open** early-late daily. **No credit cards.**
On a corner of the Grote Markt, facing the Town Hall, Den Engel is a classic Antwerp café. Customers transcend class and age barriers even if it's just for the time it takes to drink a Bolleke. Everyone in town has been here at least once. It's always open, and regulars mix comfortably with whoever happens to be passing.

L'Entrepot du Congo

42 Vlaamse Kaai, 2000 Antwerp (03 238 92 32). **Open** 8am-3am daily. **No credit cards.**
Located in the trendy southern part of Antwerp, this is a favourite meeting place of Flemish-speaking, coffee-drinking intellectuals, but it attracts an interesting and varied crowd. Merchandise from the Belgian Congo used to be stocked here and the café retains an elegant colonial look. The music is generally classical in the mornings, reggae and soul in the afternoon and evenings. It is possible to have a bite to eat here as well, and the service is both friendly and efficient.

Hard Rock Café

34-35 Groenplaats, 2000 Antwerp (03 227 05 04). **Open** 6.30-11pm Tue-Sat. **No credit cards.**
Loved and loathed around the world, the Hard Rock chain chose Antwerp as its twentieth location. In this case, the world has reason to be grateful: this is the only place where you're likely to find two floors of Flemish people looking and acting more American than Uncle Sam.

Het Swing Café

13-15 Suikerrui, 2000 Antwerp (03 233 70 75). **Open** 6.30-11pm Tue-Sat. **No credit cards.**
A popular watering hole where yuppies let their hair down. Blues, jazz and soul punctuate the air in this smoky, two-level bar. Great for people-watching.

Accommodation

Astrid Park Plaza

1 Koningin Astridplein, 2018 Antwerp (03 203 12 34/fax 03 203 12 75). **Rates** single 3,950-4,950BF (weekend rate, breakfast included).

Rubenshuis – *bought by the artist in 1611, shortly after his return from Italy. See p198.*

A relatively recent addition to this square, the exterior of the Astrid Park Plaza has all the charm of a construction made out of Lego. Fortunately the inside is much easier on the eye. The main attraction of the hotel is its central location, immediately opposite the station, the view of the city from the 'Astrid Lounge' is also quite impressive and the restaurant is worth a look. There is free access to the hotel's swimming pool, sauna and fitness room.
Hotel services *Bar. Café. Conference room. Private parking. Restaurant.* **Room services** *Mini bar. TV (Nintendo).*

Hilton
Groenplaats, 2000 Antwerp (03 204 12 12/fax 03 204 12 13). **Rates** *single* or *double* 7,000-12,200BF.
Located on a pleasant, busy square and literally a minute's walk from the Grote Markt, the Antwerp Hilton is a beautiful sand-coloured building that takes up nearly an entire side of the square. The hotel offers all the facilities and services associated with this chain but with a lot more charm than one normally expects.
Hotel services *Bar. Café. Conference room. Lounge. Restaurant.* **Room services** *Mini bar. TV.*

Ibis
Various branches (fax 03 231 88 30 for a list).
Modest, inoffensive and efficient – about half the price of a room at De Witte Leie (*see below*).

Vlaamse Jeugdherberg op Sinjoorke
(03 238 02 73/fax 03 248 19 32).
For the seriously skint traveller, this has dead-cheap rooms for four to eight persons… if you're willing to deal with a 2km hike from the city centre.

De Witte Leie
16-18 Keiserstraat, 2000 Antwerp (03 226 19 66/fax 03 234 00 19). **Rates** *single* 6,500-9,000BF; *double* 8,500-11,000BF; *suite* 15,000BF.
Modern comfort along with age-old elegance – if you are willing to spend money. De Witte Leie is composed of three

seventeenth-century townhouses. Each room is decorated in an individual style, but all have antique charm and subdued five-star luxury.

Outside Antwerp

Geel

When the Flemish say that you look as if you're from Geel, don't be too impressed with yourself at your talent for assimilation.

Geel is the famous village near Antwerp where the borderline mentally handicapped are welcomed and treated. It makes for an eye-opening visit, as they have been completely integrated into society – some are taken in by local families. The twisted legend has it that its patron saint, Dymphne, was trying to flee the come-ons of her father, the King of Ireland. He tracked her down to Geel, where he beheaded her. The church that bears her name, also the museum and hospital attached to it, you'd be crazy to miss.

Likewise Bobbejaanland, a theme park in nearby Lichtaart (45 Olensesteenweg; 014 55 78 11), a quick hop from Geel. Flemish entertainer Bobbejaan Schoepen's penchant for American country and western gear and rock 'n' roll took him to

The buildings around Antwerp's **Grote Markt**, *including the Stadthuis (Town Hall), date mainly from the Renaissance.*

Zillion *was closed by the city authorities in March 1998, but new clubs open all the time.*

Nashville in the 1950s. He claims to have been on the brink of international stardom when homesickness brought him back. In 1961, when riding his horse across a stretch of Belgian countryside, the rustic charm moved him so much that he thought: I'll destroy it to build a theme park.

Four decades on, the park has become an institution in Belgium, more for nostalgia than for any thrills and chills: for scary rides, try EuroDisney or the Belgian *autoroutes*. The surroundings are more human scale in the family-run park, which caters more to families with young children and groups of teens. The park (open 10am-5.30pm daily) allows visitors to bring picnic baskets in, so you can avoid buying the overpriced refreshments.

Getting there

By train from Gare du Nord, Gare Centrale or Gare du Midi to Berchem, switch for Geel; *by car* N2 to Leuven, switch to N19.

Tourist information

VVV Geel, Stadhuis, 2440 Geel (014 57 09 52). **Open** 8am-noon, 1-3.30pm, Mon-Fri; 10am-3pm Sat, Sun.

Lier

Featuring canals and a Grote Markt that bring to mind the much larger Bruges, this seventh-century city makes for an interesting diversion. Not to be missed is the *béguinage*, constructed in the thirteenth century, it ranks among Belgium's most beautiful. Cycling is one of the best ways to see the town – bikes can be rented at the railway station. Stop at one of the cafés on Grand Place and sample one of their tartelettes, which are renowned throughout Belgium.

Getting there

By train from Gare du Nord, Gare Centrale or Gare du Midi to Berchem (direction Antwerp), switch for Lier; *by car* N1 direction Mechelen, switch to N14 direction Lier.

Tourist information

Stadhuis, 2500 Lier (03 488 38 88/fax 03 488 13 57). **Open** 9am-12.30pm, 3.30pm-5pm, daily.

Mechelen

Although the city of Mechelen has a rich history (it was once the capital of the Netherlands during the Middle Ages), there isn't much to recommend it today, outside of the procession of Hanswijk. Taking place the Sunday before Ascension, this is the oldest historical and religious demonstration of its kind in Belgium.

There are some monuments worth visiting if you ever find yourself in Mechelen, one of which is the Speelgoed Museum (Games Museum), which is as popular with kids as it is with collectors. Puzzles and board games as well as dolls, stuffed animals and other toys are on display. And the Dierenpark Planckendael is where animals past their prime or otherwise not fit from the Antwerp Zoo spend their twilight years.

Tourist information

(015 29 76 55/fax 015 29 76 53). Guided tours arranged every weekend.

Ghent

Antwerp may be hipper, but Ghent has charm and character aplenty.

Roughly 40 minutes north of Brussels by car, Ghent – Gent in Flemish, Gand in French – is an ideal destination for a day trip. The town was a major commercial centre in the Middle Ages and this early economic success left an enduring mark on the city – the place retains a prosperous bourgeois feel, which combines surprisingly well with the relaxed atmosphere of student life. Despite its location in East Flanders, you will hear a lot of French spoken, as it was the language used by the local gentry and until relatively recently was still considered a mark of social distinction. Yet the town is also proud of its Flemish roots: in 1930 its university was the first to adopt Flemish as an academic language; the population has an impressive grasp of English.

Ghent is a city that likes spending money. Many of its commercial streets are pedestrianised, and there's a market most days of the week. Much of the place is undergoing wholesale renovation, and the fresh-painted façades add to the cheerful atmosphere. Culturally speaking, Ghent may not be as dazzling as Antwerp, but this is a town that's definitely on the move.

History

The history of Flanders in general, and Ghent in particular, has been marked by confusing changes of rulers and shifting loyalties, as the region shuttled between French, Spanish and Austrian control. Ghent was founded around AD 600 with the construction of two monasteries, St Baaf's and St Peter's, although architectural traces have been found dating back to Roman times. From around AD 900 the region was repeatedly attacked by Vikings, though local counts and administrators still managed to maintain and strengthen their power base here. However, it was only after the death of Charlemagne that Flanders began to emerge as an important commercial centre.

The death of Charlemagne, and the subsequent disintegration of his empire, gave rise to a number of principalities. After the Treaty of Verdun, Flanders, of which Ghent was part, went to Charles the Bold and came under French rule.

In the Middle Ages Flanders became wealthy – primarily because of Ghent, whose textile industry was steadily growing, and whose position near the port of Bruges was ideal for international commerce. Ghent's prosperity grew more and more closely linked to its political development. Its ruling council, or magistracy, was predominantly made up of merchants, who established their own style of political and economic despotism.

This state of affairs remained relatively unaltered until the Battle of the Golden Spurs in 1302. Allied to the French king, Ghent did not take part in the battle, but it did benefit from this unlikely victory of the Flemish people over the French aristocracy. Craftsmen and less patrician members of society were given places in the magistracy, albeit temporarily.

Throughout the Middle Ages and until the fifteenth century Ghent continued to grow, until its textile industry was the largest in Europe, and, after Paris, it was the most populated urban centre. Ghent's neutrality created a comfortable political climate in which its commercial activities could develop and thrive. It imported wool from England and sold the finished products to both England and France.

During the Hundred Years War, however, it became impossible for the city to maintain its neutrality. The Count of Flanders sided with the French – an unwise decision that led to the downturn in the city's economic fortunes.

During the fifteenth century, the fortuitous combination of premature deaths and childless marriages led to the rise of the Dukes of Burgundy. One of them, Philip the Good, managed to unite the 17 provinces in Flanders in a bid to centralise power. The Dukes were great patrons of the arts and they left their mark on all provinces. It was under their patronage that the painter Jan van Eyck worked in Ghent and Bruges.

This was the Golden Age for Brussels and Antwerp, whose industries and importance grew. The same cannot be said of Ghent, where the textile industry continued to decline because of English competition. The reign of Charles V was marked by rebellions and religious upheaval. The Reformation was sweeping across Europe, creating obvious tensions, but it was the heavy taxation needed to finance military campaigns that was responsible for much of the discontent.

Ghent remained loyal to Charles V for a long time because he had been born in the city, but this was not sufficient compensation for the city's misfortune and all feelings of loyalty eventually faded. Charles V abdicated in 1555 and power passed to his son, Philip II.

Philip II seems to have been universally despised. Unlike his father, who had been relatively tolerant of changes brought about by the Reformation, Philip II was an aggressively devout Catholic. He was so fervently committed that, although he did not spend much time in the region, he appointed the feared Count of Alva as governor. Accompanied by 10,000 soldiers, the Count ensured that the inquisition's duties were in no way hindered. Predictably there followed a period of insurrection. In 1576 the 'Pacification de Gand' was signed, uniting the 17 provinces against the Spanish. Ghent became a Calvinist city and became isolated from the other Flemish provinces, accelerating its decline.

With the death of Philip II the provinces were given quasi-autonomous status by the Archdukes Albert and Isabella. But the marriage was childless and failed to establish a dynasty. The second half of the seventeenth century was disastrous. With wars raging and certain economic restrictions being imposed, Ghent's commercial activities ground to a halt.

In 1715 power shifted once more and came into Austrian hands. Joseph II, a sort of enlightened despot, tried to push forward economic reforms, but it was only in the nineteenth century that Ghent experienced industrial success. This was due to two factors: new industrial techniques, imported from France, and the construction of the Terneuzen canal, giving Ghent access to the sea. Ghent became, and remains, Belgium's second port.

After the Congress of Vienna the provinces were brought under Dutch rule. William of Orange tried to encourage industrial development and stimulate growth. However, the Catholic Church never accepted Protestant Dutch authority. This refusal culminated in a declaration of independence that had little impact at the time but paved the way for independence.

In Ghent, the economy was booming once more. The city's bourgeoisie, impressed by the Dutch policies of industrial development, sided with William of Orange in 1830, during the struggle for Belgian independence. Ironically, in view of the bourgeois make-up of its first council, the magistracy, the growth of the textile and steel industry in the nineteenth century made Ghent a bastion of Flemish socialism.

Sightseeing

If you've arrived by train, your best bet is to hop on one of the many trams just outside the station and head straight for the city centre. It's possible

*Laurent Delvaux's rococo marble-and-oak pulpit in the **St Bavon Cathedral**, Ghent's most impressive monument.*

to rent bicycles from the station, and you will notice that, as in most university towns, cycling is the most popular mode of transport, but the historical centre is relatively small and you may find a bike more of a hindrance than a help.

Ghent is exceptionally pedestrian-friendly. Several streets are closed to traffic, and drivers are surprisingly courteous. Despite the twisting streets and unexpected squares and quays, it's almost impossible to get lost.

The St Michielsbrug Cathedral is the classic starting point for a tour of the city. One of the best views of the cathedral is from the bridge over the River Leie, which overlooks the Graslei (Herb Quay) and Korenlei (Corn Quay). Both are lined with beautiful houses, most built during the Flemish Renaissance but some dating back as far as AD 1000.

Try to visit Het Pand, a Dominican monastery that is now part of the University of Ghent, situated immediately opposite St Michielskerk. Further north, on St Veerlesplein, a bas-relief Neptune towers over the entrance of the Vismarkt (fish market). From here it only takes a few moments to reach the Vrijdagmarkt, a vast square that used to be the focal point of political life and quarrels in the Middle Ages and is still used several days a week as a market place. There are several commercial streets, of which Veldstraat is the most crowded but also the least exciting. Magaleinstraat and Koestraat are more interesting shopping areas.

There are market stalls on many squares and markets most days of the week. There's a fruit and vegetable market in Groentenmarkt every morning, and a bird market in Vrijdagmarkt on Sunday mornings. You will come across several appetising traditional bakeries and fancy cheese shops. There are plenty of cafés and tearooms where you can sample some of the city's specialities.

Although the town's historical centre is relatively compact and rich in sights, it never feels cluttered. Narrow streets around the central area naturally lead you back to open spaces – quays, canals, squares and monuments – so that the city feels airy.

Wandering around Ghent, you will come across derelict or restored buildings that once housed the city's former textile industry. The Stadthuis (Town Hall) is a good symbol of the city's changing fortunes. Initially designed to be the largest town hall in Europe, the building was begun in 1518, but had to be halted because of religious strife. Work resumed at the beginning of the seventeenth century, and a second section was added to the building. The result of this staggered construction is clearly visible in the Town Hall's split architecture. One part, decorated with countless statues, is in ornate Gothic style, while the more sober part reflects Renaissance taste.

Built over six centuries, the St Bavon Cathedral is Ghent's most impressive monument, remarkable as much for its high and late Gothic style as for the numerous works of art it contains. Laurent Delvaux's elaborate rococo pulpit, in oak and marble, is the first thing that attracts your attention as you enter, threatening for a moment to overwhelm everything else in the place.

Pieter Paul Rubens' *Entry of St Bavo into the Monastery* is displayed in the north transept in what is a sombre corner on a rainy day. The painting should be seen, but the cathedral's undisputed masterpiece is *The Mystic Lamb* by Hubert and Jan van Eyck. The painting is exhibited in the De Villa Chapel (entry is an additional 60BF), and those on guided tours are rushed in to take a long appreciative look. This means that the chapel can get crowded and you may have to wait a while to view the work properly. Don't be put off: it's worth the wait. The painting depicts a scene from the Apocalypse according to St John. The amount of detail in the painting is striking but what is most impressive is its luminosity. The colours are so bright and glistening that the painting seems to illuminate the chapel.

The twelfth-century crypt is the most ancient part of the cathedral. Although it contains tombs and a collection of the usual religious paraphernalia, it is notable mainly for its frescoes and for Justus van Gent's painting, *The Calvary Scene*.

Facing St Bavon is the Belfort. Once used to guard the city and, if necessary, to gather men to defend it, the tower was erected in the fourteenth century. If you're feeling energetic you can climb to the top to enjoy a view of the city. There's also a carillon and bell museum.

St Niklaaskerk is another outstanding piece of architecture. This church was constructed in the the thirteenth century and is by far the most elaborate example of Scheldt Gothic in the whole country. Unfortunately the church has been undergoing renovation for years and is currently closed to the public.

Surrounded by water, the Castle of Counts is Ghent's best-known attraction. Built in 1180 by Philippe d'Alsace, it is the only medieval fortress in Flanders and its fortifications have remained intact. The castle lost its original military function centuries ago and was subsequently used as a mint, a court of justice and even as a cotton mill. It is a popular destination for school trips and has enough winding staircases and dark corners to keep children amused indefinitely. There is also a modest and (unless you read the printed descriptions) relatively un-gory collection of torture instruments.

Castle apart, this is perhaps not the most appealing part of Ghent, with its motley collection of university buildings, welfare offices, bars, clubs and greasy snack emporia. But what this part of town lacks in beauty it makes up for in energy. Some of the streets, such as St Pietersnieuwstraat, are lined with bicycles chained to whatever solid object is available. Students zoom down the streets and alleyways on their clattering and clinking machines. Everyone seems to be busy, and the average age appears to be about 23, particularly in the late afternoon and evening.

If you're a keen walker or are feeling energetic, you can venture outside the historical centre and continue to explore the city. The streets may be less consistently beautiful, but there are some charming sights, especially if you take a walk by the River Leie along Lievekaal and St Antoniuskaal. This part of Ghent is quieter and more sedate, but you'll get a real feel of everyday life as it's lived in the city.

Getting there

By train from Gare du Nord, Gare Centrale or Gare du Midi; *by car* A10.

Tourist information

Stadhuis, Botermarkt, 9000 (224 15 55). **Open** 9.30am-6.30pm daily.

Museums

Museum van Hedendaagse Kunst (Museum of Contemporary Art)

Citadelpark, opposite Museum voor Schone Kunsten (09 221 17 03). **Open** 9.30am-5pm Tue-Sun.
Admission 100BF; 50BF groups; children free.
No credit cards.
This is generally thought to be Belgium's finest collection of modern art, boasting works such as Francis Bacon's *Cardinal* and masterpieces by artists from the Cobra (Copenhagen, Brussels, Amsterdam) movement. There are some fine examples of minimal and conceptual art, and the 1960s are particularly well represented, with works by Warhol, Christo and Arman.

Museum voor Schone Kunsten (Museum of Fine Arts)

3 Nicolaas de Liemaerckereplein, Citadelpark (09 222 17 03). **Open** 9.30am-5pm Tue-Sun.
Admission 100BF; 50BF groups; children free.
No credit cards.
Located near the Citadelpark on the south side of the city, this inviting and unpretentious museum contains a good selection of paintings and sculptures ranging from the fourteenth century to the first half of the twentieth century. The rooms are spacious, bright and welcoming, so, although the collection is not huge, the relaxed atmosphere makes you want to take time to enjoy it. The medieval and Renaissance sections contain works by world-renowned artists, but often the works by lesser artists are more worthwhile. Examples of this are the warm and delicate *Madonna with Carnation* by Rogier van der Weyden and *Portrait of a Young Woman* by Frans Pourbus the Elder, one of the best Flemish portrait painters of the sixteenth century. The two paintings by Hieronymus Bosch are more demanding. Painted in rich colours, *The Bearing of the Cross* is a late work by the artist.

Opposite the St Bavon Cathedral is the **Belfort** *with its fourteenth-century tower, which you may climb, and bell museum.*

The caricatures of the men surrounding Christ are reminiscent of Da Vinci's drawings. *Saint Jerome's Penance* has some of Bosch's typical quasi-surreal elements, in a simpler form. One room in this section is entirely devoted to paintings inspired by Pieter Bruegel the Elder. There is a copy of the famous *Wedding Banquet* made by Pieter Bruegel the Younger. The other paintings are based on themes typical of the Flemish master, such as village fairs.

The sixteenth- and seventeenth-century sections are a good representation of Flemish Renaissance painting, with works by Rubens, Jordaens and Van Dyck. Many of the artists included here spent time in Italy and the influence of the Italian masters, some of whom are also represented here, can be appreciated.

The modern section of the museum houses a large selection of paintings and sculptures by great Belgian artists. The museum owns the largest collection of sculptures by George Minne, and an entire room is dedicated to James Ensor, the first modern Belgian painter. The occasionally vicious drawings of Belgian bourgeoisie are typical of the artist, but his brilliant use of light is best appreciated in paintings located elsewhere in the museum, which also has works by Wouters, Spilliaerts, Permeke and Knopff.

Museum voor Sierkunst en Vormgeving (Museum of Decorative Arts & Design)

5 Jan Breydelstraat, 9000 Ghent (09 225 66 76). **Open** 9.30am-5pm Tue-Sun. **Admission** 100BF; 50BF groups; children free. **No credit cards.**

Museum voor Sierkunst en Vormgeving (Museum of Just a little way off the Korenlei, in a wonderful eighteenth-century house that was once owned by a wealthy merchant, Ghent's Museum of Decorative Arts does more than just present endless rows of carefully polished silver spoons and china in glass cases. Not all the exhibits were here originally but all of them seem to fit in naturally, giving the impression that you're looking around a private house while the owner is away. There are beautiful portraits of kings, lit by lavish crystal chandeliers, plus silk wall coverings and tapestries. The furniture, mostly French, includes baroque, rococo and Louis XVI pieces. A more modern section was recently added. This is where the 'design' part of the museum is housed and where temporary exhibitions are held. Although this new section has been cleverly arranged, it doesn't have the charm of the rest of the house, and some of the modern works are more surprising than fascinating. There are, however, some worthwhile art nouveau works by Victor Horta, Paul Hankar and Henry van de Velde.

Museum voor Volkskunde (Folklore Museum)

65 Kraanlei, 9000 Ghent (09 223 13 36). **Open** 9.30am-5pm Tue-Sun. **Admission** 80BF; groups 50BF; children free. **No credit cards.**

In Ghent they really seem to have a knack for setting museums in wonderful locations, and the Folklore Museum is no exception. It's in what used to be a group of small houses with a garden and chapel. The museum is aimed primarily at children, but parents will enjoy it as well. Its intention is to give an educational and amusing impression of life in Ghent in the nineteenth century, which it does by recreating scenes of life at home and at work. The scenes are arranged like small cinema sets, with dummies in period costume. You will see candlestick makers, cloth makers, reconstructions of sweet shops, pubs and a chemist. The museum also has a puppet theatre and there are shows for children every Saturday and Wednesday.

Most of the beautiful houses on the **Graslei** *(Herb Quay) and Korenlei (Corn Quay) were built during the Flemish Renaissance.*

Eating & drinking

Your impression of Ghent nightlife is likely to depend on the area of town you visit and the evening you happen to choose. The southern part of the city is certainly livelier and has the trendiest bars, largely because this is the student area and attracts a younger crowd. Most students, however, go home for the weekend and their big night out is usually Thursday. On Saturday the bars of the student area are still busy, but the crowd is older, calmer and somewhat smarter.

The Patershol area, right in the city's historical centre, also has plenty of restaurants and bars. With the canals and medieval streets, the atmosphere is almost magical and the streets are quieter than around St Pietersnieuwstraat and there is hardly any traffic at all. Patershol bars and restaurants tend to be rather elegant, and more subdued than in the student area.

Aba Jour

29 Oudburg, 9000 Ghent (09 234 07 27). **Open** varies. **No credit cards.**

Relaxed, unsnobby chic, with an art deco bar, cane seats and tables (some overlooking the canal) and soft lighting. Clients come here to enjoy cocktails and chat or have an apéritif.

Bar Bier

18 St Margrietstraat, 9000 Ghent (09 223 45 93). **Open** 9am-noon, 1.30-6.30pm, Tue; 11am-10pm Wed-Fri; 10am-6.30pm Sat. **No credit cards.**

Bar Bier combines hairdressing with drinking. Women and men can get their hair cut, and men can get a shave. Many students come to get their hair trimmed and drink a glass of beer. There are only three tables, so it's not a place to linger.

Brasserie Moka

46 Koestraat, 9000 Ghent (09 225 00 54). **Open** 11am-late Mon-Sat. **Credit** AmEx, DC, MC, V.

This brasserie serves generous quantities of traditional Belgian food. The lunchtime suggestions are usually varied and good, and the local specialities such as the fish *waterzooi* and *carbonnade flamande* are worth trying.

Brooderie

8 Jan Breydelstraat, 9000 Ghent (09 225 06 23). **Open** 8am-6pm Tue-Sun. **No credit cards.**

Affordable restaurant-bakery in a gabled house near the Brooderie canal. Its style is elegant and rustic, and the atmosphere pleasant and relaxed. There's a large selection of salads and vegetable pies on the menu, all served with slices of different breads (fruit and nut, rye, poppy seed). Everything is healthy and the portions generous. Brooderie also serves mouth-watering cakes, baked daily. No smoking is allowed. (*See also below* **Accommodation.**)

Greenway

42 Nederkouter, 9000 Ghent (no phone). **Open** 11.30am-9pm daily. **No credit cards.**

Healthy and tasty vegetarian snack-bar. It looks like an upmarket fast-food joint, but the jazzy music and welcoming setting make you feel anything but rushed. It serves imaginative warm sandwiches, and rice and noodle dishes that you can enjoy with fresh juices or fruity yoghurt drinks.

Het Blauwe Huis

17 Drapstraat, 9000 Ghent (09 233 10 05). **Open** noon-2pm, 6.30-10pm, Mon-Fri, Sun; 6.30-11pm Sat. **Credit** AmEx, MC, V.

Intended to be the largest town hall in Europe, Ghent's **Stadthuis** *never did quite make it.*

Formerly known as Diavolo, Het Blauwe Huis is still hard to miss: it's the only electric-blue townhouse on the block. The music and décor are the same, too, but the once-inexpensive food is a more sophisticated blend of expensive Belgian and French cuisine.

Het Waterhuis aan de Bierkant

Groenten Markt, 9000 Ghent (09 225 06 80). **Open** 11am-2am Mon-Fri; 11am-3am Sat, Sun. **No credit cards.**
A great place for beer-lovers, with an excellent range, all described on the menu. Its riverside location makes it very popular, particularly during the warmer months when tables are put out on the terrace.

Hotsy Totsy

24 Penitentenstraat, 9000 Ghent (09 234 07 08).
The Hotsy Totsy jazz bar is a Ghent institution. It attracts a varied crowd but many lawyers, politicians and media types come to enjoy strong drinks and jazz. The intimidating wooden door and heavy curtains make it look like a private club, yet it's open to all.

Lazy River Jazz Club

5 Stadhuissteeg, 9000 Ghent (09 222 23 01). **Open** varies. **No credit cards.**
Popular place to finish off the evening with drinks and music.

Pablo's

2 Kleine Vismarkt (09 233 71 51) **Open** noon-3pm, 6-11pm, Mon-Sat; 6-11pm Sun. **Credit** AmEx, MC, V.
A huge Mexican restaurant made to look like an upmarket *cantina*, Pablo's is located directly over the canal. You can eat tapas, chilli or empanadas, all served to the sound of salsa. The crowd is usually young, especially in the evening.

Pole Pole

158 St Pietersniewestraat, 9000 Ghent (09 233 21 73).
Open 6.30pm-4am Mon-Sat. **No credit cards.**
Pole pole means 'slowly slowly' in Swahili. The décor is African, with great masks and other wooden artefacts, and

the music is upbeat and enticing. The exotic cocktails and food are excellent value for money.

Rococo

57 Corduwanierstraat, 9000 Ghent (09 224 30 35).
Open 9pm-late Tue-Sun. **No credit cards.**
Located in the Patershol area and one of Ghent's moodier clubs. Artists gather around candlelit tables and a piano sits in a corner, sometimes too tempting for the would-be *chanteur* who's had a few too many.

Tête à Tête

32 Jan Breydelstraat, 9000 Ghent (09 233 95 00). **Open** noon-3pm, 7-10pm, Tue, Wed, Fri-Sun; 7-10pm Thur. **Credit** AmEx, MC, V.
New, successful and expensive, Tête à Tête serves light and beautiful cuisine. The décor is equally splendid, with soft lighting, chrome and wood fittings. Its terrace overlooks the Castle of Counts. Booking essential.

Shopping

The centre of Ghent is almost completely closed to traffic and many commercial streets are pedestrianised, making the city an ideal place for strolling around and shopping.

Veldstraat is the main shopping street, with all the usual shops (Zara, H&M, Fnac and so on) and department stores. The lack of crowds makes shopping here a pleasanter experience than in Brussels or Antwerp, but you're unlikely to find anything very original.

A large selection of beers is available at **Het Waterhuis aan de Bierkant**, *where you may sit out on the terrace in summer.*

Volderstraat, St Niklaasstraat and Magelein-straat are more interesting. The shops are attractive and elegant. You won't find great bargains here, but Ghent is not a place for bargains in general. What you get is a good selection of items and attentive individual service.

If you're looking for antiques, the areas to explore are Jan Breydelstraat and Burgstraat near the Castle of Counts, and if you enjoy food you will be constantly drawn to the bakeries, cheese shops and delicatessens. Beautiful, tempting food stalls and shops with opulent displays are to be found all over the city centre.

Every five years Ghent hosts one of the most impressive flower shows going, the Floralie Gantoise, and the city has an impressive number of florists.

Fashion

Bon-a-Tirer
8 Zuivelbrugstraat, 9000 Ghent (09 234 01 70). **Open** 10.30am-1pm, 2-6pm, Tue-Sat. **Credit** MC, V.
Women's clothing with a personal touch. There is only one of each item, and every week there are new clothes on display. The dominant colour is black but there's a choice of warm colours, too. The quality is good and so are the prices. The jewellery, laid out on a big drawing table, is interesting as well. The gigantic papier mâché turtle over one wall and scrap-metal lamps combine with the wooden beams and brick floor to create an original setting.

Bygone
12 St Niklaasstraat, 9000 Ghent (no phone). **Open** 10.30am-12.30pm, 2-5.30pm Tue-Sat. **No credit cards**.
Young and trendy women's wear ranging from casual to a little more elegant. Most items can be dressed up or dressed down, depending on the occasion. Big choice of very short skirts and sexy dresses.

First Class, Second Hand
84 St Pietersniewestraat, 9000 Ghent (09 224 21 46). **Open** 10.30am-12.30pm, 2-5pm Tue-Sat. **No credit cards**.
Second-hand designer clothes, bags and shoes. Most are in excellent condition and there are some real bargains, although it's sometimes difficult to find the right size.

Hot Couture
34 Gouvernementstraat, 9000 Ghent (09 233 74 07). **Open** 10am-6.30pm Mon-Sat. **Credit** AmEx, DC, MC, V.
The latest men's fashions and accessories by designers such as Dries van Noten, Dirk Bikkembergs and Paul Smith. The shop, arranged in several rooms, has wooden floors, leather armchairs and charming staff. Great for classy pampering.

Oona
12 Bennesteeg, 9000 Ghent (09 224 21 13). **Open** 11am-6pm Mon-Sat. **Credit** AmEx, DC, MC, V.
With its bare cement walls and light blue and grey tones, Oona's has a deliberately chilly atmosphere that suits its designer women's clothes by the likes of Jean-Paul Gaultier and D&G among others.

*The thirteenth-century **St Niklaaskerk**, currently under renovation, is the best example of Scheldt Gothic in Belgium.*

Orsacchino
13 Gouvernementstraat, 9000 Ghent (no phone). **Open** 10.30am-1pm, 2-6pm Tue-Sat. **Credit** MC, V.
Lingerie for men and women, by D&G and others. More sophisticated and daring than classical styles, and there's plenty to choose from.

Shoes

Atame
75 Henegouwenstraat, 9000 Ghent (09 233 05 88). **Open** 2-6pm Mon; 10.30am-1pm, 2-6pm Tue-Sat. **Credit** AmEx, DC, MC, V.
Women's shoes by Prada and Jill Sander. Although the choice isn't vast, the chic items are worth a look.

Obius
12 Meerseneirsstraat, 9000 Ghent (09 233 82 69). **Open** 1-6.30pm Mon; 10am-6pm Tue-Sat. **Credit** AmEx, MC, V.
Located near the Vrijdagmarkt, this is an elegant men's shop that specialises in designer shoes, many of them Belgian. It has a small choice of clothes as well.

Accessories

Au Bon Marché
94 St Pietersnieuwstraat, 9000 Ghent (09 225 47 84). **Open** 10am-noon, 1-6.30pm, Tue-Sat. **Credit** DC, MC, V.
Set in an old grocer's shop, with the original layout – high, dark wooden shelves and brass tags – Au Bon Marché sells a wide variety of accessories and bits and pieces: belts, jewellery and scarves, some shoes, and also scented candles, beautiful notebooks (made from recycled paper) and oils and fragrances for the bath.
Branch: 4 Horenstraat, 9000 Ghent.

Axes War
3 Gebr Vandeveldestraat, 9000 Ghent (09 233 42 43). **Open** 10am-noon, 1-6.30pm, Tue-Sat. **No credit cards**.
Ghent has a surprisingly large number of shops selling household gadgets. Axes War has chrome and plastic items, including all sorts of objects for the bathroom and kitchen. The merchandise is mostly fun and useless. Good for presents, though.

Siapoo
29 Sluizeken, 9000 Ghent (09 225 75 35). **Open** 10am-1pm, 2-6.30pm Tue-Fri; 11am-6.30pm Sat. **Credit** AmEx, MC, V.
Siapoo specialises in women's hats by Ria Dewilde – warm hats for winter and elegant, delicate ones for summer. The choice is tempting, but if nothing takes your fancy, hats can be made to order as well. Siapoo also sells jewellery and some women's clothes.

Children's fashion

Avandre
121 Henegouwenstraat, 9000 Ghent (09 225 21 48). **Open** 10am-6pm Mon-Sat. **Credit** AmEx, MC, V.
The entrance to Avandre is through a large iron gate that gives on to a small courtyard with a fountain, pink walls and a frieze of little ceramic tiles. The shop itself is a delight with high ceilings, polished light wooden floors and cream walls. The clothes are by designers such as Oilily and Van Notten, with colourful or more classic cuts. For babies and children up to 12.

Krokodil

5 Groot Kanonplein, 9000 Ghent (09 233 22 76). **Open**
10am-6pm Mon-Sat. **Credit** AmEx, DC, MC, V.
Two floors of soft and wooden toys, puppets and board
games. Lots of beads, wooden ovens and dolls' houses, and
a large art and crafts section with big pencils, paints and
chunky chalks.

Subliem

8 Volderstraat, 9000 Ghent (no phone). **Open** varies. **No
credit cards.**
A great choice of shoes from Banaline, Buckle My Shoe and
Italian designers. Comfortable, solid and fun, most shoes are
in suede or leather, with rubber soles.

Music

Music Mania

197 Bagattenstraat, 9000 Ghent (09 225 68 15). **Open**
11am-7pm Mon-Sat. **Credit** MC, V.
Three floors of every type of music, although Music Mania
specialises in drum 'n' bass, jungle, jazz and reggae. The
shop used to be known for its heavy metal selection, which
is still good. Although no second-hand CDs are sold here,
you should find some bargains on the third floor. Check out
the vinyl as well.

Bookshops

Herckenrath

43 Veldstraat, 9000 Ghent (09 225 35 29). **Open** 11am-
6pm Tue-Sat. **Credit** AmEx, DC, MC, V.
A vast selection of books in French. Herckenrath specialises in the French novel, but there are many other books on
philosophy, spiritualism, tourism, art and other subjects.

Intellect

1 Kaladestraat, 9000 Ghent (09 225 73 51). **Open** 9am-
noon, 1.30-6pm, Mon-Sat. **Credit** AmEx, V.
The three floors are almost entirely devoted to art books.
With books on painting, photography, decorative arts, architecture, the choice is huge. Although some novels are on sale,
there are no paperbacks.

Food

Vve Tierenteijn-Verlent

3 Groete Markt, 9000 Ghent (09 225 83 36). **Open**
8.30am-6pm Mon-Sat. **No credit cards.**
This grocery/delicatessen has been here for well over a hundred years, and much of it has been left unchanged, including the big glass and ceramic jars on the shelves, wicker
baskets and an old counter. It sells marmalades and teas and
more typical local products.

Flowers

Boone

6 Jan Breydelstraat, 9000 Ghent (09 233 14 48). **Open**
2-7pm Mon; 9am-7pm Tue-Sat; 10am-6pm Sun. **Credit**
AmEx, MC, V.
Buckets and baskets full of flowers, a large selection of
plants, and a variety of dried flowers and candles.

Dirk van Driessche

95 Gebr Vandeveldstraat, 9000 Ghent (09 223 02 39).
Open 10am-7pm Mon, Wed-Sat; noon-7pm Tue; 10am-
1.30pm Sun. **No credit cards.**
An unusual and interesting selection of plants for terraces
and gardens, plus a gorgeous selection of cut flowers. If the
display is anything to go by, the flower arrangements must
be beautiful.

Accommodation

Brooderie

8 Jan Breydelstraat, 9000 Ghent (09 225 06 23). **Rates**
single 1,300BF; *double* 2,200-2,500BF.
Charming small hotel, located in the centre of Ghent and
set in a pretty gabled house overlooking the canal. Brooderie
is also a bakery and cafe (*see above* **Eating & drinking**).
The atmosphere is informal and friendly, the staff helpful
and charming.The only inconvienience is that it only has
three rooms.

De Draecke Youth Hostel

11 St Widlostraat, 9000 Ghent (09 233 70 50). **Rates**
385-475BF.
The best bet for cheap digs.

Hotel Adoma

*St Denislaan, 9000 Ghent (09 222 65 50/fax 09 245 09
37).* **Rates** *single* 1750BF; *double* 2100BF.
A bargain – and it has the advantage of being two minutes'
walk from the station.

Hotel Gravenstein

*35 Jan Breydelstraat, 9000 Ghent (09 225 11 50/fax 09
225 18 50).* **Rates** *single* 2,900-3,850BF; *double* 3,900-
4,600BF.
Beautiful hotel set in a nineteenth-century *hôtel particulier.*
The Second Empire style is imposing and impeccable; the
elegant rooms are all equipped with modern facilities. The
hotel has its own private parking.
Hotel services *Parking.* **Room services** *Minibar.
TV.*

Hotel Sofitel

*63 Hoogpoort, 9000 Ghent (09 233 33 31/fax 09 233 11
02).* **Rates** *double* 7,250-9,150BF.
In the heart of the historic centre, the Ghent Sofitel has reasonably comfortable rooms. The modern setting is not necessarily the most charming, but the hotel is spacious and the
staff very efficient. There are no single rooms, all rooms have
either a double or twin beds.
Hotel services *Bar. Conference room.
Restaurant. Parking. Taverne.* **Room services**
Minibar. TV.

Outside Ghent

Sint Niklaas

Not exactly the most happening of towns, Sint
Niklaas's major attraction is its Thursday market,
which covers all 3.2 hectares of its Grote Markt
every week.

Worth seeing are the Mercator Museum, dedicated to the works of the sixteenth-century carto-
grapher, and the Salon des Beaux-Arts (03 778
1745), which features porcelain and furniture from
the nineteenth and early twentieth centuries in a
renovated townhouse setting.

Getting there

By train from Gare Centrale; *by car* A12 to N16, N16
to N403.

Tourist information

45 Grote Markt, 9100 Sint Niklaas (03 777 26 81).
Open 9.30am-noon, 2-4pm, Mon-Fri.

St Michielsbrug – *this bridge over the River Leie offers some of the best views in Ghent.*

Oudenaarde

The capital of the Flemish Ardennes, this pastoral brewing and textile centre was once at the border between the French and German empires, hardly an ideal location. The town's former wealth is evident in Oudenaarde's town hall, a gorgeous Gothic building finished in 1537. Its features include a golden statue of Hanske de Krijger, the town's protector. Other notable buildings in Oudenaarde include the Notre Dame de Pamèle church and the Notre Dame hospital.

The ideal time to visit is the last weekend of June, for the beer festival. Taste some of the local specialities in the interests of historical research.

Getting there
By train from Gare du Nord, Gare Centrale or Gare du Midi to Ghent, switch to Oudenaarde; *by car* A40 to Ghent, switch to N60.

Geraardsbergen

A strategically important military base in the Middle Ages, Geraardsbergen is now known to professional cyclists all over the world, sometimes by its French name Grammont. The Wall of Geraardsbergen (or Grammont) is one of the important points to pass on the yearly Tour of Flanders bicycle race.

The city also has Krakelingenstoet and Tonnekebrand, a historic festival that falls on the last Sunday of February featuring a cortège, followed by brioches being thrown into the crowd – a poor substitute for the gold coins originally employed way back when. The city also has its own version of the Manneken Pis.

Getting there
By car N8 to Ninove, switch to N255 until Denderwindeke, go west on side road.

Tourist information
Stadhuis, 9500 Geraadsbergen (054 41 41 21). **Open** 10am-1pm, 2-4pm, Mon-Fri.

Aalst

Between Ghent and Brussels, Aalst was once the capital of Imperial Flanders, a status still evident in some of the well-preserved buildings of that era. But if you can choose a period to visit, try to do so during carnival: the Sunday before Lent kicks off the festivities, including onion tossing from the Belfry. This is not as unusual as it sounds: many Belgian towns have some foodstuff that they traditionally hurl on such occasions. Comic cross-dressers also get in on the act in Aalst – some men are always looking for an excuse to get dolled up as women.

Getting there
By train from Gare Centrale; *by car* N9.

Tourist information
3 Grote Markt, 9300 Aalst (053 73 22 62). **Open** *Oct-Apr* 8.45am-noon, 1.30-6pm, Mon, Tue, Thur, Fri; 8.45-11.45am, 1.30-7pm, Wed. *Jun-Sept* 8.45am-noon, 1.30-6pm, Mon, Tue, Thur, Fri; 8.45-11.45am, 1.30-7pm, Wed; 10-11.30am, 2-5pm, Sat.

Bruges

Belgium's most beautiful city owes its appearance to a 300-year slumber.

Until the sixteenth century Bruges was an important trading centre. The Zwin gave it access to the sea and it was a point of exchange for the whole of Europe. After the Zwin silted up, trading came to a standstill and the city became Bruges la Morte for 300 years. The city was finally rediscovered by English and French romantics, who fell under the spell of its intact architecture, harmony of styles and freshwater canals.

Because of its extended hibernation, the city's historical centre has remained largely unchanged. Bruges has now become the number one destination for tourists in Belgium, visited by two million people a year. All year round, but particularly during summer, it is invaded by visitors, and the city's economy now largely depends on tourism.

There are over 100 hotels in Bruges, and more restaurants. Every shop that does not sell lace (most of it made in Asia) and disposable cameras, claims to sell the best chocolates in the country. At the height of the season one has to be armed with a certain amount of tolerance and tenacity to catch a glimpse of some of the most popular sights.

There is a positive side. All the information in the museums is in several languages; the staff in the Tourist Information Office are welcoming and helpful; and the increase in tourist-related commercial activity has only had a minimal negative impact. The town centre is well looked after and closed to traffic. Car parks have been built where the city walls once stood to provide access to the centre; most of the monuments have been restored.

Bruges is stunningly beautiful. The maze of canals and gabled houses, the paved streets and wide squares, the inner courtyards and parks are a constant surprise. More than any other city in Belgium, Bruges is a place where you can feel outside time and even forget the thousands of other visitors. Autumn, with its changing colours and light, and spring when the daffodils invade the garden of the Béguinage, are the best seasons to visit, although when the winter is cold enough you can ice-skate on the canals and during the summer you can escape to the nearby sea resorts.

History

The city of Bruges began developing around the area of the Burg, where Boudewijn I built a castle in the ninth century. The site was chosen by the Count of Flanders to protect the coast from Norman raids, and by 1134 the first set of city walls had been completed.

During the early Middle Ages the sea regularly covered the land around Bruges, creating channels. The most important of these, the Zwin, came as far as the town of Dam, founded in 1180 and connected to Bruges by a canal. Thanks to the canal, Bruges gained access to the sea, and the town began to benefit from its ideal geographical position. The port rapidly became a point of transition for ships from all over Europe.

Bruges continued to be ruled by the Counts of Flanders, although there were continual disagreements between Counts and the tradesmen. Taking advantage of this precarious situation, the French king, Philip the Good, captured Bruges in 1301. His entry into the city is remembered for the ostentatious display of wealth exhibited by the citizens. The women of Bruges were so richly adorned that they aroused the fury of Philip's wife, who felt she no longer stood out as Queen.

Bruges began to prosper rapidly. Yet, just a year after Philip's arrival, Jan Breydel and Pieter de Coninck led an uprising against him. The fight between the Clauwearts, who were tradesmen, and the Leliarts, who sided with the French, was cruel and bloody, the Flemish killing all those who could not properly reproduce the hard guttural sounds of their language. Hundreds of Frenchmen were killed after failing to pronounce the words ''s gild and vriend' (friend of the guilds). These events, known as the *Matines brugeoises*, led to the Battle of the Golden Spurs (*see chapter* **History**).

Nevertheless, with ships coming from Russia, Scandinavia, England, France, Venice and Genoa, Bruges became one of the most important trading centres in Europe. It imported wool from England and became, like its rival and neighbour Ghent, a centre of the textile industry. Italian merchants played a major part in establishing Bruges as an important financial market. One of Europe's first stock exchanges was built here.

In 1340 Bruges joined the Hanseatic League. The league was the most impressive of its kind, forging commercial links between 150 cities for half a century and facilitating exchanges between East and West.

This period of wealth coincided with one of artistic development. The fifteenth century was the Golden Age of Flemish painting. Rich merchants commissioned works from artists such as Van Eyck, Hans Memling, Hugo van der Goes and Gerard David, most of whom lived in Bruges.

Meanwhile, sailing on the Zwin was becoming increasingly difficult, and ship merchants were starting to complain. The Zwin had begun to silt up. As the city's economy was completely dependent on the canal, much effort was put into trying to rectify the situation. A second canal, the Versewater, was dug. But this provided only temporary relief. Bruges eventually lost its access to the sea and its inevitable decline swiftly ensued. Matters were not helped by the fact that Maximilian of Austria, who had been imprisoned in Bruges, deliberately favoured the development of the rival port of Antwerp. In any case, the English had by now created their own textile industry and no longer needed Bruges to weave its wools.

For the next three centuries Bruges was almost completely inactive. In the nineteenth century the Industrial Revolution passed it by. Its only activities were small family businesses or trades such as printing, brewing, laundering and shoe making. This was Bruges la Morte, as described in the novel by Georges Rodenbach.

Many townsfolk continued to hope that another canal would be dug, allowing access to the sea once more. An ambitious plan to do this had been designed by Lanceloot Blondeel in the sixteenth century, but work on the Baudouin Canal did not begin until 1887, under Léopold II, after a series of parliamentary debates. Not surprisingly, the plan had been vigorously opposed by Antwerp.

The port of Zeebrugge was opened in 1907, but its activity was cut short by World War I, when it was taken over by the Germans. Today it has the biggest fishing port in Belgium and is the chief point of entry to the country for British ferries.

Sightseeing
The historical centre

The most enjoyable way to visit Bruges is on foot or by bicycle. True, you may be tempted to hop on one of the boat tours or horse-drawn carriages, but if you do you have to be prepared to brave hordes of other visitors.

The traditional starting point for a visit to Bruges is the Markt. Facing the Halles (covered market) around the square are some of the city's finest houses; the most impressive has a golden basket poised above it. One of the oldest houses on the Markt is the Craenenburg, which dates from around the fourteenth century. It was in this house that Emperor Maximilian, captured by the people of Bruges, was held prisoner. The Craenenburg is now a popular and typical Bruges café (*see below* **Eating & drinking**).

The statues at the centre of the square are those of Jan Breydel and Pieter de Coninck, who led the people of Bruges against the French in the Matines Brugeoises. The statues were unveiled by King Léopold II, who is said to have spoken Flemish for the first time during the ceremony. The Markt is also the site where the market was traditionally held until relatively recently when it was moved to the nearby area of 't Zand.

The most striking monuments on the Markt are the Halles and the Belfry. Tall and stout, Bruges Belfry (open 9.30am-5pm Mon-Sat; admission 100BF) is possibly the finest in the country. It is over 80m (263ft) high and the climb is naturally quite tiring, although you can pause along the way to see the balcony, from which public proclamations were made, and have a look at the massive carillon and bell. The view from the top is very impressive and well worth the climb. It is the clearest way to see the timeless structure of the city.

The Halles and Belfry are symbols of the power of merchants rather than of the aristocracy. Both date from the height of the town's success, when the covered market bustled with activity and merchandise was sold from all over Europe.

From here it's a very short walk to the Burg. This beautiful square was the site chosen by Boudewijn I to build his castle, hence its name. The Stadhuis (Town Hall), with its long elaborate windows, statues and octagonal turrets, is built in a splendid and dizzying Gothic style.

Inside the Town Hall (open 9.30am-5pm Mon-Sat; admission 100BF) you will find the lavish Gothic Hall. This has beautiful wooden vaults and around it are wall paintings illustrating the history of the city. It is a history that is often related with more verve than accuracy.

The Paleis van het Brugse Vrije (Old Recorders' House), on one corner of the Burg, was built in the sixteenth century and renovated in the eighteenth. What remains of the original structure is the façade overlooking the canal. The rest is in neoclassical style. In the palace is an impressive baroque chimney piece made in black marble and oak by Lanceloot Blondeel. Charles V, sword in hand, is surrounded by Maximilian of Austria and Mary of Burgundy.

Tucked into a corner of the Burg, next to the Town Hall, is the Heiligbloed Basiliek (Basilica of the Holy Blood). Its small entrance, guarded by shining golden statues, is easily missed and hardly looks like the entrance of a church. The façade of the Basilica is one of the first examples of Italian Renaissance style in Flanders. The Lower Chapel was built in the twelfth century in honour of St Basil, and is in a pure Romanesque style. The chapel has thick walls, heavy pillars and small windows. The dark and bare interior conveys a feeling of calm and contemplation. An elegant wooden spiral staircase leads to the Chapel of the

Holy Blood. The refined sobriety of the Lower Chapel is in surprising contrast to the generous interior of the Upper Chapel.

Built in the twelfth century, this chapel has undergone substantial changes. First Romanesque, then Gothic, it was heavily altered in the nineteenth century. The decorated wooden ceiling, many of the colourful frescoes, the marvellous stained-glass windows and the pumpkin-shaped pulpit all date from this period.

It is in this Upper Chapel that the crystal phial containing two drops of holy blood is exhibited every Friday. The phial is supposed to have been given to Thierry d'Alsace by the Patriarch of Jerusalem during the Second Crusade. Legend has it that the blood contained in the phial liquefied every Friday, but the miracle apparently stopped in the fifteenth century. The Procession of the Holy Blood (*see chapter* **Brussels by Season**), a major traditional event in Bruges, takes place every year on Ascension Day. The event commemorates the procession that accompanied Thierry d'Alsace when the holy phial was first brought to the city. Today, people dressed in rich costumes walk in a similar procession, enacting biblical scenes.

From the Burg you can head on to the Vismarkt (Fishmarket), taking the narrow Blinde Ezelstraat (Alley of the Blind Donkey). The fish market still takes place here every morning from Tuesday to Saturday.

The walk along the Groenerei is one of the most popular in Bruges – not surprisingly, as the pretty gabled houses (especially the Pelican House at no.8), the trees and the water make it one of the city's favourite romantic sites. It is not, however, one of the most secluded ones: boats and people constantly pass by.

Near the Vismarkt is the Huidevettersplaats, or Tanner's Square, which leads you to the Rozenhoedkaai and to another well-known romantic spot. Rozenhoedkaai is extremely charming, but, as it's the ideal spot for a snapshot of Bruges, you're unlikely to have the place to yourself.

After the Rozenhoedkaai you come to another beautiful street, the Dijver. Along it is the College of Europe and the Groeninge Museum (*see below*). A little further up are the Arendts Gardens. These small gardens are framed by the Gruuthuse Palace (*see below*) on one side and the Onze Lieve Vrouwkerk (Church of Our Lady) at the back. In the gardens you will find four modern sculptures representing the Knights of the Apocalypse.

The Onze Lieve Vrouwkerk is an imposing brick structure with a massive tower. As the front entrance is on a busy street, it is from the garden that its solid architecture can be best appreciated. The church was built over three centuries and the combination of styles is not unanimously considered a happy one. The interior is interesting, although some of the recent alterations, including some of the glass doors and panels, divide up the structure and make it difficult to form a complete impression of the place.

The Onze Lieve Vrouwkerk is especially renowned for the works of art it houses. First and foremost among these is Michelangelo's *Madonna and Child*. The sculpture was ordered by the Piccolomini family for Siena Cathedral, but a Bruges merchant by the name of Jan Moscroent managed to buy it when the Piccolomini family failed to pay up. The sculpture is an early work by the artist and one of the few to have left Italy during his lifetime. It is delicate and tender, subtly moving rather than powerful.

In the choir are the tombs of Charles the Bold and his daughter Mary of Burgundy. Unlike her husband, Maximilian of Austria, Mary of Burgundy was loved by the people of Bruges. Tragically, she died young and beautiful after falling from a horse. Their joint mausoleum is both lavish and solemn. The golden brass glitters in the dim light of the choir; a graceful brass sculpture of the princess lies over the heavily adorned base. The monument for Charles the Bold, made at a later date, is very similar in style. In 1979 the original tomb of Mary of Burgundy was among several that were dug up. These painted stone coffins are exhibited just below the monuments.

Directly opposite the church is St John's Hospital. The hospital, one of the last remaining medieval hospitals, was still in use as late as the 1970s. It is now a conference centre. You may visit the old hospital rooms and admire some of the most puzzling surgical instruments you are ever likely to see.

Béguinage & Minnewater Park

Coming out of St John's Hospital, turn right on Katelijnestraat and walk towards the Béguinage. You can walk straight on, or take any of the side streets. The way to the Béguinage and the Minnewater Park is well signposted, so you need have no fear of getting lost.

Some of the narrow side streets around this area are very pleasant, as indeed are some of the squares, but, again, they are liable to be crowded with visitors. The Béguinage, founded in 1245 by Margaret of Constantinople, is one of the most charming locations in Bruges. The row of small white houses encircles an inner lawn, which in the spring is completely covered with daffodils. Perhaps because of the colours, the silence or the nuns walking softly by, the atmosphere of the place is calm and serene.

*The **Stadthuis** (Town Hall), located by the beautiful Burg square, is built in a dizzying Gothic style.*

There are no longer any *béguines* in Bruges (*see chapter* **Sightseeing** *page 55*); the last of them died around 1930. The women you see walking around the Béguinage are Benedictine nuns. It is possible to visit the church; one of the houses is also open to visitors.

The Béguinage and the Minnewater (or Lac d'Amour), with swans, lawns and small houses, are very picturesque. Before the Zwin silted up, barges and occasional ships would penetrate this far into the city. The sixteenth-century lock-keeper's house is still on the north side of the lake, next to the 1398 Watch Tower.

The lake is named after a woman called Minna. According to legend, Minna had fallen passionately in love with a man, but her father, as fathers often do in legends, strongly disapproved of her choice. True to her heart, however, Minna fled from her father's house and came to hide in the woods around the lake. Unfortunately, her beloved was a little slow in finding her and Minna died in his arms. The heartbroken man still found enough strength in him to change the course of the water, bury Minna's body, and let the waters flow over the grave again.

Walking back to the Markt, you can pause to look at the massive Cathedral of St Salvator, the heaviness of whose shape is slightly softened by the trees around it. The interior is less severe, but seems rather neglected compared with the pristine state of most historical buildings in Bruges. Work on the cathedral began in the tenth century, but after four fires and the Iconoclasts' Riots nothing of that period has survived except the base of the tower. These incidents are also responsible for the varied and eclectic style of the interior. The choir dates from the fourteenth century, although part of the thirteenth-century construction survives. The painted columns, similar to those in the Upper Chapel of the Basilica of the Holy Blood, are a relatively recent addition, as are the stained-glass windows. There are several paintings by Van Orley, in the right transept, but the lighting is bad and they are difficult to see.

Around St Anna

Exploring the main monuments of Bruges, its imposing palaces and succession of beautiful gabled houses, it is easy to conjure up an impression of the city's former glory. It is much harder to imagine the city during its 300 years of inactivity.

The area of St Anna, just north of the Markt, is a poorer and more populated area of Bruges, and less visited by tourists. There are fewer shops and the bars are mostly frequented by locals.

*After 300 years' slumber, Bruges was rediscovered by English and French romantics who fell for its **freshwater canals**.*

You can follow Hoogstraat, just off the Burg, and turn right on Vervedijk. The houses here are still very impressive. In Boomgardstraat you will find the Jesuit Church of St Walsburg, built between 1619 and 1641. The church is bright with tall, solid, grey Tuscan-style columns. The style is baroque and the dominant colours gold and white, yet the interior is more harmonious than over-bearing and presents a refreshing change from other monuments in the city.

Cross the little bridge between the Vervedijk and St Annarei and you'll find yourself facing the seventeenth-century Church of St Anna. This brick building, only open between April and September, looks very austere, but its luxurious interior is quite at odds with the outside.

Behind St Anna, on the corner of Peperstraat, is the curious Jeruzalemkerk (Church of Jerusalem; open 10am-5pm Mon-Fri, 10am-noon Sat), built by a rich family of Italian merchants and still belonging to its descendants. It's a small church, built on three levels, supposedly following the model of the Holy Sepulchre. Over the altar is a crucifix decorated with bones and skulls. The crypt was built as a copy of the tomb of Christ. The stained-glass windows are impressive. There's a lace museum next door.

On Karmestraat is the English Convent and its church. Although it gives the impression of being permanently closed, it is possible to visit it, although you will usually have to ring a bell.

Walking along any of the steets here, you will notice that most of the houses are far removed from the flamboyant style of the historical centre. However, the St Anna area has a lot of charm and character. You no longer have the feeling that you are walking in an open-air museum, and you finally notice that Bruges does have a life of its own. It is also possible to imagine this area when it was hard hit by poverty. Witnesses to those hard times are the numerous Maisons Dieu. The decline of Bruges began around the sixteenth century, but continued steadily well into the nineteenth. Many people abandoned the city, leaving vast spaces in the centre completely empty. Richer citizens took it upon themselves to build almshouses to shelter the poor and elderly.

There are about 30 Maisons Dieu in Bruges, and some still fulfil their original role today. The entrance is usually marked by a small statue of the Virgin. Inside is a little courtyard and anything between three and 24 identical, modest but pretty little houses, each with its individual character. The lawns are usually carefully tended and surrounded with flowers, particularly during the summer months.

One Maison Dieu is just to the right of the St John's Hospital, but if you are observant you will notice them all around Bruges, particularly in the quieter areas.

Flemish masters

The booming commercial activity in Bruges in the fifteenth century was paralleled by a flourishing of the arts. Rich merchants ordered works from painters, as did many Italian bankers living in the city at the time. While Italian painting tended to glorify humanity, the Flemish masters remained more religious in their outlook, and medieval in their complexity and spirit. The **Groeninge Museum** has an excellent selection of Flemish 'primitive' art, with numerous works by Van Eyck, Van der Weyden and Van der Goes.

Perhaps no master illustrates the concept of Flemish fifteenth-century painting better than Van Eyck. The museum's collection allows the visitor to appreciate two fundamental aspects of his work: religious painting and portrait painting. Van Eyck's improvements in the technique of oil painting are visible to this day. The colours are not only longer lasting, but the malleability of the paints enabled him to achieve an unprecedented subtlety of clarity and hue.

The results can be seen in *Madonna with Canon George van der Paele*. The realism of the work, the colours and textures, particularly of the clothes and carpet, are striking. The portraits of the Madonna and the Canon are minutely detailed and, as ever with Van Eyck, his use of light is strikingly realistic. The *Portrait of Margareta Van Eyck*, the artist's wife, is also typical of his style. Unlike many portraits by Italian artists, Van Eyck's works are not embellished. The artist paints people as they are, their faults reflections of the flaws in human nature. The accuracy of the portraits is emphasised by the elaborate and curious hats that the subjects often wear. Despite his sharp realism, Van Eyck's work often conveys a sense of mystery and divinity, communicated by the stillness in a number of his paintings.

Like many of his contemporaries, Hugo van der Goes was influenced by Van Eyck. His realism is particularly noticeable in his reproduction of the physical world. For Van der Goes, all objects had a strong symbolic import that was part of a higher reality. *The Death of Our Lady* is a work characterised by dramatic tension and strong religious feeling. The Italian banker Portinari, who was then living in Bruges, ordered a triptych from the artist for a church in Florence. The artist's composition, his use of colours, his minute reproduction of vases and flowers, were all unlike the works to be found in Italy in the same period, and the triptych made a great impact on Renaissance artists.

The *Portrait of Philippe Le Bon* emphasises the heightened realism of the works of the Flemish 'primitives', although religious tension is often very palpable in the works of the fervent Rogier van der Weyden.

The *Moreel Triptych*, by Memling, is one of his most impressive works and was ordered by the merchant Moreel. His portrait and that of his five sons is on one of the side panels, his wife and daughters on the other.

Gerard David was the last of the great Bruges artists, and became the city painter after Memling's death. The *Baptism of Christ* is one of his best works. The realism of the piece, evident in the background and plants, is the characteristic that unifies all Flemish fifteenth-century artists.

Bosch's *Final Judgement* is one of the best expressions of the artist's fantastic imagination. The work, where reality and fantasy strangely combine, is relatively small, but one could spend hours searching out details.

The ancient art section of the Groeninge Museum also has works by Pieter Bruegel the Elder, Van Orley and various mannerist and baroque works. The section devoted to modern art has paintings by Delvaux and Magritte (*see also chapter* **Surrealist Brussels**) and a beautiful sculpture by Wouters, as well as one of the largest collections of Flemish expressionist art.

Groeninge Museum

12 Dijver, 8000 Bruges (050 44 87 50). **Open** 9.30am-5pm Mon, Wed-Sat. **Admission** 200BF. **Credit** AmEx, MC, V.

The city walls

Little remains of the old city walls. Furthermore, only three of the original city doors remain, and just one of the watchtowers. Instead Bruges is now nearly entirely surrounded by a belt of parks and lawns. Many people jog around here. Walking around the entire perimeter can take a long time – it is easier to cycle. You can follow the Potterei, visit the church and seminary, then continue as far as the border of the old city. On your right you will see three impressive windmills. Only one of the three is original; the other two were taken from nearby villages and brought to Bruges.

Getting there

By train from Gare du Nord, Gare Centrale or Gare du Midi; *by car* N9 via Ghent.

*Bruges developed around the **Burg**, where Boudewijn I built a castle in the ninth century.*

Tourist information

11 Burg, 8000 Bruges (050 44 86 86). **Open** *9.30am-6.30pm Mon-Fri; 10am-noon, 2-6.30pm, Sat, Sun, public holidays.*
Website http://www.brugge.be/brugge

Museums

Brangwyn Museum

16 Dijver, 8000 Bruges (050 448 763). **Open** *9.30am-5pm Mon, Wed-Sun.* **Admission** 80BF. **Credit** AmEx, MC, V.

The museum is named after a British painter and engraver, some of whose works are exhibited in the museum. The Brangwyn exhibits lace on the ground floor, as well as glass, china, brass and crockery. There is an entire section devoted to paintings of Bruges, but the most interesting part of the collection are the sledges that were used as transport over the frozen canals.

Groeninge Museum

12 Dijver, 8000 Bruges (050 44 87 50). **Open** *9.30am-5pm Mon, Wed-Sat.* **Admission** 200BF. **Credit** AmEx, MC, V.

See p228 **Flemish masters**.

Gruuthuse Palace

17 Dijver, 8000 Bruges (050 44 87 62). **Open** *9.30am-5pm Mon, Wed-Sun.* **Admission** 130BF. **Credit** AmEx, MC, V.

The palace originally belonged to the Gruuthuse family, who had a monopoly on the making of *gruut*, a mixture of dried flowers and plants used for brewing. Louis de Gruuthuse was a diplomat and Knight of the Golden Fleece, who also invented a nastier version of the cannonball. His motto, 'Plus est en vous', is reproduced around the palace. His son, Jean Gruuthuse, allied himself with the French, leaving the palace and the country. In the seventeenth century the palace was used as a pawnshop. The city of Bruges eventually bought it and furnished it with over 2,000 exhibits.

The furniture in the reception hall dates from the sixteenth, seventeenth and eighteenth centuries, as do the silverware and ceramic exhibits. The bust of Charles V, showing a young and candid Emperor, is one of the most important pieces in the collection. Many of the other pieces are objects of daily life, some interesting and some curious. The pharmacy contains strange objects linked to healing and death; the kitchen has a big collection of wrought iron utensils for grilling meat and fish; the music cabinet has a beautiful collection of ancient musical instruments. There are also lace, tapestries and a collection of military objects, among them a guillotine.

The second floor is devoted almost entirely to lace. Lace making is a Bruges tradition that dates back to the Middle Ages, when lace was made with imported linen, always by women and often in convents and in the Béguinages. In the seventeenth century Bruges, Ghent, Brussels and Mechelen were quite unrivalled in the art of lace making.

Kantcentrum (Lace Centre)

3 Peperstraat, 8000 Bruges (050 33 00 72). **Open** *10am-noon Mon-Fri; 10am-5pm Sat.* **Closed** *public holidays.* **Admission** 60BF. **No credit cards**.

For serious lace fans. There are napkins, doilies, clothes for baptisms and communions, veils and lingerie. It's possible to see demonstrations of lace making in a room opposite the museum. Although it is a tourist attraction, the women here look as if they mean business and will get on with their work while you watch. The traditional procedure for making lace looks intricate and difficult. The lace is made on a cushion, following a pattern. The threads are held down by a series of pins or nails that are placed following the chosen pattern. The thread is wrapped around small wooden reels and the

women alternate the reels, working the strings around the pins. The older women seem to be faster than their younger colleagues, but progress is slow as lace making takes great patience and dedication.

Memling Museum

38 Mariastraat, 8000 Bruges (050 44 87 70). **Open** *9.30am-5pm Mon, Wed-Sun.* **Admission** 60BF. **Credit** AmEx, MC, V.

Born near Frankfurt, Hans Memling was one of the most acclaimed artists of his time. He studied and lived in Bruges where he created several pieces for St John's Hospital. He also undertook commissions for the English poet John Donne and the Italian banker Portinari. Memling's talent as a portrait artist and his hunger for detail are remarkable. Like all the Flemish primitives, Memling believed that the material world was a product of divine creation, and in the necessity to reproduce the work of God as faithfully and accurately as possible. His use of colours is brilliant and the scenes always carefully composed.

The relic of St Ursula was deposited in the shrine made by Memling in 1489 and is now on display in the museum. The shrine is shaped like a Gothic cathedral, and is decorated with scenes from the saint's life. The story of St Ursula and the 11,000 virgins was a popular legend. Ursula was martyred by pagans in Cologne after refusing to marry Hans, the pagan Prince of the Huns. Some of the episodes are set in Cologne. The city's cathedral, then under construction, is painted accurately, though the representations of Basle and Rome are fictitious.

The Mystical Marriage of St Cathérine is one of several similar works by Memling (another is in the Metropolitan Museum in New York). In the central panel, Jesus, sitting on Mary's lap, is sliding a ring on St Cathérine's finger. Although Memling's paintings are often said to be somewhat devoid of feeling, here the colours are vivid and passionate. Mary's cloak represents passion, in contrast with the conventional subdued blue. Episodes in the life of St John and St John the Baptist are in the background. The backs of the panels are also decorated. The rainbow structure on one of the panels is reminiscent of Bosch, although the two painters are otherwise hardly comparable.

The diptych of Marteen van Nieuwenhove has a portrait of the donor on one of the panels, while on the other Mary is depicted as giving the baby Jesus an apple. The portrait is a superb example of Memling's talent as a portrait artist. The *Sybilla Sambetha* is believed to be a portrait of Marie Moreel, who commissioned many works from Memling. (Sybils were women who announced the coming of Christ.)

Accommodation

Golden Tulip De' Medici

15 Pottererei, 8000 Bruges (050 33 98 33/fax 050 33 07 64). **Rates** *single* 4,500BF; *double* 5,500BF.

Located near the historic centre, this is, however, a modern hotel. The look of the interior is rather efficient and cold, but the rooms are spacious and comfortable. There's a recreation centre with sauna, jacuzzi, steam bath, sun beds and a gymnasium.

Hotel Die Swaene

1 Steennhouwersdijk, 8000 Bruges (050 34 27 98/fax 050 33 66 74). **Rates** *single* 4,800BF; *double* 5,800BF.

In a fifteenth-century mansion overlooking a canal, this romantic hotel is as close to Venice as you can get in Belgium.

Conservatory dining room of the romantic, fifteenth-century **Hotel de Swaene** *– see page 230.*

Chagall *on St Amandstraat – delicious seafood in a relaxed environment – see page 232.*

Hotel Jacobs

1 Baliestraat, 8000 Bruges (050 33 98 31/fax 050 33 56 94). **Rates** *single* 1,900-2,100BF; *double* 2,200-2,550BF.
More earthbound price-wise than Die Swaene, this has comfortable, practical rooms that are good value for money.

Relais Oud-Huis Amsterdam

3 Spiegelrei, 8000 Bruges (050 34 18 10/fax 050 33 88 91). **Rates** *single* 4,500BF, *double* 5,500-7,500BF; *suite* 9,500BF.
Splendid hotel set in a beautifully renovated seventeenth-century house, overlooking one of the canals. With its carved wooden staircase, chandeliers, antique furniture and bare wooden beams, the interior of the hotel has been carefully furnished and the effect is quite staggering. There is a comfortable bar and a very pretty interior courtyard.

Snuffel Travellers' Inn

47 Ezelstraat, 8000 Bruges (050 33 31 33/fax 050 33 32 50). **Rates** 300BF in a room for 12; 380BF in a room for 8; 430BF in a room for 4; supplement of 50BF for breakfast.
For bargain hunters, the Snuffel offers hostel-like accommodation in rooms for four to 12.

Het Wit Beertje

4 Witte Beerstraat, 8200 Bruges (050 31 87 62/fax 050 45 08 80). **Rates** *single* 1,000BF; *double* 1,500BF.
All rooms are ensuite and are appointed with telephone and TV. Prices include breakfast. The centre of Bruges is only a ten-minute walk away.

Eating & drinking

Bruges is full of restaurants, on every major site, on the commercial streets and down every little alleyway. All of them strive to attract tourists, some very obviously so by offering menus to suit different nationalities (English breakfasts, for instance), but most of them with tourist menus, consisting of several courses of either seafood or regional specialities. When they are in season you can eat mussels practically everywhere.

De Belegde Boteram

5 Klein St Amandstraat, 8000 Bruges (050 34 91 31).
Friendly and trendy rustic decor, with plain wooden tables for sharing. The Belegde Boteram serves salads, sandwiches and other simple dishes. It's very busy around lunchtime and customers are mostly people working in Bruges.

Cafedral

38 Zilverstraat, 8000 Bruges (050 34 08 45). **Open** 11.30am-2am; *food served* 11.30am-2pm, 6.30-11pm, daily. **Credit** AmEx, MC, V.
Brasserie in a fifteenth-century house with a church-like interior. Lovely terrace that feels like an enclosed garden.

Chagall

40 St Amandstraat, 8000 Bruges (050 33 61 12). **Open** 11am-12.30am daily. **Credit** AmEx, MC, V.
Chagall serves delicious seafood in a relaxed environment. Specialities include scampi, eels and mussels; the shellfish come highly recommended.

Craenenburg

16 Markt, 8000 Bruges (050 33 34 02). **Open** 7am-midnight daily. **No credit cards.**
The house in which Maximilian of Austria was held captive has become a typical Bruges café, with yellowed walls and wooden tables. Customers are mostly from Bruges.

De Garre

1 De Garre, 8000 Bruges (050 34 10 29). **Open** noon-midnight Mon-Thur; noon-1am Fri-Sun. **No credit cards.**
Right at the back of the shortest blind alley in Bruges, and in a sixteenth-century house, De Garre sells a huge selection of Belgian beers. Wooden beams and brick walls.

Handwritten annotations: *Bourgoensche Cryee* *La Kaddal* *La Martobubte / falstaff Pub*

De Stove

40 Klein St Amandstraat, 8000 Bruges (050 33 78 35).
Open noon-1.45pm, 6-9.30pm, daily. **Credit** AmEx, DC,
MC, V.
An elegant little restaurant, just off one of the main shopping streets, serving a variety of meat and fish dishes. Its
traditional old-time decor, with an old stove and chimney, is
simple and unpretentious.

Taverne the Hobbit

40 St Amandstraat, 8000 Bruges (050 33 55 20). **Open**
6pm-1am daily. **Credit** AmEx, MC, V.
A loyal yuppie and student following come to take advantage of the reasonably priced pasta, chicken and other standard fare, served at big round tables by candlelight.

De Witte Porte

6 Jan van Eyck Plein, 8000 Bruges (050 33 08 03).
This former wine warehouse has been done over in exquisite style, and the menu measures up to the decor's promise.
Although *waterzooi* (a chicken stew) is a Ghent speciality,
the version served here ranks with the best.

Shopping

Most tourists come the Bruges for the sightseeing,
so the majority of shops tend to sell fancy items in
lace, books on Bruges and Belgium, disposable
cameras, and T-shirts. The main shopping street
is Steenstraat, which runs from the Markt to 't
Zand. Simon Stevinplein, just off Steenstraat, has
some attractive shops, as does St Amandstraat.
Hoogstraat, north of the Markt, is less tourist-
oriented, unlike Katelijnestraat and Mariastraat.

Atelier Cocteau

8 Ziverstraat, 8000 Bruges (050 34 44 17). **Open** 10am-
6pm Mon-Thur; 9am-6pm Fri, Sat. **Credit** MC V.
Trendy and fashionable hairdresser in an old house, decorated in a modern style with bright colours and big mirrors
in golden frames. The staff are young and energetic.

Chocolate Line

Simon Stevinplein, 8000 Bruges (050 34 10 90). **Open**
10am-7pm Mon-Sat. **Credit** AmEx, MC, V.
All shops in Bruges cash in on the tourist trade, but the
chocolate shops do so unashamedly. The Chocolate Line is
a little more discreet in its presentation than other chocolate
shops, though it's doubtful that it would sell chocolate
Oscars if its customers were only from Bruges.

De Striep

42 Katelijnestraat, 8000 Bruges (050 33 71 12). **Open**
1.30-7pm Mon; 10am-12.30pm, 1.30-7pm, Tue-Sat. **Credit**
AmEx, MC, V.
Huge choice of comic books and a big selection of posters.

Dille and Kamille

Simon Stevinplein, 8000 Bruges (050 34 11 80).
Open 9.30am-6.30pm Mon-Sat; 11am-6.30pm Sun.
Credit MC, V.
This shop sells items for the garden and kitchen. The prices
are usually reasonable and the choice is interesting.

Fifty Fifty

48 Katelijnestraat, 8000 Bruges (050 34 69 87). **Open**
1.30-6.30pm Mon, Thur; 10.30am-6.30pm Tue, Wed, Fri,
Sat. **Credit** AmEx, DC, MC, V.
Fifty Fifty sells decorative American items from the 1950s,
such as replica jukeboxes, fridges and dolls. Good ideas for
presents, even if you're not a big fan of the decade.

Jos Marechal

10 Mariastraat, 8000 Bruges (050 33 00 23). **Open**
9am-12.30pm, 1.30-6pm, Mon-Sat. **Credit** AmEx, DC,
MC, V.
Immense bookshop with books exclusively in Dutch. If you
speak the language, you can lose yourself in the section
devoted to beautiful coffee-table books and art books. There
is also a large section for children.

Zazou

19-20 St Amandstraat, 8000 Bruges (050 33 46 27).
Open 10am-12.30pm, 2-6.30pm, Mon-Sat. **No**
credit cards.
Two small shops that face each other across the street. Both
sell mainly original bags, watches and jewellery, but the
selection is slightly different in the two boutiques.

Outside Bruges

If you're going to have seafood while you're in
Belgium, naturally the coast is the best area for
it: something about the sea air, combined with
the freshness of the mussels, monkfish and other
creatures fished from the North Sea, makes it
better than what might be on offer even in the
best restaurants in Brussels. But the pleasures to
be enjoyed on the Belgian coast are more than
merely piscine.

Ostende

This city is the most popular coastal destination
every summer, so attractive that even Queen
Victoria took a dip here in 1834. The site in the
early seventeenth century of battles between the
Dutch and Spanish (who left behind many offspring from liaisons with local women, evident in
the more Mediterranean complexions of some
natives), Ostende was once Belgium's answer to
Monte Carlo: beaches, museums and racetracks of
international renown.

Alas, it is now showing signs of decline. The
racetrack has ceased racing horses. But locals and
entrepreneurs are hoping that the same space will
succeed as a rock venue, to complement the famed
Casino, where many musicians that you may have
thought were long dead (Percy Sledge, Barry
White) attract sell-out crowds.

Along the coast is where the best seafood, especially shellfish, is to be had. An age-old rule of
thumb for mussels – that are to Belgium what herring is to Scandinavia – is never to eat them in
months without an 'r', that is, only from September
to April. The air here is among the best in Belgium,
and the beaches among the cleanest, although you
should avoid the water during jellyfish season.
Also, the Kleine Strand is where all the sewage
washes up, and as a result is not all that popular
with bathers.

The Kappellestraat is Ostende's high street:
Hennes & Mauritz, C&A, Leonidas and other older

shops have locations here. Upscale shops that once dotted the Adolf Buylstraat have moved on to a glass-ceilinged gallery nearby. The Lulu Shop is just about the only place women can get Vivienne Westwood, Jean-Paul Gaultier and up-and-coming Belgian designer Mieke Cosijn, and on the nearby Christinastraat, men on the lookout for Armani, Helmut Lang and Dutch designer So flock to the men's shop Jaeger. Alberdeen is the emporium for men's sportswear by such style titans as Gianni Versace and Calvin Klein, and those wanting something more alternative stop by Mandarijntje for Asian jewellery, piercings and henna tattoos.

On a more cultural note, PMMK – the Provinciaal Museum voor Moderne Kunst (Provincial Museum of Modern Art) – specialises in collections of Belgian twentieth-century artists, with symbolism and expressionism in addition to more contemporary movements well represented. Panamarenko, Permeke, Tytgat and the Cobra movement are just a few of the particular delights in the permanent collection.

James Ensorhuis (17 Vlaanderenstraat) is a former souvenir and seashell store. Inherited from his aunt, James Ensor turned it into a salon to entertain visiting artists, critics and friends until his death. The store's stock of seashells and tortoise shells, stuffed swans and carnival masks remain on permanent exhibit.

The Maritime School of the Belgian Merchant Marine, which ran from the 1930s to 1960s, sits in the Port de Plaissance near the Vindictivelaan and makes for an interesting visit.

The Paulusfeest in mid-August is the high point of the summer: local and international musicians, dancers and acting troupes converge on the city, which becomes a big carnival for a week. If you want a real understanding of Ostende, then you have to be in the audience during a performance of Lucy Loes, an Ostende folk singer who has become legendary. This is no exaggeration: the current Lucy Loes is not the original one, who died many years ago. It's unclear whether the name passed directly from the original Lucy to the reigning Lucy, or if there were Lucys in between, but, in any event, she moves the crowd to tears with her renderings of traditional folk songs in the Ostende dialect.

The Langestraat is the site of the Long Street Happening, a rougher, low-rent version of the Paulusfeest – but is still worth a look. Langestraat is lined with bars and small dance clubs that have rather lenient door policies.

The Visserplein is trendier and it is where you will find Ostende's concentration of gay bars, as well as its establishments for youngsters and yuppies. Within spitting distance is the Kaai (quay), which is renowned for its fish stands and, for those with more time on their hands, excellent fish restaurants. Among the best is 't Vistrapje.

If you want to stay in Ostend there are over 5,000 beds available in the town, so you should be able to find somewhere suitable to lay your weary head. If you're travelling on the cheap, then the De Ploate Jeugdherberg (059 80 52 97/fax 059 80 92 74) may be for you. A modern, comfortable hostel, it's also dead in the centre of town. The Hotel Thevenet (059 70 10 35/fax 059 80 94 19) has clean rooms with showers and is a short walk to the beach. And if you're in a position to spend a little more, try the Hotel Flanders (059 80 66 03/fax 059 80 16 95) across from the town's cathedral.

On a clear day, a walk along the boardwalk affords you a sea-view that stretches as far as France. At the end of the pier is Beaufort, a tavern with an interesting history. The original café on this spot was blown away in a storm. The current tenants assure patrons that things won't get so carried away in the future.

Getting there
By train from Gare du Nord, Gare Centrale or Gare du Midi; *by car* A10.

Tourist information
2 Monacoplein, 8400 Ostende (059 70 11 99). **Open** 9am-7pm Mon-Fri; 10am-7pm Sat, Sun.

De Panne

Possessing what are arguably the most beautiful dunes on the Belgian coast, De Panne also has the largest beach: over 500 hectares (1,280 acres) with more than half of that specially designated as a nature reserve. There is an ample amount of space on the beach set aside for recreation: fishing is allowed, as are windsurfing, surfing and of course swimming.

A truly touristic town that makes no bones about it, De Panne has a good range of three-star hotels, five camping grounds, and a wide selection of sports clubs where the activities range from badminton through body building to bowls. A short walk going north-east along the seafront, with the sea on your left, will bring you to St Idesbald and the Museum Paul Delvaux (*see below*), a gallery space dedicated to the late great Belgian surrealist painter. If you follow the strip along the beach in the other direction, with the sea on your right, France is just a brisk walk away.

Museum Paul Delvaux
42 Kabouterweg, 8670 St Idesbald (058 52 12 29). **Open** 10.30am-6.30 Tue-Sun. **Admission** 250BF; 180BF students, over-60s.
A large number of Delvaux's paintings and sketches are on permanent display at the Museum Paul Delvaux, situated not far from where Delvaux lived after leaving Brussels. (*See also chapters* **Surrealist Brussels** *and* **Museums**.)

Formerly a wine warehouse, **De Witte Porte** *offers a* waterzooi *to rank with the best in Belgium – see page 233.*

*In Bruges start with the **Markt** for some of the city's finest buildings and monuments.*

Getting there

By train from Gare du Nord, Gare Centrale or Gare du Midi to Ghent, switch for De Panne; *by car* A10 to Ostende, then west on N34.

Tourist information

21 Zeelaan, 8660 De Panne (058 42 18 18). **Open** *Sept-Jun* 9am-noon, 1.30-5pm, Mon-Fri; 9am-noon Sat. *Jul, Aug* 9am-noon, 1.30-5pm, Mon-Fri; 9am-noon, 1.30-5.30pm, Sat.

Blankenberghe

Blankenberghe's beach, 3km long and 3.5km wide, is another popular spot for sunlovers and others on holiday. The dunes between Blankenberghe and Zeebrugge, a less popular spot, are called the Fonteintjes, and attract many hikers and strolling couples and families. Diversion for youngsters is also provided by the modest 'Nordic' amusement park.

Getting there

By train from Gare du Nord, Gare Centrale or Gare du Midi; *by car* A10 to Ostende, then east on N34.

Bredene

Bredene has the largest camping grounds along the coastal area in Belgium. With Ostende (*see above*) and Bruges (*see above*) within spitting distance (you could even rollerblade from Bredene to the other two without breaking into a sweat), it is an ideal place to pitch your tent if you are on a camping holiday. Nature- and sports-lovers

will enjoy Paelsteenveld, a ten-hectare (25-acre) recreational park that has a mix of spectacular gardens, flowering playgrounds for children and sports facilities.

Bredene also has other attractions for sporty types: several mini-golf courses, two stables, tennis courts, bowls courts, and even a covered swimming pool for those who can't be bothered with the sea. Fishing, windsurfing and sailing are also permitted, but in designated zones.

Ieper

Ieper has been much destroyed throughout the ages, but just as ingeniously rebuilt. Once as large and renowned as Ghent and Bruges, Ieper now has an off-the-beaten-path charm and is more like real Belgium than Brussels. Beyond the usual churches and ruins, what makes Ieper memorable is its Cat festival.

Taking place on the second Sunday in May, this feline celebration stems from a medieval ritual of throwing cats off the top of the belfry. Today's politically correct climate dictates that stuffed cats be hurled instead. A cats' parade is held every three years, the next being in 2000.

Getting there

By train from Gare du Nord, Gare Centrale or Gare du Midi to Ghent, switch for Ieper; *by car* N8 via Kortrijk.

Tourist information

34 Grote Markt, 8900 Ieper (057 20 07 24). **Open** 9am-5.30pm daily.

Wallonia

From the coal mines of Charleroi to the hills of the Ardennes, the contrasting attractions of Belgium's francophone provinces are many and varied.

Liège

Liège bears the contradiction of being so close to Holland yet so far away culturally: this is what France would be like if it didn't take itself so seriously. Hilly and flat, with lush greenery and sparkling waterways, Liège offers something for everyone. It is the gateway to the Ardennes, the verdant area where every Belgian lusts to have a chalet or two. The city that gives the region its name is to Wallonia what Antwerp is to Flanders: the city everyone aspires to.

Liège

As Brussels is technically bilingual, it cannot truly claim to be the premier francophone city in Belgium: that honour belongs to Liège, a city only spitting distance away from Maastricht, but which maintains its unique Latin flavour nonetheless. From nightlife to daytime, Liège does merit your going out of your way to see it.

Its history dates back to AD 705, with the assassination of the Bishop of Tongeren-Maastricht St Lambert in the region then called Legia. In tribute to him, his successor built a sanctuary on the same spot, attracting pilgrims. The Bishop eventually took his parish elsewhere, but he left behind the beginnings of what is today Liège.

PEOPLE POWER

Craftsmen, merchants and other professionals were drawn to the city in the first centuries of its existence; these were troublesome times until the clergy and the citizens found a tenuous means of sharing governance of the city in 1316. The charter signed then made Liège one of the first slightly democratic principalities in Belgium.

But, Belgium being Belgium, Liège did have its share of the same invading forces, upheavals and intrigue that faced other cities: Charles the Bold destroyed the city (save the churches) in 1468, the French Revolution took its toll, and both World Wars have left their lasting marks.

There are four different parts to the city: the Quartier de l'Ile, an ancient island on the Meuse; the Quartier d'Outre-Meuse; the Quartier de la Pierreuse; and l'Assaut du Mont St Martin.

The traditional and historic heart of the city is St Lambert, site of the Palais des Princes-Evêques, a stately building incorporating different architectural styles, each evocative of an era of the building's history. The Palais now serves as a government building. The outer court of the building is accessible to the public, but the more intimate second court is sealed off from outside visitors.

WAFFLE, WAFFLE

Waffles, the national pastry that has more of a reputation abroad than its consumption at home merits, are the speciality of Liège. Served, with tea, either topped with chantilly and chocolate, or bought hot from vendors on the street, they are more substantial snacks than their foreign imitations. If shopping is on your agenda, take advantage of the proximity of Maastricht to hop over and hit the stores: its clothing shops offer a trendier selection than Liège.

Liège, though, does have a wealth of museums, many worth a visit, but among the most outstanding is the Musée d'Armes, the second largest of its kind in Europe, which isn't surprising when you take into account that Belgium is a major arms producer. For both the curious and the connoisseur, the museum's collection includes several pieces from Napoleon's time. The Musée de l'Art Wallon offers over 3,000 works – paintings and sculpture – that give a sample of the best of Brussels and Wallonia. For lovers of Magritte and Delvaux, this is an essential stop.

The Musée Curtius has an impressive collection displayed in an equally impressive environment: decorative objects going back to the tenth century and prehistoric artefacts going back even further, many with religious significance and in precious metals and stones, with a sumptuous seventeenth-century Renaissance *mosan* palace as its backdrop. The same building houses the Musée de Verre, where you can see thousands of glassworks from the craft's beginnings until the late 1800s – from Byzantine to baroque, the collection crosses cultures, featuring chalices, crystal and more.

In Seraing, crystal-lovers can peruse works at the Musée du Val St Lambert (041 37 09 60/fax 041 37 67 81), housed in an eighteenth-century building now completely restored. Glass-blowers and -makers show how pieces are made in an adjacent studio, while vases, candlesticks and other objects from the present collection are on display and on sale. If all this works up an appetite, Val St Lambert also has a restaurant.

Nightlife thrives in the Carré, a pedestrian area lined with cafés, discos and bars popular with teens and twentysomethings. At Le Vaudrée (041 23 18 80) you can choose from over a thousand beers, each with its own special character. The Taverne St Paul (041 23 72 17), founded more than 100 years ago, has a good selection of beers on tap. In the centre of town, try Casa Nicaragua (041 77 37 36), popular for its poetry readings and themed parties. Profits from the bar go to Nicaraguan charities. Les Caves de Porto (041 23 23 25) has another take on Latin, this time Portuguese-Brazilian. Le Pergola (041 42 57 08) is a mom-and-pop affair that has one of the warmest, most intimate dining rooms in Liège. Pasta dishes, salads and chianti are served in a discreet setting.

An old-time charm pervades L'Annexe 13, which has an authentic Liègeois ambience that makes you feel instantly at home. It's a favourite of artists, professionals and locals. The menu changes, depending on what's in season and on the market prices for the blood sausage; offal-based main courses and lots of pork – traditional, stick-to-your-ribs fare. The fact there's no telephone makes it all the more exclusive. It's in the Outre-Meuse area and is cheap. But if you're looking to impress, try Au Vieux Liège (041 23 77 88). The sixteenth-century house that is the setting for this restaurant has dining rooms full of refined charm. The seafood dishes are especially delicious, but the menu features a wider range of sophisticated French cuisine.

If you intend to stay in the city, the Hôtel le Simenon (041 41 20 20) takes its name from the Liège-born novelist who is something of a national hero. The ornate exterior of the hotel gives way to a more subdued and elegant interior, with reasonable charges for what you're getting. Passable and practical, the Hôtel l'Univers (041 54 55 55) opts for efficiency over elegance. More unusual accommodation can be found on the Bateau-péniche L'Embrun (041 21 11 20), a boat hotel.

Getting there

By train from Gare du Nord, Gare Centrale or Gare du Midi; *by car* A3.

Tourist information

92 Feronstree, 4000 Liège (041 21 92 21). **Open** *Apr-Oct* 9am-6pm Mon-Fri; 10am-4pm Sat; 10am-2pm Sun. *Nov-Mar* 9am-5pm Mon-Fri; 10am-4pm Sat; 10am-2pm Sun.
Branch: *place de Guellimins, 4000 Liège (041 52 44 19).* **Open** *Apr-Sept* 9am-noon, 12.30-5.30pm, Mon-Sat; *Oct-Mar* 10am-12.30pm, 1.30-4pm, Mon-Sat.

Province of Liège Tourism Federation

77 boulevard de la Sauvinière (041 22 42 10). **Open** 8.30am-5pm Mon-Fri; 9am-1pm Sat.

Spa

Spa, source of the world-famous mineral water, also gave its name to the word for a curative mineral spring. The town has charms that are every bit as relaxing as its name would have you believe. 'A remarkable spring that emerges in several places and tastes of iron,' is how Pliny the Elder summed it up in his *Natural History*.

Today the casino and the thermal establishment, as well as the theatres and concert halls built during the Belle Epoque (at the height of Spa's renown), look as though they've seen better days. But the Thermes de Spa (087 77 25 60/fax 087 77 50 66) still provides cures, and the town's peat baths and mineral water treatments attract even Belgians – proof that its reputation is not all hype.

If taking a dip isn't your thing, you can take advantage of the free-running springs (*pouhons*), whose high metallic content makes Spa (only 33mg of salts per litre) seem feeble. These are accessible to anyone walking along the scenic Tour des Fontaines, a trail through a quiet patch of forest. Fishing on one of the town's lakes also provides a peaceful diversion.

If you feel like splurging, the Brasserie du Grand Maur offers not only excellent traditional French cuisine but a gorgeous and elegant ambience as well. Somewhat more down-home is the Steak House (087 77 15 05).

The Hôtel Relais (087 77 40 33/fax 087 77 25 93) has a pleasant atmosphere and a lovely flowered exterior. Moderately priced, it has the added advantage of being central. And if you want to sleep among some of the most beautiful countryside in Belgium, the Parc des Sources (087 77 23 11), open from mid-March to October, is the largest camping ground in Spa, with 171 lots.

Getting there

By train from Gare du Nord, Gare Centrale or Gare du Midi to Liège, switch for Verviers, switch for Spa; *by car* A3 to A7 at Chaineux, then A27 to Sart and switch to N629 for Spa.

Tourist information

41 place Royale, 4900 Spa (087 77 25 19/fax 087 77 07 00). **Open** 9am-12.30pm, 2-6pm, Mon-Fri; 10am-12.30pm, 2-6pm, Sat, Sun.

Namur

There is no shortage of châteaux and museums for those with a thirst for historical knowledge, and there are sports activities for visitors to the province who just want to kick back. Namur is very accessible from Brussels.

Once a fortress for the Gauls, Namur has had Caesar, Charlemagne, Vikings, Normans, France, Holland, Austria and Germany each have a go at ruling it. It has weathered all this, maintaining an

Liège – *the premier francophone city in Belgium, since the capital is officially bilingual.*

ultra-unperturbable calm – at least to those on the outside. Defiant to change, Namur resisted the Industrial Revolution and, more recently, the attempts of speculators to develop it. Namur has survived both intact.

Namur

The Citadelle de Namur (081 22 68 29), in the town which shares its name with the province, is one of the largest forts still existing in Europe. Now a partly recreational, partly educational theme park, the Citadelle features rides, dioramas and museums dedicated to weaponry, both firearms and swords. It's good for children. Nearby Chevetogne has the Domaine Provincial Valery Cousin (083 68 88 21), a retreat of parks, woods and lawns. A slow train gives a guided tour of the grounds, which include an Olympic-sized swimming pool, a covered area for horse riding, fish ponds, sports fields, a miniature golf course, an amusement park, a garden of plants known for their medicinal properties, and too many other attractions to list. From

châteaux to camping grounds, this is one of the best parks Belgium has to offer.

Those with deep pockets and a hunger to match should try out La Petite Figue (081 23 13 20), an intimate two-room establishment where French cuisine is refashioned and reinterpreted for a very appreciative clientele: this is a name restaurant. But if your appetite is bigger than your finances (or if you'd just prefer to go to somewhere more typically Namurois), Le Palmier (081 22 07 39) serves a good selection of shellfish, game, meat and poultry dishes prepared as in traditional Belgian and French kitchens. The portions are more than generous.

Although the name wouldn't make you think it, L'Eblouissant (081 74 66 37) is actually an Irish pub. An eclectic selection of beers from around the world complements the expected Irish and British malts and ales on the drinks menu. But Extérieure-Nuit (081 23 09 09) is more spacious, though a touch alienating: metallic accents, videos and bare brick walls can leave you cold. It would be best visited with a large group of friends.

An old private hotel dressed up for contemporary tastes is the Hôtel St Loup (081 23 04 05). It's neither ridiculously expensive, nor exactly a bargain; the restaurant is good. The Hôtel Opéra-Le Parisien (081 23 13 90) proves the maxim 'Beware of hotels with posh names invoking foreign cities'. The sterility of the rooms may be slightly offputting, but it is clean and cheaper than the St Loup. If you are on a tight budget, the Auberge de Jeunesse (081 22 36 88) has over 100 beds with rooms accommodating from four to six in a renovated townhouse overlooking the Meuse – it's located 3km from the centre.

Geting there

By train from Gare Centrale or Schuman; *by car* N4.

Tourist information

18 rue Pieds d'Alouette, 5000 Namur (081 40 80 10). **Open** 8am-5pm Mon-Fri.

Annevoie

A few kilometres south of Namur on the N96 are the Château and Gardens d'Annevoie (082 61 15 55) in the Meuse Valley. They offer a package deal – as châteaux go, this isn't really the most impressive – and a garden alone is rarely enough to go out of your way for. Still, the late seventeenth- to early eighteenth-century château *is* a château, complete with chapel.

The garden, for which the original owners of the château devised special irrigation and a means of planting in the mid-1700s, is maintained pretty much as it was back then. This makes its delicate flower beds and well-arranged shrubbery, its lovely bubbling fountains and placid ponds, all the more impressive.

Many Belgian beers were originally brewed in monasteries such as the Abbaye de Maredsous (082 69 93 96). This monastery dates back to 1872, and now has a brewery and terrace for guests. The neo-Gothic building makes for perfect snapshots. For more beer information, the Musée des Bières Belges (081 41 11 02) has a fine collection of beer memorabilia, doodahs and objects of interest from all over the world.

Dinant

More than a speck on the map, Dinant has an easy way about it – which means it's easy to pass by. If you happen to be in the region, take advantage of the Cruises Along the Meuse, to travel to Namur, Freyr and other nearby destinations taking in the valley, woods and attempts at urbanisation that dot the shores. Do tip the guide, as they have been known to turn nasty.

Four hundred and eight steps take you to the top of the Citadelle de Dinant (082 22 36 70). Besides providing a great view of the region, there's

an arms museum, exhibits and a torture chamber in the in-house prison. It's slightly less carefree and jolly fun than the Citadelle de Namur.

Getting there

By train from Gare Centrale or Schuman to Namur, switch for Dinant; *by car* A4 to N97 near Achene, switch to N94.

Tourist information

37 rue Grande, 5500 Dinant (082 22 70 31). **Open** *Sept-Jun* 8.30am-8pm daily; *Jul-Aug* 8.30am-5pm daily.

Mariembourg

In Mariembourg, the Karting des Fagnes (060 31 26 70) offers go-karting enthusiasts what is reputed to be the longest track in Europe. Showers are available for those who want to freshen up after a session, and the canteen offers a panoramic view.

The Chemin de Fer à Vapeur de Trois Vallées (tel/fax 060 31 24 40) translates as the Three Valleys Steam Railway, which is as accurate a description as you need. It runs at a leisurely pace from Mariembourg through lush, green countryside into Givet in France. Nostalgic and fun, it's highly recommended.

Han-sur-Lesse

A tourist attraction largely because of the river Styx, an imaginatively named waterway flowing 100m below sea level. Stalactites and stalagmites, limestone bluffs, water rushing over jagged rocks are all illuminated during your ride through the Grotte de Han. An old steam train takes you to the site of the cave, slightly faster than an infant's crawl – but all the more charming for it.

Getting there

By train to Jemelle; *by car* N4 until between Hogne and Marche-en-Famenne, switch to N803.

Rochefort

The historical site of the battle between the Austrians and Lafayette, this is a hotspot for Belgian and Dutch tourists who have neither the time nor the money to make it to the Côte d'Azur but still want to bask in the sun. Best visited if you already happen to be in the area, because most of what would make the town stand out is in the past. This is evident at the Musée Archéologique du Château (084 21 25 06), in which the remains of the once-grand Château Comtal that houses the museum are actually more interesting than the artefacts on exhibit. The Grottes de Rochefort (084 21 20 80) also offers prehistoric appeal, with its tunnels, caverns, passages and streams running as deep as 60m underground.

Le Plateau du Gerny (084 22 18 08) is outside Rochefort, in the fly-speck-sized village of Humain, but it's the best restaurant in the area. Possessing a gentle country charm that is immediately relaxing, the restaurant specialises in local cuisine, with ingredients fresh from outlying farms. Should you eat so well you're unable to move on, the Hôtel le Limbourg (084 21 44 23) offers clean, quiet, affordable – if unspectacular – accommodation.

Getting there

By train from Gare Centrale or Schuman to Marloie; *by car* A4, switch to N911 near Ciergnon.

Tourist information

2 rue du Behogne, 5580 Rochefort (084 21 25 37). **Open** *Apr-Sept* 9am-12.30pm, 1-6pm, Mon-Fri; *Oct-Mar* 9am-12.30pm, 1-5pm, Mon-Fri.

Luxembourg

Far – but never too far – from the bustle of Brussels, the province that shares a border with the Grand Duchy of the same name is not short on touristic attractions. Much greener than Luxembourg you simply don't get. Lacking a major city to draw attention to it, it still attracts nature-lovers and ski enthusiasts, who flock to the Ardennes, which cover a good portion of Luxembourg. It has more animal reserves than any other province.

La Roche-en-Ardenne

World War II destroyed much of La Roche-en-Ardenne, which dates back to the Celts and the Romans and has seen the passage through it of Louis XIV, Philip II and Charles Quint. Today it has been largely rebuilt.

There are four attractions that together make La Roche a popular stop in this region. The Parc à Gibier (084 41 13 42) is a nature park featuring animals native to Belgium, of both farm and wild varieties. Children love it.

The Musée de la Bataille des Ardennes (084 41 17 25) is a more modest museum than the American Historical Center and Memorial (*see below* **Bastogne**), but it still merits a visit. It includes remnants of the era and the battle that took 114 Ardennais lives in 1944. Cars and motorcycles, photographs and mannequins dressed in period costume effectively bring the war home to you. The Ruins of Château Feodal (084 41 13 42) boast not only the big neolithic house of the former Kings of the Franks, but also its ancient Romanesque fort outside. And if you're feeling a little creative, do stop by Les Grès de la Roche pottery museum (084 41 18 78), where you can not only see some lovely ceramics, but also have a go at creating some.

Tourist information

15 place du Marché, 6980 La Roche-en-Ardenne (064 41 13 42). **Open** *Jul-Sept* 10am-noon, 2-5pm, Mon-Fri. *Oct-Jun* 10am-noon, 2-5pm, Mon, Tue, Thur, Fri.

Bastogne

The American Historical Center and Memorial in Bastogne (061 21 27 11) is dedicated to commemorating one event, the World War II Battle of Bastogne. The displays feature figures of all the principals as well as battle scenes.

Getting there

By train from Gare Centrale or Schuman to Libramont, switch for Bastogne; *by car* N4 to Semonchamps, go east on secondary road.

St Hubert

The namesake of this small town set amid woods was a young prince who ended up becoming the patron saint of hunters, due to his passion for the sport. St Hubert the town, dating back to the seventh century, is nowheresville for nightlife, but if you are in the mood for something a bit more cerebral, then it merits a visit. Among the buildings of note is the eleventh-century Basilique St Pierre St Paul St Hubert – its architectural styles are even more diverse than its name: late Renaissance, Gothic, sixteenth- and seventeenth-century classical all figure from the crypt to the steeple. The result is more harmonious in style than you would think. The old abbeys next to the basilique are somewhat less ornate, with sturdy oak doors and sedate marble hearths.

Getting there

By train from Gare Centrale or Schuman to Ciney, switch for Poix St Hubert; *by car* A4 to Forêt de Luchy, then north-west on N89.

Redu

The Village du Livre du Redu claims to have been the first village devoted completely to books, although Redu has only been devoted to books since 1984. It's more for collectors than book-lovers and avid readers – the emphasis is on rare books, though there are some lower-priced books for sale as well. In addition there are art galleries, gift shops, jewellery stores and other outlets.

Tourist information

(061 61 30 10).

Transinne

Right in the middle of the Ardennes, Transinne is the location of the Euro Space Center (061 65 64 65), which is the largest attraction of its kind in Belgium. Exhibits dedicated to the French *Ariane* and *Hermes* programmes, the *Mir* space station and the United States' Space Shuttle *Discovery*, available on video and in model form (sometimes two storeys high), make up the lion's share of the visit. Very impressive.

Ath your beck & call

The area around the city of Ath boasts several fine attractions, including the following:

Archéosites d'Aubechies

15 rue d'Abbaye, 7972 Aubechie-Beloeil (069 67 11 16). **Open** Easter-1 Nov.

The neolithic age is on display here in houses that have been recreated from that period. During the summer months, craftsmen come to give demonstrations on the different crafts of that period, such as metalwork and tanning leather. Two museums exhibiting Gallo-roman artefacts round out the educational experience.

Château d'Attre

8 avenue du Château, 7941 Attre (068 45 44 60). **Open** Apr-late Oct.

The management of the château has tried hard to avoid creating the mothballed atmosphere of most châteaux. Instead, it has succeeded in giving this eighteenth-century building a feeling of homeliness: fresh-cut flowers, framed photographs of children, newspapers left neatly behind on coffee tables, cars parked in the drive outside and desks set up in studies to look as though the person working there has just stepped away all make it seem so cosy and familial that you almost feel as if you are trespassing on someone else's hearth. Numerous lounges surround the château's park, with the original décor, well-preserved furniture and original wall coverings evoking Regency, Louis XIV and Louis XV periods. The grounds include centuries-old oak trees, which provide wonderful shade on the odd occasion that Belgium does actually have some sunshine.

Parc Paradisio

1 Domaine de Cambron, 7940 Cambron-Casteau (068 45 46 53). **Open** 10am-7pm daily.

Part nature reserve, part historic monument, this sanctuary for fowl from all over the world is contained in a thirteenth-century abbey. The abbey itself has an interesting history: it originally housed monks whose love of the finer things in life ran counter to the beliefs of most at the time – they were dubbed Cambron la Pervetie. The monks are long gone, and the area around the neoclassical tower, the crypt and the Grand Escalier inside is now home to two large ponds of waterfowl: black swans, pelicans and geese swim under tulip trees and sycamores. Elsewhere on the grounds, a wide array of parrots, macaws, parakeets and cockatoos reside in cages. All birds were bred in captivity or taken in after sustaining injuries in the wild. *Falconry exhibits throughout the day.*

Château de Beloeil

rue du Château, 7970 Beloeil (069 68 94 26). **Open** Apr-Nov.

Although the château dates back to the seventeenth century, it wasn't until war hero Charles-Joseph, a descendant of the line of royalty who had made the château their home, moved in that the Beloeil began to acquire some of the grandeur now associated with it. The park that gives on to the château was his initiative – so impressed was he by the English-style garden that he duplicated one here. Today it is private, but can be seen from afar. More accessible is the courtyard, which is especially majestic, with four round towers encircling it. Tens of rooms, lounges and chambers are turned out in tapestries, furnishings and other home accessories reaching back over the château's history. Unfortunately, as some of Charles-Joseph's heirs still live here, not all rooms are accessible to guests. The old library is especially worth a visit, with over 20,000 volumes spanning five centuries. There's a café housed in the château's chapel.

Bouillon

Bouillon is a tourists' bonanza as it offers both recreational and educational attractions for visitors. The Moulin de la Falize (061 46 62 00) has the kind of all-in-one sports facility impossible to find in major cities, because space there is at a premium. But here you can take advantage of a covered, heated swimming pool, bowling alleys, sauna, gym and camping grounds. There are mountain bikes for hire, and, in the winter, ski equipment.

The nearby Rapides du Saty are run by Moulin de la Falize and offer kayaking from March to November. A smallish go-kart racing track has just been opened at Karting (061 46 78 07), which also has a children's playground.

The nature park La Crête des Cerfs (061 46 71 52) offers an up-close look at wildlife, with bison, lynx and ostriches just a few of the animals you can inspect. Château Fort (061 46 62 57) lays claim to being the oldest and most interesting remnant of feudalism in Belgium. A glorious view of the town is afforded from the top of the château.

Getting there

By car A4 until Forêt de Luchy, then south-east on N89 until N828.

Tourist information

(061 46 62 57).

Torgny

Belgium's only real vineyard is to be found here, courtesy of the Romans' tenure in Torgny. The southernmost village in the country, blessed with a microclimate, Torgny is unapologetically small.

Getting there

By car A4 until Stockem, switch for N82 to Virton, take N811 to St Mard, switch to secondary road going south-east.

Durbury

Easy to miss on the map, Durbury has worked its quaintness over time, claiming to be the smallest town in the world to get some tourist recognition back in the 1970s. The ploy worked: busloads of

Dutch and Belgian tourists come year-round to see the medieval cobblestoned streets, ancient façades and almost Disney-like tweedom.

Getting there

By car N4 until Marche-en-Famenne, then north on N63 until Baillonville, then go east on N929.

Tourist information

(086 21 24 28).

Vielsalm

The village of Vielsalm sits amid hills and woods, offering breathtaking views as well as the Musée Coticule (080 21 57 68), which is housed in an old workshop and shows the history of *coticule*, a raw metal used in the fabrication of straight razors that, being unique to Vielsalm, was this region's bread and butter.

Disposable razors meant the end of *coticule*'s earning potential, so now the museum sits as the only testament to Vielsalm's importance.

Tourist information

(080 21 50 52).

Marche-en-Famenne

The oldest church in Belgium is located here, the eleventh-century Eglise Waha, as well as examples of Gothic and eighteenth-century architecture. Marche-en-Famenne also has a school for lace making, where lay men and women can visit the Musée de la Dentelle (084 31 21 35), a private home that has been transformed into one of the few lace museums in the country. The work of more than 800 lace makers from around Belgium, going back to the eighteenth century, as well as foreign pieces, and tools of the trade, are displayed here.

Tourist information

7 rue des Brasseurs, 6900 Marche-en-Famenne (084 31 21 35). **Open** *Oct-May* 9am-noon, 1.30-5.30pm, Mon-Sat. *Jun-Sept* 9am-noon, 1.30-5.30pm, Mon-Sat; 2-5pm Sun.

Hainaut

On the French border, this is one of the most overlooked provinces of Belgium, largely due to its lacking a major city on the same level as Ghent, Antwerp or Brussels (Charleroi, for the reasons listed below, doesn't count). Also, being in the shadow of France hasn't helped. The most Latin of Belgium's ten provinces, Hainaut follows its own time clock: don't expect to be in and out of a shop in a hurry, because Hainautiens have a habit (annoying or delightful, depending on your view) of taking their time. A large part of the Ardennes lies in Hainaut – on the whole, rather charming, if a bit slow.

Charleroi

This is the Black Country, so called because of the area's many coal mines. It may not be a popular tourist destination, but the city of Charleroi does hold some charms that, if you happen to be in the area, are worth a look.

Founded by the Romans, Charleroi is actually composed of two cities from the first conquests of Belgium and took on its present name in 1666. Louis XIV built the city up in that period, only to have the Spanish seize control in 1679. A constantly changing list of occupiers (from Austrian to Dutch to French to Spanish) wreaked havoc with Charleroi's development, until France took it under its wing for a relatively stable period of 20 years following the French Revolution. But Napoleon's defeat in Waterloo put an end to that.

The city flourished during the Industrial Revolution as its coal mines provided the resources and its people provided the manpower to sustain the economy. As social protection for workers was not yet considered important, many perished in the mines, with families being forced to work hellish hours. In 1886 a depression hit and the miners went on strike, followed by the foundries and glassworks. The owners of these businesses tried to suppress the action militarily, but lost out as grand social reforms began to be instituted.

When coal was king, everything was fine. But its decline devastated Charleroi, as the city was largely a one-industry town. As in most countries, the mines had provided work not only for the lower classes but also for the immigrant population: a look through Charleroi's telephone directories today reveals a wealth of Italian, Polish and Spanish surnames, the remnants of the influx of people from these countries coming to do the work that Belgians largely didn't want to do.

Charleroi has yet to find its feet. Like Detroit or northern coal-mining towns in the UK there is a permanent air of desperation: anyone who has the talent, luck and/or means to get out, flees. Those who stay behind are resigned, content with visits from or day trips to the outside world. This dissatisfaction is most clearly evinced in Charleroi's nightlife scene, which has a nationwide reputation as being one of the most violent and aggressive.

The city is divided into an uptown and a downtown section: downtown is tourist-central, with the higher proportion of hotels, restaurants and clubs. Of historical note is the tiny St Fiancre Chapel, a brick building from the seventeenth century that falls between uptown and downtown. More exceptional is Charleroi's Town Hall, which, built in 1936, is younger than its counterparts elsewhere in Belgium. It's a fine example of art deco architecture that can look a bit sinister in the wrong light. It also houses the Musée des Beaux Arts (071 23 02 94).

A chronologically correct presentation of the history of glass and the process of making it are on display at the Musée de Verre and the Musée Archéologique (071 31 08 38). Glass pieces from the Middle Ages to art deco and art nouveau styles are exhibited. An archaeology section takes up a small space on the ground floor, showing remnants of a Roman city from AD 2.

On the dining front, Le Trou Normand (071 32 51 34) gives you old-style Belgian and French cuisine in a pleasingly rough-hewn interior. Not a vegetarian's paradise, a good selection of meats, fish, poultry and (when in season) game is served. Moules de Zélande (071 32 50 97) is a seafood alternative, with mussels arriving daily and prepared in more than 30 different ways. Kitsch baroque is the décor of Cour de Miracles (071 30 22 71): lots of gold and red, plaster statuettes and yellow lighting give the joint a B-movie feel. Bubble Gum (071 30 28 68) is a charming take on Americana: cowskin bar stools, Budweiser and party music.

The Grand Hôtel Buisset (071 31 34 14) offers calm, modest-sized (25 rooms) accommodation that is modern and reasonably priced.

Charleroi has its annual carnival celebration just before Lent, while in nearby Jumet there is the Marché de la Madeleine parade on the Sunday closest to 22 July, when more than 2,000 men participate in a re-creation of a Napeoleonic army's descent on the city. For the acquisitive, there is the Brocante des Quais, a huge flea market that attracts bargain hunters every June.

Getting there
By train from Gare du Nord, Gare Centrale or Gare du Midi; *by car* N5.

Tourist information
by Gare Sud (071 31 82 18). **Open** 8.30am-noon, 1-5pm, Mon-Fri.

Ath

Ath is another city whose renown came after it was destroyed by marauders in the Middle Ages – they left only its Tower of Burbant standing. Today, this smallish city features little of note to interest the visitor, save the charming cafés surrounding the Grand Place, which is also the site of the impressive seventeenth-century Hôtel de Ville. *See p242* **Ath your beck & call.**

Getting there
By train from Gare du Nord, Gare Centrale or Gare du Midi; *by car* N6 to N7, then direct to Ath.

Soignies

This city known for its blue-stoned buildings has a heavily religious history. Its peak came in the fourteenth century courtesy of the textile industry, and since then its appeal has faded to an innocu-

ous charm that is easy to miss if you're driving through too fast.

Although a cemetery might seem a macabre choice of tourist sites, Le Vieux Cimitière possesses a kind of faded beauty that is strangely comforting. In the centre of the grounds is an immense chapel that, according to local authorities in such matters, is the first parish church of the twelfth century.

The rage for English gardens in Belgium is evident in the Château de Louvignies, one of the châteaux near Soignies in Chaussée-Notre-Dame-Louvignies. The other castle of note in the area is the Château d'Ecaussinnes-Lalaing (067 44 24 90), open from April to October, which is complemented by the chic but far from cheap Pilori restaurant nearby. Originally it was finished in the twelfth century in grey stone, but renovations three centuries later employed the blue stone that is characteristic of this area. From the religious objects that dominate the first floor of the château (which is also fitted with an infirmary) to the chapel on the grounds, this château is more impressive than intimate. In nearby Horrues, L'Eglise St Martin is an austere twelfth-century church that is furnished in the comparatively contemporary sixteenth-century style.

Also worth a look is the Moulin du Moulinet, a water-powered mill, which has been functioning daily for almost a century.

Getting there
By train from Gare du Nord, Gare Centrale or Gare du Midi; *by car* N6.

Tourist information
23 rue de la Régence, 7060 Soignies (tel/fax 067 33 46 93). **Open** 8am-noon, 1-4.35pm, Mon-Fri; 10am-noon, 2-5pm, Sat; 2-5pm Sun.

Tournai

Founded by Roman soldiers as a place to rest midway between Boulogne and Cologne, Tournai is the second oldest city in Belgium. Its long and complex history is fascinating: the capital of France, courtesy of Clovis (who preferred it to Paris), in the fifth century, an English cathedral city in the sixteenth century, and today again a little piece of France in Belgium.

The city still has remnants of its former occupiers: the English only left behind names such as Big Ben and the Grenadier Guards (which pubs bear as names) and an English rose gracing a fresco in the cathedral, which Henry VIII had painted. The French have fared better, influencing much of the culture largely from old allegiances – Tournai had been part of France for longer than it has been part of Belgium. French flags still fly in many parts of the town, and it's hard to tell the French from the Belgians: in fact, the citizens of Tournai are among the few Walloons who aren't insulted to be taken for French.

CLEVER MONET

The city today is either quaint or banal, depending on your tastes. More impressive for its past than its present, which is evidenced in its seven museums. The most impressive are the Musée d'Histoire Naturelle, which has a large collection of dioramas and biotopes, and the Musée des Beaux Arts, which was built by Victor Horta in the 1920s and contains works by Rubens, Monet and Van Gogh, among other greats. Horta's trademark willowy, art nouveau style is not in evidence – instead, it's his later, streamlined art deco design of galleries giving off from the courtyard that is still arguably as beautiful as any of the works displayed there. And for grandmothers and interior decorators, the porcelain of Tournai is on display at the new Musée des Arts Decoratifs. The belfry of Tournai, the oldest in Europe and a major attraction, is currently being restored.

Much of the old quarter was lost to bombing in World War II, but Romanesque churches and stone houses going back to the thirteenth century still stand in some places. The cathedral dominating the town is considered one of the finest in Belgium. The huge, sober interior is supported by sturdy Roman pillars adorned at the top with carvings of medieval faces and mythological beasts.

Other major sites include the statue of Gabrielle Petit, a local heroine who was executed by the Germans on April Fool's Day in 1916. Her final words? 'I will show them that a Belgian woman knows how to die.'

Should the hunger take you, Lapin Vert (069 23 59 39) offers rabbit with prunes and other regional dishes in the setting of a converted pharmacy. If Italian and Belgian cuisine is more your palate, then Les Trois Pommes d'Orange (069 23 59 82) is a must as much for what's on the menu as for the warm ambience. And for drinks, try the Latchodrom, which will be worth writing home about: a candlelit prehistoric grotto decorated with animal skins is the backdrop for intimate conversation. Le Purgatoire offers live music with drinks in a convivial setting.

If you want to stay, contact Agritourisme in Brussels (230 72 95) to find out about farmhouses for rent near the city by the week or the weekend. Le Panoramique (069 23 31 11/fax 069 23 33 23) provides a gorgeous view of the city from Mont St Aubert from the large bay windows that are a feature of most rooms. The small pool is even open to take a dip, weather permitting. Ultra-charming.

Getting there

By train from Gare du Nord, Gare Centrale or Gare du Midi; *by car* N6, switch to N7 at Halle, continue to Tournai.

Tourist information

14 rue Vieux Marché aux Poteries, 7500 Tournai (069 22 20 45/fax 069 21 62 21). **Open** 9am-7pm Mon-Fri; 10am-1pm, 3-6pm, Sat, Sun.

Mons

Mild, gentle and softly seductive are the best words to describe Mons (or Bergen in Flemish). This is the administrative capital of Hainaut, with a history that reaches back to the Romans. The city's existence began with a monastery founded by Waudru, who went on to become patron saint of the city. Mons prospered in the Middle Ages as the centre of the region's textile activity. Religious wars and bombings courtesy of Louis XIV brought down the city by the end of the seventeenth century. Only with Belgian independence did Mons regain some kind of social stability.

LEFT 'ERE

The Maison Van Gogh (065 35 56 11), where the Dutch master lived from 1879-80, features an audio-visual exhibit and a living space that the curators have tried to preserve as Vincent would have known it. The Collégiale Ste Waudru (065 33 55 80) is a splendid example of Brabant Gothic architecture, built and strengthened between the thirteenth and seventeenth centuries. Religious artefacts and curios are displayed throughout. The Musée des Beaux Arts (065 34 95 55) has a collection of engravings, paintings and sculpture from 1400 to the present day.

A seventeenth-century infirmary is the setting for the Musée du Folklore et de la Vie Montoise (065 31 43 57), which shows an assortment of everyday objects from the past – compasses, rulers, chairs and tables. What was considered banal in the past takes on ironic, tragic or amusing significance when looked at through modern eyes: one fascinating artefact is a window rescued from an orphanage, which served as the depository for unwanted children. The Musée François Duesberg (065 36 31 64) has a unique collection of French gold and bronze objects, including clocks and busts.

BON MONS

A new museum in town, the Musée du Château Comtal (065 33 55 80), is the former home of the Counts of Hainaut and has one of the best views of Mons and the region. Medieval icons and the like make up the majority of the collection, exhibited in the eleventh-century Chapelle St Calixte, which has recently been restored.

Outside of Mons, near the French border, is the industrial archaeological site of Grand Hornu (065 77 07 12). A notable example of the functional urbanism that in 1810 preceded the Industrial Revolution. Founder Henri du Gorge built the neo-classical, self-contained workers' complex out of nothing. It is interesting for its aesthetic appeal as well as the function of its buildings.

Back in Mons, chips – or *frites* – are served at Friterie Bily, the best friture in town. The queues can be long, but the portions are the definition of value for money. It's just 50m from the Grand

Place – anyone in Mons will be able to point you directly to it, it's so well known. A tourist trap is what No Maison (065 34 74 74) has unfortunately become: its location on the Grand Place has done it in, in terms of being a magnet for busloads of visitors. The food is standard Belgian fare, which compares well with the cuisine of other countries. If the hustle and bustle of a brasserie setting does not deter you, the prices are actually OK. Chez Henry (065 35 23 06) has an attractive brick interior that, in its sensible style, reflects its clientele: mostly city workers. The menu features grilled meat and fish and homemade soups and desserts.

Intimacy is the key to the appeal of Le Chinchin (065 84 29 15), located in the cellar of the St Georges hostel. A favourite of people to meet up in before a night on the town or to go to as the night winds down. The name is French for 'cheers'. L'Arnaque (065 36 40 16) has seen better days, but it is still a nightlife staple: you always end up there at some point in the evening. Loud and in the middle of the bar district, so there's always somewhere else to hop to if this doesn't strike your fancy.

Accommodation in Mons includes the luxurious Château de la Cense au Bois (065 31 60 00) that has large, comfortable beds, huge bathrooms and a breathtaking view of the surrounding wood: it is not cheap. Less dear is the more central Hôtel St Georges (065 31 16 29). The rooms are comfortable.

Getting there

By train from Gare du Nord, Gare Centrale or Gare du Midi; *by car* N6.

Tourist information

22 Grand Place, 7000 Mons (065 33 55 80). **Open** *Apr-Sept* 9am-6.30pm Mon-Sat; 10am-1.30pm Sun; *Oct-Mar* 9am-5pm Mon-Sat; 10.30am-1.30pm Sun.

Binche

The Golden Age of Binche came in the sixteenth century, when it was passed on to Marie of Hungary. She received emperors in the grand palace that she had constructed, becoming celebrated for her lavish parties and being the 'hostess with the mostest' until the French (as was their habit, back then) destroyed the city. Although its size would not lead you to believe it, every Belgian knows Binche. The reason? Its yearly carnival outshines others throughout the country.

Most ancient pagan rituals do possess an oddness about them when looked at through today's eyes, and Binche's carnival is no exception. This one-day event goes back to the time of Marie of Hungary and features the *gilles* de Binche, chosen participants who are supposed to be dressed like South American Indians – or at least a medieval European idea of what a South American Indian should look like. Why choose a South American Indian to be involved in a celebration to mark the beginning of Lent? South America had been discovered a few decades before, and evidently the powers-that-were decided it would be a cool idea to have participants dressing up as the latest found culture – not dissimilar to the way in which we sport ethnic tattoos and nose rings and turn saris and dashikis into western fashion statements.

In the carnival each *gille* is masked and dressed in a tunic stuffed with a pillow in the belly, trousers emblazoned with lions, elaborate hats and belts with curled-toed shoes – in short, looking as much like an Inca as the Pope. They meet in front of the Town Hall, with spectators, clowns and harlequins all ready to start the procession. Everyone dances to folk music played on tambourines and mandolins, as the *gilles* do their *chapeaux* up in plumes and toss oranges to the crowd of spectators. A large tourist contingent is always on hand for this freaky event every year, which goes to show that controlled substances were very much a part of life way back when.

At the Musée International du Carnaval et du Masque (064 33 57 41) the bronze statue of the *gille* in the front lets you know that you are entering a building dedicated to frivolity. Masks, costumes and other objects of interest from carnivals around the world are on display in this former college for monks. Some of the models are borderline scary – which means that children susceptible to nightmares should be guided very carefully. A special section is devoted to items and explanations of the carnivals of Wallonia, with displays of how the costumes are made.

ANCIENT REGIME

A short drive from Binche is the Musée Royal de Mariemont (064 21 21 93), sitting in a 50-hectare (123-acre) park once owned by Marie of Hungary. The park features ruins of the eighteenth-century château that once sat here, now overgrown with ivy. The museum stands out against the aged environment: it's a modern cinder-block of a building that has used the remains of another château partly destroyed by fire to achieve its look, with mixed results. The collections are admirable, however: ancient Egyptian, Roman and Greek pieces all figure, as do funeral masks and items from the Far East. Not the largest museum you will ever have visited, but a decent one for its size.

The Eco-Musée du Bois-du-Luc (064 28 20 00) makes for an interesting visit, but make sure you have a tour guide – otherwise, it's easy to get lost in this old industrial area. Disused trains, miners' houses and other dormant buildings that were once important parts of town life in Bois-du-Luc.

Getting there

By train from Gare du Nord, Gare Centrale or Gare du Midi; *by car* N27.

Tourist information

14 rue St Paul, 7130 Binche (064 33 37 21). **Open** 8am-noon, 12.30-4.30pm, Mon-Thur; 8am-noon Fri.

Directory

Directory

Essential information

Visas

All European Union (EU) and Swiss citizens need to show a national identity card or passport when they enter Belgium. Americans, Canadians, Australians, New Zealanders and Japanese need a valid passport; no visa is required to enter as a tourist.

Customs

For non-EU citizens and anyone bringing in duty-free goods, the following customs allowances apply when entering Belgium:

● 200 cigarettes **or** 100 cigarillos **or** 50 cigars **or** 250g (8.82 ounces) tobacco;

● 2l still table wine **and** either 1l spirits/strong liqueurs (over 22% alcohol) **or** 2l fortified wine (under 22% alcohol)/ sparkling wine/other liqueurs;

● 50g perfume;

● 250ml toilet water;

● 500g coffee **or** 200g coffee extracts/coffee essences;

● 100g tea **or** 40g tea extracts/essences;

● other goods for non-commercial use up to a maximum value of 7,300BF.

Since the EU member countries became one big happy family with the Single Market in early 1993, EU citizens over the age of 17 aren't required to make a customs declaration. That means you can bring as much duty-paid beer or wine as you can carry. There's also no limit to the amount of foreign currency that can be brought in or out of Belgium. For more information, call the Belgian Administration of Customs & Excise on 210 30 11 (9am-5pm Mon-Fri).

Insurance

As members of the European Union, both the UK and Ireland have reciprocal health agreements with Belgium. You'll need to apply for the necessary E111 form back home first. British citizens can get this by filling in the application form in leaflet SA30, available in Department of Social Security offices or at post offices. Try to get the E111 at least two weeks before you leave. Make sure you read the small print on the back of the form so you know how to obtain medical or dental treatment at a reduced charge. The E111 doesn't cover all medical costs – for example, dental treatment – so it's wise to take out private insurance. Before shelling out money on health insurance, college students should check whether their university's medical plan already provides cover. A homeowner's policy may similarly cover holidays. Non-EU citizens should take out full private insurance before they visit. In the US, STA and Council Travel and most other travel agencies offer short- and long-term coverage policies. Remember to keep all receipts for medicine or treatment that you have paid for. You'll need it to claim reimbursement from your insurance company once back home. (*See also* **Health**.)

For long-term visitors, after six months of residence you are eligible for coverage under Belgium's basic health insurance system, the *mutuelle*. It allows you to recover a large chunk of doctors' and dentists' bills, and other costs. Regular payments are automatically deducted from your salary. For contact telephone numbers look in the *Yellow Pages* under Mutualités/Ziekenfondsen.

Money matters

The unit of Belgian currency is the franc, abbreviated to BF or FB. And it's worth bearing in mind that a Belgian franc is worth much less than a French franc. Exchange rates at the time of writing were: £1 = 47BF/US$1 = 31BF. It comes in 1, 5, 20 and 50 coins. There is also a 50-centime coin (half a franc). Banknotes come in 100, 200, 500, 1,000, 2,000, 5,000 and 10,000 denominations.

Try to keep a few 5BF and 20BF coins handy. They are constantly needed, whether for a public phone, supermarket trolley deposit, toilet fee or a tip. Also be on the lookout for Luxembourg coins slipped into your change. They are on a parity with the Belgian franc and are accepted in Belgium, but are not very popular and can be a pain to dump. Belgians tend to use cash for petty transactions, and debit cards (Bancontact or Mister Cash) for more expensive purchases. Although not as widely used, credit cards are fairly common, especially in restaurants, shops and hotels. Eurocheques are best avoided, since most banks charge a 450BF fee for each one.

Banks & foreign exchange

Banks are the best places to exchange money. Generally they open from about 9am to between 3.30pm and 5pm on weekdays. A few have half-days on Saturdays. It's wise to call and check opening times beforehand as hours vary.

After banking hours you can change money and traveller's cheques at offices in Gare du Nord, Gare du Midi (7am-11pm daily) and Gare Centrale (8am-9pm daily), although they don't give advances on credit cards. However, several banks at the airport give cash advances on MasterCard (called EuroCard in Belgium) or Visa, as well as convert currency. Most open early and close around 10pm. Banque Bruxelles Lambert (BBL), for example, opens daily from 7am to 9.45pm. Kredietbank also has a branch at the airport.

American Express has two branches in Brussels, which issue traveller's cheques, replace lost or stolen cards, offer cash advances and even book flights for various fees. **American Express Gold Card Travel Service** *2 place Louise, 1050 (676 27 33). Métro Louise.* **Open** 9am-5pm Mon-Fri; 9.30am-noon Sat.
American Express Travel & Financial Services *100 boulevard du Souverain, 1170 (676 26 26/24-hour Customer Service 676 21 21). Métro Hermann Debroux.* **Open** 9am-1pm, 2-5pm Mon-Fri.

Report **lost or stolen credit cards** to the police and the 24-hour services listed below.
Diners Club *36 rue Ravenstein, 1000 (515 95 11/fax 513 52 66). Métro Gare Centrale.* **Open** 9am-5pm Mon-Fri. After hours, the above telephone number handles calls 24 hours a day.
MasterCard (EuroCard) *(24-hour toll free 0800 150 96).*
Visa International *(24-hour toll free 0800 187 56).*

Police & security

The number of violent crimes is low compared to London or New York, but one has to be on the lookout for petty theft. Pickpockets and purse-snatchers are part of the city's landscape, especially in cinema

auditoria and particularly crowded areas. The emergency number for the police is **101**.

Time & weather

Belgium is one hour ahead of British time. The Belgian climate is mild. Winters are very cold and damp, without much snow; summers are warm and often hot. Rain, however, is a force to be reckoned with all year round. The best line of defence in dealing with Brussels' fickle weather is always to bring an extra jumper or two and a collapsible umbrella. The biggest drawback to **winter** in Brussels is the shortness of the days. Much of the city stays at home or in cosy bars in the evening, since daylight only lasts from 8am to 4pm in December and January. The city starts to shake off the winter blues at Easter. **Spring** is officially welcomed as attractions open and activities, dormant during winter, start up again. In April and May, average temperatures range between 4C (40F) and 16C (60F). The heat picks up in June and July, reaching the mid-twenties (seventies) and occasionally hitting the high twenties (eighties). The flip side to depressingly short, dark winter days is the seemingly endless days of **summer** in Brussels. It's not uncommon to sit out on a café terrace at 10pm with the sky still light. **Autumn** is often rainy, with temperatures usually around 10C-16C (50F-60F) throughout October.

Tipping & VAT

Service and VAT are included in hotel and restaurant prices, though people will throw in a few extra francs when service has been exceptional. At lower-price restaurants, round up the bill by a few francs. At mid-priced restaurants customers usually kick in up to five per

cent extra. At first-class restaurants it's customary to add an extra ten per cent. Tips are also included in metered taxi fares, which are steep. Brace yourself for additional charges for baggage, Sundays and night trips.

At cinemas and theatres, tipping the attendant 20BF for a programme is expected. Although there's no charge for a public loo, it's customary to leave between 5BF and 20BF for the attendant.

Tourist information

TIB
Hôtel de Ville, Grand Place, 1000 (513 89 40/fax 514 45 38). Métro Bourse or Gare Centrale. **Open** *31 Mar-30 May, 1 Oct-31 Oct* 9am-6pm Mon-Fri; 9am-1pm, 2-6pm, Sat, Sun. *1 June-30 Sep* 9am-7pm Mon-Fri; 9am-1pm, 2-7pm, Sat, Sun. *1 Nov-30 Mar* 9am-6pm Mon-Fri; 9am-1pm, 2-6pm Sat; 1-5pm Sun.
This cramped little office is conveniently located on Grand Place. The English-speaking staff can offer tips on what to see in Brussels and how to go about it. They can also book rooms. For 80BF you can buy the *Brussels Guide and Map*, which provides complete information on sights within walking distance of the city centre. Eurocheques and traveller's cheques are accepted.

Belgian Tourist Information Office
63 rue du Marché aux Herbes, 1000 (504 03 90/fax 504 02 70). Métro Bourse or Gare Centrale. **Open** *1 Jun-30 Sep* 9am-7pm Mon-Fri; 9am-1pm, 2-7pm Sat, Sun. *1-31 Oct* 9am-6pm Mon-Fri; 9am-1pm, 2-6pm, Sat, Sun. *1 Nov-30 Mar* 9am-6pm Mon-Fri; 9am-1pm, 2-6pm, Sat, Sun. *1-31 May* 9am-6pm Mon-Fri; 9am-1pm, 2-6pm, Sat, Sun.
If you plan to make an excursion out of the city, this is the place to contact. The national tourist service, located in a handsome old building, provides information about the whole of Belgium. One of the most useful books they offer is the annual *Tourist Attractions Guide* covering the whole country. The office is broken down into Flemish and French sections. If you're planning a trip to Bruges or a weekend on the coast, ask for the Flanders Tourist Office. They sell a useful brochure, *Le Pays Flamand de Vos Vacances* (95BF), which lists over 200 quick trip ideas in Flanders. For information about the French-

speaking region, ask for the Walloon Tourist Office. They can advise on tourist attractions and have loads of info on accommodation. Book a room through BelsudReservation (504 02 80/fax 514 53 35).

Waterloo Tourist Information Centre

149 chaussée de Bruxelles, 1410 (354 99 10/fax 354 22 23). Phone for directions. **Open** *1 Nov-31 Mar* 10.30am-5pm daily; *1 Apr-31 Oct* 9.30am-6.30pm daily.

War buffs, call this centre first. They can direct you to all the key places involved in the great battle, including Napoleon's former HQ. A nearby location hosts a panorama and videos about the battle – informative but lacking historical context.

Embassies

It's advisable to phone to check opening hours. Some situations may need an appointment. In emergencies it's worth ringing after hours; staff may be on hand to deal with crises. For embassies or consulates not listed, check the *Yellow Pages*.

American Embassy *27 boulevard du Regent, 1000 (508 21 11). Métro Arts-Loi.* **Open** 9am-noon Mon-Fri.

Australian Embassy *6 rue Guimard, 1040 (231 05 00). Métro Arts-Loi.* **Open** 9am-noon, 2-5pm, Mon-Fri (visas morning only).

British Embassy *85 rue Arlon, 1040 (287 62 11). Métro Maelbeek.* **Open** 9.30am-noon, 2.30-4.30pm, Mon-Fri (passports morning only).

Canadian Embassy *2 avenue de Tervuren, 1040 (741 06 11). Métro Merode.* **Open** 9am-noon, 2-4.30pm, Mon-Fri.

Irish Embassy *89 rue Froissart, 1040 (230 53 37). Métro Schuman.* **Open** 10am-1.30pm Mon-Fri.

New Zealand Embassy *47-48 boulevard de Regent, 1000 (512 10 40). Métro Arts-Loi or Madou.* **Open** 9am-1pm, 2-3.30pm, Mon-Fri. Other enquiries, call for an appointment.

Useful numbers

Telephone **101** for the police and **100** for fire or ambulance. For non-urgent medical advice ring **105** or **479 18 18** or **648 40 14**. For out-of-hours emergency dental help ring **426 10 26**. For advice on any other emergency, from the trivial to the mundane, call the **Community Help Service**

(CHS) Helpline on 648 40 14. *See below* **Support groups**.

Other useful numbers
(Fr = French; Fl = Flemish)
Operator assistance/ reverse-charge calls
1324 *Fr*, 1224 *Fl*.
Directory enquiries (domestic)
1307 *Fr*, 1207 *Fl*; **(international)**
1304 *Fr*; 1204 *Fl (English spoken)*.
Telegrams 1325 *Fr*, 1225 *Fl*.
Time 1300 *Fr*, 1200 *Fl*.
Wake-up service 1348 *Fr*, 1248 *Fl* (or set the time yourself – eg to be woken at 6.15am, dial 1348 06 15 0).
Act Together (AIDS) *(511 33 33/fax 512 09 09)*.
Alcoholics Anonymous *(537 82 24)*.
Al-Anon English-speaking Group *(762 76 53/771 52 64)*.
Gas leaks: *244 34 54; 512 05 06*.
Overeaters Anonymous (includes anorexia and bulimia) *(502 47 71)*.
Poison control centre *(345 45 45)*.

Street names

When addressing an envelope, write the house number after the street name and place the postcode before the city, as in the following example: Monsieur Ledoux, avenue Louise 100, 1050 Bruxelles. To avoid confusion between the numbers 7 and 1, get into the habit of crossing your 7s.

Public toilets

Public toilets in Brussels, as is the case in most major cities, are not very clean. Most city centre restaurants don't mind you using their loos – though you are expected to cough up a few francs for the attendant.

Numbers

Dates are written as follows: day, month, year.

When writing figures, Belgians use commas where Americans and Britons would use decimal points and vice versa: two thousand five hundred Belgian francs is written as 2.500,00 BF.

Times are written in a 24-hour military style. For example, 4pm is 16:00.

Public holidays

New Year's Day; Easter Monday; Labour Day (1 May); Ascension Day (sixth Thursday after Easter); Pentecostal Whit Monday (seventh Monday after Easter); Belgian National Day (21 July); Assumption (15 August); All Saints' Day (1 November); Armistice Day (11 November); Christmas Day (25 December).

Although it is not an official holiday, banks and government offices usually close on 15 Nov for King's Day. And as if the country didn't have enough holidays, the Belgians make a habit of tacking on more free days to make long weekends even longer. If a holiday falls on a Tuesday or Thursday, most offices, by tradition, will 'make the bridge' (*faire le pont/de brug maken*) and observe a four-day weekend. The longest of these 'bridges' is Easter, when many Belgians embark on short trips across Europe.

As with everything in Belgium, the French and Flemish communities celebrate separate regional holidays. A day off on 11 July marks the anniversary of the Battle of the Golden Spurs in 1302 for the Flemish region of Flanders, while a holiday on 27 Sept commemorates the end of French-speaking Wallonia's revolution for independence from Holland in 1830.

Post

Post offices are generally open 9am-5pm Mon-Fri, but times can vary according to branch. If you need to post something urgently, try the central post office next to Gare du Midi on 48a avenue Fosny, 1060. It's open 24 hours daily. Letters mailed to the UK and other European countries usually take three days. Air mail to the US takes a week or so.

Postal rates

A letter weighing up to 20g costs 16BF to any EU country, and 13BF if left unsealed. Mail to non-EU countries costs 30BF up to 20g. Due to the complexity of the postage system, it's best to buy stamps at a post office rather than from a vending machine. Price is determined by the size of the envelope. Stick to using Belgian envelopes as non-standard sizes – even if different by only a fraction of an inch – can jack up the cost of postage. They *will* measure.

Sending packages

Packages up to 2kg can be mailed from any post office. Anything heavier should be taken to a post office at a railway station or the airport. All packages weighing more than 20kg must be shipped. The exception is if you use EMS Taxipost, an express delivery service offered by the Belgian postal system. Its limit is 27kg. Taxipost guarantees delivery within 24-72 hours. It's cheaper but also a bit slower than other express delivery companies. Call your local branch for prices.

DHL International

(715 50 50). **Open** 24 hours Mon-Sat. Can express deliver to most parts of the world. In the downtown area, pick-ups can be made until 8.30pm; in other areas, packages must be picked up before 5pm or 6pm. Call a day in advance if you want to send something on Saturday.

Telephones

To phone Brussels from outside Belgium, first dial the international code (00 from Britain), followed by 32 (the code for Belgium), then 2 (the code for Brussels), and finally the seven-digit number. Using the Yellow and White Pages in Brussels is a cinch, as both include an English index.

Public telephones

Public telephone booths are found at stations, post offices and other usual locations. There are several close to the Grand Place, near place de Brouckère and the Bourse. Booths sporting European flags can be used for direct-dial international calls. Coin-operated public phones accept 5BF and 20BF coins. Local calls cost a minimum of 10BF. Many public phones accept only prepaid electronic telephone cards. You can buy these at post offices, stations, newsstands and some banks and supermarkets (200BF for 20 units; 1000BF for 105 units).

Making calls

To call overseas, dial 00 then the country code and number (Australia 61; Canada 1; France 33; Germany 49; Holland 31; Ireland 353; New Zealand 64; UK 44; USA 1). To call other parts of Belgium, dial 0 plus the city code and number (Antwerp 3; Bruges 5; Ghent 91; Liège 41). To call Belgium from abroad, dial the international code then 32, and then 2 if you want Brussels.

International calls are expensive. Rates are a little lower on Sundays, holidays and between 8pm-8am. But if you plan to stay in Belgium for an extended period, the best way to save on calls is to sign on with a discount call service such as **Kallback** (call 00 1 206 216 1200 in the US for more information). For a short-term stay, a calling card with **Sprint** or **AT&T** is recommended. Despite a surcharge for each call, rates are lower than Belgacom's.

Faxes

You can always find a working telephone, buy a telecard or send a fax, telex or telegram at TT (*Telephone-Telegraphe/ Telefoon-Telegraaf*) centres.

The one on 17 boulevard de l'Impératrice is open daily from 7am-10pm.

Mobile phones & pagers

Belgium is part of the growing European mobile telephone network called GSM. Telephones on this system work in most of Western Europe and even beyond. You can rent GSMs at the airport or from some car hire agencies. The rental fee is usually low but the cost per call is high. The price to buy ranges from 10,000BF to 25,000BF. The dialling prefix for mobile phones on Belgium's only network, Proximus, is 075.

Most pagers work simply: dial the pager number and after the recording punch in your phone number and end with the # key. Pagers usually cost a few thousand francs with a monthly charge of several hundred. Some work beyond Belgium, extending to Holland and Luxembourg.

Health

Belgium has an excellent healthcare system. Most doctors are fluent in English.

Doctors

Most doctors with private practices don't have receptionists, preferring to handle the administration of payments and appointments themselves. You can walk in without an appointment during weekday office hours. If you are too sick to go in, some doctors will make house calls. After hours, you can often reach your physician (or one on call) through an answering service. Even if you're insured, expect to pay for your visit on the spot in cash or with a cheque. The same goes for pharmacies. Hang on to all receipts for reimbursement from your insurance company.

Directory

Hospitals

Outpatient clinics at private or university hospitals have an excellent reputation worldwide for their state-of-the-art technology, but often suffer from overcrowded waiting rooms and bureaucracy. Despite the drawbacks, they have a convenient concentration of specialists in one place, as well as laboratory and X-ray facilities on hand.

The following hospitals offer consultations and can provide 24-hour emergency assistance. Call first for consultation hours.

Hôpital Universitaire St Luc *10 avenue d'Hippocrate, 1200 (764 11 11/fax 764 3703). Métro Alma.*
Hôpital Erasme *808 route de Lennik, 1070 (555 31 11/fax 555 44 05). Métro Veeweyde.*
Hôpital St Pierre *322 rue Haute, 1000 (535 31 11/fax 535 40 06). Métro Porte de Hal.*
Hôpital Brugmann *2 place van Gehuchten, 1020 (477 21 11/fax 479 97 02). Métro Houba-Brugmann.*

Emergencies with children

Hôpital Universitaire des Enfants Reine Fabiola (paediatric emergency room) *15 avenue Jean Jacques Cocq, 1020 (477 31 00/477 31 01). Métro Heysel.* **Open** *emergencies* 24 hours daily; *consultations* 9-11.30am, 2-4.30pm, Mon-Fri; 9am-noon Sat.
Hôpital St Pierre *322 rue Haute, 1000 (535 43 60). Métro Porte de Hal.*

Ambulances

In an emergency, dial 100 and a medical crew will take the patient by ambulance to the nearest hospital. A doctor's approval is needed to transfer the patient to another hospital. If the situation is not so urgent, call Red Cross Ambulance Service on 105 to go to the hospital of your choice. GPs and dentists who are off duty usually have a tape recording of emergency information. Otherwise call 479 18 18 or 648 40 14 for 24-hour emergency medical assistance; and 426 10 26 for emergency

dental help (evenings 9pm-7am; weekends 24 hours; holidays 7am-9pm).

Alternative medicine

Homeopathy is still considered alternative medicine in Belgium. Listed below are two practitioners in Brussels. Call the Federation of Medical Homeopathy on 511 05 49 for further information.
Dr Dany Dejonghe *2 De Robianostraat, Tervuren 3080 (767 56 57). Tram 44.* **Open** *appointments* 8-11am, 3-5pm, Mon-Fri; *medical information* 7-8pm Mon-Fri.
Dr Paul Taub *5 avenue de la Closière, 1410 (354 12 00). Métro Albert.* **Open** 9am-5pm Mon-Fri.

Pharmacies

Pharmacies (*pharmacies/ apotheeks*) are marked with a green cross. Most are open 9am-6pm/7pm Mon-Fri. Some also open Saturday mornings or afternoons. When closed, each pharmacy displays a list of alternative pharmacies open after hours.

Dentists

Dental care in Belgium is of a high standard. The Community Liaison Office of the American Embassy (513 38 30 ext 2227) can provide a list of English-speaking dental practitioners, as can the Community Help Service Helpline (648 40 14).

Chiropractors

Belgian Chiropractors' Union
(091 221 76 58). **Open** 24 hours daily.
Contact this Ghent-based association for a list of about 20 chiropractors in the Brussels area.

Poison control centres

Centre Antipoisons/ Antigifcentrum
(345 45 45). **Open** 24 hours daily.
A group of physicians man this free helpline. They will try to determine if someone has swallowed a poisonous substance and offer advice on what measures to take.

Contraception

Condoms are sold at supermarkets and pharmacies. Birth control pills can be bought at pharmacies with a doctor's prescription.

Vets

Check *Vétérinaires/ Dierenartzen* in the Liberal Professions section of the *Yellow Pages*. Veterinary surgeries are identified by a blue cross. For an English-speaking vet, try the CHS Helpline (648 40 14) for recommendations. In an emergency (weekends and evenings) call 538 1699.

Support groups

Brussels' large foreign community has established an extensive network of support groups. Unless indicated, the groups below are for English speakers. More are listed at the back of the *Bulletin*.

Community Help Service (CHS) Helpline
(648 40 14). **Open** 24 hours daily.
A group of 42 trained English-speaking volunteers take turns manning the phones and can handle problems ranging from the critical to the mundane. They can also refer you to other specialists. There is no charge for callers. To make an appointment for a private face-to-face counselling session, call 647 67 80 (rates determined by one's means).

AIDS

Act Together
(511 33 33/fax 512 09 09).
An HIV/AIDS support group that organises referrals, arranges buddy-ing and runs a helpline on 512 05 05.

Alcoholism/eating disorders

Alcoholics Anonymous (537 82 24) offers daily meetings in English or counselling by phone. **Al-Anon English-speaking Group** (762 76 53/771 52 64) gives phone counselling to friends and relatives of alcoholics. It holds meetings every Tuesday at 8pm at the International Cultural Affairs Center, 8 rue Amédée Lynen, 1040 (Métro Madou). **Overeaters Anonymous** (502 47 71) is a self-help group for sufferers of anorexia or bulimia. Call for information.

Rape/battered women

Amazone
10 rue du Méridien, 1210 (229 38 00/fax 229 38 01). Métro Botanique or Madou/tram 92, 93, 94/bus 61, 65, 66. **Open** 9am-5pm Mon-Fri.
Various women's groups – including La Coordination des Groupes Contre la Violence Faite aux Femmes – and a restaurant are housed here. The emphasis is on sexual equality, but it is also a gay-friendly centre.

Le Refuge (Collectif pour Femmes Battues)
29 rue Blanche, 1060 (647 00 12). Tram 93, 94. **Open** 9am-7pm Mon-Fri; 9.30am-5pm Sat, Sun.
The Collective for Battered Women can be of help if you speak French. Otherwise try the CHS Helpline.

SOS Viol
29 rue Blanche, 1060 (534 36 36). Tram 93, 94. **Open** 9.30am-5.30pm Mon-Fri.
This is mainly a French-speaking support group for rape victims. A few staff members speak basic English. For after-hours assistance try the CHS Helpline.

Lost property

Report lost belongings to the nearest police inspector's office or police HQ on rue du Marché au Charbon (517 96 11). Ask for a certificate of loss for insurance purposes. If you lose your passport, contact your local embassy or consulate (*see above* **Embassies**).

Air

If you've lost an item on a flight to Brussels, you need to contact your airline. Sabena and Belgavia are the handling agents that represent most of the major airlines.

Sabena Airlines *(723 60 11).* **Open** 24 hours daily. Contact the Belgian airline for any items left on their flights. They also represent KLM, Air France, Swiss Air and Austrian Airlines.
Belgavia *(723 07 07).* **Open** 6am-11pm daily. Belgavia is the handling agent for British Airways, Lufthansa, Alitalia and Iberia among others.

Airport

If you've misplaced something at the airport, try any of the lost and found numbers below. There's usually someone on duty who speaks English.
Belgian Police (Gendarmerie/Rijkswacht) *(715 62 11).* **Open** 24 hours daily. The lost property office is in the new main terminal on the departure level near border control. Although there's no office number, directions are indicated by overhead signs.
Airport Police (Police Aeroportuaire/Luchthaven-politie) *(753 70 00).* **Open** 24 hours daily.
They have their own building next to the Sheraton Hotel and opposite the departure hall.
Airport Authorities (Regie des Voies Aerienne/ Regie der Luchtwegen) *(753 68 20).* **Open** 8am-4pm Mon-Fri.
Anything not claimed at either of the police offices ends up here, in office 418 on the departure level, in the old part of the terminal building. Follow signs for F14 – just before the entrance you'll find steps leading to the office.

Rail

For articles left on a train, enquire at the nearest railway station or check with the main rail lost property office at Gare du Nord (224 61 12).

Métro, buses & trams

STIB/MIVB *Porte de Namur, 1050 (515 23 94).* **Open** 9.30am-5pm Mon-Sat. The STIB/MIVB lost property office is inside Porte de Namur Métro station next to the Press Shop.

Opening times

Banks

Most banks open at 9am and close between 3.30pm and 5pm. Some also close for lunch.

Museums

Most museums are open 9am to 4pm Tuesday to Saturday, and sometimes on Sunday. They close on Mondays. Several are only open from Easter Sunday to September. It's wise to call the museum before visiting.

Offices

Many close early on Friday, although this is not official.

Post offices

Generally, post offices are open 9am to 5pm; some remain open until 5.30pm or 6pm.

Shops

Although there is no official closing time, most shops open from 9am to 6pm. Some groceries and supermarkets stay open till 9pm. Big department stores open till 9pm on one day a week, usually Friday. There is also a chain of (mostly) 24-hour grocer-tobacconists called White Night.

Religion

Many churches and synagogues hold services in English. There are several mosques in the city, but none of them has English services. For places away from the city centre, it is advisable to telephone for directions.

Anglican & Episcopalian
All Saints' Church *services held at Centre Notre Dame d'Argenteuil, 563 chaussée de Louvain, 1380 (384 35 56). Bus 558.* **Services** *English* 11.15am Sun.
Holy Trinity Church *29 rue Capitaine Crespel, 1050 (511 71 83/fax 511 10 28). Métro Louise.*
The Holy Communion service in English is held at 8.30am and 10.30am on Sundays, and evening praise is at 7pm. The International Christian Fellowship is held by the church's African congregation at 8pm on Fridays.

Protestant

International Protestant Church
services held at International School of Brussels, 19 mont des Chats, 1170 (673 05 81). Bus 366.
This church offers interdenominational services in English on Sundays at 10.45am (there is also a church school for children at 9.30am).

Presbyterian

St Andrew's Church of Scotland
181 chaussée de Vleurgat, 1050 (649 02 19). Métro Louise/tram 93, 94.
Services *English* 11am Sun.

Roman Catholic

Eglise St Nicolas *1 rue au Beurre, 1000 (contact Rev Phillip Sandstrom on 734 90 27 for details). Métro Bourse or De Brouckère.*
Roman Catholic Mass is held at 10am on Sundays (*see also chapter* **Sightseeing: Hidden churches**).
St Anne's Church *10 place de la Ste Alliance, 1180 (354 53 43/fax 351 23 14). Bus 43.*
Mass for the Our Lady of Mercy parish is held in English on Saturdays at 5pm, and Sundays at 10am and 1pm.

Quaker

Quaker House (Quaker Council for European Affairs) *50 square Ambiorix, 1000 (230 49 35/fax 230 63 70). Métro Schuman.* **Open** *office* 9am-5pm Mon-Fri.
Meetings for worship are held on Sundays at 11am and Wednesdays at 1-1.30pm.

Synagogues

Beth Hillel Liberal Synagogue of Brussels *96 avenue de Kersbeek, 1190 (332 25 28/fax 376 72 19). Tram 18, 52/bus 54.*
This liberal Jewish synagogue is led by an English-speaking rabbi, Abraham Dahan. Services are held on Friday evenings at 8pm and Saturdays at 10.30am. It's advisable to phone for directions.

Weights & measures

Food items are priced by the kilogram. There are 1000g (or 2.2lbs) in a kilo. *Une livre*, literally a pound, is a half-kilo or 500g. Distances are measured with the metric system. To work out miles, multiply kilometres by 0.6. To convert centimetres to inches, divide by 2.54.

Electricity

The current used in Belgium is 220V AC. It works fine with British appliances (which run on 240V), but you'll need to change the plug or buy an adapter. Both are available at most electrical goods shops.

American appliances run on 110V. To use an American hair dryer in Belgium, you'll need to buy a converter, which can be pricey. Don't bother if you're staying at a good hotel. They are often equipped with hair dryers, as well as adapter plugs to fit appliances from most countries.

Smoking

Smoking in confined public places is banned by law. This amounts to no smoking in railway stations (except on open-air platforms) and public buildings such as town halls and theatres.

The law has had little effect on restaurants, though. Very few have non-smoking sections. Recently, some of the top hotels have initiated no-smoking rooms and floors.

Water

It's safe to drink the water in Belgium. In restaurants, Belgians normally order bottled water.

Getting to Brussels

By air

Brussels' international airport is located at Zaventem, 14km north-east of the capital, with good road and rail connections to the city centre. The airport terminal building, boasts an impressive selection of shops and restaurants.

The airport information desk (7am-10pm daily) is in the check-in area of the new terminal. This terminal no longer has a tourist information desk. Instead, there's a board in the arrivals section, by the meeting point, which displays hotel information and is equipped with a telephone link for reservations. Hotel shuttle buses run from level 0. For

flight information call 753 39 13 (7am-10pm daily).

If you lose something on the plane, contact the airline via their handling agent. **Belgavia** and **Sabena** represent most of the major airlines. For property lost in the airport, try the **Belgian Police**, **Airport Police** or **Airport Authorities**.

Airport parking

Airport Park International, next to the new terminal, charges 295BF a day. There are also monitored car parks, such as **LockPark** *(720 41 91/720 63 25)* and **Car Hotel Airport Parking** *(753 53 53)*.

Connections to the city

There is a frequent shuttle **train** service – Airport City Express (753 24 40) – from Zaventem to Gare du Nord,

Gare Centrale and Gare du Midi. Tickets cost 85BF for a second class single and 120BF for a second class weekend return. The train runs three times an hour and the journey takes about 20 minutes (first train 5.25am, last train 11.46pm). If you are a woman travelling alone at night and planning to use public transport for your onward journey, it's safest to disembark at Gare Centrale.

An hourly **bus** service to Gare du Nord operates from the ground-floor level of the new terminal. The journey time is about 35 minutes and a single ticket costs 70BF.

Taxis wait directly outside the arrivals building and should display a yellow-and-blue licence emblem. The fare from Zaventem to central Brussels should cost 1000BF-1300BF. Many taxis accept credit cards. If in doubt, check the fare with the driver first. Some firms, such as Autolux, offer 25 per cent off for a return journey (see cabs with an orange-and-white aeroplane sticker). Brussels taxis have a rooftop tariff indicator system, showing 1 or 2 for single or double tariff in operation. Strictly speaking, the double tariff is only applicable outside the limits of the 19 Brussels *communes*. In practice, most drivers switch to double as soon as they're on a motorway.

By rail

EUROSTAR

The high-speed passenger train connection, which began service in November 1994, has revolutionised travel between London and Brussels. With a city-to-city journey time of 3 hours and 15 minutes (passing through the tunnel takes less than 25 minutes), it provides a reasonably priced and relaxing way of visiting Brussels. There are usually seven departures a day from Brussels Gare du Midi and London Waterloo. Check in at least 20 minutes before departure. In the UK, Eurostar information and reservations are available from selected travel agents and rail stations. In Belgium, Eurostar tickets are available at travel agents and international ticket desks in mainline stations.

Waterloo International Terminal

(01233 617575/local rate charges for callers within the UK 0345 881881). **Open** 7am-10pm Mon-Fri; 7am-9pm Sat; 9am-5pm Sun. **Credit** AmEx, DC, MC, V.
Prices from London to Brussels start at £69 for a special non-exhangeable deal and rise to £220 for an all-the-works first-class return trip.

Gare du Midi

(203 36 40/telephone sales 224 88 56). **Open** 8.15am-7pm Mon-Fri; 9.15am-4.30pm Sat, Sun, public holidays. **Credit** MC, V.
Adult prices from Brussels to London start at 3200BF for a Supersaver or Saturday day return. A second-class tourist return costs 5940BF and an Apex return is 4500BF (book at least 14 days in advance).

LE SHUTTLE

If you're driving to Brussels, Le Shuttle can transport you and your vehicle from Cheriton Park on the M20 near Folkestone to Coquelles near Calais in 35 minutes. There are good motorway connections to Brussels from there. Le Shuttle is a 24-hour service with up to four shuttles an hour departing from Folkestone. There are also facilities for the disabled. Tickets can be bought from a travel agent, Le Shuttle or (with the exception of Apex or promotional offers) on arrival at the tolls. Hertz and Le Shuttle have a Le Swap rental system so that you can drive a left-hand- and right-hand-drive car in France and the UK respectively.

Le Shuttle

(UK 0990 353535). **Open** 8.30am-6.15pm daily. **Credit** AmEx, DC, MC, V.
Five-day returns cost £70, £115, 147, or £169. Single tickets can cost £63, £109, £133 and £164.

By sea

Ostend Lines

5 Natienkaai, Ostend 8400 (059 55 99 55). **Credit** AmEx, DC, MC, V.

The ferry crossing takes 3 hours 45 minutes. An Ostend-Ramsgate standard return for one foot passenger costs 1600BF. Crossing by jetfoil is faster (1 hour 35 minutes), but carries a supplementary charge of 200BF each way.

Hoverspeed

Central Reservations, International Hoverport, Marine Parade, Dover, Kent CT17 9TG, England (01304 240241/fax 01304 240088). **Credit** AmEx, DC, MC, V.
Dover to Calais by hovercraft takes a mere 35 minutes. Return fares (including the coach from London Victoria to Dover and from Calais to central Brussels) are: £44 for an adult; £39 for under-26s; and £33 for under-16s.

By coach

Eurolines (Brussels)

(ticket sales only) 50 place de Brouckère, 1000 (217 00 25). Métro De Brouckère. **Open** 9am-6pm Mon-Fri. **No credit cards.**
Eurolines buses depart from CCN Gare du Nord (80 rue de Progrès, 1210). It also has an office for ticket sales (203 07 07).

Eurolines/National Express (Luton)

(01582 40 45 11). **Open** 8am-8pm Mon-Sat; 10am-3pm Sun; answerphone service after hours.
An adult return from London's Victoria to Brussels between 1 Sept-30 June costs £44 (1 Jul-31 Aug £49). There are reductions for youths and over-60s.

Getting around

Brussels has a modern, comprehensive, integrated and cheap public transport system. A combination of Métro, rail, bus and tram facilitates access to all parts of the Eurocapital, with the particular attraction of timed tickets that let you hop on and off as many times as you like for up to an hour.

If you prefer to walk – the city centre is so compact that it's possible to do most sightseeing on foot – but remember to take flat shoes, as many streets in the centre are cobbled.

Belgian rail

In 1835, Belgium's King Léopold I inaugurated the first railway in mainland Europe. **Société Nationale des Chemins de Fer Belges (SNCB)** now has 4,000 kilometres of track, connecting Brussels to other major European cities. Its three mainline stations – Gare Centrale (1km from Grand Place), Gare du Midi (in a zone under reconstruction and home to a popular Sunday market) and Gare du Nord (in the red-light district) – are directly

linked. Two additional rail stations, Schuman and Quartier Léopold, serve the European institutions.

Belgium is a small country and most of its tourist spots are less than an hour away by rail from Brussels. The majority of trains, although basic in terms of design, are clean and efficient. Rail travel is good value with a variety of special offers available. These include the **Eurodomino** pass, which provides: unlimited travel for periods of five or ten days in the European country of your choice; reductions for over-60s, under-26s and groups of two or more; and substantial savings during school holidays for day trippers. Tickets are generally not sold on trains, so inform the guard beforehand if boarding without a ticket (a supplement will be charged if you buy the ticket on the train). For information about Belgian railways call 0891 516 444 in the UK or 203 28 80/203 36 40 in Belgium.

There is also an excellent local rail network serving Brussels and the outlying areas. Further details and train timetables can be obtained from the stations.

Baggage facilities are available at mainline railway stations. Gare du Midi's left luggage office is next to the Eurostar terminal and charges 60BF per item per day.

TGV

The TGV (Train à Grande Vitesse) to Paris departs at least five times daily from Gare du Midi and the journey takes two-and-a-half hours. A second-class return costs 2780BF plus the TGV supplement of 120-360BF. There is also a TGV service to Nice. For further information call 203 3640.

Discount travel

Acotra World Travel Agency

51 rue de la Madeleine, 1000 (512 55 40/fax 512 39 74). Métro Gare Centrale. **Open** 10am-5.30pm Mon-Fri. **Credit** AmEx, DC, MC, V.
This agency across from Gare Centrale offers discounts on plane tickets, and can make train and room bookings. It also sells international student travel cards for 350BF.

Maps

Street names are marked in both French and Flemish. A-Z plans and maps of Brussels can be obtained from kiosks, news-agents and bookshops

throughout the city, and tourist information offices.

Transport maps and timetables are available free of charge from the STIB office and the STIB information centres at Gare du Midi, Porte de Namur and Rogier.

Métro, trams & buses

The efficient public transport network in the capital is run by STIB (Société des Transports Intercommunaux de Bruxelles). As well as the Métro, STIB has maintained and developed a tram system, providing Brussels with a non-polluting and picturesque mode of transport. The T2000 model, introduced in 1994, with gliding electric doors and low-level passenger gangways, has taken Brussels' public transport system some way into the future.

In addition to the STIB buses that serve the capital, two other bus services meet the requirements of commuters from the provinces.
De Lijn (Flanders Public Transport Service) *(526 28 11).* **Open** *phone enquiries* 8.15am-4pm Mon-Fri. Call the above number for information on services leaving from Brussels.
L'Epervier *50 place de Brouckère, 1000 (217 00 25/fax 217 31 92).* Contact this office for reservations on Europabus and Eurolines buses.
STIB *6th floor, 20 Galeries de la Toison d'Or, 1060 (general enquiries 515 20 00/bus information 515 30 64). Métro Louise or Porte de Namur.* **Open** 7.30am-5.30pm Mon-Fri; 8am-4pm Sat. Some bus routes that take in the sights are no.71 (De Brouckère – Delta), which passes through place Royale, and no.48 (Bourse – Stalle Station), which meanders around the Sablon area.
TEC (Wallonia Public Transport Service) *(010 48 04 04).* **Open** 6.30am-7pm Mon-Fri; 8am-noon Sat.

Tickets & travel passes

Tickets can be bought at Métro and rail stations, on buses and trams, at a kiosk next to the

Bourse, at STIB information centres, and at many news-agents. A one-day **Tourist Passport** is available for 220BF from the tourist information office in Grand Place and includes reductions on admission to museums. Points of sale for monthly passes are Métro Porte de Namur, Gare du Midi, the kiosk by the Bourse, SNCB stations and approved outlets. A ticket (*trajet*) entitles the user to travel on the Métro, buses and trams for one hour. Tickets must be electronically stamped by the machines at Métro stations and on trams and buses at the beginning of the journey. Controllers run random checks and can enforce a penalty of 2,000BF for being without a validated ticket. The fine increases dramatically for subsequent infractions.

The most economical way of travelling for a few days is to buy a batch of ten tickets (***une carte de dix trajets***) for 320BF. Five tickets cost 230BF, one costs 50BF and a **one-day unlimited travel pass** is 125BF. A **monthly pass** costs 1325BF. There is also a **Brussels Business Pass**, valid for one year of unlimited travel on the STIB network (for details call 515 20 54). Children under six can travel free if accompanied by an adult with a valid ticket. Public transport in the city generally operates from 5.30am to midnight.

Signs & lines

Métro stations are indicated by a white letter 'M' on a blue background, while red-and-white signs mark tram and bus stops. The first Métro started operation in 1976. Brussels is now well served by three lines and Pre-Métro trams, which run through various underground sections. Métro Line 1 is divided into Lines 1A and 1B. 1A runs from Heysel (home of the Atomium) to Hermann Debroux. 1B goes from Bizet to Stockel. Line 2 is a ring that links Simonis to Clemenceau and mirrors the inner-city ring of *boulevards* above. The main Pre-Métro line links Gare du Nord to the new station Albert in St Gilles via Gare du Midi.

The Métro system is efficient, clean and well signposted. On Line 2, you can track the progress of the train you are waiting for with computerised information boards. At night the Métro does not generally carry the same volume of passengers as the London Underground, and certain sections after 10pm can be intimidating for lone women passengers (for example, alighting at fairly deserted stations such as Yser and Porte de Hal).

Disabled travel

Public transport is not specially adapted for disabled passengers, though the latest trams with a low-level platform improve access slightly. A low-cost STIB minibus service (515 23 65) with vehicles equipped for wheelchairs is available to transport disabled travellers door-to-door. STIB has also installed facilities for blind passengers, such as Braille information panels, in at least 12 of its Métro stations.

For those travelling outside Brussels by train or on certain bus services, the disabled passenger pays and any accompanying person travels free. There are also reductions for the blind (call SNCB on 224 64 00 for details).

Taxis

Taxi ranks are situated outside mainline railway stations and at strategic locations such as Porte de Namur, the Bourse and De Brouckère. They are seldom hailed on the street. If you have a complaint to make against a taxi driver, record the

registration number of the vehicle and inform the police.

The price per km is 38BF or 76BF, depending upon whether the journey is inside or outside Brussels' 19 *communes*. Minimum fare is 95BF (plus 75BF at night). A few taxi comapnies are listed below.
Taxis Verts *54 rue des Carburants, 1190 (349 46 46).*
Autolux *1 rue du Maroquin, 1080 (411 41 42).*
Taxi Orange *37 place du Nouveau Marché aux Grains, 1000 (511 22 88).*

Bicycles

Cycling in the centre of Brussels remains a daunting prospect despite many cycle lanes and tracks. However, cycling out of town – eg along the route to Tervuren – is a scenic and relatively safe method of exploring the city's environs. Cycle lanes are designated by two broken white lines and are less secure than the cycle tracks, which are separated from the traffic.

Bike-In

18 rue Kelle, 1200 (763 13 78).
Phone for details.
If you want to explore further afield, SNCB operates a scheme whereby you can purchase a combined ticket for train journey and bike hire. A bike will be reserved for your collection on arrival at one of the 31 participating stations.

Car hire

To hire a car, you must have a full current driving licence (normally with a minimum of one year's experience) and a passport or ID card. Car rental is pricey, starting at 13500BF per week with unlimited mileage. The major car hire companies are in the airport arrivals hall and are open from 6.30am to 11pm. Hire rates at the airport are higher than in town. Special all-inclusive weekend rates (Fri pm to Mon am) are available from around 3000BF.
Avis *107 rue Colonel Bourg, 1140 (730 62 11/airport 720 09 44).*

Métro Diamant. **Open** 8am-6pm Mon-Fri. **Age requirement** over 23. **Credit** AmEx, DC, MC, V.
Budget *327 avenue Louise, 1050 (646 51 30/airport 720 80 50).*
Tram 93, 94. **Open** 8.30am-6pm Mon-Fri; 9am-noon Sat. **Age requirement** over 23. **Credit** AmEx, DC, EC, V.
Hertz *8 boulevard M Lemonnier, 1000 (513 2886/airport 720 60 44).*
Métro Anneessens. **Open** 7.30am-7pm Mon-Fri; 8am-2pm Sat; 8am-noon Sun. **Age requirement** over 25. **Credit** AmEx, DC, MC, V.

Driving – top tips

It's not easy driving around Brussels. Not only must motorists drive on the right; they must also give way to the right, even on a major road, except when marked otherwise. For example, a white sign with a yellow diamond on your road means cars from the right must stop for you. Priority must also be given to vehicles on rails.

Another factor to contend with is the aggressive behaviour of Belgian drivers, especially in tunnels. Then there's the rush hour to contend with. The cacophony of car horns and radio traffic warnings builds early on Friday afternoons when Belgians and Eurocrats alike begin their mass exodus. To enter congested traffic, you need to be ruthless. If you've survived all this, there are still the potholes. In contrast to the sleek motorways, the roads in town are riddled with flaws.

A comprehensive tunnel system links major points in the city, making it possible to traverse Brussels without seeing the light of day. The inner ring is a pentagon of boulevards (marked with signs showing a blue ring on which the yellow dot is your current location). The secondary city ring was never completed and the outer ring has ended up as an elongated pear shape with a missing base, divided into an East and West Motorway ring.

The speed limit on motorways is 120kph, on main roads 90kph and in residential areas 50kph. The drinking and driving limit is 0.2g/l (no more than two small beers or two glasses of wine). Seat belts are compulsory at the front and rear.

Officially you need an international driver's licence, but police will usually accept a valid licence from your home country. If your car is towed, go to the nearest police station to get a document releasing it. Police may give you the document free of charge or demand up to 2000BF, depending on the area of town. They will then give the address of the garage holding your car. Present the police letter there and pay another 3000-4000BF to get the car back.

The cost of fuel is similar to that in the UK. If you have a Belgian bank account, you can get a Bancontact/Mister Cash card, which allows you to buy petrol 24 hours a day at hundreds of stations across Belgium.

Driving with no traffic (a rare occurrence) and no stops, it takes about 30 minutes to Antwerp, 45 minutes to Ghent, 90 minutes to Liège and Bruges. Calais and Amsterdam are about two-and-a-half hours away and Paris three hours.

Major roads have phones along them. Seat belts are compulsory. Drink-driving penalties are stiff. And immediate fines are common if you are caught speeding and are not Belgian.

Breakdown services

In the event of a breakdown, there are two national organisations to call:
Tourist Club Belgique (TCB) *44 rue de la Loi, 1040 (24-hour emergency service 070 344 777/ enquiries 233 22 11 9am-5pm Mon-Fri).*
Royal Automobile Club de Belgique *53 rue d'Arlon, 1040 (24-hour emergency service 078 152 000/enquiries 287 09 11 9am-5pm Mon-Thur; 9am-4pm Fri).*

Repairs & services

The agents listed below can get you back on the road. Or check *Yellow Pages* under

Carrosseries (Reparations)-Autos/Carrossierieherstellingen -Auto's.
Autocenter East NV 'Toyota' *438 chaussée de Louvain, 1930 (725 12 00). Métro Meiser.* **Open** 8am-7pm Mon-Fri; 9am-6pm Sat. **Credit** AmEx, DC, MC, V.
BMW Brussels *22-38 rue du Magistrat, 1050 (641 57 11). Métro Louise.* **Open** 7.30-5.30pm Mon-Thur; 7.30am-4.30pm Fri. **Credit** AmEx, DC, MC, V.
Durieux Nissan *24 rue des Trois Ponts, 1160 (672 15 72). Métro Hankar.* **Open** 8am-noon, 1-6pm Mon-Fri; 9am-noon Sat. **Credit** AmEx, MC, V.
Rover Grand Garage St Michel *35-43 rue de l'Escadron, 1040 (732 46 00/fax 736 51 31). Métro Thieffry.* **Open** 8am-6pm Mon-Fri; *showroom* 10am-5pm Mon-Fri. **Credit** AmEx, DC, V.

<table>
<tr><td>Walking – top tips</td></tr>
</table>

Be wary at zebra crossings. Drivers do not automatically stop. If a car is bearing down on you mid-crossing, techniques to avoid certain death include looking the driver straight in the eye (often doesn't work) or looking away (suicidal body language that may not work either).

Living & working in Brussels

All British visitors need a valid passport to enter Belgium. The same goes for Swiss citizens and EU nationals, who can also use a valid national ID card. Visitors from the USA, Australia, New Zealand and Japan need only a valid passport to stay for three months as a tourist (no visa is required).

If you wish to stay longer you must participate in a maddening paper chase. For EU nationals, the process is fairly simple. You don't need to apply for a work permit, but you must register with the police. This involves a trip to the town hall of the *commune* in which you are living. Provide three photos, pay a

nominal fee, have your fingerprints taken (not all *communes* insist on this), and you'll receive a three-month residence card. This is renewable for another three months. You're then eligible to receive an ID card valid for five years, should you wish to stay. If you live or work in Belgium, you must carry your Belgian identity card (*carte d'identité/identiteitskaart*) with you at all times. If you don't have one, carry your passport. Belgian police have the right to stop you at any time to see proof of identity. If you can't produce it, they can hold you at a police station until your identity is proven, even if you haven't committed a crime.

Before starting work EU nationals should apply for forms Council Regulations 1408/71 and 574/72, which concern social security payments for those moving within the EU. For non-EU citizens the situation is more tricky. Due to high unemployment, it's becoming more difficult to get work permits (*permis de travail/ werkvergunning*). The applicant must prove that no Belgian or other EU national can do the job. Your employer must apply for the permit on your behalf. You'll also need three photos, a certificate of good health and a copy of your work contract. Processing can take up to 12 weeks.

The type of permit you get depends on how long you are planning to stay in Belgium. Most people receive B permits which are valid for one year and then must be renewed; they are not transferable from one employer to another. After three or four years with a B permit, one can apply for an A permit which is valid indefinitely with any employer in any field.

Ministère de l'Emploi et du Travail
51 rue Belliard, 1040 (233 41 11/fax 233 44 88). Métro Maelbeek. **Open** 9am-noon, 2-4pm, Mon-Fri.
Contact them for a work permit application form.

Women's Brussels

Bookshops & archives

Artemys
8-10 galerie Bortier, rue St Jean, 1000 (512 03 47). Métro Gare Centrale. **Open** noon-6pm Mon; 10am-6pm Tue-Thur; 10am-7pm Fri, Sat.
Artemys is *the* feminist bookstore in Brussels, specialising in lesbian literature in French, Flemish and English. When it opened in 1985 it sold only books, but due to lack of subsidy, it now sells calendars and cards to supplement its income. Belgium does not support its
book industry, making competition stiff and specialist bookstores a dying breed. Nevertheless Artemys has quite a following and a reputation among women's circles as a good source of information on women's topics. Upstairs there is a bulletin board advertising housing, rides, workshops and conference.

Centre de Documentation et d'Information (CEDIF)
34 rue de la Tulipe, 1050 (502 68 00). Métro Porte de Namur/bus 60, 71. **Open** 9am-noon Mon, Tue, Thur, Fri; 1-5pm Wed.
Part of the Fédération Francophone Belge pour le Planning Familial et l'Education Sexuelle, this is a good source of information on women's health and feminist issues in French. There are files on ante- and post-natal care, abortion, divorce and equal rights in the workplace.

Centre Léonie La Fontaine (Université des Femmes)
10 rue du Méridien, 1210 (229 38 33). Métro Botanique or Madou/tram 92, 93, 94/bus 61, 65, 66. **Open** 10am-5pm Mon-Fri.
Located within Amazone, a centre housing a number of women's groups, this library has a wide selection of research tools and books on feminist issues. There are also dozens of periodicals in several languages: *Feminist Review, Women's Studies International Forum, DonnaWomanFemme, Schoppenvrouw* to name a few. Anyone can use the centre and make photocopies (3BF per A4 page), but

only members are allowed to take certain books out (up to three a month). Membership is 200BF a year.

Rosa
78 & 86 Gallaitstraat, 1030 (216 23 23). Tram 52, 55, 92, 93, 94. **Open** 10am-noon, 1-5pm, Mon-Thur.
Founded in 1978, Rosa was one of the first centres for documentation and research on gender roles and feminist issues in Brussels. Today it is one of the most respected centres because of its track record and tenacity over the years. Available for consultation are documents and periodicals, as well as bibliographies on divorce, lesbian parenting and education, which the centre itself compiles. Although the centre is mostly Flemish-speaking, research materials are also available in French, English and German.

Groups & centres

International women's groups abound in Brussels – Canadian, American, South African, Sri Lankan, Swedish, British – you name it, there's one here. These groups organise charity events, excursions, social events and courses, and can be a useful way to meet other women in Brussels. The best source of information on the groups' activities is the *Bulletin*.

For a more complete list of women's organisations in Brussels, consult the *Repertoire Francophone d'Adresses pour les Femmes*. It can be found at either the Université des Femmes (which compiled the directory) or at Artemys the bookshop (*see above*) and costs 150BF.

Amazone
10 rue du Méridien, 1210 (229 38 00/fax 229 38 01). Métro Botanique or Madou/tram 92, 93, 94/bus 61, 65, 66. **Open** 9am-5pm Mon-Fri.
Amazone opened in May 1995 with the triple goal of supporting women's organisations, providing information

on women's issues to the public and offering a *'point de rencontre'* for women in Brussels. The centre is home to the following organisations: Université des Femmes, Sophia, Le Conseil des Femmes Francophones de Belgique, Nederlandstalige Vrouwenraad, Le Comité de Liaison des Femmes, Vrouwen Overleg Komitee, Stichting Vrouwen tegen Mishandeling, La Coordination des Groupes Contre la Violence Faite aux Femmes and finally La Coordination des Groupes Politiques des Femmes pour la Démocratie Paritaire. Described as 'gay friendly' but not exclusively lesbian, Amazone also houses a restaurant (228 38 37) for women and men, open for lunch. The cadre is bourgeois and the food is sandwich/salad fare.

Centre Feminin d'Education Permanente (CFEP)
1A place Quetelet, 1210 (219 28 02). Métro Botanique or Madou/tram 92, 93, 94/bus 29, 61, 63, 65, 66. **Open** 9.30am-4pm Mon-Fri.
CFEP opened in 1956 in response to growing demand among women to be active participants in Brussels' socio-economic life. Today its goal, though evolved, is much the same: to offer women training and support making them better equipped to compete in today's world. The centre's approach is one of empowerment rather than 'ladies aid'. There are courses available in computing and languages (including French conversation classes), conferences are held on topics ranging from hormone replacement therapy to advertising, and an investment club provides basic information about investing in stocks. Female entrepreneurs looking for funding can find referrals and information here on how best to get their project underway.

Focus Career Services
23 rue Lesbroussart, 1050 (646 65 30/fax 646 96 02). Tram 81, 82/bus 38, 59 60, 71. **Open** 10am-5pm Tue, Thur, Fri; 10am-8pm Wed.
While Focus Career Services is open to women and men, it is mainly used by women seeking employment in Brussels. It provides career

counselling, personal development advice, training opportunity info and job search workshops.

Health

Contraceptive pills cost an average of 200BF per month's supply. Unfortunately, they are not covered by a *mutuelle* (health insurance, which is compulsory under Belgian law). According to some women's centres, this is because the Pill is considered a 'luxury item'.

The quality of healthcare in Brussels is good and there are several women's clinics, many operating a sliding scale of payment. Some specialising in women's healthcare are listed below, but the Centre de Documentation et d'Information (*see above*), part of the Fédération Francophone Belge pour le Planning Familial et l'Education Sexuelle, can refer you to your nearest.

La Famille Heureuse

4 place Quetelet, 1210 (217 44 50). Métro Botanique or Madou/tram 92, 93, 94/bus 29, 61, 63, 65, 66. **Open** 9am-noon, 2-8pm, Mon, Tue, Thur; 9am-5pm Wed; 9am-6pm Fri. **Drop-in visits** 1-3.30pm Wed.

One of the first women's clinics to open in Brussels (1962) and one of the most comprehensive. Services include contraceptive and psychological counselling, abortion, cervical smear tests and referrals. A visit with a doctor will set you back 580BF.
Branches: St Gilles (Brussels), Mons, Tournai & Verviers.

Aimer à l'ULB

38 avenue Jeanne, 1050 (650 31 31). Bus 71/tram 23, 90, 93, 94. **Open** 9am-7pm Mon-Fri; 9.30am-12.30pm Sat.

Although located on the ULB campus, this bright and cheery clinic is open to all. The cost of medical visits is based on income so if you're on a tight budget, this is a good place to come for a check-up, prescription or cervical smear.

Collectif Contraception (Santé des Femmes)

34 avenue des Celtes, 1040 (736 13 14). Métro Merode/tram 81, 82. **Open** 9.30am-5pm Mon; noon-8pm Tue; 1-5pm Wed; 9.30am-6pm Thur; 9.30am-7pm Fri.

Services provided here include general check-ups and cervical smears, HIV testing, psychological and legal counselling, and abortions. Medical visits operate by appointment only, so call first. A basic visit costs 560BF.

Helplines

Community Help Service Helpline

(648 40 14). **Open** 24 hours daily.

This 24-hour helpline, although not specifically for women, is the only English-speaking one in Brussels. It provides general information, a listening ear and counselling/referral in emergency situations.

Le Refuge (Collectif pour Femmes Battues)

29 rue Blanche, 1060 (647 00 12). Tram 93, 94. **Open** 9am-7pm Mon-Fri; 9.30am-5pm Sat, Sun.

A refuge for victims of domestic violence, which also offers counselling and support.

SOS Harcelement Sexuel

(0800 122 32). **Open** 11am-1pm, 5-7pm, daily.

Counselling and referrals (in French) for victims of sexual harassment.

SOS Viol

29 rue Blanche, 1060 (534 36 36). Tram 93, 94. **Open** 9.30am-5.30pm Mon-Fri.

Telephone assistance for victims of sexual violence, plus psychological counselling and referrals. Volunteers accompany women to the police and to the doctor, if desired.

Safety

Not so long ago in Brussels, it was possible for a woman to hitch-hike her way round the city alone, and to bar-crawl into the early hours in relative safety. The main obstacles would be groups of lads out on the pull, who tended to be annoying rather than seriously threatening. As Brussels becomes more cosmopolitan and the population grows, it is slowly starting to gain the less desirable attributes of a big city, including increasing levels of street violence. Nowadays, a single woman hitchhiking is a rare sight indeed. You'd be well advised to avoid being alone late at night in the city centre, and try to have at least your taxi fare on you in case you can't get a lift home. Under Belgian law you are required to have 500BF as well as your ID card on you at all times.

Students' Brussels

Accommodation

Most universities have some form of student housing, but space is usually pretty limited. It might be better to rent an apartment – real estate in Brussels never really recovered from the late 1980s dive, so rents are still fairly reasonable.

One problem to be especially aware of, when seeking to rent an apartment in Brussels, is

that many bathrooms are fitted with open-flue gas water heaters. These are potentially lethal (it is absolutely vital to make sure there is sufficient ventilation). Despite increasing awareness, landlords have been slow to address the problem.

The *Bulletin* has apartment listings, though *Le Vlan* (*see chapter* **Media**) is perhaps better if you're looking for cheaper places to rent.

Universities

Académie Royale des Beaux Arts de Bruxelles

144 rue du Midi, 1000 (511 04 91). Métro Gare Centrale/tram 23, 52, 55. The Royal Academy of Fine Art has four-year courses in weaving, illustration/comic strip art, advertising and design, but is best known for painting and sculpture.

Boston University Brussels

8 St Lendriksborre, 1120 (268 00 37). Tram 23 then bus 47.

Boston University set up its campus in Brussels in 1972 and joined with VUB (*see below*) to set up an English-language Masters of Science in Management (MSM) programme. In addition to the MSM course, the university offers an MS in Administrative Studies as well as several specialised graduate certificates.

Ecole Nationale Supérieure des Arts Visuels de la Cambre

21 Abbaye de la Cambre, 1000 (648 96 19). Tram 23, 90, 93, 94/bus 71.
Brussels has two main art schools, this and the Beaux Arts (*see above*), the former being more commercially orientated and perhaps the snootier of the two. Housed in a beautiful thirteenth-century abbey in Ixelles, La Cambre has courses in fine art as well as animation, printmaking and industrial design. But the school's fortes are architecture, graphic design and fashion. Courses are taught in French.

Emerson College

240 avenue Louise, 1050 (648 58 06). Tram 93, 94.
Boston's Emerson College opened its Brussels campus in 1993 and offers a one-year MA in Global Marketing, Communication and Advertising (taught in English).

ICHEC (Institut Catholique des Hautes Etudes Commerciales)

2 boulevard Brand Whitlock, 1150 (739 37 11). Métro Montgomery/ tram 23, 44, 81, 90/bus 20, 61, 80.
Founded in 1934, ICHEC is rated as the second best business school in Brussels, after Solvay, and its students tend to be of the BCBG (*bon chic bon genre* – smart set), old money variety. Course work is extremely demanding, with between 30 and 40 class hours per week and, as with ULB, only a quarter of the initial student intake end up bringing home a degree to *maman*. On offer are four-year programmes in *sciences commerciales et financières/ consulaires* or a five-year *ingeniorat commerciale*.

Open University

38 avenue Emile Duray, 1050 (644 33 72/73). Tram 23, 90, 93, 94/bus 71.
This caters mostly for working adults who want to get a degree but don't want or can't afford to quit their jobs. Students follow a course book and audiovisual materials at their own pace, and meet regularly with a tutor at study centres either in Brussels or Antwerp. BAs and BScs take anything from four to six years to complete, depending on the student's own study plan. Degrees are offered

in the social sciences, technology, computing, mathematics, arts and sciences. There is also an MBA programme.

ULB (Université Libre de Bruxelles)

50 avenue Franklin Roosevelt, 1050 (650 21 11). Tram 93, 94/bus 71.
The Free University of Brussels was founded in 1834 by lawyer Theodore Verhaegen in order to counter the stagnant state of higher education in Brussels. At the time, the Catholic Church had a monopoly over the curricula of the country's three universities, and intellectual advancement proceeded along rigid lines. ULB began as an independent, liberal institution and received strong backing from masonic circles. Today, it is the largest university in Brussels, with over 18,000 students, of whom roughly a third are foreigners. Solbosch, ULB's main campus, is home to most faculties – Philosophy and Letters, Social Sciences, Applied Sciences, Law and European Studies – with the exception of Medicine, which is located at Hôpital Erasme. Solbosch is also home to the city's most prestigious business school, Solvay, which offers a five-year *grade d'ingénieur commercial* and a one-year MBA in English. Courses are tough at ULB. In the first year students find themselves in classrooms with upwards of 600 people, and if they make it to the second year, the numbers will have halved. By the end of the programme, only about 150 will have made it through. Student life is scattered – most students live at home or in apartments around the city – although there are a number of student associations and clubs on the Solbosch Campus.

Vesalius College

2 Pleinlaan, 1050 (629 36 26). Métro Petillon/tram 23, 90/bus 34, 95, 96.
Vesalius was created in 1987 as part of the VUB (*see below*) and in association with Boston University. Although it shares a campus with VUB (which issues Vesalius diplomas), the language of instruction is English and the style of education is decidedly American – selective admission, small classes and close faculty-student relationships, and American-style fees! Vesalius offers Bachelor's degrees in 15 subjects including economics, computer science, engineering (computer and electrical), English lit, business and human resources management. The student body is diverse, with over 50 nationalities represented, and student life is accordingly interesting.

VUB (Vrije Universiteit Brussel)

2 Pleinlaan, 1050 (629 21 11/library 629 25 05). Métro Petillon/tram 23, 90/bus 95, 96, 34.
In 1970, the Free University of Brussels split into two entities along linguistic lines, the French-speaking ULB and its Flemish-speaking counterpart, VUB. Each is funded by its respective community and educational policies are decided upon separately by the national Parliament and by each of the communities' Cultural Councils. VUB today has an enrolment of roughly 8,000 students. Although most of the courses are taught in Flemish (with the exception of Vesalius College, *see above*), there are a number of English-language postgraduate degrees.
Website: http://www.vub.ac.be

Language schools

Most *communes* offer language courses at reasonable prices and can be contacted for more details. The Chamber of Commerce and Industry also offers day and evening classes at VUB (Vrije Universiteit Brussel); a year of two three-hour sessions a week starts at 2,700BF. You can contact them on 629 27 61 for more details.

Alliance Française

59 avenue de l'Emeraude, 1030 (732 15 92). Tram 23, 90/bus 29, 63. **Open** 8.30am-noon, 1.30-6.30pm, Mon-Thur; 8.30am-noon, 1.30-5pm, Fri.
Don't want to pick up a Belgian accent? This bastion of French culture has group and private classes in French only. An intensive month-long course, meeting daily from 9am to noon, costs 10,200BF. Alternatively, there are courses that meet twice a week in the evening, which cost 3000BF per month. Classes are no larger than 15 students.

Brussels Language Studies

8 rue du Marteau, 1210 (217 23 73). Métro Arts-Loi or Madou. **Open** 8.30am-8pm Mon-Fri; 8.30am-12.30pm Sat.
This well-reputed school teaches classes in virtually every language imaginable and is extremely flexible about meeting the needs of its students. Group classes number no more than five students and cost 13,500BF for 30 hours of teaching.

CERAN Lingua

Château du Haut-Neubois, 16 avenue du Château, Spa 4900 (087 791 122). Train to Verviers then taxi/or school runs own transport – phone for details.

When the well-heeled want to brush up on a language, they pack their bags and head for this prestigious and beautiful château in the Ardennes. For a period ranging from a weekend to several weeks, students think, eat and breathe in the language of their choice, whether it's French, Italian, Japanese, German, Dutch or Spanish. A week-long stay, including texts and full room and board, starts at 47,000BF. CERAN has other language centres in Spain, France, Ireland and the US.

Fondation 9

412 avenue Louise, 1050 (640 21 92). Tram 93, 94. Open 9am-6pm Mon-Fri.

The '9' refers to the nine languages of the European Union (before Spain and Portugal joined in 1986 – it really should be Fondation 13 by now). Anyway, sponsored by ULB, the Chamber of Commerce and the City of Brussels, Fondation 9 offers group classes of up to eight students in all the official languages of the EU. An eight-week class, which meets for three hours on Saturday mornings, costs 10,500BF. Intensive 'immersion' classes cost 12,950BF per week.

Exchanges

Most universities have an office for exchange programmes, or at least their own branches of **Tempus** and **Socrates** on campus. Listed below are the main offices.

AIESEC (Association Internationale d'Etudiants en Sciences Economiques et Sociales)

50 avenue Franklin Roosevelt, 1050 (650 26 21). Tram 93, 94/bus 71.

AIESEC has offices in most universities around the world and helps students in economics or social sciences find internships abroad during their final year. The organisation also contacts companies to set up 'job days'. This address is for ULB's branch of AIESEC.

Socrates & Youth

70 rue Montoyer, 1000 (233 01 11). Métro Trône. Open 8.30am-6pm Mon-Fri.

Socrates (previously called Erasmus) is the EU agency that sets up student exchanges throughout Europe. The grants are teeny, but the experience is

well worth it. If you want to do an exchange with an institution that is not already an Erasmus member, you can set up your own programme.

Tempus (Trans-European Cooperation Scheme for Higher Education)

Ministère de l'Education de la Recherche et de la Formation Generale de l'Enseignement Supérieur et de la Recherche Scientifique, Cité Administrative de l'Etat, 204 rue Royale, 1010 (210 55 69). Métro Botanique. Open 9am-noon, 2-5pm, Mon-Fri.

EU organisation Tempus arranges educational exchanges between European member states and Eastern European countries: Albania, Bulgaria, Czech Republic, Estonia, Hungary, Latvia, Lithuania, Poland, Romania, Slovak Republic, Slovenia. Belgian francophone enquiries only.

Libraries

It can be tricky finding the book you need in Brussels, unless you have a lot of time to spare, wandering from one library to the next. If you're online, preferably with Netscape, the task is easier – log on to VUB's homepage (http:\www. vub.ac.be). From there you can search several catalogues and find out where any book is located in the country. If you don't have Netscape, you can get direct access through Telnet, an Internet service provider. Once in Telnet, type 'Open' and then the library's electronic address (biblio.vub.ac.be). One of the options is 'Other Catalogues', of which 'Antelope' can hook you in to the main libraries in Belgium. And if you're not online, no problem, VUB's library has computers that are online for you. Call them on 629 25 05.

American Documentation Center

1C square du Bastion, 1050 (512 21 29). Métro Porte de Namur/bus 71. Open 2-6pm Mon-Thur.

Part of the United States Information Service, the American Library has over 15,000 texts, most of which specialise in the area of US-Europe economic relations, environment and law. Only students doing research in

their final year can take books out on loan, otherwise there is a photocopying machine available to anyone with a copycard. The catalogue is computerised but not on the Internet yet.

Bibliothèque Royale Albert I

4 boulevard de l'Empereur, 1000 (519 53 11). Métro Gare Centrale or Parc/tram 92, 93, 94/bus 20, 34, 38, 60, 71, 95, 96. Open 9am-8pm Mon-Fri; 9am-5pm Sat.

This is the state library, holding primarily everything published in Belgium, as well as foreign journals and publications. You need a membership card to consult the vast collection of books here. Bring in a photograph, your identity card and 300BF if you're a student (if you're not a student, the yearly charge is 600BF). As usual, books cannot be taken out. The computerised catalogue lists only books that were printed after 1985. All others are still listed in the card catalogue. To consult the library's catalogue via the Internet, log on to http://www.kbr.be

Center for American Studies

3rd floor, Bibliothèque Royale Albert I, 4 boulevard de l'Empereur, 1000 (519 55 23). Métro Gare Centrale/tram 92, 93, 94/bus 20, 34, 38, 60, 71, 95, 96. Open 9am-12.30pm, 2-5pm, Mon-Fri.

Although this resource centre does not have very many primary sources, it is well stocked in American books on critical theory, history, sociology and the arts. If the book you need isn't here, staff can tell you where to find it in Belgium and beyond. Again, books cannot be taken out.

Children's Library

Centre Crousse, 11 rue au Bois, 1150 (672 48 76). Open 10am-noon Sat. Phone for directions.

Opening hours are limited, but this library is useful for kids' education. Run by a group of volunteers, it stocks over 7,000 books with a steady stream of new stock.

ULB (Université Libre de Bruxelles)

50 avenue Franklin Roosevelt, 1050 (reception 650 47 00/audiovisual department 650 43 78). Tram 93, 94/bus 71. Open 8am-10pm Mon-Fri; 10am-5pm Sat; English audiovisual section 1.30-5.30pm Mon-Fri.

Although this library is mainly for students, it's also open to non-students for 1000BF a year. It holds a surprisingly large collection of materials in English in various media. ULB bought the materials from the British Council Resources Centre when it closed down.

Business

Accountants

Arthur Andersen & Co *56 avenue des Arts, 1000 (510 42 11/fax 510 44 00 or 513 08 62). Métro Trône.* **Open** 8am-6.30pm Mon-Fri.
Coopers & Lybrand *216 avenue Marcel Thiry, 1200 (774 42 11/fax 774 42 99). Métro Roodebeek.* **Open** 8.30am-5pm Mon-Fri.
Deloitte & Touche Consultants NV-SA *6 Berkenlaan, 1831 (718 92 11/fax 718 92 04). Métro Diegem.* **Open** 8am-6pm Mon-Fri.
Ernst & Young *204 avenue Marcel Thiry, 1200 (774 91 11/fax 774 90 90). Métro Roodebeek.* **Open** 8am-6pm Mon-Fri.
KPMG Peat Marwick *Woluwe Office Park, 101 rue Neerveld, 1200 (773 36 11/fax 772 33 05). Métro Roodebeek.* **Open** 8am-6pm Mon-Fri.
Price Waterhouse *62 boulevard de la Woluwe, 1200 (773 14 11/fax 770 32 49). Métro Roodebeek.* **Open** 8am-6pm Mon-Fri.

Banks

You may want to check with your bank back home to see if they have a branch here. Many UK banks have corporate offices in Brussels, but lack personal banking services. Head offices for Belgium's biggest commercial banks are listed below. Telephone the individual branches first for opening hours, since times can vary. It's worth asking about direct debit cards which are available through the banks. The cards – known as Mister Cash and Bancontact – are accepted nearly everywhere, including supermarkets, for a mere 5BF fee per transaction.

Banque Bruxelles Lambert (BBL)
24 avenue Marnix, 1000 (547 21 11/fax 547 8800). Métro Trône. **Open** 9am-4pm Mon-Fri.

CGER Banque et Assurances
48 rue du Fossé aux Loups, 1000 (228 61 11/fax 228 71 99). Métro De Brouckère. **Open** 8.30am-3.30pm Mon-Thur; 8.30am-5.30pm Fri.
This partly state-owned bank focuses mainly on consumer banking. Also car, fire, home and life insurance.

Citibank
263g boulevard Général Jacques, 1050 (information & services 24-hour Citiphone 626 50 50/fax 626 56 18 or 626 56 19). Tram 23, 90. **Open** 9am-5pm Mon-Fri.
All the banking services available at your New York or London branch are also on offer here.

Kredietbank
7 rue d'Arenberg, 1000 (546 41 11/fax 546 42 09). Métro De Brouckère. **Open** 9am-4pm Mon-Fri.

Générale de Banque
3 rue Montagne du Parc, 1000 (information toll free 0800 12345/general 565 11 11/fax 565 4222). Métro Gare Centrale. **Open** 9am-4pm Mon-Fri.

Business information

American Chamber of Commerce
50 avenue des Arts, 1000 (513 67 70/fax 513 35 90). Métro Trône. **Open** 9am-noon, 2-5pm, Mon-Fri.
The Chamber has about a thousand members – half of whom are American and the rest European. It offers help with legal and commercial problems (though you should call for an appointment first), and organises events to maximise networking opportunities. An annual directory of all American and member companies in Brussels is free to members and costs 3500BF for non-members.

Bourse des Valeurs Mobilières de Bruxelles (Brussels Stock Exchange)
Palais de la Bourse, 1000 (information 509 12 11/public relations 509 13 48/fax 509 12 12). Métro Bourse. **Open** 9am-5pm Mon-Fri; *tours* by appointment only.
Of Belgium's two stock exchanges – the other is in Antwerp – this is the more important. Don't expect to see traders gesticulating wildly on the floor, though. All trading is computerised. Visitors can, however, hear a lecture on how the whole process works. Call Vera Moerenhout in public relations to schedule an appointment.

British Chamber of Commerce
15 rue d'Egmont, 1000 (540 90 30/fax 512 83 63). Métro Trône. **Open** 9.30am-noon, 2.30-5pm, Mon-Fri.
If you're with a British company doing business in Belgium, or a Belgium company doing business in the UK, you may want to become a member. It allows you access to the reference library and entitles you to a free copy of the directory of 300-odd members (2,500BF for non-members).

Brussels Chamber of Commerce
500 avenue Louise, 1050 (648 50 02/fax 640 93 28). Métro Louise. **Open** 9am-noon, 1.30-4pm, Mon-Thur; 9am-noon, 1-3pm, Fri.
This private club offers legal support to Brussels-based companies and advises on how economic and trade-related government policies may affect certain industries. Between 3,000 and 4,000 Belgian and foreign companies are members. Membership fees are based on company size.

Euro Info Centre – Commerce Extérieur
500 avenue Louise, 1050 (648 58 73/fax 640 93 28). Métro Louise. **Open** 9am-noon, 1-4pm, Mon-Thur; 8.30am-noon, 1-3pm, Fri.
Confused by EU legislation and how it may affect your business? The Euro Info Centre – sponsored by the EC – is designed to help small and medium-sized businesses find answers to such questions.

Ministère de la Région de Bruxelles
Services des Investissements Etranger (Foreign Investment Department), 25 rue du Champ de Mars, 1050 (513 97 00/fax 511 52 55). Métro Porte de Namur. **Open** 9am-5pm Mon-Fri.
Foreign investors looking for opportunities in Brussels will be warmly received by this office. Call for an appointment with a representative and ask about their brochures.

Office de la Propriété Industrielle (Patent Office)
Ministère des Affaires Economiques, Administration de la Politique Commerciale, 154 boulevard Emil Jacqmain, 1000 (206 41 56/fax 206 57 01). Métro Rogier or Yser. **Open** *office* 10am-noon, 2-4pm, Mon-Fri; *library* 9am-noon, 1-4pm, Mon-Fri.
For about 50BF a minute the Patent Office can do an online search to see if a patent exists in most parts of the world. After 30 minutes you should have a good idea of what's out there. The library also contains microfilm and microfiche records of patents. It costs 2,000BF to file a Belgian patent, valid for six years, and 40,000BF for 20 years' protection.

Vlaamse Dienst voor de Buitenlandse Handel (Flemish Foreign Trade Board)

80 rue Royale, 1000 (504 87 11/fax 504 88 99). Métro Parc. **Open** 9am-5pm Mon-Fri.

Foreign companies interested in importing Flemish goods or services will find all the help they need here.

Reference books

EU Committee

American Chamber of Commerce, Box 5, 50 avenue des Arts, 1000 (513 68 92/fax 513 79 28). Métro Trône. **Open** 9am-6pm Mon-Thur; 9am-5pm Fri.

The valuable EU Information Handbook contains current listings of all European Union-related committees, missions and offices. You can buy a copy for 2100BF at the American Chamber of Commerce or order it by mail.

Ernst & Young

204 avenue Marcel Thiry, 1200 (774 91 11/fax 774 90 90). Métro Roodebeek. **Open** 8am-6pm Mon-Fri.

Bogged down with Belgian bureaucracy? At no cost, E&Y will give you a useful 112-page guide, *Doing Business in Belgium.* Copies are available at all their offices worldwide.

European Report

European Information Service, 66 avenue Adolphe Lacomblé, 10306 (737 77 00/fax 732 67 57). Métro Diamant. **Open** 9am-6pm Mon-Fri.

Businessmen, lawyers and anyone else interested in detailed updates on EU activities can receive this French- and English-language publication twice a week for 46200BF a year.

Focus Career Services

23 rue Lesbroussart, 1050 (646 65 30/fax 646 96 02). Tram 81, 82/bus 38, 59 60, 71. **Open** 10am-5pm Tue, Thur, Fri; 10am-8pm Wed.

For 500BF you can get a head start on setting up a business – non-profit centre Focus produce *Getting Started... Legally: The FOCUS Guide to Working in Belgium and Starting a Business.* A reference copy is available for members. Annual membership costs 2,400BF.

Conferences

Espace Moselle

40 rue des Drapiers, 1050 (502 65 45/fax 502 66 28). Métro Porte de Namur. **Open** 9am-6pm Mon-Fri. **Credit** AmEx, DC, EC, MC, V.

For a touch of historic Brussels, Espace Moselle offers a renovated late

nineteenth-century home with high ceilings and crystal chandeliers as a meeting venue. Food and cocktails can be arranged for up to 250 people. Parking is available, as is a garden – rain permitting.

Management Centre Europe

118 rue de l'Aqueduc, 1050 (543 21 00/fax 543 24 00). Bus 54, 81. **Open** 8.30am-8pm Mon-Fri. **Credit** AmEx, DC, MC, V.

MCE is one of the top business management and training organisations in Europe, hosting a variety of large seminars and conferences. It also sets up training sessions and conferences specific to a client's request.

Palais des Congrès de Bruxelles

3 Coudenberg, 1000 (513 41 30/fax 514 21 12). Métro Gare Centrale. **Open** 8.30am-4.30pm Mon-Fri. **Credit** AmEx, DC, MC, V.

Near the Grand Place, this is one of the most convenient conference centres in Brussels. Its rooms can accommodate groups of ten for small meetings, or over 1,200 for events such as trade exhibitions.

Couriers

BTC Express

287 avenue Brugmann, 1180 (345 85 05/fax 343 63 81). **Open** 8am-7pm Mon-Fri. **No credit cards**.

Packages can be picked up and dropped off anywhere in Brussels within two hours for 325BF plus VAT.

DBXP

Box 3, 95 boulevard Louis Mettewie, 1080 (fax 469 13 71). **Open** 8am-7pm Mon-Fri (pick-ups also arranged Sat). **No credit cards**.

For 250BF, DBXP will pick up your parcel and deliver it anywhere in Brussels within two hours. Packages can also be sent to the UK and the US within a day or two.

DHL

210 Kosterstraat, 1831 (customer service 715 50 50/fax 721 45 88). **Open** customer service agents available 7.30am-midnight Mon-Fri. **No credit cards**.

Pick-ups are handled through late afternoon in most parts of the city. Packages can be dropped off at the airport in Zaventem until 10pm.

FedEx

119 Airport Building, Melsbroek, 1930 (toll free 0800 135 55/fax 752 72 80). **Open** 8am-7pm Mon-Fri. **Credit** AmEx, DC, MC, V.

If you arrange a pick-up before

2.30pm, your package will reach the US the next day. This office, based by Brussels National Airport, doesn't handle deliveries within Europe.

Electronic services

Internet access

There are dozens of Internet service providers and Internet access providers in Belgium. Consult the *Yellow Pages* for a selection.

Equipment hire

Buro Square

25 chaussée de Roodebeek, 1200 (772 41 51/fax 770 28 11). Métro Roodebeek. **Open** 9am-12.30pm, 1.30-5.30pm, Mon-Thur; 9am-12.30pm, 1.30-4.30pm, Fri. **Credit** AmEx, V.

A five-minute walk from Woluwe Shopping Centre, Buro Square carries everything from desks to fax paper. For larger equipment, call for a catalogue and to make an appointment for viewing. Buro Square's sister company Computer Square specialises in office computer systems. It has five locations in Brussels, including one in the Woluwe Shopping Centre (770 33 26).

New Telephone (Protel)

312 chaussée de Bruxelles, 1410 (354 60 98/fax 354 26 19). Bus W (Waterloo Centre stop). **Open** 9.30am-12.30pm, 2-6.30pm Mon-Fri. **Credit** AmEx, DC, MC, V.

New Telephone specialises in equipping offices with new phone systems, answerphones, voice mail, faxes and mobile phones. They also rent out photocopiers.

Papeterie IPL

635 chaussée de Waterloo, 1050 (344 89 61/fax 343 17 51). Tram 90, 94. **Open** 10am-1.30pm, 2.30-6pm, Mon-Fri. **Credit** V.

This office supplies store sells stationery ranging from the serious to the silly. It also makes up business cards for rates much lower than at many printing shops.

Estate agents

Richard Ellis

45-46 boulevard du Regent, 1000 (511 25 05/fax 511 56 16). Métro Arts-Loi. **Open** 9am-5.30pm Mon-Fri.

Healey & Baker

14 rue Montoyer, 1000 (514 40 00/fax 512 04 42). Métro Trône. **Open** 8am-7pm Mon-Fri (telephone for an appointment).

Knight Frank & Rutley

14a rue du Luxembourg, 1000 (548 05 48/fax 502 71 91). Métro Trône. **Open** 9am-6pm Mon-Thur; 9am-5.40pm Fri.

Government offices

Administration des Douanes et Accises (Customs & Excise)

Ministère des Finances, Tour Finances, 50 boulevard du Jardin Botanique, 1010 (public relations 210 30 11/fax 210 33 13). Métro Botanique. **Open** 9am-5pm Mon-Fri. Contact Mr Muylaert in public relations, who will refer you to the appropriate department.

Office National de Securité Sociale

76 boulevard de Waterloo, 1000 (509 31 11/fax 509 36 97). Métro Louise. **Open** 8am-5pm Mon-Fri (telephone for an appointment first). If you hire employees for your company, you are required to register with the ONSS for tax purposes. Translators provided free of charge.

Office de Taxe à la Valeur Ajoutée (VAT Office)

Ministère des Finances, Tour Finances, 50 boulevard du Jardin Botanique, 1010 (210 26 11/fax 210 26 35). Métro Botanique. **Open** 9am-noon, 2-4pm, Mon-Fri. All companies or individuals setting up business in Belgium must register.

Lawyers

Bugnion NV-SA

43 rue de Namur, 1000 (511 63 78/fax 513 72 41). Métro Louise. **Open** 8.30am-4pm Mon-Fri. English-speaking attorneys who specialise in patent and trademark protection within EU and beyond.

Ordre National des Avocats de Belgique (Belgian National Order of Lawyers)

Maison de l'Avocat, 65 avenue de la Toison d'Or, 1060 (534 67 73/fax 539 39 20). Métro Louise. **Open** 8.30am-5.15pm Mon-Thur; 8.30am-4.15pm Fri. This organisation can provide a list of English-speaking lawyers.

Removals

Arthur Pierre

328 chaussée de Bruxelles, 3090 (689 27 11/fax 687 46 86). **Open** 8am-5pm Mon-Fri. **No credit cards.**

Arthur Pierre has been helping families and businesses in Belgium relocate since 1898.

Maertens

5 Culliganlaan, 1831 (751 70 76/fax 751 47 18). **Open** 8am-6pm Mon-Fri. **No credit cards.** This family-owned removals company can assist in all aspects of moving but specialises in transporting art work.

Trans Euro

2b Budasteenweg, 1830 (253 25 50/fax 253 25 70). **Open** 8.30am-6pm Mon-Fri. **Credit** AmEx, DC, MC, V. Trans Euro can help you avoid lots of stress by handling the move from start to finish. The full works includes packing your belongings, loading them, getting it all through customs and reassembling the lot at the other end. A pre-move estimate is provided before any box is loaded.

Social clubs

For the thousands of wives trailing after their Eurocrat or business-oriented husbands, there are several clubs designed to make the adjustment to living in Brussels smoother.

American Women's Club *1 avenue des Erables, 1640 (358 47 53/fax 358 47 44).* **Open** 9.30am-3.30pm Mon-Fri. This long-established group maintains a busy schedule of activities for members ranging from lectures to luncheons and newcomer courses. It also publishes *Hints for Living in Belgium* (440BF), which provides detailed information on how to deal with Belgian bureaucracy and tips for setting up a household abroad. Annual membership is 3500BF with a first-year registration fee of 500BF.

British & Commonwealth Women's Club of Brussels *509 rue au Bois, 1150 (772 53 13).* **Open** 10am-3pm Mon-Fri. This club hosts several activities, from French courses to tennis lessons to outings around Belgium. It also runs newcomer classes at offices in Woluwe St Pierre. Membership costs 2000BF a year.

Canadian Women's Club *(354 22 66).* An international bilingual group with about 120 members. It holds meetings at various members' homes and plans outings in Brussels and the countryside. Ask for Claudia van der Heyden, president of the club, for more details.

Staff hire

If you don't feel like using an employment agency, you can place an ad in the Situations Vacant section in the *Bulletin*.

Manpower

523 avenue Louise, 1050 (639 10 70/fax 639 10 71). Métro Louise. **Open** 8.30am-6pm Mon-Fri. **No credit cards.** This agency can match up clients with secretaries who speak two, three or even four languages. Rates vary according to requirements.

Vedior Gregg

Riverside Business Park, 55 boulevard International, 1070 (555 16 11/fax 555 16 16). Bus 78. **Open** 8am-6pm Mon-Fri. **No credit cards.** With 90 offices throughout Belgium, One of the largest employment agencies in the country. The positions it fills range from technical to administrative. Rates for bilingual secretaries are 790-1000BF an hour.

Telecommunications

Telecom Finland International

23 rue Lozenberg, 1930 (714 86 86/fax 714 86 87). **Open** 9am-5pm Mon-Fri. Small business owners and residents making a lot of calls to Scandinavia can save up to 30 per cent on bills through this Brussels-based company.

Translators

Also check the *Yellow Pages* under *Traducteurs*.

Abetras

65-67 rue Traversière, 1210 (223 03 83/fax 223 04 15). **Open** *office* 9am-6pm Mon-Fri; *telephone enquiries* 24-hours a day. **No credit cards.** Provides simultaneous interpreters for video conferences and rents out microphones, receivers and booths. Interpreters can be hired on an à la carte basis for 18000BF per day.

BTS World Translations

Blue Tower, 326 avenue Louise, 1050 (645 16 32/fax 646 99 34). Métro Louise then tram 93, 94. **Open** *office* 9am-8pm Mon-Fri. **No credit cards.** Specialises in translating technical documents from one European language to another. For 36BF per line, you can have English documents translated into French or Dutch. Interpreters are also available.

Further Reading

Literature

Baudelaire, Charles *Amoenitates Belgicae*
Not Baudelaire's finest verse, but a scathing and often pertinent look at the Belgians and their culture. The poems are rarely published by themselves, but can be found in editions of Baudelaire's collected works.

Bertin, Eddy C
His collections are not available in English, but short stories by this Belgian writer do occasionally turn up in out-of-print horror anthologies.

Brontë, Charlotte *The Professor*
Brontë's first novel was set in Brussels, and she struggled to find a publisher for it, even after the huge success of her later works.

Brontë, Charlotte *Villette*
Brussels was the model for the town of Villette in Brontë's final novel, based on her experience of teaching there.

Christie, Agatha *The Mysterious Affair at Styles*
Allons, mes petits vol au vents… Poirot makes his début.

Claus, Hugo *The Sorrow of Belgium*
Milestone novel, set during the Nazi occupation, by a major Flemish-language novelist.

Conrad, Joseph *Heart of Darkness*
Conrad's masterpiece has early scenes in a corrupt, cheerless Brussels, unnamed but clearly identifiable.

Freeling, Nicolas *Cold Iron*
Although Freeling's most famous creation is his Amsterdam-based detective Van der Valk, many of his crime novels are also set in Belgium and France.

Gardner, Brian (ed) *Up the Line to Death*
A good collection of World War I poems, many of them written by soldiers fighting around Ypres and Mons.

Hergé *The Tintin books*
Belgium's most famous author needs no introduction, although a recent biography highlighting his willing collaboration with the Nazis has dented his reputation.

Hollinghurst, Alan *The Folding Star*
Fictional art history and sexual obsession in a dreary city in northern Belgium – fine writing, despite moony narrator.

Marlowe, Derek *A Single Summer With LB*
Marlowe's 1969 novel about 1816 – Lord Byron, Polidori and the Shellys on the shores of Switzerland's Lake Leman – begins with an evocative visit, by Byron, to the scene of the Battle of Waterloo.

Martin, Stephen (ed) *Poetry of the First World War*
Another very fine anthology, with poems about the battlegrounds of Flanders.

Royle, Nicholas *Saxophone Dreams*
Magical-realist adventures in the landscapes of Belgian surrealist Paul Delvaux, including a role for Delvaux himself. Scenes in Brussels and coastal town De Panne.

Simenon, Georges *Maigret's Revolver*
Or just about any other title by this celebrated master of the crime/detective fiction genre who was born in Liège in 1903.

Thackeray, William Makepeace *Vanity Fair*
The middle section of this sprawling novel describes the social scene in Brussels on the eve of Waterloo.

Yourcenar, Marguerite *Zeno of Bruges*
The wanderings of an alchemist in late medieval Europe. Yourcenar was born in Brussels in 1903.

Yourcenar, Marguerite *Anna, Soror*
The tragic love of a sister for her brother.

Yourcenar, Marguerite *Alexis*
The confession of a pianist to his wife, as he declares his homosexuality.

Yourcenar, Marguerite *A Coin in Nine Hands*
The story of a Roman coin which passes from one person to another. Yourcenar was the first writer to give Mussolini a bloody nose, in the above title.

History & politics

Since Belgium did not exist until 1830, few books deal specifically with its history. Instead, the determined reader will have to search for information in books about Spain, Austria, the Netherlands, Napoleon, World War I and so on. However, a few books are particularly relevant.

Parker, Geoffrey *The Dutch Revolt*
Excellent history of one of Belgium's most interesting periods, when the Spanish empire was crumbling in the sixteenth century.

Kossman, EH *The Low Countries*
Dull but informative history of Belgium from 1780-1940.

Art & architecture

Meuris, Jacques *René Magritte*
The world of the surrealist painter, in words and pictures.

Rombout, Marc *Paul Delvaux*
Excellent selection of colour plates, plus biographical text which is good in all respects except that it gives Delvaux's date of birth as 1887 instead of 1897, which would have made him 107 on his death in 1994.

Schneede, Uwe M *Surrealism*
This 1973 surrealist primer contains colour plates and text covering the major figures of the movement.

Shinomura, Junichi *Art Nouveau Architecture, Residential Masterpieces 1892-1911*
The selection of photographs of the Maison Horta would be a fine addition to anyone's coffee table.

White, Christopher *Pieter Paul Rubens: Man and Artist*
A lavishly illustrated look at the Antwerp-born artist.

Cookery

Hellon, John *Brussels Fare*
Recipes selected from Belgian restaurants.

Hezelton, Nika *Belgian Cookbook*
A cook's tour of the country.

Van Waerebeek, Ruth *Everybody Eats Well in Belgium*
Beautifully designed cookbook.

Wynants, Pierre *Creative Belgian Cuisine*
Anyone who has eaten at Wynants' Comme Chez Soi (*see* chapter **Restaurants**) will need no further encouragement.

Miscellaneous

Bryson, Bill *Neither Here Nor There*
Belgium and Brussels do not figure hugely in travel literature, but they are the subject of two amusing, if predictable, chapters in Bryson's travels around Europe.

Glover, Michael *A New Guide to the Battlefields of Northern France and the Low Countries*
Covers Waterloo as well as the World War I battlefields.

Webb, Tim *Good Beer Guide to Belgium and Holland*
One of several key books for beer lovers published by the Campaign for Real Ale (CAMRA).

Index

Advertisers' Index

Street Index

Section sponsored by

B B C WORLD SERVICE

Maps

BBC WORLD SERVICE
going abroad ?
Pack the BBC
keep up with
news
current affairs
sport
music
internet: http://www.bbc.co.uk/worldservice
e-mail: worldservice.letters@bbc.co.uk
fax: +44 (0) 171 557 1258 / 1254
phone: +44 (0) 171 240 3456
address: PO Box 76
Bush House
London WC2B 4PH
quote reference: TO.Brussels.1

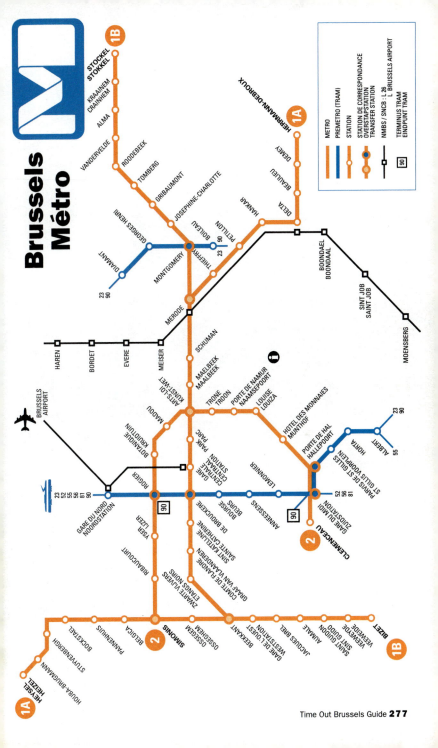

Brussels Métro

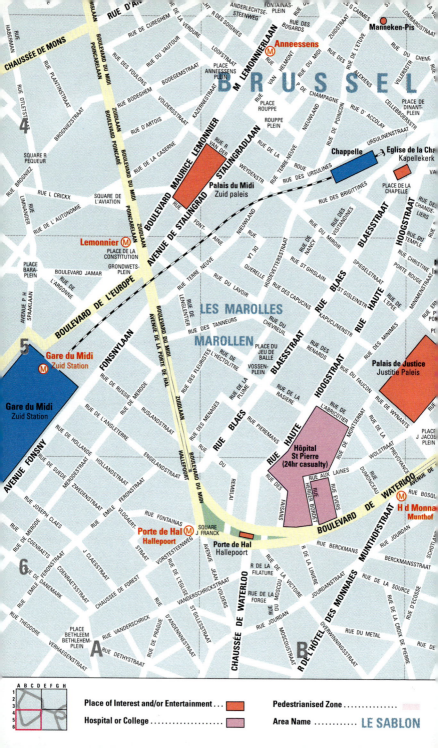

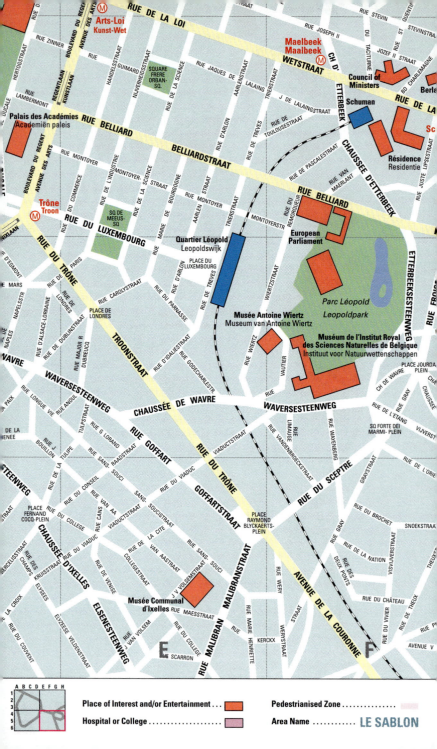

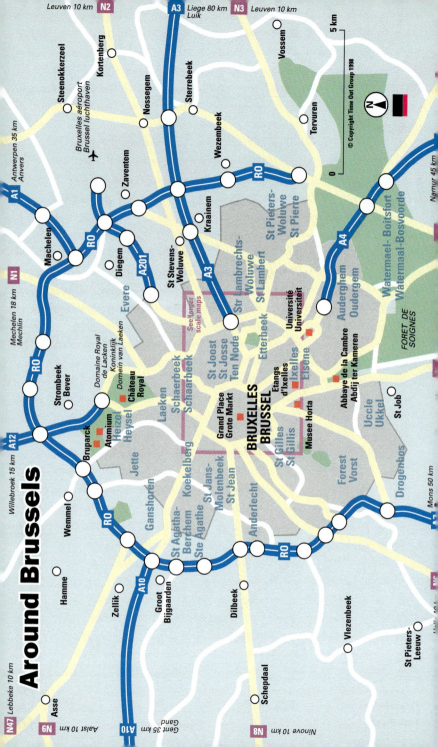

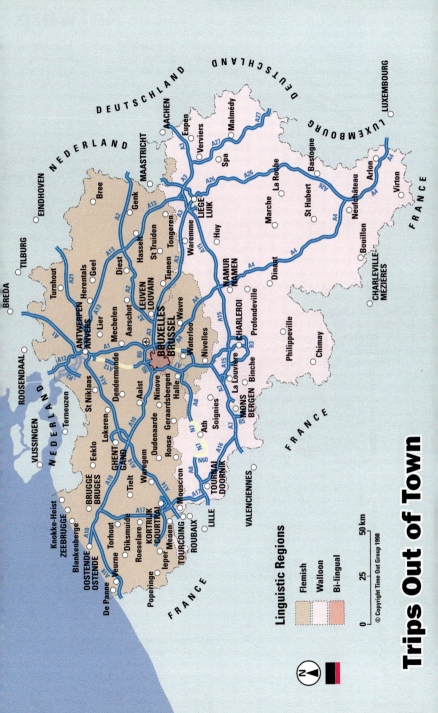

Trips Out of Town

Linguistic Regions

Flemish
Walloon
Bi-lingual

0 25 50 km

© Copyright Time Out Group 1998

N

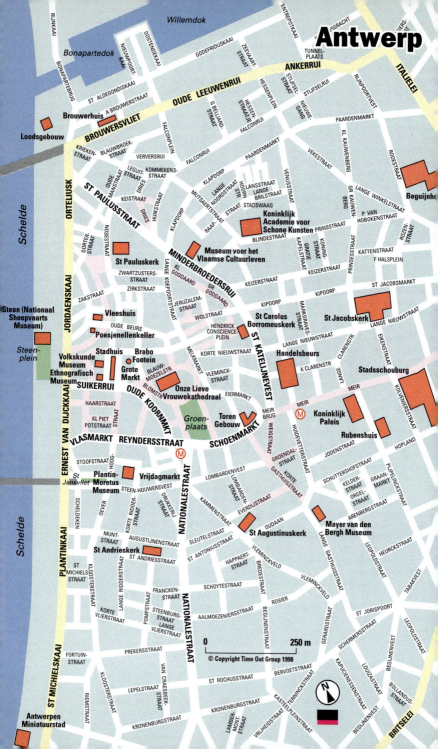

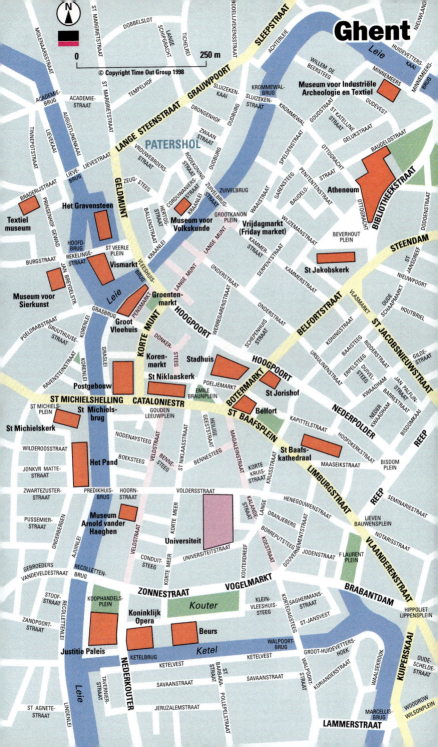

Bruges

St Walburgakerk

Korte Ridder-str

Poortersloge

Geneose Lodge

Hof Bladelin

St Jakobskerk

St Jakobs-Plein

Leeuw. Straat

Leeuwen-Brug

Boterhuis

Naaldenstraat

Sint Jansstraat

Koninklijke Stadsschouwburg

Concertgebouw

Sint Jakobsstraat

Geervlinestraat

Palmstraat

A Willaert-str

Kuipers-Straat

Vlamingstraat

Kraan-Plein

Ieper

Sint Jan-Plein

Wapenmakers Straat

Sint Walburgstraat

Ridderstraat

Oornegaard

Kandel

Hoogstraat

Peerden

Groenerei

St Pieterskapel

Philipstockstraat

Burg-Straat

Malleberg

Plein

Twijn-Straat

Kelk-Straat

Dijk

Predikheren-Straat

Muziek-conservatorium

Moerstraat

Prinsen-Hof

Ontvangerstraat

Helmstraat

Geldmuntstraat

Craenenburg

Sint Amandsstraat

Zilverstraat

Zilverstraat

Korte

Markt

Eier-Markt

Rozemarijn Straat

Provinciaal hof

Proosdij

Oude Griffie

Museum van het Vrije

Braamberg-Straat

Freren

Waalse-Str

Fonteyn-Straat

Huis Bouchoute

Kleine Amands-straat

Belfort en Hallen

Breidelstraat

Burg

Basiliek H Bloed

Stadhuis

Museum van het H Bloed

Blinde Ezelstraat

Steenhouwers-Dijk

Jozef Suvestraat

Gevangenis-Straat

Stallizerstraat

Koningin Astrid Park

Noordzandstraat

Haanstr

Giststraat

Kemelstraat

Zilverstraat

Steenstraat

Sint Niklaas-Straat

Hallestraat

Burg

Oude Kartuizerinn.

Enstraat

Wolle-Straat

Rozen-Hoed-Kaai

Pandreitje

Eekhoutstraat

Loppem-Straat

Oude Kartuizerinnenkerk

Dweersstraat

Zilverstraat

Simon Steven-Plein

Oude Burg

Nieuwe Straat

Dijver

Eekhoutpoort

Zuidzandstraat

Steenstraat

Sint Salvators-Koorstr

Hof van Watervliet

Mariastraat

Brangwyn Museum

Garenmarkt

Kathedral St Salvator

Salvatorskerkhof

Heilige Geeststraat

Gruuthusestr

Gruuthuse Museum

Groeninge Museum

Groeninge

Nieuwe Gentwe

Korte Vuldersstraat

Goezeputstraat

Prinsenhof

Mariastraat

Onze Lieve Vrouwkerk

Nieuwe Gentweg

Werkhuisstraat

Oude Gentweg

Jakobinessenstraat

Bakkers-Straat

Oostmeers

Westmeers

Sint Obrechts-straat

Memling Museum

Oud St Janshospitaal

Stoof-Straat

Walstraat

Drie Kroezen Straat

Oude Gentweg

Visspaanstraat

Boudewijn Ravestraat

Zonnekemeers

Walplein

Wijngaard Straat

Kateljinestraat

Noordstraat

Sentillenhof

Gentpoortvest

Westmeers

Oostmeers

Garsoen-Straat

Begijnhof

Wijngaard Plein

Huisbrouwerij "Straffe Hendrik"

Arsenaalstraat

Sulferbergstraat

Visspaanstraat

Kateljinestraat

Eiland

Prof Dr J Sebrechtsstraat

Minnewater

Coletijnenstraat

Bargeweg

Katelijne-Brug

N

0   250 m

© Copyright Time Out Group 1998

Buiten Begijnenvest

Begijnenvest

Begijnenvest

Minnewater Park

Buiten Katelijnevest

Buiten Katelijnevest